THE OXFORD
HISTORY OF BRITAIN

Kenneth O. Morgan is Research Professor at the University of Wales, Aberystwyth, and Honorary Fellow of The Queen's College, Oxford. From 1966 to 1989 he was Fellow and Praelector of Queen's; from 1989 to 1995 he was Vice-Chancellor of Aberystwyth, and also Senior Vice-Chancellor of the University of Wales, 1993–5. He is the author of many major works on British history including *Wales in British Politics, 1868–1922* (1963); *The Age of Lloyd George* (1971); *Keir Hardie: Radical and Socialist* (1975); *Modern Wales: Politics, Places and People* (1995); *Rebirth of a Nation: Wales 1880–1980* (Oxford paperback, 1982); *Labour in Power, 1945–1951* (Oxford paperback, 1985); *Consensus and Disunity: the Lloyd George Coalition Government, 1918–1922* (Oxford paperback, 1986); *Labour People: Leaders and Lieutenants, Hardie to Kinnock* (Oxford paperback, rev. edn., 1992); *The People's Peace: British History, 1945–1990* (Oxford paperback, 1992), reissued as *The People's Peace: British History since 1945* (Oxford paperback, 1999), and *Callaghan: a Life* (Oxford paperback, 1999). He was elected a Fellow of the British Academy in 1983.

The ten historians who have contributed to *The Oxford History of Britain* are all distinguished authorities in their field. They are:

PETER SALWAY, The Open University. *Roman Britain*

JOHN BLAIR, The Queen's College, Oxford. *The Anglo-Saxons*

JOHN GILLINGHAM, London School of Economics and Political Science. *The Early Middle Ages*

RALPH A. GRIFFITHS, University College of Swansea. *The Later Middle Ages*

JOHN GUY, University of Bristol. *The Tudor Age*

JOHN S. MORRILL, Selwyn College, Cambridge. *The Stuarts*

PAUL LANGFORD, Lincoln College, Oxford. *The Eighteenth Century*

CHRISTOPHER HARVIE, University of Tübingen. *Revolution and the Rule of Law*

H. C. G. MATTHEW, St Hugh's College, Oxford *The Liberal Age*

KENNETH O. MORGAN, The Queen's College, Oxford. *The Twentieth Century*

THE OXFORD
HISTORY
OF
BRITAIN

Revised Edition

EDITED BY
KENNETH O. MORGAN

Oxford New York
OXFORD UNIVERSITY PRESS

Oxford University Press, Great Clarendon Street, Oxford OX2 6DP

Oxford New York

Athens Auckland Bangkok Bogotá Buenos Aires Calcutta
Cape Town Chennai Dar es Salaam Delhi Florence Hong Kong Istanbul
Karachi Kuala Lumpur Madrid Melbourne Mexico City Mumbai
Nairobi Paris São Paulo Singapore Taipei Tokyo Toronto Warsaw
and associated companies in Berlin Ibadan

Oxford is a trade mark of Oxford University Press

The text of this edition first published in The Oxford Illustrated History of Britain
This edition first issued (with revisions) as an Oxford University Press paperback 1988
Updated editions 1993, 1999

British Library Cataloguing in Publication Data
Data available

Library of Congress Cataloging-in-Publication Data
The Oxford history of Britain / edited by Kenneth O. Morgan. —
Updated ed.
Includes bibliographical references and index.
1. Great Britain—History.   I. Morgan, Kenneth O.
DA30.093   1999   941—dc21   98-30644
ISBN 0-19-285349-X

15 17 19 20 18 16 14

Printed in Great Britain by
Cox & Wyman Ltd.
Reading, Berkshire

EDITOR'S FOREWORD

THE distinctiveness, even uniqueness, of the British as a people
has long been taken for granted by foreign observers and native
commentators alike. Visitors from overseas, from those
omnipresent Venetian ambassadors in the late fifteenth century,
through intellectuals like Voltaire or Tocqueville, to American
journalists in the twentieth century, have all been convinced of
the special quality of British society. This has equally been
assumed by modern native chroniclers of the British scene, as
opposed in their ideological outlooks as Sir Winston Churchill
and George Orwell, patriots both. But the nature or essence of
the Britishness of the British is far easier to proclaim than to
define, let alone to explain. Very few attempts to encapsulate its
quality have been more than marginally successful. One of the
most celebrated, addressing itself to the English people alone
and first published in 1926, came in G. M. Trevelyan's remarkable synoptic *History of England*. Trevelyan here focused on a
number of themes which he believed to have marked out the
separate experience of the English through the centuries—
geographical severance from the European continent, with the
consequent centrality of sea-power; a broad social fluidity in
which the early demise of feudalism helped generate a new
industrial and commercial enterprise; a flowing cultural continuity from the time of Chaucer and Wycliffe onwards; and
above all—a theme especially dear to the heart of an old late-
Victorian Liberal like Trevelyan—a long political and legal
evolution expressed in the durability of parliamentary institutions and the rule of law. Secure in itself, a vibrant, outward-
looking island had proceeded to colonize and civilize the world.
None of Trevelyan's themes can be dismissed. Equally, none
can be accepted uncritically in the more tormented, doubt-
ridden age of the late twentieth century, with its well-founded

suspicion of national and racial stereotypes. The problem of trying to come to grips with the essential reality of the British experience remains as pressing and as fascinating as ever.

The purpose of this book is to isolate and uncover the main elements in that experience throughout British history, from the earliest Roman period down to the later twentieth century. It is not concerned with the protean concept of 'national character', a difficult and perhaps unrewarding enterprise even when considering the English alone—and almost impossible when the distinct traditions of the Welsh, Scots, and Irish are included. It is rather intended to disentangle the main political, social, economic, religious, intellectual, and cultural features of these islands as they have revealed themselves to successive generations, and as trained scholars have tried to examine them. The question of a British 'national character', or the lack of it, will, therefore, be implicit rather than explicit. Readers will be left to draw their own conclusions, and to form their own personal visions. This is, inevitably, a multi-author volume, written by ten professional historians in close collaboration with one another. Such a collective approach is inescapable, since the days when one compendious mind such as Trevelyan's could have the capacity and the confidence to treat all aspects of British history with equal ease probably died with the Liberal intelligentsia some time after 1914. It is certainly neither practicable nor desirable, now that Renaissance men have vanished from the earth. Rather, each major phase in the history of Britain is examined here in depth by a specialist working in that field, but always directing his findings to the general reader. A basic premiss of this book is that it deals with the history of Great Britain, two partitioned, poly-cultural islands, and not merely with England alone. Indeed, the fact that the ten authors include three Welshmen and two Scots may help towards that end! Again, while the geographic and other distinctiveness of Britain from the European continent and the world beyond may constantly emerge, so too will the economic, intellectual, cultural, and religious links by which Britain and overseas nations helped shape each other's experience. The dynamic urge for exploration, colonization, and conquest from the Tudor period onwards, which led in time to the creation of the greatest empire the world had ever seen, also lent an outward-looking aspect to British historical development. Britain in this book remains the geographical island familiar to schoolchildren. But it is an island whose physical insularity was always qualified by a wider process of transmission from continental Europe, and later from North America, Africa, Asia, and Australasia, from the first arrival of the Roman legions onwards.

These chapters help to show how old clichés have dissolved in the searching light of modern research and scholarship. The 'anarchy' of the mid-twelfth century, the chaos of the Wars of the Roses, the inevitability of the Civil Wars, the serenity of Victorian England, familiar to readers of *1066 and All That*, tend to disappear like the autumn leaves at Vallombrosa. Again, the notion that British history, unlike that of less fortunate nations elsewhere, is uniquely marked by a kind of seamless, peaceful continuity emerges here as needing the most severe qualification. The history of the British people is a complex, sometimes violent or revolutionary one, full of disjunctions and abrupt changes of pace or of course. The idea of a tranquil, undisturbed evolutionary progress even for England, let alone the turbulent, fractured, schizophrenic history of the Celtic nations, comes out here as little more than a myth, fit for the refuse-heap of history, like romances of 'golden ages' over the centuries from Arthurian times onwards.

Roman Britain, as Peter Salway shows, was marked by constant, alternating phases of social upheaval and readjustment, long before the final retreat of the Romans in the early fifth century. John Blair describes the dynastic turbulence and the dramatic growth of urban life in the Anglo-Saxon period, until the final, violent end at Hastings. In the early Middle Ages, John Gillingham depicts a saga of conquest punctuated by frequent defeats on French and British soil, with an exploding society under such strain by the late thirteenth century that it is described here as being possibly on the verge of class war. Although that was avoided, in the later Middle Ages, as Ralph Griffiths writes, long wars in France were followed by aristocratic turmoil in Britain in the fifteenth century, accompanied by domestic recovery from plague and social revolt. The Tudor Age, as John Guy demonstrates, suffused in a golden glow in the patriotic effusions of later generations, was marked in fact by extreme pressure of population upon economic resources, by religious conflict, and the threat of foreign invasion. The resultant political and religious tensions inherited by the house of Stuart are analysed by John Morrill for a century in which—despite a marked decline in internal lawlessness—two civil wars, regicide, a republic, a restoration, and a revolution, followed each other in bewildering, breathless profusion. The apparent surface stability, prosperity, and cultural expansiveness of the Georgian age, as Paul Langford shows, gave way to an explosive tumult of industry, trade, and technology unprecedented in the history of the world, and also to the new revolutionary impulses surging in from the American colonies and from republican France. Somehow, the picture of Edward Gibbon, the urbane chronicler of the Rome of the Antonines and their successors, fleeing across Europe in the face of the Jacobin hordes in his beloved France, is symbolic. The early nineteenth century, as Christopher Harvie explains, did indeed manage to avoid the revolutionary malaria raging through other European states. But instead it brought massive dislocations in the social fabric and the notion of the legal community, and a seemingly unbridgeable class division that led Marx, fancifully, to see Britain as being in the forefront of the revolutionary apocalypse. The later nineteenth and early twentieth centuries, as outlined by H. C. G. Matthew, moved on rapidly from the bland self-assurance of the Great Exhibition, to the anxieties of the *fin de siècle* period, with its social tensions, imperialist neuroses, and sense of national vulnerability. The years since 1914, described by the present writer, saw two world wars, pulverizing economic pressures in the thirties and the seventies, and a forcible wrenching of Britain out of its place in the sun. The history of Britain, then, is not one of harmonious continuity, broadening from precedent to precedent, or from status to contract, as Victorian intellectuals would have it. It is a dramatic, colourful, often violent story of an ancient society and culture torn apart by the political, economic, and intellectual turmoil of human experience. Britain in many ways has been the cockpit of mankind.

And yet, a reading of these chapters may also leave the clear impression that, however elusive in definition, the sense of Britishness always survived in the post-Roman and post-Norman periods. Some elements of that consciousness, not necessarily closely related, can be clearly traced through the centuries. There were, variously, that Celtic Christian identity that survived the invasion of the Romans; the artistic flowering seen in the miniatures and sculpture of the late Anglo-Saxon era; the centralized governmental and ecclesiastical system created by the Normans and Angevins; the vivid sense of an English nationality emerging in the poetry, and perhaps even the architecture, of the fourteenth century. Even in the Tudor twilight, Shakespeare's plays testify to a growing sense of national cohesion—while the presence of that ubiquitous Elizabethan Welshman, John Dee, who invented the ambiguous term 'British Empire', indicates some wider horizons, too. Equally, the intellectual values embodied in the revolution of 1688, Macaulay's famous 'preserving revolution', suggests a social and cultural continuity beneath the surface turbulence of high politics in the seventeenth century. The communal stability of much of the eighteenth and nineteenth centuries, together with their integrative developments in industry, transport, and communication, and perhaps even the democratic advances, political and social, of the present century, have reinforced this perceptible current of national awareness. At key moments in British history, society coalesced rather than divided. Class war, however defined, did not in fact take place in the later Middle Ages; while Marx's prophecies of violent revolutionary upheaval in the modern industrial period were, fortunately, not fulfilled. That Britain was able to assimilate the strains of its political revolution as early as the seventeenth century and of its industrial revolution as early as the eighteenth, in each case long before other European nations did so, testified to the rooted strength of its institutions and its culture. Consensus, no less than conflict, is a central part of our story.

In its many forms, this rooted patriotism, embracing the Welsh, Scots, and Ulstermen over the centuries—though, significantly, never the southern Irish—endured and remained unquenchable. The visible, recognized symbols of that patriotic sense still survive—Crown, Parliament, the processes of law, the legacy of empire, the urge for individuality and domestic privacy, the collective enthusiasm for recreation and mass sport. But what is equally striking, perhaps, is the patriotism of the dissenting critics also, with their alternative scenarios. The Levellers, Daniel Defoe, William Cobbett, William Morris, R. H. Tawney, George Orwell, all in their time emerged as passionate, libertarian opponents of the social inequalities and political imbalance of their day. Yet each of them emerged, also, as deeply committed to an almost religious sense of the civilized essence of their country and its people, their history and destiny. By setting this sense of national continuity against the recurrence of disruption and crisis through the centuries, the historian derives perhaps his ultimate justification in thrusting the British people face to face with their past and with the image of themselves. We hope that general readers will understand themselves, their society, neighbours, and an encompassing world with more clarity, subtlety, enthusiasm, and even affection, after reading this book.

KENNETH O. MORGAN

Oxford,
November 1983

In this revised paperback edition, the text has been updated to take the story down to the late 1990s.

K.O.M.

Oxford,
November 1998

CONTENTS

LIST OF MAPS

The maps on pp. 211 and 243 are based on two in *English Historical Documents*, vol. iii, by H. Rothwell, by kind permission of Methuen, London; those on pp. 428 and 429 are based on two in *Transport and Economy: the Turnpike Roads of Eighteenth-Century Britain* by Eric Pawson, by kind permission of Academic Press, Inc. (London) Ltd.

1. *Roman Britain*

(*c*.55 BC–*c*. AD 440)

━━━━

PETER SALWAY

The Beginnings of British History

IN Roman times Britain had as many people as at its peak in
the Middle Ages. For four centuries it was an integral part of a
single political system that stretched from Turkey to Portugal
and from the Red Sea to the Tyne and beyond. Its involvement
with Rome started before the Conquest launched by Claudius
in AD 43, and it continued to be a part of the Roman world for
some time after the final break with Roman rule. We are
dealing with a full half-millennium of the history of Britain.

The origins of later Britain go back beyond the Roman
period. Aspects of the society the Romans found in Britain were
beginning to emerge in the Neolithic and Early Bronze Ages.
At the time of the Roman Conquest, the culture of Britain
had something like fifteen hundred to two thousand years of
development behind it—although the prehistorians are greatly
divided on the details. By the end of the pre-Roman Iron Age,
society had evolved forms of organization closely similar to
those encountered by the Romans elsewhere in north-western
Europe, and had adopted versions of the culture and language
we loosely call 'Celtic'. Outside the imperial frontiers in Britain
these continued largely unchanged; inside, the Celtic substratum persisted, assimilated and adapted by Rome in ways not
in general closely paralleled by modern colonial empires.

Why, then, are we not either starting this *History of Britain* before the Romans, or consigning Roman Britain, as some modern writers would have us do, to 'prehistory'? The answer lies in the real distinction between the Roman period and what went before. There is some truth in the assertion that the study of Roman Britain is prehistory, in the sense that we have to lean very heavily on archaeology—and this is also true of the early Anglo-Saxon period. However, our sources for Britain are by no means solely archaeological, and the interpretation of the material remains themselves cannot be divorced from the study of the written sources. It is true that the quantity of contemporary or near-contemporary literary evidence is not great in comparison with later periods but there is enough to be significant. Moreover, we have the very considerable remains of the once huge routine output of a literate society—and in a form not subject to the inevitable corruptions of the Greek and Latin literary texts, which have largely survived only by being copied and re-copied by hand down the centuries. Actual examples of writing found in Britain, mostly as inscriptions on stone but some in other forms, constitute a major primary source for the Romano-British period. They include trade marks on manufactured goods; a small but growing number of personal letters and other documents in a variety of materials, discovered in excavations; even graffiti—the everyday writing and reading matter of ordinary people. Nor can we ignore the specialized and difficult but rewarding study of Roman coinage, which had a peculiarly important part in the politics and economics of the Roman world. Not only was the currency itself manipulated by government as money, but also the wording and images upon the coins were consistently exploited as a powerful medium for mass propaganda which possessed the insistence of a television commercial repeated over and over again. The ability to read was, admittedly, very much commoner in the towns than in the Romano-British countryside but it was compulsory in the army and essential in many other walks of life. It was certainly not, as in other ages, restricted to a small or specialized class.

The critical difference between Roman Britain and what went

before is that its society was literate, perhaps more literate than at any other time till the end of the Middle Ages. Alongside and allied to this is the fact that it was a world dominated by the rule of law, which closely regulated the relations between the individual and the State and between one man and another, however corruptly or inefficiently it might often have been administered. As a society that became more and more dominated by regulations and procedures contained in official documents, the contrast between Roman Britain and the country as it was at the end of the Iron Age is startling. Then, even at the top of the social scale, where the import of Roman luxury goods was a notable feature, writing was totally absent except on the splendid but limited coinage—and even on that the language employed was almost universally Latin and the moneyers themselves often Roman.

Once Julius Caesar's expeditions of 55 and 54 BC had pointed the way, it was more or less inevitable that Rome would try her hand at conquest. Romans did not acknowledge any limit on their right to expand their rule: indeed they saw it as a divine mission. From Caesar onwards, Britain occupied a particular and significant place in the Roman consciousness. The Roman period is a turning-point, not so much in the underlying story of man's settlement of the land of Britain but in the country's emergence from prehistory into history.

The character of the physical geography of a country has a great effect on how people live, and Britain is no exception. Its outstanding permanent characteristic is the broad division between 'highland' and 'lowland'—in rough terms, between the north and west of mainland Britain and the south and east—but it is a distinction which can be overdone in historical analysis. Moreover, in Britain man has shown a considerable capacity to adapt the landscape, sometimes intentionally, often in pursuit of some other end, such as fuel. There have also been important fluctuations in the physical conditions, especially in the relative level of land and sea, with considerable effects on the coastline and inland on the pattern and level of rivers. To what extent the causes were climatic or a matter of movements in the geology is uncertain. In general, such evidence as we have for the Roman period suggests that the climate was broadly similar to present-day Britain. A period of relatively high sea-level was succeeded in the first century AD by a 'marine regression', opening up new lands for exploitation. In the third century the onset of rather wetter climatic conditions seems to be revealed by evidence of flooding in many parts of Europe, with serious problems for low-lying land, rivers, and harbours. So it would seem that climatic conditions were by no means constant throughout the period.

The once popular belief that Britain was largely covered with forest until cleared by the Anglo-Saxons is now discredited. By the Roman Conquest, although there was still a great deal of natural forest, the population had already grown to something of the order it was under the Romans, two or three times greater than during the reign of William the Conqueror (1066–87). The proportion of forest to open, settled landscape had dropped to the level of the later Middle Ages. From about 1300 BC what was to become the classic Iron Age pattern had started to take shape: hill-forts, isolated farms or groups of farms sometimes amounting to villages (often surrounded by small enclosures), larger expanses of permanent fields, woodland, and great open stretches of pasture. In the last 600 years before Caesar, Britain adopted many of the characteristics of the successive phases of the Continental Iron Age, though often with insular variations. This has led to unresolved debate among the prehistorians as to whether the changes that succeeded one another primarily reflect actual invasions on a substantial scale, the arrival of relatively small numbers of influential or conquering newcomers (as later the Normans), or the exchange of ideas through travel and trade. But whatever the mechanism, Britain had reached the point by Caesar's time where, as he himself says, the tribes he met in the parts he penetrated—the south and east—were very similar to those he encountered in Gaul. Beyond these, archaeology reveals that there were some less-advanced peoples, but all of them seem to have shared the same British version of the Celtic language and a broadly similar culture.

There is some reason to think that the tribal system we find in Britain in Claudian times was not fully developed in Caesar's, and there are other important changes in the period between the Roman invasions which we shall examine later. In southern Gaul, the native tribes had largely passed from rule by kings to elective magistracies and tribal councils, but in northern Gaul kingship was still common when Caesar arrived. In Britain it was to remain so down to Claudius, though there are some signs of joint or divided rule by pairs of kings. Society divided broadly into a warrior aristocracy and a largely agricultural commons. The priests, the druids, were a third group whose position and function is debated, though for Britain at least the evidence is against the popular notion of their having a prominent political role. The Celts were characterized by quarrelsomeness, both within the tribe and in their indulgence in inter-tribal warfare. Only on rare occasions, in the face of great danger, would Celtic tribes combine to choose a single leader; though in Gaul at least there was some tradition of periodic gatherings of prominent men from various tribes. There was little or no 'national' sentiment.

By Caesar's day, close relationships had been established between southern Britain and northern Gaul. The pattern of archaeological finds reveals two main groups of routes by which goods and people travelled between the countries. The most important at this time was between Brittany and Lower Normandy (in ancient times known collectively as Armorica) and south-west Britain, particularly through a port at Hengistbury Head in Dorset. The other routes were from Upper Normandy and the Low Countries, the lands between the mouths of the Seine and Rhine, to southern and eastern England. Caesar moreover reports that 'within living memory' a Gallic ruler had exercised power in Britain as well as his own homeland, and he was not only to find British contingents fighting alongside his Gallic enemies but to be thwarted by fugitives seeking refuge from Rome with friends or kin across the Channel.

To understand why Caesar was in Gaul and what may have prompted his campaigns in Britain we need to look briefly at the condition of Rome at this time. Rome's expansion in the third and second centuries BC from being an Italian city state to the greatest power in the Mediterranean had been under her traditional form of government. This was theoretically democratic, with assemblies of the people and annually elected magistrates, but in practice public office was held century after century by a relatively small number of aristocratic families. The senate, notionally an advisory body, came to have a dominant role, being composed of magistrates and all those who had previously been elected to the qualifying magistracies. The highest offices, the two annual consulships, were almost exclusively held by an even smaller group within the senatorial class, and its families possessed special prestige. Religious and social attitudes, closely intertwined, placed a very high value on veneration of the family ancestors and the preservation of family honour. It was a characteristic of the classical world that a man's reputation—what his peers thought of him—was of the highest importance. At Rome, the individual aristocrat was under constant pressure, both of family duty and personal ambition, to emulate his forebears by pursuing a public career and by striving for the highest office.

Reputation was won by success primarily in two fields—the law and the army. A senatorial career normally included posts in each area. Of the two, proven military prowess won the greater prestige. Holding certain senior offices, even below the consulship, brought with it eligibility to command armies and govern provinces abroad. Caesar's contemporary, the orator, politician, and moralist Cicero, states categorically what conferred the greatest personal status: there was more glory to be won by extending the empire than by administering it.

In the ancient world, wars of conquest usually showed a

handsome profit for the victor. The immense wealth brought into Rome by her conquests and the opportunities and temptations offered by her Mediterranean empire put intolerable strains on the political and social system that had been adequate for a small Italian state. By the middle of the first century BC, the Roman Republic was falling apart. The old conventions within the governing class could not cope. Ambition to join the select few at the top had been replaced by an inability to tolerate even equals in power and fame.

Part of the visible prestige of a great Roman aristocrat had long been the number of people dependent upon him. Indeed whole communities could regard themselves as among his 'clients'. Such 'patronage' was a feature of society that was to be of great importance to provinces such as Britain, otherwise far from the centre of power. By the first century BC, the old citizen armies, raised for a specific war, had been replaced by professionals. The senate made the fatal mistake of allowing these new soldiers to become dependent upon their own generals rather than the State for the rewards of service, particularly the all-important provision on retirement. The conditions for recurrent civil war were now all present and the Republic effectively doomed. Attitudes, practices, and social relationships had been set up that were to haunt Rome for the rest of her history. For Britain, it was not only the great events of the subsequent history of the empire that directly affected her destiny, but also the extraordinary success the Romans had in transmitting their values to the populations they absorbed—particularly to the native ruling classes. Indeed, the creation of a common upper-class culture, critical to the successful working of the empire itself, was in many ways also central in its downfall. The story of Britain in Roman times reflects this fundamental pattern.

Julius Caesar's conquest of Gaul must be looked at in the context of the struggle for power in the closing years of the Republic. We shall probably never know exactly why he launched his two expeditions to Britain in 55 and 54 BC nor whether he intended conquest—though there is a possible parallel in his punitive foray across the Rhine into Germany. More important were the consequences for the future. In immediate military terms the results were modest, though we do not hear of Britons fighting in Gaul again. Because of the explosive state of Gaul, Caesar was prevented from following up his victories and from taking advantage of the surrender of the temporary confederation of the British tribes. Indeed, a Roman historian writing in the next century even represented a British leader as claiming the 'repulse' of Caesar by the ancestors of his hearers.

Caesar's British enterprise made a lasting impression on Rome, however. Britain was a remote, almost fabled island across the 'Ocean', a fearsome sea to Romans as yet unaccustomed to the tidal conditions outside the Mediterranean. Britain was beyond the known world. In two brief campaigns Caesar had put Britain on the Roman map. Retaining its aura of mystery, it would henceforth always occupy an alluring place in the minds of those eager for military ambition—and Caesar had set a goal and a precedent for subsequent members of the Julian family. Moreover his experiences—he had a number of close shaves at the hands not only of the British but also of the elements—provided practical lessons for a future expeditionary commander.

Caesar had also set important precedents for intervention in Britain. He had received the surrender of powerful kings and accepted the friendship of others. A tribute—or annual tax—to be paid to Rome had been imposed. He had also installed as king of the Trinovantes of Essex a young prince who had fled to him in Gaul. The father of this prince had been killed by Cassivellaunus, the same Briton who was elected by the British confederation to lead them against Caesar—and who was now forbidden to interfere with the Trinovantes. Rome could, therefore, claim some sort of overlordship, the right to exact payments and an obligation to protect her friends, if she chose to move. (Rome rarely did so in fact, unless it was in her own interest: many small countries under her nominal protection failed to appreciate this basic fact of ancient life, with unfortunate consequences.) But precedent, we may remember, was important to the Romans, and after Caesar they had ample.

For two decades after Caesar, the attention of the Roman world was monopolized by the series of civil wars that brought the Republic to an end and put Caesar's adopted heir Octavian (later to assume the name Augustus) into power. Caesar had himself taken no action when his erstwhile Gallic friend Commius, whom he had installed as king of the Atrebates in Gaul, joined the great revolt. The crushing of that revolt saw Commius in flight to Britain—where he had earlier been used as Caesar's agent—to found a dynasty among the British Atrebates. The lack of Roman interest in Britain at this time is understandable. More interesting for us is that we are now beginning to identify tribes and plot the history of dynasties. Commius' own case is particularly intriguing. His rule over a Roman-devised 'client' kingdom of Gallic Atrebates and the Morini of the Channel coast north of the Seine had put him in control of much of the area through which the routes from the main concentration of 'Belgae', straddling the Meuse, ran towards Britain. Somewhat earlier than Caesar, there seems to have been the beginning of a movement from the Belgic part of Gaul into Britain which probably accelerated as Caesar's conquests progressed, establishing, at the least, related royal houses in Britain.

In the course of the first century BC, Belgic culture became dominant in southern Britain, even among tribes themselves not Belgic. The pattern of life was changing. The division of labour in society became more pronounced, with more and more activities, such as pottery-making, becoming the preserve of craftsmen rather than domestic. British art reached a magnificent peak, especially in metalwork, all swirling motifs and fine enamelling, but it concentrated on the equipping of warrior chiefs and possibly the adornment of shrines. In the most Belgicized areas, hill-forts tended to give way to large settlements on lower ground, sometimes with their approaches defended by

great running earthworks. These have been seen as the forerunners of Roman towns, though some were more in the nature of
royal residences than urban in the contemporary Mediterranean sense. But for the future of the British landscape the most
interesting change is the widespread emergence, particularly in
the period between Caesar and Claudius (54 BC–AD 43), of a
more permanent pattern of rural land settlement, with regular
boundaries that suggest regular tenure. There is a growing
feeling among archaeologists that this period may mark the
beginning of a framework of land-division that has persisted to
the present day. Those who worked and owned the land have
certainly changed many times. The skeleton of the landscape, in
this credible hypothesis, has survived into modern times.

In the year before his first expedition Caesar had fought and
destroyed at sea the fleet of the Veneti of Brittany, whose ships
had controlled the carrying trade between Armorica and south-
west Britain. About this time, archaeology shows a dramatic
switch in emphasis to the routes between Belgic Gaul and the
south and east of Britain. Henceforth, the sea passages from the
Seine to the Southampton area, the short crossings from
Boulogne to Kent, and the route from the Rhine and the Low
Countries to the estuaries of Essex were paramount. It is not,
perhaps, surprising to find that the greatest wealth and sophistication were now in these areas of Britain. From 12 BC, indeed,
when Augustus launched his armies on the conquest of Holland
and Germany, the new importance of the northern links with
Britain must have further sharply increased. Although in the
long run Augustus' attempt to extend the empire to the Elbe
failed, from this time large Roman armies were permanently on
the Rhine. Britain was exporting corn, hides, cattle, and iron to
the empire, all items of vital importance to the Roman military
effort. Recent research has indicated that the technologically
efficient British agriculture was producing, at least in grain, a
large surplus over the subsistence needs of its people. We may
reasonably surmise that the increasing wealth, the changes in
society, and even the new pattern of British agriculture were

stimulated, perhaps even caused, by the opportunities offered by the needs of the army of the Rhine and the emerging civil markets of the new Roman provinces across the Channel.

In his early days Augustus was acutely conscious of the legacy of Caesar's memory and the urgent need to establish a military reputation for himself. Even before his final defeat of Mark Antony he seems to have planned an invasion of Britain; and at least two more attempts were made to put it into effect. All were frustrated by more pressing demands. After 26 BC, however, he was content to let the imminent conquest of Britain remain an uncorrected impression that served as useful propaganda at Rome, while developing diplomatic relations that may have sprung out of negotiations we know were already in progress, perhaps to re-establish Caesar's taxation. Strabo, an author writing late in Augustus' reign or under his successor Tiberius, confirms that the Britons were paying heavy customs dues to Rome on their import and export trade. He seems to reflect a party line that sought to justify the shift in policy away from invasion when he claims that Rome forbore to make the easy conquest of Britain because taxation without occupation was more profitable. The Britons, he adds significantly, posed no military threat.

Commius was succeeded on his British throne by a son, Tincommius, and around 15 BC there seems to have been a reversal of attitude which put this important kingdom at the British end of the Seine-Southampton route into friendship with Rome. The reason may have been the growing power of one British tribe, the Catuvellauni, centred in Hertfordshire. Whether they had recently coalesced from smaller clans or had already been the force behind Cassivellaunus is uncertain; but the history of Britain up to the Claudian conquest is now dominated by Catuvellaunian expansion. For the time being, however, Rome chose to turn a blind eye. Even the expulsion of Tincommius and another British king, and their seeking refuge with Augustus, were only treated by Rome as support for the Augustan claim to exercise virtual sway over Britain, propaganda for internal consumption. Indeed, there is every sign the Catuvellauni were careful not to display open hostility. The balance was mutually profitable to the governing classes on both sides. British aristocrats were enjoying the imports from the empire, while the list of exports that the Roman author thinks worthy of mention shows that the Britons were not only paying for these luxuries with supplies important to the army: by ending gold, silver, slaves, and hunting dogs they had also become a source of commodities of direct interest to the emperor himself and to the rich at Rome. After disaster in Germany in AD 9, Augustus and his successor Tiberius erected non-intervention outside the empire into a principle—the absolute opposite of previous Augustan practice. It must, however, be a measure of the satisfactory nature of the working relationship that Cunobelinus, Shakespeare's Cymbeline, now king of the Catuvellauni, managed to avoid Roman retribution even when he took over the territory of Caesar's old protégés, the Trinovantes, and transferred the centre of his kingdom to Colchester. He now had command of the lucrative route to the Rhine. Within Britain he could cut the supply of their status symbols to other British princes at will; and whether by conquest or other means the power and influence of his kingdom continued to expand.

The Roman Conquest

The state of mutual toleration, satisfactory as it doubtless was for Rome and the Catuvellauni—but perhaps not so welcome to other Britons—started to crumble when the unstable Gaius (Caligula) succeeded Tiberius. At some point in this period, Cunobelinus expelled one of his sons, who eventually fled to the emperor, to whom he made a formal act of submission. Gaius not only claimed the surrender of Britain; he also gave orders for an invasion. These he subsequently countermanded, but only at the last minute, and it is this that is important. The staff work had been done, the whole massive process of build-up to an invasion had been gone through, not as manœuvres but as a real operation, and the Roman public had been reminded of unfinished business. Everything lay ready for a more determined hand.

The murder of Gaius hoisted unceremoniously to the throne his uncle Claudius, previously ignored by the rest of the imperial family under the mistaken notion that he was of defective intelligence. In fact, he combined common sense, an original mind bordering on the eccentric, a professional interest in history, and a profound veneration for Roman tradition. Faced soon after his elevation by a serious military revolt, the need to establish his reputation with the troops and gain respect at Rome must have been obvious to him. Such a man could hardly miss the chance of military glory offered by Britain and the opportunity not only to carry out the invasion cancelled by Augustus and Gaius before him but even to outdo Julius Caesar himself. Personal and family reputation could not be better served.

There was a pretext, too—and one which could be referred back to sound precedent and provided a strategic reason for intervention. Cunobelinus was now dead, and his realm had fallen into the hands of two other aggressive sons—Caratacus and Togodumnus. The eastern entrance to Britain was, therefore, unreliable. In the south, pressure on Tincommius' old kingdom had reduced it to a rump on the coast: now that entrance, too, closed when an internal coup expelled Tincommius' brother, Verica. The latter, in the time-honoured fashion, also fled to the emperor. All Britain seemed to be turning hostile, and the valuable traffic between it and the empire was threatened. Like Caesar, Claudius could respond to an appeal from a British prince.

Caesar had relied upon inspired generalship and the devotion of the troops who had served long under him. The new standing regular army that Augustus and his successors had created still depended on generalship, but was more firmly based on meticulous organization and training and the permanence of its institutions. At this period, the legions, the backbone of the army, recruited only from Roman citizens, still drew most of their men from Italy. Gradually, the citizen colonies founded in the older provinces outside Italy were to provide men for the military career. Each legion had an establishment of something over five thousand men, mostly heavy infantry, backed by small cavalry contingents, catapults, and other engines of war. The legions also provided a wide range of skilled craftsmen and administrators; and individual soldiers, all of whom were required to read and write, could be used on a vast range of government tasks. The 'auxiliary' units were, in the first half of the first century AD, evolving from native irregulars under their own chieftains into regular regiments of provincials, mostly non-citizen, but with Roman commanders. These regiments were normally five hundred strong, cavalry, infantry, or mixed, with status and pay inferior to those of the legions. Both legionaries and auxiliaries, however, enjoyed those extreme rarities in the ancient world, a regular money wage, an assured career, and provision for retirement. Education, training, and opportunities for self-advancement—not to mention self-enrichment—made the army a major force in social mobility. Both serving and retired soldiers were persons of consequence in their communities. Auxiliaries automatically received Roman citizenship on retirement and their sons were eligible to join the legions. These units thus provided a continuous process of turning unlettered barbarians into literate Roman citizens and were a major element in the assimilation of new peoples into the empire.

The force assembled to sail to Britain in AD 43 comprised four legions and about the same number of auxiliary troops, around 40,000 men in all. Facing this disciplined machine, the British forces retained their old character. The permanent warriors were the aristocracy; their favourite weapon was the chariot, which they used for rapid transport in and out of battle and in the handling of which their drivers were extremely skilled. The exact status of the cavalry is uncertain: they were probably men who could provide their own horses, but it is not clear that their prime occupation in life was fighting. The mass of the British armies was the levies, summoned from the farms. Unlike the armoured Romans, the Britons wore little or no body protection and depended on speed, impetus, and the long slashing sword. Before they could get near to Romans in battle order they were liable to lose many men to the clouds of Roman javelins; and in hand-to-hand combat their long blades were at a disadvantage faced with the closed ranks and short stabbing swords of the enemy infantry. Successes by these Celtic troops against the Romans were usually gained in surprise attacks, in ambushes, and when overwhelming detached units by sheer numbers. They could rarely match the legions in pitched battle, and Roman commanders aimed to force them out into the open or to pen them behind ramparts where Roman siegecraft and artillery could beat them down or starve them out. But perhaps their greatest disadvantage in the face of the Romans was that as farmer-soldiers they could only stay in the field for a short part of the year. If they were not sent home, the population starved. The supply system of the Roman army, on the contrary, permitted it to campaign as long as the weather permitted, and to build fortified, well-stocked camps in which to sit out each winter. Such a system permitted a war to be carried on for year after year, and provided the basis for the garrisoning required for permanent occupation. Faced with such an opponent, it is remarkable that the British resisted so long and so hard.

The invasion met with fierce resistance from some of the British tribes. Others, no doubt not sorry to see the Catuvellaunian hegemony in southern Britain destroyed, surrendered easily or joined the Romans. The campaign was crowned by the submission of eleven British kings to the emperor and his triumphant entry into Colchester, for which he had joined his advancing forces, complete with elephants. His delight was marked by the revival of ancient rituals once performed by Republican victors and the proud proclamation of the extension of empire, in which the Conquest of Ocean once more figured large (it was no hollow boast: the army had at first refused to sail).

By AD 47 the Claudian armies occupied Britain as far as the Severn and the Trent. The work of organizing Britain as a regular province was now in progress. Its governorship enjoyed high status. It was reserved for ex-consuls and carried with it the command of an exceptionally large group of legions. In its first century and a half as a province, men of particular distinction were regularly chosen. It was not only a military challenge where reputations could be won, but—though we shall never have the figures to compare income from Britain with expenditure on its defence and administration—it was regarded as a land of natural abundance as late as the fourth century. By AD 47, indeed, the exploitation of Britain's mineral resources—one of the chief objectives of victory—had begun (the silver-bearing lead of the Mendips was being mined under state control by this date). It might have saved Rome much trouble and expense if she had limited her conquest to the area she already controlled; but it is very doubtful whether Roman ambition could long have been restrained, even if the warlike and unstable tribes of the north and Wales had not been a threat to the peaceful development of the south. As it was, the events of the next two or three years committed Rome to a different course.

Roman practice in the provinces was always to shift as much of the burden of administration on to loyal locals as soon as might be. The Claudian intention seems to have been to employ 'client' kings as far as possible—the most economical method, where they were reliable. A substantial part of the south, including Verica's old kingdom, was put in the hands of one Cogidubnus, who may not have been a native Briton. The Iceni of Norfolk were kept as 'allies'; and an understanding was reached beyond the border of Roman rule with Cartimandua, queen of the Brigantes (a vast grouping of clans that encompassed most of northern England), with the object of securing the province from attack from the north. One success of this policy was when Cartimandua handed over the fugitive Caratacus to Claudius; another was the enduring loyalty of Cogidubnus, which was almost certainly of critical importance during later crises in Britain.

The rest of the province the governor would expect to administer chiefly through the tribes, reorganized as Roman local government units (*civitates*) with their nobles formed into councils and holding local magistracies—scaled-down versions of the Roman constitution, in fact, but often adapting existing institutions. In addition, throughout the province ran the writ of the chief financial secretary of Britain, the *procurator provinciae*. These provincial procurators reported direct to the emperor. This was natural enough, since they had particular responsibilities for crown land (the emperors automatically acquired the royal estates of defeated enemies, besides much else by inheritance or confiscation) and crown monopolies; but they also acted as a check on the governor, the emperor's military and judicial representative. Friction was not uncommon and not wholly unintentional.

The train of events that made it certain the province would not remain confined to the south started in AD 47 with the Roman response to raids from outside. Measures taken included not only counter-attacks but also the disarming of Britons within the province. This was bound to have come eventually, since civilians were forbidden to carry arms within the empire except in certain very limited circumstances— something that says much about everyday security in Roman times—but those who had voluntarily submitted to Rome had not expected it to apply to them. The Iceni revolted and were put down by force: the true status of the client kingdoms had now been made plain. The next step was the moving forward of the legion that had been stationed at Colchester and its replacement in AD 49 by a colony of Roman legionary veterans. This was intended as the seat of the Imperial Cult—the formal worship of Rome and the Imperial Family which focused the loyalty of the province—and the veterans were to act as a bulwark against possible revolt. In practice, Colchester was now an ungarrisoned civil city. Perhaps at the same moment, London was founded as a supply port. It is possible that from its beginning it was intended in due course to become the administrative centre of Britain as well. It was in all probability created as a deliberate act, rather than emerging out of a casual settlement of traders, as was formerly thought. The pre-eminence of the Essex coast was now challenged by the Thames, and London's position at the hub of the radiating system of main roads now being built, designed for official purposes, very soon made it also the business centre of the province.

The 50s were a decade of urban development. Only the agricultural hinterland remained largely unchanged, at least on the surface, and progress towards the universal adoption of the money economy was slow. By AD 60, however, with the governor, Suetonius Paullinus, about to subdue the troublesome tribes of North Wales, the province looked set to progress steadily. What went wrong? Why did the provincials, led by Rome's old friends the Iceni and Trinovantes, turn into a raging horde, set on destroying every trace of Rome?

We have only the Roman account, but it is enough to reveal maladministration ranging from the callously negligent to the undeniably criminal. Tacitus makes a general comment on the British character: 'The Britons bear conscription, the tribute and their other obligations to the empire without complaint, provided there is no injustice. That they take extremely ill; for they can bear to be ruled by others but not to be their slaves.' The responsibility for AD 61 cannot be confined to the procurator alone, the traditional villain of the piece. The governor has to take a share, and it cannot stop there. The young Nero, now on the throne, can hardly be blamed directly, for he was under the influence of his 'good' advisers, Burrus, the praetorian prefect, and the philosopher and dramatist Seneca. Of these two, it seems very likely that Seneca, at least, knew what was going on in Britain because he suddenly recalled, in a ruthless manner, large sums of money he had been lending to leading Britons at a high rate of interest. Reports coming out of Britain may well have indicated unrest that might put his investment at risk. In the event, the action fuelled the flames. There are two main threads to the grievances, represented respectively by the Iceni and the Trinovantes. At his death, Boudica's husband, Prasutagus, the client king of the Iceni, had left half his possessions to the emperor, expecting that this would protect his kingdom and family. Agents of the procurator and of the governor, however, had treated this as if it were the unconditional surrender of an enemy. The king's property was confiscated, nobles were expelled from their estates, and taxation and conscription enforced. The Trinovantes were suffering other insults. The main burden of the Imperial Cult, designed to promote loyalty to the emperor, had fallen on their nobles, while the Roman colonists— significantly with the encouragement of serving soldiers—seized their lands and treated them with contempt. They (and probably the aristocracies of other *civitates*) were facing financial ruin, the last straw being the reclaiming of grants made by Claudius and the recall of Seneca's loans. The Imperial Cult, as represented by the Temple of the Deified Claudius at Colchester, was, ironically, the focus of British hatred.

In answer to Boudica's protests, she was flogged and her daughters raped. Rousing her own tribe and her Trinovantian neighbours and carrying other *civitates* with her (but clearly not Cogidubnus) she swept through southern Britain, burning Colchester, London, and Verulamium (near St. Albans), torturing every Roman or Roman sympathizer she could catch, and inflicting devastating defeats on the few Roman units that had been left in that part of the country. The governor only just avoided the total loss of the province. After the eventual victory when he had brought her to battle his retribution was all the more extreme. For a while it looked as if the ruin of the province of Britain would now ironically be achieved at Roman hands. Nero, indeed, at one stage in his reign—possibly earlier, perhaps now—had been inclined to abandon Britain altogether.

In the end two factors saved the province: the intervention of a remarkable new provincial procurator, Classicianus, himself of Gallic origin, and the recall to Rome of the governor.

The recovery that occupied Britain for the decade after Boudica was genuine but unspectacular. There is some evidence that under the last governor appointed by Nero it was beginning to accelerate. But the outbreak of civil war across the empire in AD 69 ('The Year of the Four Emperors') revived the spectre of generals fighting for supremacy. However, the outcome of the wars brought in a vigorous new administration in the persons of the Flavian emperors. For Britain, this spelled provincial renewal and the expansion of Roman power. As Tacitus says, 'Now come great generals and magnificent armies, and with them the hopes of our enemies fall into ruin.'

While the Roman world had been distracted by the civil wars, a fresh outbreak of strife among the Brigantes had lost Cartimandua her kingdom and embroiled the Roman army. The north of Britain was no longer secure. The old policy of client kingship, already shaken by Boudica and previous Brigantian disturbances, was finally discredited. Within a few years even Cogidubnus was probably pensioned off to live in the splendid villa of Fishbourne. By AD 84 or 84 a succession of first-rate governors had carried Roman arms to the far north of Scotland and garrisons to the edge of the Highlands—and were pressing ahead with Romanization. Tacitus, in describing the work of his father-in-law Agricola, uses words that can characterize the Flavian period as a whole:

In order to encourage a truculent population that dwelled in scattered settlements (and was thus only too ready to fall to fighting) to live in a peaceful and inactive manner by offering it the pleasures that would follow on such a way of living, Agricola urged these people privately, and helped them officially, to build temples, public squares with public buildings (*fora*), and private houses (*domus*). He praised those who responded quickly, and severely criticized laggards. In this way, competition for public recognition took the place of compulsion. Moreover he had the children of the leading Britons educated in the civilized arts and openly placed the natural ability of the Britons above that of the Gauls, however well trained. The result was that those who had once shunned the Latin language now sought fluency and eloquence in it. Roman dress, too, became popular and the toga was frequently seen. Little by little there was a slide toward the allurements of degeneracy: assembly-rooms (*porticus*), bathing establishments and smart dinner parties. In their inexperience the Britons called it civilization when it was really all part of their servitude.

To a certain extent this urbanization under the Flavians was less than completely successful. The core of its more securely-based development can reasonably be associated with the visit of the Emperor Hadrian to Britain in person in 122, when existing schemes were revived or replaced and vast new works put in hand. But, looked at in longer perspective, the period from AD 70 to the 160s is the age when Britain truly became Roman and its lasting features as part of the empire emerged. Central to this absorption into the Roman system was the more or less universal devolution of the burden of routine administration to the local aristocracies that replaced the client kingdoms. It was crucially important to this policy to win over the native aristocracy whose confidence had been so disastrously lost in the reign of Nero, and it is in this context that Tacitus must be read.

Archaeologically, we can observe in the late first century and the beginning and middle of the second century the development of the cities and towns of Roman Britain to their full extent. The administrative centres of the *civitates* were provided with civic centres: the forum and basilica that provided market, law courts, civic offices, and council chambers; the public baths which in the Roman world provided the urban centre for relaxation and social life; engineered water supplies; public monuments honouring imperial figures and local worthies; and, in a number of cases, theatres or amphitheatres. This archaeological evidence is all the more significant in that in the empire it was normally the local notables themselves (in council or as individuals) who paid for such amenities, not State or emperor. Occasionally, a great private patron with local connections might favour the town with a benefaction or by acting as friend at court. Only in rare and well-publicized instances did emperors take a part, directly or through their representatives.

The urban expansion could not, of course, have rested solely on the basis of a relatively small native aristocracy taught to accept Roman ways. Indeed, the fact that this spread of town life was followed by the appearance of many 'villas' in the countryside—at this stage mainly modest but comfortable Roman houses, often replacing native homesteads—indicates that the British gentry retained their connections with the land. Most probably they were still chiefly resident on their estates, and many ordinary farmers shared their prosperity. In this period, too, veterans discharged from the legions were principally concentrated in the small number of cities deliberately founded to take them: Colchester, Lincoln, and Gloucester. The flourishing of the towns as a whole, therefore, depended equally on the emergence, well attested, of a lively urban population made up of officials, the professions, traders, and skilled artisans.

Some of these people, particularly among the craftsmen and traders, were immigrants or visitors from other parts of the empire, and many officials were on short-term postings to the province. Nevertheless, the population of Roman Britain remained overwhelmingly Celtic. The ranks of the Roman army, too, were increasingly recruited from the provinces in which units were stationed; gradually Britons who had been, like the mass of their fellows, without the distinctive Roman citizenship when they joined the army, must, as discharged veterans with their grants of citizenship and substantial gratuities, have formed an important part of the solid centre of the Romanized society now emerging. In the towns, slaves were set up in business by their masters; and the frequent use in the Roman world of the power to set slaves free or allow them to purchase their liberty expanded the skilled labour force and added to the

body of businessmen. Whatever the condition of the agricultural labourer, social mobility was high in the skilled and educated portion of society. Whilst the vast bulk of the ordinary
people of Britain undoubtedly remained on the land—and we
have to recall that industry too, was largely concentrated in the
countryside—the towns of the Early Empire came to provide
centres of public life, exchange and services for the rural hinterland, and wide opportunities of advancement at different levels
of society.

Hadrian's revival of flagging Flavian initiatives was thus of
major importance. But his impact on the province was great in
other ways. A man of restless and extraordinary character and
energy, much of his reign was taken up with tours of the
provinces. One of the few emperors deliberately to set himself
against the tradition of expansion of the empire, he was personally unpopular with the Roman aristocracy and many of his
vast enterprises were only partially successful, though whether
due to internal opposition or to flaws in planning is not always
clear. In Britain there are at least three major examples.
Hadrian's Wall was constructed on the line to which Roman
forces had been withdrawn in stages over the thirty years since
the extreme point of expansion, partly because of demands for
troops elsewhere, partly due to fairly serious local reverses in
the field. Such a policy suited Hadrian's general inclination to
limit the empire, and the design of the Wall was brilliantly
original. Partly because of this, however, detailed study of its
early history has revealed a remarkable series of changes of
plan within Hadrian's reign; and it must have cost many times
the original estimates of the expenditure and time required for
completion. Similarly, the agricultural colonization of the Fenlands of East Anglia involved water engineering on a grand
scale, yet many of the farms failed after only a few years.
Hadrianic London, too, saw the demolition of the substantial
Flavian forum and basilica and their replacement with a complex twice the normal size. In Gaul and elsewhere Hadrian
intervened to help cities erect public buildings. In London this

was probably related to the presence of the emperor himself during his visit to Britain in AD 122, which is supported by the erection of a permanent fort in the city at about this time—something almost unparalleled in the cities of the empire outside Rome. But when a great fire had swept through London later in Hadrian's reign the effort to reconstruct areas that had been devastated was relatively short-lived, and in the later years of the second century London shows signs of advanced urban decay.

Hadrian's frontier line from Tyne to Solway Firth represents broadly the limit within which the province settled for most of its history. Yet there were at least three major wars of conquest northwards subsequent to Hadrian, two of them commanded in person by emperors; and for long periods garrisons were maintained at points beyond the Hadrianic line and a degree of control exercised. Indeed, within months of his death in 138 plans were in hand to launch a new invasion of Scotland; and by AD 142 the armies of his generally unmilitary successor, Antoninus Pius, had, like those of Claudius, provided him with a conquest in the prestigious field of Britain. Scotland as far as the Firth of Tay was in Roman hands, and work commenced on a new, shorter, and more simply-built linear barrier to run from the Forth to the Clyde. Elaborate commemorative stone relief sculptures, set at positions along what we know as the Antonine Wall, record the confident mood of what was to be the last period of unconstrained expansion of Roman rule.

In this early Antonine period, the developments we have seen in town and country reached their first peak. Elsewhere, the empire is generally considered to have been enjoying a golden age of tranquillity and prosperity. In Britain the economic system of the Early Empire had been fully accepted, based on a money economy and large-scale, long-distance trade. Culturally, Roman fashions were dominant, and classical art and decoration widely adopted. Perhaps, historically, the most important artistic impact on the Britons of Roman conquest was the introduction of figurative styles, particularly in sculp-

Legend:
- ⊙ Provincial capital
- ■ Legionary fortresses
- ● Coloniae
- Municipia and civitas centres
- ◆ certain ◇ uncertain

0   50   100 miles
0   50   100   150 km

CALEDONIAN TRIBES

Antonine Wall

DUMNONII

VOTADINI

NOVANTAE

SELGOVAE

Hadrian's Wall

Corbridge

Carlisle

LOPOCARES
TEXTOVERDI

CARVETII

BRIGANTES

GABRANTOVICES
◇ Malton

Aldborough

York ■ PARISI

SETANTII

◇ Brough-on-Humber

● Lincoln

DECEANGLI

■ Chester

CORNOVII

ORDOVICES

◆ Wroxeter

CORITANI

◆ Leicester

ICENI

◆ Caistor by Norwich

CATUVELLAUNI

DEMETAE

◆ Carmarthen

SILURES

Gloucester ●

DOBUNNI

Cirencester ◆

Verulamium ◆

TRINOVANTES

◆ Colchester

◆ Caerleon ◆ Caerwent

ATREBATES

London ⊙

CANTIACI

◆ Canterbury

BELGAE

REGINI

Silchester ◆

◆ Winchester

DUROTRIGES

Exeter ◆   ◆ Dorchester

◆ Chichester

DUMNONII

SECOND-CENTURY BRITAIN

ture, wall-painting, and mosaic but also in a vast range of minor arts and crafts—jewellery, pottery, furniture, and household goods of every description. First-rate works of art from Roman Britain are relatively few compared with, say, southern Gaul, but they do exist. The middle range of material is, however, quite plentiful and it is abundantly clear that mass-produced articles were freely available. It is these, rather than the few works of high art that have survived, that reveal an everyday revolution in the way of life since the pre-Roman Iron Age. Roman pottery alone reveals the existence of a 'throw-away society' that is quite different from what went before or came after.

Because it affected the deepest levels of consciousness, the most telling evidence for the assimilation of Roman and native comes from religion. Roman Britain was a religious kaleido-scope, ranging from the formal rites of the Roman State—Jupiter, Juno, and Minerva, in particular—and the Imperial Cult that had more recently been grafted on to it, through a wide range of religions imported both from the neighbouring West and from the East, to the local Celtic cults. People from overseas often retained their own favourite practices: Diodora, a Greek priestess, dedicated an altar at Corbridge in her own language to the demi-god Heracles of Tyre; soldiers from the Netherlands set up others at Housesteads on Hadrian's Wall to their native goddesses the Alaisiagae, Baudihillia and Friagabis, Beda and Fimmilena. But for our purpose the most significant are the 'conflations' or amalgamations of classical and Celtic deities. This was a difficult and uncertain process, since Celtic religion identified its deities much less clearly than Roman, but it was very widespread. That its acceptance was more than superficial is clear, for example, from an altar in the great complex of temple and baths at Bath erected to Sulis Minerva—the native healing spirit of the hot springs conflated with the Roman goddess of wisdom—by Lucius Marcius Memor, *haruspex*. The function of the *haruspices* was divination of the future from the entrails of sacrificial animals. This ancient practice, held in the highest honour, went back to very early Etruscan strands in Italian religion, yet it is here related to a half-Celtic deity. Again, on Hayling Island, a major shrine of the pre-Roman Iron Age—more than likely associated with the king-ship of Verica—was rebuilt subsequently in Roman materials, probably by an architect from Roman Gaul commissioned by Cogidubnus. It is a particularly fine example of a very large class of distinctive shrines known to archaeologists as 'Romano-Celtic temples', found right across Britain, Gaul, and Roman Germany, and quite clearly the expression in Roman architectural terms of a pre-existing type peculiar to the Celtic peoples. They are instantly recognizable, being square, circular, or polygonal structures, usually box-like with a concentric 'ambulatory', and often set within enclosed precincts which may sometimes have preserved sacred groves from pre-Roman times.

At a much less formal level we find in Weardale a cavalry officer giving thanks to Silvanus (a Celtic rural god in Roman guise) for 'a remarkably fine boar no one had previously been able to catch', or at Greta Bridge two ladies setting up an altar to the local nymph. These are typical of the deep belief of both Celts and Romans that every place had its own deity. Romans found no difficulty in accepting these deities of place in the lands they conquered. Indeed, they showed real anxiety to find out their names and honour them, as a precaution if nothing else. The darker side was a belief in ghosts and the need to placate them. Here we are at the heart of Roman religion, very congenial to the Britons, the animistic belief in the localized spirits of hearth, home, family, and ancestors, and of places and objects outside, which long pre-dated the public adoption of the classical gods of Olympus. The black element is repres-ented archaeologically by written curses, some still sickening to read. From Clothall near Baldock comes a lead plate bearing a message written backwards (a practice common in magic), declaring that 'Tacita is hereby cursed, and this curse shall reveal her to be putrefying like rotting blood'. It is surely not just chance that excavation of a temple at Uley in Gloucestershire has approximately doubled the total of curse-bearing tablets known from the entire Roman world. The Britons, we are told by a classical source, were obsessed with ritual. The specifically Roman contributions were to provide new artistic and architectural forms to express religious feelings, and written language in which to make those sentiments clear and permanent. Roman religious practice, with that same sense that informed Roman law, depended on the exact performance of every act and word. The care with which the Romano-Briton phrased his dedications and curses demonstrates how well the new capacity to set wording down indelibly accorded with his own ritual inclinations.

After the invasion of Scotland, Antoninus Pius waged no more aggressive wars anywhere in the Roman world, and in the 160s the mood began to change. In Britain something had gone seriously wrong around 158. There is some evidence that the Brigantes had to be suppressed, a situation perhaps made possible by premature thinning out of troops on the ground in the Pennines under the demands of the occupation of southern Scotland; and it seems the Antonine Wall itself was temporarily lost. A brief reoccupation of Scotland, perhaps after a punitive campaign (though the chronology of this period in the north is exceptionally obscure) was followed by a definitive return to the Hadrianic line. In the reign of the next emperor, Marcus Aurelius, barbarian pressure on the frontiers of the empire generally became serious. The initiative, though Rome did not recognize it for centuries, had passed from her.

For a traveller arriving from the Continent, there was one particularly striking fashion in which Britain would have seemed different from northern Gaul, whose development it had in so many ways paralleled, allowing for the century less of time it had been under Roman rule. The permanent military presence will have made him aware that a primary concern of governors in Britain was always one of defence: there were three legions, two in the west in fortresses at Chester and at

Caerleon in South Wales, and one in the north at York, together with a very large number of auxiliary units, many occupied in containing the nominally pacified tribesmen of the hills inside the province by means of a network of forts and patrolled roads. But the most visible difference in the south was the presence of *town walls*. The building of these walls was not (other than at one period) a general response to a particular crisis. It was a leisurely process, starting in the first century with towns such as Winchester and Verulamium and still in progress in the 270s. By the early second century the three prestigious colonies had walls; and an element of civic rivalry may have stirred elsewhere. The main reason for their walls, however, had to be something sufficiently important to overcome the reluctance of Roman emperors to allow the construction of fortifications that might be held by an enemy or insurgents (locals paid for the walls, but the emperor's express permission was required); and permanent enough for the process to continue even though Britain was several times implicated in major challenges to authority. Lack of defences to the villas rules out a disorderly countryside or fear of peasant revolt. The reason must be the same factor that kept the legions in the province and the auxiliary units stationed where they were—apprehension of barbarian incursion from outside and risings in the hills within the province. The cities and towns, lying on the main roads, were the obvious targets for tribes or war parties on the move. In the ancient world city walls were more or less impregnable, except to armies with sophisticated siege machinery and the logistic support necessary to sustain a prolonged siege, or where the attackers had friends within the town. Against tribesmen, therefore, walls were a first-rate form of civic defence; and their prevalence in Britain must indicate a much greater awareness of threat than was abroad in Gaul.

The walls, however, took a long time to build, and a speedier remedy was sometimes needed. An indication of impending crisis is the appearance on a large number of urban sites in Britain of *earthwork* defences, apparently in the second half of

the second century. At Cirencester, for example, an earth ram-
part was thrown up to link monumental stone city gates and
interval towers already built, as if an urgent decision had been
taken to interrupt the leisurely construction programme and
put the defences into immediate commission. Of the various
candidates that have been proposed for this period of crisis, the
most likely seems the outbreak in the north around 180 which
included barbarian penetration of the frontier, reported widespread damage, and the death of a Roman general. A much less
likely context is the candidacy of a governor of Britain, Clodius
Albinus, for the imperial throne in the years 193-7.

The events surrounding his attempt, however, herald a new
age in the history of the empire, in the course of which Britain's
fortunes diverged much more sharply from that of neighbouring Gaul. Marcus Aurelius' great wars on the Danube, which in
the event marked the beginning of the unrelenting barbarian
pressure in the West, might, had not his death intervened, have
led to his achieving his aim of conquering Central Europe north
of the Danube. Instead, the year 180 saw the breakdown of the
system of nominating successors to the imperial throne that had
produced a century of moderate and extremely able emperors.
The accession of Marcus' dreadful son, Commodus, coincided
in Britain with the outbreak of the serious warfare in the north
mentioned above. In Britain and elsewhere, attempts to tighten
up discipline in the Roman army had ironic consequences. A
short period that saw a return to a rapid succession of murdered emperors and fresh outbreaks of civil war ended not only
with the army in a much stronger position in society but with
other profound changes in the system. The final victor, after the
defeat of Clodius Albinus in Gaul, was the immensely tough
Septimius Severus. But, far from bringing the army back to the
disciplined loyalty of the previous hundred years, Severus'
strategy for the survival of his own dynasty was to subordinate
everything to the interests of the troops.

The third-century emperors abandoned the pretence of rule
by consent. The senatorial class, which the second-century

emperors had, with varying degrees of sincerity, tried to keep involved in the responsibilities of government, both civil and military, lost ground to the career soldiers who were providing the professional officers whom the army increasingly required. The old distinction between Roman citizens and provincials without the citizenship, already fading as more and more of the latter won Roman status, was now swept away and replaced by a new class structure before the law—an upper division (*honestiores*) and a lower (*humiliores*). Significantly, soldiers fell into the former category. By the middle of the century, rampant inflation had severely damaged confidence in the currency; and the old economic pattern of major centres of production serving very large areas of the Roman world by means of long-distance trade based on a money economy was tending to be replaced by more localized industries.

For the first quarter of the third century, Septimius Severus and his dynasty seemed to offer a renewed stability, even if one based on military autocracy. But that in itself was an insecure foundation. In the middle of the century, one assassinated emperor followed another in rapid succession as army officers changed their allegiances. The old, fatal weaknesses of personal ambition and the readiness of the Roman soldier to follow his commander were unchecked. At this point almost total disaster struck as barbarians attacked in both East and West. In the East a newly-invigorated Persian Empire captured the Emperor Valerian, while successive Germanic invasions wrecked the un-walled cities of Gaul and prevented Rome from any more shielding her towns and territories across the Rhine with a permanent military presence. By 260 much of the empire was in a sorry state.

It was formerly believed that Britain had been similarly dev-astated when Clodius Albinus' unsuccessful campaign on the Continent against Severus was supposed to have stripped Britain of troops and opened the way for a major barbarian invasion. The archaeology will no longer support such a hypothesis. Problems with the tribes beyond the northern frontier towards the end of Severus' life did, however, give him a reason to choose Britain to launch a new war of conquest. There was no slackening of Roman ambition. Here the intention was the total subjugation of Scotland, to complete the conquest of the island. There is, indeed, cause to think that the interest of the Severan House in Britain revived a province that had become somewhat run down. Perhaps in connection with the imperial visit itself, London was tidied up, given new public buildings, provided with the longest circuit of walls in Britain and, at some time in the Severan period, its waterfront magnificently re-equipped with continuous quays running for more than half a mile. While the war was being planned, the imperial household itself probably settled at York. Much work had already been undertaken on the forts of the north behind the Wall, many of which seem to have been neglected, since the defeat of the barbarian intruders in the early 180s. There is some reason to think that York itself had assumed some of the governmental functions formerly located at London, perhaps when the Antonine reoccupation of Scotland extended the lines of communication. Sometime early in the third century the city that had grown up alongside the legionary fortress was dignified with the honorary rank of Roman colony. It is not, therefore, surprising to find London and York being chosen as twin capitals when, at some not entirely certain point in the Severan period, Britain was divided into two provinces. This was in line with a new policy to reduce the number of legions under the command of any one provincial governor and thus the temptation to revolt.

The planned conquest of Scotland was called off—but only after substantial successes—owing to the death of the emperor and the pressures on his successor. Security of the frontier was, however, accomplished. Britain as a whole shows every sign of having escaped the disasters of the age elsewhere. There was a slowing of new development, but the towns remained active and the villas were, if not expanded, kept up. Industry, if pottery is an indication, benefited from the problems of its

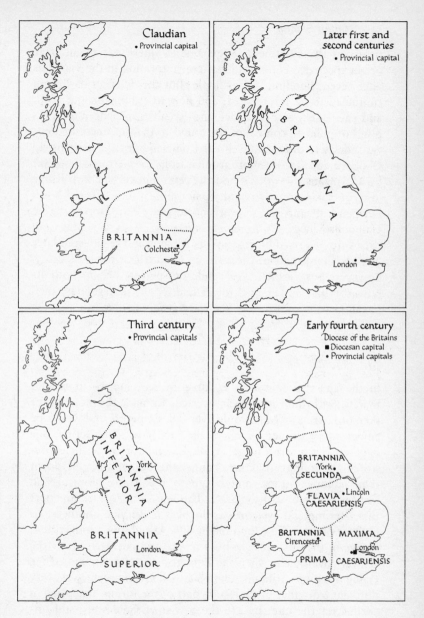

Claudian
• Provincial capital

BRITANNIA
Colchester•

Later first and second centuries
• Provincial capital

BRITANNIA

London•

Third century
• Provincial capitals

BRITANNIA INFERIOR

York•

BRITANNIA
London•

SUPERIOR

Early fourth century
Diocese of the Britains
■ Diocesan capital
• Provincial capitals

BRITANNIA
York•
SECUNDA

FLAVIA
CAESARIENSIS
•Lincoln

BRITANNIA   MAXIMA
Cirencester•
London■•
PRIMA   CAESARIENSIS

THE PROVINCES OF ROMAN BRITAIN

rivals on the Continent. Some public work that might have been expected was not undertaken: restoration in the Fenlands after severe flooding, for example. But the defences of Britain continued to be refurbished, and new forts built on the south and east coast, at Brancaster and Reculver, probably for purposes of political control of the routes to the Continent and not yet indicative of an acute threat from sea-borne barbarians. In Gaul, AD 260 saw yet more trouble from the Germans—not yet by any means the worst—and the central government in Rome lost control. Germany, Gaul, Spain, and Britain adhered to an independent emperor, comprising together the 'Empire of the Gallic Provinces' (*Imperium Galliarum*). This grouping had been foreshadowed under Clodius Albinus and re-emerged later as a structural part of the restored empire. For the time being, however, possession of peaceful, prosperous Britain with its powerful and undamaged forces and its almost legendary propaganda value must have been a considerable comfort to the Gallic emperors.

Britain under the Late Empire

In the 270s the imminent collapse of the empire—imminent, that is, with hindsight—was averted. Romans did not behave then or later as if Rome could ever fall. Emperors and would-be emperors or emperor-makers did not cease murdering one another, but a series of great soldier-emperors nevertheless restored the military balance against the barbarians, put down rival administrations, and began to repair the physical and institutional fabric of the State. This was done to such an effect that the imperial system was enabled to survive another two centuries in the West (and might have lasted much longer) and twelve in the East. In 274 Britain was brought back under the central government when the Emperor Aurelian eliminated the Gallic Empire. Britain's immediate fate, however, was very different from that of the Gallic part of the former independent north-western state. In 276 the towns of Gaul were still un-walled when, as a literary source tells us, the worst of the barbarian invasions yet saw the capture of fifty or sixty towns and their retaking by the Romans. In north-eastern France archaeology has revealed the abandonment in the late third century of villa after villa in what had been a region outstanding for its extraordinarily dense pattern of really large country houses and their estates. These houses were not to be reoccupied.

In Britain the contrast is acute. In the period 250–70 there are signs of a modest amount of building and none of universal neglect, while archaeologists are tending to date an increasing amount of new construction, particularly of villas or of enlargements and improvements to villas, to around 270–5—for example in the villas of Witcombe and Forcester Court, on the western edge of the Cotswolds. An interesting hypothesis has been advanced that there was a 'flight of capital' from Gaul to Britain. There is no positive evidence for this theory yet, but if modified a little it is attractive. It is certainly true that the great age of the Romano-British villa, long recognized as being at its peak in the fourth century, must have had its beginnings in the 270s. It seems unlikely, however, that landowners could have 'extracted their capital' from their ruined Gallic estates (in other words, sold them at a good price). When these estates were reoccupied at the end of the century it was as abandoned land given over to settlers imported by government. Behind the argument, however, lies too parochial a view of land ownership, an unspoken assumption that the typical provincial landowner possessed a single estate and lived in its villa most of the time. Possession of more than one estate was common among the upper classes of the Roman world, where wealth and status were quintessentially marked by landed property, sometimes in many parts of the empire simultaneously. For the pattern of Britain and Gaul at this period it is thus much more likely that owners with land on both sides of the Channel decided to transfer their personal residences from their Gallic villas to their properties in what must have seemed an exceptionally secure haven in an age of extreme danger; and the movement may already have started among the more cautious under the Gallic Empire. Perhaps a small piece of circumstantial evidence is that when the cities of Gaul finally were walled after 276, the circuits, though very strong, were in general short (quite unlike Britain), sometimes more like those of very powerful fortresses than walled towns. This is just what one would expect if there were no longer enough magnates with active local interests who could be tapped for the funds to defend the whole urban area.

Architecturally, the walls of these Gallic fortress cities do have close relations in Britain which are more or less contemporary, but they are not the towns. A number of new coastal fortresses were built in southern Britain—with the same pattern of very high stone walls and massive projecting towers—and older forts such as Brancaster and Reculver were modernized after the same fashion. At a much later date—in the fifth century—they are listed under a commander 'of the Saxon Shore', which has persistently suggested that they originated as a planned system of defence against Saxon sea-pirates. This is probably an anachronism. There is some reason to think that Aurelian's successor, Probus, created a tighter control of both sides of the Channel by establishing in Britain and Gaul similar strings of coastal forts; but the prime purpose has not been proven. The fact that Probus had more than once to quell serious moves against his authority in Britain may suggest that the 'Saxon Shore' had more at this stage to do with political security within the empire than frontier defence. Britain was an important asset—even more so in these straitened times—but control of the Channel was essential to its retention.

This fact was demonstrated in a remarkable fashion. In 287 a senior Roman officer named Carausius, who had been put in charge of a campaign to clear an infestation of pirates out of the Channel, came under strong suspicion of allowing the raids to happen and misappropriating the loot when it was subsequently seized by his fleet. Anticipating execution, Carausius rebelled and took control of Britain. Once again Britain was under the rule of a local emperor. This episode has attracted much romanticizing, but the fact is that neither Carausius nor other Romans before or after him who claimed the imperial title regarded Britain as something separate. Carausius is typical in blandly claiming on his coinage equality and fraternity with imperial colleagues, who, in fact, held the rest of the empire but with whom his fiction implied shared rule of the whole. The Carausian regime proved remarkably hard to dislodge, protected as it was by the sea. Carausius himself was unseated and murdered by Allectus, one of his own men, when he had lost a foothold on the Continent with the end of the siege of Boulogne in 293; but it was another three years before the central Roman government could launch a successful invasion. The Channel had proved formidable again.

Despite the fact that an element of inspired seamanship and a good deal of luck contributed greatly to the defeat of Allectus—not to mention what looks very much like lack of enthusiasm for his cause on the part of the regular garrison of Britain—in fact by 296 the rebel administration in Britain had faced a much more formidable central power. Major changes had taken place in the Roman State in those few years which move us into the period known as the 'Late Roman Empire'. The driving force was the Emperor Diocletian. Rooting himself in Roman precedent like Augustus, he initiated through his reforms a period of change that transformed the Roman State over half a century. He attempted to deal with the chronic political instability by creating a system of two senior emperors (*Augusti*) and two juniors as 'Caesars', with automatic succession. The individual provinces were once again reduced in size, and now grouped in 'dioceses', under a new tier of civilian officers known as *vicarii* to whom the governors (no longer commanding armies) were now made responsible. The frontiers were strengthened by approximately doubling the units of the army, under new commanders. Against domestic conspiracy or military revolt a deliberate attempt was made to create a greater aura around the persons of the emperors. The overall increases in the civil service were noted as phenomenal. The effects on art, fashion, and manners were hardly less pronounced.

The economic ravages of the century had been acute. Manpower shortages were now tackled by imposing rigid controls on the movement of labour, making many occupations hereditary. The problem was exceptionally severe on the land. There, the estate system which under the Late Republic had relied on a ready supply of cheap slaves from foreign wars had, in the course of the Early Empire, moved extensively to letting-out to large numbers of free tenant farmers on short leases. The disastrous economic conditions of the third century over large parts of the empire encouraged drift from the land. In reply, Diocletian virtually created a tied peasantry (the *coloni*) by law. Inflation was—ineffectually—tackled by detailed price legislation (on British duffel coats, rugs, and beer, for example). Persons in the public service were increasingly protected by being paid partially or wholly in kind. Troops, who had formerly had to buy their personal equipment out of their pay, were henceforth supplied from state factories, while officials' allowances came to be valued as much as their salaries. Taxation soared to meet the cost of reform; and the new rigidity of society had to be further tightened against attempted avoidance of the specific tax liabilities imposed on certain classes in the social hierarchy.

The new order must have arrived in full force in Britain soon after the reconquest in 296 by the Caesar in the West, Constantius I, the father of Constantine the Great. His timely rescue of London from a retreating force of Frankish mercenaries who had been in the pay of Allectus was a huge propaganda victory. It will be seen to be prophetic in more ways than one.

Most of the disorder seems to have been in the south, confined to the short campaign when Allectus was defeated. In the north, archaeological evidence for vigorous rebuilding of military installations initiated by Constantius seems more to indicate an intention for the future than repair of damage caused by enemies. The evidence suggests that a lengthy period of peace had allowed maintenance and manning to have low priority. Constantius had different ideas. Indeed, an unconvincing contemporary denial strengthens the impression that he had every intention, when opportunity offered, of launching another of those prestigious campaigns in Scotland that seem to have appealed so much to ambitious Roman emperors. Certainly, he lost no time after he became Augustus in preparing for such a war, and in 306 he was in the field. The sources claim a victory over the Picts (the first time the enemy in Scotland appears under this name); and pottery of the period found at Cramond at the eastern end of the Antonine Wall and from the old Severan fortress on the Tay suggests another sweep up the eastern side of the Highlands as his plan. Like Severus, Constantius returned to York and there died. Like Severus he had had his successor with him.

In the elevation of Constantine the Great by the army, York can fairly be said to have witnessed one of the turning-points in history. It was a curiously haphazard affair, strongly influenced by a German king called Crocus who had accompanied Constantius as one of his principal allies—and was completely contrary to the spirit of Diocletian's settlement. It set off a chain of events that ended with Constantine as sole emperor, putting into supreme power a man quite unlike Diocletian in having little adherence to the traditional past but like him capable of thinking and acting on the grandest scale. Constantine's innovations on the basis of Diocletian's conservative but immense reforms set patterns for centuries to come.

It has long been recognized that the first half of the fourth century was something of a 'golden age' for Roman Britain. We can now see that this was based on sound foundations from the previous century and continued trends already emerging in the 270s. This period of great prosperity certainly continued till the 340s, possibly till just after the middle of the century. It can legitimately be suspected that the most brilliant phase owed something to the favour of Constantine. There is some reason to suppose that, like his father, he too returned to Britain and celebrated military success here. We certainly know that for part of his reign he promoted to major status the mint at London that had been set up by Carausius. It is not impossible, too, that it was he who was responsible for changing London's name to 'Augusta'; and we may strongly suspect that the superb new river face of the walls of the fortress of York was a deliberate expression of the power of the man who had been proclaimed there, and who shared Hadrian's pleasure in vast architectural gestures.

The spirit of the age is typified by the great villas of fourth-century Britain. Socially and economically, the Late Empire in the West was marked by a polarization of wealth and to some extent power between the greater landed aristocracy on the one hand and emperor, court, and army on the other. These forces were often in conflict, but gradually tended to merge. Between them they left relatively little for the old urban middle class and the lesser gentry. Generally in the empire it was on the members of the local councils, the *curiales*, that the burden of paying for the new order fell most heavily. What had once been an honour now became a hereditary burden, and ways out were gradually sealed off by legislation.

Who, then, can have been the obviously wealthy inhabitants of the larger Romano-British villas? Some may have been rich citizens who had transferred themselves from elsewhere. If senators, or imperial officials of appropriate standing, they will have been exempt from the duties of *curiales*. Yet the curious persistence in Britain of forms of Latin indicative of educated speech but tending to be peculiar to the island does suggest that the native aristocracy remained a significant element in society. It is highly probable that they had, exceptionally, not been too badly hit in the previous century. It is tempting to wonder too, whether Constantine may not have shown them special favour.

Like the eighteenth-century English country house, to which they may in many respects reasonably be compared, these villas vary in plan, complexity, and size. Certain features are generally present—notably, construction in permanent materials, central heating (in the form of wood-, sometimes coal-fired hot-air systems), glazing, tessellated floors, and very often one or more complete bath suites. Agricultural buildings normally adjoin, and like their Georgian counterparts it is probable that most had land attached. It is clear from Roman literature that the degree and importance to the individual occupier of any particular villa of its 'economic' activity could vary enormously, from being a major source of income to little more than an amusement. Significantly, the great houses such as Wood-chester, Chedworth, or North Leigh did not stand alone, but formed the top of a very broad pyramid of villas. The modest villas that had developed in earlier times out of Iron Age farms survived, improved, or were replaced by new middle-range and small villas. This is the best evidence for the survival of a solid gentry in Britain. Some villas, it is true, disappear; but this is in the natural order of things even in a completely settled age. It is more important that in this age the villa is becoming a more prominent feature of the landscape, not less.

It has been observed that villas often display duplication in their main facilities. This has led to a somewhat complicated hypothesis to suggest that surviving Celtic custom caused a widespread shared (or divided) use of one complex by two families or two owners. An infinitely simpler explanation is that in the Roman world a gentleman of any consequence travelled with a considerable retinue of servants and friends, and that visiting one another's country houses was part of the regular social round. For journeys, the reputation of inns was so evil that anyone with the right connections preferred to travel by moving from one acquaintance's villa to another. Most Romano-British villas seem to have been connected by a drive or lane to a public road and the majority were within ten miles or so of a town. Their social relationships to the towns, and perhaps even more to one another, are therefore likely to have been as important as their economic effects.

How much the development of the large villas changed the agricultural scene we do not know. As early as the second century an occasional pattern of villa and village has been observed which seems not unlike that of manor house and village in later ages. It may be that in fourth-century Britain there were comparatively few Diocletianic *coloni*—or that changes in the law made little difference to a situation that had long existed in this relatively undisturbed region of the empire. Small, native-style farms are still much in the majority, though there are some signs of consolidation into larger units. A greater change was the encouragement given to the various trades that served the decoration of the great houses. The best known of these are the regional 'schools' of mosaicists—firms or groups of firms with workshops centred respectively on Cirencester, Chesterton (Water Newton), Dorchester (Dorset), Brough-on-Humber, and somewhere centrally in the south. Other trades, working in more perishable materials, perhaps operated in similar fashion—for example fresco-painters (of whose work just enough survives to demonstrate its importance and the quality it could reach); furniture-makers; and other suppliers of major items for the well-to-do household.

The ancient countryside was not exclusively agricultural— nor only for the pleasure of the rich. The falling-off of long-distance trade in the third century had given encouragement to more than one British industry, for example the vast potteries of the Nene Valley. In the fourth century we can observe how a similarly huge ceramic industry in Hampshire which had also expanded in the third century—mostly within the area of the later royal forest of Alice Holt—now captured the London market and flourished greatly.

In these early years of the Late Roman period the principal features of the administrative system had emerged into which the new-style provincial governors fitted. Ultimate decisions might emanate from Milan (which emperors had for some time found more convenient than Rome) or, after 324, Constantinople. But from the time of Constantius I, the central government was for routine purposes situated at Trier, on the Moselle. The head of the civil administration as far as Britain was concerned

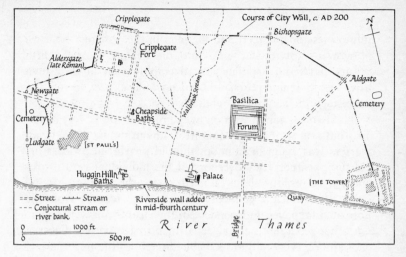

Cripplegate

Course of City Wall, c. AD 200

N

Bishopsgate

Cripplegate
Fort

Aldersgate
(late Roman)

Aldgate

Newgate

Cemetery

Basilica

Cemetery

Cheapside
Baths

Forum

Ludgate [ST PAUL'S]

Huggin Hill
Baths

Palace

[THE TOWER]

=== Street   +++ Stream
--- Conjectural stream or
    river bank

Riverside wall added
in mid-fourth century

Quay

0   1000 ft

0   500 m

River   Bridge   Thames

ROMAN LONDON

was the praetorian prefect of the Gauls, based in Trier, to
whom the *vicarius* of the British diocese was responsible. The
prefecture grouped together Britain, Spain, and northern and
southern Gaul. The headquarters of the British *vicarius* was
almost certainly in London. Under him were four provincial
governors—of Maxima Caesariensis (also probably based in
London), Britannia Prima (Cirencester), Flavia Caesariensis
(Lincoln?), and Britannia Secunda (York?), each with his own
staff. As well as normal civil duties, this structure had a vital
military role in being in charge of supply, including the new
state factories (a weaving-mill of the sort that supplied the Late
Roman army with material for uniforms is, for example, recorded in Britain). A fifth-century document, showing unusual
insignia for the *vicarius* of the Britons, may denote that by that
time at least he had, exceptionally, some troops under his
command. More important is the fact that with supply in
civilian hands there was some potential check on the army.
Socially the senior members of this new administration were
drawn from the educated middle and upper part of Roman
society. The British vicariate could be an important stage in a

fully professional career, and the men in the post of whom we know were not mediocrities. Into the beginning of the fifth century it remained policy not to employ men in their own provinces in senior posts, and most would expect to serve at some stage at the imperial court.

The financial administration of the provinces was very different from that in the Early Empire. Though the financial headquarters was again in London, the old provincial procurators had disappeared. The governors of the individual British provinces were responsible to the *vicarius* for the taxation in kind which the municipal councils were expected to raise from the individual taxpayer. Independent of the *vicarius*, however, were two other separate financial departments each with a diocesan chief officer, eventually responsible directly to the imperial secretariat. One handled taxation in cash, controlled the issue of coinage, and administered mines and certain other operations. The other was responsible for crown property throughout Britain, and to it reported the local procurators who acted as agents in charge. These two branches, however, often worked closely together and could call on the assistance of provincial governors to carry out their functions in the field.

The command structure for the army no longer had to correspond with provinces. At the same time the old distinction between legions and auxiliaries was replaced by a new one categorizing units into garrison, or frontier, troops (*limitanei*) and new, mobile field forces (*comitatenses*), the latter having higher status and remuneration. Many of the old units retained their identity, especially in Britain, where much of the old frontier remained substantially unchanged even if the internal character of units altered. At this time, the units stationed in Britain were classified as *limitanei*, emphasizing its character as a region to be defended rather than a place from which a field army might rapidly be deployed. The commander of a garrison army was entitled *dux*—the *dux Britanniarum* being one such. Mobile forces, on the other hand, tended to be led by a *comes rei militaris*, of superior rank. Under Constantine himself there was only one central field army. But under his warring sons several major field armies emerged, under generals of even higher rank. Certain of these army groups achieved permanence; and smaller task forces drawn from them became operative under such *comites rei militaris*.

The field armies contained both old units that had been retained or reformed and many new ones. Among the latter, an important proportion was raised from peoples of Germanic origin; and in the fourth century there were also many individual German recruits. Something like half the regular army in the West was German, and half Roman, including the officer corps. In 367 the *dux Britanniarum* defeated by barbarians, for example, was named Fullofaudes. By the end of the century, German generals were occupying the very highest commands. Though it was no longer fashionable for such men to adopt Roman names, they fully absorbed the attitudes and ambitions of their native-born Roman equals. However, as a group the fourth-century army officers tended to be noticeably different, culturally, from their counterparts of equivalent rank in the civil service. Important cultural prejudices, not to say dislike and contempt, appeared between certain emperors and their officers on the one hand and leading civilians on the other; and stresses between emperors, their courts, and their new capitals, and the old aristocracy that still looked towards Rome, became socially and politically important.

The final element in the Constantinian equation was the Church. The traditional public religion of the Roman State had sufficed for public purposes, but offered little to the individual. The breakdown of the Antonine peace and the crises of the third century coincided with a widespread desire for a more personal religion that offered consolation and meaning in this world and a better life in the next. Concomitantly, close contact with the East brought about the spread of various Eastern 'mystery religions', religions offering mystic revelation and personal contact with a deity. Hadrian himself had worshipped at the ancient shrine of the Eleusinian mysteries in Greece and a variety of mystery religions became respectable and accepted. The Persian cult of Mithras gained a powerful hold in military and commercial circles, where its insistence on high standards of probity and discipline and its tightly-bound brotherhood matched the ideals and interests of businessmen and officers. Unlike Christianity it was not politically suspect, and therefore not persecuted. In Britain, its chapels appear exclusively where the army or trading community were strong—at Rudchester, Carrawburgh, or Housesteads on Hadrian's Wall, and in London. Its weakness was its very exclusivity, closed to women and largely restricted to one social class. Its rites were sufficiently close to those of Christianity to make them appear blasphemous, and there are possible signs in London and at Carrawburgh, for example, of Christian attack during the Christian ascendancy, and it largely faded away during the fourth century.

Recent work on the survival of Roman Christianity in Britain after the end of Roman rule has suggested that it was more widespread and deeply-rooted than was formerly thought. It is important, however, not to read too much back from the fifth and sixth centuries into the third and fourth. It is generally agreed that Christianity had little hold in Britain before the fourth century. Third-century Britain had, indeed, its martyrs— St. Alban at Verulamium, SS Julius and Aaron probably at Caerleon. The fact that Britain fell in the part of the empire ruled by Constantius I, whose former wife was St. Helena, mother of Constantine, and who permitted the last great persecution to go no further in his area than the demolition of churches, may have had the negative effect of preventing a substantial early martyr cult in Britain. On the other hand, it may also have attracted well-to-do Christians to transfer their residences from more dangerous parts of the empire, unobtrusively increasing the villa-dwelling population.

Britain has produced the earliest set of church plate yet known from the Roman Empire (from Water Newton), almost certainly very early fourth century in date, while British bishops appear only a year after the 'Edict of Milan' legalized the Church, bearing titles indicating as their sees the capitals of the four British provinces. These facts draw our attention to the fundamental change that came with Constantine the Great. The growth of absolutism in the third century had been accompanied by sporadic imperial attempts to introduce a monotheistic state religion. From the time of Constantine the central new factor in Roman politics (and increasingly in the private sphere as well) was ideology. It was no longer sufficient to observe the customary formalities of the state religion to demonstrate loyalty: Christianity, as the new state religion, required belief. Toleration of pagan practices lasted for long. But it was gradually withdrawn, despite intense opposition during the whole of the fourth century from a powerful section of the Roman aristocracy, who both saw the old religion as central to Rome herself, and identified with it in opposition to the court. There were even to be short periods when there were pagan emperors again, sympathetic to them. Within the Church itself, however, there was a further development of immense significance for its future when the Emperor Constantius II decided that it was an imperial duty to ensure unity on doctrine. From the middle of the fourth century the hunting of heresy by the State added a new dimension to the politics of loyalty.

What must, therefore, surprise us in Britain is not that recent research has indicated a considerable amount of Christianization in the fourth century, but that there is not more. This will lead us to examine the apparent nature of the British church. The old notion of urban Christianity and rural paganism certainly cannot be sustained. Urban communities under Constantine are suggested by the bishops mentioned. A very small and unusual church excavated inside the walls at Silchester, and probable examples of the much more common cemetery churches over the graves of martyrs and other prominent Christians at Verulamium, Canterbury, and elsewhere, all point in the same direction. But the grand monuments of fourth-century Romano-British Christianity are associated with the villas:

mosaics at Frampton and Hinton St. Mary, for example, or the wall-paintings of Lullingstone. The distribution of archaeological evidence suggests that the incidence of Christianity was very patchy. A cemetery at Dorchester in Dorset indicates a large and wealthy Christian community, supported by the surrounding villas; elsewhere similar cemeteries have nothing. A remarkable series of lead baptismal fonts has not come from cities but rural locations or small settlements, likely to have been under the eye of the landowning gentry, and a very substantial proportion of them has been found in East Anglia, where there is evidence of real personal wealth in the Late Roman period.

Constantine had dealt a massive blow both to the pagan cults and to the municipalities by distributing the endowments and treasures of the temples to the Church and by diverting funds from the civic treasuries. Wealth in the fourth century increasingly fell into the hands of the greater landowners, on the one hand, and of the State and its institutions, on the other. In Britain, where the villas are such an outstanding feature of the period, it is not surprising to find them in the forefront of the development of Christianity. Nor, under these circumstances, is it surprising to find the evidence so patchy. If the strength of Christianity in a district depended on whether the local landowner was an enthusiastic Christian (or politically ambitious) or not, then this is exactly what we might predict. If the erection of churches and other Christian monuments had depended on an energetic town council, as had the provision of public temples and other civic amenities in earlier periods, then the provision might have been relatively more even. It is clear that substantially more bishops from Britain were present at the Council of Rimini in 359, but no titles survive and it is therefore not known whether they were city-based. It is perhaps significant that some, at least, were known to have had difficulty in raising the money to pay their travelling expenses. If, then, the urban Christian communities were weak—or declined over the century after an initial Constantinian boost—what does this imply for the survival of Christianity after the end of Roman rule? The clue is perhaps the eventual reconciliation to Christianity of the landowning class as a whole elsewhere in the West, if it was paralleled in fifth-century Britain. In that period, quite unlike the fourth century, we ought to see a fairly uniform spread of Christianity among the rural population. Since most of the population had, anyhow, always lived on the land, that ought to lead us to expect the general persistence of Christianity, at least as a subculture. Indeed, the fact that in Late Roman times the rural clergy, unlike their urban counterparts, were relatively poorly educated and socially obscure (in the country, even bishops could be little more than dependants of landowners), may have assisted their identification with the agricultural multitude and ensured the survival of a Church as well as a faith, whatever eventually happened to the landed proprietors themselves.

How long did the villa-based society of the fourth century retain its brilliant early prosperity, so different from so many other parts of the empire? Describing a series of raids by barbarians on places near the frontiers of Britain in AD 360, the well-informed contemporary historian, Ammianus, tells us that at that time 'a pall of fear lay over the provinces' and adds, significantly, that they 'were already exhausted by the accumulation of disaster over the years'. The opinion, moreover, has been advanced, based on the archaeology of the towns, that the latter were 'finished' by about 350 (an opinion which we shall have to interpret later). Details apart, however, the picture is startlingly different from the earlier years of the century.

There is good reason to think that the 'golden age' did not long outlive Constantine himself. His death in 337 left the empire uneasily divided between three sons, Constantius II, Constans, and Constantine II. Britain came within the dominions of the younger Constantine. Dissatisfied with his share, he attacked Constans in 340 and suffered total defeat. It was a long time since the army of Britain had been involved in a military disaster. Subsequent weakness—and possibly disaffection—are probably reflected in a most unusual and un-expected journey across the winter Channel by Constans in person in 343, the brief surviving references to which hint at pressures on the northern frontier. Border problems were cer-tainly acute by 360, the moment to which our quotation from Ammianus refers, when Scots from Ireland and Picts from Scotland had broken an agreement with Rome, implying that there had been earlier threats settled by diplomacy (and prob-ably, in the usual style, with gold). In 364 they were back time and time again, now accompanied by 'Attacotti', probably also from Ireland, and by Saxons. The great barbarian invasion of 367, to which we shall come, was therefore the culmination of a long period of trouble from outside. But events at least as bad had occurred inside the territory under Roman rule.

In 350 a palace conspiracy ended in the murder of Constans and the elevation of an officer of Germanic descent named Magnentius. The Western part of the empire was now at war with the East, under the surviving son Constantius II. The three-and-a-half-year rule of Magnentius, Christian but tolerant of pagans, proved disastrous in its consequences. Constantius II, whom we have already seen assuming the duty of suppres-sing Christian heresies, also hated paganism—indeed he rein-troduced the death penalty for its observance and scandalized the senate by removing the ancient Altar of Victory from the Senate House in Rome. With his final victory, Britain came under special scrutiny. The appointment of the head of the imperial establishment records office, one Paulus, was made with the aim of hunting down dissidents in the island. Black humour aptly nicknamed him 'The Chain'. His brief was to arrest certain military men who had supported Magnentius, but he soon extended this, unchecked, into a reign of terror in which false evidence played a dominant part, horrifying even the most loyal officers. Constantius' own *vicarius* of Britain, Martinus, sacrificed himself in a brave but unsuccessful attempt to put an end to Paulus. One cannot but suspect that many leading families which had been implicated in incidents in the past half-century were drawn into this whirlpool, in addition to those involved in current politics. Confiscations, exile, imprisonment, torture, and executions were approved by the emperor without any questioning of the evidence. The confiscations of property alone must have had a profound effect on the landed prosperity of Britain, while the devastation of morale among both civilians and army can only have left them in a weaker state to resist the barbarian troubles now pressing in on them.

The nadir came in 367. Picts, Scots, and Attacotti invaded Britain; Franks and Saxons attacked the coast of Gaul. Both the central imperial command—the Emperor Valentinian himself was in northern Gaul—and the senior officers responsible for Britain were taken by surprise. The *dux* in command of the static garrison of Britain was put out of action and the *comes* in charge of coastal defence killed. The most remarkable feature was the concerted action of such disparate barbarians. Treachery by native frontier scouts in the north is one attested part of the situation, but to account for the total operation we have to suppose an unknown barbarian with extraordinary military and diplomatic ability. Detailed knowledge of Roman dispositions and understanding of Roman military methods were not hard to come by, with so many Germans in the Roman army (though conscious disloyalty to Rome is very rarely indeed to be suspected). What convinces one of inspired barbarian leadership is the fact of simultaneous attacks by peoples with very different cultures, from homelands relatively distant from one another, with a very clever division of targets—and, perhaps most of all, with the maintenance of complete secrecy. The Romans certainly called it a conspiracy, and it is difficult not to agree with them.

Once in Britain, the barbarians ranged unchecked in small bands, looting, destroying, taking prisoners, or killing at will. The countryside near to roads must have been particularly vulnerable and not all walled towns seem to have resisted. Both civil authority and military discipline broke down. Troops deserted, some claiming—unconvincingly—to be on leave.

Political opportunists seized their chances. Britain was being used as a place of dignified exile for high-ranking offenders, and one well-documented conspiracy among them was nipped in the bud just after the Roman recovery of Britain. But there is also some evidence that one of the provinces of the British diocese (which had now been divided into five, rather than four) fell temporarily into the hands of rebels.

The response of Valentinian to the calamity was the dispatch of a small but powerful task force of élite troops under a *comes rei militaris*, Theodosius, who was the father of the later Emperor Gratian and grandfather of Theodosius the Great, and whose own father had himself served as a *comes* in Britain, under Constans. Such task forces became a frequent method of dealing with emergencies under the Late Empire: Britain had at least once already been the scene of such an expedition (in 360), possibly more than once. At this time these forces were usually made up of *comitatenses*. From the end of the fourth century, barbarian war bands under their own kings, even whole tribes, became more and more often accepted into Roman armies. Task forces thereafter tended to be made up of a mixture of whatever regular troops could be found and barbarian allies, or sometimes barbarians alone on contract for a specific campaign or operation. Looking forward, it is important to realize that in the fifth century, as military practice evolved out of that of the fourth century, 'the barbarians' were not like some hostile aliens from outer space but were a familiar fact of life. Barbarian warriors were frequently employed against other barbarians in the suppression of internal disorder, and for the prosecution of Roman civil wars.

Theodosius' conduct of the campaign and subsequent reconstruction of Britain seems to have been both brilliant and thorough. London was spectacularly relieved. Garrison troops were reassembled, deserters pardoned, and an effective army recreated. The barbarian war parties on land were picked off one by one and the Saxons defeated at sea. Goods stolen from the provincials were recovered and returned. Civil authority was restored under a new *vicarius*; the province that had been lost to rebels was regained and named Valentia in honour of Valentinian, and his eastern colleague and brother, Valens. Forts were rebuilt and damaged cities restored.

The extensive remodelling of town defences in Britain by the addition of prominent external towers, dated archaeologically to somewhere in the middle of the fourth century, is more convincingly to be attributed to Theodosius' initiative than to any other, although the variety in design and arrangement does suggest that, once again, the cost and responsibility fell on the local councillors. However, the fact that it is always the full circuit that was retained in use has very important implications for the state of the towns in the middle and late fourth century. Such wide circuits cannot have been kept solely to provide military strong points or even as refuges in time of danger for a dispersed rural population. There was something worthwhile defending with permanent works. What, then, are we to make of the notion that the towns of Britain were 'finished' by about 350? The unspoken assumption that fourth-century towns were of the same sort as those of the second is clearly mistaken. We have, of course, to be careful not to assume that all towns changed in the same ways. Yet the decay or disuse of civic public buildings is hardly surprising in the context of municipal treasuries raided by central government and councils made up of now unwilling members, Fourth-century legislation repeatedly tried to prevent members of the class that now had the hereditary obligation to serve from moving their main residences away from the towns, while those in higher social classes were exempt from municipal obligations. The new element in society was the vastly-expanded bureaucracy, and it is in their direction that we should probably be looking. Five governors, their staffs, households, companies of guards, and the many others connected with them needed housing; and there were numerous other officials with inflated establishments and life-styles supported by substantial allowances. At each level in the hierarchies, expectations existed which in the end filtered down from the lavish grandeur of the Late Roman court. Large areas of fourth-century capitals such as Trier or Arles, once normal municipalities, were given over to palaces and other associated official buildings. On a smaller scale, we ought to expect such a pattern in many towns in Britain. In fact, archaeology has demonstrated the building of large town houses in places as different as London and Carmarthen, and urban development into the middle of the fifth century at Verulamium and, of a distinctive sort, at Wroxeter. In the cultivated open spaces of this period observed within the city walls in excavations we should perhaps see the gardens and grounds of the new-style establishment rather than a decay represented by abandoned building sites. Indeed, in London and York at least we may reasonably expect the presence of emperors themselves from time to time to have made a mark on the archaeological record.

There is no reason to think that the Theodosian restoration was other than outstandingly successful. Archaeologically, it is clear that many villas continued in occupation; some were enlarged and others built from scratch. Hadrian's Wall was occupied to the end of Roman rule, even if individual garrisons were smaller than before. A new system of signal stations was established on the north-east coast. Much industry had been interrupted by the war of 367, but the many changes in pattern after it indicate vigour and new initiatives. Not surprisingly, some pagan religious sites disappear, but others continue in cult use, while still others show signs of conversion to new uses, some perhaps Christian, towards the end of the century. The forty years from 369 do not have the brilliance of the early fourth century, but the island does not provide any evidence for the sort of despair that the historians report for the 50s and 60s. In order to understand what happened in 409 it is important to realize that in the last part of the fourth century Roman Britain had not been running rapidly downhill.

This period is, in fact, marked by two more occasions on which major attempts on the imperial throne were launched from a base in Britain. In 382 a victory over the Picts by a general named Magnus Maximus (Macsen Wledig in Welsh legend) created for him a reputation that led to proclamation as emperor and the rule, for five years, of the part of the empire represented by the Gallic prefecture—Britain, Gaul, and Spain. In Britain, some forts, notably in the Pennines and Wales, were abandoned at this time and the Twentieth legion was withdrawn from Chester, but it remains still entirely uncertain whether Maximus' campaigns and eventual defeat at the hands of the Emperor Theodosius the Great had any significant overall effect on the defensive capability of the army in Britain. Between 392 and 394 Britain was peripherally involved in another palace revolt for the duration of which Theodosius lost control of the Western empire, but the significance of this incident lies more in the appearance of a general, a Frank in this case, overshadowing a compliant emperor in the West. The death of Theodosius in 395 made this new balance of power in the Western imperial government the rule, rather than the exception, for the rest of its history. The joint accession of Theodosius' sons, Honorius in the West, and Arcadius in the East, inaugurated a period in which the pattern of government in the two halves of the empire diverged fundamentally. In the East, it remained firmly in the hands of the emperor, or his chief civilian minister. In the West a powerful landed aristocracy, rooted in its estates, vied for influence with the professional soldiers who commanded the armies. After three-quarters of a century, both these parties were to come to the conclusion that they could manage without an emperor in the West.

The End of Roman Rule

The effective control of the West by the late Emperor Theodosius' chief lieutenant, Flavius Stilicho, Vandal by birth, was accompanied by a claim to the East as well. Plot, counterplot, and civil war between Stilicho, Honorius, the Western senate, and the Goths under Alaric did much to ensure in the long term the collapse of Roman rule throughout the West. In Britain, initial successes against Picts, Scots, and Saxons, and restoration of defences under Stilicho's direction were probably followed at the very beginning of the fifth century by some posting elsewhere of troops. We do not know the extent of the postings, but the cessation of bulk import of new coinage in 402 must mean that neither remaining regular troops nor civil officials were henceforth paid from central sources. It is not surprising that we find a mood of extreme discontent. In 406 the army in Britain elevated the first in a rapid succession of three emperors. On the last day of that year, large numbers of barbarians crossed the Rhine. The central government withdrew the administration of the prefecture of the Gauls to Arles, and had no time to deal with usurpers in Britain.

The third usurper ran true to form, seizing Gaul and Spain, and for some while was recognized as a legitimate colleague by the unwilling Honorius. Once again, we do not know if there was an overall reduction in the garrison of Britain, but some further withdrawal of regular units seems likely. The northwestern empire of Constantine III, however, was to be the last of its kind, and before it was finally extinguished Britain had ceased for ever to be under any sort of imperial rule.

We know tantalizingly little about the process by which this happened, but something can be pieced together. In 408 the absence of the bulk of Constantine's army in Spain left him unable to deal with heavy barbarian attacks on Britain. In 409 the mutiny of that army under its British-born commander (and his deliberate incitement of the barbarians in Gaul) coincided with renewed assaults on Britain by enemies who included Saxons. At this point, Britain, too—along with parts of Gaul—rebelled, expelling Constantine's administration. Britain successfully took on the barbarian invaders, and henceforth broke decisively with Roman rule.

How Britain expelled the invaders and what was then the state of the country can only be the subject of informed speculation. There are slight hints that Stilicho and Honorius had taken some steps to encourage local organization of, or payment for, defence. It is most unlikely that the regular army was retained when Constantine's officers were deposed, or that the elaborate administrative structure which supported it was manned and paid. Under the Late Empire, the landed class strongly resisted both the conscription of the agricultural labour force into the regular army and the payment of taxes. Elsewhere in the fifth century units whose pay stopped disbanded and dispersed or settled on the land. Indeed, from AD 455 the final running-down of the Western regular army seems to have been in progress. In Britain, with no central government, it is all the more likely that in the years from 409 groups of barbarians were paid to undertake the fighting, and some of these may already have been brought in under Constantine III or even Stilicho.

There is no sound reason for thinking that the Britons elevated any more emperors, or re-created any of the mechanisms of central government. Not only had very few of them had experience of senior office (unlike recent Gallo-Romans), but if they shared the sentiments of the landed class elsewhere in the fifth-century West, they are most unlikely to have wanted to reassume the burdens of supporting the system of imperial administration once they had been rid of it. The critical success of the Flavian governors of Britain in the first century had been to convince the native aristocracy that its advantage lay with Rome. There is no good reason to think that the events of 409 had destroyed the position of the landowning class. They are, however, very likely indeed by now to have lost confidence in the system of emperor, bureaucracy, and army as the best way of securing their still prosperous way of life. They will not have been encouraged by the ruthless political persecution in Gaul by Honorius' officers after the fall of Constantine III.

The presence of a full paper establishment of military and civil posts for Britain in the *Notitia Dignitatum* suggests that into the fifth century it was assumed centrally in the imperial ministries that Britain would be recovered—as it had so often been in the past. There was, in fact, only one short period, from 425 to 429, when a Roman military intervention in Britain was again a serious possibility. But by that time other groups of well-to-do Roman provincials, particularly in a large area of Gaul, were starting to settle down tolerably comfortably, employing, in alliance with, or under the rule of, barbarians.

Provided that the barbarians remained amenable, any of these arrangements might suit the gentry better than direct imperial rule. But for the weakened middle and artisan classes, who in the fourth century had depended more and more on the army, civil service, and urban church for jobs, patronage, or markets, the change must have been disastrous. In Britain, the Roman archaeology supports such a picture. Early in the fifth century, the massive pottery industry comes to an apparently abrupt end; by 420–30 coinage ceases to be in regular use. These facts, incidentally, make the dating of the end of the occupation of Roman sites in the fifth century much more difficult than in earlier periods. There is, however, certainly no evidence for villas having come generally to a violent end. Signs of how late towns might be active vary a good deal. At Lincoln we find a main street being resurfaced well into the fifth century; in London imported Mediterranean pottery in the ash of the heating system of one house combines with other evidence to suggest normal occupation in the early fifth century; the forum at Cirencester was being kept up after the cessation of general circulation of coins; and at Verulamium a sequence of important buildings succeeding one another on the same site is closed, strikingly, by the laying of a new water-main at a time that cannot be far short of the middle of the century.

After the break with Rome the Britons, we are told, lived under *tyranni*, or 'usurpers', best interpreted as local potentates who had filled the vacuum left by the removal of legitimate authority. Their background was probably very varied, some perhaps landowners, others military men, Roman or barbarian, who had been invited to take control or seized power. At Gloucester, a rich warrior burial is British in character rather than Saxon, and may represent a *tyrannus*, or a *condottiere* in local pay. At Wroxeter, ambitious fifth-century timber buildings may well represent the headquarters of such a leader.

In 429 St. Germanus, a prominent Gallo-Roman bishop who moved in high Roman circles, visited Britain to combat heresy, debating publicly with British magnates at Verulamium 'conspicuous for their riches, brilliant in dress, and surrounded by a fawning multitude'. The visit to Britain he repeated around 446/7, though apparently in deteriorating circumstances. At least until the 440s, therefore, something survived in Britain that was very like 'post-Roman' or 'post-imperial' life elsewhere in the West.

2. The Anglo-Saxon Period
(c.440–1066)

═══════

JOHN BLAIR

The Age of the Settlements

THE sources for the fifth and sixth centuries are so few that they can all be listed here, and so unsatisfactory that their faults must be clearly stated. On the one hand is the archaeological evidence, mainly objects from graves in pagan cemeteries. This evidence cannot lie, but the questions which it answers are strictly limited. On the other hand is a small group of texts, annals, and fragments. Of these the only substantial contemporary work is *The Ruin of Britain*, a tract written in the 540s by a British monk named Gildas whose purpose was to denounce the evils of his day in the most violent possible language. The Venerable Bede, a monk in the Northumbrian monastery of Jarrow, completed his great *Ecclesiastical History of the English People* in 731. This overshadows all other sources for the seventh and early eighth centuries, and although the invasion period was remote from Bede's own day he provides some surprisingly well-founded scraps of tradition. The only other narrative sources are fragments of chronicles preserved in later compilations, a few poems, and passing references by Continental writers. Of a very different kind are the late Saxon annals known collectively as *The Anglo-Saxon Chronicle*, which give a year-by-year summary of events in the southern English kingdoms. The early annals are much less reliable than those for later centuries, and their chronological framework is suspect before the late sixth century.

Thus there is no near-contemporary source of Anglo-Saxon origin. The reason is obvious enough: the Germanic peoples were illiterate during their first two centuries in Britain. So their early fortunes can only be glimpsed through the hostile eyes of Britons, through the ill-informed eyes of foreigners, and by means of their own half-remembered traditions. Until the late sixth century, informed guesswork must make do for history.

Archaeology provides the first clue, for it shows that there were Germanic warriors in Britain some years before 410. Late Roman cemeteries, especially along the Lower Thames Valley from Oxfordshire to the Essex coast, have produced burials with belt-fittings of a type worn by Frankish and Saxon mercenaries in the Roman army. If such troops were settled in Britain, as they certainly were in Gaul, the mid-fifth-century invaders may have joined relatives who had come two or three generations back. Sunken huts with gable-posts are characteristic of English settlement in the fifth and sixth centuries, and over two hundred of these have been found at a huge site near Mucking on the Thames estuary. It has been suggested that this complex housed mercenaries who were settled in c.400 to guard the approach to London. If so, the continuous history of Anglo-Saxon settlement begins under Roman rule.

The English of later centuries dated their ancestors' arrival some decades after this, and it does seem to have been from the 430s onwards that Germanic settlers arrived in large numbers. Before considering this remarkable process, it must be asked who the invaders were and what they were like. The first question is answered, almost as well as any modern scholar can answer it, in a startlingly well-informed passage quoted by Bede from an unknown source:

They came from three very powerful Germanic tribes, the Saxons, Angles and Jutes. The people of Kent and the inhabitants of the Isle of Wight are of Jutish origin, and also those opposite the Isle of Wight, that part of the kingdom of Wessex which is still today called the nation of the Jutes. From the Saxon country, that is, the district now known as Old Saxony, came the East Saxons, the South Saxons and the West Saxons. Besides this, from the country of the Angles, that is, the land between the kingdoms of the Jutes and the Saxons, which is called *Angulus*, came the East Angles, the Middle Angles, the Mercians, and all the Northumbrian race (that is those people who dwell north of the River Humber) as well as the other Anglian tribes. *Angulus* is said to have remained deserted from that day to this.

Archaeology confirms Bede's analysis: objects found in English graves are comparable to those from North Germany and the southern half of the Danish peninsula. Some urns from the fifth-century cremation cemeteries in East Anglia may even be work of the same potters as urns found in Saxony, and Kentish pottery and jewellery resembles material from Jutland. A district north-east of Schleswig is called to this day Angeln. To Bede's list we can probably add Frisians, mixed with Saxons who seem to have been infiltrating the coastal settlements of Frisia in the early fifth century. Even Bede's statement that some of the homeland settlements were deserted is confirmed by excavations at Feddersen Wierde, near the mouth of the Weser. Here a village of large timber buildings was abandoned in *c.*450, apparently in consequence of rising sea-levels. With the natural fertility of lowland Britain, and the evidence that its inhabitants deliberately imported mercenaries, this flooding of coastal settlements helps to provide an explanation for the Migrations.

Bede's racial division of the kingdoms of his own day is probably over-neat. The men of Kent may well have been mainly Jutish, and the other major peoples certainly thought themselves either 'Angles' or 'Saxons'. But archaeology does not suggest a very firm distinction, and by the late sixth century, when the kingdoms emerge into the light of day, there is much blurring at the edges. Thus, the finest metalwork of the East Angles resembles that of Kent, and their royal dynasty seems to have been Swedish. Sea-passage must have weakened ethnic ties, and new types of settlement and social organization apparently developed to suit the needs of pioneer colonists. It is worth noting, for instance, the contrast between the large rectangular halls at Feddersen Wierde and the formless clusters of little sunken huts which are found on English sites. What mattered was not so much that the settlers were Angles, Saxons, or Jutes, as that they belonged to the same broad culture as southern Scandinavia, Germany, and northern France. Their earliest known poems include hero-legends set in Denmark and Frisia; an early seventh-century East Anglian king possessed Swedish and Gaulish treasures; and Christianity reached England through a Kentish king's marriage with a Frankish princess. Britain exchanged the Roman Empire for another, if very different, international community.

What were these people like? Obviously they were far less civilized than the Romans, yet they had their own institutions which proved astonishingly tough. Much that the first-century historian Tacitus wrote of the *Germani* applies to their distant descendants in England. As with the *Germani*, so throughout Anglo-Saxon history, the strongest social bonds were the claims of kinship and the claims of lordship.

Kin-groups were close-knit in the homeland, and they remained so in England. The families and dependants of one man may sometimes have formed their own settlement units, with shared resources and systems of land-allotment. The influence of such extended 'affinities' on the character of the settlements is shown by the numerous place-names ending -*ing*, -*ingham*, and -*ington*. Hastings means 'the people of Haesta', Reading 'the people of Reada', Wokingham 'the farm of Wocca's people', and so on. Although it is now thought that not all of these names belong to the first settlement phase, many are early and important and refer to large tracts of land. They show that when territories came to be defined, it was often in terms of the tribal groups which had settled them. Society developed, but family loyalties remained vital. Safety lay in knowing that relatives would avenge one's death, and to neglect such vengeance meant undying shame. Already in Tacitus' day, however,

honour might be satisfied by a *wergild*, a payment by the slayer
to his victim's kin. Anglo-Saxon law codes list scales of *wergilds*
in accordance with the victim's rank, and kings increasingly
encouraged this non-violent type of retribution.

Tacitus also stresses the loyalty of the *Germani* to their lords.
Sometimes they had hereditary kings, but in battle they were
usually led by elected chiefs: 'It is a lifelong infamy and re-
proach to survive the chief and withdraw from the battle. To
defend him, to protect him . . . is the essence of their sworn
allegiance.' Nine centuries later, in 991, an Anglo-Saxon army
was defeated by Vikings at Maldon on the Essex coast. By then
England was a civilized state, long since Christianized; yet the
words which a contemporary poet ascribes to one of the defenders after his leader's death are a clear echo of Tacitus:

> 'I swear that from this spot not one foot's space
> Of ground shall I give up. I shall go onwards,
> In the fight avenge my friend and lord.
> My deeds shall give no warrant for words of blame
> To steadfast men on Stour, now he is stretched lifeless,
> —That I left the battlefield a lordless man,
> Turned from home. The irons shall take me,
> Point or edge.'

Clearly, loyalty to lord might sometimes conflict with loyalty
to kin. In the interests of good order and their own authority,
later kings tended to promote lordship: thus King Alfred's laws
allow any man to 'fight on behalf of his born kinsman, if he is
being wrongfully attacked, except against his lord, for that we
do not allow'. But on both counts, Anglo-Saxon society always
set great store by faithfulness and the keeping of oaths.

Their principal gods were those of later Norse mythology,
Tiw, Woden, and Thor. They are remembered in the day-names
Tuesday, Wednesday, and Thursday, as well as in a few place-
names (Tuesley (Surrey), Wednesbury (Staffs.), Thursley (Surrey), etc.) which presumably indicate cult centres. Even when
converted, the English named one of the main Church festivals

after their old goddess Eostre. Shrines, like those of the *Germani*, were in remote places, in woods or on hills: a few place-names include the element *hearg* (shrine), as at Peperharrow (Surrey) and Harrow-on-the-Hill. Since later Church councils forbade the veneration of 'stones, wood, trees and wells', it can be presumed that such activities featured in pagan English cults. At least in its outward forms, this religion does not look so very different from that of the pagan Britons under Roman rule.

The narrative of events before *c.*600 does not amount to much. Plagued by the Picts and Scots, says Gildas, the British under the 'proud tyrant', Vortigern, imported the first Saxons to defend the east coast. Bede and other sources add that the Saxons were led by brothers named Hengist and Horsa, who founded the kingdom of Kent, and date their landing to about 450. Although this is rather too late, the tale is very consistent with the archaeological evidence: if Germanic mercenaries were settled under Roman rule, it is entirely likely that the successor states continued the same policy. Then, according to Gildas, the mercenaries rebelled and attacked their hosts; many years of inconclusive warfare followed, culminating in a major British victory, perhaps in *c.*500, at an unidentified place called *Mons Badonicus*. Meanwhile, the *Chronicle* notes the arrival of other chieftains on the south coast, the semi-legendary ancestors of later kings: Aelle in Sussex in 477, and Cerdic and Cynric in Wessex in 495.

One figure from these years who is familiar to everyone is, of course, Arthur. Unfortunately he has only the most shadowy claims to historical reality. The two or three possible fragments of genuine tradition were written down centuries later, and the legends which have gathered around his name are romantic inventions from the twelfth century onwards. We can only say that there seem to have been memories of a British war-leader called Arthur, who was associated with the battle of *Mons Badonicus* and subsequent campaigns. Possibly there was such a chieftain or over-king, the last man to unite the former Roman province before it collapsed finally into a patchwork of

British and Anglo-Saxon states. So general is our ignorance of major political events that there seems little point in speculating further.

Gildas says that the peace won at *Mons Badonicus* lasted until his own time, fifty years later, when there were five British kingdoms ruled by wicked 'tyrants'. How far their power still extended into the future English lands is a matter for conjecture, but the re-fortification of hilltop sites in the south-west suggests many years of inconclusive skirmishing. Through all this time, as excavated cemeteries prove, the invaders were pushing steadily further inland, up the Thames Valley, westwards from East Anglia, and northwards from Wessex. The *Chronicle* shows the Wessex Saxons advancing into Wiltshire in the 550s; capturing a large block of the South Midlands in 571; and winning a decisive battle at Dyrham (Glos.) which gave them Gloucester, Cirencester, and Bath in 577. Meanwhile, other English kingdoms were emerging from the shadows: the East Angles, the East Saxons, the Mercians, and the Northumbrian kingdoms of Bernicia and Deira. By the end of the century we are again on the firm ground of some reliable facts, and find the invaders in permanent control of half the island.

What had happened to the native peoples? Sixth-century Scotland was still mainly Pictish, though the settlements of Irish (the future 'Scots') on the west coast had created a settled kingdom, Dalriada. Centuries later, a king of Dalriada was to initiate the formation of a united Scotland. There were also three northern British kingdoms: Strathclyde, centred on Dumbarton, Rheged on the Solway Firth, and Elmet in the region of Leeds. Northumbrian designs on the Picts were ended by a major defeat in 685, and expansion here was mainly at the expense of the Britons. Strathclyde survived, but Rheged and Elmet were swallowed up by Northumbria during the late sixth and seventh centuries.

The main British enclave was, of course, Wales. Refugees from the east had doubtless swelled its population. Christianity survived, and with it some distinct traces of Roman culture. Scores if not hundreds of little monasteries were probably founded there during the sixth century, and charters from south-east Wales suggest the continuance of functioning Roman estate units. The kingdoms of Gwynedd, Dyfed, Powys, and Gwent existed by *c.*550, and some minor kingdoms by the end of the century. At least two of Gildas's tyrants ruled in Wales: Maglocunus (Maelgwn) of Gwynedd, 'first in evil, mightier than many both in power and malice', and Vortipor (Gwrthefyr) of Dyfed. Vortipor's monument still remains in a Dyfed churchyard—a reassurance that some substance underlies the rantings of Gildas:

Your head is already whitening, as you sit upon a throne that is full of guiles and stained from top to bottom with diverse murders and adulteries, bad son of a good king . . . Vortipor, tyrant of the Demetae. The end of your life is gradually drawing near; why can you not be satisfied by such violent surges of sin, which you suck down like vintage wine—or rather allow yourself to be engulfed by them? Why, to crown your crimes, do you weigh down your wretched soul with a burden you cannot shrug off, the rape of a shameless daughter after the removal and honourable death of your own wife?

Cornwall, Devon, and Somerset formed the British kingdom of Dumnonia. Its king, according to Gildas, was as bad as the others: 'Constantine, tyrant whelp of the filthy lioness of Dumnonia.' The inhabitants were pushed back by the Anglo-Saxons during the seventh and eighth centuries, though Cornwall held out until 838. Thanks to this relatively late conquest, much survived. Excavation suggests that in some of the old cities, especially Exeter, Dorchester (Dorset), and Ilchester, life of a sort trickled on through the fifth and sixth centuries. Many major churches in these counties have Celtic origins: excavations at Wells in 1978–80 revealed a sequence of religious buildings from a late Roman mausoleum to the Anglo-Saxon cathedral. Here, as in Wales, smaller churches can often be traced back to a Celtic monastic enclosure (*llan*) or a cemetery around a martyr's grave (*merthyr*).

The hardest task is to estimate British survival in the regions which were firmly Anglo-Saxon by 600. From the facts that England in 1086 probably contained less than half its late Roman population, and that even this was after growth during the tenth and eleventh centuries, it is clear that depopulation in the fifth and sixth centuries was indeed drastic. Many fled westwards, or else to Brittany, and epidemic disease may have played its part. More generally, the Romano-Britons simply suffered a common fate of shattered societies; the decline in numbers is perhaps the clearest sign that their society *was* shattered. This is not to say that none remained: there are hints that the population contained substantial British elements, especially in the north and west. Sometimes (in the early Kentish laws, for instance) they appear as peasants or perhaps semi-servile estate labourers—which helps to explain how elements of Roman land organization may have passed into English society. Significantly, the English word *Wealh* ('Welshman', i.e. Briton) came to mean 'slave', making it hard to know whether the place-name Walton means 'the Britons' settlement' or 'the slaves' settlement'. However numerous, they were subservient: little of their culture passed to the Anglo-Saxons, and almost none of their language.

The early Anglo-Saxons were a non-urban people: their important places were important for hierarchical rather than economic reasons. But the view that they looked on the crumbling Roman towns with nothing but superstitious fear goes too far. The English knew what a *ceaster* was (the word is used with remarkable consistency), and often they knew its Roman name: *Mamucion* becomes *Mame-ceaster* (Manchester), *Venta* becomes *Ventan-ceaster* (Winchester), and so on. Towns occupied focal points in the road system, and their walls were strong. They were good places for chieftains to make their headquarters, and some towns may never quite have lost their local administrative functions. This does not, of course, amount to urban life: the Roman towns were not totally abandoned, but *as towns* they died.

Why was Roman Britain obliterated so much more completely than Roman Gaul? One reason is that the settlers were different: the Franks and Visigoths had come to know far more about Roman ways than the Angles and Saxons ever did. But it may also be true that the Britons themselves had changed greatly between the early fifth and mid-sixth centuries. The earliest Welsh poems show a society remarkably like that of the Saxons, dominated by the same loyalties and with the same emphasis on treasure, gift-giving, and the fellowship of warriors in their chieftain's hall. Even if no Saxon had ever set foot in Britain, it may be that its Roman civilization would have proved too fragile to last.

The Seventh Century

The first impression of early seventh-century England is that it was divided into large kingdoms: Kent, Sussex (the South Saxons), Wessex (the West Saxons), East Anglia, Essex (the East Saxons), Mercia (including the Middle Angles), and Northumbria (comprising Bernicia and Deira and, a little later, Lindsey). Reality was not quite so neat. Kingdoms were only gradually emerging from a state of flux: Middlesex, for instance, is probably the remains of a much larger Mid-Saxon territory dismembered before any surviving records could note it. There were also an unknown number of smaller peoples, lying between the big kingdoms or absorbed within them. Some, like the Hwicce of Worcestershire and the Magonsaete of the Welsh border, had their own kings who were gradually subordinated as the 'sub-kings' or 'aldermen' of greater rulers. There may have been many others: Surrey had a 'sub-king' named Frithuwold in the 670s, and it is quite possible that his ancestors had been rulers of an independent kingdom. There are also occasional hints of local separatism, and resentment against the bigger powers. Bede says that in 643 a monastery in Lindsey refused to receive the Northumbrian King Oswald's corpse, since although they knew he was a holy man 'he had

POWYS Kingdoms ruled by Celts

ENGLAND IN c.600

come from another province and had taken authority over them'. It is possible that in 600 English kings could be counted in dozens.

Even the big states experienced a shifting power balance. Bede and other sources mention a series of over-kings (*Bretwaldas* or *Brytenwaldas*), from various kingdoms but successively wielding authority over all or most of the Anglo-Saxon peoples. Whether or not the *Bretwalda*-ship was a formal office (which seems doubtful), it was certainly possible for an individual king to establish an extensive, if short-term, political dominance.

The first four in Bede's list, Aelle of Sussex, Ceawlin of Wessex, Æthelberht of Kent, and Raedwald of East Anglia, bring us to the 620s. We cannot say what their authority may have meant outside their own kingdoms, though we know that in 616 Raedwald took an army through Mercia, and defeated the Northumbrians on their own frontier. The fifth and sixth were both Northumbrian rulers, Edwin (616–32) and Oswald (633–42). These are Bede's heroes, his models of victorious Christian kingship. It is with them that we first get a clear idea of relations between the English kingdoms.

Northumbrian expansion westwards led Mercia to make common cause with the Welsh. In 632 Cadwallon, Christian British king of Gwynedd, and Penda, pagan Anglo-Saxon king of Mercia, won a short-lived victory over Northumbria, but the following year Oswald recovered power and Cadwallon was killed. The Welsh continued to support Penda, and in 642 Oswald was slain at Oswestry, campaigning far from home. This fact, and an incidental reference to his relations with the king of Wessex, show that Oswald's lordship and military activities extended far outside Northumbria. A group of early Welsh poems give the other side of the story from Bede's: his heroes are their aggressors. In the lament for Cynddylan, a nobleman from Powys who seems to have died in Penda's service, we glimpse the Northumbrians through British eyes:

> My brothers were slain at one stroke,
> Cynan, Cynddylan, Cynwraith,
> Defending Tren, ravaged town
>
> .   .   .   .   .   .
>
> More common was blood on the field's face
> Than ploughing of fallow
>
> .   .   .   .   .   .
>
> The hall of Cynddylan, dark is the roof,
> Since the Saxon cut down
> Powys's Cynddylan and Elfan . . .

In 655, Penda was defeated and killed by the Northumbrian Oswy, Bede's seventh over-king, who thereafter enjoyed great influence over the other kingdoms. None the less, the rising star was Mercia. The Mercian nobility soon expelled Oswy and chose Penda's son Wulfhere as their king. By the early 670s Wulfhere seems to have dominated the southern English kingdoms, and in 679 his successor won a victory at the Trent which finally ended Northumbrian expansionism. In the south, however, Mercian power was abruptly checked by Caedwalla of Wessex, who annexed Kent, Surrey, and Sussex during his short reign of 685–8. Caedwalla and his successor Ine built up a resilience of power in Wessex which was to determine the fate of England two centuries later.

In the world of seventh-century politics, then, it was possible to gain great power but hard to keep it for long. Why did kings rise and fall so quickly? One reason is that power and conquest depended on military forces; forces were attracted by gift-giving; gift-giving depended on wealth; and wealth in its turn was gained by power and conquest. Society was riddled with feuds, and the succession to kingdoms was fluid and uncertain; hence there were many royal and noble exiles from their own kin in search of generous and congenial lords. King Oswin of Deira, says Bede, 'was tall and handsome, pleasant of speech, courteous in manner, and bountiful to nobles and commons alike; so it came about that...noblemen from almost every kingdom flocked to serve him as retainers'. Such a system could hardly be stable: when a king grew sick, poor, or mean his retinue would collapse, and his heirs, if they survived at all, would become sub-kings or followers of a new lord.

What kingly magnificence could mean was brought to life, in 1939, by the discovery of a great royal burial at Sutton Hoo on the East Anglian coast. Since it seems to date from the 620s it was probably the tomb of King Raedwald, the fourth in Bede's list of over-kings. He was buried in a ship under a great mound, with his armour, weapons, and a mass of incomparable treasures. The gold and jewelled ornaments are perhaps the finest of their kind surviving in northern Europe, and no less remarkable is the range of countries from which items in the barrow came. An extraordinary ceremonial whetstone can scarcely be anything other than a sceptre. To judge from Sutton Hoo, poetic accounts of royal wealth contain no exaggeration: kingdoms were won and lost for treasures such as these.

From its beginnings, English society included a military aristocracy, probably with some kind of territorial base. But in the early centuries the king's followers or 'thegns' were tied less to their estates than to the king himself. They were expected to accompany him, to witness his public actions, to live in his hall, and if necessary to fight and die for him. Aristocratic life was strongly communal: the great hall as a place of good cheer, a haven in a dangerous world, is a powerful image in Anglo-Saxon writing. Nobody puts it better than Bede, in the famous words which he gives to a Northumbrian nobleman who is urging King Edwin to accept Christianity:

'This is how the present life of man on earth, King, appears to me in comparison with that time which is unknown to us. You are sitting feasting with your ealdormen and thegns in winter time; the fire is burning on the hearth in the middle of the hall and all inside is warm, while outside the wintry storms of rain and snow are raging; and a sparrow flies swiftly through the hall. It enters in at one door and quickly flies out through the other. For the few moments it is inside, the storm and wintry tempest cannot touch it, but after the briefest moment of calm, it flits from your sight, out of the wintry storm and into it again. So this life of man appears but for a moment; what follows or indeed what went before, we know not at all.'

The company in the royal or noble hall provided the audience for a literature which mirrored the age: heroic lays recited by professional bards. The surviving fragments include one major epic, *Beowulf*. As we have it, this is a relatively late and sophisticated work, perhaps written for a clerical audience. Yet it lays before us the heroic, essentially pagan world of the seventh-century aristocracy, transmuted by Christianity but not effaced. Its hero, Beowulf, is an exile who takes service with

Hrothgar, king of the Danes. A generous giver of treasure and splendid weapons, Hrothgar attracts to his court noble warriors who make him powerful. But the political world of the poem is violent and unstable: a king who loses support will quickly perish, and his kingdom with him. The ethos is one of loyalty and feud: 'It is better for everyone that he avenge his friend, rather than mourn him long . . . let he who can win glory before death.' Beowulf fights with monsters and dragons, inhabitants of a pre-Christian mental world. When he is killed, his followers lay him with rich treasures in a mound overlooking the sea, just as the East Angles had done for their king on the headland at Sutton Hoo:

> Then the warriors rode around the barrow
>
> .   .   .   .   .   .
>
> They praised his manhood and the prowess of his hands,
> They raised his name; it is right a man
> Should be lavish in honouring his lord and friend.
>
> .   .   .   .   .   .
>
> They said that he was of all the world's kings
> The gentlest of men, and the most gracious,
> The kindest to his people, the keenest for fame.

But there was more to early Anglo-Saxon society than warfare, savage loyalties, and ostentatious splendour. In some ways this was a surprisingly orderly world. The institutions which made the English state so exceptionally strong in the central Middle Ages have roots in the seventh century or even earlier: the efficiency of 'local government' was one important reason why new overlords could establish power so quickly. By the tenth century, English counties were divided for legal and administrative purposes into areas called 'hundreds'. In some at least of the early kingdoms, hundreds were formed out of larger but equally coherent districts, great blocks of fifty to a hundred square miles which apparently existed by the mid-seventh century. These have long been recognized in Kent, but recent research has detected them also in Northumbria, Mercia, Wessex, Sussex, and Surrey. The origin of this startlingly comprehensive system for dividing up the countryside is one of the great unsolved problems in early English history. Was it, as many believe, a Romano-Celtic survival? Was it created by one of the shadowy sixth-century *Bretwaldas*? Or did it develop spontaneously in the various kingdoms, reflecting common elements in the settlers' social background? Whatever the answer, it remains an oddly stable substratum in an unstable political world.

At the heart of each early district was a royal manor house or *tun*, run by a local official but visited by the king and his retinue at more or less frequent intervals. Each modern county contains several such sites, some given away by place-names such as Kingston, others less obvious. It was these 'central places', not towns or even villages, which were the main local foci of early and mid-Saxon society. The scattered inhabitants of the district looked for law and government to the king's great hall with its surrounding buildings. Here too they paid their dues and other public burdens in accordance with a complex system of assessment. Land was reckoned in 'hides', each notionally the area needed to support a free peasant cultivator and his family, and often an actual farm unit. Obligations, it seems, were assessed by the hide, and hides were grouped into multiples of twenty or more which owed obligations of a specialized kind. The king's deputy at the centre might thus receive renders of grain from some groups of hides, of calves or foals from others, and of honey, mead, or lesser commodities from others again.

Thus the early administrative districts were organized for exploitation as well as for jurisdiction. A system of economically specialized zones suited the underdeveloped countryside, with its sharp geographical contrasts and large areas of uncleared common pasture. So it is not surprising that when mid-Saxon kings granted away blocks of land, these early 'manors' often preserved the internal structure of the districts from which they were formed. Hence the 'multiple estate', the federation of distinct 'vills' or townships linked to one manorial centre, which was still prominent in many parts of England in the twelfth and thirteenth centuries. Some historians have recently argued that this type of organization (which certainly resembles that of early Wales) was of Celtic origin. Some continuity in rural organization is quite likely, but perhaps only in a sense so broad that it ceases to mean much. It was growth and social change, not conquest, which eventually made the 'multiple estate' obsolete. Granted that the British peasants were not all driven out, and that their way of life was probably not so very different from the invaders', it would be surprising if a pattern which suited existing resources had *not* continued.

This pattern also suited a peasant population which was dispersed, unstructured, and relatively small. The most prominent figure in the early sources is the free peasant farmer or *ceorl* (modern English 'churl', but without its derogatory sense), typically cultivating one hide of land. This does not mean that all seventh- and eighth-century farmers were so 'free' that they had no lord save the king. After the Conversion kings granted blocks of land to churches, as they had probably done to lay followers (at least on a temporary basis) from earlier still. The origin of the 'manor' as a private unit of jurisdiction and revenue is obscure, but some historians place it near the very beginnings of English society. The medieval division of estates into 'demesne' (exploited directly by the lord) and peasant land is recorded by the late seventh century, and much of the manpower on demesnes was provided by slaves. But in the early stages it seems likely that lesser lords, like kings, drew revenue from smallholders without greatly altering their way of life or farming methods. There is no evidence for the hierarchical, thoroughly dependent groups of tenants who existed by the tenth century; nor for the organized 'village communities' which seem so closely linked to strong lordship in the twelfth and thirteenth centuries. Archaeology suggests that most farmsteads in mid-Saxon England were either isolated or in little clusters, and even the nucleated settlements lack any sign of the orderly streets, greens, and plot-boundaries familiar from later village topography. It now seems likely that medieval common-field systems, with holdings intermixed in scattered strips, result from several centuries of evolution. In seventh-century England the integrated 'village community' was still in the future.

Into this very traditional society of kings, warriors, and farmers there came in 597 an alien influence—the Christian Church. The conversion of the English was initiated by Pope Gregory the Great, who according to tradition had seen English youths in Rome and pronounced them 'not Angles but angels'. Gregory knew that King Æthelberht of Kent had a Christian Frankish queen; thus it was to Kent that he sent the first mission, headed by a Roman monk named Augustine. Æthelberht, hesitant at first, soon converted, and Augustine founded a monastery at Canterbury. Misjudging the survival of Romano-British life, Gregory had planned archbishoprics based in London and York, but political realities were acknowledged in 601 when Augustine was enthroned as first Archbishop of Canterbury. Initially, success seemed rapid. In 604 a see was founded at Rochester; the East Saxons were converted, and a cathedral dedicated to St. Paul was built for them in London. Meanwhile several monasteries were built in Kent, their churches closely modelled on Roman prototypes.

But the skin-deep conversion of a king and his household was a shaky foundation at best. The East Saxons soon apostatized and expelled their bishop. Despite his baptism King Raedwald of the East Angles remained ambivalent, for Bede reports that he maintained simultaneously a church and a pagan shrine. In Northumbria the story is similar. King Edwin received the Roman missionary Paulinus, and was baptized with his thegns in 627. But on his defeat and death only five years later, his successors apostatized and Paulinus had to flee. The Church had speedily gained a foothold in the English courts; but a broader basis was needed if it was to rise above the ebb and flow of political fortunes.

Surprisingly, it was not the Gregorian mission which was most successful in this respect but the primitive, isolated Celtic Church. The Christians of Wales and Cornwall probably had some influence on the English, but it was scarcely very significant. Augustine, who seems to have been a rather proud, humourless man, offended the Welsh bishops and no co-operation resulted. The mission which achieved so much among the northern English came rather from Ireland to Scotland, and thence to Northumbria.

Thanks to St. Patrick and his followers, Ireland was largely Christian by the early sixth century. Monasteries multiplied, so much so that the whole Irish Church came to be organized along monastic lines. 'Provinces' were based on monasteries and were ruled by abbots; bishops performed their normal spiritual functions, but they lacked formal dioceses and were under the abbots' authority. Hence the typical Irish missionary was the wandering bishop owing obedience to a community at home. The Irish houses were to reach a level of wealth and sophistication far surpassing their counterparts in Wales, and already in the sixth and seventh centuries they were sending missionaries to Gaul, Germany, Scotland, and England. One named Columba went to Scotland, converted the northern Picts (the southern Picts were already Christian), and in *c.*563 founded a monastery on the island of Iona. When the Christian King Oswald won control of Northumbria in 633 it was naturally to Iona that he turned for a missionary, for his exile had been spent among the Irish of western Scotland.

The simple, wandering life of the Irish bishops and monks brought them in touch with the people at large. Aidan, Oswald's bishop, had the qualities needed to convert Northumbria permanently. After building a monastery on the island of Lindisfarne, he set up a church in each royal vill from which to preach to the countryside around. Bede says that he always travelled on foot, thus meeting passers-by on equal terms. Several monasteries were founded, and soon the Northumbrian Church was strong enough to branch out into other kingdoms.

Penda of Mercia remained pagan but allowed a mission from Lindisfarne to work in his realm, and his son Peada was baptized in 653. The over-kingship of Oswald and then of Oswy helped the Northumbrian Church to spread. In 635 Oswald's influence caused Cynegils of Wessex to accept baptism from a missionary named Birinus, who became first bishop of the West Saxons. Thanks to Oswy, the East Saxons re-converted and received a Northumbrian bishop named Cedd, who had been trained in the Irish Church. By 660 only the men of Sussex and the Isle of Wight remained pagan, and soon they too were converted.

The zeal of the Irish missionaries had achieved much; in the long run the authority of the Roman Church was bound to count for more. If Pope Gregory's aims were to be realized, the Celtic Church in English kingdoms had to accept the discipline of Rome. The main sticking-point was an issue which now seems absurdly trivial—on what day should Easter be celebrated? In their long isolation, the Celts had adopted computations which differed from those used at Rome. When the two Churches came into contact, the results could be inconvenient: at the Northumbrian court the Irish-trained King Oswy sometimes celebrated Easter while his Kentish-trained wife was still observing Lent. The question itself had a deep religious and symbolic importance; for the future of the English Church, resolving it was more important still. At the Synod of Whitby (664), King Oswy of Northumbria came down in favour of the Roman party, and the few Celtic die-hards returned to Iona. This was the turning-point: the Church through all the English kingdoms could now become a united and uniting force under one primate.

None the less, the Church was beset with problems in the 660s. Organization was haphazard; there were far too few bishops, and some were invalidly consecrated. Others died in a plague in 664, which also made the East Saxons apostatize again. But in 669 the pope sent a new archbishop, a native of Asia Minor named Theodore. This surprising candidate (only chosen when several others had refused) was just what was needed: a firm administrator. During his thirty-year reign, he rationalized the diocesan structure, which had been fluid everywhere and perhaps almost absent from kingdoms converted by the monastically-organized Irish. Bishops with invalid orders were disciplined, and dubious authorities either ratified or annulled: all acts of the Welsh bishops, for instance, were declared void. A synod held at Hertford in 672 established the first basic canons for Church government.

Most churchmen accepted Theodore's rulings with good grace, but not the formidable Wilfrid, bishop of Ripon and then of York. Wilfrid was firmly orthodox and had championed the Roman Easter at Whitby, but he resented any threat to his power in the Northumbrian Church. His stormy relations with Theodore and successive kings involved two expulsions, two appeals to Rome, exile, and imprisonment. Meanwhile he managed to preach to the Frisians, convert Sussex, and found monasteries in Mercia. With his retinue and huge wealth, Wilfrid seems an extraordinary mixture of saint and secular nobleman. Only a young and essentially aristocratic Church could have produced such a figure.

Theodore's reign was a golden age for monasteries. On the one hand, the great Celtic houses such as Lindisfarne and Whitby were increasingly influenced by Roman ways, though the old values lived on: in St. Cuthbert the solitude and austere devotion of the Irish missionaries was combined with Roman attitudes to monastic life and discipline. On the other hand, many new houses founded in these years would be counted for centuries among the greatest in Britain. In some ways the most important of these were Wearmouth and Jarrow, founded by Benedict Biscop, a Northumbrian nobleman turned monk. Biscop had been five times to Rome, and his twin monasteries brought to Northumbria the culture of the Mediterranean Church. Their most celebrated member, Bede himself, describes how Biscop had a church built by Gaulish masons 'in the Roman manner which he always loved', filled it with rich pictures and furnishings, and built up a great library from Continental sources.

Impressive though these achievements were, there was also a need to provide some permanent basis for the Church's work in the countryside: it is hard to believe that the conversion of the peasantry had hitherto been more than superficial. Many will find it surprising that here, too, the first stages were achieved by monastic or quasi-monastic bodies. With hindsight it seems obvious that missionary work and pastoral care are activities for priests, not monks. But in the seventh and eighth centuries this line was not quite so firmly drawn, even outside the Celtic Church. The English word *mynster* (monastery) was used for institutions ranging from true Benedictine houses to small, loose-knit communities of priests. Rules varied greatly (Biscop composed his own for Jarrow), and so did standards; we really have very little idea of what life was like in all but the greatest houses. But it is becoming clear that by 750 England contained hundreds of small 'minsters' with genuine and important pastoral functions, serving what may be called the first English parochial system.

The 'old minsters', as they came to be called, were older than the mass of ordinary local churches, and served much larger areas. Most of the sources are late, and show them as near-obsolete establishments with only residual authority. Hence we know little of their pastoral work, except that it existed. It appears that the collegiate priests, or deputies in the case of strict monks, travelled about within a defined 'parish' preaching to local communities. The 'parishioners' of the minster owed it their tithes, and were obliged to bring to it their children for baptism and their dead for burial. So complex a system could not have evolved so quickly without royal patronage. Paulinus and Aidan preached from their kings' vills (see p. 76), and it is no surprise to find many minster churches sited at royal *tuns* (see p. 75). Tithe-duty was probably based on existing tax assessments, and some kings may have founded several minsters as an act of policy, as Oswy of Northumbria seems to have

done in 655. Kings had an organized system of local government; so, therefore, did the Church. Though eventually
smothered by the thousands of little churches which sprang up
within them, minster 'parishes' moulded the whole future development of the Church in the English countryside.

If kings helped the Church to grow, the Church also enhanced the status of kings. The grandsons of pagan war-leaders
were coming to see themselves as God's appointed deputies; a
few generations later, the crowning of a new king became
something very like an episcopal consecration. With Christianity, too, came literacy: kings could revise and formulate tribal
custom to resemble the legislation of the civilized world.
Æthelberht of Kent, says Bede, made his laws 'according to
the custom of the Romans'. Æthelberht's code, and the later
seventh-century codes from Kent and Wessex, suggest a mixture of local tradition with borrowings from the Continent.
Whatever their practical usefulness (which is doubtful), the
kings who made them clearly wanted to seem sophisticated:
lawgivers in the classical mould. As the kingdoms were opened
more and more to influences from Rome and Gaul, the nature
of kingship changed. It was becoming important for rulers to
uphold justice and direct the internal affairs of their kingdoms,
not merely to win battles. Even the seventh-century codes, with
their long lists of fines and penalties, suggest an impressive
range of royal authority.

Also with the first English churches, we start to glimpse the
first English towns. Possibly sixth-century rulers had set up
headquarters in the Roman towns and forts; certainly seventh-
and eighth-century rulers favoured them as sites for cathedrals
and minsters. Canterbury, York, Winchester, and Worcester
cathedrals were all built within Roman defences, and in 635 the
first bishop of Wessex was given the Roman fort at Dorchester-
on-Thames, called by Bede a *civitas*, to found his see. Royal
halls and churches built on abandoned ruins are not in themselves towns. None the less, the most highly-organized communities of the age were surely the cathedrals and minsters;

craftsmen, tradesmen, servants, and beggars all gravitated to their doors. It is no coincidence that the first hints of reawakening urban life are associated with major churches, both in Roman towns and on the more numerous sites with no pre-English origins. The first archaeological evidence for Anglo-Saxon settlement in Canterbury is slightly later than the building of Augustine's cathedral there. At Northampton, recent excavations have shown that the nucleus of the town was an eighth-century minster church and hall, with associated buildings. A late ninth-century translation of Bede's term *urbana loca* is not, as we would expect, 'towns', but 'minster-places'. Scores of English towns began as minsters with lay settlements converging on their gates.

The Mercian Supremacy

England in the early eighth century was a more sophisticated place than it had been in the early seventh. A united English kingdom was still far away, but the English were now starting to become aware of themselves as an ethnic and cultural unity. Bede may have felt this more keenly than anyone: it is easy to forget how significant is the very title of his greatest work, *The Ecclesiastical History of the English People*. It was because he saw the common destiny of his race fulfilled in the united English Church that he could think of an 'English people'. But are there any signs that secular government was also becoming more comprehensive? This is a hard question to answer, not least because there are more sources. On the one hand, institutions and concepts which show the strong side of eighth-century kingship may not be new, but merely recorded for the first time. On the other hand, the dynastic turmoils which show its weak side may not be new either: it is possible that Bede and his contemporaries glossed over such matters. This at least can be said: as *Bretwaldas* on the old pattern the eighth-century Mercian kings were as mighty as their forerunners; and they lived in a world of greater literacy and legality, of firmer-entrenched rights, which made their power more stable and more capable of development.

Æthelbald of Mercia (716–57) inherited much of the influence won by Wulfhere. Written charters recording royal grants were now appearing in some quantity, so we can see how kings liked to style themselves. Æthelbald's titles are impressive, but perhaps not wholly new. 'King not only of the Mercians but of all the provinces called by the general name Southern English', as one charter calls him, echoes Bede's statement that the early over-kings 'held sway over all the provinces south of the River Humber'. The claim can be supported to the extent that charters show him influencing Kentish affairs and controlling London. But Wessex remained independent, as did Northumbria under Bede's patron King Ceolwulf: Mercian supremacy was never to go north of the Humber.

Æthelbald's successor Offa (757–96) was the most powerful English king before Alfred. His position once secured (which took some years), his conduct in all the kingdoms except Northumbria and Wessex seems to have been more that of a direct ruler than a remote overlord. Earlier kings had suppressed small royal dynasties, but Offa suppressed great ones. He had full control over Kent (with a brief interlude in the late 770s), and treated its king as his servant. Once he annulled a grant by King Egbert of Kent, 'saying that it was wrong that his minister should have presumed to give land ... without his witness'. After an unsuccessful coup against Offa's successor in 798, the ancient Kentish dynasty was extinguished for ever. The last king of Sussex appears as one of Offa's *duces*; in Surrey, which had been West Saxon territory, we find Offa confirming a grant by a Mercian noble. In East Anglia (though here the dynasty reappeared later), the *Chronicle* notes laconically for 794: 'In this year Offa, king of Mercia, ordered [King] Æthelberht's head to be struck off.' In Wessex, royal power and tradition were stronger: the kingdom only recognized Mercian protection between 786 and 802, and even then the lordship seems to have been of a much vaguer kind than in Kent.

Offa is the first ruler whose charters use the simple, unqualified title 'king of the English'. His status is emphasized by a
famous letter to him from the great Frankish king, Charlemagne. Charlemagne addresses him as an equal, 'his dearest
brother', and speaks of 'the various episcopal sees of your
kingdom and Æthelred's' as though Offa of Mercia and
Æthelred of Northumbria were the only kings in England. The
Frankish connection is important (though possibly too much
has been made of this one document: there had always been
plenty of contact between Gaul and the southern English). Offa
would certainly have liked to be thought another Charlemagne,
and whatever the reality of royal power, its status certainly rose
in line with developments abroad. In 787 Offa had his son
Egfrith made king of the Mercians by a solemn consecration
which Northumbria copied nine years later. The semi-sacred
character of kingship was becoming stronger.

This did not make dynasties more stable. Succession was
uncertain: long after Offa, kings would still be 'chosen' from
the royal stock. Any vaguely eligible candidate with forces
behind him could aim at the throne, and Mercia, Wessex, and
Northumbria were all torn by dynastic feuds during the eighth
century. In his efforts to secure the succession, Offa seems to
have been as ruthless towards relatives as he was towards
neighbours. When his son Egfrith died shortly after Offa himself, the Northumbrian scholar Alcuin saw it as a judgement:
'The vengeance for the blood shed by the father has now
reached the son; for you know very well how much blood his
father shed to secure the kingdom on his son.'

Much of this shows Offa in a savage light, but some important institutions did start to take shape under the Mercian
kings. The Church was now firmly established with lands and
privileges. Its assemblies were solemn affairs, recorded in
writing. Æthelbald and Offa were often involved in Church
councils and sometimes presided over them; their thegns and
ministers witnessed decisions. The way Church business was
conducted can hardly have failed to heighten the sense of

precedent and legality. Though the context is ecclesiastical, such assemblies must have helped to transform the *ad hoc* band of warriors around a seventh-century king into the formal 'Witan' or grand council which we find in late Saxon England.

The concept of 'bookland' (land for which a written charter gave legal title) was now well established. Most eighth-century charters, at least the surviving ones, are grants to churches, but they reflect a society in which rights in the land and local interests were winning ground against traditional values. The eighth-century aristocracy begin to seem a little less like warriors, a little more like country gentlemen, and evidence starts to appear for family houses and family churches. Little is known of the houses, though one has been excavated at Goltho, Lincolnshire: a mid-ninth-century defended enclosure containing a hall, kitchen, chamber, and outbuildings. For the churches there is more evidence: hereditary 'private' minsters, controlled by families of noble patrons, often figure in eighth-century sources. All this is equally true to the mightiest lord of all. Earlier kings had had their royal vills, but Offa seems to have tried to make his residence at Tamworth a kind of national headquarters or 'capital'. Near Tamworth was the Mercian cathedral of Lichfield, which Offa managed to have raised for several years into an archbishopric. If this was partly for political reasons, there was much to be said for a metropolitan church near the 'metropolis' of Offa's kingdom.

The duty of landowners to help in the building of bridges and fortifications first appears in a document of 749, and is usually stipulated in later grants of land. This is significant in an age which produced massive public works of at least two kinds: one long-famous, the other only recently understood. The first is, of course, Offa's Dyke, so called by an ancient and probably correct tradition. Recent excavations suggest that this enormous earthwork was a continuous barrier between England and Wales, running from sea to sea. Offa is known to have raided into Wales, but the Dyke must be a defensive rather than an offensive work, built to stop a Welsh counter-attack when plans for conquest had been abandoned. But the fact that it exists at all is proof of the huge resources which Offa commanded.

The charter references to 'fortress-work' imply fortified strongholds rather than dykes. It is well known that Alfred and his heirs developed a network of large communal fortresses or *burhs* to protect Wessex against the Vikings. Archaeology has recently begun to suggest that some *burhs* are a century or more older, and may have been founded to defend Mercia in its years of greatness. In most cases (for instance Bedford, where Offa is said to have been buried), the evidence is still only topographical, and therefore inconclusive. But at Hereford, excavation has revealed an eighth-century defended circuit pre-dating later Saxon enlargements, and less conclusive evidence for defences of Offa's period has been found at Tamworth. Several of the late ninth-century Wessex *burhs* may also have earlier origins; some, such as Wareham (Dorset), Dorchester (Dorset), and Oxford, are certainly on sites which were important in the eighth century or before.

We have seen two factors in the emergence of towns: churches and fortresses. The third, in the long run the biggest, is trade. Offa lived in an age when foreign and internal trade were both expanding. The clearest sign is the appearance of a systematic coinage. Until *c*.600, only foreign gold coins had circulated in England. The crude silver coins minted by seventh- and eighth-century kings were unreliable, and usually of localized circulation. A new Frankish currency of silver pennies was the model for a better coinage, and an East Anglian king seems to have used it slightly before Offa. But when Offa's beautiful pennies did appear, they quickly drove out older issues and gained a wider circulation than any currency since Roman times. Perhaps the most interesting point is that Offa's coins have been found not only in large hoards, but also in small, scattered groups. Evidently, they were used for small-scale transactions at a local level: money was becoming of general importance in the English economy.

A dispute with Offa in 789 caused Charlemagne to close Frankish ports to English merchants. Hence it seems that English merchants normally used such ports: Charlemagne's realm and Offa's were part of a growing world of international commerce. Trading centres were appearing throughout northern Europe. Excavations on the huge settlements of Hedeby in Denmark and Birke in Sweden have produced finds suggesting that in the eighth century England and the Viking lands belonged to the same international trading community. In England, commercial settlements such as these were often linked to existing royal and ecclesiastical centres, and their names often include the element *-wic* (from Latin *vicus*). *Hamwih* was the precursor of modern Southampton. It lay at the junction of the Test and Itchen near a royal vill called Hampton, and its name labels it as the *Ham-wic* associated with the *Ham-tun*. Here excavation has disclosed a settlement of at least 30 hectares, probably first occupied in about the 720s, with artefacts suggesting wide European contacts. Others were probably Ipswich (*Gips-wic*), a major pottery-producing centre, Sandwich, and Fordwich. Roman towns started to regain economic as well as hierarchical importance. A commercial suburb developed at York (*Eofor-wic*), where Frisian merchants are recorded; at Canterbury excavation has revealed eighth-century houses, and a market is mentioned in 786. Most important was London, which Bede could describe in *c.*730 as 'an *emporium* of many peoples coming by land and sea'. This commercial zone has proved hard to find, though it now seems that the Roman and medieval waterfronts at Billingsgate include a mid-Saxon clay bank. Wherever it lay, it must have been large and important: *Lunden-wic* is mentioned in the late seventh century, and eighth-century sources refer to tolls and tax-gatherers at its port.

The eighth century was a rather unsettled time for the English Church. Lay foundation and patronage of ministers had brought its own problems. Hereditary interest was not necessarily a bad thing: in the hands of a responsible family, a monastery could expect both security and prosperity. But not all proprietors were responsible; while some minsters, if we can believe Bede, were simply 'fronts' for tax evasion. Bede was not alone in worrying about lax standards. Æthelbald, Offa, and his successor Cenwulf (796–821) participated in a series of much-needed reforming synods. Monks were forbidden to live like lay nobles; drunkenness and secular songs in monasteries were condemned. In 786, Offa held the only council in the Anglo-Saxon period to be attended by papal legates. But if the growth of Church government enhanced royal dignity, it also raised the pretensions of bishops. Relations between Church and State were not always easy, especially with a king like Æthelbald who seems to have combined monastic reform with robbing minsters and seducing nuns. Dealings between the king and the Archbishop of Canterbury tended to be complicated by the strong anti-Mercian feeling in Kent. Archbishop Jaenbert was outraged when Offa raised Lichfield to an archiepiscopal see, and the scheme was abandoned after the king's death on the grounds that it had been prompted by enmity towards the people of Kent.

On the positive side, the English Church did produce one outstanding scholar, Alcuin. A product of the cathedral school at York, he was a leading figure in Charlemagne's court and took a central part in Charlemagne's great revival of classical learning and education. It is significant, especially in the context of Charlemagne's letter to Offa, that the dominant intellectual of late eighth-century Europe was an Englishman. But it must be remembered that Alcuin, like Bede before him, was a Northumbrian: we know very little about Mercian culture. Probably this simply means that much has been lost. Mercia had no Bede to record its achievements, and its greatest monasteries were sacked by the Vikings. Fragments of decorative art, such as the sculptures in the minster of Breedon-on-the-Hill, suggest sumptuous physical surroundings. A noble monument to the age of Æthelbald and Offa is the great minster church of Brixworth, Northamptonshire. It is a sign of how much we do *not* know that this monastery fails to appear in any early document, unless it is the lost *Clofesho* where the Mercian synods were held.

The most impressive fact about the eighth-century Church is that the English were now taking Christianity to their original homelands on the Continent. The mission began, oddly enough, through St. Wilfrid's quarrel with Archbishop Theodore. Setting out in 678 to state his case at Rome, Wilfrid travelled through pagan Frisia and spent a year preaching. The Frisians were well known to the English from their merchants, and Wilfrid opened the way to more ambitious missionary work. A group of Northumbrians landed in Frisia in 690. Among them was Willibrord, who took the lead and was consecrated Archbishop of Frisia in 695. He established his cathedral at Utrecht, and the organized Church of Frankish Frisia developed quickly. Willibrord's work was supplemented by a West Saxon mission led by St. Boniface. Between his arrival in 718 and his murder by pagans in 754, Boniface preached among the Frisians, Germans, and Franks, setting up a see at Maine. As well as converting pagan areas Boniface had great influence on the Frankish Church as a whole, regulating it and bringing it under papal guidance. Through his career he relied on books, recruits, and advice from England, and there survives a large correspondence with friends at home. Much of the work which transformed the stagnant Frankish Church into the expanding Church of the Carolingian revival was done by English men and women.

The Viking Invasions and the Rise of the House of Wessex

Mercian power did not long outlast Offa. His successor, King Cenwulf, kept hold of Kent and Sussex and even gained some new territory from the northern Welsh, but Wessex slipped from his grasp in 802. A new dynasty of overlords was about to appear, this time West Saxon. In 825 Egbert of Wessex won a decisive victory near Swindon, expelled a Mercian under-king from Kent, and annexed Kent, Essex, Surrey, and Sussex. Four years later, Mercia itself fell to Egbert, and even Northumbria acknowledged his lordship. The reversal is spectacular, and shows that Offa's dynasty had done little to stabilize English politics. Nor could Egbert: by his death in 839 Mercia was independent once again. The old interplay of dynasties seemed to be continuing much as ever. But under the year 789 the *Anglo-Saxon Chronicle* contains an ominous entry: the first breath of a storm that was to sweep away all rivals to the house of Wessex, and with them some of the best achievements of English civilization:

In this year Beorhtric [king of Wessex] took to wife Eadburh, daughter of King Offa. And in his days came first three ships of Norwegians from Horthaland: and then the reeve rode thither and tried to compel them to go to the royal manor, for he did not know what they were: and then they slew him. These were the first ships of the Danes to come to England.

This Viking landing was a minor affair, though there are other references soon afterwards to 'sea-borne pagans' attacking the south coast. More serious, and incomparably more distressing, were raids in the north, for they involved the successive plundering of Lindisfarne (793), Jarrow (794), and Iona (795). England had been safe from foreign attacks for two centuries; the reaction to the sudden desecration of three of its most holy places is easily imagined. These were, however, isolated incidents, and it was a generation before the Viking nuisance became a major threat. But a big raid on Kent in 835 opened three decades in which attacks came almost yearly, and which ended with the arrival of a full-scale invading army.

The dramatic expansion of the Norwegians and Danes is a European phenomenon, of which the raids on England and Ireland were only one part. Two races were involved (the word *Viking*, 'pirate', was coined by their victims and refers equally to both), and several motives. They were far from being total barbarians, and by the 840s they had been heavily involved in trade for some generations. It was, indeed, this trade which opened up regular contact with the nations to the west and south. Population grew, and it became hard to find a reasonable living at home. Many adventurers must have heard stories of the fertile lands with monasteries full of easy plunder, and it is surprising rather than otherwise that the early raids were not followed up more quickly. The fall of the Danish royal dynasty in 854 left a power vacuum, with no strong king who could unite warriors and prevent them from dispersing on foreign exploits.

These factors help to explain why raiders descended in such numbers on European countries from the 850s onwards, and why casual plundering gave way to a policy of conquest and settlement. There seem to have been two main routes: one around the north of Scotland to the Western Isles and so southwards, the other to the east and south coasts of England and to Gaul. Hence the raids and settlements in Ireland, Scotland, Wales, and Cornwall were mainly Norwegian, while those in the English and Frankish lands were mainly Danish.

In 865 the Danish 'Great Army', led by Halfdan and Ivarr the Boneless, landed in East Anglia. After a few months' stay it turned northwards into Northumbria, which happened to be split by a dynastic dispute, and captured York in 867. Both the rival kings perished, and the Danes set up their own nominee to rule Northumbria as a client state. The army then advanced into Mercia, but on meeting opposition it withdrew to York without an open fight, and in 869 descended again on East Anglia. The inhabitants were defeated in battle, and their king Edmund (soon to be venerated as St. Edmund the Martyr) became the victim of a ritual murder. Within three years, the once-great kingdoms of Northumbria and East Anglia had ceased to exist.

In 870 the Danish army camped at Reading and prepared to invade Wessex. But here the opposition was better organized. After Egbert's death the West Saxons were ruled by his son Æthelwulf, an unambitious but capable man. Æthelwulf's main achievement seems to have been to avoid the kind of family feuding which had ruined other dynasties: his four sons succeeded peacefully in order of age. When the Vikings attacked, the third son, Æthelred, was on the throne; the name of his brother and heir, Alfred, was to become the greatest in Anglo-Saxon history.

It was a combined force under Æthelred and Alfred which met the Danes on the Berkshire Downs and inflicted their first serious defeat. But the English success was short-lived. The Danes withdrew to Reading, but almost immediately advanced again and defeated Æthelred and Alfred near Basingstoke. In April 871 a new Danish army landed. Invasion of Wessex seemed imminent, and its defenders had nowhere to turn for help. In the midst of this crisis Æthelred died, and his brother became king of the West Saxons.

Alfred the Great (871–99) is known to everyone as the king who saved England against seemingly hopeless odds. This is not quite how contemporaries would have seen it. In political terms at least, 'England' still did not mean very much. The first writer known to use *Angelcynn* (literally '[the land of] the English folk') was Alfred himself, and *Englaland* does not appear for another century. It was not a foregone conclusion that the other kingdoms would accept West Saxon lordship, or even prefer it to the Danes. They might well have chosen kings of their own, and there was always a danger that English rivals, exiles, or disaffected groups would enlist Viking support. The destruction of the other dynasties did not automatically make Alfred king of all the English; he and his heirs achieved this through a mixture of military success, tactful diplomacy, and good luck.

The reign started badly, and after a year of minor defeats Alfred had to buy the Danes off. They left Wessex alone for five years, during which they invaded Mercia, expelled King Burgred, and replaced him with their own nominee: a third ancient kingdom had gone for good. The Great Army now split into two halves. One, led by Halfdan, turned north and began dividing up Yorkshire for permanent settlement. The other, led by Guthrum, Oscytel, and Anund, turned south, and in 875–6 launched another attack on Wessex. At first their success was limited; in 877 they withdrew again to partition out Mercia, and another group split off to colonize Lincolnshire, Nottinghamshire, Derbyshire, and Leicestershire.

Thus it was a much-reduced force which attacked Wessex for the third time in 878. However, a surprise attack on Chippenham gave them the upper hand; much of Wiltshire and Hampshire submitted, and Alfred was driven back to a refuge at Athelney in the Somerset marshes. The position seemed hopeless, but Alfred bided his time in his fortress and gathered troops. Early in May, says the near-contemporary writer of the *Chronicle*, 'he rode to *Ecgbrihtesstan* [Egbert's Stone] . . . and came to meet him there all the men of Somerset and Wiltshire and part of Hampshire . . . and they rejoiced to see him. And one day later he went from those camps to Iley Oak, and one day later to Edington; and there he fought against the entire host, and put it to flight.'

The victory was sudden but decisive. The Danish leader Guthrum accepted baptism with several of his captains, and the two kings settled peace terms. These recognized the Danish occupation of much of England as a *fait accompli*. The frontier ran roughly north-westwards from London to Chester; Guthrum was to withdraw with his troops behind this line, where he was to be recognized as king of an independent kingdom. By the autumn of 880 the Danes had left Wessex and begun the systematic settlement of East Anglia.

This was not the end of the conflict. In 886 Alfred captured London, apparently after defeating a Danish garrison. In 893 a big Danish army landed in the Thames estuary and raided through England during the next three years, but this time it made little impression on Wessex. Alfred had been busy, both in securing the safety of his own kingdom and in consolidating his lordship over the other territory west and south of the Danish frontier. For the first task, he seems to have improved both the army and the navy. Kings had long been entitled to levies of troops raised in accordance with the land assessment in hides. Alfred's reorganization, by which only half of the army was to be on service at any one time, foreshadows the later 'select fyrd' or militia: it must have produced a smaller but more efficient host. An obvious way of combating sea-borne raiders was with more ships, and Alfred is said to have built vessels much bigger than the Vikings', carrying sixty oars or more.

The most important element in his programme (certainly the one which saved Wessex from further inland raids) makes Alfred the first English town planner. By the late 880s Wessex was covered with a network of public strongholds, several of which have a regular grid of streets and can only be described as planned fortified towns. A document called the *Burghal Hidage* lists thirty of these *burhs*, with three more which may be later additions. Perhaps the most impressive case is Winchester, where a new grid ignoring the Roman streets was laid out within the Roman walls. The same linearity can be seen at Oxford, Chichester, Wareham, and others. Planning was remarkably systematic, and it seems that the surveyors used a standard 66-foot measure for setting out the streets. The larger *burhs* were more than just fortresses, and soon acquired an important role in the local rural economy. Manning the defences was the responsibility of neighbouring landowners, who were able in return to use the defended area for their own purposes. Often they built 'town houses' in the *burh* to store their produce for marketing: Domesday Book records several links between urban tenements and rural manors. Traders and craftsmen followed, and the strongholds of the late ninth century became the thriving towns of the tenth. Defence happened to coincide with the needs of a growing economy; thus Alfred has his unexpected but permanent memorial in the road systems of several modern towns.

One important reason for Alfred's long-term success was the tact with which he treated his neighbours. In Mercia especially, it was dangerous to wound local pride. Alfred left affairs there in the hands of the old royal council, headed by a Mercian nobleman named Æthelred who became his son-in-law, and when he took London in 886 he immediately handed it over to Mercian control. Thus treated, Æthelred was staunchly loyal to the Crown, and after Alfred's death he and his wife Æthelflaed led Mercian offensives against the Danes. If Alfred was more truly 'king of the English' than anyone before him, it was not just through military strength or because no rivals remained: people genuinely wanted him because they knew that he and his family were just and considerate rulers.

But there remained the problem of the Danes and the damage they had done. Some of it was irreparable: whatever happened now, the world of Bede and Offa had gone for ever. The size of the Danish Great Army may be disputed, but it is impossible to deny the evidence of three kingdoms destroyed, dioceses disrupted, innumerable monasteries plundered, charters and other documents almost completely lost for much of eastern England. The ruin of monasteries was perhaps the most serious, for the great houses had been the main repositories of learning and culture, while the small ones were still mainly responsible for pastoral care in the countryside.

In the Danelaw (as the area behind Guthrum's frontier came to be known) the Danish soldiers quickly established a society of their own. Yorkshire, Lincolnshire, Leicestershire, and to a lesser extent East Anglia are full of place-names ending in -*by*, -*thorp*, and other Scandinavian elements. This impact is startling: it shows both that the army was very large, and that it distributed itself widely over the countryside. Even when the Danelaw was Christianized and brought under English rule it retained striking peculiarities, with its own systems of manorial organization, land measurement, law, and social differentiation. Tenth-century kings had the problem of reconciling the claims of a united kingdom with customs very different from those of the English.

England badly needed a revival of literacy and learning, and to this Alfred devoted his last ten years. Like Charlemagne, he carried out his programme of education through a circle of court intellectuals. In some ways his own contribution to this project is the most remarkable of Alfred's achievements. He was the only English king before Henry VIII who wrote books. Lamenting the destruction of manuscripts and the decay of scholarship, he learnt Latin and translated works into English for his subjects' benefit. Among the many translations which his circle produced (and which include, significantly, Bede's *Ecclesiastical History*), three are probably Alfred's own work. It is also believed that the *Anglo-Saxon Chronicle*, as we now have it, may have been first compiled at Alfred's court. For priests, a good Latin education became once again necessary for high office. It is hard to know how well Alfred's Renaissance succeeded, but it must have provided more literate priests and a more learned laity: good foundations for the monastic reform of two generations later. Alfred was lucky that future events caused so many of his various schemes to bear fruit. Even allowing for this, he remains the outstanding figure of early English history.

The reigns of Edward the Elder (899–924), Athelstan (924–39), and Edmund (939–46) were dominated by the reconquest of the Danelaw. This half-century was the formative period for national kingship. Dynastic feuds were avoided, partly through Alfred's careful provision for the succession and partly through some lucky chances. In 902 a dangerous split was averted when Edward's cousin, who had sought Danish help to win the crown, was killed in battle. Athelstan succeeded smoothly in 924 because he was both the rightful heir to Wessex and had been educated in his Mercian aunt's household. By the mid-century there was no serious possibility that Mercia, still less any other kingdom, could revert to an older dynasty. The royal house of Wessex was the royal house of England.

The campaigns of Edward's reign were mainly directed by the king himself in partnership with his sister Æthelflaed, 'the Lady of the Mercians'. The English offensive began when a

Danish raid into Mercia was defeated in 910. Over the next eight years, Edward pushed into the Danelaw while his sister kept the Danes busy on their Mercian frontier. Æthelflaed was now threatened from two directions, for Norwegian Vikings from Ireland had begun attacking the west coast. Her main achievement was to build a series of new Mercian *burhs*: on the east frontier against the Danes, on the west frontier against the Welsh, and in the north-west to block Norwegian raids on Tamworth from the Dee and Mersey. In 917 Æthelflaed took Derby, giving Edward a chance to invade East Anglia while the enemy was occupied. By 918 all the southern Danelaw had fallen to Edward, though isolated Danish armies were holding out in Stamford, Leicester, Nottingham, and Lincoln. Leicester submitted to Æthelflaed, but her death soon afterwards forced Edward to halt the campaign while he secured Mercia. Returning swiftly, he took Stamford, Nottingham, and Lincoln, and by the end of 920 the English frontier was fixed at the Humber.

Meanwhile, Edward was forming links with his other non-English neighbours. In 918 he received the 'submissions' of the Welsh kings of Gwynedd and Dyfed. In 923, says the *Chronicle*, 'the king of Scots and the whole Scottish nation accepted him as father and lord: so also did Raegnald and the sons of Eadwulf and all the inhabitants of Northumbria, both English and Danish, Norwegians and others; together with the king of the Strathclyde Welsh and all his subjects'. These were the first in a series of such 'submissions', culminating in an extraordinary spectacle in 973 when eight 'British kings' swore fealty to Edward's grandson Edgar and rowed him on the River Dee.

It must be emphasized that these were personal submissions to the kings to whom they were made: they involved the acceptance of lordship and protection, not the permanent surrender of independence. In fact, Scotland and Wales were both advancing towards their own internal unity. In *c.*850 Kenneth Mac Alpin, king of the Scots, had annexed the Pictish kingdom, and over the next two centuries Scotland developed under Scottish (as against Pictish) rule. In Wales, politics were transformed by the sudden expansion of Gwynedd from the late ninth century onwards, leaving only Dyfed of the smaller kingdoms. The Anglo-Saxons never conquered Wales or Scotland, and in each a native power had emerged dominant by 1066. None the less, Wales was much influenced both by England and by the Vikings.

Among the many groups competing for land in tenth-century Britain was a new one—the Norwegians from Ireland. They had no fondness for the Danes, and their main object was to gain control of the northern Danelaw. In 918 a force led by Raegnald attacked Scotland, based itself in Northumbria, and the following year took York, where Raegnald established himself as king. The Norse kingdom was to last, with interruptions, for thirty-five years, during which trade grew and the twin Norse cities of York and Dublin expanded fast. Excavation at York has revealed streets of timber houses and shops, laid out by the Danes and redeveloped by Raegnald's followers. During the reigns of Athelstan and Edmund, the enemies of the English were the Norwegians more than the Danes.

In 920 Edmund had accepted Raegnald's fealty and thus acknowledged his status. But when a new Norse king tried to seize his inheritance in 926, Athelstan attacked and captured York, destroyed its defences, and received the submission of the kings of Scotland and Strathclyde. Six years later, relations between Athelstan and the Scots broke down. Fearing invasion, the various rivals of the English made common cause. But in 937 the English army under Athelstan defeated a combined force of Norse, Scots, and Strathclyde Welsh. Athelstan was now at the height of his power, king of the English and Danes and in some sense overlord of the British. He was respected by foreign powers, and formed marriage alliances with the French and German royal families. His charters show the Welsh princes regularly attending his court; Hywel Dda, king of Dyfed in Athelstan's time, imitated English silver pennies and issued laws modelled on English codes.

But much still depended on the individual king. Soon after

Athelstan's death in 939, a Norse army returned under Olaf Guthfrithson. The new king Edmund was forced to recognize Olaf as king of York and its dependent territories. Olaf died in 941, and during the next four years Edmund recovered the northern Danelaw and ravaged Strathclyde. Especially interesting here is a contemporary poem in which Edmund features as liberator of the Danes from their Norse oppressors: the great-grandsons of Alfred's enemies could identify with the English Crown rather than with their fellow Scandinavians. But in 947, the year after Edmund's death, York fell yet again to a Norse king, Eric Bloodaxe. The next six years saw a confused struggle between Eric, the new English king, Eadred, and a Norwegian rival named Olaf Sihtricson. In 954 Eadred invaded Northumbria, this time for good, and the last king of York was driven out and killed.

From nearly fifty years of complex warfare the house of Wessex had emerged triumphant. The tranquil reign of Edgar (959–75) proves that more had been created than mere military power. Edgar was not a conqueror: one historian has written that 'his part in history was to maintain the peace established in England by earlier kings'. But this was no mean achievement: the kingdom was young, and it is with Edgar that the main developments in late Saxon kingship come into focus.

From Athelstan onwards, kings made laws more frequently and went into more detail. They cover a wide range of subjects—peace-keeping, the suppression of thieves, the hierarchy of churches, the conduct of merchants and markets, to name only a few. The emphasis is on unity: Edgar's codes make allowance for local custom, especially in the Danelaw, but insist that 'the secular law shall stand in each folk as can best be established'. By the early eleventh century the trying of most serious crimes was reserved to the Crown, and there was a concept of a national peace which it was the king's duty and right to maintain. Royal authority was spread wider, and went deeper, than in any other tenth-century European country of comparable size.

Laws and charters were issued at meetings of the 'Witan' or royal council. Its development can be traced by means of the witness lists attached to charters. In the tenth century it was much bigger and probably more formal than the councils of earlier kings, and included numerous men described as 'ministers' or thegns. Some nineteenth-century historians tried too hard to see the Witan as a 'proto-parliament': it was in no sense a democratic body, nor did it impose 'constitutional' restraints on the king. But it was important. In the Witan new kings were chosen, solemn public arts were ratified, and business was discussed. It was composed of nobles, bishops, and many men of influence in their own localities. From Athelstan's reign onwards, the enlarged Witan was an established institution and a force to be reckoned with.

The king's will operated through a much-improved system of local government. During the tenth century, the regional anomalies of England were progressively reduced to a single framework of 'shires'. Some had existed for a century or more, and many were based on still older boundaries. But it was essentially under Edgar that the English counties stabilized in the form which lasted until 1974, exactly a thousand years later. The shires were entrusted to a group of leading magnates, the aldermen. In ninth-century Wessex there had been an alderman for each shire, but by a gradual process, which seems to start under Athelstan, the number of aldermen fell and their status rose. By Edgar's reign the alderman was becoming less like a local official, and more like his successor the eleventh-century earl. But he still remained in regular touch with the government of the shires under his care.

For legal and administrative purposes the shires were broken down into subdivisions, called 'hundreds' in most counties, and 'wapentakes' in the northern Danelaw. Each hundred had its own court for settling local business, and communal obligations to provide troops and oarsmen came to be assessed by the hundred. Even this was not the bottom of the ladder: for law enforcement the population was organized into groups of ten

STRATHCLYDE

LOTHIAN *Ceded to Scotland c. 975*

NORTHUMBRIA

Bamburgh

North

Carlisle

English Frontier 927

Eamont

Sea

Isle of Man

KINGDOM
OF YORK

York

Dublin

Manchester   *English Frontier, 920*
Runcorn Thelwall
Eddisbury Bakewell
Chester   Davenport
                          Lincoln
LAND OF THE   *English Frontier, 917*
ENGLISH   FIVE BOROUGHS
          Stafford
       Tamworth   EAST
MERCIA   Thetford
                                    ANGLIA
                Bedford
                        Cambridge
        Buckingham
    Cricklade   Hertford
  Malmesbury   Wallingford   Maldon
     Bath   London
                              Canterbury
W E S S E X   Winchester
Lydford   Southampton Porchester   Hastings
     Exeter   Chichester
        Wareham

▨ Norse settlements
▨ Danish settlements
━━ Boundary of Guthrum's
      Kingdom

0   50   100 *miles*
0   50   100   150 *km*

ENGLAND IN THE TENTH CENTURY

mutually-responsible households or 'tithings'. The weight of royal government reached the individual peasant through a structure of remarkable complexity. How much was new in the tenth century is hard to say. The principle of the hundred appears in earlier law codes, and it seems likely that late Saxon hundreds were often or usually based on older territories. But the system was rationalized and improved by Alfred's successors, and under Edgar it emerges clearly in its developed form.

Another mark of royal strength was the coinage. Even before Alfred, the three coin-issuing authorities (the kings of Wessex and Mercia and the Archbishop of Canterbury) had agreed on a standard currency of silver pennies. Decrees issued by Athelstan between 924 and 939 order that 'one coinage shall run throughout the land'. He and his heirs managed to maintain uniformity remarkably well, and all coins were minted by strictly-controlled moneyers in the *burhs*. In *c*.973 Edgar designed a new coinage of pennies, which remained the basis of the English currency until long after the Conquest. The excellence of the coins shows a degree of control which was, once again, unique in contemporary Europe.

Edgar's main personal achievement was his encouragement of monastic reform. True Benedictine monasticism seems to have been almost dead in early tenth-century England. Several great and innumerable small minsters had been destroyed by the Danes, while those which survived had tended more and more towards the loose, secular life-style that Bede had long ago deplored. Groups of minster priests lived in separate houses with their wives and children; in their everyday existence they came closer to cathedral canons than to monks. A successful reconstruction of the English Church would need models for the new monasticism, and money to build the new monasteries. The first was provided by the great European reform movement, of which the English reform was essentially a part; the second was provided by Edgar and his nobility. The prime movers were three great churchmen, St. Dunstan, St. Æthelwold, and St. Oswold.

The monastic reform in England began in the early 940s, and under royal patronage: Glastonbury, given to Dunstan by King Edmund, and Abingdon, given to Æthelwold by King Eadred, were the first of the 'new' houses. But Edmund and Eadred were both lukewarm, while the next king, Eadwig, had a personal grudge against Dunstan. This had productive consequences, for Dunstan was exiled abroad and gained a wide knowledge of European monasticism. Times changed with Edgar's accession in 959: Dunstan became Archbishop of Canterbury, and Æthelwold bishop of Winchester. Oswold, the youngest of the three, had spent some time in the French monastery of Fleury. Dunstan persuaded Edgar to give him the bishopric of Worcester, and soon afterwards Oswold built a monastery at Westbury-on-Trym. Over the next half-century some fifty houses were founded or refounded under the influence of Glastonbury, Abingdon, and Westbury.

The monks in the new monasteries followed a way of life based on the rule of St. Benedict, with elaborations in ritual and daily routine in line with Continental practice. In *c.*970 the various traditions were combined in the *Regularis Concordia*, one rule for all the English houses to follow. Edgar's part was crucial: he gave the weight of his authority to the movement, and all the new monasteries were under his direct patronage. The expulsion of secular priests from the old minsters to make way for monks, which first happened at Winchester in 964, would have been difficult without royal backing. Edgar gave generously, and expected others to do likewise: by the 970s there are signs that the drain on aristocratic funds was becoming resented. None the less, to found a monastery was once again a socially prestigious act.

The new houses were wealthy, respected, and endowed with treasures and fine buildings. Literary sources hint at the richness of English art under Edgar. A number of the magnificent illuminated books survive, but only fragments of the gold, enamel, and ivory ornaments, and almost none of the major buildings. Fate has been unkind to late Anglo-Saxon architecture, for all the greatest churches were rebuilt after the Conquest. As enlarged in the tenth century, the Old Minster at Winchester was 250 feet long, with side-chapels, elaborate western towers, and carved and painted friezes. But it must be stressed that this spiritual and material regeneration touched only a fraction (probably under 10 per cent) of the old communities: the others continued in their former ways. Thus at the Norman Conquest the Benedictine houses co-existed with an unknown number of small secular minsters, relics of the pre-Viking English Church.

If the new monasticism owed much to Europe, it was distinctively English in its relations with the state and society at large. By 1000 most English bishops were monks, and both bishops and abbots deliberated with lay magnates in the Witan. Great churchmen were among the most valued advisers of the last Anglo-Saxon kings. Equally, Church reform added lustre to a king who, perhaps more than any of his predecessors, set store by the sacred character of his office. Edgar's coronation in 973 was postponed until he reached thirty, the minimum canonical age for ordination to the priesthood. The climax of the ceremony was not the crowning, but the anointing with holy oil which conferred near-priestly status and set the king above human judgement. As the homilist Ælfric of Eynsham put it, 'no man can make himself king, but the people have the free will to choose him to be king who is most pleasing to them. But once he has been consecrated king he has power over the people, and they may not shake his yoke from their necks.' The frontispiece of the Winchester New Minster foundation charter shows Edgar as he wanted to be seen: crowned, standing between two saints, and offering his gift to the heavenly king through whom earthly kings rule.

Æthelred and Cnut: the Decline of the English Monarchy

The next two reigns would show that there were still great limitations on the national monarchy. A new king could not count on loyalty before he had won it, as was shown when Edgar died in 975 leaving two sons under age. The elder, Edward, became unpopular, and many nobles preferred his brother Æthelred. Edward was crowned, but four years later he was murdered at Corfe. There can be little doubt that Æthelred's supporters were responsible, and the murder was a fitting start for an unhappy reign. Æthelred 'the Unready' (979–1016) has always had a bad press (though his famous nickname has lost its original meaning, which involved the pun *Æthelræd Unræd*, 'Noble-Counsel No-Counsel'). Probably he did lack the qualities which were still so important for kingship: the knack of putting trust in the right places and commanding trust in others. On the other hand, law and justice continued to develop in his reign under the guidance of the learned Archbishop Wulfstan. If it had not been for a new problem—the return of the Vikings—the English state might have held together as well as it had done under Edgar.

The new raiders were even more dangerous than their ninth-century ancestors. By the 970s the Danish king, Harold Bluetooth, who had gained control of both Denmark and Norway, was creating a formidable army of highly-trained professional soldiers. In 988 Harold was deposed by his son Swein, who maintained his father's army and built large fortresses to house military communities. One of these has been excavated at Trelleborg in Denmark. It consists of a large circular earthwork enclosing groups of great boat-shaped halls, all planned with mathematical precision. Both Trelleborg and the Danish sagas suggest a degree of co-ordination and discipline which the English army would have found it hard to match.

The attacks began within a year or two of Æthelred's accession. At first they were on a fairly small scale, but in 991 a large Danish force defeated Alderman Byrhtnoth and the Essex militia at Maldon, and had to be bought off with a large payment. The pattern was repeated after heavy raids in 994, 997, and 1002. It is for these payments that Æthelred's reign is now so notorious. Huge numbers of his pennies have been found in

Scandinavia, and several Swedish tombstones commemorate mercenaries who went to England and enriched themselves with tribute. In the 990s, as in 1066, England's wealth was also its danger.

How was Æthelred to cope? One measure was to prevent the harbouring of Vikings by his neighbours, and for geographical reasons the young duchy of Normandy was the most important of these. The Normans were only a few generations away from their own Viking ancestors, and had sometimes opened their ports to raiders returning from England. But in 991 King Æthelred and Duke Richard made a treaty against aiding each other's enemies, and ten years later Æthelred married the duke's daughter. So began the fateful association of Normandy and England.

Hitherto the king's internal policy does not seem to have been very different from that of his predecessors. He inherited a powerful, well-established aristocracy, and his early charters show him building up support with grants of land just as Eadwig and Edgar had done. But from 1002 the Viking threat became rapidly more severe, and exposed a basic weakness in royal power. The king's lands, and probably his activities generally, were still heavily concentrated in Wessex. The resources with which he could buy support in the north and east were very limited—and these were just the areas where support most needed to be bought. They still had separatist tendencies, and contained many people who remembered their Danish origins. Æthelred's later charters show a shift of patronage into the Midlands and eastern England, and new men of non-Wessex origin become prominent. The king was struggling to hold England united and in a state of defence. His ineptitudes may have made the task harder, but nobody would have found it easy.

The strain on the government was demonstrated when, in 1002, Æthelred and his council ordered a massacre of all the Danes living in England. This extraordinary command cannot have been fully enforced—in some areas the population was largely Danish—but it hints at something approaching national hysteria. We know that, when the Danes in Oxford took refuge in St. Frideswide's minster church, the citizens burnt it down. This massacre almost certainly prompted the Danish invasion of the following year, led by King Swein himself. Swein sacked Norwich, but his East Anglian campaign involved heavy losses and in 1005 he withdrew to Denmark. Next year he returned, led his army through Berkshire, Wiltshire, and Hampshire, and once again had to be bought off with a large payment. In the ensuing respite the government built a new fleet, but early in 1009 eighty of the ships were burnt through the treason of an English captain. On the heels of this misfortune, another Danish army landed, led by Thorkill the Tall and Hemming. In 1010 they burnt Oxford, and then moved to East Anglia from which they raided into Kent the following year. The campaign ended unexpectedly in 1012 when Thorkill changed sides, disgusted by his own army's brutal murder of Archbishop Ælfheah. This brought forty-five ships into Æthelred's service; the rest of the army left England.

The feebleness of England's defences was now clear to all, and when Swein returned in 1013 it was with the intention of conquest. Disillusioned with Æthelred's government, the men of the Danelaw welcomed a Danish king and accepted Swein almost immediately. By the end of the year he had taken Oxford, Winchester, and London, and Æthelred had fled to exile in Normandy. In February 1014 Swein died; his son Harold succeeded to his Scandinavian empire, but the army in England accepted Harold's younger brother Cnut as their king. Meanwhile Æthelred had returned, and by spring he was fielding an expedition against the Danes. Caught unprepared, Cnut withdrew to Denmark. In 1015 he was back with a bigger force, to find that Æthelred's son Edmund Ironside had taken control of the northern Danelaw in defiance of his father. During the next few months Cnut recovered Northumbria and then moved towards London. But before the Danish forces arrived Æthelred was dead and Edmund had been proclaimed king. Even in

Wessex, however, many men accepted Cnut's lordship without a struggle. Edmund rallied his forces, and for a little while it seemed that the Danes might still be driven back. But in the autumn of 1016 Cnut won a decisive battle at Ashingdon in Essex. The treaty which followed left Edmund with only Wessex, and when he died shortly afterwards Cnut became king of all England.

King Cnut (1016–35) had to deal with problems which were not dissimilar to those which faced King William fifty years later. Like William, Cnut set out to rule not as a conqueror but as a rightful English king. He married Æthelred's widow, and acted ruthlessly to secure the throne: several leading English were killed, including Æthelred's eldest surviving son. Once secure, Cnut adopted with enthusiasm the traditional attributes of civilized kingship. He issued laws and founded monasteries; in the words of a chronicler of the next century, he changed himself 'from a wild man into a most Christian king'. Yet he was still a Dane, and on his brother's death in 1019 he inherited a great northern empire of which England was only part. During the 1020s he became more and more involved in Danish affairs. The breadth of Cnut's involvements is the main reason for his changes in England, which were relatively few, but in the end damaging.

Naturally he had many followers eager for rewards. There was no full-scale replacement of the English landowning class such as occurred after 1066, but a good many Danes joined the aristocracy. An alien and therefore rather insecure king, Cnut kept a regiment of household troops or 'housecarls' who were a considerable burden on the country. After thirty years of paying to keep the Danes away, landowners now had to pay to support a Danish standing army.

Cnut also had to make English government function during his long absences abroad. In 1017 he divided the kingdom into four earldoms—Northumbria, East Anglia, Mercia, and Wessex. This ran obvious risks of reviving local separatist feeling, especially since the Northumbrian and East Anglian earls were both Danes. By the end of the reign the most important figures were Siward earl of Northumbria, Leofric earl of Mercia (whose wife was Lady Godiva of Coventry fame), and Godwin earl of Wessex. Godwin's origins are obscure, but by the 1030s he and his family were the wealthiest and most powerful lay-men below the king. Cnut's earldoms are largely responsible for the power politics which dominate the last thirty years of Anglo-Saxon history.

The End of the Anglo-Saxon Kingdom

When Cnut died in 1035 there were several possible successors. The Wessex dynasty was represented by Æthelred's younger sons Edward and Alfred, now at the Norman court, and by Edmund Ironside's son who was exiled in Hungary. Cnut had two sons by two wives: Harold, by Ælfgyfu of Northampton, and Harthacnut, by Emma the widow of Æthelred. Cnut had wanted Harthacnut to succeed to his whole empire. But while Harthacnut delayed in Denmark the Witan appointed Harold as regent (despite the opposition of both Emma and Godwin), and in 1037 made him king. The previous year, the English prince Alfred had unwisely visited England and died of injuries inflicted at Godwin's instigation. Harthacnut was recalled after Harold's death in 1040, but when he died two years later the Danish royal line ended. Almost everyone now wanted to res-tore the ancient dynasty of Wessex. Æthelred's son Edward had been living for a year at the English court, and in 1042 he was elected king.

Edward 'the Confessor' (1042–66) was destined to be vener-ated as the principal English royal saint. His recent biographer, scrutinising the reality behind the pious legend, writes that 'he was not a man of great distinction. But neither was he a holy imbecile. He was, like many of his rank and time, a medioc-rity.' Whatever his strengths and weaknesses, he inherited the strongest government in eleventh-century Europe. The reason for this strength lay partly in institutions which were centuries old, partly in the very disruptions of the last sixty years.

Local government had developed since Edgar's day. On the one hand, the great earldoms consolidated under Cnut had given huge territorial power to a few men. An insecure king now had to face the threat of over-mighty subjects. On the other hand, an invaluable new official had appeared to carry out royal policy in the localities. During Æthelred's reign one of the king's local bailiffs ('reeves') in each shire had come to be known as the 'shire-reeve' or sheriff. He was the king's chief executive agent in the shire, and gradually assumed more and more of the alderman's functions. The sheriff was responsible for collecting royal revenues and the profits of justice, but he also belonged to the growing community of local thegns. In the shire court he could announce the king's will to the gentry of the shire, take a big part in day-to-day business, and add the weight of royal authority to action against oppressive magnates. The shire court and the sheriff are among the most important Anglo-Saxon legacies to later medieval government.

A highly efficient tax system had evolved as a direct result of England's weakness under Æthelred. The huge sums paid to the Danes in the 990s had to be raised from the country. The 'Danegeld', as it came to be called, was based on the ancient method of assessing land in hides, and was raised at a fixed rate of so much per hide. Between 1012 and 1051 it was levied yearly by the successive kings, though now for maintaining their standing armies. The complex system of assessment developed for this purpose is the basis of the later Domesday Book, and it is an extraordinary tribute to the early eleventh-century English bureaucracy that the Norman kings continued to raise Danegeld for nearly a century after the Conquest.

This period also saw a new type of official document: the royal writ. Writs were possibly issued by Æthelred and certainly by Cnut, but the earliest which now survive as originals are from Edward's reign. In its initial form, the writ was a brief notification to the shire-earl and the sheriff or bishop that a grant of land had been made and should be witnessed in the shire court. A typical example reads:

Edward the king greets Harold the earl and Tofi his sheriff and all his thegns in Somerset in friendly fashion. And I make known that Alfred has sold to Giso the bishop the land of Lutton peacefully and quietly: he did this in my presence at Parret, and in the presence of Edith my wife, Harold the earl and many others who were there present with us. We also wish that the same bishop shall hold that land with all its appurtenances which the bishop possesses with sac and soc as freely as any of his predecessors as bishops ever did anything. And if anything be taken away from it unjustly we ask that it may be restored. Nor shall it be done otherwise.

This combined efficiency with a new means of authentication: a pendent wax seal, stamped from a die kept in the king's household. As title-deeds, writs provided useful supplements to the old formal charters, which were unwieldy and easily forged. They also provided a means for the king to make his will known quickly and clearly in the shires. The Conqueror soon adapted the writ for issuing orders, and all the more important types of post-Conquest royal document are descended from it.

When ordering a taxation or issuing a writ, the king would have consulted his secretariat. Edward the Confessor, like kings since Alfred at the latest, had a clerical staff of priests, headed by a chief clerk whose office developed into that of the medieval chancellor. One of their duties was to keep records: from the late Anglo-Saxon period comes evidence of very detailed surveys recording land-tenure, numbers of hides, and tax obligations. Some remarks by Bede suggest that even the seventh-century Northumbrian kings had enough precise information to grant land in exact numbers of hides; while from the eighth century a document called the *Tribal Hidage* lists the names and hidages of the peoples, provinces, and tribes dependent on Mercia. So we can be confident that ninth- and tenth-century kings had fiscal records of some kind, though how detailed is impossible to say. By Edward the Confessor's reign, the royal secretariat possessed rolls which listed the hidages of shires and hundreds, the amount of royal land they contained, and perhaps even the names, owners, and values of individual manors. We know this not from the documents themselves (though a few fragments survive), but from Domesday Book. The great survey of 1086 could scarcely have been compiled so quickly and so thoroughly if the commissioners had not had access to earlier lists. The loss of the pre-Conquest public records is tragic, but the mere knowledge that they existed says much for the quality of Edward's administration.

If English government changed greatly between the reigns of Alfred and Edward, so too did English society. The mid-ninth to mid-eleventh centuries saw rapid growth in the population and economy. Before Domesday Book there are no statistics, but written, archaeological, and topographical evidence gives some strong hints that many aspects of later English society crystallized in these years. Not surprisingly, more people meant bigger towns. By the Conquest there were English towns in a sense that we would understand today: large concentrations of people with markets and tradesmen, groups of craftsmen in specialized quarters, guilds and regulations, numerous churches, and in some cases rapidly expanding suburbs. The late Saxon law codes recognize trading centres or 'ports' (not necessarily coastal) and large boroughs, rated according to the number of moneyers they were allowed to contain. The towns included most of the *burhs* and many minster centres, but they were not confined to places of ancient importance. We cannot even guess at the number of local markets, but a good many which first appear in the thirteenth century may be older than they seem.

The countryside was also changing, though it is hard to trace the changes clearly. Topographical studies suggest a process of settlement nucleation in the more populous areas, with the inhabitants of scattered farms clustering into villages. At the same time, agriculture was becoming more complex and more integrated, so that by 1066 many parts of England had 'common fields', farmed by peasants with intermingled holdings, and therefore probably with corporately-agreed cropping patterns. The early development of field systems is now a controversial subject, but it is in the tenth century that we can first detect the basic contrast between the open-field zone of Midland England and the surrounding 'wood-pasture' areas. Much remains uncertain about the relationship between changes in settlement form, agriculture, and land-holding, but it seems that the process went through several stages and continued well beyond the Conquest. There are also suggestions that sometimes these were not spontaneous developments, but rearrangements planned from above. Peasant society was becoming more stratified and cohesive, and lords were making greater demands on their tenants.

One reason is that there were more manors and more manorial lords. Except in retarded areas, most of the old 'multiple estates' had fragmented by the eleventh century into units corresponding in size to modern rural parishes. Population grew, cultivation expanded, and the components of the old 'extensive' systems became self-contained entities. Many more charters survive from the tenth century than from the eighth and ninth together; most of them grant smaller units of land, and the proportion in favour of laymen is higher. The class of small thegns had broadened into a rural squirearchy, and Domesday Book shows that in 1066 England contained hundreds of manorial lords.

This is the context in which most parish churches were founded. Just as kings and bishops had built minsters in the seventh and eighth centuries, so thegns built manorial churches in the tenth and eleventh. There were *some* private churches from a relatively early date (Bede mentions a bishop consecrating one in the 690s), but both documents and archaeology suggest that the majority were founded after 900, perhaps even after 950. Pastoral organization must have been chaotic: the minster parishes were slowly decaying, and more and more of the manors within them were acquiring rival churches of their own, served by manorial priests. Eleventh-century churches (both before and after the Conquest) were in effect 'owned' by their lords, and their functions were determined on tenurial rather than pastoral lines: the church's function was to serve the needs of the lord, his household, and tenants. We can scarcely speak of anything so formal as a 'parochial system', though the raw materials were there: probably more than half the parish churches existing in 1700 were founded before 1066.

So the familiar landmarks of rural England—villages, manor houses, churches—took shape mainly in the late Saxon period. For Archbishop Wulfstan, writing in c.1010, the last two were normal marks of thegnhood: 'If a *ceorl* prospered so that he possessed fully five hides of land of his own, a church and a kitchen, a bell and a fortress-gate, a seat and special office in the king's hall, he was worthy thereafter to be called a thegn.' The 'fortress-gate' in this famous passage leads to a question which has become needlessly controversial: were there castles in pre-Conquest England? One writer, equating private castles with feudalism and convinced that late Saxon England was non-feudal, argues that it contained no fortresses beyond the communal *burhs*. But if a strongly-fortified manor house counts as a castle, the existence of castles says little about a society except that it included a land-based aristocracy of some status. In fact excavation now proves that fortified houses *did* exist, and complex manorial buildings surrounded by banks and ditches of c.1000–20 have been found at Sulgrave, Northamptonshire, and Goltho, Lincolnshire. These sites show that ordinary late Saxon thegns' residences could be as imposing as most manor houses of the twelfth and early thirteenth centuries.

Warfare was becoming more professional, and equipment consequently more expensive. By the end of the tenth century, a system of military service had developed in which every five hides was responsible for providing and equipping one man for the *fyrd* (militia). This acknowledged that the average farmer could not reasonably be expected to kit himself out from his own resources, and by implication raised the status of the fighting man. Five hides, according to Wulfstan, was a thegn's minimum estate, and armour and weapons had become another mark of thegnhood. The fully-armed late Saxon warrior was something more than a *ceorl* turned soldier.

By Æthelred's reign the monastic reform was running out of steam. Burton Abbey in Staffordshire (1004) and Eynsham Abbey in Oxfordshire (1005) were the last great foundations, and the general political disruption and draining of resources soon put a stop to large-scale patronage and building. Edward's piety did, however, produce one building project, the most ambitious that England had ever seen. In about 1050 he began to rebuild the old minster church at Westminster on a scale worthy of the English monarchy. Architecture in England was stagnant, but in Normandy its development during the last forty years had been spectacular: the finest buildings of Edgar's day would have looked unimpressive beside the abbey churches of Bernay and Caen. So for Westminster Abbey Edward naturally looked to Norman architects, though his church as eventually built was magnificent and innovative even by their standards, and probably owed something to English decorative traditions. It is somewhat ironic that the last great monument of the house of Wessex was mainly a product of Norman culture.

The final years of Anglo-Saxon history are dominated by Godwin's family and the problem of the succession. Edward had married Godwin's daughter, but by the early 1050s it had become clear that he would never produce an heir. Edward, son of Edmund Ironside, returned from Hungary with his infant son in 1057 but died almost immediately. The young prince Edgar was the legitimate heir, but nobody can have viewed with much enthusiasm the prospect of a child on the throne. The Norwegian king, Magnus, and after him his son Harold Hardrada, saw themselves as the heirs to Cnut's empire, including England. Neither candidate is likely to have appealed much to King Edward: his eyes, if they were turned anywhere, were turned across the Channel. The duchy of Normandy, where he had lived in exile for twenty-five years, had developed fast in strength and internal organization. In 1035 Duke Robert had been succeeded by his bastard son William, then a boy of seven. We will never know for certain if Edward promised his throne to William, but we can say that this is exactly the course which we might expect of him.

Edward had never forgiven Godwin for his brother's murder, and the tension between them came to a head in 1051. One of Edward's Norman friends became involved in a brawl at Dover, and several men were killed. Edward ordered Godwin, as earl of Wessex, to sack Dover in retribution. Godwin refused and raised troops against the king, who summoned the Mercian and Northumbrian earls with their full forces. Conflict was avoided; as a contemporary put it, 'some of them considered it would be great folly if they joined battle, because wellnigh all the noblest in England were present in those two companies, and they were convinced they would be leaving the country open to the invasion of our enemies'. Godwin's support crumbled, and he and his family went into exile. Over the next year Edward increased the Norman element at court, but in 1052 Godwin returned with a large fleet and the king was obliged to be more compliant. The Norman archbishop fled home, and several of his fellow countrymen were banished at Godwin's request.

Godwin now enjoyed virtually supreme power, but in 1053 he died. His successor in the earldom of Wessex was his son Harold, destined to be the last Anglo-Saxon king. When Earl Siward of Northumbria died two years later, his earldom went to Harold's brother Tostig. Thanks to the activities of King Gruffydd of Gwynedd, the standing of Godwin's sons soon rose yet higher. Gruffydd, who had recently made himself supreme in Wales, allied with the exiled heir to the Mercian earldom and launched a series of attacks into English territory, in the course of which Hereford was sacked and burnt. The combined forces of Harold and Tostig drove Gruffydd back into

Wales, and in 1063 caused his downfall and death. With this success behind him, Harold was the outstanding figure in England. Despite his lack of royal ancestry, he seemed an obvious candidate for the throne.

But in 1064, or perhaps early in 1065, Harold visited Duke William in Normandy. He went, say the Norman sources, as Edward's ambassador, to swear an oath confirming an earlier promise of the English crown. It is possible, but on the whole unlikely, that the story of the oath is a Norman invention. But there is a third explanation, the one which the English artists of the Bayeux Tapestry may secretly be trying to give us: Harold falls into William's hands by mischance, is forced to swear the oath, and returns shamefacedly to a horrified King Edward. Whichever version is true (and on balance the Norman one may have the best claim after all), many contemporaries believed that William had right on his side as well as might.

The events of the last two years moved quickly. During 1065 Northumbria rebelled against Earl Tostig. Harold mediated, but the local nominee was upheld: Tostig went into exile, henceforth his brother's enemy. On 5 January 1066 King Edward died. Urgent military need overrode legality, and the Witan elected Harold as king. This was the signal for his two adult rivals. Harold Hardrada of Norway was the first to move: aided by the exiled Tostig, he invaded Northumbria during the summer and occupied York. Harold, who was awaiting the expected invasion from Normandy, was forced to move north. At Stamford Bridge near York he met and defeated the Norwegian forces on 25 September. Hardrada and Tostig were both killed, and King Harold recovered Northumbria.

Meanwhile Duke William's fleet, which had been delayed by bad weather, landed at Pevensey on 28 September. Harold rushed southwards; but the preparations which he had made two months earlier had fallen apart, and the core of his army was exhausted. On 14 October 1066, the English and Norman armies met near Hastings. Harold's forces gathered on the crest of a hill and formed a wall of shields. The battle lasted all day, and at first the English position seemed strong. Apparently it was lost through lack of discipline rather than lack of force. Sections of Harold's army seem to have been enticed down the slope in pursuit of real or feigned retreats, and then cut off and overwhelmed. Gradually the English troops were broken up; the centre held until dusk, but the outcome was already clear when Harold fell on the spot marked in later centuries by the high altar of Battle Abbey.

William advanced to Dover and then to Canterbury, where he received the submission of Winchester. But his main objective was London, for there the core of the English resistance had gathered under Edgar Atheling. Meeting opposition at London Bridge, William encircled the city leaving a trail of devastation. Meanwhile the Atheling's party was crumbling, and when William reached Berkhamsted the English nobles, headed by Edgar himself, met him and offered their fealty. Alfred's family had survived Danes, Norsemen, and Danes again, but at last a foreign dynasty had supplanted it for good.

3. The Early Middle Ages
(1066–1290)

JOHN GILLINGHAM

1066 and All That

ON Christmas Day 1066 Duke William of Normandy was acclaimed king in Westminster Abbey. It was an electrifying moment. The shouts of acclamation—in English as well as in French—alarmed the Norman guards stationed outside the abbey. Believing that inside the church something had gone horribly wrong, they set fire to the neighbouring houses. Half a century later, a Norman monk recalled the chaos of that day. 'As the fire spread rapidly, the people in the church were thrown into confusion and crowds of them rushed outside, some to fight the flames, others to take the chance to go looting. Only the monks, the bishops and a few clergy remained before the altar. Though they were terrified, they managed to carry on and complete the consecration of the king who was trembling violently.'

Despite his victory at Hastings, despite the surrender of London and Winchester, William's position was still a precarious one and he had good reason to tremble. It was to take at least another five years before he could feel fairly confident that the conquest had been completed. There were risings against Norman rule in every year from 1067 to 1070: in Kent, in the south-west, in the Welsh marches, in the Fenland, and in the north. The Normans had to live like an army of occupation, living, eating, and sleeping together in operational units. They had to build castles—strong points from which a few men could dominate a subject population. There may well have been no more than 10,000 Normans living in the midst of a hostile population of one or two million. This is not to say that every single Englishman actively opposed the Normans. Unquestionably there were many who co-operated with them; it was this which made possible the successful Norman take-over of so many Anglo-Saxon institutions. But there is plenty of evidence to show that the English resented becoming an oppressed majority in their own country. The years of insecurity were to have a profound effect on subsequent history. They meant that England received not just a new royal family but also a new ruling class, a new culture and language. Probably no other conquest in European history has had such disastrous consequences for the defeated.

Almost certainly this had not been William's original intention. In the early days many Englishmen were able to offer their submission and retain their lands. Yet by 1086 something had clearly changed. Domesday Book is a record of a land deeply marked by the scars of conquest. In 1086 there were only two surviving English lords of any account. More than 4,000 thegns had lost their lands and been replaced by a group of less than 200 barons. A few of the new landlords were Bretons and men from Flanders and Lorraine but most were Normans. In the case of the Church we can put a date to William's anti-English policy. In 1070 he had some English bishops deposed and thereafter appointed no Englishman to either bishopric or abbey. In military matters, the harrying of the north during the winter of 1069–70 also suggests ruthlessness on a new scale at about this time. In Yorkshire this meant that between 1066 and 1086 land values fell by as much as two-thirds. But whenever and however it occurred it is certain that by 1086 the Anglo-Saxon aristocracy was no more and its place had been taken by a new Norman élite. Naturally this new élite retained its old lands on the Continent; the result was that England and Normandy, once two separate states, now became a single cross-Channel political community, sharing not only a ruling dynasty, but also a single Anglo-Norman aristocracy. Given the advantages of water transport, the Channel no more divided England from Normandy than the Thames divided Middlesex from Surrey. From now on, until 1204, the histories of England and Normandy were inextricably interwoven.

Since Normandy was a principality ruled by a duke who owed homage to the king of France this also meant that from now on 'English' politics became part of French politics. But the French connection went deeper still. The Normans, being Frenchmen, brought with them to England the French language and French culture. Moreover, we are not dealing with a single massive input of 'Frenchness' in the generation after 1066 followed by a gradual reassertion of 'Englishness'. The Norman Conquest of 1066 was followed by an Angevin conquest of 1153–4; although this did not involve the settlement of a Loire Valley aristocracy in England, the effect of the arrival of the court of Henry II and Eleanor of Aquitaine was to reinforce the dominance of French culture.

Whereas in 1066 less than 30 per cent of Winchester property owners had non-English names, by 1207 the proportion had risen to over 80 per cent, mostly French names like William, Robert, and Richard. This receptiveness to Continental influence means that at this time it is the foreignness of English art that is most striking. In ecclesiastical architecture, for example, the European terms 'Romanesque' and 'Gothic' describe the fashionable styles much better than 'Norman' and 'Early English'. Although churches built in England, like manuscripts illuminated in England, often contain some recognizably English elements, the designs which the architects and artists were adapting came from abroad, sometimes from the Mediterranean world (Italy, Sicily, or even Byzantium), usually from France. It was a French architect, William of Sens, who was called in to rebuild the choir of Canterbury Cathedral after the fire of 1174. Similarly Henry III's rebuilding of Westminster Abbey was heavily influenced by French models. Indeed so great was the pre-eminence of France in the fields of music, literature, and architecture, that French became a truly international rather than just a national language, a language spoken—and written—by anyone who wanted to consider himself civilized. Thus, in thirteenth-century England, French became, if anything, even more important than it had been before. Throughout most of the period covered by this chapter a well-educated Englishman was trilingual. English would be his mother tongue; he would have some knowledge of Latin, and he would speak fluent French. In this cosmopolitan society French was vital. It was the practical language of law and estate management as well as the language of song and verse, of *chanson* and romance. The Norman Conquest, in other words, ushered in a period during which England, like the kingdom of Jerusalem, can fairly be described as a part of France overseas, *Outremer*; in political terms, it was a French colony (though not, of course, one that belonged to the French king) until the early thirteenth century and a cultural colony thereafter.

It is hardly surprising, then, that generations of patriotic Englishmen should have looked upon the battle of Hastings as a national catastrophe. Yet even if we do not, as E. A. Freeman did, describe Paris as 'beastly', it can still be argued that the Norman Conquest was the greatest disaster in English history. Not because it was predatory and destructive—though, of course, like any conquest it was both—but because of the problem of '1066 and All That'. With 1066 as the most famous date in English history the Norman Conquest is a 'blessedly well-known landmark'. It is devastatingly easy to see it as a 'new beginning' or a 'significant turning-point'. Almost everything that happened in late eleventh-century England has been discussed in terms of the impact of the Norman Conquest. But the second half of the eleventh century was a period of rapid development throughout Europe. Countries which suffered no Norman Conquest were, none the less, transformed. So there is the problem. In some respects 1066 wrought great changes; in other respects, great changes occurred but can hardly be ascribed to the Conquest; in yet others, the most striking feature is not change at all, but continuity.

The main problem facing the historian of this period, however, is posed not by a single dramatic event, but by a social and cultural process of great complexity. This is the tremendous proliferation of written records which occurred during the twelfth and thirteenth centuries. Many more documents than ever before were written and many more were preserved. Whereas from the whole of the Anglo-Saxon period about 2,000 writs and charters survive, from the thirteenth century alone there are uncounted tens of thousands. Of course the 2,000 Anglo-Saxon documents were only the tip of the iceberg; many more did not survive. But this is true also of the thirteenth century. It has, for example, been estimated that as many as eight million charters could have been produced for thirteenth-century smallholders and peasants alone. Even if this were to be a rather generous estimate, it would still be true that whole classes of the population, serfs for example, were now concerned with documents in ways that previously they had not been. Whereas in the reign of Edward the Confessor only the king is known to have possessed a seal, in Edward I's reign even serfs were required by statute to have them. At the centre of this development, and to some extent its motor, lay the king's government. The king possessed permanently organized writing offices, the chancery, and then the exchequer too: they were becoming busier and busier. In Henry III's reign, we can measure the amount of sealing wax which the chancery used. In the late 1220s it was getting through 3.63 lb. per week; by the late 1260s the amount had gone up to 31.9 lb. per week. Not only was the government issuing more documents than ever before; it was also systematically making copies and keeping them. Here the key date is 1199. In that year the chancery clerks began to keep copies, on rolls of parchment, of most of the letters—and certainly of all the important ones—sent out under the great seal. The survival of the chancery enrolments means that from 1199 historians know a great deal more about the routine of government than ever before.

These are developments of fundamental importance. The proliferation of records involved a shift from habitually memorizing things to writing them down. It meant that the whole population was now, in a sense, 'participating in literacy'; even if they could not themselves read they became accustomed to seeing day-to-day business transacted through the medium of writing. Clearly this development of a literate mentality is closely linked with the cultural movement commonly known as the twelfth-century Renaissance. At first the power-houses of the new learning all lay abroad in the towns and cathedrals of Italy and France; but by the late twelfth century there were some schools of higher learning in England and by the 1220s two universities, first at Oxford and then at Cambridge, had been established. At Oxford there were schools where men could learn severely practical subjects such as conveyancing, administration, and elementary legal procedure. And throughout England the signs point to an increasing number of schools at all levels.

But are these profound developments associated with revolutionary changes in other aspects of social organization? Clearly, the production of all these written records means that society is becoming more bureaucratic, but does this mean that the relationships between classes are being conserved or being altered? Is the economic system changing? Is the political system changing? Or are both merely being more elaborately recorded?

These are not questions which it is easy to answer. The cumulative nature of the evidence tends to deceive. For example, a particular form of relationship between men may first be clearly documented in the thirteenth century. But does this mean that the relationship itself originated in that century? Or that these types of relationship were first fixed in writing then?

Or only that this is the earliest period from which the relevant documents happen to have survived? A case in point is the fact that the earliest known examples of a type of document known as the 'indenture of retainer' date from the thirteenth century. The indenture records the terms on which a man was engaged to serve his lord; it would normally specify his wages and, if it was a long-service contract, his retaining fee. On the basis of these documents, historians have decided that the 'indentured retainer' and the 'contract army' both came into existence towards the end of the thirteenth century, and that they were characteristic of the later Middle Ages, the period of 'bastard feudalism'. Yet there is clear, though indirect, evidence that both contract armies and retainers receiving fee and wages were in existence at least as early as 1100. And in general in this chapter it will be argued that there was a much higher degree of continuity in economic, political, and social organization than is often supposed. But first, before going any further, it will be useful to give a brief outline of the main events, concentrating on those events which were of greatest concern to kings.

William I (1066–1087)

After 1071, William's hold on England was fairly secure. The Welsh and the Scots gave him little trouble. Scandinavian rulers continued to look upon England with acquisitive eyes but the ever-present threat of another Viking invasion never quite materialized. From 1071 to the end of his reign most of William's attention was taken up by war and diplomacy on the Continent. Normandy was his homeland and far more vulnerable to sudden attack than was his island kingdom. Several of William's neighbours were alarmed by his new power and took every opportunity to diminish it. At their head were King Philip of France, and Count Fulk le Rechin of Anjou. Their best opportunities were provided by William's eldest son Robert (b. 1054). Recognized as the heir to Normandy as long ago as 1066, he had never been allowed to enjoy either money or power, and from 1078 onwards he became involved in a series of intrigues against his father. In quarrels between the king of France and the duke of Normandy the natural battlefield was the Vexin, a disputed territory lying on the north bank of the Seine between Rouen and Paris. The county of Maine, which William had conquered in 1063, played a similar role in the hostilities between Normandy and Anjou. Maine was to remain a bone of contention for the next two generations; the Vexin for much longer still (until 1203). Thus already in William's reign it is possible to see the political pattern which was to dominate the next century: the intermingling of family dissension and frontier dispute. In this context the circumstances of William's death are revealing. The garrison of the French fortress of Mantes made a raid into Normandy. William retaliated and while his troops sacked Mantes (July 1087) he received the injury from which he died. Robert was in rebellion at the time and chose to remain at the court of King Philip, while his younger brother William dutifully, and pointedly, was to be found in attendance at his father's bedside. On 9 September 1087, William I died. His body was carried to his great church of St. Stephen at Caen. Towards the end of his life he had grown very fat and when the attendants tried to force the body into the stone sarcophagus, it burst, filling the church with a foul smell. It was an unfortunate ending to the career of an unusually fortunate and competent king.

William II (1087–1100)

Whatever William's last wishes may have been, there was a strong presumption that the eldest son should have his father's patrimony, that is those lands which the father himself had inherited. Thus, despite his rebellion, Robert succeeded to Normandy. But a man's acquisition, the land he himself had obtained whether by purchase, marriage, or conquest, could more easily be used to provide for other members of his family. Thus England, the Conqueror's vast acquisition, was used to provide for his younger son, William. Naturally, Robert objected to this and perhaps, if it had not been for his rebellion, he would have succeeded to England as well.

What is clear is that the customs governing the succession to the throne were still flexible; they could—should—be bent in order to take account of political realities, for example the characters of the rival candidates. Thus those influential men, Archbishop Lanfranc of Canterbury among them, who decided to accept William Rufus as king of England, may well have judged that he would make a better ruler than his elder brother. In view of Robert's record both before and after 1087 this would have been a reasonable judgement, yet within a few months of his accession Rufus found himself opposed by a powerful coalition of great barons, the magnates. According to the Anglo-Norman chronicler Orderic Vitalis, the rebels' object-ive was to reunite England and Normandy, not for the sake of some principle of constitutional law but in order to ease their own political problems. Their dilemma was summed up in the words which Orderic placed in the mouth of the greatest of them, Odo of Bayeux. 'How can we give proper service to two distant and mutually hostile lords? If we serve Duke Robert well we shall offend his brother William and he will deprive us of our revenues and honours in England. On the other hand if we obey King William, Duke Robert will deprive us of our patrimonies in Normandy.' This was an argument which appealed to powerful vested interests and could very easily have unseated Rufus. If there were to be just one ruler of the joint Anglo-Norman realm then the elder brother's claim was dif-ficult to deny. Fortunately for Rufus, his brother's case went almost by default: Robert stayed in Normandy, leaving his supporters in the lurch. None the less the 1088 revolt, despite its swift collapse, does reveal just how precarious was the position of a king of England who was not also duke of Normandy.

Taking the forty-eight years (1087–1135) of the reigns of William II and Henry I as a whole, it can be seen that the rebellions (1088, 1095, 1101, 1102) cluster in the two periods (some fifteen years in all) when the king was not duke, that is 1087–96 and 1100–6. Obviously, it was not in the king's interest that England and Normandy should be under separate rulers. But neither was it in the interest of the aristocracy. As Odo of Bayeux's speech makes plain they had too much at risk to welcome instability. Whenever the cross-Channel kingdom did break up into its constituent parts this ushered in a period of conflict which was only settled when one ruler ousted the other. Thus the primary concern of a king of England was to win and hold Normandy.

In 1089 Rufus laid claim to the duchy. With English silver he was able to buy support and he campaigned there with some success. But his hold on England still remained insecure; he faced a conspiracy in 1095. Next year the tension was resolved, at any rate temporarily, in a totally unforeseeable manner. The astonishing success of Pope Urban II's preaching tour created a climate of opinion in which thousands decided to join an expedition aimed at recovering Jerusalem from the Muslims. For Robert Curthose this offered an honourable and exciting way out of his increasingly difficult domestic political position. In order to equip himself and his retinue for the long march, he pawned Normandy to William for 10,000 marks.

The new duke's next task was to recover Maine and the Vexin, lost during Robert's slack rule. By 1099, this had been successfully accomplished. Rufus had restored his father's kingdom to its former frontiers; indeed in Scotland, by installing Edgar on the throne in 1097, he intervened more effectively than even his father had done.

Yet for all his success as a generous leader of soldiers, William's reputation has remained consistently low. Unfortunately for him, the history of the time was written almost entirely by monks and they did not like him. Serious-minded churchmen, accustomed to the conventional piety and sober discretion of his father's court, were appalled by Rufus's, by its ostentatious extravagance, by its gaiety, and by the new fashions—long hair for example—which seemed to them to be both effeminate and licentious. Rufus never married. According to the Welsh *Chronicle of Princes*, 'he used concubines and because of that died without an heir'. He may have been sceptical of the claims of religion—at any rate this is how contemporaries portrayed him; undoubtedly he treated the Church as a rich corporation which needed soaking. He was rarely in a hurry to appoint bishops and abbots, for during vacancies he could help himself to the Church's revenues. In carrying out these profitable policies Rufus relied on the ingenious aid of a quick-witted and worldly clerk, Ranulf Flambard, whom he eventually made bishop of Durham.

Above all Rufus's reputation has suffered because in 1093, when he thought he was dying, he appointed a saintly scholar Anselm of Bec as Archbishop of Canterbury (after having kept the see vacant for four years). What made this appointment so disastrous from William's point of view was the fact that it occurred at a time when a European movement for Church reform—the Gregorian reform—had created a controversial atmosphere in which holy men were only too likely to become political radicals. In 1095 William called a council at Rockingham to deal with the matters in dispute between him and Anselm. To the consternation of all, Archbishop Anselm appealed to Rome, arguing that as Archbishop of Canterbury he could not be judged in a secular court. The rise of the Papacy in the second half of the eleventh century, with its claim to the first loyalty of prelates, had brought a new and disturbing element on to the political stage. If churchmen were to believe that their obligations to God, as defined by the vicar of St. Peter, were to override their duty to the king, then the customary structure of the world would have been turned upside down.

Anselm's case in favour of an autonomous spiritual hierarchy was a well-reasoned one; in this respect he can be said to have had the better of the argument. But Rufus had a case too; not only that, he had power—pitted against the material resources available to a masterful king, a scholarly Archbishop of Canterbury was in a very weak position indeed. William continued to harass the archbishop, and never showed any sympathy for his attempts to reform the Church. Eventually Anselm could bear it no longer. In 1097 he sailed from Dover, leaving the estates of Canterbury to be taken into the king's hand. In the short run the king had gained from the quarrel. In 1100 he enjoyed the revenues of three bishoprics and twelve abbeys. Nor was there as yet any sign that the arguments had undermined men's belief in the awesome powers of an anointed king. Even Eadmer, the Canterbury monk who wrote a *Life of Anselm*, remarked of Rufus that 'the wind and the sea seemed to obey him'. Indeed, Eadmer went on, 'in war and in the acquisition of territory he enjoyed such success that you would think the whole world smiling upon him'. Whether, in reality, William II's position in 1100 was quite so strong is another matter; it suited moralistic chroniclers to portray him as a self-confident, boastful king who was struck down just when he seemed to be at the very pinnacle of success. During the summer of 1100 everyone must have known that the peaceful interlude of Duke Robert's absence was about to end. The crusader was on his way home, accompanied by a rich wife and basking in the prestige due to a man who had fought his way into the Holy City. When Curthose reclaimed his inheritance, who could tell what would happen or what line the Anglo-Norman magnates would take? As it happened, on 2 August 1100 a hunting accident in the New Forest brought the life of this forceful and much-maligned king to an abrupt end. Also, as it happened, William's younger brother was in the New Forest on the day the king died.

Henry I (1100–1135)

As soon as he knew Rufus was dead Henry moved fast. He rode to Winchester and took possession of the treasury. Then he went straight on to Westminster where he was crowned on 5 August. This speed of action has prompted speculation that

Henry knew that his brother was going to die, that he had 'arranged the accident'. But no contemporary makes the charge and if Henry had planned so cold-blooded a crime his timing is likely to have been different. The impending war between Rufus and Curthose could be expected to end with the defeat and perhaps the elimination of one of them. In other words a delayed assassination would have opened up to the assassin the prospect of obtaining *both* England *and* Normandy. As it was, Rufus's death in August 1100 meant that Henry had to act with phenomenal speed merely to seize control of just one of the two parts of the Anglo-Norman realm. A man capable of waiting for so long before he struck would surely have waited a year or two longer.

A few weeks later, Robert arrived back in Normandy. Henry had to prepare to meet the inevitable invasion. His policy was to buy support by granting favours and wide-ranging concessions. This was a policy proclaimed on the day of his coronation, when he issued a charter of liberties denouncing his brother's oppressive practices and promising good government. On the other hand the urgent need to organize his defences meant that Henry could not afford to cause too much confusion. This was a time for gestures and manifestos, but it was not the moment to overturn a whole regime. The reality of the situation was that his elder brother had left him a ready-made court and administration and Henry had little choice but to take them over.

When Duke Robert landed at Portsmouth in July 1101, many of the greatest barons in England, led by Robert of Bellême and his brothers, flocked to his side. But Rufus's court circle, Robert of Meulan at their head, remained loyal to Henry; so also did the English Church. Both sides drew back and negotiated. Henry was to keep England and pay his brother a pension of £2,000 a year.

Having survived the crisis of 1101, Henry set about ensuring that it would not recur. The essential first step was the overthrow of the house of Montgomery (Bellême). In 1102 he captured Robert of Bellême's chief strongholds in the Welsh marches and then banished him. Two years later he confiscated the lands of William of Mortain. But Earls Robert and William, like others in their position, possessed in their Norman properties a base from which to organize the recovery of their English lands. By perpetuating the separation of England and Normandy the treaty of 1101 had ensured the continuance of political instability. So in a rerun of the history of the previous reign we find a king of England, first on the defensive, then going over to the attack. At the battle of Tinchebray (1106) the issue was decided. Duke Robert himself was captured and spent the last twenty-eight years of his life as his brother's prisoner.

Although in the first years of his reign Henry was preoccupied with Norman affairs, he was not as free to concentrate on them as he would have liked. Traditional royal rights over the Church were threatened by the new ideas associated with the Gregorian reform movement. The reformers did not only wish to purify the moral and spiritual life of the clergy; in order to do this, they believed that it was also necessary to free the Church from secular control. The most hated symbol of this control was lay investiture, a ceremony in which a new abbot or bishop received the ring and staff of office from the hands of the secular prince who had appointed him. Although the first papal decree against lay investiture had been issued as long ago as 1059 and more prohibitions had been published since, no one in England seems to have been aware of their existence until Anselm returned in the autumn of 1100. While in exile he had learned of the papal attitude to lay investiture. Thus although he himself had been invested by Rufus in 1093 he now refused either to do homage to Henry or to consecrate those prelates whom Henry had invested. This placed the king in a difficult position. Bishops and abbots were great landowners and key figures in central and local administration; he needed their assistance and had to be sure of their loyalty. On the other hand, unlike Rufus, he was unwilling to provoke a quarrel, so for years he found it more convenient to postpone the problem rather than try to solve it. Not until 1107 was the matter settled.

Henry renounced lay investiture, but prelates were to continue to do homage for their fiefs. In practice, the king's wishes continued to be the decisive factor in the making of bishops. To some extent, it can be said that Henry gave up the form but preserved the reality of control. When Anselm died in 1109 he kept the see of Canterbury vacant for five years. Yet he had lost something and he knew it. In the fierce war of propaganda which accompanied the 'Investiture Contest' the Gregorians had insisted that the king was a layman, nothing more, and as such he was inferior to all priests, for priests were concerned with the soul and the king only with the body. The Church could no longer tolerate the old idea that anointed kings were sacred deputies of God. In giving up lay investiture Henry was acknowledging the secular nature of his office. It was an important moment in the history of kingship.

Once Normandy had been conquered and a compromise solution found to the investiture dispute, Henry's main concern was to hold on to what he had. Recognizing the threat that could come from an alienated aristocracy, he was careful to close the gap between court and magnates which Rufus had allowed to develop. In Orderic's words, 'he treated the magnates with honour and generosity, adding to their wealth and estates, and by placating them in this way, he won their loyalty.' A direct threat to Henry's position came from the claim of Curthose's young son, William Clito (b. 1102) that he, not Henry, was the rightful duke of Normandy. This rival claim, coupled with Normandy's long land frontier, meant that the duchy remained the most vulnerable part of his empire. After 1106 Henry spent more than half the rest of his reign there in opposition to the traditional enemies of the Norman dukes, notably Louis VI of France (king 1108–37), and Fulk V of Anjou (count 1109–28). He organized a protective ring of alliances—no less than eight of his illegitimate daughters were married to neighbouring princes, from Alexander of Scotland in

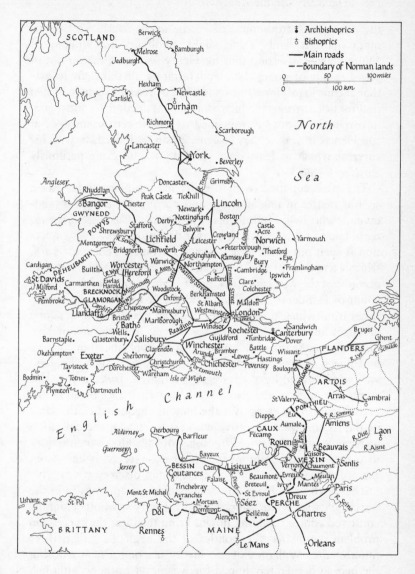

THE ANGLO-NORMAN REALM 1066–1154

the north to Rotrou count of Perche in the south. This diplomatic pattern lends some slight credibility to William of
Malmesbury's assertion that for Henry sex was a matter not of
pleasure but of policy. The end result of all this activity was
that Henry kept Normandy and for this reason, since it turned
out to be a struggle which only maintained the status quo,
historians have not been inclined to take it very seriously. But
for Henry it was a very serious business indeed, a war for
survival which at least once, in 1118–19, he came perilously
close to losing.

The preoccupation with the defence of Normandy was a
serious matter in England too, and not just for the great landowners who held estates on the Continent. Castles, garrisons,
diplomacy, and war all cost a great deal of money. The connection is spelt out in the *Anglo-Saxon Chronicle*'s entry for 1118.
'King Henry spent the whole of this year in Normandy on
account of the war with the king of France, count of Anjou and
count of Flanders ... England paid dearly for this in numerous
taxes from which there was no relief all year.' The king's long
absences and his urgent need for money were the motors behind the increasing elaboration and sophistication of the
machinery of government. While the king was away, England
was administered by a vice-regal committee. Twice a year this
committee met 'at the exchequer', that is, it met to audit the
accounts of the sheriffs over the famous chequered cloth. Most
of the routine administrative work, in particular the collection
of revenue, was supervised by Roger of Salisbury, a man who—
in contrast to the flamboyant Flambard—seems to have been
the archetypal bureaucrat, competent and discreet.

The death of William, his only legitimate son, in 1120 in the
wreck of the White Ship brought Henry's whole carefully
contrived edifice tumbling down. From then on, the succession
problem dominated the politics of the reign. Less than three
months after William's death, Henry married a new wife but
the heir so desperately hoped for was never born. So although
Henry is said to have acknowledged more than twenty bastards, he was survived by only one legitimate child, his

daughter Matilda. When her husband, Emperor Henry V of Germany, died in 1125, Henry recalled her to his court and made the barons swear to accept her as heir to the Anglo-Norman realm. Then in 1127 Henry received a fresh shock. William Clito was recognized as count of Flanders. If he were able to employ the wealth of Flanders in pursuit of his claim to Normandy, then the outlook for his uncle was black indeed. At this critical juncture Henry approached Fulk V of Anjou with a proposal for a marriage alliance between Matilda and Fulk's son and heir, Geoffrey Plantagenet. In June 1128 Matilda, somewhat against her will, was married to the fourteen-year-old youth. Unquestionably, Count Fulk had scored a diplomatic triumph: the first vital step in the Angevin take-over of the Anglo-Norman realm.

By 1135 Henry I was quarrelling openly and violently with Geoffrey and Matilda. This had the effect of driving those magnates who were loyal to Henry into opposition to the Angevins. When the old king died these magnates would inevitably find it difficult to come to terms with his designated heirs. In this sense it was Henry himself who provoked the succession dispute which followed his death. Even at the end of his life he still wanted his daughter and son-in-law to succeed, but he had been unable to bring himself to take the measures which would have enabled them to do so. Henry I had been an outstandingly able and successful king, the master politician of his age, but even he failed to cope with the tensions of the succession question. It was for this reason that Henry of Huntingdon portrayed Henry as a king in a permanent state of anxiety. 'Each of his triumphs only made him worry lest he lose what he had gained; therefore though he seemed to be the most fortunate of kings, he was in truth the most miserable.'

Stephen (1135–1154)

When the news came that Henry I lay dying, the old king's chosen heirs were in their own dominions, either in Anjou or in Maine. But his nephew, Stephen of Blois, was in his county of

Boulogne. From there, it was but a day-trip to the south-east of England. This accident of geography gave Stephen a head start. Having first secured the support of the Londoners he then rode to Winchester, where his brother, Henry of Blois, was bishop. With Henry's help he obtained both the treasury at Winchester, and Roger of Salisbury's acceptance of his claim to be king. Then all that remained was to persuade the Archbishop of Canterbury to anoint him. This was done by arguing that the oath to Matilda—which they had all sworn—was void because it had been exacted by force, and by spreading a fictitious story about the old King's deathbed change of mind. On 22 December 1135, Stephen was crowned and anointed king at Westminster.

The political structure of the Anglo-Norman realm meant that once Stephen had been recognized as king in England, he was in a very strong position in Normandy as well. From then on, the Norman barons could give their allegiance to someone else only at the risk of losing their English estates. Above all those with most to lose felt that they had to support Stephen. So, right from the start of their campaign to win their inheritance, Geoffrey and Matilda found themselves opposed by the most powerful magnates of the Anglo-Norman state.

The first two and a half years of Stephen's reign passed peacefully enough: indeed they were rather more trouble-free than the opening years of both his predecessors' reigns had been. The first serious blow came in the summer of 1138 when Robert of Gloucester decided to join his half-sister's cause. Robert's defection not only meant that Stephen lost control of some important strong points in Normandy, it was also a signal that the Angevins were on the point of carrying the struggle to England. As Stephen waited for the blow to fall he began to lose his grip on the situation.

He offended his brother Henry of Blois by not making him Archbishop of Canterbury; he arrested three influential 'civil service' bishops, including Roger of Salisbury, and thus enabled Henry of Blois to claim that ecclesiastical liberties had been infringed. In the autumn of 1139, when the Empress—as Matilda was commonly known—landed at Arundel and seemed to be in Stephen's grasp, he allowed her to go free to join Robert of Gloucester at Bristol when the ruthless, if unchivalrous, thing to do was to imprison her. From now on there were two rival courts in England. The civil war was well and truly joined.

In February 1141 Stephen rashly accepted battle at Lincoln, and fought on bravely when he might have escaped. As a result, he was captured and put in prison in Bristol. Henry of Blois, now acting as papal legate, openly went over to the Empress's side and in the summer she was able to enter London. But she spurned the peace terms worked out by the legate and offended the Londoners by her tactless behaviour. When Stephen's queen, Matilda of Boulogne, advanced towards the city, the Londoners took up arms and drove the Empress out. Thus, the planned coronation at Westminster never took place. Matilda never became queen of England. A few months later Robert of Gloucester was captured and since he was the mainstay of her party Matilda had to agree to an exchange of prisoners: Stephen for Robert. The Empress had thrown away a won position; England remained a divided country.

In Normandy, events had taken a very different course. Geoffrey of Anjou stayed behind to maintain the pressure on the duchy—and to look after his own interests in Anjou. A series of campaigns from 1141 to 1144 ended with the surrender of Rouen and Geoffrey's formal investiture as duke. But the count of Anjou's single-minded concentration on the conquest of Normandy led to him turning his back on England.

Here the civil war settled down into a kind of routine. Neither side could make much headway at a time when the art of war revolved around castles, and the defenders generally held the advantage. In October 1147 Robert of Gloucester died. Disheartened, the Empress left England early in 1148, never to return.

In 1150 Geoffrey of Anjou associated his son Henry with him in the rule of the duchy. Next year this arrangement was legitimized when Louis VII (king of France 1137–80), in return for concessions in the Vexin, decided to recognize Henry as duke. At this point, it must have looked as though the old link between England and Normandy had at last been broken. Yet neither side would give up its claims and though there seemed to be a stalemate in England, on the Continent the situation turned out to be remarkably fluid. Geoffrey of Anjou died, still under forty, leaving his eldest son in control of both Normandy and Anjou. In March 1152 Louis VII divorced his wife, Eleanor of Aquitaine. Eight weeks later she married Henry Plantagenet, who in consequence could now add control of the vast duchy of Aquitaine to his other Continental possessions.

Henry's marriage was a great coup—yet it also gave fresh hope to Stephen. Louis VII organized a grand coalition of all Henry's rivals. As a result, the summer of 1152 saw Henry fighting on four fronts at once—in Aquitaine, in Normandy, against rebels in Anjou, and against Stephen in England. One well-informed Norman chronicler tells us that the betting was that Henry would not survive. At this juncture, his decision to sail to England and carry the fight to Stephen impressed contemporaries by its sheer audacity. Even so there was little Henry could do to break the stalemate in England and his whole position was still precariously over-extended when the death of Stephen's heir, Eustace, in August 1153 transformed everything. Stephen's second son, William, had never expected to be king and so the way was opened for a negotiated settlement.

The barons on both sides had long been anxious for peace. Their landed estates made them too vulnerable to the ravages of war for them to be in favour of protracted hostilities. At times they had ignored the wishes of the chief protagonists and made local truces of their own. So there was a general sense of relief when Stephen and Henry bowed to the wishes of their advisers.

By the treaty of Westminster (December 1153) it was agreed that Stephen should hold the kingdom for life and that he should adopt Henry as his heir. William was to inherit all Stephen's baronial lands. This, in essence, was a repeat of the peace terms proposed by Henry of Blois in 1141. Matilda's inability to be magnanimous in victory had cost the country another twelve years of civil war. Now at last Stephen could rule unchallenged but he was a tired man and did not live long to enjoy it. On 25 October 1154 he died and was buried by the side of his wife and elder son in the monastery they had founded at Faversham.

Stephen must take some responsibility for the troubles of his reign. He was a competent army commander and a brave knight—but perhaps too gallant for his own good. It is true that he was faced by a disputed succession, but then so were all his predecessors; disputed successions were the norm. Stephen of Blois was a more attractive character than any of the Norman kings: but he lacked their masterfulness. Without it he was unable to dominate either his court or his kingdom. Moreover he spent very little time in Normandy; only one visit, in 1137, during his entire reign. This stands in marked contrast to the itineraries of his predecessors and, in view of the 'cross-Channel structure' of the Anglo-Norman aristocracy, was certainly a mistake. In this sense the ruler from the house of Blois can be said to have failed because he was too 'English' a king to realize that England was only a part of a greater whole.

Henry II (1154–1189)

Henry took over without difficulty; it was the first undisputed succession to the English throne for over a hundred years. As lord of an empire stretching from the Scottish border to the Pyrenees he was potentially the most powerful ruler in Europe, richer even than the emperor and completely overshadowing the king of France, the nominal suzerain of his Continental possessions. Although England provided him with great wealth as well as a royal title, the heart of the empire lay elsewhere, in Anjou, the land of his fathers.

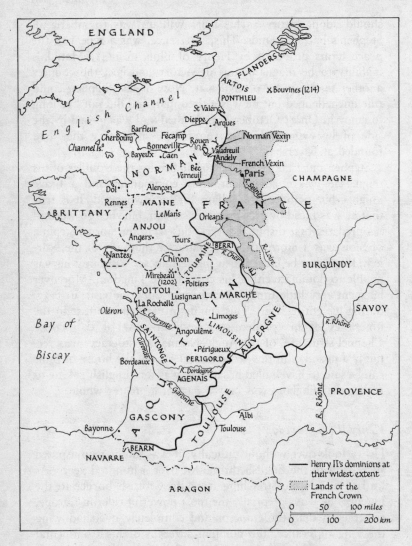

ENGLAND

English Channel

FLANDERS

ARTOIS

PONTHIEU

✕ Bouvines (1214)

St Valéry

Dieppe

Arques

Barfleur

Fécamp

Cherbourg

Bonneville

Rouen

Norman Vexin

Channel Is°

Bayeux

Caen

Vaudreuil

Andely

French Vexin

Bec

Paris

CHAMPAGNE

NORMANDY

Verneuil

Dol

Alençon

FRANCE

Rennes

MAINE

BRITTANY

Le Mans

Orleans

ANJOU

Angers

Tours

Nantes

TOURAINE

Chinon

BERRY

R. Cher

Mirebeau

(1202)

Poitiers

AQUITAINE

BURGUNDY

POITOU

Lusignan

LA MARCHE

La Rochelle

R. Loire

Oléron

R. Charente

Limoges

SAVOY

Bay of

LIMOUSIN

AUVERGNE

R. Rhône

Biscay

Angoulême

SAINTONGE

Périgueux

R. Dordogne

PERIGORD

Bordeaux

AGENAIS

R. Garonne

PROVENCE

R. Rhône

GASCONY

Albi

TOULOUSE

Bayonne

Toulouse

BEARN

—— Henry II's dominions at
their widest extent

⠿ Lands of the
French Crown

NAVARRE

ARAGON

0   50   100 miles

0   100   200 km

THE CONTINENTAL DOMINIONS OF HENRY II

In England his first task was to make good the losses suffered during Stephen's reign. By 1158 this had been achieved. The most dramatic example came in 1157 when he used diplomatic pressure to force the young king of Scotland, Malcolm IV, to restore Cumberland, Westmorland, and Northumbria to the English Crown. In Wales, however, Henry found in Owain of Gwynedd and Rhys of Deheubarth two well-established princes whom it was impossible to browbeat. In 1157 and 1165, force of arms proved equally unavailing in the face of a combination of Welsh guerrilla tactics and torrential summer rain. After 1165 Henry's attitude to the Welsh princes was much more accommodating. As early as 1155 he had toyed with the idea of conquering Ireland. Not until 1169–70, however, did the move into Ireland take place, first by some lords from the Welsh march and then (in 1171–2) by Henry himself. As the long delay makes plain, in the king's eyes there were matters much more urgent than the Irish question.

Out of the thirty-four years of his reign, Henry II spent twenty-one on the Continent. Socially and culturally England was a bit of a backwater compared with the French parts of the Angevin dominion. The prosperous communities which lived in the valleys of the Seine, Loire, and Garonne river systems were centres of learning, art, architecture, poetry, and music. Aquitaine and Anjou produced two of the essential commodities of medieval commerce: wine and salt. These could be exchanged for English cloth and this trade must have brought great profit to the prince who ruled over both producers and consumers. As duke of Normandy, duke of Aquitaine, and count of Anjou Henry had inherited the claims of his predecessors to lordship over neighbouring territories. These claims led to intervention in Nantes (1156) where he installed his brother, Geoffrey, as count; an expedition against Toulouse in 1159 which resulted in the capture of Cahors and the Quercy; the recovery of the Norman Vexin in 1160; and finally, as a result of repeated invasions after 1166, the occupation of Brittany and the installation of his son Geoffrey as duke.

Yet ironically it is not for his successes that Henry is best remembered, but for his dubious part in the murder of Thomas Becket. In June 1162 Becket was consecrated Archbishop of Canterbury. In the eyes of respectable churchmen Becket, who had been chancellor since 1155, did not deserve the highest ecclesiastical post in the land. He set out to prove, to an astonished world, that he was the best of all possible archbishops. Right from the start, he went out of his way to oppose the king who, chiefly out of friendship, had promoted him. Inevitably it was not long before Henry began to react like a man betrayed. In the mid-twelfth century Church-State relations bristled with problems which could be, and normally were, shelved by men of goodwill but which could provide a field-day for men who were determined to quarrel. Henry chose the question of 'criminous clerks' as the issue on which to settle accounts with his archbishop. Like many laymen, Henry resented the way in which clerks who committed felonies could escape capital punishment by claiming trial in an ecclesiastical court. At a council held at Westminster in October 1163 Henry demanded that criminous clerks should be unfrocked by the Church and handed over to the lay courts for punishment. In opposing this, Becket carried his episcopal colleagues with him but when Pope Alexander III asked him to adopt a more conciliatory line, Henry summoned a council to Clarendon (January 1164). He presented the bishops with a clear statement of the king's customary rights over the Church—the Constitutions of Clarendon—and required from them a promise to observe these customs in good faith. Taken by surprise, Becket argued for two days and then gave in. But no sooner had the rest of the bishops followed his example than Becket repented of his weakness. Thoroughly exasperated, Henry now decided to destroy Becket. He summoned him before the royal court to answer trumped-up charges. The archbishop was found guilty and sentenced to the forfeiture of his estates. In a hopeless position Becket fled across the Channel and appealed to the pope. By taking a stand on principle and then wavering Becket had reduced the English Church to confusion.

With Becket in exile Henry concentrated on more important matters for the next five years: Brittany was conquered and the English judicial system overhauled. Then in 1169 the question of the coronation of the heir to the throne, Prince Henry, led to the interminable negotiations between king, pope, and archbishop being treated as a matter of urgency. In 1170 Becket returned to England determined to punish those who had taken part in the young king's coronation. His enemies lost no time in telling Henry of the archbishop's ostentatious behaviour. 'Will no one rid me of this turbulent priest?' Henry's heated words were taken all too literally by four of his knights. Anxious to win the king's favour they rushed off to Canterbury; and there, on 29 December 1170, Becket was murdered in his own cathedral. The deed shocked Christendom and secured Becket's canonization in record time. In popular memory the archbishop came to symbolize resistance to the oppressive authority of the State, but in reality everyone was better off with him out of the way. Once the storm of protest had died down it became apparent that the king's hold on his vast empire had in no way been shaken by the Becket controversy. In the early 1170s Henry stood at the height of his power.

By this date Henry II had already decided that after his death his dominions should be partitioned between his three eldest sons. Henry was to have his father's inheritance, namely Anjou, Normandy, and England; Richard was to have his mother's inheritance, Aquitaine; Geoffrey was to have the acquisition, Brittany. For the moment there was nothing for John but later, in 1185, he was granted his father's other major acquistion, Ireland. By then Henry II's partition plans had already run into difficulties. The trouble was that they aroused expectations which, while he retained all real power in his own hands, he could not satisfy. Thus from 1173 onwards Henry was plagued by rebellious sons. The rebels, moreover, could always count on a warm welcome at the court of the king of France. After 1180 this was a serious matter for in that year the mild-mannered Louis VII was succeeded by his son Philip II Augustus, an unscrupulous politician determined to destroy the

Angevin Empire. The deaths of two of his sons, the young King Henry in 1183 and Geoffrey in 1186, ought to have simplified Henry's problems, but this was offset by the old King's obvious preference for John, a preference which alarmed Richard. An alliance between Richard and Philip brought Henry to his knees and, defeated, the old king died at Chinon on 6 July 1189.

Only in the last weeks of his life had the task of ruling his immense territories been too much for Henry. He rode ceaselessly from one corner of his empire to another, almost giving an impression of being everywhere at once—an impression that helped to keep men loyal. Although the central government offices, chamber, chancery, and military household, travelled around with him, the sheer size of the empire inevitably stimulated the further development of localized administrations which could deal with routine matters of justice and finance in his absence. Thus in England, as elsewhere, government became increasingly complex and bureaucratic. This development, taken together with Henry's interest in rational reform, has led to him being regarded as the founder of the English common law, and as a great and creative king, but in his own eyes these were matters of secondary importance. To him what really mattered was family politics and he died believing that he had failed. But for over thirty years he had succeeded.

Richard I (1189–1199)

Richard's alliance with Philip Augustus meant that his position as heir to all his father's rights and dominions was unchallengeable. John remained lord of Ireland; in time, Brittany would belong to Geoffrey's posthumous son Arthur, now two years old. The rest was at Richard's disposal.

But Richard had no wish to stay long in England. He had been made duke of Aquitaine in 1172 and since then had spent most of his life on the Continent. Even after he became king of England he was well aware that he ruled much more than England. In consequence he, like his father, had wider interests

and greater responsibilities. One aspect of this was the assistance he gave to the kingdom of Jerusalem, a kingdom ruled by
a daughter of the junior branch of the house of Anjou now
married to one of his Aquitanian vassals. In November 1187, as
soon as he heard the news of Saladin's overwhelming victory at
Hattin, Richard took the cross. Delayed by his involvement in
the family quarrels at the end of his father's reign, he was now
determined to leave for the East as soon as he had raised
enough money and arranged for the secure government of all
his dominions during a prolonged absence.

In July 1190 he and Philip Augustus set out on the Third
Crusade. Not until March 1194 did Richard again set foot on
English soil. In the mean time he had taken both a fleet and an
army to the other end of the Mediterranean. Although unable
to recapture Jerusalem, he achieved an astonishing amount
against a great opponent, Saladin. On crusade Richard tackled
and solved far greater logistical problems than ever confronted
other warrior-kings of England, William I, Edward III, or
Henry V. The treaty of Jaffa which he negotiated in 1192 enabled
the crusader states to survive for another century.

During his absence on crusade there had been some disturbances in England in 1191 but his contingency plans restored
stable government. King Philip, after his own return to France,
tried to take advantage of Richard's continued absence, but
without success. If Richard had returned from crusade as he
expected in January 1193 he would have found his empire
intact.

The damage was done while he was held captive in Germany.
He stayed in prison for more than a year (December 1192–
February 1194) and—for all anyone knew in 1193—might have
had to stay there much longer. Even in these inauspicious
circumstances Richard's agents in England were able to contain
his younger brother's treacherous revolt. The real losses were
suffered on the Continent, in particular in Normandy where
Philip overran the Vexin and came close to capturing Rouen
itself.

Richard was released in February 1194 after payment of

100,000 marks, the first two-thirds of the king's ransom. After a brief visit to England (March–May 1194) he returned to the Continent and devoted the next five years to the hard grind of recovering the territory lost so rapidly while he was in prison. By the end of 1198 Richard's skilful diplomacy, fine general-ship, and, above all, his greater resources meant that he had succeeded in recapturing almost everything that had been lost. Then, in April 1199, Richard died as the result of a wound suffered at the siege of Chalus-Chabrol (near Limoges) where he was engaged in suppressing a rebellion led by the count of Angoulême and the viscount of Limoges. In the Angevin-Capetian struggle this was to be the decisive turning-point.

One of the marks of Richard's greatness had been his ability to choose ministers, above all, Hubert Walter in England. As justiciar, Archbishop of Canterbury, and papal legate Hubert Walter stood for harmonious co-operation between king and Church. In England, as in the other provinces of the Angevin Empire, Richard's long absences meant the continuing develop-ment, under Walter's supervision, of an effective machinery of central government. From the point of view of Richard's sub-jects, this meant increasingly heavy taxation, but there is no evidence to suggest that the financial burdens of war had brought the Angevin Empire to the point of economic collapse.

John (1199–1216)

Richard left no legitimate children, and when he died the differ-ent parts of the Angevin Empire chose different successors. The barons of England and Normandy opted for John; Anjou, Maine, and Touraine preferred Arthur of Brittany, now twelve years old; Aquitaine continued to be held—on John's behalf—by his mother, Eleanor (d. 1204). By May 1200 John had ousted Arthur and had established himself as lord of all the Angevin dominions, though at a heavy price—the cession of the Vexin and Evreux to King Philip (treaty of Le Goulet, January 1200). Later that year his first marriage was annulled and he married

Isabella of Angoulême. There were great strategic advantages to be gained from marrying the heiress to Angoulême and had John given her fiancé, Hugh of Lusignan, adequate compensation, all might yet have been well. As it was, this marriage set in motion a train of events which led to Hugh appealing to the court of France and, in 1202, to Philip's declaration that all John's Continental dominions—the lands which he held as fiefs of the king of France—were forfeit. The sentence still had to be enforced. In 1152 Henry II had resisted Louis VII's attempt to execute a similar verdict. In 1203–4, however, John failed where his father had succeeded. By his tactless treatment of the leading barons of Anjou and Poitou he threw away all the advantages he won when he captured Arthur at Mirebeau (July 1202); the well-founded rumour that he was responsible for his nephew's murder (April 1203) further undermined an already shaky reputation. In an atmosphere of suspicion and fear John found it impossible to organize an effective defence. In December 1203 he threw in the towel and withdrew to England. Philip overran Normandy, Anjou, Maine, Touraine, and all of Poitou except for La Rochelle. These humiliating military reverses earned for John a new nickname. 'Lackland' now became 'Softsword'.

Until December 1203 John, like his father and brother, spent most of his reign in his Continental possessions. After that date he became, by force of circumstances, an English king. Not since Stephen's reign had the country seen so much of its ruler, but there was little pleasure or profit to be got from a king who constantly suspected that men were plotting against him. The weight of John's presence was even felt in the north where men were not accustomed to visits from kings of England. The extent of their resentment can be measured by the number of northerners who opposed John in 1215–16. Undoubtedly he faced genuine problems. He was duty-bound to try to recover his lost inheritance, but the conquests of 1203–4 meant that the French king was now a much more formidable opponent. An unusually high rate of inflation meant that many families and religious houses were in financial difficulties and they found it easier to blame the king than to understand the underlying economic forces. Inflation tended to erode the real value of royal revenues. As a result, John levied frequent taxes and tightened up the laws governing the forest (a profitable but highly unpopular source of income).

John also quarrelled with the Church. A disputed election to the see of Canterbury in 1205 led to a clash with Innocent III. In 1208 Innocent laid an interdict on England and Wales; all church services were suspended and remained so for six years. In 1209 John himself was excommunicated. Neither John nor lay society in general seem to have been very worried by this state of affairs; indeed since John's response to the interdict was to confiscate the estates of the Church it even helped to ease his financial problem. But in 1212 a baronial plot and Philip's plans to cross the Channel served to remind John that an excommunicated king was particularly vulnerable to rebellion and invasion. So he decided to make peace with the Church in order to have a free hand to deal with his more dangerous enemies. By agreeing to hold England as a fief of the Papacy in May 1213 he completely won over Innocent and assured himself of the pope's support in the coming struggles.

All now turned on the outcome of John's attempt to recover his lost lands. In 1214 he led an expedition to Poitou but the defeat of his allies at the battle of Bouvines (July 1214) entailed both the failure of his Continental strategy and the onset of rebellion in England. But rebels had genuine problems too. Leadership was normally provided by a discontented member of the royal family. After the elimination of Arthur, John faced no such rivals. His own sons were too young. The only possible candidate was Louis, son of Philip Augustus, but a Capetian prince was hardly an attractive anti-king. So the rebels devised a new kind of focus for revolt: a programme of reform. In June 1215, after they had captured London, the rebels forced John to accept the terms laid out in a document later to be known as Magna Carta. In essence it was a hostile commentary on some of the more objectionable features of the last sixty years of Angevin rule. As such it was clearly unacceptable to John who regarded the agreement made at Runnymede merely as a means of buying time. Attempts to implement Magna Carta only led to further quarrels. In the end the rebels had to invite Louis to take the throne. In May 1216 he entered London. When John died, in October 1216, shortly after losing part of his baggage train in quicksands in the Wash, the country was torn in two by a civil war which was going badly for the Angevins.

John possessed qualities which have endeared him to some modern historians. He took a close interest in the details of governmental and legal business, but in his own day this counted for little. It is a mistake to see him as a busier king than his predecessors. The survival of chancery records from 1199 onwards permits historians to look, for the first time, into the daily routine of the king's government at work. As a result they have sometimes given the impression that John was unusually competent. In fact he was a very poor king, incompetent where it really mattered, in the management of his more powerful subjects.

Henry III (1216–1272)

The minority council which governed in the name of John's nine-year-old son, Henry, was soon vouchsafed that success in war, both on land (the battle of Lincoln, May 1217) and at sea (battle of Dover, August 1217), which had been denied his father. Under the impact of these defeats, support for Louis dwindled rapidly. In September 1217 he accepted the treaty of Lambeth and withdrew.

It was not until 1232 that Henry began to rule in his own right. Minorities tended to be periods of unstable government; but, on the whole, the men, above all Hubert de Burgh, who kept Henry in political tutelage until he was in his mid-twenties, did remarkably well. Most of the struggles for power took place in the council chamber; appeals to arms were rare and very brief. As part of a series of conciliatory moves Magna Carta was amended and reissued. But while the lords of the council concentrated on their own rivalries and on events in England and Wales, they were understandably less concerned about the king's overseas inheritance. None of them had estates in Poitou and Gascony. In 1224, during one such domestic quarrel, their old Capetian enemy, now King Louis VIII, walked into Poitou, captured La Rochelle, and threatened Gascony. An expedition in 1225 consolidated the position in Gascony but made no serious attempt to recover Poitou. Subsequent expeditions, in 1230 and 1242, were on a more ambitious scale but ended ingloriously. After 1224, only Gascony remained of the lands which Henry III's ancestors had once held in France. The effect of this was to reverse the territorial balance of the twelfth century. Once England had been one of the provinces in the Angevin orbit; now it became the indisputable centre of the Plantagenet dominions. Eventually, by the treaty of Paris (1259), Henry gave up his claims to Normandy, Anjou, and Poitou, and did homage to Louis IX for Gascony.

Realistically speaking, the treaty of Paris was Henry III's greatest political success but he accepted the generous terms offered by Louis IX only with great reluctance and in the hope of extricating himself from his other difficulties. Chief among these was the fact that a sworn confederation of the most powerful magnates in the country was threatening to take up arms against him. Henry had faced opposition on and off since 1233. Time and again, the bone of contention had been his choice of friends and advisers; these were the men who obtained the lion's share of the patronage at the king's disposal. The problem was aggravated by the fact that many of his favourites were not English—this at a time when English politics were becoming increasingly insular. Henry was a good family man, happily married (since 1236) to Eleanor of Provence, and ready to provide generously for his wife's relatives. Then, when life in France became difficult for his half-brothers, the Lusignans—his mother's children by her second marriage—

he welcomed them to England and from 1247 onwards they constantly soured the atmosphere.

Equally controversial was the king's scheme for providing for Edmund, his own second son. In 1252 the pope offered the kingdom of Sicily to Henry and in 1254 he accepted on Edmund's behalf. Unfortunately, Sicily was actually held by Manfred, an illegitimate son of the Hohenstaufen Emperor Frederick II. Not only did Henry agree that he would finance the island's conquest, he also promised to meet the pope's existing debts—and the pope had already spent a fortune, some 135,000 marks, in fighting Manfred. It was an absurd commitment and in 1258 it ended with the barons taking the government out of the king's hands and initiating a far-reaching programme of reform: the Provisions of Oxford (October 1258) and the Provisions of Westminster (October 1259). But taking power out of the hands of an adult king, and handing it to an elected aristocratic council, was a revolutionary step. For the next five years England teetered on the brink of civil war. When, in the spring of 1264, war finally came, the issues at stake had been narrowed down to one question. Was, or was not, the king free to choose foreigners to be his counsellors? Ironically, the man who had been most adamant in insisting that in the last resort it was the barons, acting in the name of 'the community of the realm', who should decide, was himself born a foreigner, Simon de Montfort. By this time, Simon had long been a powerful member of 'the community': earl of Leicester since 1231, husband of the king's sister since 1238. In 1264 Earl Simon won the battle of Lewes, but next year was himself defeated, killed, and dismembered at the battle of Evesham. In the last years of Henry III's reign the full restoration of royal authority was combined with the recognition, in the statute of Marlborough (1267), that the 'customs of the realm' including both Charters of Liberties and even some of the Provisions of Westminster, should be upheld. Feeling uncomfortable in this atmosphere of moderation, the victor of Evesham, Edward, the heir to the throne, went off on crusade, leaving his father free to concentrate on rebuilding Westminster Abbey.

Edward I (1272–1307)

In 1272 Edward I was in Sicily, on his way back from crusade, when he heard the news that his father had died and that he had been proclaimed king. He returned home at a leisurely pace. In Paris, choosing his words carefully, he did homage to Philip III for his lands in France: 'I do you homage for all the lands which I ought to hold of you.' He then turned south to Gascony where he stayed in 1273–4. He visited Gascony again in 1286–9. He was the last Plantagenet king to hold court at Bordeaux and when he left, in July 1289, it marked the end of an era. Yet the history of English rule in Gascony is by no means a straightforward story of decline. In 1279, for example, the French at last handed over the Agenais, as they were bound to do under the terms of the treaty of Paris. The Agenais was an important wine-growing area and its cession further strengthened the rapidly-developing commercial links between Bordeaux and London. The Bordeaux wine customs, farmed for only £300 a year in the 1240s, were worth over £6,000 sixty years later. In return the Gascons imported English cloth, leather, and corn. A mutual interest in an expanding trade riveted the two communities together.

In October 1274, soon after his return to England, Edward launched an inquiry into the activities of both royal and baronial officials. Like similar earlier investigations it uncovered an enormous number of grievances and in trying to remedy some of these, the king's advisers, headed by his chancellor, Robert Burnell, were led on to issue new laws on a wide range of subjects. But even in the most prolific period of legislation (1275–90) there was no attempt to codify English law in the manner of a Justinian and the statutes were quite as much concerned with the rights of the king as with the liberties of the subject.

From 1276 to 1284 Edward's main preoccupation was with

Wales. Initially his plan was to cut Llywelyn ap Gruffydd down to size and then hand the Welsh prince's lands to his brothers Dafydd and Gruffydd. But after the victorious campaign of 1277 he imposed a peace treaty which the Welsh found humiliating and failed to give Dafydd the rewards he had expected. In 1282 the Welsh rebelled. In the war of 1282–3 Llywelyn was killed and Dafydd captured. He was then put on trial and executed as a traitor, the first man since 1076 to forfeit his life for rebellion. Unlike the campaign of 1277, the war of 1282–3 had been intended as a war of conquest; given Edward's enormous preponderance of resources, it was not too difficult a task.

Whereas the conquest of Wales can be seen as the culmination of centuries of warfare, relations between the kingdoms of England and Scotland were exceptionally good for most of the thirteenth century. But in 1286 Alexander III was killed by a fall from his horse and his only granddaughter, Margaret, the 'Maid of Norway', was recognized as heir to the throne. Edward I proposed that she should marry his own son and heir, Edward. The Scottish magnates agreed to this proposal (treaty of Birgham, July 1290) but at the same time insisted that Scotland should retain its own laws and customs.

Sadly, the six-year-old Margaret died in Orkney (September 1290). Edward seized the opportunity to assert his overlordship and his right to adjudicate between the contenders for the throne. After complicated legal arguments he decided in favour of John Balliol; on St. Andrew's Day 1292 the new king was enthroned at Scone. Up to this point Edward was justified in claiming that his actions had helped to maintain peace and order in Scotland; but from now on his domineering treatment of the Scots was to provoke a long and disastrous war.

Wales and the Marches

Eleventh-century Wales was a collection of small kingdoms in a mountainous country. These were kingdoms without stable borders. They expanded and contracted in accordance with law (the custom of sharing the inheritance between sons) and politics (the ambitions and military fortunes of individual rulers). Although English kings traditionally claimed an overall supremacy here, they had done little to transform that ill-defined overlordship into lasting military and administrative control. At first it looked as though the impetus of the Norman Conquest of England would carry the newcomers right through Wales. The Norman earls of Hereford, Shrewsbury, and Chester were, in effect, licensed to take whatever they could. But after a period of rapid advance in 1067–75, they found their progress impeded by the nature of the terrain. As a result, their colonizing efforts were long confined to the lowlands and river valleys, particularly in the south. There were indeed periods when Welsh princes recovered the initiative and resumed control of lands they had earlier lost. Not until the reign of Edward I was the Norman Conquest of Wales complete. Thus throughout this period Wales was a land of war, a land of castles. Welsh princes and Anglo-Norman marcher lords made war and peace and both therefore enjoyed what later constitutional lawyers would call 'sovereign' powers.

For most of this period the conquest was a piecemeal affair, undertaken and carried through by individual Anglo-Norman baronial families: the Clares, the Mortimers, the Lacys, the Braoses. The lands which they conquered were, in effect, 'private' lordships, outside the normal framework of English governance. Nonetheless, these families remained subjects of the king of England and occasionally they were reminded of this fact in summary fashion. In 1102 Henry I broke the sons of Roger of Montgomery, earl of Shrewsbury, and dismembered their father's marcher 'empire'. In 1208–11 John drove William de Braose to destruction. The groundwork of conquest and colonization was left to the marcher lords, but the overall strategy remained in royal hands. It was, for example, the kings who determined what relations with the native princes should be: a matter which became increasingly vital as some Welsh kingdoms were eliminated and the surviving ones became increasingly consolidated.

By the second half of the twelfth century the rulers of Deheubarth, particularly the Lord Rhys, and of Gwynedd were outstanding. In the thirteenth century two princes of Gwynedd, Llywelyn the Great and his grandson, Llywelyn ap Gruffydd, managed, by force and diplomacy, to bring all the other Welsh dynasties under their authority. Indeed in the treaty of Montgomery (1267) Llywelyn ap Gruffydd was able to persuade a reluctant English king, Henry III, to acknowledge both his territorial gains and his new title, 'Prince of Wales'.

But eight years earlier another treaty had sealed the fate of Wales. In 1259 by the treaty of Paris Henry III accepted the loss of most of his Continental possessions. Peace with France meant that for the first time a king of England could, if he wanted to, concentrate his attention on his British neighbours. There followed Edward's conquest and a massive programme of castle building. By the statute of Wales (1284) the newly-acquired lands were divided into shires on the English model: Flint, Anglesey, Merioneth, and Caernarfon. As for Welsh laws and customs, Edward announced: 'certain of them we have abolished; some we have allowed, some we have corrected, others we have added'. What this meant in effect was that English common law had been introduced into Wales.

There were revolts in 1287 and 1294–5 but the castles proved their worth. Flint, Rhuddlan, Aberystwyth, Builth, Conway, Caernarfon, Criccieth, Harlech, and Beaumaris—resounding names, and resoundingly expensive to build and maintain. This was the high premium Edward paid to insure his conquests against the fire of rebellion.

The contrast between, on the one hand, the piecemeal conquest of the south and east and, on the other, the sudden defeat which overwhelmed the north and west left an enduring mark on the political geography of Wales. The Edwardian conquests were largely retained in Crown hands; the rest remained divided into the numerous large lordships collectively known as the march of Wales. As for Prince Llywelyn, killed in an English trap at Irfon Bridge in 1282, his fate was to become a cult figure for some twentieth-century Welsh nationalists.

Scotland

In contrast to fragmented Wales, in the eleventh century much of Scotland, in particular the south and east—the wealthiest part—was ruled by one king, the king of the Scots. Ever since Athelstan's reign, the king of the Scots had occasionally recognized English overlordship, but that was as far as the connection went—or was likely to go. On the one hand the king of the Scots was too powerful to have much to fear from the kind of 'private enterprise' invasions which marked the advance of Anglo-Norman barons into Wales and even Ireland. On the other, his land was too poor and he was generally too distant a figure to be of much interest to the kings of England. Besides, although it might not be too difficult to launch a successful expedition against the Scots, the dual problem of conquering and controlling so remote a country seemed—and probably was—insoluble to kings whose own bases lay in the Thames Valley and further south.

Nor were the Scots obsessed by the problem of the English. Apart from a temporary success when King David (1124–53) took advantage of the civil war of Stephen's reign to acquire Northumbria (held from 1149 to 1157), the border with England effectively remained where it had been established in the eleventh century. Much more significant was the kingdom's extension to include the far north and much of the western seaboard (Caithness, Ross, Moray, Argyll, Galloway). The culmination of this expansionist policy came when the king of Norway ceded the Western Isles (treaty of Perth, 1266). Scottish advance here was materially assisted by the stability and continuity of leadership provided by three successive kings: William I (1165–1214), Alexander II (1214–49), and Alexander III (1249–86).

Territorial expansion in the Highlands was matched by internal development in the Lowlands. Here, burghs, abbeys, and cathedrals were founded; castles were built and royal sheriffdoms formed in order to reduce the kingdom to manageable administrative units; royal moneyers began to mint silver pen-

nies (enjoying parity with English sterling) and import duties were collected. The marriages made by its rulers show that in the twelfth and thirteenth centuries Scotland was increasingly becoming part of a 'European' political scene. What was most remarkable about all these developments was that they involved very little war. So long as no English king conceived the unrealistic ambition of conquering Scotland, there was no reason for that to change.

Government

The most important component of government remained the king himself. His character still counted for more than any other single factor—as is obvious from the contrast between Edward I's reign and the reigns of both his father and son. But naturally the king could not govern alone. Wherever he went he was followed by a great crowd: courtiers, officials, servants, traders, petitioners, and hangers-on of every description.

At the centre of the crowd that followed him was the king's household. In part this was an elaborate domestic service: cooks, butlers, larderers, grooms, tent-keepers, carters, pack-horse drivers, and the bearer of the king's bed. There were also the men who looked after his hunt, the keepers of the hounds, the horn-blowers, the archers. Then there were the men whose work was political and administrative as well as domestic. Some of them had fairly well-defined functions. The chancellor was responsible for the king's seal and the chancery clerks. Treasurer and chamberlains looked after the king's money and valuables. Constables and marshals were in charge of military organization. But the household, like the king, was omnicompetent and any great household officer, the steward for example, was likely to find himself entrusted with essential political and military tasks.

Some of these officials were clerks. Until the 1340s the chancellor and the treasurer always were. But many of them were laymen: the chamberlains, the stewards, the constables, the marshals—as also, at a local level, were the sheriffs. Medieval kings of England did not depend exclusively, or even primarily, upon clerks for the administrative skills necessary to rule a country. Nor did they rely on a group of royal officials whose interests were pitted against the interests of the great land-holders, the magnates. On the contrary, the king's household normally included some of the most powerful barons. Servants in the king's household, they were also lords of great estates and masters in their own houses. Through their influence the authority of the Crown was carried into the localities. This in-formal power system was often reinforced by the appointment of members of the household to local offices. Under Rufus, Hamo 'the steward' was sheriff of Kent; Urse d'Abetôt was constable of the household and sheriff of Worcester. Throughout the twelfth and thirteenth centuries household knights continued to be employed as sheriffs.

Here, in the king's household, lay the mainspring of govern-ment. This is as true of 1279, the year of Edward I's Household Ordinance, as it is of 1136, the approximate date of the earliest surviving description of the king's household, the *Constitutio domus regis*. Moreover there is no reason to believe that the household of the *Constitutio* was significantly different from William I's household, or indeed, from Cnut's household.

Similarly the king's household was the hub of military organ-ization. It has long been accepted that the armies of Edward I's reign were essentially 'the household in arms'. The house-hold cavalry constituted a professional task force capable of responding quickly if trouble blew up unexpectedly. In the event of a major campaign, it could be rapidly expanded. Household knights were often made responsible for mobilizing and commanding large infantry contingents. The household men, the *familiares*, were paid annual fees and then daily wages according to the number of days they served. This, it used to be thought, was a far cry from the Norman period when armies were basically 'feudal hosts', made up of the quotas of knights which tenants-in-chief mustered when summoned to perform their military service to the Crown. But close study of the much more fragmentary evidence for the period around 1100 has demonstrated that not only is it difficult to find the 'feudal host' in action, but also that all the essential features of the Edwardian system were already in existence—the retaining fees, the daily wages, the framework for planned expansion, the use of household troops both as garrisons for key castles and as the main field armies (composed of knights and mounted archers), the employment of household knights as commanders of supplementary forces. There is no reason to believe that the tasks which Cnut's housecarls were called upon to perform were fundamentally different.

For practical purposes there was an upper limit on the size of the royal household in peacetime; transport and catering problems were alone sufficient to see to that. To some extent, forward planning of the royal itinerary helped; when they knew in advance where the household was going to be then merchants could arrange to be there with their wares. But the presence of the king imposed a near-intolerable burden on any district through which he passed. The demands made by the household had a dramatic effect on local foodstocks and prices; it created a situation wide open to abuse. This is how Eadmer, a monk of Canterbury, described the household of William Rufus, a king of whom he disapproved. 'Those who attended his court made a practice of plundering and destroying everything; they laid waste all the territory through which they passed. Consequently when it became known that the king was coming everyone fled to the woods.' In Edward I's reign there is still the same combination of planning and plunder. An official letter announcing that he intended to spend Easter at Nottingham asked that local people should be comforted by being assured that the king would go as fast as he had come.

Thus it was both for political reasons—in order to make his presence felt—and for economic reasons—to make his presence no longer felt—that the king travelled constantly. The sheer size of their dominions meant that in this respect the Angevins had to work harder than their predecessors, though John's political failures did at least have the effect of easing his travel problems. After 1203 the royal itinerary became increasingly confined to England and, in Edward I's case, to North Wales as well. After 1289 no king visited Gascony. At the same time the roads leading in and out of London became gradually more important. By 1300 the king's itinerary was no longer dominated, as John's had still been, by the restless move from palace to hunting lodge in 'central Wessex', the old heartland of the West Saxon kings.

Yet while political and economic considerations made the court mobile, there was another feature of the age which pointed in the opposite direction: the seemingly inexorable development of bureaucracy. Given the practical limitations on household size, what would happen as the king's secretarial and financial officers grew ever more numerous? Inevitably not all of them could continue to travel everywhere with their lord. Some were bound to settle down in a convenient place. By 1066 indeed this point had already been reached. There was already a permanent royal treasury at Winchester, a depository for fiscal records as well as for silver, and this required a permanent staff to guard and oversee it. By 1290 there were many more settled officials, both clerks and laymen, in the chancery and exchequer, and they were settled at Westminster, not Winchester. But this bureaucratic growth had not altered the fundamental political facts of life: the king still itinerated; he still took with him a seal, a secretariat, and financial experts—and it was within this mobile group, not at Westminster, that the most important political and administrative decisions were taken. In 1290, as in 1066, the saddle remained the chief seat of government, both in war and in peace. There was still no capital but the king's highway.

Nor had bureaucratic growth altered the basic fact that the political stability of the realm still depended primarily on the king's ability to manage the small, but immensely powerful, aristocratic establishment—as is made clear by the events of Henry III's and Edward II's reign. On what terms did the tenants-in-chief hold their estates from the king? They were expected—as they had been in Anglo-Saxon England—to serve and aid the king: essentially this meant political service and, in times of war, military service; in certain circumstances they could be asked to give him financial aid. In addition, a tenant-in-chief's heir had to pay a duty, known as a relief, in order to enter into his inheritance, while if he—or she—were under age then the king took the estates into his custody, to do with them very much as he pleased (subject to certain conventions). In these circumstances the king controlled his ward's marriage. If there were no direct heirs, then after provision had been made for the widow—whose re-marriage was also subject to Crown control—the king could grant the land out again to whomever he pleased. This degree of control over the inheritances and marriages of the wealthiest people in the kingdom meant that the king's powers of patronage were immense. He not only had offices at his disposal, he also had heirs, heiresses, and widows. Thus, for example, when Richard I gave William Marshal the heiress to the earldom of Pembroke, he, in effect, made William a millionaire overnight. No political leader in the Western world of today has anything remotely approaching the power of patronage in the hands of a medieval king. It is not surprising that the king's court was the focal point of the whole political system, a turbulent, lively, tense, factious place in which men—and a few women—pushed and jostled each other in desperate attempts to catch the king's eye. Not surprisingly it was a twelfth-century literary convention to describe a courtier's life as sheer hell—but standing at the mouth of hell there were hundreds only too keen to enter. In these circumstances patronage was one of the strongest cards in the king's hand. It mattered how he played it, and a king who played it badly would soon find himself in trouble.

The essential features of this patronage system were already in existence during the reign of William Rufus. This much is clear from the terms of the Coronation Charter issued by Henry I in 1100. It is also clear that the system was still in existence during the reign of Edward I. Magna Carta had clarified it and, to some extent, even modified it. After 1215, for example, baronial reliefs were fixed at a rate of £100. None the less, the laws governing inheritance, wardship, and marriage could still be manipulated to suit a king's personal predilections, whether it was to provide for his own family, as with Edward I, or to enrich favourites, as with Edward II. What is less clear is whether the system was already there in 1066. Most historians would probably say that it was not. But it is surely significant that Cnut and, probably, Æthelred the Unready were already making promises broadly similar to those contained in the charter of 1100.

Patronage was lucrative. Men offered money in order to obtain what the king had to offer: offices (from the chancellorship down), succession to estates, custody of land, wardship, and marriage—or even nothing more concrete than the king's goodwill. All of these were to be had at a price, and the price was negotiable. Here was an area in which a king could hope to raise more money by consistently driving harder bargains. In these circumstances any document which told the king how rich his tenants were would naturally be immensely valuable. Domesday Book is just such a record—and it showed that half the value of the whole country was in the hands of less than two hundred men. By fining these men heavily when they were in political trouble or by offering them what they wanted, though at a price, the king had found a practical method of soaking the rich. Of course the information had to be kept up to date and throughout the twelfth and thirteenth centuries the Crown found ways of ensuring that it was. For example, one of the surviving documents produced by Henry II's administration is the delightfully named 'Roll of Ladies, boys and girls'. Thus to a hostile observer like Gerald of Wales the king appeared to be 'a robber permanently on the prowl, always probing, always looking for the weak spot where there is something for him to steal'. Gerald was talking of the position under the Angevins but it may be that Lucy, widowed countess of Chester, offering

Henry I 500 marks for the privilege of remaining single for five years, would have concurred. The fact that most of the influential people in the realm were semi-permanently in their debt gave kings a powerful political lever—and one which they regularly employed. In 1295, for example, Edward I used the threat of debt collection to force a group of reluctant magnates to go to Gascony.

The earliest surviving detailed account of royal revenues, the pipe roll of 1129–30, shows just how lucrative patronage could be. In this financial year Henry I is recorded as having collected about £3,600 from agreements of this kind. This is about 15 per cent of his recorded revenue and more than he got from taxation. But the arithmetic of the pipe roll tells us a good deal more than this. In 1129–30 the total sum due as a result of agreements made in this and previous years was almost £26,000, that is only 14 per cent of the amount due was actually collected. William de Pont de l'Arche, for example, had offered 1,000 marks for a chamberlainship and in 1129–30 he paid 100 marks. This meant that if the king were satisfied with William's behaviour, then payment of further instalments might be suspended or pardoned. The expectation that the exchequer would not press too hard had the effect of encouraging men to bid highly. But a man who fell out of favour would find that he had to pay up promptly—or get into even worse trouble. This, for example, was the fate which befell William de Braose in John's reign. In other words, collecting only a small proportion of the amount due was not an indication of chronic government inefficiency but rather of a further refinement of an infinitely flexible system of patronage.

Masterful kings always had their hands in their subjects' pockets. Edward I was known as *Le Roi Coveytous* just as William I had 'loved greediness above all'. At a more abstract level, as early as the twelfth century it was asserted that royal power can be measured in financial terms. In the words of Richard FitzNeal, bishop of London, Treasurer of England, and author of *The Dialogue of the Exchequer*, a work dating from the 1170s, 'the power of princes fluctuates according to the ebb and flow of their cash resources'. The pipe roll of 1129–30—a record of the accounts presented at the exchequer by sheriffs and other officials in that year—shows an exchequer system already working very much along the lines described in *The Dialogue*. But the financial system itself certainly pre-dated the pipe roll. In broad outline—annual renders made by sheriffs to the treasury—it is an Anglo-Saxon system. In 1066 and 1086 the renders produced by some large royal manors were still paid in kind. By 1129–30 it is clear that a widespread commutation into money rents had taken place. This was in line with general European development. The more the sheriffs' renders were made in cash, the greater the need for an easily followed but quick method of making calculations in pounds, shillings, and pence. Thus the chequered table cloth (from which the word exchequer is derived) served as a simplified abacus, on which the king's *calculator* did sums by moving counters from square to square like a croupier. The earliest reference to the exchequer dates from 1110. Twice a year a group of the most powerful and trusted men in the realm met in order to audit the sheriffs' accounts. When the king was in Normandy they would meet, as the vice-regal committee 'at the exchequer', in the king's absence. Presumably a similarly composed committee had met for a similar purpose when Cnut was in Denmark.

But this is speculation. It is only when we reach 1129–30 that some degree of precision is possible. Even here, however, we have to be careful. An exchequer record, a pipe roll, tells almost nothing about those sums which were paid into and out of the chamber. Certainly these sums cannot be quantified, though in view of the fact that the chamber was the financial office of the itinerant household it is likely that they were large. For example it was estimated that by 1187 Henry II had paid 30,000 marks into his Jerusalem bank account though there is no sign of this money in the pipe rolls of his reign. In the absence of twelfth-century chamber records, it is not easy to estimate total royal revenue. Thus, the low pipe roll totals in the early years of Henry II's reign may be very largely a reflection of the new king's preference for chamber finance, a very natural preference for an Angevin prince, all of whose forefathers had managed perfectly well without an exchequer. After all, when it came to minting coins the Angevins introduced Angevin practice into both England and Normandy. But, whatever the difficulties, analysis of the only surviving pipe roll of Henry I's reign is undoubtedly revealing.

In 1129–30, £22,865 was paid into the treasury. Out of this total almost £12,000 comes under the heading of 'land and associated profits'. Just under £3,000 can be described as taxation, nearly all of this (almost £2,500) being Danegeld, as the geld (see p. 168) was commonly called in the twelfth century. Another £7,200 can be described as the profits of feudal lordship and jurisdiction: this included about £1,000 from ecclesiastical vacancies; £2,400 from judicial fines; and the £3,600 from agreements mentioned earlier. Thus over half the recorded revenue came from land; about a third from lordship and jurisdiction; and only some 13 per cent from taxation. If we compare this with the state of royal revenues in the early years of Edward I's reign then some significant differences emerge. In very rough terms, land accounted for about a third of the total; lordship and jurisdiction may well have provided less than 10 per cent, while taxation (including customs duties) accounted for over a half. Land, lordship, and jurisdiction became relatively less important; taxation became much more important. Even allowing for the likelihood that tax revenue in 1129–30 was rather less than usual (because the geld was the only tax levied that year), this broad generalization would still hold.

Though the royal lands were immensely lucrative in 1130, a comparison with Domesday Book suggests that they were already a declining asset. In 1086 the total recorded value of the king's lands and boroughs was almost £14,000, while by 1129–30 it had gone down to less than £10,700. It seems that the stock of royal lands was dwindling faster than it was being replenished by forfeitures and reversions to the Crown (escheats). Kings had to grant land to powerful men. They did so in order to reward and encourage loyalty, particularly early in their reigns when faced with the problems of disputed succession. This process continued, but was to some extent offset by attempts to manage the royal estates more efficiently. The success of these managerial reforms, begun under Hubert Walter, then continued by John's and Henry III's ministers, can be measured by the fact that Edward I was still able to enjoy a revenue from land of some £13,000 a year. (In view of the inflation in the previous one hundred and fifty years, however, this means that real income from this source was a good deal less than it had been in 1129–30. Equally £20,000 under Henry I was probably worth more than £40,000 under Edward I.)

The geld, the hide—the unit of land on which the geld was assessed—and the fiscal machinery through which the geld was collected, are all further examples of those rights which the Norman kings inherited from the Anglo-Saxons. Even though at two shillings on the hide the geld contributed only 10 per cent of Henry I's recorded income, it was clearly a valuable royal asset. By 1129–30 it had become an annual tax and one which could occasionally be levied at a higher rate (moreover geld exemptions could be granted as political favours, adding yet another string to the bow of royal patronage). But the geld was levied only twice by Henry II, in 1155–6 and 1161–2. Instead he developed other levies, the aid of knights (scutage: assessed on knights' fees) and the aid of boroughs and cities (tallage: assessed on a valuation of movable property). By John's reign, scutages and tallages between them constituted a more or less annual tax which adequately compensated the Crown for the withering away of the geld. But the geld was not quite dead. Under a new name, carucage, and a revised assessment it was revived and levied four times between 1194 and 1220.

By this date, however, the government had discovered a new and altogether more productive form of tax, assessed not on land but on an estimate of a man's revenues and movable property. Probably based on the ecclesiastical tithe, it was initially used in 1166, 1185, and 1188 for a pious purpose—the financial support of the Holy Land. John certainly levied this tax on movables in 1207, and may have done so in 1203. An account of the 1207 tax survives and the figures which it discloses are astonishing. Levied at the rate of $\frac{1}{13}$ it produced no less than £60,000—a sum far and away in excess of the yield of other taxes. (Yet in 1194 this same tax had been levied at the rate of $\frac{1}{4}$—the heaviest rate in the long history of the tax—in order to contribute to Richard's ransom). In the mid-1190s the first national customs system was introduced. These developments suggest that royal revenues reached new high levels during Richard's and John's reign. By 1213–14 John had accumulated some 200,000 marks. But these large accumulations were soon spent. These were years of war, of the Third Crusade and of the defence of the Angevin Empire. John's final failure in 1214 ushered in a long period of relative peace. Not until 1294 would the English taxpayer once again find himself paying for a major European war.

In the mean time, however, there were two other significant thirteenth-century innovations—the development of taxation of the clergy, and the establishment of a customs system. Since 1199 the Church had been made subject to an income tax imposed by the pope. Initially intended to finance crusades, it was later used for a variety of 'good causes'—as defined by the pope. Thus in 1217 Honorius III ordered bishops and prelates to help out the boy-king Henry III. From then on the Church was frequently required to subsidize the king, particularly if he had taken the cross, as Henry III did in 1250 and Edward I did in 1287. In 1291, for example, Edward received no less than 100,000 marks out of the proceeds of a papal crusading tax. By the mid-thirteenth century it had already become clear that the English Church was prepared to give financial aid to the king—though, naturally, assemblies of clergy haggled over the amount and took the opportunity of their meeting to discuss other matters which they felt needed remedying. Hardly surprising then that Henry III should go one step further in 1254 and ask for a clerical grant without first seeking papal consent. This precedent was followed in 1269, and then on three occasions by Edward I (1279/80, 1283, and 1290) in the years before 1294.

The customs duty in Richard's and John's reigns had been a war measure; it lapsed when John sought a truce with Philip Augustus in 1206. The importance of the duty on wool exports established in 1275 was that it became a permanent addition to the Crown's peacetime revenue. Its yield varied according to the fortunes of the wool trade but at the rate agreed in 1275, half a mark (6s. 8d.) per sack, it brought in between £8,000 and £13,000 per annum in the years before 1294. These new measures, papal taxation of the English Church and the customs duty on wool, were both related to the presence of Italian mercantile and banking houses in England. On the one hand, it was the ubiquitous Italian businessman that enabled the thirteenth-century Papacy to operate as an international finance corporation. On the other, credit finance came to play an increasingly large part in government. Edward I's debt to the Ricciardi of Lucca for the years from 1272 to 1294 totalled nearly £400,000; 48 per cent of this debt was repaid out of the customs receipt from a trade in which the Italians were increasingly involved. Kings, of course, had borrowed before. In the 1250s, Henry III owed the Ricciardi over £50,000; in the 1150s, Henry II used loans from a Flemish businessman, William Cade, to finance the making of the Angevin Empire. What was significant in the late thirteenth century was both the scale of the operations and the linkage between credit and customs. Compared with the sums obtainable from these new sources, the amounts to be derived from traditional levies, scutages, tallages, and feudal aids, were hardly worth the trouble of collecting and they gradually fell into disuse.

The customs system of 1275 had been granted in Parliament after discussion between the king's advisers and the merchants. Characteristic of all these taxes was that someone else's consent was required: either the pope's, or the merchants', or the clergy's, or the country's. By contrast land, lordship, and juris-diction were revenue-producing rights which did not require meetings of influential men to approve their exploitation—indeed all influential men enjoyed similar rights (though on a smaller scale) and presumably took them for granted—so long as they were not abused. Whereas 85 per cent of Henry I's recorded revenue came from land, lordship, and jurisdiction, they provided less than 40 per cent of Edward I's. The higher the proportion of Crown revenue that came from taxation, the greater was the need for political mechanisms that enabled that consent to be obtained. This is the process known as the growth of representative institutions; in the case of the tax on movables it is the growth of Parliament.

During the long years of freedom from foreign war after 1214 the tax on movables remained an occasional resource of the Crown. War was occasional and other acceptable justifica-tions for the tax were rare, so consent was only occasionally forthcoming—certainly not as often as Henry III would have liked. But the growing potential of the tax was revealed by the last of the seven levies collected between 1208 and 1293: the assessed yield of the $\frac{1}{15}$ of 1290 was over £116,000. How was consent to this extraordinary tax obtained? The king's advisers would have had to make a case. Presumably, they pointed to the expenses of his recent stay in Gascony (1286–9) and of his future crusade; they may well have pointed out that in the interests of Christian piety he was sacrificing a lucrative source of revenue in deciding to expel the Jews—although by 1290 the Jewish community had been squeezed so hard by royal financial demands that it had little more to give. But to whom did they make the case? They made it to the men who represented 'the community of the realm' and, in the first instance, these were the magnates—the sorts of influential men who always had attended major political assemblies, whether Anglo-Saxon, Norman, or Angevin. The assembly of 1290, 'Parliament' as it was now called, met from April to July and in its first ten weeks

it got through a great deal of business, including some important legislation. In mid-July another group of men arrived,
knights of the shire. Less than a week later Parliament was
dissolved. Why had the knights been so belatedly summoned to
attend? Because the magnates were reluctant to approve the
tax. They agreed to it but 'only insofar as they were entitled to'.
Yet they had not been similarly reluctant to deal with other
kinds of parliamentary business, judicial, political, legislative.
In other words the magnates still adequately represented 'the
community of the realm' in most fields—but not when taxation
was on the agenda. From the late twelfth century onwards,
kings had grown accustomed to bargaining with individual
shire communities, so it was an obvious step to require these
local communities to choose men to speak for them on some of
those occasions when the king wanted to summon an assembly
to represent the community of the whole realm. Assemblies of
magnates were being reinforced in this way from the 1250s
onwards and gradually the knights, yeomen, and burgesses who
represented shires and boroughs—the Commons—were being
accorded a more prominent role. As the proceedings of the
Parliament of 1290 make clear it was above all else the king's
need for taxation which stimulated this development.

Was the process also the result of social change? Was there a
thirteenth-century 'rise of the gentry' which meant that traditional political institutions had to be reshaped? Did the gentry
now count for more in the localities so that if kings wanted
their needs widely understood and their taxes efficiently collected they had to offer them a place in the main political
forum of the realm? These are difficult questions, so difficult
indeed to answer in the affirmative that some historians have
argued that, on the contrary, the thirteenth century was a
period of crisis for the knightly class. One of the problems is a
familiar one: the growing volume of evidence. We know much
more about the thirteenth-century gentry than we do about
their predecessors. But did Simon de Montfort and his friends
court the gentry more assiduously in the period 1258–65 than

John and the rebel barons had done in 1212–15? Magna Carta contains clauses which appeal to wider social groups than the barons, but so too does Henry I's Coronation Charter. To whom was Edward the Confessor appealing when, in 1051, he decided not to collect the *heregeld*? Neither in the twelfth century nor in Anglo-Saxon times did society consist only of barons and peasants. The sort of men who got themselves chosen to be knights of the shire in the late thirteenth century were exactly the sort of men who always had attended the great political assemblies. True, they had come then in the retinues of the magnates, but it was in their retinues that sensible magnates found their best advisers—and presumably they had listened to them. The knights of the late thirteenth century were not coming to these meetings for the first time; they were simply coming under another guise. It may be that the evidence of political change—the more elaborate representative institutions of the thirteenth century, the larger share of taxation in crown revenue—still has to be set within a framework of underlying social continuity.

Law and Justice

From the reign of Henry II onwards, royal judges began to hold local sessions (assizes) so frequently that it becomes possible to speak of the application over almost the entire country of a common body of customary law, the 'common law', the custom of the king's court as described in treatises such as 'Glanvill' and 'Bracton'. The previous system had been one in which, generally speaking, local courts had applied local custom. Kings, of course, had long been held to be responsible for law and order; in particular they were expected to deal with serious offences, the pleas of the Crown, but until a regular, centrally-directed machinery of justice was established, their activity in this field could only be sporadic. They intervened when influential people were involved and they launched occasional drives against theft, especially cattle-rustling. In this respect, the

Anglo-Saxon system of justice survived the Norman Conquest. The change came in 1166 with the Assize of Clarendon, reinforced in 1176 by the Assize of Northampton. These assizes introduced regular measures for the trial by royal judges of those suspected of serious crimes. At first Henry II's judges were simply men whom the king trusted—they might be earls, barons, bishops, abbots, or counsellors from the royal household, exactly the sort of people whom earlier kings had sent out on specific commissions of justice or inquiry—the biggest and most famous of such inquiries being the Domesday survey. For men such as these, holding courts of law was just one of the many tasks, administrative, diplomatic, and military, which they carried out on the king's behalf. But the introduction of frequent circuits meant an ever-increasing burden of judicial work and by the end of the twelfth century we can identify a group of men, most of them laymen, who specialized in legal business, in effect professional judges. There were, of course, lower courts dealing with less serious offences, but the 'professional' courts increasingly came to dominate the field. For one thing the lower courts had no authority to innovate, whereas the king could, and did, create new offences. For example the crime of conspiracy was 'invented' in 1279 when Edward I ordered the itinerant judges to inquire into confederacies to defeat the ends of justice. Since the king's courts dealt not only with crime but also with disputes concerning property they were clearly felt to be performing a useful service. Magna Carta criticized many aspects of royal government, but not this one. Indeed it asked that the king's judges should visit each shire four times a year, more frequently than was in practice possible.

The judges were men learned in the law; being learned, they naturally responded to shifts in attitudes and ideas prevailing within educated opinion. One such shift was in the direction of a self-consciously rational approach to intellectual problems—an approach typified by Abelard's dictum: 'By doubting we come to inquiry, by inquiring we come to perceive the truth.'

When applied to the law, this was a dictum which could have far-reaching implications. For example, if the guilt or innocence of a suspect could not readily be determined, it had for centuries been customary to send him to the ordeal, usually the ordeal of hot iron or the ordeal of water. This system worked well enough while men believed in it—it relied on the same psychological insight as the modern lie-detector—but was highly vulnerable to doubt. If an innocent man came to doubt the ordeal's efficacy as the means whereby God would prove his innocence then he was all the more likely to fail the ordeal. Once raised, these doubts could not be stilled. At first they seemed shocking—as when voiced by William Rufus—but eventually they became conventional. Finally, in 1215 Pope Innocent III forbade the participation of priests in the ordeal and, in England at least, this meant that the system came to an abrupt end. After an initial period of confusion, trial by ordeal was replaced by trial by jury: this was a method which had already been used with some success in settling disputes about possession of land. In 1179 Henry II had ordered that, in a case concerning property rights, the defendant might opt for trial by jury rather than trial by battle—the method which had been introduced into England by the Normans and the efficacy of which, like the ordeal, was vulnerable to doubt. But this rule when applied to criminal justice meant that there was a trial only when the accused opted for one. Obviously he came under great pressure. By a statute of 1275 he was condemned to a 'prisone forte et dure' until he did opt for trial. In consequence, many men died in prison, but because they had not been convicted, their property was not forfeited to the Crown. For this reason some chose to die rather than risk trial. Not until the eighteenth century was this right to choose taken away.

At first, and particularly in property litigation, juries had been called upon to settle straightforward questions to which they might reasonably be expected to know the answer. But problems arose when more complicated cases came before them and when trial by jury replaced the ordeal. For, unlike God, a jury was not omniscient. So efforts were made to cut through the complexities of any given dispute in order to isolate a specific question which the jury could fairly be expected to decide. But to do this well required specialized knowledge and skill; in other words it needed professional lawyers. And so, in the course of the thirteenth century, a legal profession developed, with its own schools, its own literature, and its own language (law French).

Despite all these changes, in many fundamental respects Anglo-Saxon attitudes towards justice continued to flourish. In the Anglo-Saxon and Anglo-Norman periods, serious offences had been dealt with under a procedure which ended with the guilty party being required to pay compensation to the victim or his family. The new machinery of justice established by the Angevins tended to impose punishment without compensation. In many cases, homicide, wounding, and rape for example, this was felt to be intolerable, so despite the impression given by writers such as 'Glanvill' and 'Bracton' who would have us believe that the new principles had effectively displaced the old, it seems that in reality the old procedures survived; they were adapted and grafted on to the new. What this meant was that those who could afford it escaped punishment but paid compensation to the victim or his kin, while those who could not, suffered the consequences.

Church and Religion

Domesday Book suggests that the village priest was usually reckoned to be a member of the peasant community. His church belonged to the local lord. If an estate were divided then the profits of the church which went with that estate might also have to be divided. In many ways, the village priest shared the life-style of the ordinary villager. He was very unlikely to be celibate; indeed, he was probably married and may well have inherited his position from his father. Given this basic situation, one can only admire the temerity of those eleventh-century reformers who aimed to abolish both lay control of the Church and the family life of the clergy. Under papal stimulus, the campaign for reform reached England in 1076. In subsequent decades, it was gradually stepped up and in the long run it even had a kind of success. By the late thirteenth century, married clergy were exceptional. On the other hand, plenty of them—including some of the most powerful—continued to have mistresses. Ranulf Flambard of Durham and Roger of Salisbury had their counterparts almost two hundred years later in Walter Langton of Coventry, who was accused of strangling his mistress's husband, and Robert Burnell, Edward I's chancellor, whom the king twice tried to have translated from Bath and Wells to Canterbury. As far as lay patronage and family connection were concerned, these two aspects of church life were hardly touched. 'The Lord deprived bishops of sons, but the devil gave them nephews.'

Yet even the limited success of the campaign against clerical marriage is remarkable—given how ineffective decrees on this subject had been in the seven hundred years from the fourth century onwards. It may well be linked with the general improvement in education in the twelfth and thirteenth centuries. If society at large became more literate then the clergy could more readily be recruited from the laity; they did not have to remain what they had come close to being, a hereditary caste. The more people went to school, the more they learned to know, and some of them to respect, the ancient law of the Church. Certainly there is reason to believe that in thirteenth-century England a higher proportion of the population was celibate than had been in the eleventh century. Quite simply, there were far more people who had taken vows of chastity. Everywhere in Europe monasticism flourished and England was no exception. In 1066 there were some fifty religious houses in England and perhaps 1,000 monks and nuns. By 1216 there were approximately 700 houses and some 13,000 monks, nuns, canons, and canonesses. A century later, the total was nearer 900 houses and 17,500 members of the religious orders. Seen in the context of an overall tripling of the population these are impressive figures. Even so they fail to make plain the extent to which religious life had become diversified and enriched. In the eleventh century, all the houses were Benedictine in type. By the mid-thirteenth century not only were there several hundred Benedictine houses, there were also a number of new orders from which a man or woman could choose—regular canons, Cistercians, Gilbertines (the one peculiarly English order), Templars, Hospitallers, Carthusians, Dominicans, Franciscans, Carmelites, and Austin friars. Within this framework, almost every conceivable variety of religious life, rural, urban, contemplative, ascetic, active, was now catered for. What is more, most of those who entered the religious life now did so because they chose to. Whereas the old Benedictine houses had recruited their monks largely from the children given by their aristocratic parents to be brought up in the cloister (oblates), from the mid-twelfth century onwards those who entered both the new and the old orders were adults. The Cistercians, who established the new pattern, prohibited entry for anyone under the age of sixteen and insisted upon a year's noviciate. Conscripts had been replaced by volunteers.

During the course of the twelfth century, the English Church established the diocesan and parochial organization under which it was to live for centuries. The last new dioceses to be created were Ely (in 1108) and Carlisle (1133). Dioceses were divided into archdeaconries, and archdeaconries into rural deaneries. In the Norman period, as before, new parishes were created almost at will—the will of the local lord; but thereafter it became much harder. The territorial organization of the Church became, as it were, frozen in its twelfth-century state. This was certainly not because demographic and economic expansion was now levelling off. On the contrary, new settlements continued to be founded and the old ones continued to grow. What was happening was that the development of canon law and of papal jurisdiction was tending to protect innumerable vested interests. The rise of the lawyer, itself the result of change in one sphere of life, made it harder to change things in others. Where this created a real pastoral problem was in the towns. Bishops wrestled with the problem but much of their effort was frustrated by the proprietary interests of patrons, churchmen as well as laymen. The thirteenth century found a solution, but it needed a radical departure, a new form of religious life, to make it possible. This new form was provided by the mendicant orders, the friars—mobile missionaries whose international organization cut clean through diocesan and parochial boundaries. The first friars to come to England were the Dominicans. They arrived in 1221 and headed for Oxford. Three years later, the Franciscans arrived; their earliest friaries were in Canterbury, London, and Oxford. The Carmelites and Austin friars arrived in the 1240s. By 1300 the friars had founded some 150 houses in England.

The coming of the friars, like the growth of canon law, is a movement which reflects one of the basic circumstances of the English Church. Although its growing material wealth was firmly rooted in English soil, in its spiritual, intellectual, and corporate life as a Church it was simply a part of Latin Christendom. This was particularly true of the period from the late eleventh century onwards. Even though the Anglo-Saxon Church had always been open to Continental influences, the fact that, after 1066, it became French in its speech and emphatically Latin in its learning tended to accentuate this receptiveness. Still more important was the Gregorian reform movement and the associated development of canon law and papal jurisdiction over the entire Latin Church. The reformers' demand for *libertas ecclesiae*, the privileged freedom of the Church, undeniably had some dramatic consequences; but in the end it turned out to be unobtainable. While liberty was linked with privilege and the continued possession of great corporate wealth, kings and other secular patrons could not afford to renounce some of their crucial powers, in particular the power to appoint, even though by the thirteenth century they were having to work through the legal machinery of the Roman curia in order to obtain their ends. The fact was that the spiritual weapons at the Church's disposal, excommunication and interdict, were ultimately insufficient to deter the secular power. They tended, moreover, to become blunted through over-use. In areas which really mattered to the lay world, not just patronage but also war, tournaments, and business practice, the heroic days of the Gregorian reform gradually, in the course of the twelfth and thirteenth centuries, gave way to a period of accommodation. But where the reformers did succeed was in translating the theory of papal headship of the Church into the fact of a centralized system of government. To a quite remarkable extent, the clergy learned to do what the pope told them to do. Thus when Pope Innocent III, in pursuit of his quarrel with King John, laid an interdict on England, the clergy obeyed. For six years, from 1208 to 1214, the church doors were closed and the laity were locked out; they were denied the sacrament of the altar, solemnization of marriages, burial in consecrated ground. Even when the pope, beginning in 1199, ordered the taxation of the Church, the clergy grumbled but paid up. From 1228 onwards we can trace a continuous series of resident collectors in England; they bore the title of *nuncio* and almost all of them were Italians. Here too there was accommodation. It seemed realistic to win the king of England's approval and so, by 1300, it was the king who received the lion's share of the proceeds.

Throughout this period, Catholic Christianity remained the unchallenged religion of the country. It was taken for granted. When the churches were closed for six years there was hardly a murmur of public protest—but neither was there an upsurge of interest in alternative religions. In the twelfth and thirteenth centuries, heresy was no more of a threat to the English Church than it had been in the eleventh: in this respect England was different from many parts of Europe. Throughout this period there were a few non-Christians—Jews—in the country, but their position was always precarious, at times painfully so, and in 1290 they were expelled. Most Christians rejoiced.

Economy 181

Economy

The basic outline of the English economy in 1086 emerges very clearly from the repetitive, laconic phrases of Domesday Book. This was a fundamentally agrarian economy. Over 90 per cent of the people lived in the country and earned their daily bread and ale from the resources of the land. The land was already well settled—some 13,000 settlements are named—and much cultivated. As much as 80 per cent of the arable acreage of 1914 had been under the plough in 1086. Pasture, woodland, and fen were also exploited. Most men were farmers and fishers. Neither trade nor industry could offer a major alternative source of employment. Domesday statistics—though they have to be used as cautiously as any other statistics—can help to fill out the picture. People called *villani* comprised the most numerous class (41 per cent of the total recorded population). Their land holdings came to about 45 per cent of all the land. The next largest number (32 per cent) were the people known as 'bordars' or 'cottars'; they held only 5 per cent of the land. Thus, although there were enormous individual variations, it is clear that we are dealing with two distinct classes: those who had a substantial stake in the village fields and those who possessed hardly more than a cottage and its garden. In addition there were the 14 per cent of the total who were described either as 'free men' or 'sokemen'. Since they held a fifth of the land they seem to belong, economically speaking, to the same class as the *villani*. Finally there were the slaves, 9 per cent of the recorded population, who held no land.

At the other end of the social scale were the king and a tiny group of powerful men, all of them *rentiers* who lived in style on the revenues of their great estates. Less than two hundred laymen and roughly one hundred major churches (bishoprics, abbeys, and priories) held between them about three-quarters of the assessed value of the whole country. These men—in legal terminology they were known as the king's tenants-in-chief—had tenants of their own. A wealthy baron like William de

Warenne, for example, had granted out holdings worth about £540 out of an estate valued at over £1,150. Some of these subtenants were men described as knights and their tenancies as knights' fees. (Although many of the knights were no richer than the richest *villani* the fact remains that they lived in closer association with their lords and therefore belonged to a different social group.) The rest of a tenant-in-chief's estates— usually between a half and three-quarters of them—were kept 'in demesne', and it was from these demesne lands that a lord drew the bulk of his income and food. A monastic house, with a fixed centre, needed regular supplies of foodstuffs, but other great landlords, who were more peripatetic, would probably be more interested in money. Most demesnes therefore were leased—'farmed' was the technical term—in return for a money rent. Most of the lessees came from exactly the same range of social ranks as did the holders of knights' fees; together they constituted a landowning 'middle class', a gentry.

What happened to the English economy in the two hundred years after 1086? Even over so long a period as this it can be argued that, in many fundamental respects, there was little change. England was no more urbanized in 1286 than in 1086. True, there were more and larger towns but then there were more people altogether. There were undoubtedly striking improvements in ship design—a continuing feature of northern Europe from the eighth century onwards. In this period it meant, above all, the development of the 'cog', a large, tubby bulk-carrier with a stern-post rudder and a deep draught. This meant economies of scale in the maritime trade which had long linked the east coast with the Scandinavian world and the west with the Atlantic coast of France. Presumably the volume of trade in wool, cloth, timber, salted fish, and wine was increasing and merchants' profits may well have been increasing too. Even so there was no English commercial revolution, no development of banks and credit facilities of the kind that can be claimed for thirteenth-century Italy. One consequence of this relative backwardness was that in the thirteenth century an increasingly high proportion of England's foreign trade came to be in Italian hands. Their reserves of liquid capital enabled Italian companies to offer attractive terms. They could not only buy an abbey's entire wool clip for the current year; they could also buy it for years in advance. By lending large sums to Henry III and Edward I, they obtained royal patronage and protection. In a very real sense late thirteenth-century England was being treated as a partially developed economy. Much of its import–export business was handled by foreigners (Gascons and Flemings as well as Italians). Its main exports were raw materials—wool and grain—rather than manufactured goods. There had been, in other words, no industrial revolution.

Throughout this period the major industries remained the same ones: cloth, building, mining and metalworking, salt production, and sea fishing. Moreover, despite the claims sometimes made for the cloth fulling-mill, there were no significant advances in industrial technology. Nor was there anything to compare with the highly-capitalized development of the Flemish cloth industry in the twelfth and thirteenth centuries. On the other hand growing Flemish demand for English wool did help to preserve the favourable balance of trade which, throughout this period, ensured an inflow of bullion sufficient to maintain the one coin, the silver penny, at a consistently fine standard. (Whereas in more rapidly developing and more highly monetized regions, people used a much debased coinage to perform the economic function of small change. In this sense too the English economy saw comparatively little change.)

Above all there was no agricultural revolution. Despite the fact that thirteenth-century experts on estate management, men such as Walter of Henley or Henry of Eastry, approached their job in a rational and scientific manner, the technical limitations under which they worked meant that no significant increase in yields was possible, neither from sheep in terms of weight of fleece, nor from seed in terms of yield of grain. Though the use of the horse as a draught animal was spreading, this was of marginal importance. The main problems lay not in ploughing, but in sowing, reaping, and maintaining soil fertility. Sowing and reaping by hand was wasteful and slow. Marl and most other types of fertilizer were either expensive or unobtainable. Only animal dung was generally available and it was widely and systematically used. But the high costs of feeding flocks and herds through the winter meant that there were upper limits to the amount of dung that could be produced. And unless there were basic improvements in primary production—as there were not—improvements at the second stage of production, for example the introduction of windmills around 1200, could only be of marginal economic importance. Thus in many respects England remained a stagnant economy. It can indeed be argued that, by comparison with some of its neighbours, especially Flanders and Italy, England was less advanced in the thirteenth century than it had been in the eleventh.

But having said all this, it must be made clear that in one vital respect there had been considerable change. By the late thirteenth century there were far more people living in England than there had been in 1086—notwithstanding the fact that men and women were familiar with *coitus interruptus* as a method of birth control. Exactly how many people there were, it is impossible to say. Estimating population at the time of the Domesday survey is an extremely difficult task. Most historians would put it at between one and a quarter and two and a quarter millions. Estimating the late thirteenth-century population is even more hazardous. Some historians would go as high as seven millions; others would put it much lower, perhaps five millions. But almost all agree that the population more than doubled and most would accept that it probably trebled. The hypothesis of slow growth from the eleventh (or perhaps indeed from the tenth) century, followed by an acceleration from the end of the twelfth century onwards seems to be a plausible one. But not only did rates of growth vary (probably) over time; they also varied (certainly) in space. Thus the population of the

North Riding of Yorkshire probably increased some twelvefold in the two hundred years after 1086; elsewhere, and particularly in those areas which were already relatively densely settled by the time of the Domesday survey, that is along the south coast and in some parts of East Anglia, the growth rate was very much smaller, though it was particularly high in the silt belt around the Wash.

What were the economic consequences of this increase of population? They can best be summed up by the phrase, 'expansion without growth'. Thus the immediate consequence was the physical expansion of settlement and cultivation. The expansion of settlement was a fairly straightforward matter. Indeed, there are plenty of signs of what the citizen of the modern world is inclined to call progress. Towns flourished. Their main function was to act as local markets. Where we know the occupations of their inhabitants, the predominance of the victualling trades and of craftsmen-shopkeepers in leather, metal, and textiles is striking. Even for the big towns—and by European standards England contained only one genuinely big town, London, assessed in 1334 at four times the wealth of its nearest rival, Bristol—long-distance and luxury trade remained less important. An increasing density of rural population meant that towns increased both in size and in number. Between 1100 and 1300, some 140 new towns were planted and, if it is not just a trick of the evidence, it would seem that the decades between 1170 and 1250 saw the greatest number, Portsmouth, Leeds, Liverpool, Chelmsford, Salisbury, for example. Mostly they were founded by local lords who expected to make a profit out of the money rents and tolls they planned to collect. Some were sited where they could take advantage of the expansion of maritime commerce, as larger ships meant that coastal ports such as Boston, King's Lynn, and Hull (all new foundations) did better than up-river ports such as Lincoln, Norwich, and York.

In the countryside, too, the hand of the planner is sometimes visible, particularly in the regular-form villages which were laid out in those northern areas which had been laid waste by the Normans. Elsewhere, in already densely settled East Anglia for example, villages sometimes moved to new sites straggling along the edge of common land, presumably in order to free good arable land from the 'waste' of being built upon.

But finding room to live was one thing; growing enough food to live on quite another. In general the expansion of farmland took place not so much through the establishment of new settlements as through piecemeal increase around existing centres. Huge acreages of forest, fen, marsh, and upland were cleared, drained, and farmed. Some of this was on potentially good soil—the silt belt around the Wash is the classic example—but much of it, like the clearings in the Sussex Weald, would always remain poor. This is 'the journey to the margin'—men moved out to the margins of cultivation and farmed land that was indeed marginal: it produced returns which were barely worth the labour expended. So pressing was the demand for food, bread above all, that even other 'necessities'—fuel and building timber—were having to give way.

Naturally attempts were made to farm the existing arable more intensively. In the thirteenth century the three-field, instead of the two-field, system came to be more widely adopted. This meant that a third rather than a half of the land was left fallow each year. But more intensive land use required a correspondingly more intensive application of fertilizers if soil quality were to be maintained. Unfortunately, the expansion of arable was sometimes at the expense of both pasture and woodland. The effect of this on livestock numbers could hardly have permitted increased manure production and may have actually led to a decrease in droppings. This in turn could have led to soil exhaustion and lower, rather than higher yields. Whether or not yields did decline towards the end of the thirteenth century, one thing that does seem clear is that, if the physical limit of cultivation were reached and population still continued to grow, then one of two things would have to happen.

Either more food would be imported or the average standard of living would have to fall. There is no evidence that grain imports rose. If anything the trend was probably in the opposite direction. English grain dealers took their merchandise in bulk-carrying ships to regions such as Flanders, Gascony, and Norway, that is, to places where industrialization or specialization had reached a higher pitch than in England and where regional economies were geared to the import of basic foodstuffs in return for cloth, wine, and forest products. Moreover the abundant estate records of thirteenth-century England make it clear that the average size of tenant holdings was shrinking. In this period more people means less land per head.

Despite this gloomy picture many thirteenth-century villagers may have been better off than their predecessors at the time of Domesday Book. They were relatively free from the devastation caused by war. None of them was a slave. Slavery is a feature of economies characterized by labour shortage; as population, and therefore the supply of labour, rose so slavery declined. True, many of them were serfs (or villeins)—perhaps as much as half the total population—whereas the *villani* and cottagers of Domesday Book (three-quarters of the listed population) were free. But although the *villani* and cottagers were free inasmuch as they were not slaves, it is clear that they were not very free—thus the existence of the much smaller Domesday class (only 14 per cent of those listed) called precisely 'free men'. What made life difficult for the *villani* and cottagers was that their lords were free too—free and powerful. They were free to manipulate custom in order to impose as many burdens as they could, and in a period of relative labour shortage this is likely to have meant a heavy regime of labour services: at times like this lords would not be content to pay wages at levels set by the market. Only as supply rose would lords increasingly turn to the alternative of wage labour. In the twelfth century, many tenants found their obligations converted from labour service to payment of a money rent. At this point, the development of the legalistic outlook becomes important. In the decades either side of the year 1200, the king's judges formulated rules to determine who had the right to have their disputes heard in the royal courts and who had not. They decided that those who had the right were 'free', while those who had not were 'servile'. The effect of this classification of society into two distinct categories was to enserf half the population: to make them legally unfree. But what the lawyers took with one hand they gave with the other. The more everything came to be defined and written down, the more customary tenures tended to become 'frozen' in that state in which they were written down. It became less easy to manipulate custom; more effectively than before custom tended to protect the status quo. In this sense, even unfree tenants in the thirteenth century were less vulnerable to the arbitrary exactions of individual lords than many free tenants of the eleventh century had been. Thirteenth-century lords who tried to manipulate custom often found themselves involved in long legal battles with well-organized village communities.

But although customary law may have offered a poor tenant some protection from his lord's demands, it could do nothing to protect him from the grim realities of economic change. In the years either side of 1200, half the villagers of England may have been enserfed, but this mattered little compared with the fact that poor villagers became still poorer. Those who really suffered towards the end of the thirteenth century were not servile tenants as such, but those tenants, whether free or servile, who were poor and those who had no land at all. We know something about tenants. Mortality rates on the Winchester manors suggest that from 1250 onwards the poorer tenants were becoming increasingly 'harvest-sensitive'—a euphemistic phrase meaning that, with each bad harvest, more of them died, either of starvation or of the diseases attendant upon malnutrition. Study of the West Midlands manor of Halesowen suggests that poor tenants there—the successors of the cottagers of Domesday—had a life expectancy some ten years less than the better-off tenants, the successors of the Domesday *villani*. What happened to the landless we can only guess; the nature of the evidence is such that they rarely find themselves mentioned in thirteenth-century records. Labourers on great estates customarily received not only cash but also an allowance of grain sufficient to sustain a family. But what about those landless labourers who became 'surplus to the economy'? Presumably they also became 'harvest-sensitive'.

But the economic clouds which brought misery for the poor were nicely lined with silver for the rich. The growth of population meant an increasing demand for food. Prices rose, particularly around 1200 and in the late thirteenth-century. On the other hand, a plentiful supply of labour meant that money wage rates, both for piece-work and for day-work, remained stable throughout the century. Real wages, in other words, fell. In these circumstances, wealthy landowners could do very well. Selling their surplus produce on the market brought increasing profits. Markets proliferated. Between 1198 and 1483 some 2,400 grants of market were made by the Crown and of these over half came in the period before 1275. Equally a rising demand for tenancies meant growing rent-rolls. To take just one example, the bishop of Ely's net income rose from £920 in 1171–2 to £2,550 in 1298. But this does not quite mean that all the fortunate possessor of a great estate had to do was sit back and let the laws of supply and demand do their work for him. In the twelfth century, as before, most of the manors belonging to a wealthy tenant-in-chief were in fact held by his tenants, either as knights' fees or leased out at fixed rents to 'farmers'. At a time of stability or gradual expansion, this made good sense; from the lord's point of view it kept his administrative costs down to a minimum. The stability of the system is indicated by the fact that long-term leases for a life or for several lives were common, and that these long-term grants tended to turn into hereditary tenures.

But the steep rise in prices around 1200 created severe problems for the lord living on fixed rents. If he, rather than his tenants, were to take advantage of the market economy, then he had to switch to direct management of his manors. To abandon an age-old system was not easy and many lords encountered fierce resistance from their tenants, but gradually it was done. The most famous description of the process can be read in Jocelin of Brakelond's account of the business-like life of Abbot Samson of Bury St. Edmunds (abbot 1182–1211). The landlord took his estates into his own hands, appointed bailiffs and reeves to run them and sell the surplus on the open market. Under this new regime, the lord's expenses and profits were going to vary from year to year. This would have made it very easy for his officials to cheat him unless a close check were kept on their activities. So a detailed record of the manorial year was drawn up and then sent, together with similar returns from the other manors, to be checked by auditors who represented the central administration of a great estate. (The survival of masses of these accounts means that we know a great deal about some aspects of the thirteenth-century English rural economy.) The auditors had a policy-making as well as a fraud-detecting role. They fixed targets for each manor, the levels of production of grain and livestock which had to be reached. They took investment decisions, whether to build new barns, whether to buy fertilizers, and so on. Inspired by these concerns a whole new literature was born, treatises on agriculture and estate management, of which Walter of Henley's *Husbandry* is the most famous. All these changes presupposed the existence of widespread practical literacy: without this it would not have been possible to carry through the managerial revolution—for that is what it was—of the early thirteenth century.

The whole point of the new system was to maximize the lord's profits, and to do so in as rational a way as possible. It seems unlikely that this was an approach which was going to concern itself with the problems facing the poor, the lame ducks of the economic system, nearly all of whom were born lame. At a manorial level there are innumerable cases of resistance to a lord's demands, both passive resistance and direct, sometimes legal, action. In the towns, too, there is increasing evidence of a struggle between rich and poor. By the 1290s England was a country choked with people, a traditional economy unable to cope with the strains of population pressure, even perhaps a land on the brink of class warfare.

4. The Later Middle Ages
(1290–1485)

=====

RALPH A. GRIFFITHS

To those who lived at the time, and to many historians since, the fourteenth and fifteenth centuries seemed a dangerous, turbulent, and decadent age. England's civil and foreign wars—especially those in Scotland, France, and the Low Countries—lasted longer, extended further afield, cost more, and involved larger numbers of men than any it had fought since the Viking Age. Within the British Isles, Welshmen were distrusted by the English, despite Edward I's conquests; uprisings culminating in Owain Glyndŵr's rebellion (from 1400) seemed to justify this distrust and recall prophecies that foretold of the expulsion of the English from Wales. Celtic prejudice against Englishmen flourished with all the bitterness and resentment of which the defeated or oppressed were capable: 'The tyranny and cruelty of the English', claimed a Scot in 1442, 'are notorious throughout the world, as manifestly appears in their usurpations against the French, Scots, Welsh, Irish and neighbouring lands.' Famine, disease, and (from 1348) plague drastically reduced England's population by the early fifteenth century, perhaps by as much as a half, and this severely disrupted English society. Towards the end of the fifteenth century, French statesmen were noting with disapproval Englishmen's habit of deposing and murdering their kings and the children of kings (as happened in 1327, 1399, 1461, 1471, 1483, and 1485) with a regularity unmatched anywhere else in Western Europe. Spiritual uncertainty and the spread of heresy led the choleric Chancellor of Oxford University, Dr Thomas Gascoigne, to conclude that the English Church of his day was decayed, and its bishops and clergy failing in their duty. One popular poet, writing about 1389, thought that this seemingly decadent age was all too appropriately reflected in the extravagant and indecent fashion for padded shoulders, tightly-drawn waistbands, close-fitting hose, and long pointed shoes.

There are, of course, dangers in taking contemporaries at their own estimation, particularly if they lived at times of special tension or turmoil. It is now accepted that wars can have a creative side, in this case giving Englishmen a sharper sense of national identity; that famine and disease need not utterly prostrate a society, or economic contraction necessarily mean economic depression; that the growth of heresy and criticism of religious institutions may spur men to greater personal devotion; that, as with the evolution of Parliament, political crises have constructive features; and, finally, that literary and artistic accomplishments are rarely extinguished by civil commotion or social ferment. From the vantage point of the late twentieth century, the later Middle Ages now appear as an age of turbulence and complexity, sure enough, but also as an age of vitality, ambition, and, above all, fascination.

England at War, 1290–1390

The king and his court, with the royal family and household at its centre, were the focus and fulcrum of English government and politics. Central to both was the relationship between the king and his influential subjects: the barons or magnates first and foremost, but also country knights and esquires who often aspired to join the baronial ranks, wealthy merchants, and the bishops and talented clerks—all of whom sought patronage, position, and promotion from the Crown. A successful king was one who established a harmonious relationship with all or most of these influential subjects, for only then could political stability, effective government, and domestic peace be assured. This was no simple or easy task. The growing emphasis on the king's sovereign authority in his kingdom, reinforced by the principle (from 1216) that the Crown should pass to the eldest son of the dead monarch and by the extension of royal administration in the hands of a network of king's clerks and servants, was bound to be at the expense of the feudal, regional power of the great landowners. Yet that very principle of hereditary monarchy, while it reduced the likelihood of royal kinsmen squabbling over the Crown, made it more likely that unsuitable kings (by their youth, character, or incapacity) would sometimes wear it. Above all, the persistent warfare of the fourteenth and fifteenth centuries imposed heavier obligations on England's kings. From Edward I's reign onwards, there was no decade when Englishmen were not at war, whether overseas or in the British Isles. Every generation of Englishmen in the later Middle Ages knew the demands, strains, and consequences of war—and more intensely than their forebears.

After the civil war of Henry III's reign, a successful effort was made to reconcile England and restore domestic peace whereby the king and his subjects could re-establish a stable relationship that gave due regard to the rights and aspirations of both. The new monarch, Edward I (1272–1307), showed himself to be capable, constructive, and efficient in his government, and also determined to emphasize his position as sovereign. But his unrelenting insistence on asserting his sovereignty in all the territories of the British Isles, even those beyond the borders of his realm, began the era of perpetual war.

In Wales, he overwhelmed Gwynedd, the most vigorous and independent of the surviving native lordships, and with Llywelyn ap Gruffydd's death in 1282 the conquest of Wales was successfully completed after two hundred years of intermittent warfare. The Crown thereby expanded its territories in North and West Wales to form a principality that covered half the country; in 1301 this was conferred on the king's eldest son as the first English-born Prince of Wales. It was a notable achievement, if a costly one. Material damage had to be made good; an imaginative plan for future security included a dozen new and half-a-dozen reconstructed fortresses, most of them complemented by new walled boroughs peopled by loyal immigrants; and a permanent administration was devised for the conquered lands. This administration (announced in the statute of Rhuddlan, 1284) began as a military regime but soon established peace and stability by a judicious combination of English innovation and Welsh practice. Firmness, tempered by fairness and conciliation, was the hallmark of relations between the new governors and the Welsh population, and rebellions in 1287, 1294–5, and 1316 were not widespread or dangerous threats. Yet the costs of conquest were prodigious. Soldiers and sailors, architects, craftsmen, and labourers were recruited in every English county and beyond to serve in Wales. At least £75,000 was spent on castle-building between 1277 and 1301 alone (when a skilled mason earned less than 2s. a week), whilst the suppression of the 1294–5 revolt cost about £55,000. Fortunately, royal government in Wales proved eminently successful: by the mid-fourteenth century it was producing a profit for the royal exchequer and the Welsh gentry prospered in co-operation with an alien regime.

No sooner had Llywelyn been eliminated than Edward I turned to the lords of the Welsh march (or borderland)—mostly English magnates—to establish his sovereign rights over them and their subjects too; and he brought the Welsh Church and bishops more directly under his control. The whole enterprise of Edwardian conquest showed an imagination and determination and a grasp of strategy that went far beyond the military campaigns. But the feelings of bitterness among the conquered, who were ruled in Church and State by an alien hierarchy, could not easily be removed. If English domination were to become oppressive, if the economic benefits of stable rule dried up, or if relations between native and immigrant deteriorated, serious problems would be created for the English state, and colonial rule would be threatened.

Edward I was equally intent on exerting his superior lordship over Scotland. This was an exceptionally ambitious undertaking because Scotland, unlike Wales, had its own monarch (of the house of Canmore) and Scotsmen's sense of independence was fierce, especially in the remoter Highlands. But, as with Wales, an opportunity to assert England's overlordship had arisen in Edward's reign in 1286 on the death of King Alexander III and of his granddaughter and heiress four years later. Edward accepted the invitation of the Scottish 'guardians of the realm' to settle the succession question, and he took advantage of this 'Great Cause' (1291–2) to secure recognition of himself as 'lord superior' of Scotland. Scottish resistance and Edward's efforts to make his claim a reality began a barren period of mutual hostility between the two countries that lasted well into the sixteenth century. The Scots sought French aid (1295) and papal support, and they generated a vigorous patriotism in defence of their political independence under the leadership of William Wallace (executed 1305) and Robert Bruce (King Robert I, 1306–29). A score of English invasions in the half-century after 1296 succeeded in establishing an uneasy military and administrative presence in the Lowlands, but it was difficult to sustain in poor and hostile country and had to be financed largely from England. Nor did the English command the northern seas or subdue and control the north and west of Scotland. Thus, the English had none of the advantages—or success—that attended their ventures in Wales, and even in battle (notably at Bannockburn, 1314) their cavalry forces suffered humiliating defeat at the hands of more mobile Scotsmen. The treaty of Northampton (1328), which recognized King Robert and surrendered the English claim to overlordship, was quickly disowned by Edward III when he took personal charge of the government in 1330. Anglo-Scottish relations thereafter were a sad catalogue of invasion, border raids, unstable English occupation of southern shires, Franco-Scottish agreements that hardened into the 'Auld Alliaunce'—even the capture of King David II at Neville's Cross (1346). Scotland proved a persistent and expensive irritation after English claims and ambitions were thwarted by determined and united resistance by the Scots.

After Bannockburn, Robert I tried to forestall further English operations in Scotland by exploiting the situation in Ireland. During 1315–18 his brother, Edward Bruce, secured the support of Anglo-Irish magnates and Gaelic chiefs, and in 1316 he was declared High King of Ireland. Soon afterwards, Robert himself visited Ireland and this may have been designed to stimulate a 'pan-Celtic' movement against Edward II of England (1307–27). This Scottish intervention was a severe shock to the English government and revealed the weakness of its regime in Dublin. No English king visited Ireland between 1210 and 1394—not even Edward I, conqueror of the Welsh and 'hammer of the Scots'. Instead, Edward I ruthlessly stripped the country of its resources of men, money, and supplies, especially for his wars and castle-building in Wales and Scotland. Harsh exploitation and absentee rule led in time to administrative abuse and the decay of order, of which the Anglo-Irish magnates and Gaelic chiefs took full advantage. The king's officials presided over an increasingly feeble and neglected administration, whilst a Gaelic political and cultural revival had taken root in the thirteenth century. This contributed to the success of Edward Bruce, during whose ascendancy Ireland, said a contemporary, 'became one trembling wave of commotion'. The English lordship never recovered and henceforward was unable to impose its authority throughout the island. Instead of being a financial resource, Ireland became a financial liability, with a revenue after 1318 that was a third of what it had been under Edward I and therefore quite inadequate to sustain English rule. Periodic expeditions led by minor figures could do little to revive the king's authority and the area under direct rule consequently contracted to the 'pale' around Dublin. It was a confession of failure when the government resorted to racial and cultural separation, even persecution, by a series of enactments culminating in the statute of Kilkenny (1366). The 'lord of

Ireland' had a perfunctory lordship in the later Middle Ages that was costly, lawless, hostile to English rule, and open to exploitation by the Scots, the French, and even by Welsh rebels.

The recognition of overlordship which English monarchs demanded of the Welsh, Scots, and Irish was denied to the French king in Gascony, where these same English kings, as dukes of Aquitaine, had been feudal vassals of the Crown of France since 1204. Gascony lay at the heart of Anglo-French relations both before and during the so-called Hundred Years War (1337–1453): it replaced Normandy and Anjou as the main bone of contention. At Edward I's accession, this prosperous, wine-producing province was England's only remaining French territory, and the political link with England was reinforced by a flourishing export trade in non-sweet wine which was complemented by the transport of English cloth and corn by sea to Bordeaux and Bayonne: in 1306–7 the duchy's revenue was about £17,000 and well worth fighting for. Friction with the French king over Gascony's frontier and the rights of Gascons was gradually subsumed in the larger issues of nationhood and sovereignty posed by an assertive, self-conscious French state bent on tightening its control over its provinces and vassals (including the English duke of Aquitaine). For their part, Edward I and his successors were reluctant to see French royal rights emphasized or given any practical meaning in Gascony. The result was a series of incidents, peace conferences, 'brush-fire' wars in which French armies penetrated Gascony and the duchy was periodically confiscated, and English expeditions—even a visit by Edward I himself (1286–9).

Relations between England and France might have continued to fester in this fashion had it not been for two other factors. The English government resented the Franco-Scottish alliance (from 1295) and was angered by the refuge offered by the French (1334) to the Scottish King David II after Edward III had invaded Scotland. Even more contentious were the consequences of the approaching extinction of the senior male line of the French royal house of Capet. The deaths, in rapid succession, of four French kings between 1314 and 1328, requiring the swearing of homage for Gascony on each occasion, were irritating enough, but the demise of the last Capet in 1328 raised the question of the succession to the French throne itself. At that point, the new English king, Edward III (1327–77), was in no position to stake his own claim through his French mother, Isabella, but in 1337, when the Gascon situation had deteriorated further, he did so. His action may have been primarily tactical, to embarrass the new Valois monarch, Philip VI, though for an English king to become king of France would have the undeniable merit of resolving at a stroke the difficult Gascon issue: the political stability and economic prosperity of Gascony would be assured. Thus, when a French fleet was sighted off the Norman coast *en route* (so the English believed) for Scotland in 1337, war began—and would last for more than a century.

England's war aims were neither constant nor consistently pursued. Especially in the fourteenth century, its war diplomacy was primarily dictated by a series of immediate problems, notably, of how to maintain independent rule in Gascony and how to deter Scottish attacks across the northern border in support of the French. Even after Edward III claimed the French Crown in 1337, he was prepared to ransom John II, the French king captured at the battle of Poitiers (1356), and to abandon his claim in the treaty of Brétigny (1360) in return for practical concessions. Nevertheless, dynastic ties, commercial and strategic considerations, even differing attitudes to the Papacy, which was installed at Avignon from 1308 to 1378, combined to extend the Anglo-French conflict to the Low Countries, to Castile and Portugal, as well as to Scotland, Ireland, and even Wales. To begin with, the wars (for this was a disjointed series of conflicts rather than one war) were fought by sieges in northern France in 1338–40; then there was more intensive campaigning by pincer movements through the French provinces of Brittany, Gascony, and Normandy in 1341–7 (resulting in the English victory at Crécy and the capture of Calais).

This was followed by bold marches or *chevauchées* by Edward III's eldest son, Edward the Black Prince, from Gascony in 1355–6 (culminating in the great victory at Poitiers) and by the king himself in 1359 to Rheims, the traditional coronation seat of French kings. The renewal of war in Castile (1367) inaugurated a period of more modest and fitful campaigning in Portugal, Flanders, and France itself, with both sides gradually exhausting themselves.

The advantage in the war lay initially with England, the more united and better organized of the two kingdoms. Its prosperity, based especially on wool production, and its experience of warfare in Wales and Scotland, were invaluable foundations for larger-scale operations on mainland Europe. The existence of highly independent French provinces dictated English strategy. Edward III's campaigns in the Low Countries in 1338–40 relied on the support of the cloth-manufacturing cities of Flanders which, though subject to the French king, had vital commercial links with England. In the 1340s a succession dispute in Brittany enabled English forces to intervene there and even to garrison certain castles; while Gascony, though far to the south, afforded direct access to central France.

The wars within the British Isles gave the English government a unique opportunity to develop novel methods of raising substantial forces. Supplementing and gradually replacing the traditional feudal array, the newer paid, contracted armies, recruited by indentured captains, were smaller, better disciplined, and more dependable and flexible than the loosely organized and ponderous French forces. English men-at-arms and archers, proficient in the use of the longbow and employing defensive tactics in battle, had a decisive advantage which brought resounding victories against all the odds in the early decades of the war (most notably at Crécy and Poitiers). The war at sea was a more minor affair, with naval tactics showing little novelty or imagination. It was usually beyond the capability of fourteenth-century commanders to stage a naval engagement and the battle of Sluys (which the English won in 1340) was incidental to Edward III's expedition to Flanders. The English never kept a fleet permanently in being, but the Valois, learning the expertise of their Castilian allies, later constructed dockyards at Rouen which in time gave them an edge at sea (witness their victory off La Rochelle in 1372).

English investment in the French war was immense and unprecedented. Expeditions were organized with impressive regularity and were occasionally very large (over 10,000 men in 1346–7, for instance). The financial outlay was prodigious and tolerated so long as the war was successful; but as the margin of England's military advantage narrowed after 1369, so the government resorted to newer and more desperate expedients, including poll taxes. Shipping for defence and expeditions could not be supplied solely by the traditional obligation of the southern Cinque Ports, and hundreds of merchant vessels (735 for the siege of Calais in 1347, for example) were impressed and withdrawn from normal commercial operations. Coastal defence against French and Castilian raiders, who grew bolder after 1369, was organized by the maritime shires of the south and east, supported by others inland—but even this could not prevent the sacking of Winchelsea (1360), Rye (1377), and other ports. The costs of war were indeed high. It is true that conquered French estates were enjoyed by many a fortunate soldier, and ransoms were profitable during the victorious years (King John II's ransom alone was fixed at £500,000). But the lives and occupations of thousands of Englishmen, Welshmen, and Irishmen were disrupted by war service; supplies of food, materials, and equipment were diverted to operations that were entirely destructive; and the wool and wine trades were severely hampered. What is remarkable is that England was able to engage in these enterprises overseas for decades without serious political or social strains at home, and at the same time to defend the Scottish border, keep the Welsh calm, and avoid Irish uprisings. This achievement owed much to the inspiration, example, and leadership of Edward III and the Black Prince, both of whom embodied the chivalric virtues vaunted by the

nobility and admired by society at large. To Jean Froissart, the
Hainaulter who knew them both and kept a record of the most
inspiring chivalric deeds of his age, the king was 'gallant and
noble [whose] like had not been seen since the days of King
Arthur'. His son appeared as 'this most gallant man and chival-
rous prince' who, at his death in 1376, a year before Edward III
himself died, 'was deeply mourned for his noble qualities'. King
Edward presided over a regime in England that was less harsh
than Edward I's and far more capable than Edward II's.

These wars were a catalyst of social change, constitutional
development, and political conflict in England which would
otherwise have occurred more slowly. Moreover, along with
the rest of Europe, England in the fourteenth century experienced population and economic fluctuations that increased tension and uncertainty. The result was a series of crises which
underlined how delicately balanced was the relationship between the king and his subjects (especially his magnates, who
regarded themselves as representing the entire 'community of
the realm') and how crucial to a personal monarchy was the
king himself. Able and determined—even far-sighted—Edward
I and his advisers may have been, but the king's obstinate and
autocratic nature seriously strained relations with his influential
subjects. Between 1290 and 1297, the propertied classes, the
merchants, and especially the clergy were subjected to extraordinarily heavy and novel demands for taxes (four times as
frequently as in the first half of Edward's reign) for the king's
enterprises in France and the British Isles. There was resistance
and a property tax of 1297 produced only a fraction (£35,000)
of what had been anticipated. Further, armies had been summoned by the king for prolonged service outside the realm.
Edward's attempts to silence resistance shocked the clergy and
embittered the merchants. The leading magnates, including
Welsh marcher lords who resented Edward's invasion of their
cherished franchises, reacted by resuming their time-honoured
role as self-appointed spokesmen of the realm, and they presented grievances to the king in 1297 and again in 1300. They

deployed Magna Carta as their banner against taxation without the payers' consent, and against oppressive and unprecedented exactions. Yet, when Edward died in the arms of his attendants at Burgh-by-Sands on 7 July 1307, just as he was about to cross the Solway Firth on his sixth expedition to Scotland, the problems of wartime remained. He bequeathed to his son and successor, Edward II (1307–27), an expensive war in the north that was nowhere near a victorious conclusion, and political unrest in England compounded by a dwindling of trust between monarch and subject. These two preoccupations—political stability and war—dominated public affairs during the following 200 years and had a profound effect on the kingdom's social and political cohesion and on its economic prosperity. The new king would need exceptional tact if a further crisis of authority were to be avoided.

Tact was not Edward II's outstanding quality. Starved of affection during childhood, ignored by his father in adolescence, and confronted by unsolved problems at his accession, Edward II sought advice, friendship, even affection, from ambitious favourites such as Peter Gavaston and Hugh Despenser who were unworthy of the king's trust and whose influence was resented by many magnates. These facts, together with the determination of the magnates (led by Thomas, earl of Lancaster) to extract from Edward concessions and reforms which Edward I had been unwilling to confirm, turned the formidable difficulties of ruling a kingdom that was facing setbacks in Scotland, Ireland, Wales, and France into a struggle for political reform and personal advancement. An extended and more specific coronation oath (1308) bound the new king more firmly to observe English law and custom, and ordinances drawn up by the magnates in 1311 sought to limit the king's freedom of action; these ordinances were announced in Parliament in order to gain wide support and approval. Edward II had all the stubbornness of his father (though without his ability) and Gavaston's murder (1312) converted this quality into an unshakeable resolve not to be dominated by his friend's murderers.

Meanwhile, the burdens of war and defence on the king's subjects were scarcely less heavy than they had been during Edward I's conquests, and this at a time of severe social distress and poverty caused by a succession of disastrous harvests and livestock diseases during 1315–22. Civil war (1321–2) and the king's deposition (1326–7) were the fateful outcome of the failure of king and governed to co-operate to mutual benefit. Edward denounced the ordinances in 1322, again in a Parliament (at York), and after the defeat of his opponents at Borough-bridge in 1322, he executed Lancaster. By 1326, Edward's deposition in favour of his namesake son and heir seemed the only alternative to a mean, oppressive, and unsuccessful regime that engendered civil strife. This awesome step, engineered with Queen Isabella's connivance, the acquiescence of Prince Edward, and with substantial magnate and other support, demonstrated in a Parliament, was unprecedented: since the Norman Conquest, no English king had been deposed from his throne. In 1327, therefore, every effort was made to conceal the unconcealable and justify the unjustifiable. Browbeaten, tearful, and half-fainting, the wretched king was forced to assent to his own abdication, and a meeting of Parliament was used to spread the responsibility as widely as possible. Although the accession of Edward's son ensured that the hereditary principle remained intact, the inviolability of anointed kingship had been breached.

Although only fifteen in 1327, Edward III was soon a parent and proved far more capable than his father and more sensitive than he to the attitudes and aspirations of his magnates—indeed, he shared them, particularly in warfare and in accepting the chivalric obligations of an aristocratic society. At the same time, the new king's grandiose and popular plans in France raised issues similar to those posed by Edward I's enterprises in the British Isles and Gascony. Should these plans ultimately prove unsuccessful, the implications for England might well be similar to those that had surfaced in Edward II's reign. The outbreak of prolonged war in 1337 meant increased taxation at a level even higher than that of Edward I's last years, and Edward III showed the same ruthlessness towards merchants, bankers, and landowners as Edward I had done. Moreover, the absences of the king on campaign, in the thick of the fighting which he and his magnates relished, posed serious questions for a sophisticated administration normally under the personal direction of the king. Edward's ordinances (issued at Walton-on-Thames, 1338) for the government of England from abroad caused friction between the king and his advisers in northern France on the one hand, and those councillors remaining in England on the other. Some even feared that, if the war were successful, England might take second place in King Edward's mind to his realm of France. Thus, in 1339–43 another crisis arose in which magnates, merchants, and the Commons in Parliament (now the forum in which royal demands for taxation were made) protested to the king. Edward was induced to act more circumspectly and considerately towards his magnates, clergy, and subjects generally. The eventual reconciliation, and the re-establishment of the trust in the king that had proved so elusive since the 1290s, was possible because Edward III was a sensible and pragmatic monarch, with a self-confidence that did not extend to arrogance. He appointed ministers acceptable to his magnates, he pandered to the self-importance of Parliament, and he developed a remarkable *rapport* with his subjects which sustained his rule in England and his ambitions in France for a quarter of a century. Further crisis was avoided, despite England's involvement in its most major war yet.

There was an enormous contrast with the situation in the 1370s and 1380s. For the generation of Englishmen alive then, the frustrations of the resumed war in France (from 1369) and of debilitating skirmishes in Ireland and on the Scottish border were unsettling; and renewed taxation, after a decade when England had enjoyed the profits of war and a respite from taxes, was resented. Raids on south-coast ports were frequent, uncertain naval control of the Channel imperilled trade and upset the merchants, and expensive *chevauchées* in France were occasionally spectacular but rarely profitable. Yet the abrupt reversal of English policy in 1375, involving a humiliating truce with France and payments to the mistrusted pope, only served to affront and exasperate Englishmen. Moreover, after the death (1369) of Queen Philippa, a paragon among queens, Edward III lapsed gently into a senility that sapped his strength and impaired his judgement. The Black Prince, too, began to suffer from the effects of his wartime exertions; in fact, he predeceased his father in June 1376. Yet the financial, man-power, and other burdens on England's population were not eased. Questions were raised, especially by the Commons in Parliament, about the honesty as well as the competence of the king's advisers and officials. Strengthened by a rising tide of anti-clericalism in an age when the reputation of the Papacy and the Church was severely tarnished, the outcry had swept Edward III's clerical ministers from power in 1371 and others were accused of corruption, even treason. Another political crisis had arisen. In the 'Good Parliament' of 1376, the longest and most dramatic assembly yet held, the allegedly corrupt and incapable ministers—even the old king's influential mistress, Alice Perrers—were accused by the Commons and tried before the Lords in a novel and highly effective procedure (impeachment) which henceforward enabled persons in high places to be held publicly to account for their public actions.

The crisis entered a new phase when King Edward himself died in June 1377. He was succeeded by the Black Prince's only surviving son and heir, Richard II (1377–99), who was ten years of age. England was faced with the prospect of only the second royal minority since 1066 and the first since 1216. On the latter occasion there had followed a period of political turbulence centring on the young Henry III; a similar situation developed after 1377 and played its part in precipitating the Peasants' Revolt (1381) in eastern and south-eastern England. A series of poll taxes was imposed during 1377–80 to finance the war. These taxes were at a rate higher than was usual and the tax of

1379 was popularly known as 'the evil subsidy'. They sparked off violence in East Anglia against the tax-collectors and the justices who tried to force compliance on the population. But what turned these irritations into widespread rebellion was the prolonged dislocation of unsuccessful war, the impact of recurrent plagues, and the anticlerical temper of the times. Hopes of remedy placed by the rebels in the young King Richard proved to be vain, though he showed considerable courage in facing the rebels in London during the summer of 1381.

Richard was still only fourteen, and the aristocratic rivalries in the ruling circle continued, not least among the king's uncles. This and the lack of further military success in France damaged the reputation of the council that governed England in Richard's name and even affected the king's own standing in the eyes of his subjects. Richard, too, was proving a self-willed monarch whose sense of insecurity led him to depend on unworthy favourites reminiscent of Edward II's confidants. As he grew older, he naturally wanted to expand his entourage and his household beyond what had been appropriate for a child. Among his friends and associates were some who were new to the ranks of the aristocracy, and all were generously patronized by the king at the expense of those (including his uncle Gloucester) who did not attract Richard's favour. In 1386 Parliament and a number of magnates attacked Richard's closest associates and even threatened the king himself. With all the stubbornness of the Plantagenets, Richard refused to yield. This led to further indictments or appeals of his advisers by five leading 'appellant' lords (the duke of Gloucester, and the earls of Warwick, Arundel, Nottingham, and Derby, the king's cousin), and a skirmish took place at Radcot Bridge in December 1387 when the king's closest friend, the earl of Oxford, was routed. At the momentous 'Merciless Parliament' (1388), the king was forced to submit to aristocratic correction which, if it had been sustained, would have significantly altered the character of the English monarchy. Once again, the pressures of war, the tensions of personal rule, and the ambitions of England's

magnates had produced a most serious political and constitutional crisis. The institution of hereditary monarchy emerged
largely unscathed after a century and more of such crises, but
criticism of the king's advisers had reached a new level of
effectiveness and broader sections of opinion had exerted a
significant influence on events. These were the political and
personal dimensions of more deep-seated changes that were
transforming England's social and economic life in the later
Middle Ages.

Wealth, Population, and Social Change

England's wealth in the later Middle Ages was its land, the
exploitation of which engaged most Englishmen: growing corn,
producing dairy goods, and tending livestock. England's most
important industry, textiles, was indirectly based on the land,
producing the finest wool in Europe from often very large sheep
flocks: St. Peter's Abbey, Gloucester, owned over 10,000 sheep
by 1300, when the total number in England is thought to have
been in the region of fifteen to eighteen millions. The wealthiest
regions were the lowlands and gently rolling hill-country of the
midland and southern shires, with extensions into the borderland and southern littoral of Wales. Other industries were less
significant in creating wealth and employing labour, but Cornish tin-mining was internationally famous and the tin was
exported to the Continent. Lead, iron, and coal mining was
quite modest, though the coastal traffic in coal from the Tyne
Valley and the neighbourhood of Swansea reflected its growing
domestic and industrial use. As for financial and commercial
services, the economy gained little from what became, in modern times, one of the nation's prime sources of wealth. Few
English merchants—the de la Poles of Hull were an exception—
could compete with the international bankers of Italy, with
their branches in London, despite the fact that Edward I and
Edward III were slow to honour their war debts to these Italian
companies. England's mercantile marine was generally out-

classed, except in coastal waters, by foreign shipping; but the Gascon wine-run and woollen shipments to the Low Countries did fall increasingly into the hands of English merchants and into the holds of English vessels. The thousand and more markets and fairs dotted about the English and Welsh countryside—more numerous by 1350 than in the past—served mainly their local community within a radius of a score or so miles. Most of these small towns and villages—Monmouth, Worcester, and Stratford among them—were integrated with their rural hinterland, whose well-to-do inhabitants frequently played a part in town life, joining the guilds, buying or renting town residences, and filling urban offices. A small number of towns, including some ports, were larger and had broader commercial horizons: Shrewsbury's traders travelled regularly to London by the fifteenth century, and merchants from the capital and Calais (after 1347) visited the Welsh borderland in search of fine wool. Bristol, with its vital link with Bordeaux, was rapidly becoming the entrepôt of late medieval Severnside; whilst York, Coventry, and especially London were centres of international trade.

From this wealth sprang the prosperity of individuals, institutions, and the Crown. The greatest landowners were the lay magnates (small in number, like 'skyscrapers on a plain'), bishops, monasteries, and other religious institutions. In 1300 these still benefited handsomely from a market boom created by the expanding population of the previous century. Prices were buoyant and landed incomes substantial: after the earl of Gloucester died at Bannockburn (1314), his estates were estimated to be worth just over £6,000 a year, whilst those of Christ Church Priory, Canterbury, produced in 1331 a gross annual income of more than £2,540. Landowners therefore exploited their estates directly and took a personal interest in their efficient management. They insisted on their rights as far as possible, squeezing higher rents out of tenants and carefully recording in manor courts the obligations attached to holdings. Such landed wealth was the foundation of the political, administrative, and social influence of the aristocracy, many of whom had estates in several counties as well as Wales and Ireland: Humphrey, earl of Hereford and Essex, for instance, inherited property in Essex, Middlesex, Huntingdonshire, Hertfordshire, and Buckinghamshire, and also in Brecon, Hay, Huntington, and Caldicot in the Welsh march. Land was equally the basis of the gentry's fortunes, albeit on a more local, shire level; whilst it gave ecclesiastical landowners an earthly authority that complemented their hold on men's minds and souls. This wealth could support pretensions and ambitions on a more national stage, as in the case of Thomas, earl of Lancaster, the richest earl in the England of his day.

The peasantry in 1300 were living in a world where land was scarce and opportunities for economic advancement were limited by the tight controls of the landowners. Prices were high—the price of wheat after 1270 was consistently higher than it had been earlier in the century—and there was little cash to spare after food, clothing, and equipment had been bought. Wages in an over-stocked labour market were low and reduced the purchasing power of skilled and unskilled alike: a carpenter earned 3*d.* a day (without food) and a labourer 1*d.* or 1½*d.* Grumbles, complaints, and spasms of violence were directed at landowners and their officials, and rent strikes and refusals to perform customary labour services were not uncommon.

The merchants of 1300, most notably the exporters of wool and importers of wine, thrived in an expanding market from the Baltic to Spain, Portugal, and, especially after the opening of the sea-route from the Mediterranean, to northern Italy. During 1304–11 wool exports averaged annually 39,500 sacks (each containing at least 250 fleeces) and only 30–40 per cent of these cargoes was shipped by foreigners. The rising antipathy towards alien merchants in English trade reflects the self-confidence and assertiveness of native (or denizen) merchants. Edward I legislated (1280s) in their interest, notably to facilitate the recovery of debts at law, which was essential to the expansion of trade. But when war came, merchants were among the

MAIN ROADS IN MEDIEVAL ENGLAND AND WALES

first to resist heavy taxation, especially the *maltolt* (or 'evil tax') of 1294, and the impressment of their ships.

The king was the largest landowner of all, even before Edward I acquired a principality in Wales and the estates of the house of Lancaster merged with the Crown's in 1399. The growth of national taxation under Edward I and his successors enabled the Crown to tap the wealth of private landowners and merchants, too. Not even the peasantry escaped, as was well appreciated by those who sang the popular lament, 'Song of the Husbandman', in Edward I's reign. Then, in 1327, all who had goods worth at least 10s. a year were required to pay 1s. 8d. in tax, and doubtless the less well-off had the burden passed on to them indirectly. The preoccupation with war made the king heavily dependent on the wealth and forbearance of his subjects. If that wealth ceased to grow, or if the prosperity of individuals and institutions were punctured, then the king's extraordinary commitments might eventually be beyond his means and his subjects' tolerance wear dangerously thin.

By the mid-fourteenth century the prosperous period of 'high farming' was almost over. Prices were falling, making cultivation for a market less profitable. Wages were rising, more so for agricultural labourers than for craftsmen, and there was no advantage in employing women, who were paid the same as men—indeed, in bear-baiting they were paid more! The principal reason why large-scale farming was losing some of its attraction was that the population boom came to an end and went, full throttle, into reverse. As the pool of available labour shrank, wages rose; as the population declined so did the demand for food and supplies, and prices followed suit.

England's population reached its peak, perhaps over four millions, about the end of the thirteenth century. At that time, there was insufficient cultivable land to ensure that all peasant families had an adequate livelihood. A high population coupled with low living standards inevitably meant poverty, famine, and disease, and a mortality that crept upwards and brought the demographic boom to a halt. The plight of those living at or below the poverty-line was made worse by a series of natural disasters related to over-exploitation of the land and exceptionally bad weather in the opening decades of the fourteenth century. Poor harvests were calamitous for a society without adequate storage facilities: there was less to eat and no cash to buy what now cost much more. The harvests of the years 1315, 1316, 1320, and 1321 were exceptionally bad; cattle and sheep murrains were especially prevalent in 1319 and 1321, and on the estates of Ramsey Abbey (Cambs.) recovery took twenty years; and in 1324–6 parts of England had severe floods which drowned thousands of sheep in Kent. Famine and disease spread, and on Halesowen Manor (Worcs.) 15 per cent of males died in 1315–17. Agricultural dislocation was widespread, grain prices soared (from 5s. 7¼d. to 26s. 8d. per quarter in Halesowen during 1315–16), and wool exports collapsed. However, it was a temporary calamity and England gradually recovered during the 1320s; but the vulnerability of the poor in particular had been starkly demonstrated.

Longer lasting and more profound were the consequences of plague. The first attack, known since the late sixteenth century as the Black Death but to contemporaries as 'the great mortality', occurred in southern England in 1348; by the end of 1349 it had spread north to central Scotland. Geoffrey le Baker, a contemporary Oxfordshire cleric, described its progress from the ports, where it arrived in rat-infested ships, and men's helplessness in diagnosing its cause and dealing with its effects.

And at first it carried off almost all the inhabitants of the seaports in Dorset, and then those living inland and from there it raged so dreadfully through Devon and Somerset as far as Bristol and then men of Gloucester refused those of Bristol entrance to their country, everyone thinking that the breath of those who lived amongst people who died of plague was infectious. But at last it attacked Gloucester, yea and Oxford and London, and finally the whole of England so violently that scarcely one in ten of either sex was left alive. As the graveyards did not suffice, fields were chosen for the burial of the dead . . . A countless number of common people and a host of monks and nuns and clerics as well, known to God alone, passed away. It was the young and strong that the plague chiefly attacked ... This great pestilence, which began at Bristol on [15 August] and in London about [29 September], raged for a whole year in England so terribly that it cleared many country villages entirely of every human being.

While this great calamity was devastating England, the Scots rejoicing thought that they would obtain all they wished against the English ... But sorrow following on the heels of joy, the sword of the anger of God departing from the English drove the Scots to frenzy ... In the following year it ravaged the Welsh as well as the English; and at last, setting sail, so to speak, for Ireland, it laid low the English living there in great numbers, but scarcely touched at all the pure Irish who lived amongst the mountains and on higher ground, until the year of Christ 1357, when it unexpectedly and terribly destroyed them also everywhere.

At a stroke, the Black Death reduced England's population by about a third. By 1350, Newcastle upon Tyne was in desperate financial straits 'on account of the deadly pestilence as by various other adversities in these times of war', and Carlisle was 'wasted and more than usually depressed as well by the mortal pestilence lately prevalent in those parts as by frequent attacks' (by the Scots). Seaford (Sussex) was reported even in 1356 as 'so desolated by plague and the chances of war that men living there are so few and poor that they cannot pay their taxes or defend the town'. Tusmore (Oxon.) was another victim of the plague: by 1358 permission was given to turn its fields into a park because every villein was dead and the village no longer had any taxpayers. Nevertheless, the Black Death's effects were not immediately or permanently catastrophic. The behaviour of a Welshman living in Ruthin was not uncommon: he 'left his land during the pestilence on account of poverty', but by 1354 he had returned 'and was admitted by the lord's favour to hold the same land by the service due from the same'. In any case, in a well-populated country, dead tenants could be replaced and landowners' incomes over the next twenty years were cut by no more than 10 per cent. It was the recurrence of plague over the following century—particularly the attacks of 1360–2, 1369, and 1375—which had lasting effects, even if these outbreaks were more local and urban. The population steadily declined to about $2\frac{1}{2}$ millions—or even less—by the mid-fifteenth century.

For those who survived an ugly death, life may not have been as wretched in the late fourteenth and fifteenth centuries as it undoubtedly was before. For many peasants, this became an age of opportunity, ambition, and affluence: Chaucer was able to portray his pilgrims in the *Canterbury Tales* with good-humoured optimism, not in an atmosphere of gloom and despondency. The peasant in a smaller labour market was often able to shake off the disabilities of centuries, force rents down, and insist on a better wage for his hire; and with the collapse in prices, his standard of living rose. The more successful and ambitious peasants leased new property, invested spare cash by lending to their fellows and, especially in the south and east, built substantial stone houses for the first time in peasant history.

Landowners, on the other hand, were facing severe difficulties. Market production in wheat, wool, and other commodities was less profitable, the cultivated area of England contracted, and agricultural investment was curtailed. Wages and other costs climbed and it seemed advisable to abandon 'high farming' techniques in favour of leasing plots to enterprising peasants. Entire communities were deserted—the 'lost villages' of England—and many of these were abandoned as a result of the twin afflictions of demographic crisis and prolonged war: among the English regions with the highest number of 'lost' villages' are Northumberland, close to the Scottish border, and the Isle of Wight, the goal of enemy marauders. Only in the last decades of the fifteenth century—from the 1460s in East Anglia—did England's population begin to rise at all significantly, and it is likely that the level of 1300 was not reached again until the seventeenth century.

England's economy had contracted markedly in the late four-teenth century, but it was not universally depressed. After men came to terms with the psychological shock of the plague visitations, society adjusted remarkably well, though not with-out turmoil. Landowners had the most painful adjustment to make and they reacted in several ways, not all of which were calculated to preserve domestic peace. Some, including the more conservatively-minded ecclesiastical landlords such as the abbot of St. Albans, resorted to high-handed measures, even to oppression and extortion, to preserve their hold on their re-maining tenants. Some exploited their estates ruthlessly in order to conserve their incomes, and the harsh attitudes of magnate families such as the Mortimers, with extensive estates in Wales, may have helped cause the Glyndŵr rebellion (1400). Others, such as the dukes of Buckingham later in the fifteenth century, adopted more efficient methods of management to improve the profitability of their estates. Yet others saw the enclosure of fields and commons for pasture and cultivation as less costly and an alternative means of buttressing unsteady rent-rolls; enclosure gathered speed especially in the north and west in the later fifteenth century. Large and small, the landowners as a group acted 'to curb the malice of servants, who were idle, and not willing to serve after the pestilence, without excessive wages'. Edward III's ordinance (1349) to restore pre-plague wage levels and discourage mobility among an emancipated labour force was quickly turned into a parliamentary statute (1351). Moreover, the well-placed magnate or gentleman had supplementary sources of wealth available to him: royal pat-ronage in the form of grants of land, money, and office (as the Beaufort relatives of King Henry VI well knew); family inherit-ance, which enabled Richard, duke of York (d. 1460) to be-come the richest magnate of his age; and fortunate marriage with a well-endowed heiress or a wealthy widow. Others pros-pered in the king's service, not least in war. Henry V's spec-tacular victories enabled the capture of ransomable prisoners and the acquisition of estates in northern France, and as late as

1448 the duke of Buckingham was expecting more than £530 a year from the French county of Perche. Some invested the profits of service and war in the mid-fifteenth century in the grandest manner, building imposing and elegant castles: witness Sir John Fastolf's at Caister (Norfolk), or the Herberts' huge fortress-palace at Raglan (Gwent), or Sir Ralph Botiller's castle at Sudeley, Gloucestershire. Such means and resources as these facilitated the emergence of aristocratic lines that were every whit as powerful as those of earlier centuries and often with entrenched regional positions like those of the Nevilles and Percies in the north and the Staffords and Mortimers in the west.

Similar adjustments were taking place in English towns and trade. Wool-growing remained the main pastoral occupation, but the pattern of its industry was transformed during the fourteenth century. Partly as a result of the war and its disruption of Flemish industry, and partly as a result of changes in English taste and demand, cloth manufacture absorbed growing quantities of wool previously exported; a number of the wool ports, such as Boston and Lynn in eastern England, began to decline. Leading cloth-manufacturing centres such as Stamford and Lincoln were overtaken by a host of newer ones sited in villages and towns near fast-flowing streams and rivers that ran the fulling mills. York found itself upstaged by Leeds, Halifax, and Bradford; further south, East Anglia, the west country, and even Wales developed a flourishing cloth industry, with Bristol as the main outlet in the west. London was in a class of its own: the only medieval English town with a population probably in excess of 50,000 in the late fourteenth century. It was an entrepôt for the kingdom, a terminal of the Baltic, North Sea, and Mediterranean trades; it attracted immigrants from the home counties and East Anglia, and especially from the East Midlands; and its suburbs were creeping up-river towards Westminster. No less than in the countryside, these changes unsettled life in a number of towns, whose burgess oligarchies strove to maintain their control in a changing world. The landowners of England thus strove to counter the economic crisis, but it was often at the price of straining relations with an increasingly assertive peasantry and established urban communities.

The cumulative effect of economic, social, political, and military strains in fourteenth-century England is seen most graphically in the Peasants' Revolt (1381). It was exceptional in its intensity, length, and broad appeal, but not in its fundamental character which was revealed in other conspiracies and insurrections in the years that followed. Widespread violence was sparked off in 1381 by yet another poll tax, this one at 1s. a head, three times the rate of 1377 and 1379. People responded with evasion, violence towards the collectors and the justices who investigated and, ultimately, in June 1381, with rebellion. Agricultural workers from eastern and south-eastern England were joined by townsmen and Londoners; the grain- and wool-growing countryside of East Anglia had felt the full impact of the contraction and dislocation of the economy and the social contradictions of an increasingly outmoded feudal society. Moreover, the rebels were disillusioned by the political mismanagement of the 1370s and the recent dismal record in France, and they feared enemy raids on the coast. Although heretics played no major role in the rebellion, radical criticism of the doctrines and organization of the English Church predisposed many to denounce an establishment that seemed to be failing in its duty.

Pressure on the government and an appeal to the new king ('With King Richard and the true-hearted commons' was the rebels' watch-word) held out the best hope for remedy of grievances, and the populace of London offered a pool of potential sympathizers. The rebels accordingly converged on London from Essex and Kent (where Wat Tyler and a clerical demagogue, John Ball, emerged as leaders). They threw prisons open, sacked the homes of the king's ministers, ransacked the Tower, and tried to frighten Richard II into making far-reaching concessions which, if implemented, would have broken the remaining bonds of serfdom and revolutionized landholding in Church and State. But the rebellion was poorly planned and organized and more in the nature of a spontaneous outburst of frustration. By 15 June the rebels had dispersed to their homes.

Still at War, 1390–1490

In 1389, when Richard II was twenty-two years old, he declared: 'I am of full age to govern my house, and my household, and also my realm. For it seems unjust to me that the condition which I am now in should be worse than the condition of the least of my kingdom.' The events of 1386–8, when the appellant lords sought to dictate the choice of the king's friends and ministers and to regulate his political actions, had poisoned relations between the unforgiving king and his critics. Among these were some of the most powerful magnates in the realm, with estates in central and southern England that together rivalled in size the remoter franchises of the Crown in Wales, Cheshire, and Cornwall. After 1389, however, Richard cautiously asserted himself as king of England, and with intelligence and courage he tried to deal with the consequences of his predecessors' ambitions and policies during the previous century. In a period of comparative political calm, Richard carefully constructed a party of loyalists, based on his household and the distant franchises, particularly Cheshire and North Wales. The earl of Arundel's forfeited lordships gave him an enhanced royal power in the Welsh march, where aristocratic lordships were at their most independent. The large and expensive expedition to Ireland in 1394–5, the first by an English king since 1210, was successful in revitalizing English rule and bringing Gaelic and Anglo-Irish lords to heel by a skilful mixture of firmness and conciliation; Richard may even have had the final and long-delayed conquest of the island in mind. This venture certainly strengthened his power in yet another royal lordship and demonstrated what his household organization and resources could achieve, albeit temporarily. Towards Scotland, following the English defeat at Otterburn (1388), Richard took the more traditional paths of encouraging dissident Scottish magnates and planning military campaigns; but in the 1390s he came to appreciate the benefits of peace. A treaty with France in 1396 and Richard's marriage to Isabella of Valois halted an even more debilitating war; if the cessation of hostilities had run its intended course (to 1426), it would have provided the longest period of peace in the entire Hundred Years War. At home, the king was able to concentrate on restoring royal government which had been so seriously damaged by the personal and political weaknesses of the 1370s and 1380s. To this end, ceremony and visual symbolism were creatively used as royal propaganda.

Richard was imaginative, shrewd, and masterful. Other of his attributes were less desirable in a king. His upbringing and adolescent experiences bred an insecurity that led to over-confidence, a lack of proportion, and arbitrariness. Wilfully extravagant towards his friends, he could be capricious, secretive, and harsh towards his enemies, and in 1397–8 he exiled the earl of Warwick, executed Arundel, murdered Gloucester, and then exiled Derby and Nottingham too. Ruthlessly deploying the monarch's personal powers ('He threw down whomsoever violated the Royal Prerogative' was part of the inscription he composed for his own tomb), Richard's last two years have been justly termed tyrannous. The pope was induced to threaten excommunication against any who 'attempts anything prejudicial against the right of our Crown, our regality or our liberty, or maliciously defames our person', while Richard's treaty with France promised French aid against his own subjects should the need arise. His second visit to Ireland in May 1399 presented Henry Bolingbroke, earl of Derby and now duke of Hereford and Lancaster, with the opportunity to return to England, retrieve his position, and recover the duchy of Lancaster estates of his father that had recently been seized by Richard. The king's methods had outrun English law and custom—and the tolerance of his greater subjects. But his de-

position later in the year (29 September) ended the most coherent attempt yet to lift the burden of war from Englishmen's
shoulders.

The dethronement of Richard II was a momentous decision.
Despite the precedent of 1327, the situation in 1399 was different in one important respect. It was the first time since Richard
the Lionheart's death that an English king had ended his reign
without leaving a son and heir, and the realm now faced the
possibility of a disputed succession. Custom since 1216 had
vested the succession in the senior male line, even though that
might mean a child-king (as in the case of Henry III and
Richard II himself). But there was as yet no acknowledged rule
of succession should the senior male line fail. In 1399 the choice
by blood lay between the seven-year-old earl of March, descended through his grandmother from Edward III's second
son, Lionel, and Henry Bolingbroke, the thirty-three-year-old
son of King Edward's third son, John. Bolingbroke seized the
Crown after being assured of support from the Percy family
whom Richard had alienated. But in the extraordinary
circumstances created by Richard II's dethronement and imprisonment, neither March nor Bolingbroke had obviously the
stronger claim. No amount of distortion, concealment, and
argument on Bolingbroke's part could disguise what was a
coup d'état. Hence, as in the twelfth century, an element of
dynastic instability was injected into English politics which
contributed to domestic turmoil, and encouraged foreign intrigue and intervention in the following century.

England, meanwhile, could not escape the consequences of
its earlier attempted subjugation of the 'Celtic' peoples in the
British Isles. After the failure of Richard II's imaginative policies, a more stable relationship was needed to ensure security
for the realm now that further conquest and colonization were
patently beyond its resources. In practice, English kings abandoned all serious intention of implementing their claims to
overlordship in Scotland and much of Ireland. In the fifteenth
century, they were on the defensive against the Scots, partly

because of the renewal of war in France and partly because of England's internal difficulties in Henry IV's reign (1399–1413) and after 1450; the Scots even sent substantial reinforcements to aid the French in 1419. For a brief time (1406–24), the captivity in England of King James I deterred major hostilities across the border, but thereafter the Scots became more daring, hoping to recover Roxburgh Castle and also Berwick, which they achieved in 1460–1. Raids, sea skirmishes, and piracy, together with ineffective truces, combined to produce a state of interminable 'cold war'. Only after the end of the Hundred Years War (1453) and the establishment of the Yorkist regime in England (1461) was there a really purposeful search for a more stable relationship. An Anglo-Scottish treaty was sealed in 1475, and a 'perpetual peace' in 1502, despite misgivings in France and the occasional English campaign in Scotland, such as Richard, duke of Gloucester's seizure of Berwick in 1482. This marked a significant shift in relations between the two countries, although border society continued to thrive on raids and disorder was a way of life.

The equilibrium reached in relations with Ireland was less satisfactory for England than for the Gaelic population and the Anglo-Irish nobility. Richard II's bold assertion of royal authority had failed, and was not repeated in the Middle Ages. The king's lordship of Ireland, though heavily subsidized from England, was consistently weak: the Gaels enjoyed independence and comparative prosperity, and the Anglo-Irish cherished their own power and came to terms with their Gaelic counterparts. The English government's main concern was security ('Ireland is a buttress and a post under England', declared a contemporary in the 1430s), and only when this was threatened during the Welsh rebellion (1400–9) and in the 1450s was more interest shown in Irish affairs. Internal political fragmentation and separation from England were the result. The greater Anglo-Irish magnates were the only source of power on which the government could rely to preserve some semblance of its authority: most Englishmen were reluctant even to go to

Ireland, effective rule from Dublin was impossible, and the resources for conquest simply did not exist. The real rulers of fifteenth-century Ireland were magnates such as the earls of Ormond and Kildare; even if the government had wanted to dislodge them, it could not. An equilibrium in Anglo-Irish relations was reached, but at the cost of surrendering effective English control.

In Wales, the heritage of complete conquest brought its own problems, notably a resentment which, in the unsettled economic climate of the late fourteenth century, was focused on the Anglicized boroughs and directed against officials in Church and State who were mostly from the English border shires or even further afield. This resentment was channelled into rebellion by Owain Glyndŵr from 1400, and after this unpleasant experience most Englishmen regarded Wales with suspicion and fear. One contemporary urged:

> Beware of Wales, Christ Jesus must us keep,
> That it make not our child's child to weep,
> Nor us also, if so it go this way
> By unwariness; since that many a day
> Men have been afraid of there rebellion....

Wales, then, posed a security problem and one much closer to hand. It not only provided a landfall for enemies from overseas (as at the height of Glyndŵr's rebellion and repeatedly during the Wars of the Roses), but was a land marred by misgovernment and disorder. Henry V showed firmness tempered by conciliation in dealing with Welshmen immediately after the rebellion collapsed, and marcher lords were ordered to attend to their lordships. But later on, neither the Crown nor the marcher lords were capable of sustaining vigorous rule, and the Welsh squirearchy, brothers-in-arms of the English gentry, showed less and less responsibility. Yet these Welsh squires were needed by the Crown and the marcher lords to govern Wales, for the Crown became immersed in civil war and by the fifteenth century the smaller number of lords were deterred from living in their lordships by falling incomes and Welsh hostility. The country, which by 1449 'daily abundeth and increaseth in misgovernance', consequently presented a problem of order—and therefore of security—for much of the century. Successive English regimes, from Henry VI to Henry VII, sought to keep the Welsh peaceful, improve the quality of government, and control the local squirearchy, for only then could the threat to the border shires and to the stability of the kingdom be lifted. In the first half of the century, the aim was to tighten up the existing machinery of law enforcement, relying on royal officers and marcher lords to fulfil their responsibilities. More radical and constructive solutions were eventually adopted, especially by Edward IV, who settled his son, the Prince of Wales, at Ludlow in the 1470s with a supervisory power in the principality of Wales, the marcher lordships, and the English border shires. This was a bold act of devolution that gave future princes responsibility throughout Wales.

The territorial power of the English magnates (the barons, viscounts, earls, marquesses, and dukes in ascending order of status) was crucial to the peace of the realm and the success of royal government. They became in the fifteenth century a strictly-defined and hereditary social group that was practically synonymous with the parliamentary peerage sitting in the House of Lords. The monarch could create peers (as Henry VI and Edward IV readily did) and could elevate existing ones to higher rank, while the king's patronage was essential to maintain magnate wealth and influence. Monarchs who did not appreciate this risked serious conflict with their magnates (as Richard II and Richard III discovered to their cost). Though few in number—at most sixty families, and perhaps half that figure after decades of civil war—they were vital not only because of the independent lordships which some of them held in the Welsh march and the dominance of the Nevilles and Percies in the north, but also because of their social and political control of the English provinces. They were a more effective buttress of the Crown than its own bureaucracy or civil service.

This was especially true in a century when three dynasties seized the Crown by force and had formidable military commitments at home and overseas to which the magnates made a notable contribution. The humiliation of defeat in France and the loss of English territories there was directly felt by the magnates and was something which Edward IV and Henry VII later strove to avoid.

These magnates had an identity of interest with the gentry of England—the 6,000 to 9,000 gentlemen, esquires, and knights who sought the 'good lordship' of the magnates and provided 'faithful service' in return. The magnates gave fees, land, and offices, and the gentry advice, support, and military aid: in 1454 the duke of Buckingham gave his badge to 2,000 of his retainers. Towns and townsmen were part of this relationship of mutual interest and service which historians have unflatteringly dubbed 'bastard feudalism'. The behaviour of the magnates and the gentry and townsmen in two distinct Houses of Parliament—the Lords and Commons—was another aspect of this interlocking relationship.

The co-operation of the magnates and their clients was especially vital to the usurping dynasties of the fifteenth century. The Lancastrians were well placed because Henry IV inherited the network of interests created by his father, John of Gaunt. At £12,000 a year, Gaunt was the richest magnate in late medieval England and his extensive estates and patronage were now at the disposal of his descendants as kings of England (1399–1461). The Yorkists (1461–85), as heirs of the earl of March, the alternative candidate in 1399, were less well endowed, except in the Welsh march. Their failure to enlist the support of most magnates was a serious weakness in a dynasty which survived for just twenty-four years. Henry VII, who inherited the estates, territorial influence, and patronage not only of Lancaster and York, but also of Neville, Beaufort, and other casualties of civil war, established the firmest control of all over the English magnates and gentry.

The first usurper, Henry IV, had the advantage of displacing a king who had alienated many and whose noble sympathizers were discredited. Henry's drive, perseverance, and powers of conciliation—not to say his generosity—and his Lancastrian connections enabled him to overcome the most daunting combination of enemies that any English king had faced. Richard II's die-hard supporters were foiled in their plot to assassinate Henry and his sons at Windsor Castle, and these rebels were apprehended and killed at Cirencester (December 1399). The danger from such 'Ricardians' led to Richard's own mysterious death in Pontefract Castle soon afterwards. The Percy earls of Northumberland and Worcester, virtual kingmakers in 1399, were so disenchanted by 1403 with the king's aim to win over all shades of opinion that they plotted several risings. Northumberland's son Hotspur, while marching to join the Welsh rebels, was defeated and killed near Shrewsbury. A Percy alliance with Archbishop Scrope of York raised the north of England, but Henry again acted quickly and in 1405 executed the prelate. Northumberland's last strike, with Scottish aid, collapsed at Bramham Moor, where the earl was slain (1408).

The Welsh rebellion had deeper roots in the soil of a colonial society. The distress experienced by a plague-ridden people, oppression by alien landowners bent on maintaining their incomes, a tendency to close the doors to opportunity against aspiring Welshmen, even resentment at Richard II's removal, combined to throw the country into revolt (1400). The variety of rebel motives and the divisions in Welsh society meant that this was no purely national, patriotic rising. Yet it was the most serious threat that Henry IV had to face and the most expensive to suppress. From his estates in north-east Wales, Owain Glyndŵr laid waste castles and Anglicized towns. He and his guerrilla forces exploited the mountainous terrain to harass and exhaust the enemy and then disappear 'among rocks and caves'. Their success can be measured by the length of the rebellion, the absence of decisive battles, and the fruitlessness of royal expeditions. Glyndŵr could occasionally muster 8,000 men, and he sought aid from France (1403) and fellow 'Celts' in

Scotland and Ireland (1401). In 'parliaments' in 1404 and 1405, he produced grand schemes for an independent Wales, with its own ecclesiastical organization and universities (aims which were not finally realized for another four centuries), and his alliance with the Percies was intended as a prelude to the dismemberment of Henry IV's realm.

The English, led by the king and his eldest son, Prince Henry, conducted several Welsh campaigns (1400–5), whose strategy was akin to that adopted in France—with pincer movements, destructive *chevauchées*, and co-ordinated supply by land and sea. The burden fell most heavily and frequently on the border shires and the West Midlands, which time and again were ordered to array men for service in Wales. These armies were substantial ones—4,000 strong—especially when one recalls that the armies sent to France rarely exceeded 5,000–6,000 men. But service in Wales was nothing like as popular as service in the lusher fields of France; there was difficulty in raising enough cash to pay the soldiers and garrisons, and in September 1403 Henry IV was told that 'you will not find a single gentleman who will stop in your said country'.

Generally secure in the north and west, Owain had his own problems of manpower, supply, and money, and the failure of his march on Worcester in 1405 caused his star to wane. He lost his Scottish ally when James I fell into English hands (1406), and an Anglo-French truce was arranged in 1407.

By 1408, the greatest dangers for Henry IV had passed: by perseverance, decisiveness, and a readiness to live in the saddle, as he pursued his enemies across England and Wales and to Edinburgh beyond, Henry overcame them all. By conciliation, he obtained Parliament's support without surrendering any significant part of his royal powers, and his four sons, Henry, Thomas, John, and Humphrey, were a maturing asset. Only two further threats to the dynasty occurred after his death in 1413. When the anticlericalism of certain courtiers turned to heresy the following year, Henry V did not hesitate to condemn even his old friend, Sir John Oldcastle. The last revolt before

1450 to be justified by the usurpation of 1399—that in favour of the earl of March in 1415—was suppressed just before King Hal left for France. Henry IV could claim considerable success in establishing his dynasty on firm foundations. International acceptance was won by alliances in Germany, Scandinavia, Brittany, and Burgundian Flanders.

Henry V inherited a realm that was sufficiently peaceful, loyal, and united for him to campaign extensively in France (from 1415) and to spend half of the next seven years abroad. With experience of war and government as Prince of Wales, he proved a capable, fearless, and authoritarian monarch who abandoned the careful ways of his father. Even during his absences in France, his kingship was firm and energetic, enabling him to wage a war that was as much a popular enterprise as Edward III's early campaigns had been. His reign was the climax of Lancastrian England.

Henry prepared for war by conciliating surviving Ricardians and renewing foreign alliances. The condition of France, with an insane king and quarrelsome nobles, encouraged his dreams of conquest. By 1415 he felt able to demand full sovereignty over territories beyond Edward III's vision and even to revive Edward's claim to the French Crown. Henry's ambitions coincided with his subjects' expectations. Large armies were raised under the leadership of enthusiastic magnates and knights; the realm voted taxation frequently and on a generous scale, and the king was able to explain his aims publicly so as to attract support. He even built a navy to dominate the Channel. This enthusiasm hardly faded at all before his death, though the parliamentary Commons expressed (1420) the same unease about the consequences for England of a final conquest of France as had their forebears to Edward III.

Henry V's strategy was Edward's—to ally with French nobles to exploit their divisions and press his own dynastic claim. Throughout the war, Burgundy's support was essential to English success. Quite soon, however, the invader's aims broadened into conquest and colonization on an unprecedented

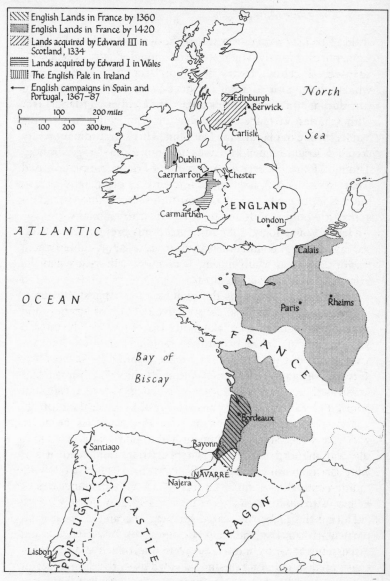

English Lands in France by 1360
English Lands in France by 1420
Lands acquired by Edward III in Scotland, 1334
Lands acquired by Edward I in Wales
The English Pale in Ireland
English campaigns in Spain and Portugal, 1367-87

100   200 miles
100 200 300 km

North

Sea

Edinburgh
Berwick
Carlisle

Dublin
Caernarfon
Chester

ENGLAND

Carmarthen

London

ATLANTIC

Calais

OCEAN

Paris
Rheims

FRANCE

Bay of

Biscay

Bordeaux

Santiago

Bayonne

NAVARRE
Najera

PORTUGAL

CASTILE

ARAGON

Lisbon

ENGLISH MILITARY ENTERPRISES IN WESTERN EUROPE IN
THE LATER MIDDLE AGES

scale. The 1415 expedition tested the water and the victory at Agincourt strikingly vindicated traditional English tactics. In 1417–20, therefore, Henry set about conquering Normandy which, along with adjacent provinces, was the main theatre of war during and after Henry's reign. The treaty of Troyes (1420) with Charles VI made him regent of France and heir to the Valois throne in place of the Dauphin. This extraordinary treaty dictated Anglo-French relations for more than a generation. Though Henry V never became king of France (he predeceased Charles VI in 1422), his baby son, Henry VI of England and, to the Anglophiles, Henry II of France, inherited the dual monarchy. It would require unremitting effort to maintain it.

Henry V and John, duke of Bedford, his brother and successor as military commander in France, pushed the Norman frontier east and south during 1417–29 and they defeated the French successively at Agincourt (1415), Cravant (1423), and Verneuil (1424). This was the high point of English power in France. Under Bedford, a 'constructive balance of firmness and conciliation' sought to make both the conquered lands and further campaigns (southwards in Anjou and Maine) pay for themselves. But the French resurgence inspired by Joan of Arc and the coronation of Charles VII at Rheims (1429) foiled this plan, and the English advance was halted after the defeat at Patay. Thereafter, the Normans grew restless under their foreign governors, England's Breton and Burgundian allies began to waver, and the English Parliament had to find yet more cash for the war in northern France where garrison and field armies were an increasingly heavy burden. The English were in a military as well as a financial trap—and without the genius of Henry V to direct them.

During the 1430s the search for peace became more urgent, particularly in England. The Congress of Arras (1435) and discussions at Gravelines (1439) were unproductive, largely because English opinion remained divided as to the desirability of peace and the wisdom of significant concessions. But the recovery in Charles VII's fortunes, the mounting cost of English expeditions to defend Lancastrian France, Bedford's death in 1435, and especially the defection of Burgundy were decisive factors. The government freed the duke of Orléans (a captive in England since Agincourt) to promote peace among his fellow French princes (1440), though he did not have much success. In 1445 Henry VI married the French queen's niece, Margaret of Anjou, but even that only produced a truce, and a proposed meeting of kings never took place. Eventually, Henry VI promised to surrender hard-won territory in the county of Maine as an earnest of his personal desire for peace. His failure to win the support of his subjects for this move—especially those magnates and gentry who had lands in France and had borne the brunt of the fighting—led to the exasperated French attacking Normandy in 1449. Their onslaught, supported by artillery, was so spectacularly successful that the English were defeated at Rouen and Formigny, and quickly cleared from the duchy by the end of August 1450. '. . . never had so great a country been conquered in so short a space of time, with such small loss to the populace and soldiery, and with so little killing of people or destruction and damage to the countryside,' reported a French chronicler.

Gascony, which had seen few major engagements under Henry V and Henry VI, was invaded by the triumphant French armies, and after their victory at Castillon on 17 July 1453, the English territories in the south-west were entirely lost. This was the most shattering blow of all: Gascony had been English since the twelfth century, and the long-established wine and cloth trades with southwest France were seriously disrupted. Of Henry V's 'empire', only Calais now remained. The defeated and disillusioned soldiers who returned to England regarded the discredited Lancastrian government as responsible for their plight and for the surrender of what Henry V had won. At home, Henry VI faced the consequences of defeat.

Within three weeks of Castillon, Henry VI suffered a mental and physical collapse which lasted for seventeen months and from which he may never have fully recovered. The loss of his

French kingdom (and Henry was the only English king to be crowned in France) may have been responsible for his breakdown, though by 1453 other aspects of his rule gave cause for grave concern. Those in whom Henry confided, notably the dukes of Suffolk (murdered 1450) and Somerset (killed in battle at St. Albans, 1455), proved unworthy of his trust and were widely hated. Those denied his favour—including Richard, duke of York and the Neville earls of Salisbury and Warwick— were bitter and resentful, and their efforts to improve their fortunes were blocked by the king and his court. Henry's government was close to bankruptcy, and its authority in the provinces and in Wales and Ireland was becoming paralysed. In the summer of 1450, there occurred the first popular revolt since 1381, led by the obscure but talented John Cade, who seized London for a few days and denounced the king's ministers. The king's personal responsibility for England's plight was inevitably great.

Henry VI was a well-intentioned man with laudable aspirations in education and religion; he sought peace with France and wished to reward his friends and servants. But no medieval king could rule by good intentions alone. Besides, Henry was extravagant, over-indulgent, and did not have the qualities of a shrewd and balanced judge of men and policies. He was intelligent and well educated, but he was the least experienced of kings and never shook off the youthful dependence on others which had been the inevitable hallmark of his long minority (1422–36). Many of his problems were admittedly unavoidable. The dual monarchy created by his father made heavier and more complex demands than those placed on a mainly military conqueror such as Edward III or Henry V. His minority was a period of magnate rule which created vested interests that were not easily surrendered when the king came of age—particularly by his uncle, Humphrey, duke of Gloucester, and his great-uncle, Henry Beaufort, cardinal-bishop of Winchester. Moreover, after Gloucester's death in 1447, Henry was the only surviving descendant of Henry IV in the senior male line, a fact which led him to distrust the duke of York, the heir of that earl of March who had been passed over in 1399. There was, then, ample reason for disenchantment with late Lancastrian rule, and in Richard of York there was a potential leader of the discontented.

Despite the king's illness, the birth of a son to his abrasive queen in October 1453 strengthened the Lancastrian dynasty, but it hardly improved the immediate prospect for the realm or for Richard of York. As England's premier duke and Henry's cousin, York was twice appointed protector of the realm during the king's incapacity (1454-5, 1455-6). But as such he aroused the queen's fierce hostility which erupted in the battles of Blore Heath and Ludford Bridge (September-October 1459), and in the subsequent Parliament at Coventry which victimized York, the Nevilles, and their supporters. This alienation of powerful men by a regime with a disastrous record at home and abroad led York to claim the Crown in October 1460. After his death at Wakefield soon after, his son Edward took it for himself on 4 March 1461, with the aid of the earl of Warwick. The period of dynastic war that is popularly known as the Wars of the Roses was now well under way amid conditions that had been ripening during the 1450s.

The new Yorkist monarch, Edward IV, suffered from a cardinal disadvantage: the deposed king, his queen, and his son were still at large. They thus provided a focus for their adherents and their Scots and French sympathizers, who were only too eager to embarrass a weak English regime. After Henry's capture in the north (1465), Edward felt more secure, though even then the former king was kept a prisoner in the Tower of London and his queen and son received shelter in Scotland and then in France. More serious still was Edward's failure to gain broad support from the English magnates and their clients. Furthermore, in the late 1460s he gradually alienated his powerful 'kingmaker', the earl of Warwick, who (like Northumberland after 1399) came to resent Edward's growing independence. Edward was also deserted by his feckless brother, George, duke of Clarence. These various elements combined to plot rebellion (1469) and, with encouragement from Louis XI of France, came to an uneasy agreement in July 1470 with the exiled Lancastrian Queen Margaret. Warwick, Clarence, Lancastrians, and dissident Yorkists returned to England and sent Edward IV fleeing to his ally, the duke of Burgundy. They promptly restored (or 'readepted') Henry VI, the first English king to have two separate reigns (1470–1). When Henry's Parliament assembled in November 1470, the chancellor was appealing beyond Westminster to the country at large when he took as the text of his opening sermon, 'Return O backsliding children, saith the Lord'.

But the deposed Edward, like Henry VI before him, was at liberty and he was able to raise a force with Burgundian help. Moreover, Henry's restored regime was undermined by a series of conflicting loyalties and mutually exclusive interests. Thus, when Edward returned to England in March 1471, he was able to defeat and kill Warwick at Barnet before marching west to vanquish at Tewkesbury the Lancastrian queen and prince, who had only just returned from France. At last Edward IV was dynastically secure: Queen Margaret was captured after Tewkesbury, her son was slain in the battle, and on the very night Edward returned triumphantly to London (21 May) Henry VI died in the Tower, most probably murdered. The main Lancastrian royal line was extinct. The Yorkist dissidents were either cowed or dead, and Clarence, though for a time reconciled with his brother, was subsequently executed for further indiscretions in 1478.

The relative political security which Edward enjoyed in the 1470s allowed him to attempt a period of constructive rule. He tried to repair England's reputation abroad by alliances with Brittany, Burgundy, and Scotland, and also by retracing the steps of previous kings to France. His expedition of 1475 was a near-disaster when his Breton and Burgundian allies proved fickle, but in the treaty of Picquigny Louis XI provided him with a handsome financial inducement to retire to England.

Edward's attempts to reorganize the government's financial administration were on lines suggested during the Lancastrian period. If he pleased Parliament by declaring his readiness to rule without special taxes, his desire to reward friends and attract political supporters meant that he could embark on no consistent programme of increasing his revenues. He curried favour with merchants and Londoners, participating in trade on his own account and maintaining good relations with Flanders and the Hanse League of German ports. Above all, the stability of his later years owed much to the continuity of service of several able and loyal officers of state.

Why, then, did the Wars of the Roses not come to an end and why did not posterity come to know of a Tudor dynasty only among the squirearchy of North Wales? The Yorkists fell victim in 1483–5 to two of the most common hazards to afflict a personal monarchy: a minority and a ruthlessly ambitious royal kinsman. When Edward IV died on 9 April 1483, his son and heir, Edward, was twelve. His minority need not have been long, and in any case England had weathered previous minorities without undue difficulty. But the degeneration of political behaviour since the 1450s, especially the often arbitrary, ruthless, and illegal actions of Edward IV, Warwick, and Clarence, made Edward V's accession particularly perilous. The Yorkist brothers, Edward, Clarence, and Gloucester, seem to have been unable to outgrow aristocratic attitudes to embrace the obligations of kingship in the short time their dynasty was on the throne. Edward relied on a circle of magnates, most of them linked with his own or his wife's Woodville family, to extend his authority in the kingdom: Gloucester in the north, the Woodvilles in Wales, and Lord Hastings in the Midlands. It worked well enough while Edward lived, but in 1483 the dangers of relying on an exclusive faction surfaced. Mistrust, particularly between Gloucester and the Woodvilles, undermined the ruling circle, and those outside it—not least the long-established Percies in the north and the duke of Buckingham in Wales and the West Midlands—saw their opportunity.

In these circumstances, the character and ambition of the sole remaining Yorkist brother, the thirty-year-old Richard of Gloucester, led him to contemplate seizing his young nephew's Crown for himself. He usurped the throne on 26 June, imprisoned (and probably murdered) Edward V and his brother, 'The Princes in the Tower', and executed the queen's brother and Lord Hastings. His only concession to customary rules of inheritance of the Crown was his unprincipled declaration that Edward IV and his sons were bastards; he ignored the children of Clarence. Richard III's actions and methods led to a revival of dynastic warfare. In October 1483, the duke of Buckingham, who was descended from Edward III's fifth son, Thomas, rebelled. More successful was the landing from France in August 1485 of Henry Tudor, though his claim to the throne through his mother, representing the illegitimate Beaufort line of Edward III's son, John, was tenuous. Nevertheless, at Bosworth Field on 22 August 1485 he vanquished and slew King Richard III. By then, Richard's own royal line seemed bankrupt: his wife and his only son were already dead.

A number of factors enabled Henry VII to keep his Crown after Bosworth. Alone among the usurpers of the fifteenth century, he was fortunate to have slain his childless predecessor in battle. The support which he received from the disillusioned Yorkists was crucial, especially that of Edward IV's queen. Also England's magnates were war-weary: their ranks were depleted, and in some cases their territorial power was either weakened or destroyed. As a result, attempts to dethrone Henry were poorly supported in England and the Yorkist pretenders (such as Lambert Simnel in 1487) failed to carry conviction. The actual fighting during 1455–85 may have amounted to only fifteen months, and the size of the armies involved may not have been very large; but the significance of a battle need bear no relation to the numbers engaged or the casualties sustained. The Wars of the Roses came close to destroying the hereditary basis of the English monarchy and Henry Tudor's seizure of the Crown hardly strengthened it. Henry posed as the representative and inheritor of both Lancaster and York, but in reality he became king, and determined to remain king, by his own efforts.

Towards a Nation

English kings enjoyed a mastery in their kingdom which French monarchs might have envied, and the Crown embodied the unity of England. Its wearer was not as other men. The coronation ceremony stressed his semi-spiritual quality, which seemed proven by the alleged power of the royal touch to cure the skin disease scrofula. Richard II insisted that those who approached him should bend the knee, and 'Majesty' became the common address in the fifteenth century.

The tentacles of royal administration—enabling decisions, grants of taxation, and legal pronouncements to be implemented—stretched to the extremities of the British Isles in every direction but the north and west. The franchises of the bishop of Durham and the earl of Chester stood outside the shire system of England and had a special independence. But there was no question of their being beyond the reach of the king's government: the bishops of Durham were almost always the king's choice and, like Anthony Bek (d. 1311) and Thomas Langley (d. 1437), often royal councillors; whilst after 1301 the earl of Chester was also Prince of Wales and the king's eldest son, and for most of the later Middle Ages the king administered Cheshire because there was no adult earl.

The king's administration was a co-operative affair. In each county the sheriffs and the newer justices of the peace functioned best with the aid of the nobility and local gentry, whose interests in turn were securely tied to the monarch, the greatest single source of wealth and patronage in the realm. Parliament, with its commons' representatives from counties and towns between Carlisle and Cornwall, Shrewsbury and Suffolk, came to play an essential part in late medieval government. By Edward I's reign, war and domestic upheaval had fortified the king's need to consult his subjects ('the community of the realm', as contemporaries termed them) and to seek their advice in reaching and implementing decisions affecting the realm at large. It also seemed wise, from time to time, to include local representatives as well as lay and ecclesiastical lords in a central assembly that was Parliament. The wish to tap the wealth of townsmen and smaller landowners as well as the nobility; the need for material aid and expressions of support in war and political crises; and the advisability of having the weight of a representative assembly behind controversial or novel changes in the law or in economic and social arrangements—all these factors combined to give Parliament a frequency (it met on average once a year during 1327–1437), distinctive functions, and established procedures, and to give the commons' representatives a permanent role in it from 1337 onwards. This institution, unique among the parliaments of medieval Europe, discussed both important matters of business and minor matters raised by individuals. It won a monopoly of taxing Englishmen; it was the highest court in the land; and it made new law and modified existing law through legislation. Even the commons' representatives won privileges for themselves, not least free speech and freedom from arrest during parliamentary sittings. It remained essentially an instrument of government at the king's disposal, but it could sometimes criticize his policies and ministers (as in the 1370s and 1380s and the 1440s), though almost never the king himself. When the practical needs that had brought Parliament into existence and encouraged its development disappeared, it met far less often: only once in every three years on average between 1453 (the end of the Hundred Years War) and 1509.

The commons' representatives had to be informed, courted, and persuaded before they returned home to their constituents, considerable numbers of whom desired information about affairs. It was, after all, they who paid taxes, served in war and defence, and who were asked for their co-operation and obedience. The government was, therefore, well advised to weigh carefully the news it transmitted to the realm and the opinions it hoped the king's subjects would adopt. Well-developed methods of communication and propaganda were used to this end. The preambles of official proclamations could popularize a policy and justify a practice: Edward IV's proclamation against Margaret, queen of the deposed Henry VI, made much of the memory of Archbishop Scrope of York, who had been executed by Henry's grandfather and had since taken on the aura of a martyr. This was skilful propaganda to sustain opposition to the Lancastrian dynasty, for proclamations were sent to every shire for public reading and display. Songs and ballads reached wide audiences too, and some that were officially inspired stressed the glories of Agincourt out of all proportion. Sermons were no less effective in moulding opinion and mobilizing support: in 1443 Henry VI requested that good, stirring preachers be sent through every diocese to reinforce from the pulpit royal appeals for money for yet another French campaign. Corona-tions, royal progresses, and the formal entries of kings and queens into York, Bristol, and Gloucester (as well as London) were occasions for lavish displays of official propaganda, harnessing mythology, Christianity, and patriotism. In 1417, Henry V was portrayed for all to see at his reception by London as a soldier of Christ returning from crusade against the French. If any citizen harboured lingering doubts about the justice of his invasion of France, this was calculated to remove them.

The circulation of letters to inform, persuade, and justify was as near as the pre-printing age came to publication; such letters soon found their way into popular chronicles. In this way, Henry V reported to his subjects the progress of his French campaigns. Even fashionable writers of the day became official propagandists. In the fifteenth century, authors rarely produced their works unsolicitedly. Thomas Hoccleve was a humble gov-ernment bureaucrat who was paid by Henry V to produce laudatory verses about Agincourt and the English siege of Rouen (1419). John Lydgate was patronized by Henry VI and his court over a long period, implanting in the popular mind all the jingoism that could be wrung out of the successful defence of Calais against Burgundian attack in 1436.

The king, his court, and his ministers—the principal exploiters of these channels of communication—resided most often at Westminster, London, or Windsor. The shrine of English monarchy was Westminster Abbey, and Parliament usually met at Westminster (all thirty-one Parliaments did so between 1339 and 1371, and none met elsewhere after 1459). The departments of government gradually settled into permanent offices at Westminster or, to a lesser extent, London, which was the largest and wealthiest city in the land. In the later Middle Ages, it became the undisputed capital of the kingdom in every sphere except the ecclesiastical (where Canterbury remained the seat of the primate of All England). Along with Westminster and the growing riverside suburb in between, London became the administrative, commercial, cultural, and social focus for the kingdom. Government increased in extent, sophistication, and tempo in the later Middle Ages, particularly in wartime: regular taxes had to be collected and managed, frequent meetings of Parliament were held, the customs service was developed, the practicalities of war and defence had to be organized, and law and order throughout the kingdom was supervised there. Concentrated, co-ordinated, and sedentary government was the result. York lost its claims as a rival centre when the persistent war with Scotland in the first third of the fourteenth century was overtaken by the much greater preoccupation with France. Moreover, the absence of Edward III and Henry V on campaign abroad emphasized the trend towards a fixed, centralized governmental headquarters that could operate without the participation of the king himself. The crisis of 1339–41 brought home to Edward III that he could no longer take the machine of government with him, as Edward I and his predecessors had done. By 1340 the exchequer had returned to Westminster, which it never left again. The bureaucracy of the king's chancery, exchequer, and law courts expanded in the capital and, as a group of ambitious small landowners, in the neighbouring counties. Magnates, bishops, and abbots acquired inns or houses in or near the city, and the surnames of London's inhabitants and the language they spoke suggest that many humbler folk were migrating to the capital from every part of the kingdom—and from Wales and Ireland too.

The English character of the Church in England was its second most significant and enduring quality in the later Middle Ages. Its first was the Catholic faith and doctrine which it shared with other Latin churches. But it was widely accepted that this universal Church, headed by the pope in Rome as spiritual father, was a family of individual churches, each with its own character and autonomy. The Englishness of the Church in England became more pronounced in the later Middle Ages as the ecclesiastical dimension of English nationhood. This owed something to the English language and the separate experience of the English people, and a good deal to English law and custom, the framework within which Englishmen (including the clergy) lived and which the king swore to uphold in his coronation oath. Moreover, the Church of England, including its buildings, had been established, encouraged, and patronized by English kings, noblemen, gentry, and townsmen, giving them a personal and family interest in individual churches and their priests. The bishops were great landowners—the bishop of Winchester had an annual income of £3,900 in the mid-fifteenth century—who sat in Parliament and were among the king's councillors. They, and lesser dignitaries too, were usually promoted because they were trusted by, and useful to, the Crown and could be rewarded in the Church without cost to the exchequer. There were, then, good practical reasons why Englishmen should control the English Church and mould its character and personnel. This seemed the more urgent during the French wars. In 1307 and regularly thereafter, the pope's role in the organization and administration of the English Church, even in the appointment of bishops, was bitterly opposed. After all, most popes in the fourteenth century were French-born, and during 1308–78 they lived at Avignon, where they were in danger of becoming lap-dogs of the French (or so it was widely believed). By contrast, only one pope had been an Englishman (in the mid-twelfth century) and none had ever visited England—and would not do so until 1982.

The trend towards an Anglicized Church can be illustrated in several ways. Church law, based on the codes of the early Fathers and replenished by papal legislation, was received and generally applied in the Church courts of England, and the pope's ultimate jurisdiction in ecclesiastical matters was acknowledged. But in practice, Church law was limited by royal authority, particularly when clerks accused of crimes tried to claim 'benefit of clergy'. From Edward I's day, the pope's ability to tax the English clergy was severely curtailed and most papal taxes found their way into the king's coffers instead of fuelling the enemy's war effort (as many believed). More serious still were the limitations on the pope's power to appoint bishops and other important members of the English Church from the mid-fourteenth century onwards, and during the Great Schism (1378–1417, when there were two, sometimes three, popes simultaneously claiming Christendom's allegiance), the pope whom England supported was in no position to resist. The anti-papal statutes of Provisors (1351, reissued 1390) and *Praemunire* (1353, extended 1393) were used by English kings to impose a compromise on the pope whereby the initiative in appointments rested with the king. As a result, very few foreigners were appointed in the English Church by the fifteenth century unless, as with Henry VII's nomination of three Italian bishops, they had the government's specific approval.

Few clergymen in England protested at this state of affairs. The bishops did not do so because of the men they were and the way in which they were appointed. The Church did not do so corporately because it feared papal taxation. The clergy did not do so because English kings were the protectors of the faith against heretics and a buttress against anticlerical attack. In 1433, even an abbot of St. Albans could declare that 'the king knows no superior to himself within the realm'.

THE PRE-REFORMATION DIOCESES OF ENGLAND AND WALES
(THIRTEENTH CENTURY)

Predominantly English in character were two expressions of religious fervour outside the institutional church of late medieval England: the devotional fashion was strictly orthodox in theology, whereas the Lollard movement inspired by John Wycliffe was heretical. The fourteenth century saw a burgeoning interest in mystical and devotional writings, most of them in English from the latter part of the century and appealing to a growing literate public. Such people took for granted the teachings and practices of the Church but preferred a personal, intuitive devotion focused on the sufferings and death of Christ, the Virgin Mary, and the Lives of Saints, collected in the *Golden Legend*. The writers were frequently solitary figures commending the contemplative life to their readers. By far the most popular devotional works were by Richard Rolle, a Yorkshire hermit, and, later, by the recluse, Dame Juliane of Norwich. The *Book of Margery Kempe*, the spiritual autobiography of the wife of a Lynn burgess, exemplified the virtues which lay men and women sought, and the revelations, visions, and ecstasies by which they came to possess them. Laymen such as Henry, duke of Lancaster (who in 1354 wrote a devotional work of his own in French), and devout women such as Lady Margaret Beaufort, mother of Henry VII, turned to this intense spiritual life as a reaction to the arid theological discussions of scholars, though they did not stray into the unorthodoxy of Lollardy whose spiritual roots were not dissimilar.

Lollardy (probably a name derived from *lollaer*, a mumbler— of prayers) was the only significant heretical movement to sweep through medieval England, and Wycliffe was the only university intellectual in the history of medieval heresy to inspire a popular heretical movement against the Church. It was a largely indigenous English scheme of thought that laid great store by books and reading. Though Wycliffe is unlikely to have written in English, he inspired a series of English polemical works and also the first complete translation of the Bible by 1396. To begin with, he appealed to the anticlerical temper of his times and gained reputation and support among noblemen, courtiers, and scholars for his criticism of the Church's wealth and the unworthiness of too many of its clergy. But his increasingly radical theological ideas, placing overwhelming confidence in Holy Scripture, led to his condemnation and withdrawal from Oxford. The sympathy which he had received from influential men ebbed away when confronted with the strict orthodoxy of Henry IV (who added burning in 1401 to the armoury of the persecutors of heresy) and almost disappeared when Lollardy became tinged with rebellion in Sir John Oldcastle's rising. Deprived of its intellectual spring and its powerful protectors, Lollardy became a disjointed, unorganized but obstinate movement of craftsmen, artisans, and poor priests in the Welsh borderland and industrial towns of the Midlands. Their beliefs became more and more disparate and eccentric, but their basic hostility to ecclesiastical authority, their devotion to the Scriptures, and their belief in an English Bible prefigured the Reformation and were to be central convictions in later English Protestantism.

The spread of literacy and the increased use of the English language were twin developments of the late fourteenth and fifteenth centuries. They were symptomatic of Englishmen's growing awareness of public affairs, and reflect feelings of patriotism and nationhood.

It is easier to be persuaded of all this than to prove it in detail. There are no contemporary estimates of how rapidly and how far literacy spread; nor is it possible for us to quantify it with the data provided by largely innumerate contemporaries. A rough index of its growth becomes available if the statutes of 1351 and 1499 defining the legal privilege of 'benefit of clergy' (then the literate class) are compared. In 1351 it was stated that all laymen who could read should be accorded 'benefit of clergy'. One hundred and fifty years later, the situation had so changed that a distinction was drawn between mere lay scholars and clerks in holy orders, and only to the latter was 'benefit of clergy' now to be extended. Maybe the literate class had expanded to the point where 'clerical' was a meaningless adjective to apply to it, though the statute of 1499 attributed the need for change to abuse rather than to the expansion itself.

An equally generalized indication is provided by comparing the two popular risings of the later Middle Ages—the Peasants' Revolt (1381) and John Cade's rebellion (1450). In 1381 the complaints of the peasantry from Kent and Essex were (as far as we know) presented to Richard II orally, and all communications with the king during the revolt appear to have been by word of mouth; at the Tower of London, Richard had to ask that the rebels' grievances, hitherto roared at him by the insurgents outside, be put in writing for him to consider. Compare this with 1450, when the demands of Cade's followers, also drawn from Kent and the south-east, were submitted at the outset in written form of which several versions were produced and circulated. They are long documents, with a coherent and comprehensive argument, expressed in English, sometimes of a colloquial kind. The business of publishing manuscripts was extending its range at this very time. John Shirley (d. 1456) is known to have run his business from four rented shops near St. Paul's Cathedral and to have produced, for sale or loan, 'little ballads, complaints and roundels'. Twenty years later, customs accounts document the importation of large quantities of manuscript books through London—over 1,300 in 1480–1 alone.

One may cautiously introduce some figures to indicate that late medieval literacy was not confined to the noble, clerical, or governmental classes. As was probably the case with Cade's rebels, some artisans and craftsmen could now read and write. Eleven out of twenty-eight witnesses in a legal suit of 1373 described themselves as *literatus* (or capable of understanding Latin and therefore, one presumes, English too); and a mid-fifteenth century will provided a similar proportion of 'literates' among witnesses who included merchants, husbandmen, tailors, and mariners. There were doubtless others whom, literate or not, one would never dream of employing as witnesses, but we are undeniably moving towards Sir Thomas More's enthusiastic estimate at the beginning of the sixteenth century that more than 50 per cent of Englishmen were literate.

If we cannot accept such figures with complete confidence, we can at least observe literate men—rarely women—at work in a variety of occupations. They filled some of the highest political offices in the land hitherto reserved for clerics: from 1381, laymen frequently became Treasurer of England, an office for which a command of reading and writing—if not of figures—was an essential qualification. Literate laymen were employed as clerks in government service, a niche which the poet Thomas Hoccleve occupied for over thirty-five years. It is also clear that by 1380 tradesmen were keeping written bills; soon afterwards country yeomen were writing—certainly reading—private letters, and even peasants who served as reeve on their manor were functioning in an administrative environment whose business was increasingly transacted on paper and parchment. By Edward IV's time, the rules and regulations of some craft guilds were insisting on a recognized standard of literacy for their apprentices.

The reading habits of at least well-to-do laymen reflect the same thing. Reading chronicles was very popular, and not only in London; the surviving manuscripts alone run into hundreds and show signs of being produced in increasing numbers as the fifteenth century wore on—most of them in English. Merchants and others took to owning 'common-place books', those personal, diminutive libraries of poems, prophecies, chronicles, and even recipes, through which they browsed at leisure. They possessed books and carefully disposed of them—particularly the religious and devotional ones—in their wills.

This literate world was increasingly an English world. The facility to speak and understand French (and therefore to read and write it) was in marked decline before the end of the fourteenth century; even for official and formal business in government and private organizations, English was becoming at least as common. Discussions in Parliament were taking place in English by the middle decades of the century, and the first written record of this dates from 1362. Although only a rough and ready guide, it is worth noting that the earliest known property deed drawn up in English is dated 1376, the earliest will 1387. The proceedings of the convocation of Canterbury were conducted in English quite often by the 1370s, and Henry IV spoke to Parliament in English in 1399 and had his words carefully recorded. The reasons for this quiet revolution are complex, but among them may be numbered the patriotism generated by the long French war; the popularity of Lollardy, which set great store by English books and sermons; the lead given by the Crown and the nobility; and, of course, the greater participation of the English-speaking subject in the affairs of the realm, not least in Parliament. The triumph of the written language was assured.

Before that happened, one major problem had to be faced: that of regional dialects. Only then could the full potential of English as a written and spoken tongue be realized. It must be admitted that in this first century or so of popular, literate English, quaint Cornish, wilfully foreign Welsh, and such unintelligibilities as the Yorkshire dialect could not be fully absorbed into a common idiom; but much headway was made. The spreading tentacles of government helped, developing and extending the use of a written language for official communication throughout the realm during the first half of the fifteenth century. A further factor was the emergence in the fourteenth century of London as the settled capital of the kingdom, with York as a subsidiary administrative centre and Bristol as the second commercial metropolis, each evolving a dialect that inevitably became comprehensible to the others and gradually fused in a standardized English. This dialect was predominantly midland English, which triumphed at the expense of a city-bound tongue; and for this reason it was the more easily adopted in rural shires. That the victor was a midland dialect was in large part due to the substantial migration of midlanders and easterners to London in the fourteenth and fifteenth centuries. Lollardy was partly responsible too, for it was especially vigorous in the Midlands and West Country, and most of its written works were in varying forms of the midland tongue. By capturing London, this midland dialect in speech and writing captured the kingdom.

Geoffrey Chaucer had serious misgivings as to whether his writings would be understood across England—and he wrote for a limited, charmed circle.

> And for there is so great diversity
> In English and in writing of our tongue
> So pray I God that none miswrite thee,
> Nor thee mismetre for default of tongue.
> And read whereso thou be, or else sung
> That thou be understood, God I beseech.

In a legal case of 1426, it was stated that words were pronounced differently in different parts of England 'and one is just as good as the other'. Half a century later, William Caxton could be more optimistic that his printed editions of several hundreds would, with care, be quite comprehensible from one shire to another. He realized that 'common English that is spoken in one shire varieth from another'; but by using 'English not over rude, nor curious, but in such terms as shall be understood by God's grace', he anticipated little difficulty. The greater ease of understanding, in both speech and writing, that had developed meanwhile was crucial to the effectiveness of communication, the common expression of opinion, and the forging of a sense of nationhood.

English had become 'the language, not of a conquered, but of a conquering people'. The self-confidence of its writers reached the heights of genius in Chaucer, and it attracted patronage from the wealthiest and most influential in the realm—from kings, noblemen, gentlemen, and townsmen. English prose in the fourteenth and fifteenth centuries was far outshone in quality and popularity by English verse in all its forms: lyric and romance, comedy and tragedy, allegory and drama. Much of this poetry fell squarely in the northern European tradition, and the literary revival of the north-west and the Midlands in the fourteenth century was mainly of alliterative, unrhymed verse. But it was sponsored by local gentry and magnates such as the Bohuns (earls of Hereford) and the Mortimers (earls of March), and could produce works of considerable imaginative power in *Sir Gawain and the Green Knight* and *Piers Plowman*. In the same region, ritual Christian drama in the English Miracle Play Cycles was developed during the fourteenth century and achieved great popularity in northern towns such as York, Beverley, Wakefield, and Chester, where the plays were organized and performed by the town guilds.

At the same time, in the south and east, a newer mode of verse was appearing which owed more to current fashions of style and content in French and early Renaissance Italian writing. Through the pen of Chaucer, and to a lesser extent his friend John Gower, it created masterpieces of English literature. These were unequalled in their richness of thought and vocabulary, their imagination and depth of human understanding, and in their sheer artistry. *Troilus and Criseyde*, written about 1380–5, and especially the immensely ambitious and complex panorama of *The Canterbury Tales* (written 1386–1400 but never completed), decisively extended English literary accomplishment. They displayed a wisdom, worldliness, and inventiveness, and a mastery of contemporary English idiom in all its variety, which earn Chaucer his place as the greatest English medieval writer.

Gower, a Kentishman, was patronized by Richard II and, later, by Henry Bolingbroke. Chaucer, who came of London merchant stock, grew up in aristocratic and royal circles, and he was one of the most lionized and richly rewarded poets of any age. This reflects both the extraordinary quality of his writing, and also the recognition which influential contemporaries were prepared to give to the English language which he enriched. If Chaucer's disciples, Hoccleve and Lydgate, seem second-rate in comparison with their master, at least the royal, court, and city patronage which these authors received assured a bright future for what was essentially the English literary school of the capital.

The same sources of wealth and taste were placed at the disposal of England's architects and builders. Developing their ideas from the predominant Gothic style of much of Europe, of which the pointed arch is the symbol and most characteristic feature, they created architectural styles which have a good claim to be regarded as distinctively English. Since the nineteenth century, these have been termed Decorated (more accurately free-flowing and curvilinear) and Perpendicular (or rather vertical and rectilinear), and they are best identified in the window and arch design of England's cathedrals, larger parish churches, and colleges. In so far as any new architectural development can be explained with precision, it is thought that renewed diplomatic and crusader contacts with the Muslim and Mongol worlds of Egypt and Persia towards the end of the thirteenth century transmitted knowledge of Eastern building styles and techniques to the far West. The delicate tracery and luxuriant naturalistic motifs which are a feature of the new Decorated style appear on the three surviving Eleanor Crosses that Edward I erected in the 1290s to mark the stages in the journey of his wife's body from Lincoln to its burial at Westminster. Eastern influences have also been observed in the hexagonal north porch and doorway of St. Mary Redcliffe, Bristol, dating from early in the fourteenth century. After only half a century (1285–1335) of these extravagant complexities, which were unparalleled in Gothic Europe and have been hailed as 'the most brilliant display of sheer inventiveness in the whole history of English medieval architecture', a reaction set in. This reaction produced the most English style of all, the Perpendicular. In an age when England was at war, this was rarely imitated on the European mainland. Its simpler, cleaner lines and larger, lighter spaces may have appeared first in the royal chapel of St. Stephen, Westminster (destroyed 1834), or in the city cathedral of St. Paul (burned 1666). Either way, it quickly spread to the West Country, through courtly influence focused on Edward II's shrine at Gloucester. It can still be admired on the grand scale in the choir of Gloucester Cathedral, dating from the mid-1330s, as well as in the later naves of Canterbury (from 1379) and Winchester (from 1394). Decoration was now concentrated English-style in roof vaulting, culminating in the fan vaults of Hereford's chapter house (now destroyed) and the cloisters at Gloucester, which were built after 1351.

Yet Perpendicular building is found most frequently and at its best in the greater parish churches of England such as Cirencester, Coventry, and Hull. Not even plague and warfare, which may have inhibited large-scale projects for a while in the fifteenth century, could deter clothiers and landowners in East Anglia and the West Country from lavishing their wealth on these monuments to English taste and skill. Perpendicular architecture experienced an exuberant resurgence in the latter part of the fifteenth century in some of the most famous of English buildings, most of them sponsored by the Crown—Eton College, St. George's Chapel, Windsor (from 1474), King's College Chapel, Cambridge, and Henry VII's Chapel in Westminster Abbey. It was incontestably 'the Indian Summer of English medieval architecture'.

Incomparably English were the Perpendicular towers of late medieval parish churches, ranging from the sturdy St. Giles Church, Wrexham, to the soaring shaft of St. Botolph's, Boston, and the elegance of Taunton, St. Stephen's, Bristol, and St. John's, Cardiff. So, too, were the carved timber roofs of the fourteenth and fifteenth centuries, beginning with the timber vault planned for the chapter house at York after 1291, and the replacement of the tower of Ely Cathedral, which collapsed in 1322, by a timber vault and lantern tower. This roof work culminated in the great hammer-beam oak roof of Westminster Hall (1394–1400), commissioned by Richard II and judged to be 'the greatest single work of art of the whole of the European middle ages'. Masons, carpenters, and architects were patronized by kings, courtiers, noblemen, and others from the thirteenth century onwards, and not simply for religious building;

they also worked on royal and private castles and manor houses. Although forming a profession largely based in London and connected with the office of king's works, these craftsmen were assigned duties throughout England and Wales. They placed their expertise and experience at the disposal of noblemen and bishops and thereby created a national style to suit national tastes.

Englishmen's sense of nationhood and their awareness of their own Englishness are not easily gauged. But they sometimes compared themselves—and were compared by others—to peoples of different race, language, country, or cultural and political tradition. In the later Middle Ages, Englishmen confronted, frequently violently, other peoples both in the British Isles and in mainland Europe. These confrontations were a forcing-house of nationhood and self-conscious Englishness. Such experiences gave rise to a number of emotions, which made English people aware of their nature, unity, and common traditions and history.

So long as England was ruled by Norman dukes or Angevin counts, and Anglo-Norman barons held estates on both sides of the Channel and others did so in both England and Scotland, it was impossible for the ruling élite to think of itself as exclusively English. But this became possible once Normandy and Anjou were overrun by the French and formally surrendered to them in 1259, for the cross-Channel nobility had then to decide where its prime allegiance lay. It became more likely, too, with the growing self-consciousness of the Scottish kingdom, particularly when Edward I's wars made land-holding across the border a thing of the past. Thereafter, the separateness of England was identified with its encircling seas. In the mid-1430s a pamphleteer advised:

> Keep then the seas about in special;
> Which of England is the round wall,
> As though England were likened to a city
> And the wall environ were the sea...

English kings from Edward I were more truly English in up-bringing and outlook than any since King Harold. Indeed, Henry VI in his thirty-nine-year reign never visited Scotland or Ireland; he only once set foot in Wales—a day at Monmouth—and never again went to France after his coronation visit at the age of nine.

As to foreigners, the dominance of Flemings and then Italians in England's overseas trade in the thirteenth century fostered resentment of their commercial success. In Henry VII's reign Englishmen were said to 'have an antipathy to foreigners, and imagine that they never come into their island but to make themselves master of it and to usurp their goods...'. After all, natives of a country at war with England might, like the alien priories attached to French monasteries, send money to an enemy, or, like the servants of Henry IV's queen, the duchess of Brittany, act as spies for France. Not for nothing did the king's clerks scratch 'Do not show to aliens!' on state papers at the outset of the Hundred Years War.

England's wars, waged successfully by humble bowmen as well as knights and noblemen, created among all ranks a self-confidence that warmed English hearts. A well-informed obser-ver said in 1373 that 'the English are so filled with their own greatness and have won so many big victories that they have come to believe they cannot lose. In battle, they are the most confident nation in the world.' Pride in their victories seemed unbounded, and individual kings embodied the achievements. Under Edward III, 'the realm of England has been nobly amended, honoured and enriched to a degree never seen in the time of any other king', whilst Henry V's reputation among his subjects reached even greater heights. Englishmen's belief in their superiority—a short step from pride and self-confidence—remained unshaken even in the mid-fifteenth century, by which time England's fortunes seemed far less golden. The wild Gaels were treated as 'mere Irish' and the Flemings in 1436 with undisguised scorn:

Remember now, ye Flemings, upon your own shame;
When ye laid siege to Calais, ye were right still to blame;
For more of reputation, be Englishmen than ye,
And come of more gentle blood, of old antiquity.

An Italian visitor around 1500, when England's overseas 'empire' was all but lost, could still report that 'the English are great lovers of themselves and of everything belonging to them. They think that there are no other men than themselves, and no other world but England; and when they see a handsome foreigner they say that "he looks like an Englishman", and that "it is a great pity that he should not be an Englishman".' Feelings of superiority easily turned to disdain or even hate. After decades of war with the French, Francophobia was common and matched only by the Anglophobia of the French, who came to regard the English as 'a race of people accursed'. At no time was this distaste for things French stronger than during the reign of Henry V. He may have claimed the French crown, but in England he discouraged the use of the French language in government and literate society. The London brewers took their cue from their admired king, and when they wrote their ordinances in English they noted that 'our mother tongue, to wit, the English tongue, hath in modern days begun to be honourably enlarged and adorned ... and our most excellent lord, King Henry V, hath procured the common idiom ... to be commended by the exercise of writing'.

Tales of a British past and practical feelings of insecurity had combined with the vigour and ambition of English kings down to Edward I—perhaps Edward III—to take the English into Scotland, Wales, and Ireland. Their success in absorbing these territories was limited; and try as they might to Anglicize the Welsh and Irish in culture, language, and habit, the English with their dependent dominions were denied political nationhood in the later Middle Ages. The English delegation to the Church's Council at Constance (1414–17) declared:

whether a nation be understood as a people marked off from others by blood relationship and habit of unity, or by peculiarities of language (the most sure and positive sign and essence of a nation in divine and human law) . . . or whether a nation be understood, as it should be, as a territory equal to that of the French nation, England is a real nation . . .

But they spoilt their political case by adding that Scotland, Wales, and Ireland were part of the English nation.

5. The Tudor Age
(1485–1603)

JOHN GUY

Population Changes

THE age of the Tudors has left its impact on Anglo-American minds as a watershed in British history. Hallowed tradition, native patriotism, and post-imperial gloom have united to swell our appreciation of the period as a true golden age. Names alone evoke a phoenix-glow—Henry VIII, Elizabeth I, and Mary Stuart among the sovereigns of England and Scotland; Wolsey, William Cecil, and Leicester among the politicians; Marlowe, Shakespeare, Hilliard, and Byrd among the creative artists. The splendours of the Court of Henry VIII, the fortitude of Sir Thomas More, the making of the English Bible, Prayer Book, and Anglican Church, the development of Parliament, the defeat of the Armada, the Shakespearian moment, and the legacy of Tudor domestic architecture—these are the undoubted climaxes of a simplified orthodoxy in which genius, romance, and tragedy are superabundant.

Reality is inevitably more complex, less glamorous, and more interesting than myth. The most potent forces within Tudor England were often social, economic, and demographic ones. Thus if the period became a golden age, it was primarily because the considerable growth in population that occurred

between 1500 and the death of Elizabeth I did not so dangerously exceed the capacity of available resources, particularly
food supplies, as to precipitate a Malthusian crisis. Famine and
disease unquestionably disrupted and disturbed the Tudor economy, but they did not raze it to its foundations, as in the
fourteenth century. More positively, the increased manpower
and demand that sprang from rising population stimulated
economic growth and the commercialization of agriculture,
encouraged trade and urban renewal, inspired a housing
revolution, enhanced the sophistication of English manners,
especially in London, and (more arguably) bolstered new
and exciting attitudes among Tudor Englishmen, notably individualistic ones derived from Reformation ideals and Calvinist
theology.

The matter is debatable, but there is much to be said for the
view that England was economically healthier, more expansive,
and more optimistic under the Tudors than at any time since
the Roman occupation of Britain. Certainly, the contrast with
the fifteenth century was dramatic. In the hundred or so years
before Henry VII became king of England in 1485, England had
been underpopulated, underdeveloped, and inward-looking
compared with other Western countries, notably France. Her
recovery after the ravages of the Black Death had been slow—
slower than in France, Germany, Switzerland, and some Italian
cities. The process of economic recovery in pre-industrial
societies was basically one of recovery of population, and
figures will be useful. On the eve of the Black Death (1348),
the population of England and Wales was between 4 and 5
millions; by 1377, successive plagues had reduced it to 2.5
millions. Yet the figure for England (without Wales) was still
no higher than 2.26 millions in 1525, and it is transparently
clear that the striking feature of English demographic history
between the Black Death and the reign of Henry VIII is the
stagnancy of population which persisted until the 1520s.
However, the growth of population rapidly accelerated after
1525:

English population totals 1525–1601

Year	Population total in millions
1525	2.26
1541	2.77
1551	3.01
1561	2.98
1581	3.60
1601	4.10

(Source: E. A. Wrigley and R. S. Schofield, *The Population History of England, 1541–1871*, London, 1981)

Between 1525 and 1541 the population of England grew extremely fast, an impressive burst of expansion after long inertia. This rate of growth slackened off somewhat after 1541, but the Tudor population continued to increase steadily and inexorably, with a temporary reversal only in the late 1550s, to reach 4.10 millions in 1601. In addition, the population of Wales grew from about 210,000 in 1500 to 380,000 by 1603.

While England reaped the fruits of the recovery of population in the sixteenth century, however, serious problems of adjustment were encountered. The impact of a sudden crescendo in demand, and pressure on available resources of food and clothing, within a society that was still overwhelmingly agrarian, was to be as painful as it was, ultimately, beneficial. The morale of countless ordinary Englishmen was to be wrecked by problems that were too massive to be ameliorated either by governments or by traditional, ecclesiastical philanthropy. Inflation, speculation in land, enclosures, unemployment, vagrancy, poverty, and urban squalor were the most pernicious evils of Tudor England, and these were the wider symptoms of population growth and agricultural commercialization. In the fifteenth century farm rents had been discounted, because tenants were so elusive; lords had abandoned direct exploitation of their demesnes, which were leased to tenants on favourable terms. Rents had been low, too, on peasants' customary holdings; labour services had been commuted, and servile villeinage had virtually disappeared from the face of the English landscape by 1485. At the same time, money wages had risen to reflect the contraction of the wage-labour force after 1348, and food prices had fallen in reply to reduced market demand. But rising demand after 1500 burst the bubble of artificial prosperity born of stagnant population. Land hunger led to soaring rents. Tenants of farms and copyholders were evicted by business-minded landlords. Several adjacent farms would be conjoined, and amalgamated for profit, by outside investors at the expense of sitting tenants. Marginal land would be converted to pasture for more profitable sheep-rearing. Commons were enclosed, and waste land reclaimed, by landlords or squatters, with consequent extinction of common grazing rights. The literary opinion that the active Tudor land market nurtured a new entrepreneurial class of greedy capitalists grinding the faces of the poor is an exaggeration. Yet it is fair to say that not all landowners, claimants, and squatters were entirely scrupulous in their attitudes; certainly a vigorous market arose among dealers in defective titles to land, with resulting harassment of many legitimate occupiers.

The greatest distress sprang, nevertheless, from inflation and unemployment. High agricultural prices gave farmers strong incentives to produce crops for sale in the dearest markets in nearby towns, rather than for the satisfaction of rural subsistence. Rising population, especially urban population, put intense strain on the markets themselves: demand for food often outstripped supply, notably in years of poor harvests due to epidemics or bad weather. In cash terms, agricultural prices began to rise faster than industrial prices from the beginning of the reign of Henry VIII, a rise which accelerated as the sixteenth century progressed. Yet in real terms, the price rise was even more volatile than it appeared to be, since population growth ensured that labour was plentiful and cheap, and wages low. The size of the work-force in Tudor England increasingly exceeded available employment opportunities; average wages and living standards declined accordingly. Men (and women) were prepared to do a day's work for little more than board wages;

able-bodied persons, many of whom were peasants displaced by rising rents or the enclosure of commons, drifted in waves to the towns in quest of work.

The best price index hitherto constructed covers the period 1264–1954, and its base period is most usefully 1451–75—the end of the fifteenth-century era of stable prices. From this index, we may read the fortunes of the wage-earning consumers of Tudor England, because the calculations are based on the fluctuating costs of composite units of the essential foodstuffs and manufactured goods, such as textiles, that made up an average family shopping basket in southern England at different times. Two indexes are, in fact, available: first the annual price index of the composite basket of consumables; secondly the index of the basket expressed as the equivalent of the annual wage rates of building craftsmen in southern England. No one supposes that building workers were typical of the English labour force in the sixteenth century, or at any other time. But the indexes serve as a rough guide to the appalling reality of the rising household expenses of the majority of Englishmen in the Tudor period.

Indexes (1451–75 = 100) of (1) price of composite unit of consumables; (2) equivalent of wage rate of building craftsman

Year	(1)	(2)
1450	102	98
1490	106	94
1510	103	97
1530	169	59
1550	262	48
1570	300	56
1590	396	51
1610	503	40

(Source: E. H. Phelps Brown and S. V. Hopkins, *Economica*, no. 92, Nov. 1956, n.s. vol. xxiii)

It is clear that in the century after Henry VIII's accession, the average prices of essential consumables rose by some 488 per cent. The price index stood at the 100 or so level until 1513, when it rose to 120. A gradual rise to 169 had occurred by 1530, and a further crescendo to 231 was attained by 1547, the year of Henry VIII's death. In 1555 the index reached 270; two years later, it hit a staggering peak of 409, though this was partly due to the delayed effects of the currency debasements practised by Henry VIII and Edward VI. On the accession of Elizabeth I, in 1558, the index had recovered to a median of 230. It climbed again thereafter, though more steadily: 300 in 1570, 342 in 1580, and 396 in 1590. But the later 1590s witnessed exceptionally meagre harvests, together with regional epidemics and famine: the index read 515 in 1595, 685 in 1598, and only settled back to 459 in 1600.

The index expressed as the equivalent of the building craftsman's wages gives an equally sober impression of the vicissitudes of Tudor domestic life. An abrupt decline in the purchasing power of wages occurred between 1510 and 1530, the commodity equivalent falling by some 40 per cent in twenty years. The index fell again in the 1550s, but recovered in the next decade to a position equivalent to two-thirds of its value in 1510. Apart from 1586–7, it then remained more or less stable until the 1590s, when it collapsed to 39 in 1595, and to 29 in 1597. On the queen's death in 1603 it had recovered to a figure of 45—which meant that real wages had dropped by 57 per cent since 1500.

These various data establish the most fundamental truth about the age of the Tudors. When the percentage change of English population in the sixteenth century is plotted against that of the index of purchasing power of a building craftsman's wages over the same period, it is immediately plain that the two lines of development are opposite and commensurate (see graph). Living standards declined as the population rose; recovery began as population growth abated and collapsed between 1556 and 1560. Standards then steadily dropped again, until previous proportions were overthrown by the disasters of 1586–7 and 1594–8—though the cumulative increase in the size of the wage-labour force since 1570 must also have had distorting effects.

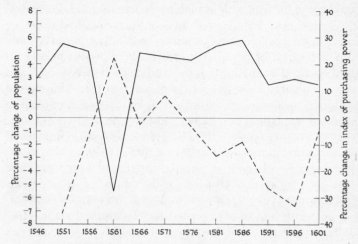

—— Percentage change of population since last total (Source: E. A. Wrigley and R. S. Schofield, *The Population History of England, 1541–1871*, London, 1981)

--- Percentage change since last total (averaged over three years) in index of purchasing power of building craftsman's wages as compared to index of his purchasing power in 1510 (Source: E. H. Phelps Brown and S. V. Hopkins, *Economica*, no. 92, Nov. 1956, n.s. vol. xxiii)

In other words, population trends, rather than government policies, capitalist entrepreneurs, European imports of American silver, the more rapid circulation of money, or even currency debasements, were the key factor in determining the fortunes of the British Isles in the sixteenth century. English government expenditure on warfare, heavy borrowing, and debasements unquestionably exacerbated inflation and unemployment. But the basic facts of Tudor life were linked to population growth.

In view of this fundamental truth, the greatest triumph of Tudor England was its ability to feed itself. A major national subsistence crisis was avoided. Malthus, who wrote his historic *Essay on the Principle of Population* in 1798, listed positive and preventive checks as the traditional means by which population was kept in balance with available resources of food. Preventive checks included declining fertility, contraception, and fewer, or later, marriages; positive ones involved heavy mortality and abrupt reversal of population growth. Fertility in England indeed declined in the later 1550s, and again between 1566 and 1571. A higher proportion of the population than hitherto did not marry in the reign of Elizabeth I. Poor harvests resulted in localized starvation, and higher mortality, in 1481–3, 1519–21, 1527–9, 1544–5, 1549–51, 1554–6, 1586–7, and 1594–7, the most serious crop failures being in 1555–6 and 1596–7. In fact, as the effect of a bad harvest in any particular year lasted until the next good or average crop was gathered, the severest dearths lasted from 1555 to 1557, and from 1596 to 1598. Yet devastating as dearth and disease proved for the affected areas, especially for the towns of the 1590s, the positive check of mass mortality on a national scale was absent even during the influenza epidemic of 1555–9. True, in addition to its other difficulties, Mary's regime faced the most serious mortality crisis since the Black Death: the population of England dropped by 200,000, or by six per cent. But since some regions were relatively lightly affected, it is not proved that this was a national crisis in terms of its geographical extent. Also, population growth was only temporarily interrupted. Indeed, the chronology, intensity, and restricted geographical range of famine in the sixteenth century suggest that starvation crises in England were abating, rather than worsening, over time, while epidemics took fewer victims than before in proportion to the expansion of population. The countryside escaped crisis during two-thirds of Elizabeth's reign and the rural population remained in surplus. When the towns suffered an excess of deaths over births, this surplus was sufficient both to increase the numbers who stayed on the land and to compensate for urban losses by migration to towns.

So there is much to be said for an optimistic view of the age of the Tudors. The sixteenth century saw the birth of Britain's pre-industrial political economy—an evolving accommodation between population and resources, economics and politics, ambition and rationality. England abandoned the disaster-oriented framework of the Middle Ages for the new dawn of low-pressure equilibrium. Progress had its price, unalterably paid by the weak, invariably banked by the strong. Yet the tyranny of the price index was not ubiquitous. Wage rates for agricultural workers fell by less than for building workers, and some privileged groups of wage-earners such as the Mendip miners may have enjoyed a small rise in real income. Land-owners, commercialized farmers, and property investors were the most obvious beneficiaries of a system that guaranteed fixed expenses and enhanced selling prices—it was in the Tudor period that the nobility, gentry, and mercantile classes alike came to appreciate fully the enduring qualities of land. But many wage-labouring families were not wholly dependent upon their wages for subsistence. Multiple occupations, domestic self-employment, and cottage industries flourished, especially in the countryside; town-dwellers grew vegetables, kept animals, and brewed beer, except in the confines of London. Wage-labourers employed by great households received meat and drink in addition to cash income, although this customary practice was on the wane by the 1590s.

Finally, it is not established that vagabondage or urban population outside London expanded at a rate faster than the general rate of increase in national population. It used to be argued that the English urban population climbed from 6.2 per cent of the national total in 1520 to 8.4 per cent by the end of the century. However, London's spectacular growth alone explains this apparent over-population: the leading provincial towns, Norwich, Bristol, Coventry, and York, grew slightly or remained stable in absolute terms—and must thus have been inhabited by a reduced share of population in proportional terms.

Henry VII

Yet if the new dawn was marked by low-pressure equilib-rium, the quest for political stability at the end of the fifteenth century remained of paramount importance to future progress. No one now thinks that the thirty years' internal commotion known·as the Wars of the Roses amounted to more than an intermittent interruption of national life, or that Henry VII's victory at Bosworth Field (22 August 1485) rates credit beyond that due to luck and good fortune. Bosworth Field was, indeed, conclusive only because Richard III, together with so many of his household men and supporters, was slain in the battle; because Richard had eliminated in advance the most plausible alternatives to Henry VII; and because Henry was ingenious enough to proclaim himself king with effect from the day before the battle, thus enabling the Ricardian rump to be deemed traitors. By marrying Elizabeth of York, daughter of Edward IV, Henry VII then proffered the essential palliative to those Yorkist defectors who had joined him against Richard in the first place—the ensuing births of Arthur in 1486, Margaret in 1489, Henry in 1491, and Mary in 1496 achieved the 'Union of the Two Noble and Illustrious Families of Lancaster and York' upon which the pro-Tudor chronicler Edward Hall lavished the praise echoed by Shakespeare.

But the need for stability went far beyond Henry VII's accession and marriage. The victor of Bosworth Field could found a new dynasty; it remained to be seen whether he could create a new monarchy. The essential demand was that someone should restore the English Crown to its former position above mere aristocratic faction. The king should not simply reign; he should also rule. For too long, the king of England had been 'first among equals', rather than 'king and emperor'. The Wars of the Roses had done negligible permanent damage to agriculture, trade, and industry, but they had undermined confidence in monarchy as an institution: the king was seen to be unable, or unwilling, to protect the rights of all his subjects. In particular, royal government had ceased to be politically neutral, having been excessively manipulated by individuals as an instrument of faction. All aspects of the system, especially the legal system, had been deeply permeated by family loyalties, aristocratic rivalries, favouritism, and a web of personal connections.

In fairness to Edward IV, whom Sir Thomas More thought had left his realm 'in quiet and prosperous estate', the work of reconstruction had already been started. Edward IV's failure to make sufficient progress was primarily due to his excessive generosity, his divisive marriage to Elizabeth Woodville, and his barely-controlled debauchery. His premature death had become the cue for the usurpation of Richard III, who was leader of a large and unusually powerful northern faction. Henry VII was, by contrast, dedicated and hard-working, astute and ascetic, and financially prudent to the point of avarice, or even rapacity, as some have maintained. Yet Henry's ace in the campaign for stability was that his good luck in sweeping the board at Bosworth, as in the case of William the Conqueror in 1066, had freed him, temporarily at least, from dependence on any one group or faction. Henry's continued independence and security naturally had to be earned, consolidated, and defended—a formidable task that absorbed many years. In fact, the first of the Tudor kings had specifically to combine the task of restoring the monarchy with that of protecting its flank from hyperactive Yorkist conspiracy.

Of the two Yorkist impostures, that of Lambert Simnel as earl of Warwick in 1487, although the more exotic, was, thanks to Irish support, the more menacing; that of Perkin Warbeck, as Richard of York during the 1490s, was more easily contained despite Scottish involvement. Simnel was routed at Stoke (16 June 1487); his promoters were killed or pardoned, and the young imposter was taken into the royal household as a servant. Warbeck fell into Henry's hands in August 1497; before long he had abused the king's leniency and was hanged in 1499. His demise was then made an occasion for executing the real earl of Warwick. But it was another seven years before the incarceration in the Tower of Edmund de la Pole, duke of Suffolk, completed the defensive process.

By that time, it was clear that Henry VII, if not to be

distinguished as the inventor of new methods of government, had, nevertheless, mastered the art of streamlining the old. The touchstone of his policy was enforcement—the enforcement of political and financial obligation to the Crown, as much as of law and order. In achieving the restoration of the monarchy, the Tudors practised their belief that ability, good service, and loyalty to the regime, irrespective of a man's social origins and background, were to be the primary grounds of appointments, promotions, favours, and rewards. This belief was most evident in Henry VII's use of royal patronage and in his appointments of ministers and councillors. Patronage was the process by which the Crown awarded grants of offices, lands, pensions, annuities, or other valuable perquisites to its executives and dependants, and was thus its principal weapon of political control, its most powerful motor of political management. Subjects, from great peers of the realm to humble knights and gentry, vied with each other for a share of the spoils—no nobleman was too high to join in the undignified scramble. Henry VII gradually restructured the patronage system to reflect more realistically the Crown's limited resources, and next ensured that the values of grants made under the great seal were fully justified in terms of return on expenditure. The resources of Tudor monarchy were relatively meagre in the years before the Dissolution of the Monasteries, and again in the later part of Elizabeth I's reign. Henry VII set the pace and the standards for distributing royal bounty for much of the sixteenth century; indeed, the only danger inherent in the Tudor model of cash efficiency was that it might veer towards meanness or excessive stringency. The level and flow of grants might become so far diminished in relation to expectations as to ferment impatience, low morale, and even active disloyalty among the Crown's servants and suitors.

Henry VII's ministers were all personally selected by the king for their ability, assiduity, shrewdness, and loyalty—again a pattern for the most part emulated by his Tudor successors. Yet at first sight, Reynold Bray, Richard Empson, and Edmund

Dudley seemed to hold quite minor offices. Bray was Chancellor of the duchy of Lancaster; soon after he died, in 1503, Empson succeeded him; Dudley was 'president of the Council', which effectively meant minister without portfolio. But Bray and the rest exercised control, under the king, far in excess of their apparent status. For Henry VII managed in an absurdly short space of time to erect a network of financial and administrative checks and blueprints, the records of which never left the hands of himself and the selected few, and the methods of which were equally of their own devising. Financial accounting, the exploitation of the undervalued resources of the Crown lands along the most modern lines known to the land-holding aristocracy, the collection of fines and obligations, and the enforcement of Henry VII's morally-dubious but probably necessary system of compelling political opponents, or even apparent friends, to enter into coercive bonds for good behaviour—these vital matters were dealt with only by the king and his inner ring. It was a system that owed nothing to Parliament; it owed something to the Council in so far as Bray and the others sat there as Henry's most trusted councillors; but it owed everything to the king himself, whose vigilance and attention to detail were invincible. Nothing slipped past Henry's keen eye, least of all money through his twitching fingers. The extant Chamber books, the master-documents of the early Henrician nexus of administrative co-ordination, are signed, and thus checked, on every page, and even beside every entry, by the king who was the best businessman ever to sit on the English throne.

Tudor government, however, was as much a question of partnership as of dictatorship. England lacked a police force and a standing army. Revenues increasingly failed to match the expanding functions of central bureaucracy and costs of warfare. James Harrington wrote in *Oceana*, first published in 1656, that government could be based either upon a nobility or upon an army. He was right; in the absence of the permanent militia, the Crown ruled in part through its territorial magnates. It was for Henry VII and his successors at best to subdue, at worst to preside over, aristocratic faction, while steering the private resources of the peerage along lines compatible with royal interests. In short, 'overmighty subjects', whose persistence was lamented by Sir John Fortescue in the fifteenth century, and Francis Bacon in the seventeenth, were essential to the running of the country. For it was less 'overmighty subjects' that led to disorder than 'undermighty kings'. Both Henry VII and Henry VIII appreciated this: between them, they tamed the nobility in order to ride upon its back.

Henry VII's methods here were a judicious combination of carrot and stick. In his large and active King's Council, the first of the Tudors practised consultation in a way that inspired, alternately, participation and boredom. All noblemen might be councillors before the reform of the Council by Henry VIII in late 1536, and political identity depended on attending Council meetings from time to time. At Westminster the Council sat in Star Chamber (literally *camera stellata*, the room's azure ceiling being decorated with stars of gold leaf), which was both a meeting place for the working Council and a court of law. When Parliament was not in session, Star Chamber formed the chief point of contact between the Crown, its ministers, and the nobility until Wolsey's fall in 1529, and under Henry VII it discussed those issues, such as internal security, the armed defences, and foreign affairs, which, of necessity, had to secure the support of the magnates, who were also the muster-men and captains of armies. The Council never debated fiscal or enforcement policies under Henry VII, matters which remained firmly vested in the hands of ministers and those of two tribunals known as the Council Learned in the Law and the Conciliar Court of Audit. But by making conciliar involvement a dimension of magnate status, Henry VII went far towards filtering out the threat of an alienated nobility that sprang from lack of communications and isolation in the political wilderness.

Next, Henry VII made an overtly determined bid to concentrate the command of castles and garrisons, and, as far as possible, the supervision of military functions, in the members of the royal Household, and he launched direct attacks on the local, territorial powers of the magnates, if he felt that those powers had been exercised in defiance of perceived royal interests. Such attacks normally took one of two forms, either that of prosecutions and fines at law for misfeasance, or the more drastic resort of attainder and forfeiture.

George Neville, Lord Bergavenny, for instance, was tried in King's Bench in 1507 on a charge of illegally retaining what amounted to a private army. He pleaded guilty (people did under Henry VII, for it was cheaper), and was fined £70,650, being the price, at the rate of £5 per man per month, for which he was liable for having hired 471 men for 30 months from 10 June 1504 to 9 December 1506. It seems that the 'army' comprised 25 gentlemen, 4 clerics, 440 yeomen, one cobbler, and one tinker—the Tudors got details right. But Henry VII was not opposing retaining on principle on the occasion of this prosecution; he *valued* Bergavenny's force, down to that last Kentish tinker, just as much as did its true territorial proprietor—it was even better that Bergavenny was footing the bill. Despite Henry VII's peaceful foreign policy, England was within the mainstream of European affairs, quite apart from her fluctuating relations with Scotland. The all-too-brief marriage of Prince Arthur to Catherine of Aragon in 1501 considerably raised Henry VII's stature in Europe, while his treaty with Anne of Brittany obliged him briefly to invade France in 1492. England, or rather the king of England, had virtually no army beyond that recruited on demand from the royal demesne, and that provided on request by the nobility. Thus, in Bergavenny's case, which was exemplary and admonitory, it was especially relevant that the accused was by birth a Yorkist, and that he had been implicated in an unsuccessful rising of Cornishmen in 1497.

Yet far more drastic, and effective, was the weapon of attainder and forfeiture. Acts of attainder were parliamentary statutes proclaiming convictions for treason, and declaring the victim's property forfeit to the king and his blood 'corrupted'. The method almost always involved execution of the victim, but did not necessarily lead to the total forfeiture of his lands. Most attainders were by tradition repealed later in favour of the heirs, though not always with full restoration of property. Henry VII's reign saw 138 persons attainted, and 86 of these attainders were never reversed. Only 46 were reversed by Henry VII, and six by Henry VIII. These figures compare unfavourably with those of the reigns of Henry VI, Edward IV, and even Richard III— reflecting the toughness of Tudor policy. Henry VII realized that attainders were not simply a tool of faction and dynastic intrigue: they could be used to excise 'overmighty' or hostile magnates, while at the same time significantly augmenting the Crown's own power and income. In similar fashion, Henry VIII, after the Pilgrimage of Grace (1536), and Elizabeth I, after the Northern Rising (1569), used attainders to bolster the Crown's territorial strength and eradicate magnate resistance. Finesse was, however, required if the method was not to back-fire. Its excessive use, and repeated failure to reverse attainders in favour of heirs, could spark resentment among the peerage, whose partnership with the monarchy was thus impaired. Attainders could also do serious damage if they left a power vacuum in a particular local area, as occurred in East Anglia when the third duke of Norfolk was attainted by Henry VIII in 1547. His attainder, reversed by Mary in 1553, created instability which the Crown could not easily correct, and paved the way for Ket's Rebellion in 1549.

Historians suspect that Henry VII overdid his policy of enforcement in the latter part of his reign. In 1506, he commissioned one Polydore Vergil, who was a visiting collector of papal taxes, to write a history of England, and it was Polydore who opined that the first of the Tudors had practised financial rapacity after 1502.

For he began to treat his people with more harshness and severity than had been his custom, in order (as he himself asserted) to ensure that they remained more thoroughly and entirely in obedience to him. The people themselves had another explanation for his action, for they considered they were suffering not on account of their own sins but on account of the greed of their monarch. It is not indeed clear whether at the start it was greed; but afterwards greed did become apparent.

The debate concerning Henry's rapacity still rages. Whatever the eventual outcome, three points are proven. First, Henry VII used penal bonds in sums ranging from £100 to £10,000 to enforce what *he* considered to be acceptable behaviour on his subjects. These bonds aimed to hold the political nation, especially the nobility, at the king's mercy, and to short-circuit due process of common law in case of offence by the victims. If a man was deemed to have misbehaved, he would simply be sued for debt on his bond—it was not possible to litigate over the nature or extent of the alleged offence. In other words, Henry VII used bonds to defeat the law in the way that King John and Richard II had used blank charters. Second, Empson and Dudley corrupted juries to find verdicts in favour of Henry VII's feudal rights. The best example is the case of the estates of the earl of Westmorland. A conciliar inquiry had to be launched to rectify this matter in Henry VIII's reign. Lastly, Henry VII sold offices, including legal ones. He twice sold the chief justiceship of the Court of Common Pleas, and at high prices. He also sold the posts of Attorney-General, Master of the Rolls, and Speaker of the House of Commons.

Henry VIII

Henry VIII's accession in 1509 was greeted with feasting, dancing, and rejoicing. He succeeded at barely eighteen years of age, because his elder brother, Arthur, had died in 1502. Under pressure from his councillors, essentially his father's executors, Henry began his 'triumphant' reign by marrying his late brother's widow, Catherine of Aragon—a union that was to have momentous, not to say revolutionary, consequences. He continued by executing Empson and Dudley, who were thrown to the wolves to win popularity. The trick worked—no one complained that the Council omitted to cancel the last batches of outstanding bonds until well into the 1520s. Yet Henry VIII had started as he meant to go on; a glimpse of his vindictiveness was revealed.

Henry VIII's character was certainly fascinating, threatening, and sometimes morbid. His egoism, self-righteousness, and capacity to brood sprang from the fusion of an able but second-rate mind with what looks suspiciously like an inferiority complex. Henry VII had restored stability and royal authority, but it may have been for reasons of character, as much as policy, that his son resolved to augment his regal power. As his reign unfolded Henry VIII added 'imperial' concepts of kingship to existing 'feudal' ones; he sought to give the words 'king and emperor' a meaning unseen since the days of the Roman empire. He was eager, too, to conquer—to emulate the glorious victories of the Black Prince and Henry V, to quest after the golden fleece that was the French Crown. He wished, in fact, to revive the Hundred Years War, despite the success of Valois France in consolidating its territory and the shift of emphasis of European politics towards Italy and Spain. Repeatedly the efforts of his more constructive councillors were bedevilled, and overthrown, by his chivalric dreams, and by costly wars that wasted men, money, and equipment. If, however, humanist criticism of warfare by Colet, Erasmus, and Thomas More is well known, it should not be forgotten that 'honour' in the Renaissance was necessarily defended in the last resort by battle. 'Honour' was the cornerstone of aristocratic culture; sovereign rulers argued that unlike their subjects they lacked 'superiors' from whom redress of grievances might be sought, and so had no choice but to accept the 'arbitrament' of war when diplomacy failed. Also war was the 'sport of kings'. By competing dynastically and territorially with his European counterparts, especially Francis I, Henry VIII acknowledged settled convention and, even more obviously, popular demand. His reign saw the boldest and most extensive invasions of France since the reign of Henry V. In fact, only a minority of contemporaries had any sense of the serious long-term economic damage that Renaissance warfare could inflict.

Evaluation is always a matter of emphasis, but on the twin issues of monarchic theory and lust for conquest, there is everything to be said for the view that Henry VIII's policy was consistent throughout his reign; that Henry was himself directing that policy; and that his ministers and officials were allowed freedom of action only within accepted limits, and when the king was too busy to take a personal interest in state affairs.

Cardinal Wolsey was Henry VIII's first minister, and the fourteen years of that proud but efficient prelate's ascendancy (1515–29) saw the king in a comparatively restrained mood. Henry, unlike his father, found writing 'both tedious and painful'; he preferred hunting, dancing, dallying, and playing the lute. In his more civilized moments, Henry studied theology and astronomy; he would wake up Sir Thomas More in the middle of the night in order that they might gaze at the stars from the roof of a royal palace. He wrote songs, and the words of one form an epitome of Henry's youthful sentiments.

> Pastime with good company
> I love and shall until I die.
> Grudge who lust, but none deny;
> So God be pleased, thus live will I;
> > For my pastance,
> > Hunt, sing and dance;
> > My heart is set
> > All goodly sport
> > For my comfort:
> > Who shall me let?

Yet Henry himself set the tempo; his pastimes were only pursued while he was satisfied with Wolsey. Appointed Lord Chancellor and Chief Councillor on Christmas eve 1515, Wolsey used the Council and Star Chamber as instruments of ministerial power in much the way that Henry VII had used them as vehicles of royal power—though Wolsey happily pursued uniform and equitable ideals of justice in Star Chamber in place of Henry VII's selective justice linked to fiscal advantage. But Wolsey's greatest asset was the unique position he obtained with regard to the English Church. Between them, Henry and Wolsey bludgeoned the pope into granting Wolsey the rank of legate *a latere* for life, which meant that he became the superior ecclesiastical authority in England, and could convoke legatine synods. Using these powers, Wolsey contrived to subject the entire English Church and clergy to a massive dose of Tudor government and taxation, and it looks as if an uneasy compromise prevailed behind the scenes in which Henry agreed that the English Church was, for the moment, best controlled by a churchman who was a royal servant, and the clergy accepted that it was better to be obedient to an ecclesiastical rather than a secular tyrant—for it is unquestionably true that Wolsey protected the Church from the worst excesses of lay opinion while in office.

The trouble was that, with stability restored, and the Tudor dynasty apparently secure, England had started to become vulnerable to a mounting release of forces. It used to be argued that anti-clericalism was a major cause of the English Reformation, but this interpretation has lately been challenged. Recent research has established that the majority of late medieval English clergy were not negligent or unqualified: Church courts were not usually unfair; probate, mortuary, and tithes disputes were few; pluralism, absenteeism, nepotism, sexual misconduct, and commercial 'moonlighting' by clergy were less serious than once was thought. On the other hand, there *were* priests who failed to hold services at the proper times, who did not preach, and whose habits were aggressive—the rector of Addington in Northamptonshire, cited before the Lincoln consistory court in 1526, had two children by his cook and marched about the village in chain-mail. In fact, it was all too easy for a priest to behave like other villagers: to make a mistress of his house-keeper, and to spend the day cultivating his glebe. Although the English Church was free of major scandals, such abuses as non-residence, pluralism, concubinage, and the parochial clergy's neglect to repair chancels, where these occurred, continued to attract attention. Also tithes disputes, probate and mortuary fees, charges for saying mass on special occasions, and the trial and burning of heretics could become flash-points. In particular, it was pointed out by prominent writers, notably the grave and learned Christopher St. German (1460–1541), that the Church's procedure in cases of suspected heresy permitted secret accusations, hearsay evidence, and denied accused persons the benefit of purgation by oath-helpers or trial by jury, which was a Roman procedure contrary to the principles of native English common law—a clerical plot to deprive Englishmen of their natural, legal rights. Such ideas were manifestly explosive; for they incited intellectual affray between clergy and common lawyers.

Late medieval religion was also sacramental and institutional: it could appear to be dominated by 'objective' ritual and ceremony at the expense of 'subjective' religious experience based on Bible reading at home. As the expectations of the educated laity mirrored those of the Renaissance, many people sought to found their faith on texts of Scripture and Bible stories (preferably illustrated ones), but vernacular Bibles were illegal in England—the Church authorities believed that the availability of an English Bible, even an authorized version, would ferment heresy by permitting Englishmen to form their own opinions. Sir Thomas More, Wolsey's successor as Lord Chancellor, declared in his proclamation of 22 June 1530 that 'it is not necessary the said Scripture to be in the English tongue and in the hands of the common people, but that the distribution of the said Scripture, and the permitting or denying thereof, dependeth only upon the discretion of the superiors, as they shall think it convenient'. More pursued a policy of strict censorship: no books in English printed outside the realm on *any* subject whatsoever were to be imported; he forbade the printing of Scriptural or religious books in England, too, unless approved in advance by a bishop. But More and the bishops were swimming against the tide. The invention of printing had revolutionized the transmission of new ideas across Western Europe, including Protestant ideas. Heretical books and Bibles poured from the presses of English exiles abroad, notably that of William Tyndale at Antwerp. The demand for vernacular Scriptures was persistent, insistent, and widespread; Henry VIII was enlightened enough to wish to assent to it, and publication of an official English Bible in Miles Coverdale's translation was first achieved in 1535, the year of More's death.

Of the forces springing from the European Renaissance, Christian Humanism and the influence of Greek learning came first. The humanists, of whom the greatest was Erasmus of Rotterdam (1467–1536), rejected scholasticism in favour of simple biblical piety, or *philosophia Christi*, which was founded on primary textual scholarship, and in particular study of the Greek New Testament. Erasmus made several visits to England, and it was in Cambridge in 1511–14 that he worked upon the Greek text of his edition of the New Testament.

But the renaissance of Greek learning owed as much to a native Englishman, John Colet, the gloomy dean of St. Paul's and founder of its school. Colet, who was also young Thomas More's spiritual director, had been to Italy, where he had encountered the neoplatonist philosophy of Marsilio Ficino and Pico della Mirandola. He had mastered Greek grammar and literature, which he then helped to foster at Oxford and at his school, and the fruits of his philosophical and literary knowledge were applied to Bible study—especially to the works of St. Paul. The result was a method of Scriptural exegesis that broke new ground. Colet emphasized the unity of divine truth, a literal approach to texts, concern for historical context, and belief in a personal and redemptive Christ. These exciting ideas inspired both Erasmus and the younger generation of humanists.

The humanists first challenged the English establishment in 1512 when, preaching before Convocation, Colet attacked clerical abuses and demanded reform of the Church from within.

His sermon caused resentment but the humanists continued to call for spiritual renewal. Erasmus embellished his evangelism with racy criticisms of priests and monks, Catholic superstition, and even the papacy. He published his *Handbook of a Christian Knight* (1503), *Praise of Folly* (1511), and *Education of a Christian Prince* (1516) before Luther challenged the papacy. Also in 1516 he published his Greek New Testament together with a revised Latin translation. Scholars and educated laymen were delighted; at last they drank the pure waters of the fountain-head.

More's *Utopia* (1516) was more complex. It wittily idealized an imaginary society of pagans living on a remote island in accordance with principles of natural virtue. The Utopians possessed reason but lacked Christian revelation, and by implicitly comparing their benign social customs and enlightened attitudes with the inferior standards, in practice, of Christian Europeans, More produced an indictment of the latter based largely on deafening silence. For the irony and scandal was that Christians had so much to learn from heathens.

Yet the humanism of Erasmus and More was fragile. Even without Luther's challenge it would have become fragmented because faith and reason in its scheme were at odds. More's solution was to argue that faith was the superior power and that Catholic beliefs must be defended because God commanded them, but Erasmus trusted human rationality and could not accept that God tested people's faith by making them believe things that Renaissance scholarship had thrown into question. Even Luther regarded Erasmus as an enemy because of his emphasis on reason. So these fissures weakened humanism and new exponents of reform caught public attention. In England, the influence of Lutheranism exceeded the small number of converts: the rise of the 'new learning', as it was called, became the most potent of the forces released in the 1520s and 1530s. Luther's ideas and numerous books rapidly penetrated the universities, especially Cambridge, the City of London, the inns of court, and even reached Henry VIII's Household through the intervention of Anne Boleyn and her circle. At Cambridge, the young scholars influenced included Thomas Cranmer and Matthew Parker, both of whom later became Archbishops of Canterbury. Wolsey naturally made resolute efforts as legate to stamp out the spread of Protestantism, but without obvious success. His critics blamed his reluctance to burn men for heresy—for Wolsey would burn books and imprison men, but shared the humane horror of Erasmus at the thought of himself committing bodies to the flames. However, the true reason for Luther's appeal was that he had given coherent doctrinal expression to the religious subjectivity of individuals, and to their distrust of Rome and papal monarchy. In addition his view of the ministry mirrored the instincts of the laity, and his answer to concubinage was the global solution of clerical marriage.

Into this religious maelstrom dropped Henry VIII's first divorce. Although Catherine of Aragon had borne five children, only the Princess Mary (b. 1516) had survived, and the king demanded the security of a male heir to protect the fortunes of the Tudor dynasty. It was clear by 1527 that Catherine was past the age of childbearing; meanwhile Henry coveted Anne Boleyn, who would not comply without the assurance of marriage. Yet royal annulments were not infrequent, and all might have been resolved without drama, or even unremarked, had not Henry VIII been a proficient, if mendacious, theologian.

The chief obstacle was that Henry, who feared international humiliation, insisted that his divorce should be granted by a competent authority in England—this way he could deprive his wife of her legal rights, and bully his episcopal judges. But his marriage had been founded on Pope Julius II's dispensation, necessarily obtained by Henry VII to enable the young Henry VIII to marry his brother's widow in the first place, and hence the matter pertained to Rome. In order to have his case decided without reference to Rome, in face of the papacy's unwillingness to concede the matter, Henry had to prove against the reigning pope, Clement VII, that his predecessor's dispensation was invalid—then the marriage would automatically terminate, on the grounds that it had never legally existed. Henry would be a bachelor again. However, this strategy took the king away from matrimonial law into the quite remote and hypersensitive realm of papal power. If Julius II's dispensation was invalid, it must be because the successors of St. Peter had no power to devise such instruments, and the popes were thus no better than other human legislators who had exceeded their authority.

Henry was a good enough theologian to know that there *was* a minority opinion in Western Christendom to precisely this effect. He was enough of an egoist, too, to fall captive to his own powers of persuasion—soon he believed that papal primacy was unquestionably a sham, a ploy of human invention to deprive kings and emperors of their legitimate inheritances. Henry looked back to the golden days of the British imperial past, to the time of the Emperor Constantine and of King Lucius I. In fact, Lucius I had never existed—he was a myth, a figment of pre-Conquest imagination. But Henry's British 'sources' showed that this Lucius was a great ruler, the first Christian king of Britain, who had endowed the British Church with all its liberties and possessions, and then written to Pope Eleutherius asking him to transmit the Roman laws. However, the pope's reply explained that Lucius did not need any Roman law, because he already had the *lex Britanniae* (whatever that was) under which he ruled both Church and State:

For you be God's vicar in your kingdom, as the psalmist says, 'Give the king thy judgments, O God, and thy righteousness to the king's son' (Ps. lxxii: 1)...A King hath his name of ruling, and not of having a realm. You shall be a king, while you rule well; but if you do otherwise, the name of a king shall not remain with you ... God grant you so to rule the realm of Britain, that you may reign with him for ever, whose vicar you be in the realm.

Vicarius Dei—vicar of Christ. Henry's divorce had led him, incredibly, to believe in his royal supremacy over the English Church.

With the advent of the divorce crisis, Henry took personal charge of his policy and government. He ousted Wolsey, who was hopelessly compromised in the new scheme of things, since his legatine power came directly from Rome. He named Sir Thomas More to the chancellorship, but this move backfired owing to More's scrupulous reluctance to involve himself in Henry's proceedings. He summoned Parliament, which for the first time in English history worked with the king as an omnicompetent legislative assembly, if hesitatingly so. Henry and Parliament finally threw off England's allegiance to Rome in an unsurpassed burst of revolutionary statute-making: the Act of Annates (1532), the Act of Appeals (1533), the Act of Supremacy (1534), the First Act of Succession (1534), the Treasons Act (1534), and the Act against the Pope's Authority (1536). The Act of Appeals proclaimed Henry VIII's new imperial status— all English jurisdiction, both secular and religious, now sprang from the king—and abolished the pope's right to decide English ecclesiastical cases. The Act of Supremacy declared that the king of England was supreme head of the Church of England— not the pope. The Act of Succession was the first of a series of Tudor instruments used to settle the order of succession to the throne, a measure which even Thomas More agreed was in itself sound, save that this statute was prefaced by a preamble denouncing papal jurisdiction as a 'usurpation' of Henry's imperial power. More, together with Bishop Fisher of Rochester, and the London Carthusians, the most ascetic and honourable custodians of papal primacy and the legitimacy of the Aragonese marriage, were tried for 'denying' Henry's supremacy under the terms of the Treasons Act. These terms made it high treason maliciously to deprive either king or queen of 'the dignity, title, or name of their royal estates'—that is to deny Henry's royal supremacy. The victims of the act, who were in reality martyrs to Henry's vindictiveness, were cruelly executed in the summer of 1535. A year later the Reformation legislation was completed by the Act against the Pope's Authority, which removed the last vestiges of papal power in England, including the pope's 'pastoral' right as a teacher to decide disputed points of Scripture.

Henry VIII now controlled the English Church as its supreme head. Yet why did bishops who held crucial votes in the House of Lords and Convocation permit the Henrician Reformation to occur? The answer is partly that Henry coerced his clerical opponents into submission by threats and punitive taxation; but some bishops actually *supported* the king, albeit sadly. They preferred to be ruled by the Tudors personally, with whom they could bargain and haggle, than be subordinated to Parliament, which was the alternative. As early as 1532 Cromwell had sought to make the Tudor supremacy parliamentary. But Parliament's contribution was cut back to the mechanical, though still revolutionary, task of enacting the requisite legislation. In Henry's view, the models for statecraft were the late Roman emperors, especially Constantine and Justinian, who governed both Church and State. Henry held his supremacy to be 'imperial' despite the use of Parliament. Royal supremacy was 'ordained by God'; all Parliament had done was belatedly to recognize the fact. Also it was not until 1549, 1552, and 1559 that the full implications of the break with Rome became clear, when the royal supremacy became the vehicle of the Protestant Reformation. Not everyone realized what was happening in the 1530s. Many saw the Acts of Appeals and Supremacy as a temporary squabble between king and pope, a cause unworthy of martyrdom.

Before 1529 Henry had ruled his clergy through Wolsey; after 1534 he did so personally, and through his second minister, Thomas Cromwell. A former aide of Wolsey, Cromwell had risen to power as a client of the Boleyn interest. By January 1532 he had taken command of the machinery of government, especially the management of Parliament. And by exploiting the offices of Master of the Jewels, King's Secretary, Lord Privy Seal, and Henry's (lay) vicegerent in spirituals, he became chief policymaker under Henry until he fell in June 1540. Indeed, some historians have argued that Cromwell was the architect of a Tudor 'revolution in government'. While this has never been proved, it remains true that he attempted the reform of the

King's Council and of Tudor financial institutions. In 1536 the large, unwieldy Council known to Henry VII and Wolsey was turned into an executive board of some nineteen persons and renamed the Privy Council. Forging ahead after 1540, the Privy Council made and enforced policy under the Crown, supervised the law courts, managed Exchequer finance, and co-ordinated the localities. Proceeding by state paper rather than royal writ, it became a partner of the Crown as much as a corporate servant. Cromwell's financial reforms also started to separate the financing of the royal family and household from that of national government, though this important process was not fully complete until the 1570s.

Yet Cromwell's major assignment was the Dissolution of the Monasteries. For three invincible forces merged after 1535 to dictate their removal. First, religious houses almost invariably owed allegiance to parent institutions outside England and Wales—this was juridically unacceptable after the Acts of Appeals and Supremacy. Secondly, Henry VIII was bankrupt. He needed to annex the monastic estates in order to restore the Crown's finances. Thirdly, Henry had to buy the allegiance of the political nation away from Rome and in support of his Reformation by massive injections of new patronage—he must appease the nobility and gentry with a share of the spoils. Thus Thomas Cromwell's first task as vicegerent was to conduct an ecclesiastical census under Henry's commission, the first major tax record since Domesday Book, to evaluate the condition and wealth of the English Church. Cromwell's questionnaire was a model of precision. Was divine service observed? Who were the benefactors? What lands did the houses possess? What rents?— and so on. The survey was completed in six months, and Cromwell's genius for administration was shown by the fact that *Valor Ecclesiasticus*, as it is known, served both as a record of the value of the monastic assets, and as a report on individual clerical incomes for taxation purposes.

The lesser monasteries were dissolved in 1536; the greater houses followed two years later. The process was interrupted by a formidable northern rebellion, the Pilgrimage of Grace, which was brutally crushed by use of martial law, exemplary public hangings, and a wholesale breaking of Henry's promises to the 'pilgrims'. But the work of plunder was quickly completed. A total of 560 monastic institutions had been suppressed by November 1539, and lands valued at £132,000 per annum immediately accrued to the Court of Augmentations of the King's Revenue, the new department of state set up by Cromwell to cope with the transfer of resources. Henry's coffers next received £75,000 or so from the sale of gold and silver plate, lead, and other precious items; finally, the monasteries had possessed the right of presentation to about two-fifths of the parochial benefices in England and Wales, and these rights were also added to the Crown's patronage.

The long-term effects of the dissolution have often been debated by historians, and may conveniently be divided into those which were planned, and those not. Within the former category, Henry VIII eliminated the last fortresses of potential resistance to his royal supremacy. He founded six new dioceses upon the remains of former monastic buildings and endowments—Peterborough, Gloucester, Oxford, Chester, Bristol, and Westminster, the last-named being abandoned in 1550. The king then reorganized the ex-monastic cathedrals as Cathedrals of the New Foundation, with revised staffs and statutes. Above all, though, the Crown's regular income was almost doubled—but for how long? The bitter irony of the dissolution was that Henry VIII's colossal military expenditure in the 1540s, together with the laity's demand for a share of the booty, politically irresistible as that was, would so drastically erode the financial gains as to cancel out the benefits of the entire process. Sales of the confiscated lands began even before the suppression of the greater houses was completed, and by 1547 almost two-thirds of the former monastic property had been alienated. Further grants by Edward VI and Queen Mary brought this figure to over three-quarters by 1558. The remaining lands were sold by Elizabeth I and the early Stuarts. It is

true that the lands were not given away: out of 1,593 grants in
Henry VIII's reign, only 69 were gifts or partly so; the bulk of
grants (95.6 per cent) represented lands sold at prices based on
fresh valuations. But the proceeds of sales were not invested—
quite the opposite under Henry VIII. In any case, land *was*
the best investment. The impact of sales upon the non-parliamentary income of the Crown was thus obvious, and there
is something to be said for the view that it was Henry VIII's
dissipation of the ex-monastic resources that made it difficult
for his successors to govern England.

Of the unplanned effects of the dissolution, the wholesale
destruction of fine Gothic buildings, melting down of medieval
metalwork and jewellery, and sacking of libraries were acts of
licensed vandalism. The clergy naturally suffered an immediate
decline in morale. The number of candidates for ordination
dropped sharply; there was little real conviction that Henry VIII's
Reformation had anything to do with spiritual life, or with
God. The disappearance of the abbots from the House of
Lords meant that the ecclesiastical vote had withered away,
leaving the laity ascendant in both Houses. With the sale of
ex-monastic lands usually went the rights of parochial presentation attached to them, so that local laity obtained the bulk of
Church patronage, setting the pattern for the next three centuries. The nobility and gentry, especially moderate-sized gentry
families, were the ultimate beneficiaries of the Crown's land
sales. The distribution of national wealth shifted between 1535
and 1558 overwhelmingly in favour of Crown and laity, as
against the Church, and appreciably in favour of the nobility
and gentry, as against the Crown. Very few new or substantially
enlarged private estates were built up solely out of ex-monastic
lands by 1558. But if Norfolk is a typical county, the changing
pattern of wealth distribution at Elizabeth's accession was that
4.8 per cent of the county's manors were possessed by the Crown,
6.5 per cent were episcopal or other ecclesiastical manors, 11.4 per
cent were owned by East Anglian territorial magnates, and 75.4
per cent had been acquired by the gentry. In 1535, 2.7 per cent

of manors had been held by the Crown, 17.2 per cent had been owned by the monasteries, 9.4 per cent were in the hands of magnates, and 64 per cent belonged to gentry families.

Without Henry VIII's preparatory break with Rome, there could not have been Protestant reform in Edward VI's reign—thus evaluation can become a question of religious opinion, rather than historical judgement. However, it is hard not to regard Henry as a despoiler; he was scarcely a creator. Thomas Cromwell did his utmost, often behind the king's back, to endow his contemporaries with Erasmian, and enlightened, idealism: the Elizabethan Settlement owed much to the eirenic side of Cromwell's complex character. But Cromwell's reward was the block. When Henry became convinced that his viceger-ent was protecting Protestants at Calais, he withdrew his support and allowed Cromwell to fall victim to his factional enemies. And without Wolsey or Cromwell to restrain him, Henry resolved to embark on French and Scottish wars, triggering a slow-burning fuse that was extinguished only by the execution of Mary Stuart in February 1587.

Yet if Henry turned to war and foreign policy in the final years of his reign, it was because he felt secure at last. Crom-well had provided the enforcement necessary to protect the supreme head from internal opposition; Jane Seymour had brought forth the male heir to the Tudor throne; Henry was excited about his marriage to Catherine Howard, and had settled Church doctrine by the Act of Six Articles (1539).

The matrimonial adventures of Henry VIII are too familiar to recount again in detail, but an outline may conveniently be given. Anne Boleyn was already pregnant when the king mar-ried her, and the future Elizabeth I was born on 7 September 1533. Henry was bitterly disappointed that she was not the expected son, and when Anne miscarried a deformed male foetus in January 1536, he was convinced that God had damned his second marriage. He therefore destroyed Anne in a palace coup (May 1536) and married Jane Seymour instead. But Jane's triumph in producing the baby Prince Edward was Pyrrhic, for she died of Tudor surgery twelve days later. Her successor was Anne of Cleves, whom Henry married in January 1540 to win European allies. But Anne, gentle but plain, did not suit; divorce was thus easy, as the union was never consummated. Catherine Howard came next. A high-spirited flirt, she had been a maid of honour to Anne of Cleves, and became Henry's fifth queen in July 1540, a month after the coup that destroyed Cromwell. She was executed in February 1542 for adultery. Finally, Henry took the amiable Catherine Parr to wife in July 1543. Twice widowed, Catherine was a cultivated Erasmian, who did much to preserve the cause of humanist reform until it could re-emerge in the reign of Edward VI.

Henry VIII's new plans for war, which hardened when he learned of Catherine Howard's infidelity, resurrected youthful dreams of French conquests. Wolsey had largely organized the king's early campaigns in 1512 and 1513; Henry led in person a large army from Calais in 1513, seizing Thérouanne and Tournai after the battle of the Spurs (16 August). True, the captured towns were costly to defend and Thomas Cromwell called them 'ungracious dogholes' in Parliament, but they delighted the king. Another invasion was planned, but Henry's allies were unreliable and Wolsey negotiated an Anglo-French *entente* (August 1514). This crumbled on the death of Louis XII and accession of Francis I (1 January 1515). But in 1518 Wolsey agreed new terms with France which were transformed into a dazzling European peace treaty. The pope, emperor, Spain, France, England, Scotland, Venice, Florence, and the Swiss forged, with others, a non-aggression pact with provision for mutual aid in case of hostilities. At a stroke Wolsey made London the centre of Europe and Henry VIII its arbiter. This *coup de théâtre* was the more remarkable in that it was the pope's own plan that Wolsey snatched from under his nose. At the Field of Cloth of Gold in 1520, Henry vied with Francis at a vast Renaissance tournament that was hailed as the eighth wonder of the world. Further campaigns in 1522 and 1523 brought Henry's army to within fifty miles of Paris. Then the best chance of all arose:

Henry's ally the Emperor Charles V defeated and captured Francis at the battle of Pavia (24 February 1525). But the opportunity could not be exploited owing to England's financial exhaustion. So Henry made peace with France. And when the divorce campaign began, he became insular in outlook, fearing Catholic invasion. Certainly he was in no position to resume warfare until the reverberations of the Pilgrimage of Grace had died away.

By 1541 Henry was moving towards a renewed amity with Spain against France, but he was prudent enough to hesitate. Tudor security required that, before England went to war with France, no doors should be open to the enemy within Britain itself. This meant an extension of English hegemony within the British Isles—Wales, Ireland, and Scotland. Accordingly Henry undertook, or continued, the wider task of English colonization that was completed by the Act of Union with Scotland (1707).

The Union of England and Wales had been presaged by Cromwell's reforming ambition, and was legally accomplished by Parliament in 1536 and 1543. The marcher lordships were shired, English laws and county administration were extended to Wales, and the shires and county boroughs were required to send twenty-four MPs to Parliament at Westminster. In addition, a refurbished Council of Wales, and new Courts of Great Sessions, were set up to administer the region's defences and judicial system. Wales was made subject to the full operation of royal writs, and to English principles of land tenure. The Act of 1543 dictated that Welsh customs of tenure and inheritance were to be phased out, and that English rules were to succeed them. Welsh customs persisted in remoter areas until the seventeenth century and beyond, but English customs soon predominated. English language became the fashionable tongue, and Welsh native arts went into decline.

Tudor Irish policy had begun with Henry VII's decision that acts of Parliament made in England were to apply to Ireland, and that the Irish Parliament could only legislate with the king of England's prior consent. By 1485 English authority did not in practice extend much beyond the Pale (the area around Dublin). But Ireland was generally quiet before 1534, even if the Gaelic chiefs held the balance of power. The Tudors ruled largely through the Anglo-Irish nobility before the Reformation, but a crisis erupted in 1533 when Irish politics began to merge with those of the Reformation. Surprised by the Kildare revolt (July 1534), Henry VIII could only parley with the rebels until a relief army was organized. Then the defeat of the rebels in August 1535 was followed by a major switch of policy: direct rule. For Cromwell's aim was to assimilate Ireland into the unitary realm of England under the control of an English-born deputy. Yet this policy required the backing of a standing army controlled from Westminster. Next, Henry VIII changed his style from 'lord' to 'king' of Ireland (June 1541). His assumption of the kingship was justified on the grounds that 'for lack of naming' of sovereignty the Irish had not been as obedient 'as they of right and according to their allegiance and bounden duties ought to have been'. But the move committed England to a possible full-scale conquest of Ireland, should the chiefs rebel, or should the Irish Reformation, begun by Cromwell, fail. It even militated *against* the idea of a unitary state. For a subordinate superstructure had been created for Ireland: the later Tudors ruled technically two separate kingdoms, each with its own bureaucracy. In future ideological terms, it became possible to conceive of Anglo-Irish nationalism, as opposed to English or Gaelic civilization. Lastly, despite the confiscation of Kildare's estates and the dissolution by Henry VIII of half the Irish monasteries, the Irish revenues were insufficient to maintain either the Crown's new royal status or its standing army. And since the army could not be withdrawn, the case for the conquest of Ireland was reinforced.

Yet the linchpin of Tudor security was the need to control Scotland. James IV (1488–1513) had renewed the Auld Alliance with France in 1492 and further provoked Henry VII by offering support for Perkin Warbeck. But the first of the Tudors declined to be distracted by Scottish sabre-rattling, and forged

THE UNION OF ENGLAND AND WALES

a treaty of Perpetual Peace with Scotland in 1502, followed
a year later by the marriage of his daughter, Margaret, to King
James. However, James tried to break the treaty shortly after
Henry VIII's accession; Henry was on campaign in France, but
sent the earl of Surrey northwards, and Surrey decimated the
Scots at Flodden on 9 September 1513. The élite of Scotland—the
king, three bishops, eleven earls, fifteen lords, and some 10,000
men—were slain in an attack that was the delayed acme of
medieval aggression begun by Edward I and Edward III. The
new Scottish king, James V, was an infant, and the English

interest was symbolized by his mother, Henry VIII's own sister. But Scottish panic after Flodden had, if anything, confirmed the nation's ties with France, epitomized by the regency of John duke of Albany, who represented the French cause and urged Francis I to sponsor him in an invasion of England.

The French threat became overt when the mature James V visited France in 1536, and married in quick succession Madeleine, daughter of Francis I, and on her death Mary of Guise. In 1541 James agreed to meet Henry VIII at York, but committed the supreme offence of failing to turn up. By this time, Scotland was indeed a danger to Henry VIII, as its government was dominated by the French faction led by Cardinal Beaton, who symbolized both the Auld Alliance and the threat of papal counter-attack. In October 1542 the duke of Norfolk invaded Scotland, at first achieving little. It was the Scottish counterstroke that proved to be a worse disaster even than Flodden. On 24 November 1542, 3,000 English triumphed over 10,000 Scots at Solway Moss—and the news of the disgrace killed James V within a month. Scotland was left hostage to the fortune of Mary Stuart, a baby born only six days before James's death. For England, it seemed to be the answer to a prayer.

Henry VIII and Protector Somerset, who governed England during the early years of Edward VI's minority, none the less turned advantage into danger. Twin policies were espoused by which war with France was balanced by intervention in Scotland designed to secure England's back door. In 1543 Henry used the prisoners taken at Solway Moss as the nucleus of an English party in Scotland; he engineered Beaton's overthrow, and forced on the Scots the treaty of Greenwich, which projected union of the Crowns in form of marriage between Prince Edward and Mary Stuart. At the end of the same year, Henry allied with Spain against France, planning a combined invasion for the following spring. But the invasion, predictably, was not concerted. Henry was deluded by his capture of Boulogne; the emperor made a separate peace with France at Crépi, leaving England's flank exposed. At astronomical cost the war continued until June 1546. Francis I then finally agreed that England could keep Boulogne for eight years, when it was to be restored to France complete with expensive new fortifications. He also abandoned the Scots, endorsing by implication the terms of the treaty of Greenwich. But it was too late: Henry's 'rough wooing' of Scotland had already backfired. Beaton had trumped Henry's English party and repudiated the treaty; the earl of Hertford, the future Protector Somerset, was sent north with 12,000 men. Hertford's devastation of the border country, and Lothian, was successful, but was culpably counterproductive. In particular, the sack of Edinburgh united Scottish resistance to English terrorism. Henry VIII had thus engineered exactly what he wished to avoid—simultaneous conflict with France and Scotland. Hertford returned to Scotland in 1545, but the French faction remained ascendant, even after Beaton was murdered in May 1546 by a group of Fife lairds.

Edward VI

The death of Henry VIII in 1547, and the Protectorate until 1549 of the obsessional, vacillating Hertford as duke of Somerset left a power vacuum at the centre. This was paralleled locally by the temporary inability of county governments to contain outbreaks of violence and rebellion springing mainly from the decline in living standards in the 1540s. Riot and commotion were virtually ubiquitous from 1548 to 1550, save in the north where memories of the ill-fated Pilgrimage of Grace were perhaps still fresh. Coinage debasements designed to help pay for the French war had caused rampant inflation, and the most abrupt decline in the purchasing power of money coincided with Somerset's enclosure commissions and sheep tax, a platform that fermented rumours that the Protector supported the poor against the rich. The most serious uprisings took place in Devon and Cornwall, and in East Anglia, culminating in formal sieges of Exeter and Norwich by rebels. Somerset's equivocation, and inability to end this domestic crisis, prompted the earl of Warwick's coup against him in October 1549.

Yet Somerset's most spectacular failure was his continued adherence to the defunct treaty of Greenwich. His desire to realize Henry VIII's plan to subdue French influence in Scotland and achieve the union of the Crowns became an obsession. His victory at the battle of Pinkie (10 September 1547) was justified as an attempt to free Scotland from the Roman clergy, but the Scottish Reformation was hardly helped by a policy that pushed Scotland ever closer into the embrace of France. In June 1548, 6,000 French troops landed at Leith, and Mary Stuart was removed to France. When Somerset continued to threaten Scotland, Henry II of France declared war on England. Boulogne was blockaded; French forces in Scotland were strengthened. The Scots then agreed that Mary should eventually marry the Dauphin, heir to the French throne. That provision hammered the last nail into Somerset's coffin.

The earl of Warwick's coup, and realignment of the Privy Council, was completed by February 1550. Warwick shunned the title of Protector; instead he assumed that of Lord President of the Council, an interesting choice, since it revived an office effectively obsolete since the fall of Edmund Dudley, Warwick's father. Posthumous tradition has vilified Warwick as an evil schemer—a true 'Machiavel'. But it is hard to see why, for expediency in the interests of stability was the most familiar touchstone of Tudor policy. Three episodes allegedly prove Warwick's criminal cunning: his original coup against Somerset, the subsequent trial which ended in Somerset's execution in January 1552, and the notorious scheme to alter the succession to the throne in favour of Lady Jane Grey, Warwick's daughter-in-law. However, only the last of these charges seems justifiable by Tudor standards, and even this would be regarded differently by historians had the plot to exclude the Catholic Mary actually succeeded.

Warwick, who created himself duke of Northumberland in October 1551, made, in fact, a laudable effort to reverse the destabilization permitted, or left unchecked, by Somerset. Domestic peace was restored by the use of forces which included

foreign mercenaries; England's finances were put back on
course by means of enlightened reforms and retrenchments.
Above all, Somerset's disastrous wars with France and Scotland
were quickly terminated. Northumberland sought peace with
dishonour—a humiliating but attractive alternative to fighting.
Boulogne was returned to France at once; English garrisons in
Scotland were withdrawn, and the treaty of Greenwich was
quietly forgotten. It thus became inevitable that Mary Stuart
would marry the Dauphin, but considerations of age ensured
that the union was postponed until April 1558.

The English Reformation had meanwhile reached its crossroads. After Thomas Cromwell's execution, Henry VIII had
governed the Church of England himself: his doctrinal conservatism was inflexible to the last. But Somerset rose to the
Protectorate as leader of the Protestant faction in the Privy
Council, and the young Edward VI—he was nine years old in
1547—mysteriously became a precocious and bigoted Protestant too. In July 1547, Somerset reissued Cromwell's Erasmian
injunctions to the clergy, followed by a Book of Homilies, or
specimen sermons, which embodied Protestant doctrines. He
summoned Parliament four months later, and the Henrician
doctrinal legislation was repealed. At the same time, the chant-
ries were dissolved. These minor foundations existed to sing
masses for the souls of their benefactors; as such, they encouraged beliefs in purgatory and the merits of requiems, doctrines
which Protestants denied. Somerset thus justified their abolition
on religious grounds, but it is plain that he coveted their property even more to finance his Scottish ambitions. Next, the
Privy Council wrote to Archbishop Cranmer, ordering the
wholesale removal of images from places of worship, 'images
which be things not necessary, and without which the churches
of Christ continued most godly many years'. Shrines, and the
jewels and plate inside them, were promptly seized by the
Crown; the statues and wall-paintings that decorated English
parish churches were mutilated, or covered with whitewash. In
1538 Henry VIII had suppressed shrines which were centres of

pilgrimages, notably that of St. Thomas Becket at Canterbury. Protector Somerset finalized the destruction already begun, ensuring that the native art, sculpture, metalwork, and embroidery associated with Catholic ritual were comprehensively wiped out.

The danger was always that Protestant reform would overreach itself—in the Cornish rebellion of 1549, opposition to the first of Cranmer's Prayer Books provided the chief rallying point. The system for licensing public preachers had broken down by September 1548, and Somerset was obliged, temporarily, to ban all preaching, whether licensed or not, in favour of readings of the official homilies. The Protector, though, promised 'an end of all controversies in religion' and 'uniform order', and Cranmer also aspired to this ideal. He wrote to Albert Hardenberg, leader of the Bremen Reformed Church:

We are desirous of setting forth in our churches the true doctrine of God, neither have we any wish to be shifting and unstable, or to deal in ambiguities: but, laying aside all carnal considerations, to transmit to posterity a true and explicit form of doctrine agreeable to the rule of the scriptures; so that there may be set forth among all nations a testimony respecting our doctrine, delivered by the grave authority of learned and pious men; and that all posterity may have a pattern which they may imitate. For the purpose of carrying this important design into effect we have thought it necessary to have the assistance of learned men, who, having compared their opinions together with us, may do away with doctrinal controversies, and establish an entire system of true doctrine.

Protestant theologians who responded to Cranmer's call included John Knox from Scotland, Martin Bucer from Strasbourg, John à Lasco from Poland, Peter Martyr Vermigli from Italy, and Bernardino Ochino, the controversial ex-vicar-general of the Capuchins, who had made a sensational conversion to Protestantism in the early 1540s.

Yet Protestants were even less capable of consensus than were Catholics. John Knox, to whom Northumberland inadvertently offered the bishopric of Rochester (fortunately Knox refused), was particularly atavistic; he thrived on crisis. Cranmer soon came to see that unity could only be achieved at the price of uniformity—this was the fundamental lesson of the English Reformation. Accordingly the two editions of his Book of Common Prayer (1549, 1552), which enshrined the pure and Scriptural doctrines for which the primate had craved since 1537, not only had to be approved by Parliament; they had to be enforced by Acts of Uniformity. The advantages from Cranmer's viewpoint were that the Books were in English, and the second was unambiguously Protestant; the drawback was that the Prayer Books were first published as schedules to the Uniformity Acts, so that the doctrines and ceremonies of the English Church now rested on parliamentary authority, rather than on the independent legislative power of the supreme head. This constitutional amendment marked the final triumph of the Tudor laity over the Church, for Elizabeth I, in fashioning the religious settlement of 1558–9, took Cranmer's Prayer Books as a precedent.

Queen Mary

Northumberland's patronage of Knox, who in exile during Mary's reign scandalized Europe by theorizing upon the rights of subjects to rebel against idolatrous rulers, illustrates how far the duke had linked his future to the Protestant cause. Edward VI had never enjoyed good health, and by the late spring of 1553 it was plain that he was dying. By right of birth, as well as under Henry VIII's will, Mary, Catherine of Aragon's Catholic daughter, was the lawful successor. But Northumberland's attempted *putsch* in July 1553 needs more than a casual explanation. The facts are that Northumberland bound his family to the throne on 21 May by marrying his eldest son to Lady Jane Grey. Jane was the eldest daughter of the marquis of Dorset, and residuary legatee of the Crown, after the Princesses Mary and Elizabeth, under Henry VIII's will. Next, a documentary 'device' was drafted, by which Edward VI disinherited his sisters and bequeathed his throne to Jane and her heirs. Edward died on 6 July 1553; Northumberland and the Council proclaimed Jane queen four days later. The duke's treachery seems proved. Yet the plot may have been Edward's. The Protestant boy-bigot hated his sisters, especially Mary; the 'device' was drafted in his own hand, and corrected by him. At the very least, Edward had been Northumberland's willing collaborator.

Jane Grey ruled for nine days. Knox preached on her behalf, and threatened popery and tyranny should Mary enforce her claim. But the *putsch* was doomed. Mary was allowed to escape to Framlingham, the walled fortress of the Catholic Howard family. Proclaimed by the East Anglian gentry, she marched south. London changed sides; Northumberland, Jane, and their principal adherents eventually went to the block.

Yet Mary triumphed because she cheated. The Norfolk gentry were persuaded of her Tudor legitimism; they learned the terrible extent of her Catholicism only after she was safely enthroned at Westminster. Even so, we should beware of the bias of John Foxe and other Protestant polemicists writing in Elizabeth's reign, who would prefer us to believe that Mary did nothing but persecute. It is true that Mary burned a minimum of 287 persons after February 1555, and others died in prison. But the leading Protestant martyrs, Bishops Hooper, Ridley, Latimer, and Archbishop Cranmer were as much the victims of straightforward political vengeance. Stephen Gardiner, the failed conservative manipulator of Henry VIII's reign, who had been outwitted by Thomas Cromwell in the 1530s, was abandoned by the king in the 1540s, and had languished in the Tower during Edward's reign, had become Lord Chancellor in 1553; he had bitter scores to settle. Secondly, we should appreciate that many of the Marian 'martyrs' would have been burnt as anabaptists, or Lollards, under Henry VIII. By sixteenth-century standards there was nothing exceptional about Mary's reign of terror beyond the fact that, as in the case of More when he had persecuted Protestants as Lord Chancellor, she regarded her work as well done. Even the scale of Mary's persecution may have been exaggerated, for the figures come from the biased Foxe, who reported the same examples twice whenever possible, and who conveniently forgot that the un-persecuted Lollards of Edward's reign had created a backlog.

Mary's true goal was always England's reunion with Rome; persecution was a minor aspect of her programme. It was thus to her advantage that the parliamentary landed laity were, by this date, thoroughly secular-minded, for they repealed the Henrician and Edwardian religious legislation almost without comment, and re-enacted the heresy laws—all the time their sole condition was that the Church lands taken since 1536 should not be restored. Yet Mary needed papal assistance; she could not work alone. In November 1554, Cardinal Pole, an English Catholic exile of Plantagenet lineage, landed in England, absolved the kingdom from sin, and proclaimed papal reunion. Pole, who was appointed Archbishop of Canterbury, then attempted to implement intelligent ecclesiastical reforms in the spirit of the Counter-Reformation: these covered such areas as the liturgy, clerical manners, education, and episcopal supervision. But Pole's approach was visionary. He saw people not as individuals but as a multitude; he emphasized discipline before preaching; and he sought to be an 'indulgent' pastor who relieved his flock of choices they were too foolish to make for themselves. Yet heresy could not be contained by such methods. Dubbing himself the 'Pole Star', Pole thought his mere presence could guide lost souls. And he was afforded neither the time nor the money needed to accomplish his tasks: three years, and virtually no money, were not enough. The ecclesiastical machine ground slowly; standards of clerical education could not be raised without the augmentation of stipends, especially in the north.

Mary's short reign was, nevertheless, surprisingly successful in other spheres. The financial reforms of Northumberland were completed; the Exchequer was revitalized and reorganized; a blueprint for recoinage was prepared, and was adopted under Elizabeth. In 1557, a committee was named to investigate 'why customs and subsidies be greatly diminished and decayed'.

The outcome was a new Book of Rates in May 1558, which increased customs receipts by 75 per cent. Nothing on this scale would be tried again until James I's reign, when the Great Contract of 1610 proved such a disastrous failure.

Yet Mary made two bad mistakes. The first was to allow some 800 English Protestants to emigrate to Frankfurt, Zurich, and Geneva. For not only did these exiles launch a relentless crusade of anti-Catholic propaganda and subversive literature against England, which the government was obliged to suppress or refute as best it could; they also flocked home again upon the accession, in 1558, of Elizabeth, the Protestant Deborah, as they believed her to be, when some were appointed bishops, despite the inherent tension between the Anglican ceremonials they became obliged to enforce, and the Genevan distaste for popish rituals and vestments they had so recently shared. Mary's second mistake was her Spanish marriage. Her union with Philip, son of the Emperor Charles V, was her own idea, celebrated in July 1554 despite the pleas of privy councillors and Parliament. Philip was styled king jointly with Mary as queen during her lifetime; however, his rights in England were to expire if Mary died childless, as proved to be the case. Yet even these terms did not appease opponents of the match: four simultaneous rebellions were planned for 1554, of which Sir Thomas Wyatt's, in Kent, began prematurely in January. Wyatt led 3,000 men to London, proclaiming that 'we seek no harm to the Queen, but better council and counsellors'. But Wyatt declined to pillage London; he removed his force to Kingston—a fatal diversion. His army was defeated, and 100 rebels, including Wyatt, were executed as traitors. The other projected rebellions came to nothing.

Wyatt's fear that England would become a Spanish pawn was, none the less, justified. In 1556, Philip became king of Spain, following Charles V's abdication. Within a year, he had dragged his wife into a war with Henry II of France, which culminated in the recapture of Calais by the duke of Guise (7 January 1558). Calais, apart from its commercial value as the wool Staple, was symbolic of the glorious French campaigns of the Black Prince and Henry V: its loss was more than bad luck. Mary's death in November 1558 was thus unmourned, and the fact that Cardinal Pole died within a few hours of the queen was a positive fillip. Henry II meanwhile exulted with Te Deum and bonfires, and the marriage of Mary Stuart to the Dauphin, the perilous consequence of the aggression of Henry VIII and Somerset, was expedited.

Elizabeth I

Elizabeth I, daughter of Henry VIII and Anne Boleyn, ascended her throne on 17 November 1558. Ruler of England for forty-four years, she has won a reputation far in excess of her achievements. It is plain that her own propaganda, the cult of Gloriana, her sheer longevity, the coincidence of the Shakespearian moment, and the defeat of the Armada have beguiled us into ignoring the many problems of her reign.

Yet whatever fables have been peddled, Sir Robert Naunton was right when he said: 'Though very capable of counsel, she was absolute enough in her own resolution, which was apparent even to her last.' She knew her mind and controlled her policy; her instinct to power was infallible. Councillors attempted to concert their approaches to her on sensitive matters, but they were rarely successful; she would lose her temper whereupon the matter would rest in abeyance. But she postponed important decisions: unless panicked, she could delay for years. On the other hand, her attitude has to be offset against her financial position and the conservatism of most of her subjects who were far from being Protestant 'converts' before the outbreak of war with Spain. Possibly her greatest asset was *lack* of preconceptions; she was not a conviction-politician like Sir Francis Walsingham or the earl of Leicester, though her taste for *realpolitik* exceeded Lord Burghley's. Apart from her concern to recover Calais as revealed by her French campaign of 1563, she ignored conventional royal ambitions. Her father's expansionist dreams were absent; her sister's ideological passions were eschewed; and despite negotiations conducted until 1582, a dynastic marriage was avoided. For although the second half of the sixteenth century saw the rise of ideological coalitions in Europe, England did not possess sufficient resources to wage open war until the 1580s; therefore a passive stance that responded to events as they occurred, while shunning obvious initiatives, was appropriate.

At first, though, the emphasis was on religious settlement. The efforts of Northumberland and Mary to reverse the destabilization of 1547–9 were flatly contradictory. Hence Elizabeth's coronation slogan was 'concord'. Her personal *credo* remains elusive, but she may originally have aimed to revive Henry VIII's religious legislation, to re-establish her royal supremacy and the break with Rome, and to permit communion in both kinds (bread and wine) after the reformed fashion— but nothing else. If so, she was 'bounced' by her chief councillor, William Cecil, for the only time in her reign. For when Parliament assembled in January 1559, he introduced bills to re-establish royal supremacy and full Protestant worship based on the 1552 Prayer Book. And when these were opposed by the Marian bishops and conservative peers, he baited a trap for the Catholics. A disputation was begun at Westminster Abbey (31 March) which restricted debate to what was justified by Scripture alone. When the Catholics walked out, Cecil had a propaganda victory: two bishops were even imprisoned. True, Elizabeth was styled 'supreme governor' of the English Church in an effort to minimize the impact of the supremacy. But when the Acts of Supremacy and Uniformity finally passed, they did so without a single churchman's consent, thereby making constitutional history. The cry of 'foul' was taken up by Catholic apologists, who accused Cecil of coercion 'partly by violence and partly by fear'. And another act returned to the Crown such ex-monastic property as Mary at her own expense had begun to restore to the Church, while a final act strengthened the Crown's estates at the expense of the bishops. The Elizabethan Settlement was completed in 1563, when Convocation approved Thirty-nine Articles defining the Anglican Church's doctrine—these were based on forty-two articles drafted by Cranmer in Edward VI's reign. Lastly, in 1571, the Settlement gained teeth sharper than the Act of Uniformity, when a Subscription Act required the beneficed clergy to assent to the Thirty-nine Articles.

The Anglican Church eventually became a pillar of the Elizabethan state. Despite its faults, the framework that John Jewel defended in his *Apology of the Church of England* (1562), and to which the 'judicious' Richard Hooker gave rational credibility in *The Laws of Ecclesiastical Polity* (1594–1600), the 'Church by law Established' saved England from the religious civil war that afflicted other European countries at the time, notably France. Yet while the Settlement meant that England became officially Protestant in 1559, a huge missionary effort to win the hearts and minds of parishioners (especially those in remoter counties and borderlands) lay ahead. Outside London, the South East, parts of East Anglia, and towns such as Bristol, Coventry, Colchester and Ipswich, Catholicism predominated at Elizabeth's accession: the bishops and most parochial incumbents were Marians, and committed Protestants were few. Whereas Elizabeth and Cecil inherited all the negative and destructive elements of Henrician anti-papalism and Edwardian Protestantism, they had inadequate resources to build the Anglican Church, though it is false to see their task purely in confessional terms. For by this stage, inertia was strong among those who had come to regard the Church as a rich corporation to be asset-stripped, or as a socio-political nexus whose leaders were local governors and whose festivals characterized the communal year. In addition, Protestantism, with its emphasis on 'godly' preaching and Bible study, was an academic creed, unattractive to illiterate villagers steeped in the oral traditions and symbolic ritualism of medieval England.

The decline of Catholicism in the parishes during Elizabeth's reign was due partly to its own internal changes and partly to the success of committed Protestants in marketing a rival evangelical product. One dynamic change sprang from mortality.

For the post-Reformation English Catholic community owed everything to Henrician and Marian survivalism, and relatively little to the missions of seminary priests and Jesuits after 1570. Over 225 Marian priests who saw themselves as Roman Catholics and who had separated from the Anglican Church were active in Yorkshire and Lancashire before 1571, supported by a fifth column within the official Church that remained willing to propagandize for Rome. By 1590, however, barely a quarter of the Marian clergy were still alive, and no more than a dozen by 1603. It is important not to forget the conditions in which the Catholics had to work. The penal laws became savage as fears of Spanish invasion increased. In 1584–5, Parliament enacted that if a priest had been ordained by papal authority since 1559, no additional proof was needed to convict him of treason. Furthermore, 123 of the 146 priests executed between the passing of this act and Elizabeth's death were indicted under its terms, and not under those of earlier treason laws. But it was the challenge of Anglicanism, rather than the threat of persecution, that succeeded in forcing Catholicism into minority status. Protestant evangelism was largely based on preaching, though Elizabeth's personal views and lack of resources precluded a full government programme for the propagation of Protestant preaching. What was achieved was often due to voluntary 'puritan' efforts. For whereas under Henry VIII and Edward VI the impetus for the Reformation had come largely from the regime, under Elizabeth, by contrast, the 'primary thrust' of Protestant evangelism came from below.

A term of abuse, 'puritan' was used to index the nature and extent of opinions of which conservatives disapproved. It meant a 'church rebel' or 'hotter sort' of Protestant; but the core of puritanism lay in the capacity of 'godly' Protestants to recognize each other within a corrupt and unregenerate world. Men of conviction, many of them former Marian exiles, the 'puritans' sought to extirpate corruption and 'popish rituals' from the Church (the cross in baptism, kneeling at the Communion, wearing of copes and surplices, the use of organs, etc.), but

Elizabeth consistently refused to adjust the Settlement even in detail. The most she was prepared to do was to refer petitions of which she approved to the bishops. In fact, when points were tested by puritan clergy, strict conformity was required. Archbishop Parker's *Advertisements* (1566), issued in response to disputes over clerical dress and ceremonies, enforced the rubrics of the Prayer Book. And when Edmund Grindal (Archbishop of Canterbury, 1576–83), who shared the puritan desire for reformation, dared to tell Elizabeth he was subject to a higher power, he was suspended from office. His successor, John Whitgift (1583–1604), required all clergy to subscribe to the royal supremacy, Prayer Book, and Thirty-nine Articles, or else be deprived.

Yet the need to graft the Anglican Church into English national consciousness was only the first of several tests faced by the regime. In April 1559, the peace of Cateau-Cambrésis (between Spain, France, and England) ended Mary's French war and Philip II briefly joined the queue of suitors for Elizabeth's hand. During the 1560s, Spain sought to preserve the amity with England, not least to ensure free traffic through the English Channel to the Spanish Netherlands. Yet Catholics, the papacy, Spain, and France were potential foes: the real danger was the threat of a Catholic coalition against England. And by 1569 the Catholic cause was linked to intrigue which, in its more innocent variety, sought to recognize Mary Stuart's right as Elizabeth's successor, but in more dangerous forms plotted to depose Elizabeth and enthrone Mary.

Mary had married the Dauphin in April 1558, and seven months later the Scottish Parliament agreed to offer him the crown matrimonial in exchange for support for the Scottish Reformation. Mary Tudor's death unleashed new French intervention in Scotland; there was sporadic fighting, which was overtaken by full-blooded Protestant revolution. When John Knox returned from exile in Geneva to preach at Perth in May 1559, he lit the fuse of a delayed explosion. Mary Stuart's husband succeeded to the French throne as Francis II in July

1559, but when he died in December 1560 the Scottish queen was forced to return to Edinburgh—she was back by August 1561. By then Elizabeth and Cecil had intervened on Knox's side: the Scottish Reformation had become the vehicle for the expulsion of Continental influence from the British Isles, and the assertion of the hegemony sought by Henry VIII.

Elizabeth meanwhile declined to marry or name her successor. Her obstinacy drove Cecil and the Privy Council to distraction. By contrast Mary Stuart's supporters hoped that she would succeed Elizabeth in a Catholic coup. For Mary's grandmother had been Henry VIII's sister, Margaret. But Mary made mistakes in Scotland; she alienated her friends as well as enemies, lost the battle of Langside, and fled to England in May 1568. Elizabeth, in effect, imprisoned her. A chain of intrigues took shape, in which Catholic, papal, and pro-Spanish ambitions allied, threateningly, with anti-Cecil factionalism at Court. But the Northern Rising of 1569, led by the disillusioned Catholic earls of Northumberland and Westmorland, was incoherently attempted and easily crushed. By 1572, Elizabeth and Cecil had passed another major test. Stability had been preserved: Cecil was ennobled as Lord Burghley.

The Northern Rising and Mary's imprisonment began a new phase in Tudor politics. Throughout Europe, opinion was polarizing on religious grounds: England's role as a Protestant champion was highlighted. Relations with Spain deteriorated when Cecil seized Philip II's treasure-ships *en route* for the Netherlands (December 1568). Then Pope Pius V issued a bull, *Regnans in Excelsis* (February 1570), that declared Elizabeth excommunicated and urged loyal Catholics to depose her. There followed the massacre of Protestants in Paris on St. Bartholomew's Day 1572 and outright revolt in the Netherlands—both fired Protestant consciences and inspired Englishmen to volunteer aid to the Netherlands. Lastly, Elizabeth's *entente* with France as a counter against Spain, which was twice taken to the point of marriage negotiations, was regarded as hostile by Philip II. On these matters the Privy

Council was divided. But these divisions were not pro- and anti-Spanish but between *realpolitik* and religion. With few exceptions, members of the Privy Council were united against Spain and committed to the European Protestant cause. In particular, Burghley, the earl of Sussex, Leicester, and Walsingham agreed on the broad aims of a Protestant foreign policy in the 1570s and 1580s. Their differences centred only on the extent to which England should become militarily committed. For Leicester and Walsingham wanted direct English intervention in the Netherlands, but the queen and Burghley were adamant that England alone could not survive war with Spain.

Yet when war with Spain came in 1585, England was isolated. After 1572 Elizabeth assisted France against Spain in the Netherlands, trying to reconcile conflicting political, religious, and commercial interests at minimum cost. She backed Francis duke of Anjou, her most plausible suitor, brother and heir of Henry III of France. But Anjou died in June 1584 having failed to halt Spanish recovery in the Low Countries. And since the Protestant Henry of Navarre now became heir to the French throne, the Wars of Religion resumed in France: the Guise Court party allied with Spain (secret treaty of Joinville, December 1584). So France was divided while Philip II prospered. He annexed Portugal (1580) and the Azores (1582-3): the size of his combined fleets exceeded those of the Netherlands and England combined. At this point the Marquis of Santa Cruz proposed the 'Enterprise of England'—an Armada to overthrow Elizabeth. Observers debated only whether the Netherlands or England would be reduced first.

The pivotal event was the assassination of the Dutch leader, William of Orange (10 July 1584). This created panic among English politicians who feared that Elizabeth, too, might fall victim. In May 1585, Philip felt confident enough to seize all English ships in Iberian ports; Elizabeth responded by giving Leicester his head, allying with the Dutch States General in August, and dispatching the earl to Holland with an army. But Leicester's mission was a fiasco; his ignominious return in

December 1587 was shortly followed by his death. Only Sir Francis Drake and other naval freebooters enjoyed success. And
outright war followed Mary Stuart's execution in February
1587. For new Catholic plots, at least one of which involved
Elizabeth's attempted assassination, hardened the Privy Council's attitude. Elizabeth stood indecisive and immobile; Mary
had been tried and convicted, but she was of the royal blood.
But the Council could wait no longer: the sentence was put
into effect. Scotland fulminated, but the twenty-one-year-old
James VI was appeased by subsidies and enhanced prospects
of the greatest of glittering prizes—succession to the English
Crown. (In any case, James had no illusions about Spanish support for the Scottish Reformation.)

The Armada was sighted off the Scilly Isles on 19 July 1588:
the objective was the conquest of England, which would itself
assure the reconquest of the Netherlands. Philip's plan was to
win control of the English Channel, to rendezvous with the
duke of Parma off the coast of Holland, and to transport the
crack troops of Philip's Army of Flanders to England. The main
fleet was to cover Parma's crossing, and then unite forces carried by the Armada itself with Parma's army in a combined
invasion of England. The Armada was commanded by the duke
of Medina Sidonia; the English fleet was led by Lord Howard
of Effingham, with Drake as second in command. Effingham
sailed in the *Ark Royal*, built for Sir Walter Raleigh in 1581;
Drake captained the *Revenge*, commissioned in 1575. In England the local militias were mobilized; possible landing places
were mapped, and their defences strengthened. But had Parma
landed, his army would have decimated English resistance: the
effectiveness of English sea-power was vital.

In the event, the defeat of the Armada was not far removed
from traditional legend, romantic games of bowls excepted.
The key to the battle was artillery: the Armada carried only 19
or 20 full cannon and its 173 medium-heavy and medium guns
were ineffective—some exploded on use which suggests that
they were untested. And whereas the Spanish had only 21
culverins (long-range iron guns), the English had 153; whereas

the Spanish had 151 demi-culverins, the English had 344. In brief, Effingham and Drake outsailed and outgunned their opponents. The battered Armada fled north towards the Firth of Forth, trailing back to Spain via the Orkneys and the west coast of Ireland. In August 1588 Protestant England celebrated with prayers and public thanksgiving. But the escape was narrow; Elizabeth never again committed her whole fleet in battle at once. Moreover, although later generations boasted that she kept Spain at bay at minimum cost by avoiding foreign alliances and relying on the royal navy and part-time privateers who preyed on enemy shipping, the supremacy of the naval over the Continental land war is a myth. The war at sea was only part of a struggle that gripped the whole of western Europe and centred on the French civil war and revolt of the Netherlands. Since Elizabeth lacked the land forces, money, and manpower to rival Spain, she was obliged to help Navarre and the Dutch. The Catholic League was strongest in Picardy, Normandy, and Brittany; these regions and the Netherlands formed what amounted to a continuous war zone. Elizabeth dispatched auxiliary forces annually to France and the Netherlands in 1589–95; cash subsidies apart from the cost of equipping and paying these troops cost her over £1 million. By comparison, English naval operations were heroic sideshows of mixed strategic value.

Yet late Elizabethan policy was damaging from several viewpoints. For the aims of Navarre and his partners diverged, and when in July 1593 he converted to Catholicism to secure his throne as Henry IV, he soured hopes of a European Protestant coalition. Elizabeth, however, continued to support him, since a united France restored the balance of power in Europe, while his debts ensured continued Anglo-French collaboration in the short term. Next, the queen quarrelled with the Dutch over their mounting debts and the cost of English garrisons and auxiliary forces. Thirdly, the cost of the war was unprecedented in English history: even with parliamentary subsidies, it could only be met by borrowing and by sales of Crown lands. Lastly, the war, in effect, spread to Ireland. The Irish Reformation had not succeeded: Spanish invasions as dangerous as the Armada were attempted there. These, combined with serious internal revolt, obliged the Privy Council to think in terms of the full-scale conquest of Ireland logically induced by Henry VIII's assumption of the kingship. Elizabeth hesitated—as well she might. At last her favourite, the dazzling but paranoid earl of Essex, was dispatched in 1599 with a large army. But Essex's failure surpassed even Leicester's in the Netherlands; he deserted his post in a last-ditch attempt to salvage his career by personal magnetism, and was executed in February 1601 for leading his faction in a desperate rebellion through the streets of London. Lord Mountjoy replaced him in Ireland, reducing the Gaelic chiefs to submission and routing a Spanish invasion force in 1601. The conquest of Ireland was completed by 1603. Yet the results were inherently contradictory: English hegemony was confirmed, but the very fact of conquest alienated the indigenous population and vanquished hopes of advancing the Irish Reformation, and thus achieving cultural unity with England.

Such contradictions were not, however, confined to Irish history. Internal tension became inexorably pronounced in Elizabethan government and society. If the English Deborah had constructed the Anglican Church, thwarted rebellion, defeated the Armada, and pacified Ireland, the Tudor stability thus restored, and preserved, was none the less vulnerable to structural decay. Problems that were at first relatively minor gained momentum as the reign progressed, but the queen's caution and immobility prevented her from taking remedial action in time. It was as if the sheer effort of making the Settlement of 1559 had sapped away Elizabeth's creative powers, or perhaps the extent to which she had been pushed into Protestantism then had dissuaded her from permitting further changes in any sphere. Perhaps she was simply too much her father's daughter? In any event, her constancy, so admired in her youth, deteriorated with age into indecisiveness, inertia, and benign neglect.

The most obvious area of decline was that of government.

Did Elizabethan institutions succumb to decay during the war with Spain? Criticism centres on the inadequacy of taxation, local government, and military recruitment; an alleged 'slide to disaster' in the provinces caused by alienation of less exalted 'country' gentlemen from the Court; the rise of corruption in central administration; the abuse of royal prerogative to grant lucrative 'monopolies' or licences in favour of courtiers and their clients, who might also enforce certain statutes for profit; and the claim that the benefits of the Poor Laws were negligible in relation to the rise in population and scale of economic distress in the 1590s.

It is true, Elizabeth and Burghley allowed the taxation system to decline. Not only did the value of a parliamentary subsidy fail to increase in line with inflation despite soaring levels of government expenditure, but receipts dropped in cash terms owing to static tax assessments and widespread evasion. Rates became stereotyped, while the basis of assessment became the taxpayer's unsworn declaration. And whereas Wolsey had attempted to tax wage-earners as well as landowners in Henry VIII's reign, Elizabeth largely abandoned the effort. Although the yield of a subsidy was £140,000 at the beginning of Elizabeth's reign, it was only £80,000 at the end. In Sussex, the average tax assessment of seventy leading families fell from £61 in the 1540s to £14 by the 1620s; and some potential taxpayers escaped altogether. In Suffolk 17,000 taxpayers were assessed for the subsidy of 1523 but only 7,700 for that of 1566. True, the Privy Council ordered subsidy commissioners to ensure that assessments were made impartially and 'answerable to the meaning of Parliament' and 'not so underfoot as heretofore hath been used'. Yet Burghley himself evaded tax, despite holding office as Lord Treasurer after 1572. He grumbled hypocritically in Parliament about tax cheating, but kept his own assessment of income static at £133. 6s. 8d.—his real income was approximately £4,000 per annum. Lord North admitted that few taxpayers were assessed at more than one-sixth or one-tenth of their true wealth, 'and many be 20 times, some 30, and

some much more worth than they be set at, which the commissioner cannot without oath help'. And when arguing in
Parliament for exemption of lesser taxpayers in 1601, Raleigh suggested that while the wealth of a person valued in the subsidy
books at £3 per annum was close to his true worth, 'our estates
that be £30 or £40 in the Queen's books are not the hundredth
part of our wealth'.

The initiative, however, had to come from the Crown. And
the striking feature of Elizabeth's strategy is that while elsewhere European rulers were inventing new taxes under the
pressure of war or threat of invasion, Elizabeth stuck to precedent. She resisted fiscal innovation, extracting some three per
cent of England's national income for the war, whereas Philip II
appropriated 10 per cent of Castile's. She exacted multiple
subsidies after 1589, but these were subject to the law of diminishing returns: the same few taxpayers were assessed using the
same stereotyped valuations, though not even the humblest
taxpayer was charged at modern rates of income tax.

The failure of Elizabethan government to maintain the yield of
the subsidy was the biggest weakness of the late-Tudor state. Yet
Elizabeth left an accumulated debt of only £365,000. Since Mary
had left a debt of £300,000, the comparison (allowing for inflation) is entirely to her sister's credit. Within six years James I
had paid all but £133,500 of this debt, though his own deficits
dwarfed anything envisaged by Elizabeth. But Elizabeth bridged
the gap between receipts and expenditure by sales of Crown
land and borrowing. Lands worth £267,800 were sold between
1560 and 1574, and £608,000 was raised from land sales between 1589 and 1603. Also £461,500 was borrowed during the
war with Spain. Such expedients reduced future revenue and
deprived the Crown of security against loans. Yet how many
early-modern rulers took a long-term view, especially in wartime? It is easy to accuse Elizabeth of mismanagement, but we
tend to forget that she was not accountable to an electorate.

Another point to note is that local taxation escalated under
Elizabeth, especially for poor relief, road and bridge repairs,

and militia expenditure, all of which compensated to some extent for the inadequacy of national taxation. Although this subject is relatively unexplored, it is clear that the recruitment and training of the militia was very expensive and burdened the localities with additional rates which were authorized by Justices of the Peace and collected by hundred and parish constables. Training cost considerable sums by the 1580s; the localities were responsible, too, for providing stocks of parish arms and armour; for paying muster-masters; for repairing coastal forts and building beacons; and for issuing troops mustered for the foreign service with weapons and uniforms, as well as conveying them to the required port of embarkation. In Kent the cost of military preparations borne by the county between 1585 and 1603 exceeded £10,000. True, a proportion of 'coat-and-conduct' money required to equip and transport troops was recoverable from the Exchequer, but in practice the localities met roughly three-quarters of the cost. Also whereas merchant ships (except customarily fishing vessels) had traditionally been requisitioned from coastal towns and counties to augment the royal navy in time of war, the Crown in the 1590s started demanding money as well as ships, and impressed fishermen for service in the royal navy and aboard privateers to the detriment of the local economy. And when the ship money rate was extended to inland areas such as the West Riding of Yorkshire, it aroused opposition to the point where the Crown's right to impose it was questioned.

While, however, the needs and agencies of defence, military recruitment, and finance assumed prominence in Elizabethan government, the backbone of the system remained the local magistracy. The key officials were unsalaried JPs, whose numbers increased from on average fewer than ten for each county in 1500, to forty or fifty by the middle of Elizabeth's reign, and up to ninety by 1603. But the main Tudor innovation in local government was the lieutenancy system made permanent in 1585. Whereas earlier appointments had been temporary, designed to subordinate the shire levies to a single official, the outbreak of war with Spain prompted a new departure. Lieutenancy commissions were issued for nearly all the English and Welsh counties, and the length of the war meant that in many cases the appointees continued in post for life. In general, the lord-lieutenant was the senior resident nobleman or privy councillor in a district, though there were some exceptions. According to his commission, he was to put his district into the best possible state of defence, to which end he was authorized to muster everyone eligible for service overseas or in the trained bands, arm them, drill them, and if necessary discipline them by invoking martial law. If martial law were needed, a provost marshal was to be appointed to execute it. Lastly, all other local officials were to obey and assist lieutenants and their deputies.

Throughout, the Crown's policy was *ad hoc* and reflected military and political needs. But the appointments assisted stability for two reasons. First, lieutenants were given direct lines of communication to the Privy Council; second, the function matched military needs to aristocratic traditions. The defence of the realm against the Crown's enemies was the ancient role of the nobility, satisfying their honour and justifying their privileges. Yet whereas under Henry VII's and Henry VIII's military system the nobility mustered their feudal retinues as quasi-independent territorial magnates, Elizabeth's lieutenants were agents of the Crown who could be dismissed or summoned to answer for their conduct. And since so many were privy councillors, they responded more readily to central government initiatives than did JPs. They sent a steady flow of information from the localities back to the Privy Council, forging a bilateral chain of communication between central and local government. The tempo visibly quickened in local administration as better records were kept, ordnance depots were established, new transport facilities were provided, members of the trained bands began to be recruited for overseas service alongside the forced levies, and elaborate arrangements were made for one county to send its men to defend another.

Yet the strain of a war economy was cumulative: 105,800

men were impressed for service in the Netherlands, France, Portugal, and Ireland during the last eighteen years of the reign. Conscription for Ireland after 1595 aroused the greatest resentment. In 1600 there was a near mutiny of Kentish cavalry at Chester as they travelled to Ulster. So pressure on the counties led to administrative breakdowns and opposition to central government's demands, while disruption of trade, outbreaks of plague (much of it imported by soldiers returning from abroad), ruined harvests in 1596 and 1597, and acute economic depression caused widespread resentment. Yet the idea of an Elizabethan 'slide to disaster' remains unproven. In the 1590s tension between 'Court' and 'country' was neither as ideological as it was under Charles I, nor did it represent much more than war-weariness and dislike of fiscal burdens. Even in 1598–1601, local resistance to official demands remained largely passive, with exceptions only in coastal counties such as Norfolk.

At the level of central government, however, rising corruption signalled the drift towards venality. In particular, the shortage of Crown patronage during the long war and log-jam in promotion prospects encouraged a traffic in offices. Corruption was not inevitable: official salaries had been raised by Henry VIII, while improved methods of provisioning and the possibility of taking subsistence allowances in either cash or kind compensated to an extent for the rising cost of living. So corruption sprang less from poverty than from increased tolerance of dishonesty during the 1590s. On the other hand, the patronage log-jam was genuine. Whereas the Crown possessed 1,200 or so offices worthy of a gentleman's standing in Elizabeth's reign, Henry VIII had enjoyed similar patronage at a time when aspiring gentry were fewer and official pluralism less pronounced. Also the Reformation had ended the system whereby many of the Crown's bureaucrats were rewarded by preferment as non-resident clergy. Yet research suggests that Elizabeth staved off the worst abuses of the patronage system during her reign. She vetted candidates for office, while contriving to ensure that her discretion was not undermined by collusion between suitors and courtiers. If she suspected deceit, she would invoke her talent for procrastination. Competition at Court, especially during the war years, nevertheless created a 'black market' in which influence was bought and sold. Offices were overtly traded, but unlike Henry VII's sales, the Crown rarely profited financially. Payments were made instead to courtiers to influence the queen's choice: benefit to the Crown was restricted to the increase in New Year's gifts Elizabeth received when appointments were pending. So for a minor post £200 or so would be offered, with competitive bids of £1,000 to £4,000 taken for such lucrative offices as the receivership of the court of wards or treasurership at war. And bids were investments, since if an appointment resulted, the new incumbent would so exercise his office as to recoup his outlay plus interest, for which reason the system was corrupt by Tudor as well as modern standards because the public interest was sacrificed to private gain.

Where late Elizabethan government aroused more vocal dissent was in the matters of licences and monopolies. Clashes in 1597 and 1601 were the ugliest in Parliament during the Tudor period. They signalled unequivocal resentment of abuses promoted by courtiers and government officials. True, some monopolies or licences were genuine patents or copyrights, while others established trading companies with overseas bases which also provided valuable consular services for merchants abroad. But many were designed simply to corner the market in commodities for the patentees, or to grant them exclusive rights which enabled them to demand payments from manufacturers or tradesmen for carrying out their legitimate businesses. They had doubled the price of steel; tripled that of starch; caused that of imported glasses to rise fourfold; and that of salt elevenfold. Courtiers enforced them with impunity, since patents rested on royal prerogative—the common-law courts lacked the power to vet them without royal assent. Indignation was first vented in Parliament in the 1570s, but it was the late Elizabethan mushrooming of monopolies that provoked the backlash. When the young lawyer, William Hakewill, cried, 'Is not bread there?', Elizabeth had personally to intervene to neutralize the attack. And in 1601 she averted the crisis at the expense of the patentees: a proclamation annulled twelve monopolies condemned in Parliament and authorized subjects grieved by other patents to seek redress in the courts of common law.

The final criticism levelled against late Elizabethan government is that the benefits of the Poor Laws were crushed by the rise of Tudor population and economic distress of the 1590s. Although this question raises problems, a Malthusian diagnosis can be eliminated. The Elizabethan state profited from a steadily rising birth-rate that coincided with increased life expectancy. In particular, mortality emergencies of 1586–7 and 1594–8 were not national in geographical extent. The death-rate jumped by 21 per cent in 1596–7, and by a further 5 per cent in 1597–8. But fewer parishes experienced crisis mortality than during the influenza epidemic of 1555–9. And later economic depressions in 1625–6 and 1638–9 were more severe. On the other hand, agricultural prices climbed higher in real terms in 1594–8 than at any time before 1615, while real wages plunged lower in 1597 than at any time between 1260 and 1950. Perhaps two-fifths of the population fell below the margin of subsistence: malnutrition reached the point of starvation in the uplands of Cumbria; disease spread unchecked; reported crimes against property increased; and thousands of families were thrown on to parish relief.

So in a material sense the Poor Laws must have been inadequate. The estimated cash yield of endowed charities for poor relief by 1600 totalled £11,700 per annum—one-quarter of one per cent of national income. Yet the estimated amount raised by poor rates was smaller. If these figures are correct, what was audible was not a bang but a whimper. Yet food and enclosure riots were markedly fewer than might be expected. At a different level the Poor Laws operated as a placebo: the 'labouring poor' were persuaded that their social superiors shared their view of the social order and denounced the same 'caterpillars of the commonwealth'—chiefly middlemen.

The pessimism of the Tudor twilight is partially balanced by positive advances, notably in domestic housing. The years from 1570 to 1610 have no formal significance, but they nevertheless mark the first key phase of the English housing revolution. Probate inventories suggest that from 1530 to 1569 the average size of the Tudor house was three rooms. Between 1570 and the end of Elizabeth's reign it was four or five rooms. The period 1610–42, which was the second phase of the revolution, saw the figure rise to six or more rooms. After 1570, prosperous yeomen might have six, seven, or eight rooms; husbandmen might aspire to two or three rooms, as opposed to the one-room cottages ubiquitous in 1500. Richer farmers would build a chamber over the open hall, replacing the open hearth with a chimney stack. Poorer people favoured ground-floor extensions: a kitchen, or second bedchamber, would be added to an existing cottage. Kitchens were often separate buildings, probably to reduce the risk of fire. A typical late Elizabethan farmstead might be described as 'one dwelling house of three bays, one barn of three bays, one kitchen of one bay'. Meanwhile there were corresponding improvements in domestic comfort. The average investment in hard and soft furniture, tableware, and kitchenware in Tudor England prior to 1570 was around £7. Between 1570 and 1603 it rose to £10. 10s., and in the early Stuart period it climbed to £17. The value of household goods of wealthier families rose by 250 per cent between 1570 and 1610, and that of middling and lesser persons slightly exceeded even that high figure. These percentages were in excess of the inflation rate.

In the upper echelons of society, Elizabethan great houses were characterized by innovations founded on Tudor stability and rising standards of comfort. English architecture after about 1580 was inspired by Gothic ideals of chivalry as much as by Renaissance classicism. The acres of glass and towering symmetry of Hardwick Hall, Derbyshire, built in 1591–7 by Robert Smythson for Elizabeth, countess of Shrewsbury, paid homage to the Perpendicular splendour of King's College Chapel, Cambridge. But if Elizabethan Gothic architecture was neo-medieval in its outward profile, the aim was for enhanced standards of sophistication within. In any case, the neo-medieval courtyards, gatehouses, moats, parapets, towers, and turrets of Tudor England were ornamental, not utilitarian. The parapets at Hardwick incorporated the initials E.S. (Elizabeth Shrewsbury)—the decorative device that proclaimed the parvenue. Brick chimneys became a familiar feature of Tudor mansions, and they signified the arrival of the kitchen and service quarters within the main house, either into a wing or a semi-basement. As time progressed, basement services became fairly common, and were particularly favoured in town houses built on restricted sites. Household servants began to be relegated to the subterranean caverns from which it took three centuries to rescue them.

Yet this was not coincidental. The Elizabethan mansion was the first of its genre to equate privacy with domestic comfort. The great hall of the medieval manor house was not abandoned, but it gave way to the long gallery, hung with historical portraits, where private conversations could be conducted without constant interruption from the traffic of servants. In fact, these Elizabethan long galleries were modelled on those erected in Tudor palaces earlier in the century. An interesting early example was Wolsey's gallery at Hampton Court, where in 1527 Henry VIII and Sir Thomas More had paced uneasily together as they first discussed the terms of the king's proposed divorce. In similar fashion, ground-floor parlours replaced the great hall as the customary family sitting and dining-rooms—at least for normal daily purposes. The family lived in the ground-floor parlours and the first-floor chambers; the servants worked on both these floors and in the basement, and slept in the attics or turrets. Staircases were revitalized as a result: the timber-framed structure gradually became an architectural feature in itself. Finally, provision of fresh-water supplies and improved sanitary arrangements reflected the Renaissance concern with private and public health. In the case of town houses, the family would often go to immense lengths to solve drainage

problems, sometimes paying a cash composition to the municipal authorities, but frequently performing some service for the
town at Court or at Westminster in return for unlimited water
or drainage.

These improvements in Tudor housing were complemented
by technical progress in the fields of art and music. Nicholas
Hilliard became the most influential painter at the Elizabethan
Court on the strength of his ravishing miniatures. Trained as a
goldsmith, Hilliard earned renown for his techniques as a 'lim-
ner', or illuminator of portrait gems that captured the 'lovely
graces, witty smilings, and these stolen glances which suddenly
like lightning pass, and another countenance taketh place.' Intimacy was the key to this style, combined with a wealth of
emblematic allusion that added intellectual depth to the mirror-
like image portrayals. In Hilliard's hands, the miniature was far
more than a mere reduced version of an easel painting—but
that was thanks to his creative invention. To enhance the techniques learned in the workshops of Ghent and Bruges, where
the miniature was painted on fine vellum and pasted on to card,
Hilliard used gold as a metal, burnishing it 'with a pretty little
tooth of some ferret or stoat or other wild little beast'. Dia-
mond effects were simulated with utter conviction, and Hilliard's jewel-bedecked lockets were often worn as talismans, or
exchanged as pledges of love between sovereign and subject or
knight and lady. Hilliard's techniques were passed on to his
pupil, Isaac Oliver, and finally to Samuel Cooper. The miniature was ultimately confounded by the invention of photo-
graphy.

Tudor music was invigorated by royal and noble patronage,
by the continued liturgical demands of the Church, and by the
steady abandonment of the strict modal limitations of the
medieval period in favour of more progressive techniques of
composition and performance. The Tudor monarchs, together
with Cardinal Wolsey, were distinguished patrons of music
both sacred and secular. An inventory of Henry VIII's musical
instruments suggests that as lavish a selection was available in

England as anywhere in Europe—the king himself favoured the lute and organ. His and Wolsey's private chapels competed to recruit the best organists and singers to be found in England and Wales. In Mary's reign, England was exposed to the potent artistry of Flemish and Spanish music, while the seminal influence of Italy was always present in the shape of Palestrina's motets and the works of the Florentine madrigalists. Elizabeth I retained a large corps of Court musicians drawn from Italy, Germany, France, and England itself. But her Chapel Royal was the premier conservatoire of Tudor musical talent and invention, for Thomas Tallis, William Byrd, and John Bull made their careers there. The Protestant Reformation happily encouraged, rather than abandoned, composers—the Edwardian and Elizabethan injunctions left liturgical music intact, and many of the gentlemen of the Chapel discreetly remained Catholics, including Byrd and Bull. Yet it was the technical advances that really mattered. Byrd and Bull gradually freed themselves from the old ecclesiastical modes, or ancient scales. Tallis and Byrd gained a licence for music printing that enabled them to pioneer printed musical notation, albeit unsuccessfully. Melody, harmony, and rhythm became as important to music as plainsong and counterpoint, and the arts of ornamentation and extemporization thrived among the virginalists, and among the lute and consort players. Such developments presaged the music of seventeenth-century English and Continental composers, and ultimately that of J. S. Bach.

The age of the Tudors ended on an equivocal note, which is best discerned in its literature. Erasmus's wit and More's satirical fiction expressed (though in Latin) the intellectual exuberance of pre-Reformation Europe. Sir Thomas Elyot, Sir John Cheke, and Roger Ascham translated Renaissance ideals into pedestrian but tolerable English prose. Sir Thomas Wyatt, Henry Howard, earl of Surrey, and Sir Philip Sidney reanimated English lyric poetry and rekindled the sonnet as the vehicle of eloquent and classical creativity. But it was Edmund Spenser who rediscovered to perfection what English prosody had lacked since the time of Chaucer. Once again, music tutored the ear, and the connections between ear and tongue were fully realized. Spenser attained an impeccable mastery of rhythm, time, and tune—his work was no mere 'imitation of the ancients'. In particular, his harmonious blend of northern and midland with southern dialects permitted verbal modulations and changes of diction and mood akin to those of lute players. His pastoral sequence, *The Shepheards Calendar* (1579), was a landmark in the history of English poetry, its melodious strains encapsulating the pains and pleasures of pastoral life.

> Colin, to heare thy rymes and roundelayes,
> Which thou wert wont on wastfull hylls to singe,
> I more delight then larke in Sommer dayes;
> Whose Echo made the neyghbour groves to ring,
> And taught the byrds, which in the lower spring
> Did shroude in shady leaves from sonny rayes,
> Frame to thy songe their chereful cheriping,
> Or hold theyr peace, for shame of thy swete layes.

Spenser's masterpiece was *The Faerie Queene* (1589 and 1596), an allegorical epic poem, which examined on a dazzling multiplicity of levels the nature and quality of the late-Elizabethan polity. The form of the poem was Gothic as much as Renaissance: the Gothic 'revival' in architecture after 1580 was paralleled by its episodic sequences, within which details took on their own importance, decorating the external symmetry without damaging the total effect. The poem above all, though, was an allegory. As Spenser explained in a dedicatory epistle to Sir Walter Raleigh, 'In that Fairy Queen I mean glory in my general intention, but in my particular I conceive the most excellent and glorious person of our sovereign the Queen, and her kingdom in Fairy land. And yet, in some places else, I do otherwise shadow her.' In other words, Spenser's allegory was part moral, part fictional—there was no easy or straightforward correspondence of meaning. Yet the allegory had a single end; as in *Piers Plowman* before it, and *Pilgrim's Progress* afterwards, *The Faerie Queene* led the reader along the path upon which truth was distinguishable from falsehood. To this end, the ambition, corruption, intrigue, and secular-mindedness of Elizabethan power politics were sublimated into the 'delightful land of Faerie', clothed in the idyllic garments of romance, and exalted as the fictional realization of the golden age of Gloriana.

It was inevitable that Spenser should fail to impress the Elizabethan establishment. He informed Raleigh that his 'general end' was 'to fashion a gentleman or noble person in virtuous and gentle discipline'. Yet the ambiguities were pervasive: Spenser saw his goal as already archaic. Chivalry had been soured by Renaissance politics and statecraft; the 'verray parfit, gentil knyght' of Chaucer's age had been displaced by the Tudor courtier. The golden age had passed, if it had ever existed:

> So oft as I with state of present time
> The image of the antique world compare,
> When as mans age was in his freshest prime,
> And the first blossome of faire vertue bare;
> Such oddes I finde twixt those, and these which are,
> As that, through long continuance of his course,
> Me seemes the world is runne quite out of square
> From the first point of his appointed sourse;
> And being once amisse growes daily wourse and wourse.

Spenser's allegory in *The Faerie Queene* was unquestionably over-complex; his attempt to fuse worldly and idealized principles of behaviour into a single dramatic epic was bound to prove unmanageable. Moreover, the reader was obliged to unriddle endless personifications of Elizabeth as the moon-goddess Diana (or Cynthia or Belphoebe), of Sir Walter Raleigh as Timias, of Mary Stuart as Duessa, who also doubled as Theological Falsehood—and so on. However, Spenser's failure to convince, as opposed to his poetic ability to delight, actually *heightens* our impression of his disillusion and despair. We are taught to debunk the myth of Gloriana; art has held 'the mirror up to nature' and shown 'the very age and body of the time his form and pressure'.

Another faithful mirror of the Tudor age was that held by the immortal William Shakespeare. Author of thirty-eight plays that included *Hamlet* (1600–1), *King Lear* (1605–6), and *Othello* (1604), and of 154 Sonnets (1593–7), together with *Venus and Adonis* and *The Rape of Lucrece* (1593–4), Shakespeare has exerted greater influence on English literature and European drama than any other single writer. The sheer vitality, power, and virtuosity of his work remain unmatched in any European language; his genius exceeded that of Chaucer or Tennyson—it need not be justified or explained. We should, however, remember that Shakespeare was not an 'intellectual' or 'élitist' writer, like Milton or Voltaire. His orbit centred on Stratford and London, not Oxford and Cambridge. His was the everyday world of life, death, money, passion, stage business, and the alehouse—such matters became the stuff of peerless drama and poetry. The rich variety of his experience is perhaps the chief reason for the universality of his appeal; certainly there is no hint of the bigot or intellectual snob in his work.

Shakespeare's experience was, nevertheless, that of a writer at the cultural crossroads of Europe. After about 1580, European literature explored increasingly the modes of individual expression and characterization associated with modern processes of thought. Authors and the fictional characters they created displayed awareness both of experience in general, and of themselves as the particular agents of unique experiences. Shakespeare's *Hamlet* and Christopher Marlowe's *Doctor Faustus* (1592) epitomize the dramatic depiction of individual experience in Elizabethan literature. Of the two plays, *Hamlet* is the more advanced. Shakespeare took a familiar plot and transformed it into a timeless masterpiece. But Marlowe's *Faustus* was not far behind. Both dramatists were eager to pursue psychology, rather than ethics. The difference is that Faustus does not pass beyond the bounds of egotism and self-dramatization to realize self-analysis, whereas Hamlet's subjective introspection and self-doubts are the keystones of the action.

What a piece of work is a man! how noble in reason! how infinite in
faculties! in form and moving, how express and admirable! in action,
how like an angel! in apprehension, how like a god! the beauty of the
world! the paragon of animals! And yet to me, what is this quintes-
sence of dust?

(Hamlet, ii. ii. 323–9)

Neoplatonist philosophy as practised at the dawn of the
sixteenth century by John Colet and his circle had dealt with
the objective appreciation of senses, natures, and truth—this
reflected the medieval cast of mind. Eighty or so years later, the
emphasis had shifted towards subjectivity and self-expression,
paradoxically under the influence of Calvinist theology, which
so stressed the inflexibility of God's predestined Word that a
person's quest for grace necessarily came to depend on systematic self-scrutiny. Calvinism was also replacing the medieval
ideal of chivalry with the notion of the permanent spiritual
warfare of God's elect against worldly thraldom.

Marlowe and Shakespeare dominated Elizabethan drama,
although they did not monopolize it. The allegories and morality plays of the fifteenth century flourished until suppressed,
especially in such provincial towns as Chester, Coventry, and
York. But the Brave New World was symbolized by Shakespeare's Globe Theatre in London, where the impact of the
Protestant Reformation had combined with the enhanced
sophistication of metropolitan life to give distinctive shape to
the preferred drama of modern Britain. Self-expression, individuality, and the soliloquy were the cultural developments that
paralleled the expansion of education and literacy, the birth of
the nonconformist conscience, and the growth of cosmopolitan
attitudes.

Yet Hamlet's melancholy defeated his self-knowledge. He
remained uncertain of his destiny, and of the reason for his
existence:

To be, or not to be: that is the question:
Whether 'tis nobler in the mind to suffer

> The slings and arrows of outrageous fortune,
> Or to take arms against a sea of troubles,
> And by opposing end them? To die: to sleep;
> No more; and, by a sleep to say we end
> The heart-ache and the thousand natural shocks
> That flesh is heir to, 'tis a consummation
> Devoutly to be wish'd.
>
> (*Hamlet*, III. i. 56–64)

Such sentiments were equally applicable to the dusk of Tudor England. When the bell tolled for the age of Gloriana, on 24 March 1603, Elizabeth had already lost her will to survive, Burghley was five years dead, and a newly ambitious and less scrupulous generation of courtiers was ascendant. It is easy to romanticize or eulogize such Tudor triumphs as stability, economic expansion, the Reformation, the repulse of Spain, the defeat of Protestant and Catholic extremism, and the unification of Britain—finally attained on Elizabeth's death. But reality is more abrasive. Stability had begun to breed instability through structural decay. By the 1620s England would be unable to fight a protracted war without engendering domestic political friction. When Clarendon later began his *History of the Rebellion and Civil Wars* he wrote: 'I am not so sharpsighted as those, who have discerned this rebellion contriving from (if not before) the death of Queen Elizabeth.' He knew that if we read history backwards, Elizabeth's inertia and immobility in the 1590s, combined with the rise of 'venality' at Court, could be said to have established a pattern that precluded comprehensive reform. But history is properly read forwards. When this is done, it is clear that a 'slide to disaster' was unlikely in the sixteenth century. Elizabeth controlled her own policy; the Privy Council was a tightly organized body; communications with the localities were good; a Protestant consensus had emerged. Yet the Tudor legacy of meagre public revenue and endemic corruption in the central bureaucracy was ultimately ameliorated *by* the events of the Civil War and Interregnum.

6. *The Stuarts*
(1603–1688)

JOHN MORRILL

THE Stuarts were one of England's least successful dynasties. Charles I was put on public trial for treason and was publicly beheaded; James II fled the country fearing a similar fate, and abandoned his kingdom and throne. James I and Charles II died peacefully in their beds, but James I lived to see all his hopes fade and ambitions thwarted, while Charles II, although he had the trappings of success, was a curiously unambitious man, whose desire for a quiet life was not achieved until it was too late for him to enjoy it. Towering above the Stuart age were the two decades of civil war, revolution, and republican experiment which ought to have changed fundamentally the course of English history, but which did so, if at all, very elusively. Whilst kings and generals toiled and failed, however, a fundamental change was taking place in English economy and society, largely unheeded and certainly unfashioned by the will of government. In fact, the most obvious revolution in seventeenth-century England was the consequence of a decline in the birth-rate.

Society and Economic Life

The population of England had been growing steadily from the early sixteenth century, if not earlier. It continued to grow in the first half of the seventeenth century. The total population of England in 1600 was probably fairly close to 4.1 million (and Scotland, Ireland, and Wales, much more impressionistically, 1.9 million). By the mid-century, the population of England had reached a peak of almost 5.3 million, and the total for Britain had risen from roughly 6.0 to roughly 7.7 million. Thereafter, the number stabilized, or may even have sagged to 4.9 million in England, 7.3 million in Britain. The reasons for the rise in population, basically a steady progression with occasional set-backs resulting from epidemics before 1650, and the subsequent relapse, are very puzzling. The best recent research has placed most emphasis on the family-planning habits of the population. Once the plague had lost its virulence, a country like England, in which land was plentiful and extremes of weather never such as to wipe out entire harvests, was likely to see population growth. Each marriage was likely to produce more than enough children who would survive to adulthood to maintain the population. The rate of population growth was in fact kept rather low by the English custom of late marriage. In all social groups, marriage was usually deferred until both partners were in their mid-twenties and the wife had only twelve to fifteen childbearing years before her. The reason for this pattern of late marriage seems to be the firm convention that the couple save up enough money to launch themselves as an independent household before they wed. For the better off, this frequently meant university, legal training, an apprenticeship of seven years or more; for the less well off a long term of domestic service, living in with all found but little in the way of cash wages.

This pattern continued into the late seventeenth century with even later marriages; perhaps the real earnings of the young had fallen so that sufficient savings took longer to generate. At any rate the average age of first marriage seems to have risen by a further two years to over twenty-six, with a consequent effect on fertility. More dramatic still is the evidence of a will to restrict family size. Steps were clearly taken in families with

three or more children to prevent or inhibit further conceptions. For example, mothers would breast-feed third or subsequent children for many more months than they would their
first or second child, with the (effective) intention of lowering
fertility. Crude contraceptive devices and sexual prudence were
also clearly widespread. Some studies of gentry families even
suggest that celibacy became much more common (the growth
of the Navy may be partly responsible for this unexpected
development!). In South Wales, one in three of all heads
of leading gentry families remained unmarried in the late
seventeenth century compared with a negligible proportion one
hundred years earlier; while the average numbers of children
per marriage declined from five to two and a half (which, given
the high rate of child mortality, meant that a high proportion
of those families died out). It is not known whether this was
typical of the gentry everywhere or of other social groups. But
it does graphically illustrate changing demographic patterns.

The economic, social, and political consequences were
momentous. In the century before 1640, population was growing faster than food resources. One result of this was occasional
and localized food shortages so severe as to occasion hunger,
starvation, and death. It is possible that some Londoners died
of starvation at the end of the sixteenth and at the beginning of
the seventeenth-centuries and quite certain that many did so in
Cumbria in the early 1620s. Thereafter, famine disappears as
a visible threat, in England at least. Increased agricultural production, better communication and lines of credit, and the
levelling off of population solved the problem. England escaped
the periodic dearths and widespread starvation that were to
continue to devastate its continental neighbours for decades to
come.

A more persistent effect of population growth was price
inflation. Food prices rose eightfold in the period 1500–1640,
wages less than threefold. For most of those who did not
produce their own food, and enough of it to feed themselves
and their household with a surplus to sell in the market, it was

a century of financial attrition. Above all, for the growing proportion of the nation who depended upon wage-labouring, the century witnessed a major decline in living standards. In fact, a large section of the population—certainly a majority— had to buy much of their food, and these purchases took up an increasing proportion of their income. It became a central concern of government to regulate the grain trade and to provide both local machinery and an administrative code, backed up by legal sanctions, to ensure that whenever there was harvest failure, available stocks of grain and other produce were made widely available at the lowest extra cost which could be achieved.

A growing population put pressure not only on food resources but on land. With families producing on average more than one son, either family property had to be divided, reducing the endowment of each member for the next generation, or one son took over the family land or tenancy while the others had to fend for themselves. The high prices of agricultural produce made it worth while to plough, or otherwise to farm marginal lands hitherto uneconomic, but in most regions by the early seventeenth century there was little unoccupied land left to be so utilized. The way forward lay with the more productive use of existing farmed land, particularly in woodland areas or in the Fenland where existing conditions (inundations by the sea or winter rain) made for only limited usage. The problem here was that the drainage of the Fens or the clearing of woodland areas was costly, had to be undertaken by those with risk capital, and had to be at the expense of the life-style, livelihood, and modest prosperity of those who lived there. Once again, government was forced to be active in mediating (or more often vacillating) between encouraging higher productivity and guarding against the anguish and protest of those adversely affected.

A growing population also put pressure on jobs. By the early seventeenth century there was widespread underemployment in England. Agriculture remained the major source of employment, but the work in the fields was seasonal and hundreds of thousands found lay labouring sufficient for part but not all of the year. Because, however, labour was plentiful and cheap, because most manufacturing relied exclusively on muscle power rather than a form of energy that would draw workers to its source, because raw materials walked about on, grew up out of, or lay dormant within the land, 'industry' in the seventeenth century took place in cottages and outbuildings of rural village communities. For some, especially in the metal-working and building trades, 'manufacturing' would be the primary source of income. For others, as in some textile trades, it could be a primary or secondary source of income. Textiles were by far the largest 'manufacture' with perhaps 200,000 workers scattered throughout England, above all in the south-west, in East Anglia, or in the Pennine region. It was a particularly volatile industry, however, with high food prices dampening the domestic market and war and foreign competition sharply reducing foreign markets in the early seventeenth century. Tens of thousands of families, however, could not balance the household budget whatever they tried. Injury, disability, or death made them particularly vulnerable to a shortfall of revenue. There was chronic 'under-employment': a structural problem of too many part-time workers seeking full-time work.

At Aldenham in Hertfordshire, about one in ten households needed regular support from the poor rate but a further one in four (making over one-third in all) needed occasional doles or allowances (for example of fuel or clothes) to ease them through difficult patches. For a large number of families, achieving subsistence involved scrounging or scavenging fuel or wild fruit and vegetables and seeking periodic help from local charities or the rates—what has been called the 'economy of makeshifts'. One effect of the difficulties of rural employment was to drive large numbers of men and women into the cities—above all to London—where the problems were no less but rather more volatile. There was a large amount of casual unskilled labour in the towns, but casual work could shrink rapidly in times of recession or harvest failure. High food prices meant less demand for other goods and this in turn meant less scope for non-agricultural wages. Those who most needed additional wages for food were most likely to find less work available. Once more, the government had been drawn in to organize and superintend a national scheme of poor relief, and ancillary codes of practice governing geographical mobility, house building, and the promotion of overseas trade. Thus a growing population greatly increased the duties and responsibilities of the government, arguably beyond the Crown's resources and capacity. Those who produced and sold goods, those who could benefit from the land hunger in increased rents and dues, and those who serviced an increasingly complex and uncertain market in lands and goods (notably the lawyers) wanted to enjoy the fruits of their success; others looked to the Crown to prevent or to mitigate the effects of structural change. A dynamic economy is one in which government has to arbitrate between competing and irreconcilable interests. No wonder the Crown found itself disparaged and increasingly distrusted.

By contrast, the late seventeenth-century saw the easing, if not the disappearance, of these problems. The slight population decline in itself prevented the problems from getting worse. The upsurge in agricultural productivity was more important. The nature and extent of agricultural change in the seventeenth century is still much disputed. What is clear is that England ceased from about the 1670s to be a net importer of grain and became an exporter; indeed, bounties had to be introduced to ensure that surplus stocks were not hoarded. This remarkable turn-around may have been the result of a massive extension of the acreage under the plough—either by the ploughing of land not hitherto farmed or by land amelioration schemes. But it might also be the result of the introduction of new methods of farming which dramatically increased the yield per acre. By skilful alternation of crops and more extensive use of manure and fertilizers, it is possible to increase yields of grain and to sustain much greater livestock levels. Almost all the ideas which were to transform English agriculture down to the early nineteenth century were known about by 1660; indeed most of them had been tried and tested in the Netherlands. The problem is to discover how rapidly they were taken up. There was stubborn conservatism, especially among the yeomen; the good ideas lay mingled in the textbooks with some equally plausible ones which were in fact specious; the most effective methods required considerable rationalization of land use and some of them required high capital outlay. In the early part of the century, it seems likely that the most widespread innovations were not those which increased yields, but those which soaked up cheap surplus employment—especially 'industrial' cash crops that had to be turned into manufactures: dye crops, tobacco, mulberry trees (for silkworms). It was only when a falling population raised real wages and lowered grain prices that the impetus to increase productivity replaced the desire to extend the scale of operation as a primary motivation of the farmer. Changes in the way land was rented out also gave the landlord better prospects of seeing a return on the money he invested in land leased out. The new farming probably consolidated the position established earlier by the simple device of increasing the acreage under the plough. Either way, government action in the grain market and the regulation of wages became far less frequent and necessary.

In 1600, England still consisted of a series of regional economies striving after, if not always achieving, self-sufficiency. Problems of credit and of distribution hindered the easy exchange of produce between regions. Most market towns, even the large county towns, were principally places where the produce of the area was displayed and sold. By 1690 this was no longer the case. England had for long been the largest free trade area in Europe and had the Crown had its way at most points in the century, the full integration of Ireland and Scotland into a customs-free zone would have been achieved or brought nearer. That it was not owed most to the narrow self-interest of lobbyists in the House of Commons, especially in the 1600s and the 1660s. No point in England was (or is) more than seventy-five miles from the sea, and as a result of the schemes to improve river navigation, few places by 1690 were more than twenty miles from water navigable to the sea. Gradually, a single, integrated national economy was emerging. No longer did each region have to strive for self-sufficiency, producing low-quality goods in poor-grade soil or inhospitable climate. Regional specializations could emerge, taking full advantage of soil and climatic conditions, which could then be exchanged for surplus grain or dairy products from elsewhere. Hence, the spread of market-gardening in Kent.

Exactly the same could be said for manufactures. One consequence of and further stimulus to this was a retailing revolution—the coming of age of the shop. The characteristic of market towns was the market-stall or shambles, in which the stall-holders or retailers displayed their own wares which they had grown, made, or at least finished from local raw materials. By 1690, most towns, even quite small ones, had shops in the modern sense: places which did not distribute the produce of the region but which met the variegated needs of the region. The shopkeeper met those needs from far and wide. One particularly well-documented example is William Stout who, in the 1680s, rented a shop in Lancaster for £5 per annum. He visited London and Sheffield and bought goods worth over £200, paid for half in cash (a legacy from his father), half on credit. Soon he was purchasing goods from far and wide and offering the people of Lancaster and its environs a wide variety of produce: West Indian sugar, American tobacco, West Riding ironmongery, and so on. None the less, once towns became centres for the distribution of the produce of the world, people would tend to bypass the smaller towns with little choice and make for the bigger centres with maximum choice. This is why most seventeenth-century urban growth was concentrated in existing large market towns. The proportion of the population living in the twenty or so towns which already had 10,000 inhabitants rose sharply; the proportion living in the smaller market towns actually fell slightly. Some small centres of manufacturing (metalworking towns such as Birmingham and Sheffield, or cloth-finishing towns such as Manchester or Leeds, or ship-building towns such as Chatham) became notable urban centres. But the twenty largest towns in 1690 were almost the same as the twenty largest in 1600. All of them were on the coast or on navigable rivers.

Large towns, then, prospered because of their changing role in marketing. But many of them—and county towns especially —increasingly concentrated not only on the sale of goods; they began to concentrate on the sale of services. The pull of the shops and the burgeoning importance of county towns as local administrative centres in which hundreds gathered regularly for local courts and commissions, encouraged the service and leisure industries. Gentlemen and prosper-ous farmers came to town for business or for the shops, and would stop to take professional advice from lawyers, doctors, estate agents; or bring their families and stay over for a round of social exchanges linked by visits to the theatre, concerts, or new recreational facilities. The age of the spa and the resort was dawning.

Paris, the largest town in France, had 350,000 inhabitants in the mid-seventeenth century. The second and third largest were Rouen and Lyons with 80,000–100,000 inhabitants. In Europe, there were only five towns with populations of more than 250,000, but over one hundred with more than 50,000 inhabit-ants. In England, however, London had well over half a million inhabitants by 1640 or 1660; Newcastle, Bristol, and Nor-wich, which rivalled one another for second place, had barely 25,000 each. London was bigger than the next fifty towns in England combined. It is hard to escape the conclusion that London was growing at the expense of the rest. Its stranglehold on overseas trade, and therefore on most of the early banking and financial activity, was slow to ease; in consequence much of the trade from most of the outports had to be directed via London. In the seventeenth century the major new 're-export' trades (the importation of colonial raw materials such as sugar and tobacco for finishing and dispatch to Europe) were concentrated there. London dominated the governmental, legal, and political world. While rural England flourished under the opportunities to feed the capital and keep its inhabitants warm, urban growth was probably slowed. By 1640, 10 per cent of all Englishmen lived in the capital, and one in six had lived part of their lives there. By 1690 the richest one hundred Londoners were among the richest men in England. No longer was wealth primarily the perquisite of the landed.

If goods moved more freely within a national economy, people may have become more rooted in their own community. Both before and after the Civil War, more than two-thirds of all Englishmen died in a parish different from the one in which they were born. But both before and after the wars, most did not move far; most stayed within their county of birth. It is possible to distinguish two patterns of migration. The first is 'betterment migration' as adolescents and young adults moved to take up apprenticeship or tenancies of farms. This migration throughout the century was essentially local except for movement from all over the country to London for apprenticeships. The second is 'subsistence migration', as those who found no work or prospect of work at home took to the road, often travelling long distances in the hope of finding employment elsewhere. Such migration was far more common in the first half of the century than in the second, partly because demographic stagnation and economic development created a better chance of jobs at home, partly because the general easing of demands on poor relief made parish authorities more sympathetic to the able-bodied unemployed, and partly because tough settlement laws inhibited and discouraged migration. An Act of Parliament in 1662 gave constables and overseers power to punish those who moved from parish to parish in search of vacant common land or wasteland on which to build cottages.

The seventeenth century is probably the first in England history in which more people emigrated than immigrated. In the course of the century, something over one-third of a million people—mainly young adult males—emigrated across the Atlantic. The largest single group made for the West Indies; a second substantial group made for Virginia and for Catholic Maryland; a very much smaller group made for Puritan New England. The pattern of emigration was a fluctuating one, but it probably reached its peak in the 1650s and 1660s. For most of those who went, the search for employment and a better life was almost certainly the principal cause of their departure. For a clear minority, however, freedom from religious persecution and the expectation that they could establish churches to worship God in their preferred fashion took precedence. An increasing number were forcibly transported as a punishment for criminal acts or (particularly in the 1650s) simply as a punishment for vagrancy. In addition to the transatlantic settlers, an unknown number crossed the English Channel and settled in Europe. The largest group were probably the sons of Catholic families making for religious houses or mercenary military activity. Younger sons of Protestant gentlemen also enlisted in the latter. Many hundreds were to return to fight the English Civil War. Thus, whereas the sixteenth century had seen England become a noted haven for religious refugees, in the seventeenth century Europe and America received religious refugees from England. The early seventeenth century probably saw less immigration from abroad than for many decades before. The only significant immigration in the seventeenth century was of Jews who flocked in after the Cromwellian regime had removed the legal bars on their residence, and of French Huguenots escaping from Louis XIV's persecution in the 1680s.

Fewer men set up home far from the place of their birth. But many more men travelled the length and breadth of England. There was a tripling or a quadrupling of the number of packmen, carriers, and others engaged in moving goods about. The tunnage of shipping engaged in coastal trading probably rose by the same amount. The roads were thronged with petty chapmen, with their news-sheets, tracts, almanacs, cautionary tales, pamphlets full of homespun wisdom; pedlars with trinkets of all sorts; and travelling entertainers. If the alehouse had always been a distraction from that other social centre of village life, the parish church, it now became much more its rival in the dissemination of news and information and in the formation of popular culture. In the early years of the century, national and local regulation of alehouses was primarily concerned with ensuring that not too much of the barley harvest was malted and brewed; by the end of the century, regulation was more concerned with the pub's potential for sedition.

In the century from 1540 to 1640 there was a redistribution of wealth away from rich and poor towards those in the middle of society. The richest men in the kingdom derived the bulk of their income from rents and services, and these were notoriously difficult to keep in line with inflation: a tradition of long leases and the custom of fixed rents and fluctuating 'entry fines'—payments made when tenancies changed hands—militated against it. Vigilant landowners could keep pace with inflation, but many were not vigilant. Equally, those whose farms or holdings did not make them self-sufficient suffered rising (and worse, fluctuating) food prices, while a surplus on the labour market and declining real wages made it very hard for the poor to make good the shortfall. The number of landless labourers and cottagers soared. Those in the middle of society, whether yeomen farmers or tradesmen, prospered. If they produced a surplus over and above their own needs they could sell dear and produce more with the help of cheap labour. They could lend their profits to their poorer neighbours (there were after all no banks, stocks and shares, building societies) and foreclose on the debts. They invested in more land, preferring to extend the scale of their operations rather than sink capital into improved productivity. Many of those who prospered from farming rose into the gentry.

Only two groups had 'social' status in seventeenth-century England—the gentry and the peerage. Everybody else had 'economic' status, and was defined by his economic function (husbandman, cobbler, merchant, attorney, etc.). The peerage and gentry were different. They had a 'quality' which set them apart. That 'quality' was 'nobility'. Peers and gentlemen were 'noble'; everybody else was 'ignoble' or 'churlish'. Such concepts were derived partly from the feudal and chivalric traditions in which land was held from the Crown in exchange for the performance of military duties. These duties had long since disappeared, but the notion that the ownership of land and 'manors' conferred status and 'honour' had been reinvigorated by the appropriation to English conditions of Aristotle's notion of the citizen. The gentleman or nobleman was a man set apart to govern. He was independent and leisured: he derived his income without having to work for it, that income made him free from want and from being beholden to or dependent upon others, and he had the time and leisure to devote himself to the arts of government. He was independent in judgement and trained to make decisions. Not all gentlemen served in the offices which required such qualities (justice of the peace, sheriff, militia captain, high constable, etc.). But all had this capacity to serve, to govern. A gentleman was expected to be hospitable, charitable, fair-minded. He was distinguished from his country neighbour, the yeoman, as much by attitude of mind and personal preference as by wealth. Minor gentry and yeomen had similar incomes. But they lived different lives: the gentleman rented out his lands, wore cloth and linen, read Latin; the yeoman was a working farmer, wore leather, read and wrote in English. By 1640, there were perhaps 120 peers and 20,000 gentry, one in twenty of all adult males. The permanence of land and the security of landed income restricted gentility to the countryside; the prosperous merchant or craftsman, though he may have had a larger income than many gentlemen, and have discharged, in the government of his borough, the same duties, was denied the status of gentleman.

He had to work, and his capital and income were insecure. Younger sons of gentlemen, trained up in the law or apprenticed into trade, did not retain their status. But they were put into professions through which they or their sons could redeem it. The wealthy merchant or lawyer had some prospect of buying a manor and settling back into a gentler life-style at the end of his life.

This pattern shifted in the late seventeenth century. Conditions were now against the larger farmer: he had high taxation, higher labour costs, and lower profits, unless he invested heavily in higher productivity, which he was less able to do than the great landowners (for whom there were economies of scale). Few yeomen now aspired to the trappings of gentility, while many minor gentlemen abandoned an unequal struggle to keep up appearances. On the other hand, professional men, merchants, and town governors became bolder in asserting that they were as good as the country gentleman and were entitled to his title of respect. The definition of 'gentility' was stretched to include them without a prior purchase of land. This 'pseudo-gentility' became increasingly respectable and increasingly widely recognized, even by the heralds. It was not, however, recognized by many country gentlemen who bitterly resented this devaluation of their treasured status. They responded to the debasement of the term 'gentry' by sponsoring and promoting a new term which restored their exclusiveness and self-importance: they called themselves squires and their group the 'squirearchy'.

The century between 1540 and 1640 had seen the consolidation of those in the middle of society at the expense of those at the bottom and, to some extent, of those at the top. The century after 1640 saw some relief for the mass of poor householders, increasing difficulties for large farmers and small landowners, rich pickings for those at the top. There was emerging by 1690 (though its great age was just beginning) a group of men whose interests, wealth, and power grew out of, but which extended far beyond, their landed estates. They invested in trade, in government loans, in the mineral resources of their land, as well in improved farming and in renting out farming land. They spent as much time in their town houses as in their country seats; they were as much at home with the wealthy élite in London as with their rural neighbours. They constituted a culturally cosmopolitan élite of transcendent wealth, incorporating many of the peerage, but not confined to them. This new phenomenon was recognized at the time and needed a label, a collective noun. It became known as the aristocracy (a term hitherto a preserve of political thinkers, like democracy, rather than of social analysis). The invention of the term 'squire' and adaptation of the word 'aristocrat' in the late seventeenth century tells us a great deal about the way society was evolving. The integration of town and country, the spread of metropolitan values and fashions, the fluidity of the economy and the mobility of society are all involved in the way men categorized one another. By 1690, England already had a flexible and simple moneyed élite; access to wealth and power was not restricted by outdated notions of privilege and obsessions with purity of birth as in much of Europe.

Government and Law

Stuart governments had little understanding of these structural changes and less ability to influence them. The resources of Stuart government fell far short of those required to carry out the ambitions and expectations which most people had of their king and which kings had of themselves.

The financial and bureaucratic resources at the disposal of kings remained limited. James I inherited an income of £350,000 a year. By the later 1630s this had risen to £1,000,000 a year and by the 1680s to £2,000,000 a year. This is a notable increase. It meant that, throughout the seventeenth century, the Stuarts could finance their activities in peacetime. As the century wore on, revenues from Crown lands and Crown feudal and prerogative right fell away to be an insignificant part of royal revenues. The ordinary revenues of the Crown became predominantly those derived from taxing trade: customs duties on the movement of goods into and out of the country and excise duties, a sales tax on basic consumer goods (above all beer!). Only during the Civil Wars and Interregnum (when a majority of state revenues came from property taxes) did direct taxation play a major part in the budget. Over the period 1603–40 and 1660–89, less than 8 per cent of all royal revenues came from direct taxation—certainly less than in the fourteenth or sixteenth centuries. This, in part, reflects landowner domination of the tax-granting House of Commons; but it also reflects an administrative arthritis that hindered improvements in the efficiency and equity of tax distribution.

The buoyancy of trade, especially after 1630, was the greatest single cause of the steady growth in royal income—well ahead of inflation—that made Stuart monarchy at almost every point the least indebted in Europe. Both James I and Charles II suffered from fiscal incontinence, buying the loyalty and favour of their servants with a rashness that often went beyond what was necessary. However, the problems of the Stuarts can fairly be laid at Elizabeth's door. All over Europe in the sixteenth and seventeenth centuries, princes used the threat of invasion by tyrannical and/or heretical foreigners to create new forms of taxation which were usually made permanent when the invasion scare had receded or was repulsed. William III was to make just such a transformation in the 1690s when England was under siege from the absolutist Louis XIV and the bigoted James II. Since the Stuarts never faced a realistic threat of invasion, they never had a good excuse to insist on unpalatable fiscal innovations. Elizabeth I had a perfect opportunity in the Armada years but she was too old, conservatively advised, too preoccupied even to attempt it. Instead she paid for the war by selling land. Although this did not make James I and Charles I's position as difficult as was once thought, it did have one major consequence: it deprived the king of security against loans.

The Stuarts, then, whenever they put their mind to it, had an adequate income and a balanced budget. Almost alone amongst the rulers of the day they never went bankrupt, and only once, in 1670, had to defer payment of interest on loans. But they never had enough money to wage successful war. Since, throughout the century up to 1689, no one ever threatened to invade England or to declare war on her, this was not as serious as it sounds. England waged war on Spain (1624–30, 1655–60), on France (1627–30), and on the Netherlands (1651–4, 1665–7, 1672–4), but always as the aggressor. It cannot be said that these wars achieved the objectives of those who advocated them, but none was lost in the sense that concessions were made on the status quo ante. While rivalries in the colonial spheres (South Asia, Africa, North, Central, and South America) were intensifying, no territories were ceded and expansion continued steadily. There was a growing recognition of the futility of major armed interventions on the Continent which led to gradual increases in the proportion of resources devoted to the navy, while all Continental countries found that the costs of land warfare hindered the development of their navies. By 1689 the British navy was the equal of the Dutch and the French, and the wars of the next twenty-five years were to make it the dominant navy in Europe. For a country which could not afford an active foreign policy, England's standing in the world had improved remarkably during the century.

The monarchy lacked coercive power: there was no standing army or organized police force. Even the guards regiments which protected the king and performed ceremonial functions around him were a Restoration creation. In the period 1603–40 the number of fighting men upon whom the king could call in an emergency could be counted in scores rather than in thousands. After 1660 there were probably about 3,000 armed men on permanent duty in England and rather more in Ireland and Tangiers (which had come to Charles II as a rather troublesome part of the dowry of his Portuguese wife). There were then also several thousand Englishmen regimented and in permanent service with the Dutch and with the Portuguese

armies who could be recalled in emergency. But there was no
military presence in England, and apart from pulling up illegal
tobacco crops in the west country and occasionally rounding
up religious dissidents, the army was not visible until James II's
reign.

It had not been so, of course, in the aftermath of the Civil
War. At the height of the conflict, in 1643–4, there were probably 150,000 men in arms: one in eight of the adult male
population. By the late 1640s, this had fallen to 25,000. The
number rose to 45,000 in the third Civil War, waged against the
youthful Charles II and the Scots (1650–1), and then fell to
remain at between 10,000 and 14,000 for the rest of the decade
(although between 18,000 and 40,000 more were serving at any
particular moment in Scotland and Ireland). The troops in
England were widely dispersed into garrisons. London had a
very visible military presence, since 3,000 or so troops were
kept in very public places (including St. Paul's Cathedral, the
nave of which became a barracks). Everywhere troops could be
found meddling in local administration and local politics (and
perhaps above all in local churches, for garrisons very often
protected and nurtured radical, separatist meeting-houses). The
army was at once the sole guarantor of minority republican
governments, and a source of grievance which hindered long-
term acceptance of the Regicide and Revolution by the population at large.

Throughout the rest of the century, then, the first line of
defence against invasion and insurrection was not a standing
army but the militia: half-trained, modestly equipped, often
chaotically organized local defence forces mustered and led by
local gentry families appointed by the Crown but not subservient to the Crown. They saw active service or fired shots in
anger only as part of the war effort in 1642–5.

There was no police force at all. Few crimes were 'investigated' by the authorities. Criminal trials resulted from accusations and evidence brought by victims or aggrieved parties to
the attention of the justices of the peace. Arrests were made by

village constables, ordinary farmers or craftsmen taking their turn for a year, or by sheriffs (gentlemen also taking their turn) who did have a small paid staff of bailiffs. Riots and more widespread disorders could only be dealt with by the militia or by a 'posse comitatus', a gathering of freeholders specially recruited for the occasion by the sheriff.

The Crown had little coercive power; it also had little bureaucratic muscle. The total number of paid public officials in the 1630s was under 2,000, half of them effectively private domestic servants of the king (cooks, stable boys, etc.). The 'civil service' which governed England, or at any rate was paid to govern England, numbered less than 1,000. Most remarkable was the smallness of the clerical staff servicing the courts of law and the Privy Council. The volume of information at the finger-tips of decision-makers was clearly restricted by the lack of fact-gatherers and the lack of filing cabinets for early retrieval of the information which was available. In the course of the seventeenth century there was a modest expansion of the civil service with significant improvements in naval administration and in the finance departments (with the emergence of the Treasury as a body capable of establishing departmental budgets and fiscal priorities). Two invaluable by-products of the Civil War itself were the introduction of arabic numerals instead of Roman ones in official accounts and of the printed questionnaire. Although the Privy Council trebled in size in the period 1603–40 and doubled again under Charles II, there was a steady decrease in efficiency, and the introduction of subcommittees of the Council for foreign affairs, trade, the colonies, etc. did not improve on Elizabethan levels of efficiency.

Government in seventeenth-century England was by consent. By this we usually mean government by and through Parliament. But, more important, it meant government by and through unpaid, voluntary officials throughout England. County government was in the hands of 3,000 or so prominent gentry in the early seventeenth century, 5,000 or so in the late seventeenth century. They were chosen by the Crown, but that freedom of choice was effectively limited in each county to a choice of fifty or so of the top eighty families by wealth and reputation. In practice all but heads of gentry families who were too young, too old, too mad, or too Catholic were appointed. In the 200 or so corporate boroughs, power lay with corporations of 12–100 men. In most boroughs these men constituted a self-perpetuating oligarchy; in a large minority, election was on a wider franchise. Only in the 1680s was any serious attempt made to challenge the prescriptive rights of rural and urban élites to exercise power.

The significance of the government's dependence on the voluntary support of local élites cannot be overestimated. They controlled the assessment and collection of taxation; the maintenance, training, and deployment of the militia; the implementation of social and economic legislation; the trial of most criminals; and, increasingly, the enforcement of religious uniformity. Their autonomy and authority was actually greater in the Restoration period than in the pre-war period (the Restoration settlement was a triumph for the country gentry rather than for king or Parliament). The art of governing in the seventeenth-century was the art of persuading those who ruled in town and country that there was a close coincidence of interest between themselves and the Crown. For most of the time, this coincidence of interest was recognized. Crown and gentry shared a common political vocabulary; they shared the same conception of society; they shared the same anxieties about the fragility of order and stability. This constrained them to obey the Crown even when it went against the grain. As one gentleman put it to a friend who complained about having to collect possibly illegal taxes in 1625: 'we must not give an example of disobedience to those beneath us'. Local élites were also engaged in endless local disputes, rivalries, conflicts of interest. These might involve questions of procedure or honour; they might involve the distribution of taxation or rates; or promotion to local offices; or the desirability of laying out money to improve highways or rivers. In all these cases the crown and the Privy Council was the obvious arbitrator. All local governors needed royal support to sustain their local influence. None could expect to receive that support if they did not co-operate with the Crown most of the time. The art of government was to keep all local governors on a treadmill of endeavour. In the period 1603–40 most governors did their duty even when they were alarmed or dismayed at what was asked of them; after 1660 the terrible memories of the Civil War had the same effect. Only when Charles I in 1641 and James II in 1687 calculatingly abandoned the bargain with those groups with the bulk of the land, wealth, and power, did that coincidence of interest dissolve.

In maintaining that coincidence of outlook we should not underestimate the strength of royal control of those institutions which moulded belief and opinion. The Crown's control of schools and universities, of pulpits, of the press was never complete, and it may have declined with time. But most teachers, preachers, writers, most of the time upheld royal authority and sustained established social and religious views. This is perhaps most clearly seen in the speed with which the ideas of Archbishop Laud and his clique (which, as we shall see, sought to revolutionize the Church of England) were disseminated at Oxford and Cambridge, through carefully planted dons, to a whole generation of undergraduates. Equally the strength of divine-right theories of monarchy was far greater in the 1680s amongst the graduate clergy than in the population at large, again as a result of the Crown's control over key appointments in the universities. At the Restoration, the earl of Clarendon told Parliament that Cromwell's failure to rgulate schoolmasters and tutors was a principal reason why Anglicanism had thrived in the 1650s and emerged fully-clad with the return of the king: he pledged the government to ensure the political loyalty and religious orthodoxy of all who set up as teachers, and there is evidence that this was more effectively done in the late seventeenth century than at any other time. Even after 1689 when the rights of religious assembly were conceded to Dissenters, they were denied the right to open or run their own schools or academies.

The Early Stuarts

The Crown, therefore, had formidable, but perishable, assets. There was nothing inexorable either about the way the Tudor political system collapsed, causing civil war and revolution, or about the way monarchy and Church returned and re-established themselves. Fewer men feared or anticipated, let alone sought, civil war in the 1620s or 1630s than had done so in the 1580s and 1590s. Few men felt any confidence in the 1660s and 1670s that republicanism and religious fanaticism had been dealt an irrevocable blow.

Throughout Elizabeth's reign, there was a triple threat of civil war: over the wholly uncertain succession; over the passions of rival religious parties; and over the potential interest of the Continental powers in English and Irish domestic disputes. All these extreme hazards had disappeared or receded by the 1620s and 1630s. The Stuarts were securely on the throne with undisputed heirs; the English Catholic community had settled for a deprived status but minimal persecution (they were subject to discriminatory taxes and charges and denied access to public office), while the Puritan attempt to take over the Church by developing their own organizations and structures within it had been defeated. A Puritan piety and zeal was widespread, but its principal characteristic was now to accept the essential forms and practices of the Prayer Book and the canons but to supplement and augment them by their own additional services, preachings, prayer meetings. Above all, they sought to bring a spiritualization to the household that did not challenge but supplemented parochial worship. These additional forms were the kernel and the Prayer-Book services the husk of their Christian witness, but the degree of confrontation between Puritans and the authorities decreased, and the ability of Puritans to organize an underground resistance movement to ungodly kings had vanished. Finally, the decline of internal tensions and the scale of conflicts on the Continent itself removed the incentive for other kings to interfere in England's domestic affairs. In all these ways, England was moving away from civil war in the early seventeenth-century. Furthermore, there is no evidence of a general decline into lawlessness and public violence. Quite the reverse. Apart from a momentary spasm induced by the earl of Essex's attempts to overturn his loss of position at court, the period 1569–1642 is the longest period of domestic peace which England had ever enjoyed. No peer and probably no gentleman was tried for treason between 1605 and 1641. Indeed, only one peer was executed during that period (Lord Castlehavon in 1631, for almost every known sexual felony). The number of treason trials and executions in general declined decade by decade.

Early Stuart England was probably the least violent country in Europe. There were probably more dead bodies on stage during a production of *Hamlet* or *Titus Andronicus* than in any one violent clash or sequence of clashes over the first forty years of the century. Blood feuds and cycles of killings by rival groups were unheard of. England had no brigands, bandits, even groups of armed vagabonds, other than occasional gatherings of 'Moss Troopers' in the Scottish border regions. While the late sixteenth-century could still see rivalries and disputes amongst county justices flare up into fisticuffs and drawn swords (as in Cheshire in the 1570s and Nottinghamshire in the 1590s), respect for the institutions of justice was sufficient to prevent a perpetuation of such violence into the seventeenth century.

Englishmen were notoriously litigious, but that represented a willingness to submit to the arbitration of the king's courts. There was still much rough justice, many packed juries, much intimidation and informal community sanctions against offenders. But it stopped short of killings. A random fanatic stabbed the duke of Buckingham to death in 1628, but few if any other officers of the Crown—lord-lieutenants, deputy lieutenants, justices of the peace, or sheriffs—were slaughtered or maimed in the execution of their duty. A few bailiffs distraining the goods of those who refused to pay rates or taxes were beaten up or chased with pitchforks, but generally speaking the impression of law and order in the early decades is one of the omnicompetence of royal justice and of a spectacular momentum of obedience in the major endeavours of government. It even seems likely that riots (most usually concerned with grain shortages or the enclosure of common land depriving cottagers and artisans of rights essential to the family economy) were declining in frequency and intensity decade by decade. Certainly the degree of violence was strictly limited and few if any persons were killed during riots. The response of the authorities was also restrained: four men were executed for involvement in a riot at Maldon in 1629 just weeks after the quelling of a previous riot. Otherwise, the authorities preferred to deploy minimum force and to impose suspended sentences and to offer arbitration along with or instead of prosecutions. Riots posed no threat to the institutions of the State or to the existing social order.

The fact that few contemporaries expected a civil war may only mean that major structural problems went unrecognized. England may have been becoming ungovernable. Thus, the fact that neither crew nor passengers of an aircraft anticipate a crash does not prevent that crash. But while planes sometimes crash because of metal fatigue or mechanical failure, they also sometimes crash because of pilot error. The causes of the English Civil War are too complex to be explained in terms of such a simple metaphor, but it does seem that the English Civil War was more the consequence of pilot error than of mechanical failure. When, with the wisdom of hindsight, contemporaries looked back at the causes of the 'Great Rebellion' they very rarely went back before the accession of Charles I in 1625. They were probably right.

James I was, in many ways, a highly successful king. This was despite some grave defects of character and judgement. He was the very reverse of Queen Elizabeth. He had a highly articulate, fully-developed, and wholly consistent view of the nature of monarchy and of kingly power—and he wholly failed to live up to it. He was a major intellectual, writing theoretical works on government, engaging effectively in debate with leading Catholic polemicists on theological and political issues, as well as turning his mind and his pen to the ancient but still growing threat of witchcraft, and to the recent and menacing introduction of tobacco. He believed that kings derived their authority directly from God and were answerable to him alone for the discharge of that trust. But he also believed that he was in practice constrained by solemn oaths made at his coronation to rule according to the 'laws and customs of the realm'. However absolute kings might be in the abstract, in the actual situation in which he found himself, he accepted that he could only make law and raise taxation in Parliament, and that every one of his actions as king was subject to judicial review. His prerogative, derived though it was from God, was enforceable only under the law. James was, in this respect, as good as his word. He had several disagreements with his Parliaments, or at any rate with groups of members of Parliament, but they were mostly unnecessary and mostly of temporary effect. Thus he lectured the Commons in 1621 that their privileges derived from his gift, and this led to a row about their origins. But he was only claiming a right to comment on their use of his gift; he was not claiming, and at no point in relation to any such rights and liberties did he claim, that he had the right to revoke such gifts. It was this tactlessness, this ability to make the right argument at the wrong moment that earned him Henry IV of France's *sobriquet*, 'the wisest fool in Christendom'.

His greatest failings, however, were not intellectual but moral and personal. He was an undignified figure, unkempt, uncouth, unsystematic, and fussy. He presided over a court where peculation and the enjoyment of perquisites rapidly obstructed efficient and honest government. Royal poverty made some remuneration of officials from tainted sources unavoidable. But under James (though not under his son) this got out of hand.

The public image of the court was made worse by a series of scandals involving sexual offences and murder. At one point in 1619 a former Lord Chamberlain, a former Lord Treasurer, a former Secretary of State, and a former Captain of the Gentlemen Pensioners, all languished in the Tower on charges of a sexual or financial nature. In 1618, the king's latent homosexuality gave way to a passionate affair with a young courtier of minor gentry background, who rose within a few years to become duke of Buckingham, the first non-royal duke to be created for over a century. Buckingham was to take over the reins of government from the ailing James and to hold them for the young and prissy Charles I, until his assassination in 1628. Such a poor public image cost the king dear. His lack of fiscal self-restraint both heightened his financial problem and reduced the willingness of the community at large to grant him adequate supply.

James I was a visionary king, and in terms of his own hopes and ambitions he was a failure. His vision was one of unity. He hoped to extend the Union of the Crowns of England and Scotland into a fuller union of the kingdoms of Britain. He wanted full union of laws, of parliaments, of churches; he had to settle for a limited economic union, a limited recognition of joint citizenship and for a common flag. The sought-after 'union of hearts and minds' completely eluded him. James's vision was expressed in flexible, gradualist proposals. It was wrecked by the small-mindedness and negative reflexes of the parliamentary county gentry. He also sought to use the power and authority of his three crowns—England, Scotland, and Ireland—to promote the peace and unity of Christian princes, an aim which produced solid achievements in James's arbitration in the Baltic and in Germany in his early years, but which was discredited in his later years by his inability to prevent the outbreak of the Thirty Years War and the renewed conflict in the Low Countries. Finally, he sought to use his position as head of the 'Catholic and Reformed' Church of England, and as the promoter of co-operation between the Presbyterian Scots and episcopal English churches, to advance the reunion of Christian churches. His attempts to arrange an ecumenical council and the response of moderates in all churches, Catholic, orthodox, Lutheran, and Calvinist to his calls for an end to religious strife, were again wrecked by the outbreak of the Thirty Years War. But they had struck a resonant chord in many quarters.

James's reign did see, however, the growth of political stability in England, a lessening of religious passions, domestic peace, and the continuing respect of the international community. His 'plantation policy' in Ulster, involving the dispossession of native Irish Catholic landowners and their replacement by thousands of families from England (many of them in and around Londonderry settled by a consortium of Londoners) and (even more) from south-west Scotland, can also be counted a rather heartless short-term success, though its consequences are all-too-grimly still with us. He left large debts, a court with an unsavoury reputation, and a commitment to fight a limited war with Spain without adequate financial means.

He had squabbled with his Parliament and had failed to secure some important measures which he had propounded to them: of these, the Act of Union with Scotland and an elaborate scheme, known as the Great Contract, for rationalizing his revenues were the only ones that mattered. But he had suffered no major defeat at their hands in the sense that Parliament failed to secure any reduction in royal power and had not enhanced its own participation in government by one jot. Parliament met when the king chose and was dismissed when its usefulness was at an end. Procedural developments were few and had no bearing on parliamentary power. Parliament had sat for less than one month in six during the reign and direct taxation counted for less than one-tenth of the total royal budget. Most members recognized that its very survival as an institution was in serious doubt. No one believed that the disappearance of Parliament gave them the right, let alone the opportunity, to resist the king. James was a Protestant king who ruled under law. He generated distaste in some, but distrust and hatred in few if any of his subjects. Charles I's succession in 1625 was the most peaceful and secure since 1509, and arguably since 1307.

Just as there is a startling contrast between Elizabeth I and James I so there is between James I and Charles I. Where James was an informal, scruffy, approachable man, Charles was glacial, prudish, withdrawn, shifty. He was a runt, a weakling brought up in the shadow of an accomplished elder brother who died of smallpox when Charles was twelve. Charles was short, a stammerer, a man of deep indecision who tried to simplify the world around him by persuading himself that where the king led by example and where order and uniformity were set forth, obedience and peace would follow. Charles I was one of those politicians so confident of the purity of his own motives and actions, so full of rectitude, that he saw no need to explain his actions or justify his conduct to his people. He was an inaccessible king except to his confidants. He was a silent king where James was voluble, a king assertive by deed not word. He was in many ways the icon that James had described in *Basilikon Doron*.

Government was very differently run. Charles was a chaste king who presided over a chaste court; venality and peculation were stanched; in the years of peace after 1629 the budgets were balanced, the administration streamlined, the Privy Council reorganized. In many respects, government was made more efficient and effective. But a heavy price was paid. In part this was due to misunderstandings, to failures of communication. The years 1625–30 saw England at war with Spain (to regain the territories seized from Charles's brother-in-law the elector Palatine and generally to support the Protestant cause) and with France (to make Louis XIII honour the terms of the marriage treaty uniting his sister Henrietta Maria to Charles I). Parliament brayed for war but failed to provide the supply to make the campaigns a success. A mercenary army was sent in vain into Germany; naval expeditions were mounted against French and Spanish coastal strongholds. Nothing was achieved.

The administrative and military preparations themselves, together with financial devices resorted to in order to make good the deficiencies of parliamentary supply, were seen as oppressive and burdensome by many and as of dubious legality by some.

Throughout his reign, however, Charles blithely ruled as he thought right and did little to explain himself. By 1629, king and Parliament had had a series of confrontations over the failure of his foreign policy, over the fiscal expedients needed to finance that policy, over the use of imprisonment to enforce those expedients, and over the king's sponsorship of a new minority group within the Church, whose beliefs and practices sharply diverged from the developing practice and teachings of the Anglican mainstream. In 1629, passions and frustrations reached such a peak that Charles decided that for the foreseeable future he would govern without calling Parliament. He probably believed that if the generation of hotheads and malcontents who had dominated recent sessions was allowed to die off, then the old harmony between king and Parliament could be restored. It was as simplistic as most of his assessments. But the decision was not in itself self-destructive. The three Parliaments of 1625–9 had been bitter and vindictive. But they represented a range of frustrations rather than an organized resistance. They also demonstrated the institutional impotence of Parliament. There was much outspoken criticism of royal policies, but no unity of criticism. Some MPs were anxious about the Crown's religious and foreign policies, others with the legal basis of the fiscal expedients. There was little that men such as John Pym, Sir Edward Coke, Sir Thomas Wentworth, Sir John Eliot, Dudley Digges (to name perhaps the most vociferous royal critics in those sessions) shared in common beyond a detestation of Buckingham and the belief that the misgovernment of the present was best put right by their own entry into office. All were aspirant courtiers both because of the rewards and honours that would flow from office, and because of the principles and policies they would be able to advance. No change of political institutions and no change in the constitution was envisaged. They were not proto-revolutionaries; they lacked the unity of purpose even to stand forth as an alternative government team.

So in the 1630s the king ruled without Parliament and in the absence of any concerted action, peaceful or otherwise, to bring back Parliament. The king raised substantial revenues, adequate for peacetime purposes, and he faced obstruction, and that largely ineffective obstruction, in only one instance—the Ship Money rates used to build a fleet from 1634 onwards. Most of this obstruction was based on local disputes about the distribution of the rate, and over 90 per cent of it was collected, if rather more slowly than anticipated. Arguments about the legality of the measure were heard in open court and after the king's victory payments were resumed at a high level. By 1637 Charles was at the height of his power. He had a balanced budget, effective social and economic policies, an efficient council, and a secure title. There was a greater degree of political acquiescence than there had been for centuries.

He was, however, alienating a huge majority of his people by his religious policies, for his support for Archbishop William Laud was re-creating some of the religious passions of the 1570s and 1580s. But it was not leading to the development of an underground church or of subversive religious activity. Indeed, those who found the religious demands of Laud unacceptable now had an option not available to previous generations: they could and did emigrate to the New World. There, freed from the persecution of the Anglican authorities, they set about persecuting one another in the name of Protestant purity.

There were, however, two things about Laud which dangerously weakened loyalty to the Crown. One was that the teachings of many of those sponsored by the archbishop, and many of the practices encouraged by Laud himself and his colleagues, were reminiscent of Roman Catholic beliefs and ritual. With Laud himself maintaining that the Roman Church was a true church, though a corrupt one, it became widely believed that popery was being let in by a side door, that the Church was being betrayed and abandoned. Laud's own priorities were not, in fact, intended to change the liturgy and observances of the Church, but to restrict Englishmen to a thorough conformity to the letter of the Prayer Book. The 1559 Prayer Book was not only necessary, it was sufficient. Thus the wide penumbra of Puritan practices and observances which had grown up around the Prayer Book was to be curtailed or abolished. This programme incensed all Puritans and worried most other men. Just as bad was Laud's clericism, his attempt to restore the power and authority of the bishops, of the Church courts, of the parish clergy by attacking lay encroachments on the wealth and jurisdiction of the Church. Church lands were to be restored, lay control of tithes and of clerical appointments restricted, the clergy's power to enforce the laws of God enhanced. The most notable visual effect of Laud's archiepiscopate was the removal of the communion tables from the body of the church to the east end, where they were placed on a dais and railed off. At the same time, the rich and ornamental pews set up by the status-conscious clergy were to be removed and replaced by plain, unadorned ones. In the House of God the priest stood at the altar raised above the laity who were to sit in awed humility beneath his gaze. Sinful man could not come to salvation through the word of God alone, or at all, but only through the sacraments mediated by His priesthood. Only a priesthood freed from the greed and cloying materialism of the laity could carry out the Church's mission. Such a programme committed Laud to taking on almost every vested secular interest in the State.

Despite this, in 1637 Charles stood at the height of his power. Yet five years later civil war broke out. Only a catastrophic series of blunders made this possible. The most obvious lesson the king should have learnt from the 1620s (if not the 1590s) was that the Tudor-Stuart system of government was ill-equipped to fight successful wars, with or without parliamentary help. This did not matter since no one was likely to make war on England in the foreseeable future, giving the Crown time in an increasingly favourable economic climate (the great inflation petering out and foreign trade booming). What Charles had to avoid was blundering into an unnecessary war. In 1637, however, he blundered into civil war with his Scots subjects. Governing Scotland from London had proved beyond Charles, whose desire for order and conformity led him first to challenge the autonomy of the Scots lords in matters of jurisdiction and titles to secularized Church lands, and then to attempt to introduce religious reforms into Scotland similar to those advocated by Laud in England. Protests over the latter led to a collapse of order and the king's alternating bluster and half-hearted concession led to a rapid escalation of the troubles. Within twelve months, Charles was faced by the ruin of his Scottish religious policies and an increasing challenge to his political authority there. He therefore decided to impose his will by force. In 1639 and again in 1640 he planned to invade Scotland. On both occasions the Scots mobilized more quickly, more thoroughly, and in greater numbers than he did. Rather than accept a deal with the Short Parliament (April-May 1640) which was willing to fund a campaign against the Scots in return for painful but feasible concessions (certainly for less than the Scots were demanding), Charles preferred to rely on Irish Catholics, Highland Catholics, and specious offers to help from Spain and the Papacy. Poor co-ordination, poor morale, and a general lack of urgency both forced Charles to abandon the campaign of 1639 and allowed the Scots to invade England and to occupy Newcastle in the autumn of 1640. There they sat, refusing to go home until the king had made a treaty with them, including a settlement of their expenses, ratified by an English Parliament.

A unique opportunity thus arose for all those unhappy with royal policies to put things right: a Parliament was called which could not be dismissed at will. The ruthlessness of the way the opportunity was taken was largely the result of that unique circumstance. Within twelve months those institutions and prerogatives through which Charles had sustained his non-parliamentary government were swept away. The men who had counselled the king in the 1630s were in prison, in exile, or in disgrace. But the expected return to peace and co-operation did not occur. Instead, the crisis rapidly deepened amidst ever greater distrust and recrimination. Civil war itself broke out within two years to the dismay and bewilderment of almost everyone. The reasons why Charles's position collapsed so completely, so quickly, and so surprisingly are necessarily a matter of dispute amongst historians. But two points stand out. One is that once the constitutional reforms which were widely desired were achieved, Charles's palpable bad grace, his obvious determination to reverse his concessions at the earliest opportunity, and his growing willingness to use force to that end, drove the leaders of the Commons, and above all John Pym, to contemplate more radical measures. In 1640 almost without exception the members favoured a negative, restrained programme, the abolition of those powers, those prerogatives, those courts which had sustained non-parliamentary government. No one had intended to increase the powers of the two Houses, but only to insist that Parliament be allowed to meet regularly to discharge its ancient duties: to make law, to grant supply, to draw the king's attention to the grievances of the subjects, and to seek redress. By the autumn of 1641 a wholly new view had emerged. It was that the king himself was so irresponsible, so incorrigible, that Parliament, on the people's behalf, had a right to transfer to themselves powers previously exercised by the king. Specifically, this meant that the Houses should play a part in the appointment and dismissal of Privy Councillors and principal officials of State and court, and that the Privy Council's debates and decisions should be subject to parliamentary scrutiny. Such demands were facilitated by the fact that Charles had made very similar concessions to the Scots in his treaty with them in July 1641, and such demands were given new urgency by the outbreak of the Irish rebellion in October.

The Catholics of the north of Ireland, fearful that the English

Parliament would introduce new repressive religious legislation, decided to take pre-emptive action to disarm those Ulster Protestants who would enforce any such legislation. With the legacy of hatred built into the Ulster plantations, violence inevitably got out of hand and something like 3,000 (that is, one in five) of the Protestants were slaughtered. Reports in England credibly suggested even larger numbers. Fatally for Charles I, the rebels claimed to be acting on his authority and produced a forged warrant to prove it. This reinforced rumours of Charles's scheming with Irish Catholics, of his negotiations with Catholic Spain and with the pope for men and money to invade Scotland in 1640, and it followed on from the discovery of army plots in England and Scotland earlier in the year to dissolve Parliament by force. Within weeks it was emphatically endorsed by Charles's attempt, with troops at his back, to arrest five members of the Commons during a sitting of the House. In these circumstances, to entrust Charles with recruiting and commanding the army to subjugate the Irish, an army available for service in England, was unthinkable. John Pym now led a parliamentary attack on Charles I as a deranged king, a man unfit to wield the powers of his office. In the eighteen months before the outbreak of civil war, a majority of the Commons and a minority of the House of Lords came to share that conviction. When Charles I raised his standard at Nottingham and declared war on his people, the question of his judgement, of his trustworthiness was one which divided the nation.

The first point about the outbreak of the war is, then, that Charles's actions in 1640–2 forced many men into a much more radical constitutional position that they had taken or anticipated taking. But the constitutional dynamic was a limited one. The question of trust arose in relation to an urgent non-negotiable issue: the control of the armed forces to be used against the Irish rebels. This turned attention on a further related question, the king's control of the militia and of those who ran it, the lord-lieutenants and their deputies. These constitutional issues together with the accountability of the king's ministers and councillors to Parliament proved to be the *occasion* of the Civil War. But they were not the prime considerations in the mind of those who actively took sides. Certainly the question of trust drew some men to the side of the Houses; but the palpably new demands now being made by Pym and his colleagues were wholly unacceptable to many others. If the king's flirtations with Popery drove some into the arms of Pym, so Pym drove others into the arms of the king by his reckless willingness to use mass picketing by thousands of Londoners to intimidate wavering members of both Houses to approve controversial measures. But for everyone who took sides on the constitutional issue in 1642, there were ten who found it impossible to take sides, who saw right and wrong on both sides, and who continued to pray and to beg for accommodation and a peaceful settlement. In a majority of shires and boroughs, the dominant mood throughout 1642 was pacifist, neutralist, or at least localist. That is, attempts were made to neutralize whole regions, for demilitarization agreements to be reached between factions or to be imposed by 'peace' movements on both sides, or for the county establishments to impose order and discipline in the name of king or Parliament but without doing anything to further the larger, national war effort. Constitutional issues, however much they pressed them upon those at Westminster who experienced royal duplicity and the London apprentices' politics of menace, were not in themselves weighty enough to start a civil war.

By 1642, however, a second factor was crucial: religion. The religious experiments of Archbishop Laud reactivated Puritan militancy. By 1640 substantial numbers of clergy, of gentry, and especially prosperous farmers and craftsmen had decided that the system of Church government, so easily manipulated by a clique of innovators and crypto-Catholics such as they deemed the Laudians to be, had to be overthrown. The office of bishop must be abolished, the Prayer Book, which, said some, 'is noisome and doth stink in the nostrils of God', must be suppressed, the observance of 'popish' festivals such as Christmas and Easter must be stopped. A majority in Parliament initially favoured a more moderate reform—the punishment of Laud and his henchmen and legislation to reduce the autonomy and jurisdiction of the bishops. But the Scots' pressure for more change, a carefully orchestrated petitioning campaign for reform of the Church 'root and branch', and outbreaks of popular iconoclasm (the smashing of stained glass and the hacking out of communion rails was reported from many regions) led to a rapid polarization of opinion. Since many of those who campaigned against bishops also campaigned against rapacious landlords and against tithes (with implications for property rights in general), the defence of the existing Church became a defence of order and hierarchy in society and the State as well as in religion.

There was an Anglican party before there was a royalist party, and those who rushed to join the king in 1642 were those clearly motivated by religion. On the other side, those who mobilized for Parliament were those dedicated to the overthrow of the existing Church and to the creation of a new evangelical church which gave greater priority to preaching God's word, greater priority to imposing moral and social discipline. It was a vision reinforced by the return of exiles from New England who told of the achievements of the godly in the Wilderness. Like the Israelites of the Old Testament led out of bondage in Egypt to the Promised Land, so God's new chosen people, the English, were to be led out of bondage into a Promised Land, a Brave New World. While the majority of Englishmen dithered and compromised, the minority who took up the armed struggle cared passionately about religion.

Those who hesitated were, then, sucked inexorably into the Civil War. Faced by escalating demands and threats from the minority who had seized the initiative, most men had to choose sides. Many, maybe most, followed the line of least resistance and did what they were told by those in a position immediately to compel obedience. Others, deciding reluctantly and miserably, examined their consciences and then moved themselves and their families to an area under the control of the side which they thought the more honourable. But fear of the king's 'popish' allies and of Parliament's religious zealots made that decision unbearable for many.

The Civil Wars

The first Civil War lasted from 1642 until 1646. It is impossible to say quite when it began: the country drifted into war. In January 1642 the king left London and began a long journey round the Midlands and the north. In April he tried to secure an arsenal of military equipment at Hull (left over from his Scottish campaign). The gates were locked against him and he retired to York. Between June and August, Charles and the two Houses issued flatly contradictory instructions to rival groups of commissioners for the drilling of the militia. This led to some skirmishing and shows of force. By the end of August both sides were recruiting in earnest and skirmishing increased. The king's raising of his standard at Nottingham on 20 August was the formal declaration of war. But the hope on all sides remained either that negotiations would succeed or else that one battle between the two armies now in the making would settle the issue. But that first battle, at Edgehill in South Warwickshire on 23 October, was drawn and settled nothing. Although the king advanced on London and reached Brentford, he did not have the numbers or the logistical support to take on the forces blocking his path. He retreated to Oxford as the winter closed in and the roads became impassable. Only after a winter of fitful peace and futile negotiation did the real war break out. Those first armies had been cobbled together and paid on a hand-to-mouth basis. By the spring, it was clear that the nation had to be mobilized. Armies had to be raised in every region and the money and administrative apparatus to sustain those armies created. The country may have stumbled into war; but the logic of that war and its costs would turn civil disturbance into bloody revolution.

It is probable that at some moments in 1643–5 more than one in ten of all adult males was in arms. No single army exceeded 20,000 men, and the largest single battle—Marston Moor near York in June 1644, which saw the conjunction of several separate armies—involved less than 45,000 men. But there were usually 120,000 and up to 140,000 men in arms during the campaigning seasons of 1643, 1644, and 1645. Both sides organized themselves regionally into 'associations' of counties, each with an army (at least on paper) whose primary duty was to clear the association of enemies and to protect it from invasion. Both sides also had a 'marching army' with national responsibilities. In these circumstances the war was essentially one of skirmishes and sieges rather than of major battles. Some regions saw little fighting (for example, East Anglia, the south coast, mid-Wales); others were constantly marched over and occupied by rival armies (the Severn and Thames valleys were amongst the worst, but the whole of the Midlands was a constant military zone). Parliament's heartland was the area in the immediate vicinity of London. Proximity to the capital and to the peremptory demands of the Houses, and the rapid deployment of thousands of Londoners in arms (the unemployed and the religiously inclined joining up in uncertain proportions) ensured that the lukewarm and the hesitant accepted parliamentary authority. Equally, the king's initial strength lay in the areas he visited and toured: the North and East Midlands in a swathe of counties from Lancashire to Oxfordshire. The far north and the west were initially neutral or confused. Only gradually did royalists gain the upper hand in those areas.

The King had several initial advantages—the support of personally wealthy men, a naturally unified command structure emanating from the royal person, a simpler military objective (to capture London). But Parliament had greater long-term advantages: the wealth and manpower of London, crucial for the provision of credit; the control of the navy and of the trade routes with the result that hard-headed businessmen preferred to deal with them rather than with the king; a greater compactness of territory less vulnerable to invasion than the royalist hinterlands; and the limited but important help afforded by the invasion of 20,000 Scots in 1644 in return for a commitment by the Houses to introduce a form of Church government similar to the Scottish one.

It was always likely that the parliamentary side would wear down the royalists in a long war. So it proved. Purely military factors played little part in the outcome. Both sides deployed the same tactics and used similar weapons; both had large numbers of experienced officers who had served in the armies of the Continental powers in the Thirty Years War. In 1645 both sides 'new modelled' their military organizations to take account of the changing military balance, the king setting up separate grand commands on Bristol and Oxford, Parliament bringing together three separate armies depleted in recent months: an army too large for its existing task, the defence of East Anglia, the unsuccessful southern region army of Sir William Waller, and the 'marching army' of the commander-in-chief, the earl of Essex. This New Model Army was put under the command of an 'outsider', Sir Thomas Fairfax, to avoid the rival claims of senior officers in the old armies, and all MPs were recalled from their commands to serve in the Houses; but otherwise commands were allocated more or less according to existing seniority. The New Model was not, by origin, designed to radicalize the parliamentary cause and it was not dominated by radical officers. Professionalization, not radicalization, was the key; the army's later reputation for religious zeal and for representing a career open to the talents was not a feature of its creation. The great string of victories beginning at Naseby in June 1645 was not the product of its zeal, but of regular pay. In the last eighteen months of the war, the unpaid royalist armies simply dissolved, while the New Model was well supplied. The Civil War was won by attrition.

The last twelve months of the war saw a growing popular revolt against the violence and destruction of war. These neutralist or 'Clubmen' risings of farmers and rural craftsmen throughout west and south-west England sought to drive one or both sides out of their area and demanded an end to the war by negotiation. Again, as the discipline of royalist armies disintegrated they were the principal sufferers. But the hostility of the populace to both sides made the fruits of victory hard to pick.

To win the war, Parliament had imposed massive taxation on the people. Direct taxation was itself set at a level of 15–20 per cent of the income of the rich and of the middling sort. Excise duties were imposed on basic commodities such as beer (the basic beverage of men, women, and children in an age just prior to the introduction of hot vegetable drinks such as tea, coffee, and chocolate) and salt (a necessary preservative in that period). Several thousand gentry and many thousands of others whose property lay in an area controlled by their opponents had their estates confiscated and their incomes employed wholly by the State except for a meagre one-fifth allowed to those with wives and children. By the end of the war, Parliament was allowing less active royalists ('delinquents') to regain their estates on payment of a heavy fine; but the hardliners ('malignants') were allowed no redress and were later to suffer from the sale of their lands on the open market to the highest bidder. All those whose estates were not actually confiscated were required to lend money to king or Parliament; refusal to lend 'voluntarily' led to a stinging fine. In addition to those burdens, both sides resorted to free quarter, the billeting of troops on civilians with little prospect of any recompense for the board and lodging taken. Troops on the move were all too likely to help themselves and to point their muskets at anyone who protested. Looting and pillaging were rare; pilfering and trampling down crops were common. All this occurred in an economy severely disrupted by war. Trade up the Severn was seriously affected by the royalist occupation of Worcester and parliamentarian occupation of Gloucester; or up the Thames by royalist Oxford and parliamentarian Reading. Bad weather added to other problems to make the harvests of the later 1640s

Map labels:

SCOTLAND

NORTHUMBER-LAND

CUMBERLAND

DURHAM

WESTMOR-LAND

North Sea

× Major battles
⊙ Major sieges

0   50 miles
0   50   100 km.

YORKSHIRE

Marston Moor (2·7·44) × ⊙ York

Preston⊙ ×*Preston*   Hull⊙
    (17–19·8·48)

LANCASHIRE

Chester⊙   CHESHIRE   DERBY-SHIRE   LINCOLN-SHIRE

×*Nantwich* (25·1·44)   NOTTINGHAM-SHIRE   ⊙Newark

SHROPSHIRE   STAFFORD-SHIRE   LEICESTER-SHIRE   RUTLAND

WARWICK-SHIRE   ×*Naseby* (14·6·45)   NORTHAMPTONSHIRE   HUNTS   NORFOLK

Worcester× (3·9·51)   *Edgehill* (23·10·42)×   CAMBRIDGE-SHIRE   SUFFOLK

WALES   HEREFORD-SHIRE   BEDFORD-SHIRE

⊙Gloucester   OXFORDSHIRE   BUCKINGHAMSHIRE   HERTFORD-SHIRE   ESSEX

GLOUCESTER-SHIRE   Oxford⊙   MIDDX

⊙Bristol   *Newbury* (20·9·43)×   Reading   SURREY   KENT

BERKSHIRE   *Newbury* (27·10·44)×

WILTSHIRE   HAMPSHIRE   SUSSEX

SOMERSET   ×*Langport* (10·7·45)

DEVON   DORSET   Portsmouth ⊙

CORNWALL   ×*Lostwithiel* (1·9·44) ⊙Plymouth

English Channel

MAJOR BATTLES AND SIEGES OF THE ENGLISH CIVIL WARS
1642–1651

the worst of the century. High taxation and high food prices depressed the markets for manufactures and led to economic recession. The plight of the poor and of the not-so-poor was desperate indeed. The costs of settlement, of the disbandment of armies, and of a return to 'normality' grew.

In order to win the Civil War, Parliament had to grant extensive powers, even arbitrary powers, to its agents. The war was administered by a series of committees in London who oversaw the activities of committees in each county and regional association. Committees at each level were granted powers quite at variance with the principles of common law: powers to assess people's wealth and impose their assessments; to search premises and to distrain goods; to imprison those who obstructed them without trial, cause shown and without limitation. Those who acted in such roles were granted an indemnity against any civil or criminal action brought against them, and (after mid-1647) that indemnity was enforced by another parliamentary committee. Judgments reached in the highest courts of the land were set aside by committee decree. Only thus had the resources to win the Civil War been secured. But by 1647 and 1648 Parliament was seen as being more tyrannical in its government than the king had been in his. The cries for settlement and restoration were redoubled.

In order to win the Civil War, Parliament promised the Scots that the Elizabethan Church would be dismantled and refashioned 'according to the word of God, and the example of the best reformed churches' (a piece of casuistry, since the Scots wrongly assumed that must mean their own church). By 1646 this was accomplished, on paper at least. Episcopacy, cathedrals, Church courts, the Book of Common Prayer and the Kalendar (including the celebration of Christmas and Easter) were abolished and proscribed. In their place a 'Presbyterian' system was set up. Ministers and lay 'elders' from a group of neighbouring churches were to meet monthly to discuss matters of mutual concern. Representatives of all such meetings or 'classes' within each county were to meet regularly. The activities at parish, classical, and provincial level would be co-ordinated by a national synod and by Parliament. No one was exempt from the authority of this new national Church any more than they had been from the old Church. The new national faith would be based upon a new service book ('the Directory of Public Worship', emphasizing extempore prayer and the preaching of the Word), new catechisms, and new articles of faith. At every level, the 'godly' were to be empowered to impose moral duties, a 'reformation of manners', and strict spiritual observance through ecclesiastical and secular sanctions. But this Puritan experiment was stillborn. It gave the laity far too much control to please many strict Presbyterian ministers. It gave too little authority to the individual parishes and too much to classes, provinces, and synods to please many others. The precise doctrinal, liturgical, and disciplinary requirements were too rigid for others or just plain unacceptable in themselves. While there was 'Puritan' unity in 1642 against the existing order, the imposition of one particular alternative created a major split in the movement. Many 'Independents' refused to accept the package and began to demand liberty of conscience for themselves and a right of free religious assembly outside the national Church. Some began to refuse to pay tithes. The disintegration of Puritanism preceded any attempt to impose the Presbyterian system. At the same time, this system was bitterly opposed by the great majority of ordinary people. Over four generations they had come to love the Prayer Book and the celebration of the great Christian festivals. They resented the loss of both, and also the Puritan doctrine that forbade anyone to come to receive holy communion without first being approved by the minister and his self-righteous henchmen and given a certificate of worthiness. Throughout much of England, therefore, including East Anglia, the decrees against the Prayer Book and the celebration of Festivals were a dead letter. Ministers who tried to impose change were opposed and even thrown out, and although one in five of the clergy were ejected by parliamentary commissions for spiritual, moral, or political unfitness, a majority of their replacements sought secret episcopal ordination. The Puritan experiment was ineffective but added to popular hatred of an arbitrary Parliament.

But if the great majority, even on the winning side, became convinced that the Civil War had solved nothing and had only substituted new and harsher impositions on pocket and conscience for the old royal impositions, a minority, equally dismayed by the shabby realities of the present, persuaded themselves that a much more radical transformation of political institutions was necessary. God could not have subjected his people to such trials and sufferings without a good purpose. To admit the futility of the struggle, to bring back the king on terms he would have accepted in 1642, would be a betrayal of God and of those who had died and suffered in His cause. Once again it was the religious imperative which drove men on. Such views were to be found in London, with its concentration of gathered churches and economic distress, and in the army, with its especially strong memories of suffering and exhilaration, many soldiers aware of God's presence with them in the heat of battle. Furthermore a penniless Parliament, bleakly foreseeing the consequences of seeking to squeeze additional taxes from the people, enraged the army in the spring of 1647 by trying to disband most of them and to send the rest to reconquer Ireland without paying off the arrears of pay which had been mounting since the end of the war. In the summer of 1647 and again in the autumn of 1648 a majority in the two Houses, unable to see the way forward, resigned themselves to accepting such terms as the king would accept. His plan since his military defeat, to keep talking but to keep his options open, looked likely to be vindicated.

On both occasions, however, the army prevented Parliament from surrender. In August 1647 it marched into London, plucked out the leading 'incendiaries' from the House of Commons, and awed the rest into voting them the taxation and the other material comforts they believed due to them. In doing so, they spurned the invitation of the London-based radical group known as the Levellers to dissolve the Long Parliament, to decree that all existing government had abused its trust and was null and void, and to establish a new democratic constitution. The Levellers wanted all free-born Englishmen to sign a social contract, an Agreement of the People, and to enjoy full rights of participation in a decentralized, democratic state. All those who held office would do so for a very short period and were to be accountable to their constituents. Many rights, above all freedom to believe and practice whatever form of Christianity one wanted, could not be infringed by any future Parliament or government. The army, officers and men, were drawn to the Levellers' commitment to religious freedom and to their condemnation of the corruption and tyranny of the Long Parliament, and officers and 'agitators' drawn from the rank and file debated Leveller proposals, above all at the Putney debates held in and near Putney Church in November 1647. But the great majority finally decided that the army's bread-and-butter demands were not to be met by those proposals. Instead the army preferred to put pressure on the chastened Parliament to use its arbitrary powers to meet their sectional interests.

The outcome was a second Civil War, a revolt of the provinces against centralization and military rule. Moderate parliamentarians, Clubmen, whole county communities rose against the renewed oppressions, and their outrage was encouraged and focused by ex-royalists. The second Civil War was fiercest in regions little affected by the first war, insufficiently numbed by past experience—in Kent, in East Anglia, in South Wales, in the West and North Ridings. It was complicated by the king's clumsy alliance with the Scots, who were disgusted by Parliament's failure to honour its agreement to bring in a Church settlement like their own, and who were willing, despite everything, to trust in vague assurances from the duplicitous Charles. If the revolts had been co-ordinated, or at least contemporaneous, they might have succeeded. But they happened one by one, and one by one the army picked them off. With the defeat of the Scots at Preston in August, the second Civil War was over.

It had solved nothing. Still the country cried out for peace and for settlement, still the army had to be paid, still the king prevaricated and made hollow promises. As in 1647, the Houses had to face the futility of all their efforts. By early December there were only two alternatives: to capitulate to the king and to bring him back on his own terms to restore order and peace; or to remove him, and to launch on a bold adventure into unknown and uncharted constitutional seas. A clear majority of both Houses, and a massive majority of the country, wanted the former; a tiny minority, spearheaded by the leaders of the army, determined on the latter. For a second time the army purged Parliament. In the so-called Pride's Purge, over half the members of the Commons were arrested or forcibly prevented from taking their seats. Two-thirds of the remainder boycotted the violated House. In the revolutionary weeks that followed, less than one in six of all MPs participated, and many of those in attendance did so to moderate proceedings. The decision to put the king on trial was probably approved by less than one in ten of the assembly that had made war on him in 1642.

In January 1649, the king was tried for his life. His dignity and forbearance made it a massive propaganda defeat for his opponents. His public beheading at Whitehall took place before a stunned but sympathetic crowd. This most dishonourable and duplicitous of English kings grasped a martyr's crown, his reputation rescued by that dignity at the end and by the publication of his self-justification, the *Eikon Basilike*, a runaway best seller for decades to come.

Commonwealth and Protectorate

From 1649 to 1660 England was a republic. In some ways this was a revolutionary period indeed. Other kings had been brutally murdered, but none had previously been legally murdered.

Monarchy was abolished, along with the House of Lords and the Anglican Church. England had four separate constitutions between 1649 and 1659, and a chaos of expedients in 1659–60. Scotland was fully integrated into Britain, and Ireland subjugated with an arrogance unprecedented even in its troubled history. It was a period of major experiment in national government. Yet a remarkable amount was left untouched. The legal system was tinkered with but was recognizably the old arcane common law system run by an exclusive legal priesthood; local government reverted to the old pattern as quarter sessions returnd to constitute veritable local parliaments. Exchequer reasserted its control over government finance. Existing rights of property were protected and reinforced, and the social order defended from its radical critics. There was a loosely structured national Church. If no one was obliged to attend this national Church, they were required to pay tithes to support its clergy and to accept the secular and moral authority of parish officers in the execution of the duties laid upon them in Tudor statutes. In practice, the very freedom allowed to each parish in matters of worship, witness, and observance, permitted Anglican services and the Anglican feasts to be quietly and widely practised.

Institutionally, it was indeed a decade of uneven progress back towards a restoration of monarchy. From 1649 to 1653, England was governed by the Rump Parliament, that fragment of the Long Parliament which accepted Pride's Purge and the Regicide and which assumed unto itself all legislative and executive power. Despite the high-minded attempts of some MPs to liken themselves to the assemblies of the Roman Republic, the Rump in practice was a body that lived from hand to mouth. Too busy to take bold initiatives and to seek long-term solutions, let alone to build the new Jerusalem, the Rump parried its problems. By selling the Crown's lands, Church lands, and royalist lands, it financed the army's conquest of Ireland, which included the storming of Drogheda and Wexford and the slaughtering of the civilian population, acts unparalleled in England, but justified as revenge for the massacres of 1641, and its gentler invasion of Scotland. By the establishment of extra-parliamentary financial institutions and by the restoration of pre-war forms of local government, the Rump wooed enough men in the provinces into acquiescence to keep going and to defeat the royalists in a third Civil War. By incoherent and contradictory pronouncements on religion, it kept most men guessing about its ecclesiastical priorities, and drove none to desperate opposition. The Rump even blundered into a naval war with the Dutch and captured enough Dutch merchantmen in the ensuing months to double Britain's entrepôt trade. A demoralized royalist party licked its wounds and tried to pay off its debts; a dejected majority of the old parliamentarian party grudgingly did what they were told but little more. The Rump stumbled on.

By the spring of 1653 the army was ready for a change. With fresh testimonies of divine favour in their victories in Scotland and Ireland and over Charles II at the battle of Worcester, its leaders, above all its commander (since 1649) Oliver Cromwell, demanded the kind of godly reformation which the Rump was too preoccupied and too set in its ways to institute.

Disagreements between Rumpers and army commanders led finally to the peremptory dissolution which the latter had ducked in 1647 and 1648. Fearful that free elections would provoke a right-wing majority, Cromwell decided to call an 'assembly of saints', a constituent assembly of 140 hand-picked men drawn from amongst those who had remained loyal to the godly cause, men who shared little beyond having what Cromwell called 'the root of the matter in them', an integrity and intensity of experience of God's purpose for his people, whose task it was to institute a programme of moral regeneration and political education that he hoped would bring the people to recognize and to own the 'promises and prophecies' of God. Cromwell's vision of 140 men with a fragment to contribute to the building up of a mosaic of truth was noble but naïve. These 140 bigots of the Nominated or Barebones Parliament, leaderless and without co-ordination, bickered for five months and then, by a large majority, surrendered their power back into the Lord General's hands. Cromwell's honest attempts to persuade others to govern while he stood aside had failed. The army alone propped up the republic and could make and break governments. The army must be made responsible for governing.

From December 1653 until his death in September 1658, Oliver Cromwell ruled England as Lord Protector and Head of State. Under two paper constitutions, the *Instrument of Government* (1653–7, issued by the Army Council) and the *Humble Petition and Advice* (1657–8, drawn up by a Parliament), Cromwell as head of the executive had to rule with, and through, a Council of State. He also had to meet Parliament regularly. Cromwell saw himself in a position very similar to that of Moses leading the Israelites to the Promised Land. The English people had been in bondage in the Land of Egypt (Stuart monarchy); they had fled and crossed the Red Sea (Regicide); they were now struggling across the Desert (current misfortunes), guided by the Pillar of Fire (Divine Providence manifested in the army's great victories, renewed from 1656 on in a successful war against Spain). The people, like the Israelites, were recalcitrant and complaining. Sometimes they needed to be frog-marched towards the Promised Land, as in 1655–6 when Cromwell became dismayed by the lack of response in the people at large during an abortive royalist uprising (few royalists participated but many turned a blind eye, and few beyond the army rushed to extinguish the flames of rebellion). He then instituted a system of government placing each region under the supervision of a senior military commander. These 'Major Generals' were responsible for security but also interfered in every aspect of local government and instituted a 'reformation of manners' (a campaign of moral rearmament). At other times Cromwell tried to wheedle the nation towards the Promised Land with policies of 'healing and settling', playing down the power of the sword and attempting to broaden participation in government and to share power with local magistrates and with Parliament.

If Cromwell had settled for acquiescence and a minimum level of political acceptance, he could have established a secure and lasting regime. But he yearned for commitment and zeal, for a nation more responsive to the things of God, more willing to obey His commands. Cromwell was an orthodox Calvinist in his belief in the duty of God's elect to make all men love and honour Him, and in his belief that God's providence showed His people the way forward. He was unusual in believing that, in this fallen world, the elect were scattered amongst the churches. Toleration was a means to the end of restoring the unity of God's word and truth. This religious radicalism went along with a social conservatism. The hierarchical ordering of society was natural and good, its flaws and injustices not intrinsic but the consequence of sin. It was not society but man's behaviour within society that must be reformed.

By executing Charles, Cromwell cut himself off from justifications of political authority rooted in the past; by acknowledging that a free vote of those who held the franchise would restore the king, that is by refusing to base his authority on consent, Cromwell cut himself off from arguments of the present. His self-justification lay in the future, in the belief that he was fulfilling God's will. But because he believed that he had such a task to perform, he had a fatal disregard for civil and legal liberties. To achieve the future promised by God, Cromwell governed arbitrarily. He imprisoned men without trial. When George Cony, a merchant, refused to pay unconstitutional customs duties, Cromwell imprisoned him and his lawyer to prevent him taking his case to court. When Parliament failed to make him an adequate financial provision, he taxed by decree. When the people would not respond voluntarily to the call to moral regeneration, he created Major-Generals and set them to work. Hence the supreme paradox. Cromwell the king-killer, the reluctant head of state, the visionary, was begged by his second Parliament to become King Oliver. He was offered the

Crown. Ironically he was offered it to limit his power, to bind him with precedents and with the rule of law. Because such restrictions were irrelevant to the task he believed he was entrusted to perform, because God's Providence did not direct him to restore the office that He had set aside, he declined the throne.

While Cromwell lived, the army (who had the immediate military muscle) and the country gentry (who had the ultimate social authority) were kept in creative tension. Cromwell was a unique blend of country gentleman and professional soldier, of religious radical and social conservative, of political visionary and constitutional mechanic, of charismatic personal presence and insufferable self-righteousness. He was at once the only source of stability and the ultimate source of instability of the regimes he ran. If he could have settled for settlement, he could have established a prudent republic; if he had not had a fire in his belly to change the world, he would never have risen from sheep farmer to be head of state. With his death, the republic collapsed. His son lacked his qualities and succumbed to the jealousy of the senior military commanders. They in turn fell out amongst themselves and a national tax strike hastened the disintegration of the army. Eighteen months after Cromwell's death, one section of the army under General Monck decided that enough was enough. Free elections were held and Charles II was recalled.

Restoration Monarchy

Charles was restored unconditionally. His reign was declared to have begun at the moment of his father's death; those Acts of Parliament to which his father had assented were in force, all the rest were null and void (which meant, for example, that all Crown and Church land sold off by the republic was restored, but also that those royalists who had paid fines or who had repurchased their estates under Commonwealth legislation went uncompensated). Parliament assured itself of no greater role in the government than it had possessed under Elizabeth and the early Stuarts (except for a toothless act requiring a triennial session of Parliament, an Act Charles II ignored without popular protest in 1684). Since the Long Parliament and those of the Interregnum had abused their authority as freely as Charles I had done, it seemed pointless to build them up as a counterpoise to the Crown. Rather the Restoration Settlement sought to limit royal power by handing power back from the centre to the localities. Charles I had agreed to the abolition of the prerogative courts, to the restriction of the judicial power of the Privy Council (now emasculated and thus unable to enforce policy), to the abolition of prerogative taxation. The local gentry were freer than ever before to run their own shires. What is more, with remarkable nerve and courage, Charles set out to build his regime on as broad a base as possible. He refused to give special positions of favour and trust to his own and his father's friends. There was to be power-sharing at every level of government: in the council and in the distribution of office at court, in the bureaucracy, in local government. Old royalists, old parliamentarian moderates who had shunned the Interregnum regimes, Cromwellian loyalists, all found places. Indeed, the group who did least well were the royalist exiles. Charles defeated parliamentary attempts at a wide proscription and punishment of the enemies of monarchy. Only those who signed Charles I's death warrant and a handful of others were exempted from the general Act of Indemnity and Oblivion (one bitter cavalier called the Restoration an 'act of indemnity to the King's enemies and of oblivion to his friends'). It took courage to determine that it was better to upset old friends (who would not send the king on his travels again) than to upset old enemies. Plots against Charles II were few and restricted to radical religious sects. Even a government with less than 3,000 men in arms could deal with such threats.

Charles had hoped to bring a similar comprehensiveness to the ecclesiastical settlement. He sought to restore the Church of England, but with reforms that would make it acceptable to the majority of moderate Puritans. To this end, he offered bishop-rics to a number of such moderates and he issued an interim settlement (the Worcester House Declaration) which weakened the power and autonomy of the bishops and made the more contentious ceremonies and phrases of the Prayer Book op-tional. He also wanted to grant freedom of religious assembly (if not equality of political rights) to the tiny minority of Puritans and Catholics who could not accept even a latitudinarian national Church. For eighteen months he fought for this mod-erate settlement only to be defeated by the determination of the rigorist Anglican majority in the Cavalier Parliament, by the lukewarmness of his advisers, and by the self-destructive be-haviour of Richard Baxter and the Puritan leaders. They re-fused the senior positions in the Church offered them, they campaigned against toleration, and they persisted in unreason-able demands at the conference held to reform the Prayer Book. Their Scottish colleagues, more flexible and pragmatic, achieved a settlement acceptable to a majority of their brethren.

Charles finally abandoned the quest for a comprehensive Church and assented to the Act of Uniformity which restored the old Church, lock, stock, and barrel, and which imposed a number of stringent oaths and other tests on the clergy. In consequence about one in five of the clergy were ejected by the end of 1662, and many of them began to set up conventicles outside the Church. Charles then set about promoting the cause of religious toleration for all non-Anglicans. Even though his first attempt in January 1663 was a failure, he had the consola-tion of knowing that he had reversed traditional roles. The pre-war Puritans had looked to Parliament for protection from the king; the new non-conformists had to look to him for protection from Parliament. For fifteen years this made his position in relation to the majority of them politically safe. None the less, it was the single greatest weakness of the Res-toration settlement. A comprehensive political settlement was set against a narrow, intolerant religious settlement. Few local governors were Dissenters; but many were sympathetic to them and reluctant to impose the full strictures of the vindictive laws which Parliament went on to pass against their religious assemblies.

In general, Charles's problems did not arise from the settlement but from his preferred lines of policy. In some ways, he was a lazy king. His adolescence and early manhood had been dominated by the desire to gain the throne and once he had returned from exile all his ambition was spent. He was the only one of the Stuarts not to be a visionary, not to have long-term goals. This made it easy for him to back down whenever his policies were strongly opposed. But while he lacked vision, he did not lack prejudices and preferences. He was a man with a strong rationalist streak—a worldly man with many mistresses and seventeen acknowledged bastards, a cynic with regard to human nature, an intellectual dilettante who took a lively if spasmodic interest in the affairs of the Royal Society launched at his accession. But this intellectual empiricism was joined with an emotional and spiritual mysticism which he got from his parents. He believed that he possessed semi-divine powers and attributes (no king touched so much for the king's evil, that class of unpleasant glandular and scrofulous disorders that kings were reputed to be able to cure). He was also strongly drawn to Roman Catholicism. His mother, wife, brother, and favourite sister were all Catholics and while he had a *bonhomie* which made him accessible to many, it was superficial, and he was only really close to his family. He knew that wherever Catholicism was strong, monarchy was strong. The Catholics had remained conspicuously loyal to his father. If any theology of Grace made sense to Charles it was Catholic doctrine (of his mistresses, Charles said that he could not believe that God would damn a man for taking a little pleasure by the way). He was drawn to Catholicism and twice revealed that preference (in a secret treaty with France in 1670 and in his deathbed reception into the Catholic Church). He was much too sensible politically to declare himself except on his deathbed. But it did lead him to make clear his commitment to toleration. Both this and his obvious admiration for his cousin Louis XIV of France caused growing alarm in England.

Charles was given a generous financial settlement in 1660–1 (£1.2 million per annum), principally from indirect taxation. Bad housekeeping made this inadequate in his early years, and in general it left him with little flexibility. He had no ability to raise emergency taxation without recourse to Parliament and limited access to long-term credit. Thus although Charles had sole responsibility for foreign policy and for making war and peace, Parliament clearly would not vote the necessary revenues without a consideration of the cause for which the money was needed.

The period needed a great administrative reformer in the mould of Henry VIII's Thomas Cromwell, and it did not find one. Decision-making and policy enforcement needed restructuring and formalizing. The Council was too large and amorphous to be effective, and decisions were too often made at one *ad hoc* meeting in the king's chambers and unmade at a subsequent *ad hoc* meeting. This led to real uncertainty and eventually to panic about who was in charge. With the Council emasculated, enforcement of policy was left to individual ministers and departments without co-ordination. Patronage was chaotically handled. Equally, Parliament was inefficient and increasingly crotchety. Charles, feeling that those elected in 1661 were as loyal a group of royalists as he was likely to meet, kept the 'Cavalier' Parliament in almost annual sessions for eighteen years. In part, its inefficiency was due to a growing rivalry between the two Houses, especially over the Lords' claim to take over much of the jurisdiction of the defunct conciliar courts, and a number of sessions were wrecked by deadlock on such issues. In part, its inefficiency was due to there being no government programme for it to get its teeth into. A body of several hundred members without recognized leadership spent much time discussing what to discuss. With most senior ministers in the Lords, and a predisposition to resist management by the court, the 1660s and 1670s were years of drift. Charles ruled without serious threat to his position at home or abroad. The early euphoria gave way to a mild polit- ical depression as the final ravages of plague, the humiliating Dutch incursions up the Medway during the second Dutch war (1665–7), and the Great Fire of London (1666) sapped the self-confidence of 1660–1 that God would bless a land that had come to its senses.

There were many political embarrassments, such as the defeat of a major attempt to introduce religious toleration (1672–3), the suspension of interest payments on his loans (1672), and the political brawls in Parliament as the discredited ministers of the 'Cabal' administration blamed each other for their collect- ive failure (1674–5). But the only challenge to his authority came in the Exclusion crisis of 1678–81. This was triggered by the revelations of Titus Oates, Israel Tonge, and other desper- adoes of a popish plot to murder Charles and put his Catholic brother on the throne. This was more lucid and more plausible than many similar tales, but was just as mendacious. The mysterious death of an investigating magistrate and the discov- ery of conspiratorial letters in the possession of James's private secretary also heightened tension. The result was a full-scale attempt to place a parliamentary bar on the accession of James and thereby to shatter Charles's divine-right theories of govern- ment.

In fact the political leaders of the Exclusion movement were at least as concerned to use the crisis to clip Charles's wings as James's. For the first twelve months their target was not James but Charles's Cavalier-Anglican chief minister, the earl of Danby. This appears odd, but it is clear that Shaftesbury, the leader of the Opposition, saw Danby's regime as just as much a threat to liberties as James might be. Danby's principles were the very antithesis of Shaftesbury's, in that he had developed sophist- icated techniques of parliamentary management, had centralized financial control, had upset the balance of interests in local government to the advantage of Cavalier-Anglicans, seemed willing to develop a standing army in peacetime, and had allied with the Dutch against the French. Shaftesbury, a turncoat in the Civil War, a member of Barebones Parliament and of Cromwell's council of state, who had served Charles as Chancellor of the Exchequer and Lord Chancellor, had a consistent record of supporting free and unfettered Parliaments, decentralization, religious toleration, a horror of standing armies, and a distaste for the Dutch. Danby's policies amounted in fact to nothing more than a programme to give Charles II a quiet life: to Shaftesbury it looked like incipient absolutism. By now there was such a conjunction in people's minds between Popery and arbitrary government, that even Danby could be portrayed as a secret agent of the papists, despite his impeccable Anglicanism. Only when Danby was imprisoned in the Tower did Shaftesbury turn to Exclusion, as an end in itself and as a means to other ends. These included shattering the theoretical basis of divine right and creating the need for continued political action and cohesion (to secure Exclusion on Charles's death, for James would hardly accept it without a fight). To secure Exclusion, Shaftesbury created the first political party in English history. His 'Whigs' produced a mass of propaganda, organized petitions and demonstrations, and co-ordinated campaigns in three successive general elections (1679–81).

They failed. Charles held all the trump cards. The Whigs were fatally divided over who should take James's place as heir—Monmouth, the favoured royal bastard, or Mary, James's Protestant daughter. Almost without exception, the Whigs were committed to lawful, peaceful action only. The memories of civil war were too strong to allow violent councils to hold sway. Charles could, and did, use his power to summon and dissolve Parliament to his own advantage; he had a solid majority in the House of Lords that would vote down the Exclusion Bill time after time; a trade boom enhanced royal revenues on trade and freed Charles from financial worry; and his policy of offering concessions short of Exclusion bought off many moderates. Shaftesbury fatally assumed that Charles would weaken under pressure. He never grasped that Charles would always concede matters of policy, but never matters of principle. He would never have surrendered his divine right. His ultimate sacrifice would have been to divorce the barren queen he respected if he did not cherish, to remarry, and to solve the succession crisis via the marriage bed. It would have been the supreme demonstration of his political style.

As it was, the same iron nerve, pragmatism, and easy good-will to all, which he had demonstrated in 1660, won him the day. A nation racked by political deadlock for three years backed off, took stock, and rallied to him. In his last years he was able to pick off those who had crossed him, reward those who had stood by him, enjoy a quiet life at last. He left a nation governed by and for those who believed in the divine right of kings, the divine right of the Church of England, and the divine right of the localities to run their own affairs. The complacency of the Tory-Anglicans knew no bounds, as they welcomed James II to the throne, the king whose rights they had protected. Such complacency was in for a rude shock.

James was in fact a bigot. His government of Scotland in the early 1680s had seen a most severe repression and extensive use of judicial torture against Protestant Dissenters ('conventic-lers'). Worse still, James believed himself to be a moderate. He had no deliberate plan to set himself up as an absolutist king on the Continental model. But since a trade boom greatly en-hanced royal revenues (and his first Parliament, meeting under threat of a military bid for the throne by Charles's favoured bastard, the duke of Monmouth, voted higher rates in addi-tion), he was able to maintain an army of 20,000 men. The army's most striking characteristic was its professionalism and the apolitical views of its career commanders. James had twice urged Charles to use his tiny army to get rid of troublesome Parliaments. He would not have hesitated to use his army against a recalcitrant assembly, but he did not intend to rule without Parliament. Indeed, at the time of his fall, he was engaged in the most elaborate operation ever attempted, to 'pack' Parliament with sympathizers. Until early 1688 James's second marriage, more than a decade old, was childless. James—already fifty years old—expected to be succeeded by his Protestant daughter Mary and her Dutch husband, William of Orange. He intended to secure for all time a religious and civil equality for his co-religionists. This meant not only removing from them all the penalties and disabilities under the Penal Laws (fines for non-attendance at Anglican worship) and Test Acts (barring them from all offices and paid employments under the Crown), but also allowing the Catholic Church to be set up alongside the Anglican Church. This meant establishing a Catholic hierarchy and diocesan structure and public places of worship. It also meant allowing Catholics a share in the universities (maybe even the take-over—or 'restoration'—of some colleges to serve as Catholic seminaries). It would probably have led on to granting Catholics exemption from tithes and the authority of Anglican courts. James honestly believed that once the ban on Catholic evangelism was lifted, once the civil and religious disabilities were removed, the return of hundreds of thousands to the Faith was certain. He believed that this granting of 'equal status' to Catholics was a humane and moderate programme. If, in the short term, a certain amount of positive discrimination was necessary to favour Catholics in appointments to national and local office, this too was only fair as a correcting exercise.

It need hardly be said that the Tory-Anglican political nation was outraged. Their loyalty to the Church proved greater than their loyalty to their anointed king. James soon discovered that no Tory-Anglican Parliament would repeal the anti-Catholic legislation and while a packed judiciary would uphold his suspension of that legislation, it would come back into force the moment he died and his Protestant heir took over. He therefore made a desperate bid to jettison the Tory squirearchy and to build an alternative power base in an alliance of Catholics and Protestant Dissenters. Three-quarters of all JPs were sacked, together with most lord-lieutenants. The new men were of lower social origin, and James's purge constituted a greater social revolution in local government than had been attempted even in the years 1646–60. James called in the charters of most towns and reorganized their governments to give Dissenters control (this was especially vital if he was to get a sympathetic parliamentary majority). To win over the Dissenters, a Declaration of Indulgence was issued giving them full religious freedom.

The Tory-Anglicans were stung, but initially pacific. The whirlwind would blow itself out; James would die and Mary succeed him; they would take their revenge. Passive disobedience would limit James's success. Thus seven bishops petitioned him explaining why they would not obey his order to instruct their clergy to read the Declaration of Indulgence to their flocks. They also committed the Church to a future Anglican toleration of Protestant Dissenters. James had the bishops tried for seditious libel, but even his judges summed up against him and they were acquitted. However, the Tory complacency of 1687 ('we are not to be laughed out of our doctrine of Non-Resistance and passive obedience on all occasions' wrote the marquis of Halifax) turned to stunned horror in June 1688 with the birth of a son and heir to James II. Now indeed the possibility of a dynasty of rabid Catholics appeared to stretch out before them.

Ironically, while many Anglican leaders came to put their religion before their political principles, many Dissenters chose to put political principles first. They had little doubt that James was using them for present purposes only. Thus leaders of both parties joined in the desperate expedient of inviting William of Orange to come to England, suitably protected with armed men, to remonstrate with James. Perhaps they really believed that this would lead to James agreeing to William's humiliating terms: the recall of the writ designed to produce a packed Parliament and new writs to return a 'free' Parliament; a declaration of war on France; and a commission to investigate the legitimacy of the infant Prince of Wales. Only a minority were willing to join William's invasion by taking up arms; but even fewer were willing to lift their little fingers to help James.

Whatever those who invited William may have expected, William himself almost certainly intended to depose James. He was taking a quite outrageous risk, justified only by the necessity of harnessing the whole of Britain's military, naval, and financial resources to the struggle against Louis XIV. But how he expected to secure the throne is less clear. In the event, he was able to get himself proclaimed joint ruler with Mary within a matter of weeks because James had what can only be called a complete mental collapse. His army and William's never met. William landed at Torbay on 5 November and moved east. James brought his army as far as Salisbury where incessant nosebleeds held him up. As his behaviour became more and more bizarre and manic, many of his professional officers and commanders deserted him. James then fled back to London and was quickly in William's hands. Even then, his position was not hopeless. A series of vague undertakings and promises would have ensured that he retained the loyalty of most peers and leading gentry. But he was beyond reason. He twice escaped (on the first occasion, to William's annoyance, being captured on the Kent coast by well-meaning fishermen and sent back). His flight to France, the public promises of Louis XIV to use French arms to restore him, and William's clear statement that he would not protect the realm unless he shared the throne with his wife, left the political nation no choice. Almost all Whigs and most Tories, rationalizing their conduct as best they could, and in a variety of ways, agreed that James had vacated his throne and that the Crown be offered jointly to William and Mary. The Glorious Revolution of 1688 was even more unanticipated and unplanned than the Great Rebellion of 1642; its consequences probably more momentous.

Had the English Revolution had any lasting effects on the power of the Crown? The answer is that it had surprisingly little. In the 1680s the Crown was far better endowed financially, it had a growing but still inadequate civil service, and an unprecedented opportunity to create a standing army. Parliaments had shown themselves quite unable to defeat the king, in the sense of imposing on him restrictions and conditions that he disliked or taking away from him powers he had hitherto enjoyed. The royal prerogatives in the 1680s were little different from those of the 1600s. The king could veto bills he did not approve; he could dispense individuals from the operation of statutes; he could pardon whomsoever he chose. He selected his own councillors, judges, senior administrators, and he could dismiss most of them at will. He was not bound to take anyone's advice. If he had lost most of his feudal revenues and his 'discretionary' powers to raise money, he had been amply compensated by parliamentary taxes, some in perpetuity, others for life.

The only really major weakening of royal power had come in the legislation of 1641 which abolished those courts and councils which were particularly susceptible to royal control. The most important restriction was the one which took away from the Privy Council its judicial power. Its teeth removed, the Council ceased to be an executive, active body, monitoring, cajoling, and directing the work of local government, and reverted to what it had begun as: a talking shop, a place where the king sought advice. It probably never functioned as well under the Stuarts as under the Tudors; James I allowed factionalism to spill over from the Council to the floor of Parliament; Charles I did not want to hear alternative proposals from groups within the Council. He wanted puppets to confirm his own preconceptions. Charles II enjoyed policy-making in secret, summoning ministers to hasty meetings in his private quarters, so that no one knew what was going on. For different reasons, each of these monarchs encouraged the growth of secret committees of the Council comprising the holders of key offices. Here was the seed of the Cabinet councils of the eighteenth century. Other conciliar courts abolished in 1641 included Star Chamber, High Commission, Requests, and—more by chance than design—the Regional Councils of the north and in the marches of Wales. Charles II was restricted at the Restoration not by the gentry in Parliament, but by the gentry in the provinces. Almost all the methods by which Tudor and early

Stuart kings could bring recalcitrant county communities to heel had been taken away. Government was more than ever by their active consent. In the 1660s all taxation except the customs, all ecclesiastical legislation (such as the Act of Uniformity, the Conventicle Acts, and the Five Mile Act), and most security matters, were entrusted to the gentry magistrates with no appeal from their decisions to the central courts.

The abolition of the monarchy and the experience of republican rule thus had a very limited direct impact. Even the memory of Charles I's public trial, conviction, and decapitation did not change the monarchy's pretensions to rule by divine right nor make them more respectful of Parliaments. After all, the political nation knew that regicide had cost them dear, that it had added to, rather than removed, their oppressions. The problems of matching resources to responsibilities had become clearer; but the problems themselves had neither increased nor diminished. The alternatives for England were to see either a strengthening of the central executive and administration at the expense of the independent county gentry; or else a further withering away of the centre, turning England into a series of semi-autonomous county-states, self-governing, undertaxed, stagnant. The latter was the preference of a range of 'Country parties' visible in the Parliaments of the 1620s, the neutralist groups in the Civil War, and many Whigs in the 1670s and 1680s. It was also the preference of republicans such as John Milton, who admired the Dutch republic and longed to see the same oligarchic civic humanism develop in England. Most dramatically, it was the ideal of democratic groups such as the Levellers, who wanted to make governors more accountable, government subservient to the liberties of a sovereign people, and who therefore urged devolution of power to elected local magistrates and juries. But these 'Country' ideologies were incompatible with the development of a global empire. The expansion into the West Indies and along the eastern seaboard of North America (from Carolina to the St. Lawrence); into extensive trade networks with South America, West Africa, India, and Indonesia; even the protection of the vital trades with the southern and eastern Mediterranean all required strong naval and military power. This could only be sustained by a massive increase in the ability of the State to tax and to wage war. It was the combined threat of Louis XIV and the exiled James II after 1689 to introduce Popery and arbitrary government which finally forced through the necessary constitutional and political changes, as the following chapter will show. The Stuart century was one of unresolved tensions.

Intellectual and Religious Life

For the Church of England, if not for the monarchy, the seventeenth century was an age of disillusionment. By the time of the Glorious Revolution of 1688–9 it had lost the intellectual, moral, spiritual authority it had acquired by 1603. Intellectually, Anglicanism was on the offensive at the beginning of the century. The generation living through the events of 1559 witnessed a settlement cobbled together to meet political necessities, a hybrid of Protestant doctrine and Catholic practice. The criticisms of the first generation of Puritans were the more telling because their Marian exile allowed them to speak from experience of the purity of the Continental reformed churches. The new generation of the 1590s and 1600s had known no other Church, and had come to love the rhythms of the Anglican liturgical year and the cadences of Cranmer's liturgy. The work of Jewel, Hooker, and Andrewes presented the Church of England as the best of all Churches, claiming an apostolic descent and an uninterrupted history from the Celtic Church which gave it a greater authority than the schismatic Protestant Churches, and a superiority over Rome in that it had sloughed off the corruptions and failings of the Roman Catholic Church just as it had sloughed off the usurped authority of the bishops of Rome. The Church of England had an authority as ancient and as apostolic as Rome's, and a practice more true to the injunctions of Christ. These were claims which the Puritans did not find easy to meet.

Puritans displayed an increasing willingness to work within the Church. Their response to James I's accession, the Millenary Petition, called only for modifications within the existing framework. At the Hampton Court Conference of 1604, in which James presided over a meeting of bishops and Puritans, discussion was entirely about how to make the episcopal national Church more effectively evangelical. Puritans yearned for a godly prince who, like the Emperor Constantine 1,200 years before, would bring good order to his State, and promote and protect true religion. They chafed for more to do, rather than for less. They worked within the Church and not against it. Even the 5 per cent of the nation who made up the Catholic recusants succumbed to an intellectual onslaught led by Anglican divines. The greatest single debate on any issue in the first quarter of the century was over the duties of Catholics to take the oath of allegiance and to eschew papal claims to command their political allegiance. Anglican arguments prevailed and the Catholics, while holding to their faith, abandoned political resistance. The Gunpowder plot was the last real popish plot. As English Catholicism became controlled less by militant clergy and more by a prudent peerage and gentry, its pacifism and political acquiescence grew.

Protestant unity, if not uniformity, was retained until the Long Parliament. Puritans added their own practices to those of the Church, but the number who opted out and set up conventicles or assemblies in defiance of the Church was extremely few. Some hundreds, perhaps thousands, moved to New England rather than submit to the narrow interpretation of Anglican practice required by Archbishop Laud. But there was no schism.

The Civil War and Interregnum years saw the disintegration not only of Anglicanism, but of English Puritanism. The structure of the Church of England was abolished (bishops, church courts) or proscribed (the Prayer Book, the celebration of Christmas or Easter). Cathedrals were turned into preaching centres or secularized (used as barracks, prisons, shopping arcades). In thousands of parishes the old services and celebrations were carried on despite the proscriptions. But the Church leaders lost their nerve. The bishops fled, hid, remained silent. They were not replaced as they died. By 1660 the survivors were all over seventy years of age, and Church of England bishops were an endangered species.

But those who dreamed of replacing Anglicanism by a Calvinist church like those of Massachusetts, Scotland, or Geneva were disappointed. The Presbyterian system conceived by Parliament was stillborn. The chaos of the Civil War created a bewildering variety of sects and gathered churches. The Baptists, one of the few strong underground churches before 1640, spread widely via the army. Many new groups denied Calvinist notions of an Elect predestined to salvation, and proclaimed God's Grace to be freely available. Some even proclaimed universal salvation. Such groups were most evident in London and other provincial cities. The largest of all the sects was the Quakers, whose informal missionary evangelism in the countryside gained thousands of adherents in the 1650s: denouncing the formalization of religion, and the specious authority of 'hireling priests' in their 'steeple houses', the Quakers urged men to find the divine spark within themselves, the Holy Spirit which came direct to the Christian, mediated neither by the Church nor Scripture. Their hatred of formal worship and of tithes led them into widespread campaigns of militant passive disobedience. One of their leaders, James Nayler, was tried for blasphemy by the second Protectorate Parliament in 1656. Although he escaped the sentence of death, he was subject to a variety of severe physical punishments, Parliament taking several hours to contemplate which bits of him should be sliced or cut off.

There was no recovering the old triumphalism after 1660. The Church might be outwardly restored to its ancient forms at the Restoration, but it had neither the self-assurance nor the power to reimpose a general uniformity. Anglican apologetic was defensive and edgy. With the disappearance of High Commission and the rust of disuse settled in its diocesan courts, it lacked the weapons to punish defaulters. The ignominy of its abolition left it institutionally enfeebled. In 1660 the celebration of Easter and the ubiquitous return of maypoles may have been spontaneous and have shown signs of its deep roots in popular culture. But those who chose to defy it were not going to be forced back into its assemblies. The decision in 1662 not to broaden its appeal by adapting its liturgy and by softening episcopal pretensions drove two thousand clergy out of the Church. Despite the attempts to prevent unlawful conventicles, the Baptists, Quakers, and other radicals were not to be up-rooted. Even more important, the tens of thousands of 'Dissenters' of 1662 who were within the moderate Puritan tradition re-examined whether their desire to be part of a national Church (though not the one on offer) outweighed their desire for a pure worship of God. In the 1580s and the 1600s they had preferred to 'tarry for the magistrate', to stay in the Church and to wait for better times. In Restoration England, they came more and more to opt for separation. In the early seventeenth century they found 'much piety in Babylon'; now they abandoned such temporizing and went into schism. The Toleration Act of 1689 was the formal recognition of the fact of religious pluralism. Unable to punish those who were not its members, and unable to compel men and women to be its members, the Church of England was a spent spiritual force.

In the early and mid-seventeenth century, most intellectuals and most governors believed that there was a divine imperative to bring godliness, good discipline, and order to the English nation. God was guiding His people towards a Promised Land of peace and justice in which men would love and worship him as it was their duty to do. The vision of a better world that could be built by man's response to the divine challenge was shared by James and Charles I, by Wentworth and Laud, by Pym and Cromwell. All political writings were suffused by the immanence of God in his Creation, by a deep sense of God's activity in human history and in His providences, His signs of Himself. Shakespeare's plays, Donne's poems, the thoughts of

Henry Parker and the young John Milton all proclaim the same point: the plays of Marlowe are the exceptions that prove the rule.

No such hopes survived the Interregnum. The trauma of regicide left few royalists with faith in the providences of God; the much deeper sense of betrayal experienced by the radicals in 1660 largely explains their political quiescence thereafter. Psychologically, the pain of betrayal after such visible testimonies of divine favour was too great. Instead, most of the Puritans and their heirs internalized the kingdom of God. They accepted the world as the domain of sin and of imperfectibility. Within this vale of tears, each person must seek personal peace by building a temple of grace within himself or herself. This acceptance of the limits of what Church and State could achieve dominated the ideology of the late seventeenth century. It is apparent in the way Charles II's jaundiced view of the world was combined with his deep personal mysticism, in the latitudinarianism of the bishops and of the clerical establishment; in the Dissenters' abandonment of the quest for a national Church. A few men continued to seek the millennium (Sir Isaac Newton combined his successful search for physical laws with an unsuccessful search for the dating of the Second Coming from the runes in the Book of Revelation), but most settled for making the most of things as they were. John Milton heroically confronted a God who appeared to have guided his people in the 1640s and 1650s only to betray them in 1660. *Paradise Lost* looked at the Omnipotent Creator who let man fall, *Paradise Regained* looked at the temptation of Christ in the wilderness, at the false worldly ways in which Man might proclaim the gospel. Perhaps republicans had been tempted into the wrong paths. *Samson Agonistes*, most poignantly of all, studied a man given great gifts by God who failed to use them in His service. Just as Samson dallied with Delilah and was shorn of his strength, so the republicans had been distracted by the things of the flesh in the 1650s and had missed their chance to do God's will. But the more typical Puritan work of the Restoration is

Bunyan's *Pilgrim's Progress* which concerns the individual's personal search for peace and salvation.

Christianity was being depoliticized and demystified. The characteristic Anglican tracts of the late seventeenth century had titles like *The Reasonableness of Christianity* and *Christianity not Mysterious*. Where God had been in the very warp and woof of nature and life, he now became the creator who set things going, and the spirit who worked within the individual and kept him obedient to moral rules. Sermons stressed the merits of neighbourliness and charity. Ministers were encouraged to preach that religious duties meant being kind to old people and animals rather than preaching about the transformation of the world. From the Dissenting side, John Locke, pleading for religious toleration, defined a church as a voluntary society of men, meeting together to worship God in such fashion as they deemed appropriate. Religion had become an unthreatening matter, almost a hobby. The authorities need not concern themselves with what consenting adults did in private meetings. The Puritans of previous generations could not have conceived anything so anaemic.

This dilution of religious energies, this breakdown of a world-view dominated by religious imperatives can be seen in literature and in science. Restoration theatre differs from Jacobean not in its vulgarity or even in its triviality so much as in its secularism. Metaphysical poetry, which rooted religious experience in the natural world, gave way to a religious poetry either more cerebral and coolly rational, or else more ethereal and other-worldly.

Secularization was also an aspect of change in the visual arts. Tudor and Stuart country houses emphasized paternalistic Christian values, being built around a great hall in which the household and a wider community gathered to do business and to eat together. There might be a 'high table', reflecting hierarchy and degree, but there was an easy informality of social relations. By the late seventeenth century, new houses had 'withdrawing' rooms and private dining-rooms, while servants and other members of the household were given separate quarters. Houses were set in spacious parks surrounded by high walls and patrolled by gamekeepers. Royal palaces showed the way in these developments.

The seventeenth century, like the sixteenth, saw little church building. Perhaps a majority of all new churches were those needed in London after the Great Fire of 1666. There was, however, a stark contrast between the intensity and devotional emphasis of early Stuart churches and chapels such as the one at Peterhouse, Cambridge, and the coolness, light, rationalist air of Wren's London churches. Allegorical stained glass and dark wood panelling gave way to marble. The recumbent effigies of souls at rest gave way to an upright statuary of men and women reflecting on their moral duties.

In all the visual arts, the influence of the Counter-Reformation art of Spain, Spanish Italy, Spanish Netherlands—an ornateness that bound together the natural and the supernatural worlds—gave way to the influences of Louis XIV's France—self-indulgent, revelling in its own material extravagance. In the early seventeenth century, artists, musicians, and poets joined forces to produce the Masque, an entertainment that sought to bring together the world of classical civilization and Christian values, of audiences drawn into the action as performers, a merging of fantasy and reality. The power of the illusion was so great in the case of Inigo Jones and Ben Jonson's Masques for Charles I, that the king came to believe that his own piety and virtue would soon infect his subjects and that order and uniformity could be as easily achieved in the State as on the stage. No such illusion bedevilled the artifice of the opera, the equivalent art-form of the late seventeenth century. While early Stuart writers wrestled with the heroic and the tragic, late Stuart writers turned to the domesticated homiletics of the novel and to the mock epics of Dryden and later of Pope.

Restoration science was just as secularized. In the 1640s and 1650s, scientists had sought what they termed 'a great instauration'. Drawing on the ideas of Francis Bacon, and led by visionary social engineers such as Samuel Hartlib and the Bohemian exile Comenius, the scientific establishment were lionized by the Puritan politicians and undertook to build a Brave New World. Man would tame and gain dominion over the natural world. Medical advances would vanquish disease, agricultural advances would conquer hunger and want. The reformation of justice and of education would bring man into peaceful enjoyment of the new order. It was yet another facet of Protestant eschatology, and the scientific Zion, like other Zions, evaporated in 1660. The later seventeenth century in the Royal Society was not an age of visions but of piecemeal enquiry and improvement. Francis Bacon's principles of exact observation, measurement, and of inductive reasoning, refined by the Frenchman Descartes, allowed major advances in the classification and study of plant and animal life. Harvey's discovery of the circulation of the blood, just before the Civil War, led on to a series of advances in the knowledge of anatomy and physiology in the second half of the century. Isaac Newton's *Philosophiae Naturalis Principia Mathematica* (1687) was the basis of understanding of the physical laws for two hundred years, and the work of Robert Boyle in chemistry and Robert Hooke in geology created new disciplines on the basis of extensive experimentation and measurement. The advance of the physical sciences hit hard at the older mysteries. The discovery of the geometrical movement of heavenly bodies destroyed the credibility of astrology in intellectual circles. It is astonishing how quickly the discovery of natural laws bred a confidence that *everything* had a natural explanation. The realm of magic, of witches and spells, was abandoned by the educated. Within a generation of 1640 the prosecution of witches almost ceased. This was not because the people at large ceased to believe in curses and in magic, but because it was impossible to secure convictions from sceptical judges and jurors. Science and technology did not in fact advance on all fronts. The economy remained almost wholly dependent on human and animal muscle-power. No progress was made towards harnessing steam, let alone gas or electricity as energy sources. The extraction of minerals from the ground and the smelting of ore contributed another technological bottle-neck. Science was changing attitudes, not transforming the economy.

Political thought was being secularized too. Thomas Hobbes stripped sovereignty of its moral basis; in *Leviathan* (1651) the concept of legitimacy as the justification of political authority was replaced by a concentration on *de facto* power and the ability to afford protection to the subjects who lived under this power. Machiavelli remained an odious name but his ideas became more and more persuasive as a counter to the divine-right pieties of Robert Filmer and of Stuart apologists.

The English Revolution does, then, stand as a turning-point. It may have achieved little that any of the parties sought after or fought for. It may have done even less to transform political and social institutions. But it deeply affected the intellectual values, at least of the political élite. An age which derived its momentum from Christian humanism, from chivalry, from a reverential antiquarianism, gave way to an age of pragmatism and individualism. When John Locke wrote in his second *Treatise of Government* (1690) that 'all men are naturally in a state of perfect freedom to order their actions and dispose of their possessions and persons as they think fit without asking the leave or depending upon the will of any man' he was proclaiming a message only made possible by the disillusionment with old ideals, but a message which was to make much possible in the decades to come.

7. The Eighteenth Century
(1688–1789)

═══

PAUL LANGFORD

Revolution and its Repercussions

THE historical importance of the Revolution of 1688—the 'Glorious Revolution'—has inevitably fluctuated in the process of constant reinterpretation by successive generations. It has fared particularly badly at the hands of the twentieth century, and threatens to disappear altogether under the demands of modern historical scholarship. The decisive triumph of the liberal and democratic spirit, beloved of Macaulay and the Victorian Whigs, has dwindled into the conservative reaction of a selfish oligarchy. Especially when compared with modern revolutions, it seems rather to resemble a palace coup than a genuine shift of social or political power. This impression is reinforced, perhaps, by what was seen at the time as one of its most creditable features—the relative absence of physical violence. Yet this aspect can be exaggerated. In Scotland, the supporters of the deposed king had to be crushed by force of arms, a process which was completed in 1689. In Ireland there was positively a blood-bath, one which still holds a prominent place in Irish myths and memories. When the siege of Londonderry was lifted, and James II decisively defeated at the battle of the Boyne, Ulster Protestants certainly considered their salvation to be glorious, but they can hardly have thought of it as bloodless.

The story might easily have been the same in England. The

former royalist Nicholas L'Estrange testified that only chance, the disarray of James II's friends, and above all the king's surprising failure to raise the royal standard in his own realm, prevented a civil war as ferocious as those of the mid-century. Yet L'Estrange's very relief that his family had been saved further sacrifices in the cause of the Stuarts perhaps provides a clue to the comparative tranquillity associated with the making of the revolution in England. A perceptible sense of compromise, of the need to step back from the brink, carries over the centuries from the debates of the assembly which met in London in January 1689. The Convention, which transformed itself into Parliament by the simple expedient of passing an Act to that effect, displayed an understandable desire to legitimize what was manifestly illegitimate by following as far as possible the procedural forms employed at the Restoration in 1660. On matters of substance, the priority was plainly to find a common core of agreement rather than to test the more extreme solutions offered by either side. William of Orange was made king, with Mary as queen. Tories, led by Danby, would have preferred Mary as sole monarch, or some species of regency ruling technically in the name of James II. But the Protestant saviour would accept nothing less than the crown, and so it was. None the less, every effort was made to conceal the revolutionary nature of what was being done. Though James's supposedly illegal acts—particularly his reliance on a standing army and his recourse to the dispensing and suspending powers—were formally condemned, the Bill of Rights went out of its way to pretend that the deposed king had in effect abdicated, leaving a deserted realm no alternative but to seek the protection of the House of Orange. Implausible though this appeared, it was sufficient to secure the assent of a majority of the ruling class. There were, inevitably, exceptions. Some churchmen, led by Sancroft, the Archbishop of Canterbury, and two of the bishops who had helped bring James II down in the Seven Bishops Case, declined to take even the cautiously worded oaths designed by the Convention. Others, like the Nottingham

Tories, old champions of the court in the reaction of 1681–7, wrestled with the concept of a rightful king who owed his title to a *de facto* decision of Parliament, but not to the *de jure* ordinance of heaven.

Yet the substantive acceptance of parliamentary monarchy was achieved. The profound importance of this achievement was obscured not merely by conscious attempts to avoid dogmatic prescriptions in 1689 but by the long agonies which followed. Passive obedience and non-resistance continued to be influential concepts, buttressed as they were by elaborate arguments stressing the providential nature of the Protestant Wind in 1688, and the duty of every citizen to co-operate with any form of authority rather than submit to anarchy. For a generation, these notions continued to work on men's minds, bestowing a sense of legitimacy on the rage and despair felt by many who had seen the necessity for what had happened in 1688 but found it difficult to live with all the consequences. Beyond that, they sank into the Anglican orthodoxy of the eighteenth-century mind and helped secure the underlying authoritarianism which was to remain an important element of political ideology in the age of the American and French Revolutions. But, with this reservation, the major change of course carried out in 1688 can be seen to have been truly revolutionary. The Bill of Rights clearly overrode the hereditary right which formed the basis of the restored constitution of 1660 and replaced it with the will of the nation expressed through Parliament. First William and Mary, then Mary's sister Anne, and finally, after the death of the latter's son the duke of Gloucester in 1700, the Electors of Hanover (descended from James I through the female line) all owed their title to the determination of the propertied classes. At a time when absolutism, both in theory and practice, seemed to be in the ascendant in the Western world, the importance of this transformation should not be underestimated. Eighteenth- and nineteenth-century Whigs exaggerated the coherence and completeness of the contract theory which seemed to have triumphed in 1689 and they underrated the tensions, contradictions, and conflicts which it entailed. But they were fundamentally correct in seeing it as a historic turning-point involving the decisive rejection of an entire conception of government.

The status of the monarchy was very much the conscious concern of the revolutionaries of 1688. It is doubtful whether many of them foresaw the consequences of their actions in terms of England's relations with foreign powers. In this respect, indeed, the importance of the Revolution is undenied and undeniable. Before 1688, the policy of successive rulers, Cromwell, Charles II, and James II, had been largely pro-French and anti-Dutch. After 1688 France was to become a more or less permanent enemy, and certainly a constant rival in the battle for supremacy overseas. The scale of conflict was also novel. The Nine Years War (1688–97) and the War of Spanish Succession (1702–13) involved Britain in both Continental and colonial warfare as she had not been involved since the Elizabethan struggle with Spain, and in the interim the technological and strategic complexity of war-making had vastly increased. The part of Englishmen in this unexpected, if not unpredictable, consequence of the Revolution was affected by various considerations. In terms of grand strategy, the priority was to combat Louis XIV's expansionist policies in the Low Countries, and to prevent the erection of a mighty new Bourbon empire comprising the Spanish as well as French monarchy. The interests of commerce, which once had required protection against Dutch economic enterprise, could now be said to dictate an aggressive stance towards the more sustained challenge of French competition, and especially the assertion of Britain's right to a share in the trade if not the territory of the Spanish empire. These arguments were woven by the Whigs into a systematic case for an interventionist foreign policy, expressed most clearly in the Continental campaigns of William III and Marlborough. But such considerations would not have led many Englishmen to approve the formidable outlay of expenditure and resources in these years if it had not been for the dynastic issue. The Nine

Years War has appropriately been called the War of the English Succession. William would hardly have set sail for Torbay in 1688 if he had not assumed that the English alliance against France would follow logically from his own intervention in English affairs. Yet in fact diplomatic and military support from his new subjects was made much more likely by Louis XIV's imprudent championship of James II. French backing for the Jacobite camp was withdrawn when an uneasy peace was negotiated in 1697. But four years later, with the Spanish Succession at stake, and Europe on the verge of war once more, it was again Louis's support for the Stuarts, this time in the shape of James's son the Old Pretender, which convinced many reluctant Englishmen of the case for involvement in a Continental conflict.

One of the most startling aspects of the wars was the sheer success of English arms, particularly under Marlborough in the War of Spanish Succession. It was not just that the Protestant Succession was effectively secured at least for the present. More striking still was the new reputation earned by a country widely regarded as little more than a pensioner of France only a short time before. Marlborough's triumphs at Blenheim and Ramillies, not to say Rooke's at Gibraltar and Stanhope's at Minorca, established Britain as a major force in Continental politics, a substantial power in the Mediterranean, and a worthy competitor for France overseas. The latter stages of the war, in which military progress seemed to diminish in direct proportion to national expenditure, removed the loftier ambitions suggested by the dazzling victories of the Blenheim period, but when peace was made at Utrecht in 1713 sufficient was secured to retain the essential impact of the successes, and even to create the impression of what French diplomatic historians have termed the 'English hegemony' in Europe.

Hardly less important was the domestic impact of warfare. The cost of the wars amounted to almost £150 million in an age when peacetime expenditure was thought excessive at two millions per annum. This vast outlay required a corresponding rise in levels of taxation, with widespread political repercussions. But more interesting in retrospect is the fact that a large proportion of the bill, approximately one-third, was met by borrowing. Sums of this order could only be found in a buoyant and flexible money market, such as that created by the economic conditions of the late seventeenth century. Though land values were seriously affected by agrarian recession, trade had enjoyed a great upsurge in the 1680s and the investment surpluses released were to wash over the economy for a good many years. A post-revolution government, sorely in need of cash and prepared to mortgage the incomes of unborn generations of taxpayers to permit a competitive interest rate, offered promising investment possibilities. The financiers whose initiative eventually led to the foundation of the Bank of England in 1694 were not, in principle, engaging in anything new. As long as wars had been undertaken, governments had been forced to rely on loans from the business community. What was new was the political infrastructure which was necessitated by the exceptionally heavy borrowing of this period. The credit-worthiness of the new regime, based as it was on a parliamentary title, was negligible without the clear understanding that the propertied classes would ultimately be prepared to foot the bill. Without a matching recognition on the part of the regime that it must closely collaborate with those classes and their representatives, no such understanding could exist. The National Debt and all it entailed was built on this essential nexus of interest linking an illegitimate dynasty, the financial world, and the taxpaying public.

As war followed war and decade followed decade the burden of debt grew. Successive governments found it ever harder to avoid borrowing, and the main function of those taxes which were raised was often merely to pay the interest charges on the debt. With hindsight, the advantages of this system, without precise parallel in contemporary Europe, are obvious. The political security of an otherwise somewhat shaky regime was much enhanced, and national resources in wartime much boosted by this machinery for channelling private wealth into public expenditure. At the time, the disadvantages attracted more attention. The pretence that the National Debt could actually be repaid and the nation released from the threat of bankruptcy became increasingly thin. The anxieties of a society traditionally ill-disposed to taxation in general and new forms of taxation in particular made the task of the Treasury and the Committee of Ways and Means increasingly harrowing. Yet, even at the time, there were those who had a shrewd perception of one quite priceless political advantage of the new system. This arose from its impact on Parliament, and especially on the House of Commons. For everything depended on Parliament's part in this elaborate process, and Parliament was understandably jealous of its rights in matters of finance. The land tax, the basic guarantee of the taxpayer's commitment to the National Debt, was cautiously voted for a year at a time. Even the customs and excise duties, granted for much longer periods, were extended and renewed only after the most prolonged debate and haggling. The 'budget' was nominally an achievement of the mid-century, when the term was first used during Henry Pelham's time as First Lord of the Treasury (1743–54). But its essential features can be traced back to the Revolution, and it is this aspect of 1689 which more than anything else finally secured Parliament's central place in constitutional development. At times in the seventeenth century it had been possible to see the legislature as a faintly absurd and decidedly irritating survival of England's medieval past, an irrational obstruction to efficient monarchical government which might profitably be dispensed with altogether. Now its future was secure; since 1689 Parliament has met for a substantial period every year. In this sense the Revolution gave a novel twist to an old problem: eighteenth-century politicians asked themselves not how to do away with the need for Parliament, or even how to crush it. Rather they had to consider how to manipulate it. The arts of management were to provide the key to the conduct of Georgian politics.

It was impossible in the late seventeenth century to engage in political revolution without raising the prospect or the spectre (depending on one's viewpoint) of ecclesiastical revolution. In this respect the Revolution of 1688 was perhaps important not merely for what it did but for what it failed to do. Many contemporaries hoped for a radical revision of the Church settlement of the 1660s. There was talk of a truly comprehensive national Church, and for some Dissenters, particularly the Presbyterians, the possibilities of reconcilation to the establishment seemed stronger than at any time since Hampton Court in 1604. In the event, however, their hopes were dashed. As in 1662, the Anglican squirearchy would permit no weakening of the hierarchical and episcopalian structure of the Church. It would be inappropriate to talk of a Laudian or high-church reaction at this time. But any sign of genuine *rapprochement* with the Dissenters was quickly extinguished. Instead, the latter were offered the least that could be offered against the background of recent events, a grudging toleration. The Toleration Act of 1689 in effect granted freedom of worship to Protestant nonconformists in premises licensed by Anglican bishops, provided that those concerned shared the basic doctrines laid down in the Thirty-nine Articles and sanctioned by the Act of Uniformity. This seemed a far cry from the prospect held out to Dissenters of all kinds by James II.

No doubt for this reason, it has been customary to play down the full significance of the Toleration Act. An extremely qualified liberty permitted to those whose beliefs were defined in strictly qualified terms seemed a poor reward for men who had resisted the temptations offered by the Declarations of Indulgence and had welcomed William of Orange. But such judgements depend heavily on the point of view. For Dissenters who had been vigorously persecuted as recently as the early 1680s, the Toleration Act provided an unprecedented statutory security. From the vantage point of anxious churchmen it was no less important to maintain the substance of the Restoration Settlement. The Prayer Book of 1662 was to remain the liturgical basis of Anglican worship until the twentieth century; but in 1689 it seemed to offer a precarious platform of doctrine without which established Protestantism might be lost. Paradoxically, the resulting exclusiveness of the Church had much to do with England's eighteenth-century reputation as a civilized society in a barbarous world. A comprehensive national Church embracing all but a small number of sectaries and papists would have been a very different matter from a restricted religious establishment, co-existing with large numbers of nonconformists. The difference was perhaps a tolerant, pluralist society. The legal recognition of liberty of worship went far beyond what had been achieved in most of Europe, and Voltaire was to hold it up as the crucial element in the development of a free society. If so, it was to a large extent the consequence of the Revolution.

The achievements of these years had a price in the social tensions and political conflicts which marked the Augustan era. Pre-eminent among the signs of strain was indeed the plight of the religious establishment. The great cry of the period was 'The Church in Danger'. Whether it was truly in danger seems doubtful in retrospect. Toleration was obviously a fearful blow to those who dreamed of reviving a Laudian church. But the swelling tide of latitudinarian theology and sentiment made it seem innocuous enough to most. Moreover, the political monopoly enjoyed by Anglicans under the Test and Corporation Acts was left intact by the Revolution Settlement. Here, however, was the rub. For in practice there was every indication that Dissenters were able to challenge and evade this monopoly. The readiness of many nonconformists to resort to occasional conformity, annually taking the sacraments according to the Anglican rite in order to meet the requirements of the statutes, and for the rest worshipping in their own meeting houses, was a constant source of irritation to their enemies. Whether the actual practice of occasional conformity grew in this period is uncertain. But it was unquestionably more noticeable now that Dissenting chapels were publicly recognized, and now that the double standard apparently observed by those who attended them was plain to all. Moreover, the general climate of the 1690s and 1700s provoked anxiety and even hysteria on the part of churchmen. Theological speculation and deistic tendencies were much discussed and much feared. John Toland's *Christianity Not Mysterious*, one of the earliest and most systematic attempts to popularize the case for 'natural' against 'revealed' religion, began a torrent of polemical debate on such matters in 1697. Nor did it help that some of the worst offenders were themselves clergy of the established Church. Samuel Clarke, the Whig sceptic whose assault on Trinitarianism brought the wrath of Convocation upon his head in 1712, and Benjamin Hoadly, who held three bishoprics in succession but denied the divine nature both of his office and of the Church itself, were only the more spectacular examples of the heretical spirit which seemed to mark the progress of the early Enlightenment in England.

The high-church reaction to these trends reached its peak under Queen Anne when the presence on the throne of a pious and theologically conservative queen provided an additional impulse. But its force derived much from other developments, many of them connected with party politics. The Tories, who frequently described themselves as 'The Church party', depended heavily for their appeal on the sense of crisis in the Church. They also drew extensively on the emotional support of the backwoods Anglican squirearchy. For the latter, the world opened up by the Revolution brought nothing but ill. The wars of the period necessitated the heaviest direct taxation since the 1650s. A land tax of four shillings in the pound came as a heavy burden on estates already afflicted by agricultural depression. Moreover, the war for which such sacrifices were required seemed designed to benefit precisely the enemies of the gentry—the merchants, manufacturers, and above all 'monied men' most active in the commercial and financial expansion of late Stuart England. Such men, it seemed, were often religious Dissenters, escaped all but indirect taxes, and invariably pursued Whig politics. The link between the old and new party systems was sometimes tenuous. The new Tories of Anne's reign were often drawn from families with a Puritan or Whiggish background; their leader, Robert Harley, was himself one such. On the other side, the Whig Junto, whose ruthless pursuit of place and power earned them an unenviable reputation for placing party before principle, seemed unlikely descendants of the Country Whigs of 1679. But there was no doubt about the intensity of party feeling in the early eighteenth century. It perhaps reached its height in 1710 when the Whigs impeached the Tory divine, Dr Sacheverell, for preaching the old doctrine of non-resistance. The popular convulsions which followed clearly revealed the potential for political instability which the Revolution had incidentally created. The Triennial Act of 1694 had principally been designed to compel the Crown to summon Parliament regularly, in which respect it proved unnecessary. But it also provided for frequent elections, and the consequence was a period of the most intense and unremitting electoral conflict, involving ten general elections in twenty years and exceeding anything which had gone before. Moreover, the effective abolition of state censorship, with the lapsing of the Licensing Act in 1695, ensured a large and growing forum for public debate. It is no coincidence that these years witnessed the decisive stage in the establishment of Grub Street, in the emergence of the periodical press, and in the growth of a genuinely popular political audience. In general, the reign of Anne has been seen by historians as the natural backdrop to the achievement of political stability. But on the evidence available to contemporaries it seemed rather to suggest that the price of limited monarchy and financial security was political chaos.

The Rise of Robinocracy

The Hanoverian Accession in 1714 brought new tensions to an already strained situation. While Anne lived, it had been possible, in terms of sentiment if not of logic, to consider her as a true Stuart occupying the throne in some sense in trust for her family. With the arrival of a German-speaking Elector of Hanover, strongly committed to intervention abroad and Whiggism at home, such pretences became difficult to sustain. From a dynastic standpoint everything was to play for in 1714. Many urged the Pretender to consider that London was worth the abandonment of the mass; had James III returned to the Anglican fold he would plainly have strengthened the chances of a second Stuart Restoration. Without this personal sacrifice, the Jacobite Rebellion of 1715 proved a damp squib. France, after the death of Louis XIV in the same year, was in no position to involve herself in English adventures. Even in Scotland, where the rebellion had its seat and indeed its heart, the prospects for the Stuarts were not particularly promising. 'The Scottish Union, concluded in 1708 in an atmosphere of considerable urgency, had taken much of the sting out of the succession problem. Many Scots mourned the loss of their national Parliament and thereby their independence. But the Union was shrewdly designed to preserve Scottish legal and ecclesiastical institutions, while simultaneously offering real commercial benefits through incorporation in England's imperial system. In these circumstances, the failure of the '15 was to all intents and purposes a foregone conclusion.

If the Old Pretender missed his chance, so in a different sense did his apparently successful rival, George I. By the latter part of Anne's reign, the unpopularity of the war, the electoral appeal of the 'Church in Danger', and not least the queen's own irritation with the Junto Whigs, had placed the Tories firmly in the saddle. For most of them the interests of the established Church took precedence over sentimental attachment to the Stuart dynasty. A judiciously bipartisan policy on the part of the new regime, on the lines of William III's tactics in 1689, would have done much to ease the transition of 1714. Instead, George I displayed all too clearly his readiness to make the Hanoverian succession the exclusive property of the Whigs. The years 1714–21 witnessed a campaign for Whiggish dominance which comprehensively alienated the Tories, made the dangers of the Jacobite Rebellion greater than they need have been, and generally threatened to reshape the Revolution settlement. First the Septennial Act was passed, ensuring that the new Whig government would not have to face an unmanageable electorate until the greater part of its work was complete. It was rumoured that, when that time came, the Whigs would remove all statutory restraints on the duration of Parliaments, making possible the revival of 'long' or 'pensioner' Parliaments. At the same time, the means by which the Tories of Anne's reign had endeavoured to shackle Dissent, the Occasional Conformity and Schism Acts, were first suspended and then in 1718 repealed altogether. A Universities Bill was designed to give the Crown complete control of Fellowships and Scholarships in Oxford and Cambridge, with a view to transforming the principal nurseries of the Church and the professions into Whig preserves. Above all the Peerage Bill of 1719 was projected to restrict the House of Lords to approximately its existing size. This would have ensured permanent Whig hegemony in the Upper House, regardless of any change of mind on the part of the monarch, and provided the Whigs with a built-in check on legislation affecting their interests. With this programme, there went a steady, systematic purge of Tories in the lord-lieutenancies and commissions of the peace, in the armed forces, and in the civil service at all levels.

Complete success in this great enterprise would have created a system much like that which emerged in Sweden at this time, and which condemned that country to fifty years of national impotence and aristocratic factionalism. It would have established an oligarchy as unlimited as that absolute monarchy which generations of seventeenth-century Englishmen had so dreaded. It would also have made virtually impossible one of the eighteenth century's most characteristic achievements, a stable yet flexible political structure. That it failed owed much to the divisions among the Whigs themselves. Their plans proceeded relatively smoothly while the great Whig families united to crush their opponents during the early years of George I's reign. But this union proved short-lived. The new king's foreign policy caused severe strains by its blatant use of England's naval power to secure Hanover's Baltic ambitions. There was also an increasingly bitter struggle for pre-eminence within the ministry. The eventual result, in 1717, was the Whig split, which placed Walpole and Townshend in opposition and left Stanhope and Sunderland more firmly ensconced at court than ever. Palace politics were also subject to upheaval. The king's son, the future George II, and his wife Princess Caroline, clearly indicated their intention of siding with Townshend and thereby began a long tradition of political intrigue by Hanoverian heirs to the throne. In this situation there was little hope of completing the grandiose plans of Stanhope for the promised land of Whiggism. In the House of Commons Walpole himself played a leading part in defeating the Peerage Bill and forcing the abandonment of the Universities Bill. Any hope the ministry had of saving something from the wreckage of their plans was lost soon after in the South Sea Bubble.

In retrospect, there is a certain inevitability about the South Sea Bubble and the general financial crash which went with it. It seems to bring to a fitting conclusion the intense and inflated commercialism which had accompanied the rise of the 'monied interest' in the preceding years. Yet initially there was much to be said for the scheme which caused this convulsion. The financial interests represented in the Bank of England had enjoyed a more than favourable return on their investments during the wars, and there was obviously room for greater competition between the nation's creditors. The Tory ministers of Queen Anne's reign had indeed encouraged the formation of the South Sea Company in 1711 with a view to providing an effective alternative to the Whig Bank. Moreover, there was little doubt that the funds existed, not merely in the City, but among smaller savers generally, for a more extended and more equitable investment in the public debt. The South Sea Company's scheme of 1719 seemed well calculated to redistribute the National Debt while offering better terms to the national

Exchequer. The difficulties began not with the essential logic of the scheme but with the many and varied interests involved in it. For the Directors of the Company, and especially the inner group which initiated the project, there was the need to make a substantial profit not merely for themselves but for the many courtiers, ministers, and MPs whose support was politically essential to secure acceptance of their proposals. That support was bought at a high price in terms of stock supplied on favourable terms, or even stock granted by way of open bribery. In short, many of those involved in the management of the South Sea Scheme had a strong interest in quick profits, which could only be achieved by boosting the Company's potential far beyond competing investment possibilities. Such an exercise depended heavily on the attractions of the Company's trade in the south seas. The Anglo-Spanish treaty of 1713 had given the Company a monopoly of the Spanish slave-trade and a valuable share in the Spanish American market for European goods. In theory, this offered the most promising prospects. In practice, the difficulties of managing this far-flung trade from London were to prove immense, and they were not rendered less by the often bitter conflicts between the British and Spanish governments. The trade could not have proved profitable in the short run, and even with time it could hardly fulfil the wild expectations raised in 1719. But realities were quickly forgotten in the mania for speculation which prevailed in the early months of 1720. Provided the stock was rising, new speculators were constantly encouraged to invest, permitting those who had already purchased to unload their holdings at a handsome profit. The constant inflow of funds justified new issues of stock and increasingly vociferous assertions of the durability of the investment, not to say still more generous pay-offs to the politicians. In this situation, created by a corrupt regime, a naïve investing public, and a well-established National Debt, the inevitable happened. The bubble grew steadily, encouraging still more fraudulent bubbles in ever more implausible projects as it grew. When confidence eventually failed and the bubble burst the consequences were catastrophic, particularly for those who had sold substantial assets in land or other forms of property to buy at absurdly inflated prices. Little could be done for these sufferers, by no means drawn only from the wealthiest classes. Parliament rushed through a statute severely restricting joint-stock companies for the future, but this was shutting the stable door after the horse had bolted. More dramatic action was needed to minimize the damage to the regime. The king and the Prince of Wales were publicly reconciled. The opposition Whigs were welcomed back into office, Townshend to set about cultivating the goodwill of the king's mistress the duchess of Kendal, Walpole to push through the Commons a solution for the Bubble crisis which would at least protect the National Debt and save the face of the court. In this task, which earned him an enduring reputation for 'screening' corruption and fraud in high places, Walpole was in one sense aided by the very gravity of the situation. Many of those implicated in the murky transactions of 1720 were Tories who had no more enthusiasm than their Whig counterparts for public exposure. Moreover the Bubble was part of an international crisis with matching disasters in Paris and Amsterdam; it was not implausible to lay some of the blame on impersonal financial forces unconnected with individuals in the City or at court. In any event the king's ministers were, with the exception of two or three suitable scapegoats, permitted to get away with their crimes. For Walpole all this represented a great political triumph, fittingly capped by the fortuitous elimination of his rivals. Within two years, both Stanhope and Sunderland had died, leaving the way open for a new era of Walpolian supremacy, or as his opponents were to term it 'Robinocracy'.

Contemporaries, of course, could not be expected to foresee the relative stability which lay ahead. The 1720s were troubled years, not least in the most basic terms of human health and survival. The decade began, not merely with the Bubble, but with fears of a visitation from the plague which was currently devastating the south of France and which could readily be transmitted to London by way of Marseilles and the shipping lanes. In the event, the panic proved unjustified; the strains of the disease which had periodically ravished so much of Europe since the first onset of the Black Death nearly four hundred years earlier were approaching dormancy if not extinction. But this was not obvious at the time and in any case there were less exotic, home-grown maladies which continued to exert a tenacious hold on the vital statistics of demography. The later 1720s were particularly harrowing in this respect. The first three years of George II's reign, which began in 1727, were afflicted by successive waves of smallpox and influenza-like infections, imprecisely and variously described by contemporaries as agues and fevers. The demographic consequences were clearly serious. Much of the slow and slender gain in population which had occurred since the 1670s seems to have been wiped out in what was evidently the worst mortality crisis since the 1580s. By 1731 the total population stood at about 5,200,000, a figure probably lower than that for Cromwell's England in the mid-1650s.

The sense of sickness which pervaded the period was more than physiological. The greed, fraudulence, and hysteria which had characterized the South Sea Bubble were denounced both in the press and from the pulpit as the ruling vices of the years which followed. Luxury and lavish living were seen as the causes, moral decay and dissolution as the consequences. There seemed to be striking evidence of this in the great scandals which disfigured public life at this time. A whole series of parliamentary investigations uncovered extensive corruption in high places. The trustees of the Derwentwater estates were found to have connived at the sale of forfeited Jacobite property to some of their own number at artificially low prices. The directors and officials of the Charitable Corporation, whose duty it was to provide employment and assistance for the poor, were convicted of jobbery, misappropriation, and even outright peculation. In both cases, prominent MPs and supporters of the government were implicated. More sensational still was the impeachment of the Lord Chancellor, Lord Macclesfield, for organizing the sale of judicial offices. Even his ministerial colleagues declined to defend him when it emerged that this flourishing branch of commercial law had been financed from the proceeds of private property entrusted to the care of Chancery. That the guardians of equity should thus be caught in the act of infringing it seemed peculiarly shocking to an age which entertained a profound respect for rights of property. Moreover, public misdeeds could readily be matched by private ones. Crime, a distorting mirror of society, but a mirror none the less, seemed to become ever more organized, more commercial, and more cynical. Jonathan Wild, the master thief-taker, was a fitting representative of his time. Most of his profits were gained by restoring to their owners the goods stolen by his own minions. His success depended heavily on the corrupt collaboration of JPs and their officers in the metropolis. His was only one growth sector in the flourishing economy of crime. Poachers in the royal forests were often well-organized, systematic suppliers to the London market. The smugglers of the south and east coasts pursued market principles and economies of scale, again with the frequent co-operation of officials and the public at large. The authorities made somewhat desperate attempts to combat these threats. Wild was brought to justice on a technicality. His execution in 1725 was to ensure his place in popular mythology. The poachers of Windsor Forest and elsewhere were the subject of new legislation, the draconian Black Act of 1723. They have had to wait until the twentieth century to achieve the status of folk-heroes, in their case bestowed by historians intent on treating them as authentic representatives of a popular culture. The smugglers seemed to flourish almost in proportion to the government's efforts to suppress them; at their most active in the 1730s they were capable of mounting pitched battles with George II's dragoons in their heroic service to a consumer society.

For this was what was emerging in early Hanoverian England. In this respect the South Sea Bubble is best seen not as the grand finale of post-Revolution England, but rather as a spectacular curtain-raiser to the prosperity, vulgarity, and commercialism of the mid-eighteenth century. The theatrical metaphor is peculiarly appropriate, for the period has a special significance in the history of the performing arts. The 1720s and 1730s witnessed a considerable expansion in the London theatre and an increasingly political role for it. Until the court took action to obtain extensive powers of censorship in 1737 it was the forum, along with the press generally, for a mounting campaign of criticism of the kind of society which seemed to have emerged during and after the Bubble. Nothing expressed such criticism more effectively than John Gay's *Beggar's Opera*, the great success of 1728. Whether the opera was actually intended as a political satire is uncertain, but it is significant of the contemporary climate of opinion that it was instantly accepted as such. Gay's message fitted well into the prevailing concern with illusion and unreality. It clearly depicted the court of George II as a kind of thieves' kitchen; the morality of the ruling class was put on par with that of the London underworld. It was a point which Fielding was to reinforce by means of his unflattering comparison of Jonathan Wild with Sir Robert Walpole. It also had closely matching themes in Pope's *Dunciad*, Swift's *Gulliver's Travels*, and Bolingbroke's *Craftsman*, all products of a remarkable decade of polemical satire. Many of its elements were familiar ones: the retreat into classicism, the appeal to country values, the attraction of the rural idyll, above all the incessant criticism of the supposedly synthetic, moneyed world of early eighteenth-century commercialism. In these respects the literary and journalistic invective of the Walpole era can be seen, indeed, as the final, most violent surge of a tide which had been flowing for many years. But in inspiration for the future, or constructive analysis of alternative possibilities, it was manifestly deficient.

When Gay's audience glimpsed in Macheath the very essence of Walpolian politics, they seized upon one of the most significant aspects of the period—the close connection, seen if not established, between the political character of the Hanoverian regime and the supposed ills of contemporary society. With a few exceptions (notably the cartoonist William Hogarth, who reserved most of his energies for satirizing manners and morals), the intellectual and artistic élite of London was remarkably unanimous in its view that Walpole was the arch-villain of the piece. His characteristic image was that of a *parvenu* Norfolk placeman, enriched by a career of systematic corruption (he had been prosecuted by the Tories for official peculation in 1712) and elevated to supreme power for his utter lack of principle and total submission to the views of the court. Before 1727, his brother-in-law, Lord Townshend, had shared both his power and his unpopularity. But the death of George I and the accession of a new king placed him clearly in the full glare of public attention. By his adroit management of George II and more especially Queen Caroline, Walpole elbowed out all rivals for power, including, in 1730, Townshend himself. As a result he soon achieved a lonely eminence such as none had enjoyed, perhaps, since Danby in the 1670s. His hegemony inevitably drew the full fire of Grub Street on his personal position. He was the Great Man, the English Colossus, the Man Mountain. He also appeared as the perfect representative of the politics of illusion—the Norfolk trickster, the Savoy Rareeshowman, Palinurus the magician, Merlin the wizard, the Screenmaster-General and so on. Both his mastery of the irascible and unpredictable George II and his control of a previously unmanageable Parliament were protrayed in countless broadsides and prints as the arts of a veritable political conjuror.

At the time and ever since, the true basis of Walpole's success has been traced to his skilful use of influence and even bribery. The stability which seems to mark the period and to separate it from the political chaos of earlier years can be viewed, on this reading, as the natural culmination of forces working in favour of the executive. The expansion of government as a result of the wars, especially the vast machinery created to operate the new financial system, plainly generated a considerable quantity of new patronage. Moreover, the overwhelming necessity for post-revolution governments to obtain a working majority in the Commons provided a strong incentive to use this patronage for the purposes of parliamentary management. Hence the emergence of a much larger, much more disciplined Court and Treasury party, capable of bridging the ancient gap between Crown and Commons and inaugurating a new era of harmony between executive and legislature. It is an attractive theory, but not all the premisses are secure and not all the conclusions inescapable. Walpole's principles of management were far from novel. At least since the reign of Charles II, they had been employed by successive ministers to maintain a substantial court party in the House of Commons. Placemanship and careerism, not to say widespread evidence of corruption, had marked the reign of Anne as much as that of her successors. In some respects, indeed, the peaceful years of Walpole's ministry reduced the amount of patronage available. It is true enough that both Walpole himself and his effective successor Henry Pelham were adroit managers, and that both welded the court party into an exceptionally efficient instrument of control. But it needed more than patronage to create the classical parliamentary system of Georgian England.

This is not to deny Walpole's own inimitable talents. As a courtier he was without compare. His manipulation of the queen and (partly through her) of the king was a consummate mixture of flattery, cajolery, and bullying, brilliantly described in the memoirs of Lord Hervey, whose intimacy with Queen Caroline gave him ample opportunity to witness it. But winning courtiers were nothing new. What was more striking was the unusual combination of gifts which permitted him to handle MPs with equal skill. His decision to remain in the House of Commons as first minister was quite critical in this respect. Where previous ministers had traditionally departed to the Lords Walpole made a point of remaining in the chamber which ultimately controlled the purse-strings of government. As a debater he was somewhat crude (not necessarily a disadvantage), skilled, and extremely effective. As a conciliator, his capacity for ascertaining and implementing the views of the typical country gentleman was outstanding. But most important of all were his policies, which differed profoundly from the partisan programme of his old Whig colleagues. His desire to avoid exacerbating ancient animosities was particularly marked in his treatment of the Church. With the assistance of Indemnity Acts the Dissenters were left to enjoy their freedom of worship and even some measure of local power. But there was no serious attempt to break the Anglican monopoly in principle, and the repeal of the Test and Corporation Acts had to wait another hundred years. Nor was there any serious talk of wholesale changes elsewhere, in the corporations, the universities, or indeed in Parliament itself. The new Whig policy of peace with France became under Walpole a policy of peace with everyone, carrying with it the priceless advantage of low taxation. In theory the Whig supremacy continued unabated. In practice Walpole subtly transformed the basis of the Hanoverian regime. The politics of coercion gave way to those of consensus; the objective of an exclusive oligarchy was replaced by the uninspiring but solid appeal of a ruling coalition open to anyone prepared to pay lip-service to undefined 'Revolution principles'.

Even without Walpole the Hanoverian regime would eventually have had an important impact on the pattern of politics. For simply in terms of corruption it was not the novelty of Walpole's management which counted, but rather the extent to which patronage was channelled in one direction. Before 1714, uncertain or inconsistent policies on the part of the court had made the calculations of placemen and patrons exceedingly difficult. From the boroughmonger at the apex of the electoral pyramid to the humble exciseman or common councillor at its base, it was far from clear where the means to profit and power lay. Much of the instability of party politics under Queen Anne arose from the resulting oscillations. After 1715 this problem was resolved for more than a generation by one simple and central fact of public life. Both George I and George II objected to the inclusion of Tories in their ministries, and with the exception of the short-lived Broad Bottom Administration in 1743, a product of the instability which followed Walpole's fall, the Tory party remained in the wilderness for more than forty years. Paradoxically, this proscription made ministerial stability more secure. Court Tories were more determinedly courtiers than they were Tories, and the prospect of permanent exclusion from place and profit was more than many could bear. Moreover, Walpole's form of Whiggism was exceptionally undemanding and there were many whose families had previously sided with the Tories who found little difficulty in subscribing to the new Whig principles. This particularly was the case with those who from interest or instinct gravitated naturally towards the politics of courts. By the 1730s the close boroughs of Cornwall, divided between Whigs and Tories at the beginning of the century, were dependable Whig preserves. In the Lords only a handful of Tory peers continued loyal to their friends in the Commons, though in 1712 Harley had achieved a Tory majority there. The change was not sudden or spectacular but it was steady and sustained, and some of the most important political names of the eighteenth century were part of it, including both the Pitt and the Fox families.

The stability of the political scene under Walpole and Pelham was unquestionably a major achievement of the Hanoverian system; but it is important not to exaggerate its extent. Politics in George II's reign did not descend into the torpor with which they are often associated. For the price of Hanoverian identification with Whiggism, albeit a somewhat watery Whiggism, was the permanent alienation of the die-hard 'country' Tory families. These families, though they rarely produced politicians of the first rank, maintained a certain resilience in opposition and provided an important focus for other potentially hostile elements. They made life difficult and unpleasant for those of their comrades who did defect; for example, when one of their aristocratic leaders, Earl Gower, joined Henry Pelham, the result at the general election of 1747 was rioting of almost unparalleled ferocity in Gower's home county of Staffordshire. In the counties, indeed, the Tories had their heartland. Among the forty-shilling freeholders of the county electorates, particularly in the Midlands, the west country, and Wales, they received consistent and even increasing support. Elsewhere they were influential if not dominating. The Toryism of the Church was bound to be diluted by the persistent drip of Whig jobbery, but one of the great seminaries of the Church, the university of Oxford, remained loyal to the Anglican gentry, and there was sufficient ecclesiastical patronage in the hands of the Tory families to maintain a powerful interest. In substantial cities there were also promising reservoirs of potential opposition to the regime. In London, Bristol, Norwich, and Newcastle, for instance, there was a long tradition of popular participation in politics, and much combustible material for Tory incendiaries. The Walpole system was too widely based to be considered a narrow oligarchy, but while a significant portion of the landed and clerical classes and a large body of middle- and lower-class opinion in the towns opposed it, the stability of the age could be more apparent than real.

Naturally enough, the conditions for genuine crisis were created only when the regime itself was divided. By the early 1730s Walpole was faced by a dangerous alliance of rivals at court. Their opportunity came with his celebrated attempt to extend the excise system, a project which was financially sound but which awakened the deepest and most violent antipathy among those numerous Englishmen who detested new taxes and feared the expansion of the government's bureaucracy. Only Walpole's readiness to withdraw his scheme in 1733 and the solid support of George II against his court rivals saved his administration; even so, the general election of 1734 produced a widespread reaction against him and a severely reduced majority in the House of Commons. An even more serious situation arose four years later. The powerful out-of-doors agitation which demanded an aggressive stance towards the Spanish Empire in 1738 and 1739 was all the more dangerous because it had support from Frederick Prince of Wales. The consequent alliance of alienated Tories, discontented Whigs, hostile business men, popular politicians, and the heir to the throne was dangerous indeed and eventually it was not only to force Walpole into a war which he profoundly disliked, but even to bring him down. The problem of the reversionary interest was particularly alarming; it was, until Frederick's death in 1751, to pose Pelham the same problems which it posed Walpole.

Even without these internal strains, the Whig supremacy faced considerable opposition. The Jacobite threat was probably exaggerated; it may be doubted whether many of those who toasted 'the king over the water' would actually have risked either their property or their lives for the House of Stuart. None the less, the more committed among them had some encouragement. The War of Austrian Succession (1740–8) found Britain involved, not merely against Spain overseas, but against a powerful Bourbon coalition on the Continent. In that war George II seemed primarily concerned to protect his beloved electorate; the consequent clash with domestic interests, and above all the unpopularity of investing British money and British blood in Germany and the Netherlands, gave patriot politicians ample ammunition for attacks on the regime. Walpole had predicted long before that warfare would mean a struggle for the English succession on English soil, and so it proved. When the Jacobite invasion came in 1745, it revealed the full extent of the danger to the Hanoverian dynasty. By European standards, the British standing army was tiny; even the small and ill-assorted force which the Young Pretender brought right into the heart of the English Midlands in December 1745 plainly stretched the defenders to the limit. An effective militia, without Tory support, had long since been abandoned; many of the country gentry offered at best sullen neutrality. The ferocious terror which was deployed against the Scottish Highlanders after the Jacobite army had been pushed back and finally crushed at Culloden was a measure of the alarm and even panic which had gripped the authorities in

London. In these respects, as in others, the crisis of 1745 provides a useful corrective to excessively bland portrayals of the essential complacency of the Whig system. The customary picture of political apathy and aristocratic elegance can be a misleading one. It hardly fits the ragged but bloody progress of the rebels in 1745, nor do the relatively sedate years of the early 1750s altogether bear it out.

Pelham, for example, whose adroit management had steered his country safely if somewhat ignominiously out of the war and whose financial acumen did much to put the National Debt on a more secure basis thereafter, proved capable of misjudging the political climate. His Jew Bill of 1753, designed to soften the civil disabilities of the Jewish community in Britain, provoked a torrent of high-church hostility and intolerance and compelled him to repeal the offending measure before he could be punished for it in the general election of 1754. Again, the Jacobite alarms and excursions were far from over. As late as 1753 London was regaled with the spectacle of a Jacobite rebel being publicly hanged; in some respects, no doubt, politics in the eighteenth century was more polite, but it was not invariably so.

Industry and Idleness

The death throes of Jacobitism coincided chronologically with the passing away of pre-industrial society, for conventional accounts of the immense economic growth and change described as the Industrial Revolution locate its birth firmly in the mid-eighteenth century. Yet the period which in retrospect seems to have provided the platform for industrial take-off was widely regarded at the time as one of worrying recession, and continues to present problems of evaluation. In the 1730s and 1740s agricultural prices were exceptionally low; some important manufacturing regions, particularly the old textile centres, suffered serious unemployment and unrest. But there were also more promising developments. Low food prices permitted

higher spending on consumer goods and thereby encouraged the
newer industries, particularly in the Midlands. If agriculture
was frequently depressed by these prices it was also stimulated
by them, in East Anglia for example, to increase production.
The improved techniques of mixed farming often associated
with the age of 'Turnip' Townshend do not belong exclusively
to this period, but their importance was certainly more widely
appreciated. In other sectors there was very marked advance.
For instance, the 1730s witnessed one of the most striking
developments in the history of transport—the construction of a
nation-wide turnpike system. Before 1730, only a handful of
turnpike trusts had been established. Most main roads, including the Great North Road beyond Northamptonshire and
almost the whole of the Great West Road, depended for their
maintenance on those unfortunate parishes which happened to
lie in the immediate vicinity. The roads of early Georgian
England, subjected to the immense strain of rapidly-growing
passenger traffic and ever more burdensome freight services
between major centres of consumption, were rightly considered
a national disgrace. Turnpike trusts were a neat, if not always
popular, solution, which permitted the injection of substantial
sums of locally raised capital into repair and maintenance, on
the security of a carefully graduated system of tolls. The heyday
of the trusts lay in the four middle decades of the century. They
testified strongly to the vitality of the provinces, with a large
proportion of the new roads in the north and in the West
Midlands; by 1770, when the canals were beginning to offer
stiff competition for freight, they offered a genuinely national
network of relatively efficient transport. The effect on journey
times was dramatic. Major provincial centres such as York,
Manchester, and Exeter were well over three days' travel from
London in the 1720s; by 1780 they could be reached in not
much more than twenty-four hours. Significantly these reduc-
tions, which applied to almost all important routes, seem to
have stretched contemporary transport technology to the limit;
they were subject to little further improvement until about

1820, when Macadam and Telford were to achieve further striking savings.

The development of the turnpikes would not have been possible without a great expansion of inland consumption, trade, and capital. But the internal growth implied in these years was more than matched by expansion overseas. Again contemporary appearances could be misleading. Patriot politicians continued to hold before the public an essentially old-fashioned view of empire. Colonies still tended to be seen primarily as valuable sources of raw materials, as dumping grounds for surplus population, or as means of adding to the nation's stock of bullion. The jewels in the imperial crown were the West Indies, with their sugar plantations; the Anglo-Spanish War of 1739, like its predecessors, was seen as a means of breaking into the eldorado of South America, with enticing prospects of gold, silver, and tropical products. Yet in retrospect it is clear that Britain's overseas trade was being recast in the direction of a quite new kind of empire. The dynamic export markets lay increasingly outside Europe, notably in North America. Textiles, the traditional staple, benefited by this redirection, but the growth was still more marked in the newer manufacturing sectors associated particularly with the metal industries, in the production of household commodities, tools, weapons, and all kinds of utensils—in short in the vastly expanding demand for 'Birmingham goods'.

Mercantilist theories were capable of adaptation to accommodate the new trends but it took a time for the process to register clearly with contemporaries. By the 1750s, the full importance of the thirteen American colonies was beginning to be appreciated, and the eyes of businessmen and administrators alike were beginning to turn towards competition with France for dominance of the North Atlantic world. The changing emphasis also had important implications in domestic terms. The growth of Georgian London was rapid, and its place as the greatest and most dynamic city in the Western world was already secure. But the fact was that in strictly comparative terms London was less important. A large share of the new trade in the Americas went to new or growing ports in the west, notably Liverpool, Bristol, Glasgow, and for a short but spectacular burst of commercial activity, Whitehaven. The industrial hinterland of these ports, the Severn Valley and West Midlands, the Yorkshire and Lancashire regions, and the west of Scotland, were decisively shifting the industrial base of the country away from the south, east, and west, towards the north and Midlands.

This shift is clearly seen in the demographic trends of the period. After the disasters of the 1720s, population had started growing again, albeit on a very gently rising plateau in the 1730s. The abortive Census proposed in 1750, had it been conducted, would probably have identified a total of about 5.8 million, half a million more than twenty years previously. By 1770 it stood at about 6.4 million, and by 1790 it was approaching 8 million. By nineteenth-century standards this was not a very impressive rate of growth. None the less it represented the crucial turning-point in modern demographic history. Much the same could be said of industrial and urban growth generally. There was no shortage of important innovations and new enterprises in the late seventeenth and early eighteenth century. But between the age of Abraham Darby and the age of Josiah Wedgwood there lay a world of difference. In this respect, the mid-century was again a watershed. The familiar giants of the early industrial revolution, Boulton and Watt, Garbett, Arkwright, Wedgwood himself, made their mark on the national consciousness in the 1760s and 1770s, and it was at the time of the Seven Years War, in the early 1760s, that the full excitement of what was occurring for instance at Birmingham and Manchester began to register. Urban improvement itself reflected the economic growth and the widespread interest in it. Contemporaries who could remember the reign of Queen Anne and who were to live on into the last quarter of the eighteenth century cited the 1760s and 1770s as a time of extraordinary change and improvement in the material life of the cities, and

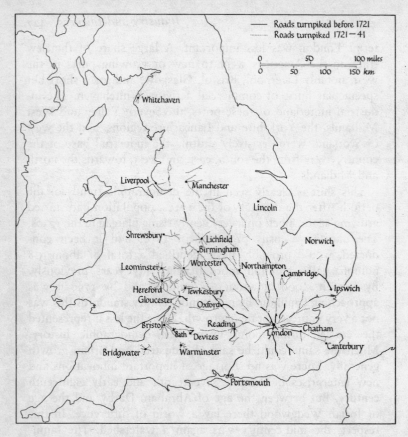

Roads turnpiked before 1721
Roads turnpiked 1721 — 41

0		50		100 miles
0	50	100	150 km	

Whitehaven

Liverpool Manchester

Lincoln

Shrewsbury Lichfield Norwich
Birmingham
Leominster Worcester Northampton
Hereford Tewkesbury Cambridge
Gloucester Oxford Ipswich
Bristol Reading London Chatham
Bath Devizes Canterbury
Bridgwater Warminster

Portsmouth

THE TURNPIKE ROAD NETWORK IN 1741

also to some extent of the smaller towns. The emphasis was
always on space, hygiene, and order. The expanding towns of
Manchester and Glasgow were much admired by visitors for
their spacious squares, and neat rows of houses and ware-
houses. By comparison, the cluttered townscape of the older
centres, with its narrow streets and timber and thatch housing,
seemed outdated and even barbarous. No town with civic self-
respect neglected the chance to obtain parliamentary authority
for an improvement commission, equipped with extensive powers

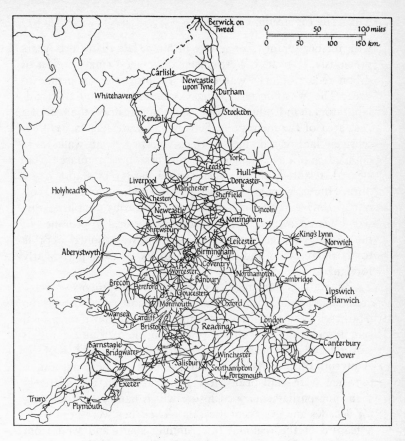

THE TURNPIKE ROAD NETWORK IN 1770

of rebuilding. Many of the better-preserved Georgian towns
of today owe their character to this period of urban redevelopment. Perhaps the most spectacular example of imaginative
town-planning occurred north of the border; Edinburgh's New
Town continues to testify to the vigour of the City fathers in
this respect. The capital of South Britain was not far behind.
In a symbolic as well as practical act of modernization, the City
of London's medieval gates were demolished in 1761. One of
them, Ludgate, had been confidently restored and embellished,

with further centuries of service in mind, less than thirty years previously. In nearby Westminster the biggest single project of urban redevelopment was begun at almost the same time in 1762. The Westminster Paving Commissioners and their collaborators in individual parishes were to transform the face of a vast area of the metropolis. Sewers and water-mains were extensively laid or redesigned. Streets and pedestrian walks were cobbled and paved, many for the first time. Squares were cleared, restored, and adorned with a variety of statuary and flora. Houses were systematically numbered; the old signs, colourful, but cumbersome and even dangerous to passers-by, were cleared away. By the 1780s the physical appearance of the capital, with the exception of its slums, was a source of pride to its inhabitants, and of wonder to its visitors, particularly foreigners.

Change was not restricted to cities and towns. Village architecture changed more gradually in most cases, but on the land itself new patterns were emerging. The most celebrated symptoms of the agricultural revolution, the parliamentary enclosure acts, were heavily concentrated in the second half of the eighteenth century. Their economic impact can be exaggerated, for they were statistically less significant than the relatively silent non-parliamentary enclosure which had been proceeding for decades and even centuries; moreover they were principally a feature of the regional belt running south and west from Yorkshire to Gloucestershire. But as pointers to the profitability of agriculture on marginal or convertible land, they are powerful evidence, and in their impact on the landscape they deeply impressed contemporaries. By the time of Adam Smith's *Wealth of Nations*, published in 1776, they suggested a confidence amounting almost to complacency about the continuance of economic growth. Curiously Smith himself did not altogether share this confidence. But Smith was an academic, his work was essentially one of theory rather than practical observation, and much of it had ben conceived before the more spectacular developments of the 1760s and 1770s. His countryman John

Campbell, whose *Political Survey* (1774) was an unshamed panegyric of Britain's economic progress, is in this respect a surer guide.

The gathering pace of material growth had an inevitable impact on the character of English society. To some extent the results were in line with the trends suggested by commercial diversification and the general advance of capitalism in preceding periods. In terms of social structure, therefore, the principal effect was, so to speak, to stretch the social hierarchy. Because wealth was distributed so unevenly, and because the levels and nature of taxation did so little to redistribute that wealth, real living standards rose much more dramatically in the middle and at the top of the social scale than at the bottom. In principle, this was by no means new. For example, the development of agriculture in the course of the sixteenth and seventeenth centuries had already noticeably altered the structure of the typical rural community. Enclosure, engrossing, improvement in general were gradually turning village society, characterized by the small property-owner, the freeholder or yeoman beloved of enthusiasts for Old England, into something quite new. Substantial capitalist farmers, frequently tenants of gentry landlords rather than landowners themselves, were coming to dominate an agrarian world in which all below them were increasingly reduced to landless labourers. The process has sometimes been exaggerated, for its actual incidence depended heavily on local conditions. But it certainly speeded up during the eighteenth century, and, most importantly, had a close counterpart in the development of industrial and urban society.

In this sense at least eighteenth-century England was growing into a more polarized society. Worse, the damaging consequences of polarization were far more apparent. Increased mobility, not to say the large contemporary improvement in literacy and communications generally, made worrying comparisons of rich and poor ever more obvious. The extravagant life-style of a ruling élite which seemed to live in a blaze of conspicuous consumption, and also the more modest but cumulatively more influential rise in middle-class standards of living, made the inequalities of a highly commercial, cash-based economy glaringly plain. The *malaise*, if it was a *malaise*, was at its most conspicuous in the capital. Conditions in London, with its relative shortage of well-established social restraints and conventions, its constant tendency to throw the wretchedly poor into close, but profitless, contact with the comfortably bourgeois and even the immensely rich, inevitably gave rise to moral outrage and social criticism of the kind which lives on in Fielding and Hogarth.

How much of the concern reflected an actual worsening of living conditions, it is difficult to judge. Before 1750, very low food prices, combined with the wage stability of a relatively static population, probably increased the real earnings of the poor. The fearful problems arising from the Londoner's thirst for gin—and the less damaging but at the time equally criticized liking of the poorer sort for tea—suggest that at least there was no shortage of disposable income at this time. After the mid-century, however, conditions seem to have deteriorated for many. A return to the older cycle of indifferent and even deficient harvests, together with the episodic slumps and unemployment characteristic of industrial economies, made life at the bottom of the heap a hazardous and harrowing business. Moreover, rapid population growth together with mechanical innovation helped to keep wages relatively low, and ensured that the advantages of industrial expansion were not necessarily shared with the humbler members of an emerging proletariat.

The eighteenth century was more sensitive to social problems than it has sometimes seemed, though it had no easy or comprehensive answers. The poor themselves fought back, mainly with traditional weapons in defence of an embattled economic order. Against dearth and high prices, they appealed to ancient laws restricting middlemen and monopolies. Against wage-cutting and the introduction of machinery, they organized combinations to defeat their masters, and clubs to provide an element of social insurance. In extremity, they rebelled and rioted with regularity and enthusiasm. This was a losing battle, although they were not without their victories. The landed gentry had some sympathy with popular resentment of the activities of moneyed and mercantile entrepreneurs. But the growth of a specialized market for the products of an improving agriculture was as essential to the landlord as to the provisions merchant. Similarly with the antiquated machinery of industrial relations: attempts to enforce the old apprenticeship laws were ineffective against the joint efforts of capitalist manufacturers and unskilled labourers to cheat them. A corporation which succeeded in operating such restrictive practices merely ensured that it did not share in new investment and industry. Associations received even shorter shrift. The friendly clubs, intended purely to provide pensions and sickness benefits, were encouraged by the upper orders. But combinations (or trade unions), even when directed against the more manifest injustices of eighteenth-century employers, such as the use of truck in the west-country clothing industry, were frequently repressed. Where they sometimes succeeded, as in the London tailoring trade, or in the royal dockyards, it was a tribute to the determination of well-established industrial groups. In most of the new industries the manufacturer swept all before him.

The most extreme manifestation of lower-class discontent was in some respects the most tolerated, no doubt because it was seen by paternalistic rulers as a necessary if regrettable safety valve. The measures used to suppress riots were rarely excessive, and punishment was used in an exemplary way on a small number of those involved. Even then, it was often surprisingly light if the provocation seemed extreme and there were no serious implications. Election riots, indeed, were regarded for most of the period as largely unavoidable; in a tumultuous town such as Coventry, with a large electorate and active involvement by those who were not even electors, they were a predictable feature of every election. The recurrent food riots associated with periods of dearth like the mid-1750s and the mid-1760s were also treated as a more or less necessary, if unwelcome, aspect of country life. Within certain limits, there was a wide tolerance in such matters. For instance, the fury of the Spitalfields silk weavers in London in 1765 (when it was believed that the duke of Bedford had worsened their plight by his support for the importation of French silks) brought about something like a full-scale siege of Bedford House. The riots were serious enough to warrant the use of troops, yet even polite London society saw nothing incongruous in treating them as an interesting diversion, worthy of personal inspection from the sidelines. Persistence, of course, was liable to lead to sterner consequences. Thus, the initial riots against turnpikes in the 1730s were treated with relative good humour, and even a hint of encouragement from some among the propertied classes who resented tolls as much as their lowlier compatriots. But exemplary sentences inevitably followed. Moreover, from the 1760s there were hints of a changing attitude towards popular disturbances. John Wilkes's protracted and controversial campaign in defence of electoral rights and the freedom of the press produced violent demonstrations on the streets. The consequent clashes with authority in the name of 'Wilkes and Liberty' had too many political implications to be viewed with complacency. The anti-papist Gordon riots of 1780, which for the first time produced a real state of terror in London, marked a further important stage in this process. It needed only the French Revolution in the following decade to complete the destruction of the old tolerance and to install the popular riot among the bugbears of the propertied mind.

There were no permanent solutions to the problems engendered by the quantitative growth and qualitative impoverishment of the lowest sort. Poor relief in the eighteenth century continued to be operated on the basis of the Elizabethan Poor Law and the 1662 Act of Settlements. At their worst, these would have put the life of a poor labourer and his family on a par with or perhaps below that of an American slave or a Russian serf. Poor relief might involve the barest minimum of subsistence dependent on ungenerous neighbours, or sojourn in a poor house with consequent exposure to a ruthless master who drew his income from the systematic exploitation of those in his charge. The laws of settlement provided for compulsory residence in the parish of birth for those not occupying a house worth at least £10 per annum, a not insubstantial sum. In practice, these draconian regulations were less forbidding. Poor relief was a major item in the expenditure of most parishes and by the late eighteenth century was already growing at an alarming rate. If frequently extended to regular outdoor relief and to some extent took account of the rising cost and the rising standard of living. The settlement laws were enforced only to a limited extent. Unhappily their chief victims were women, children, and the old, precisely those who were likely to be a burden on the parish to which they fled. But, even so, restrictions on movement by the second half of the century in reality were slight. The immense labour requirements of industry could hardly have been met if there had been any serious attempt to implement them.

Propertied people felt strongly about the poor in this as in other ages. But they felt still more strongly about crime. For a commercialized society provided ever more temptations, and ever more provocation by way of encouragement to lawlessness. The flashier forms of criminality, such as highway robbery, or the most sociologically interesting, such as offences against the game laws, have traditionally attracted most attention. But the vast majority of crime was one form or another of petty theft, an offence against propertied values which seemed to present a constantly growing threat, particularly in the urban areas. Against this tide of illegality, exaggerated no doubt, but real enough for all that, property in this period had few defences. Urban crime cried out for effective police forces offering a high chance of detection and conviction (if it did not cry out for kinder cures!). But a police force would have presented many dangers, not least its potential use in terms of political patronage. Moreover the continuing threat represented by any organized force at the command of government was taken very seriously. Few would have seen the point in keeping a standing army to the minimum while permitting a more novel and no less sinister force to spring up in its stead. In consequence, with few and partial exceptions, for example the efforts of the Fielding brothers in London, the period witnessed no significant improvement in this area. Rather, the authorities were driven back on sheer deterrence, the threat of transportation or death even for relatively insignificant offences. This was the period of the proliferation of capital sentences for minor crimes, against which early nineteenth-century reformers were to fulminate. It was in fact the only logical means to stem the flow of crimes against property. Even so it proved self-defeating. For juries would not convict and judges would not condemn in any but the clearest cases. The statistics of conviction are small compared with the actual numbers of offences. Even when the death sentence had been pronounced there was a strong chance of a reprieve at the request of the judge, or at the behest of a highly-placed patron. In this way, the processes of justice inevitably sank into the general welter of inconsistent policy and political manipulation which marked the period.

If the poor looked to the State in vain, they looked to the Church with but faint hope. The Church of the eighteenth century has a poor reputation for what would today be called social policy. Entrenched as it was in the patronage structure of the Georgian world, it could hardly be expected to offer a systematic challenge to prevailing attitudes. But it does not altogether deserve its reputation. The sheer volume of eighteenth-century charity is sometimes forgotten. No doubt this is largely because it was overwhelmingly voluntary, and informal. Without the official or state papers which accompany the exercise of charity in a later or even an earlier age it can easily vanish from sight. Yet in terms of the endowment and maintenance of a host of institutions for education, health, and recreation the record is a striking one. It was marked by a frequently patronizing attitude, and motivated in part by an anxiety to keep at bay the social and political threat of the dispossessed. But this is not uncharacteristic of other periods, and the sheer quantity remains surprising. Subscription and association—the central features of this process—built schools, endowed hospitals, established poor houses, supervised benefit societies. In this the Church, or rather the churches, were heavily involved. Not the least active was a class reviled by later reformers, the dignitaries of the Anglican Establishment—its bishops, archdeacons, deans, and canons.

There was, however, a paradox about the Church's position in the eighteenth century. The influence of 'natural' religion in the early part of the century had produced a growing emphasis on works rather than faith. Christians were those who behaved like Christians, and charity was the most obvious expression of religious devotion. But rational religion, however benevolent, did not offer much spiritual consolation to those who lacked the education or the intellect to be rational. The spiritual energy of all the main churches manifestly wilted under the impact of latitudinarian tendencies. Mainstream Dissent, tortured by the theological tensions which arose from the deist challenge to the doctrine of the Trinity, visibly declined as a force in popular life and retreated for the moment at least to its traditional support among the urban middle class. The Church in the rural areas continued its somewhat erratic work, dependent as ever on the residence and personal commitment of a portion of its clergy. In the towns it was all too prone to withdraw, or to appeal, like Dissenters, to the polite middle-class congregations who could afford to supplement the poor town livings and to beautify or rebuild churches.

It was left to that rebellious daughter of the Church, the Methodist movement, to offer the poor recompense in the next world for their sufferings in this. The many facets and connections of Wesleyan Methodism make it difficult to generalize about its importance. John Wesley himself was an Oxford don of high-church views and unenlightened politics. Yet to many his influence seemed to express something of the Puritan spirit of seventeenth-century religion. His own spiritual journey was

tempestuous and marked by the highest degree of what could
easily be seen as recklessness and self-will. But the organization
and discipline which he bestowed on his followers verged on
despotism. In theological terms, Wesley was an Arminian; but
Calvinism exercised a far-reaching effect on the Methodist
movement. Indeed Wesley was preceded in the field by Calvin-
ists such as Griffith Jones and Howell Harris in Wales, and
George Whitefield in England. To their enemies, all such men
seemed dangerous, even seditious characters. Field-preaching
could be seen as an open attack on the parish clergy's monopoly of the pulpit; from the vantage point of lay authority, Wesley's readiness to preach his saving message to all ranks and
degrees made squires and shires shake. Yet his political views
were positively authoritarian, and he offered no challenge to
social order. Through his attitudes and those of his followers
ran only one concern: the total availability of the evangelist's
salvation to all, above all to the poor, to the outcast communities of mining and manufacturing England, neglected by more
fashionable divines. It is possible to exaggerate his achievement,
for at his death there can hardly have been more than about
seventy to eighty thousand committed Methodists. Yet the
alarm and controversy to which his turbulent life and travels
gave rise suggests the extent of his impact on Georgian society.
Methodists were accused of an infinity of sins, some of them
mutually incompatible. Their preachers were both papists and
Puritans, Jacobites and republicans; they ravished wives or
influenced them to give up all fleshly pleasures; they coveted
other men's goods or denied them the use of worldly possessions. The sheer multiplicity of the charges against Methodism
makes it obvious that Wesley touched a tender spot on the contemporary conscience and exposed an embarrassing deficiency in
its pattern of beliefs.

The Making of Middle England

The impression confirmed by the early history of the Methodist
movement is very much one of considerable social strains and

problems. But it is possible to over-colour the general picture. For one thing it was widely believed at the time that English society avoided the worst of extremes. Foreigners were struck by the flexibility and cohesion of the English social fabric, not by its tensions and rigidities. A succession of French visitors, from Voltaire to the Abbé Grosley, testified in print to the lack of 'caste' in this country, and especially to the ease with which individuals could move up and down the social ladder. In particular the absence of aristocratic privileges and advantages compared with the Continent earned their applause. Peers might be tried by the House of Lords, but when they went to the gallows they suffered publicly like common criminals. When Lord Ferrers was executed for murdering his servant in 1760 his fate was widely construed as clear evidence that in crime and in death alike the law of England made no distinctions. In a matter of less moment but perhaps no less significance, Grosley was astonished to discover that the tolls on the new turnpikes were paid regardless of rank and without remission for noblemen. Moreover the degradation and dearth which threatened the lives of the urban poor seemed preferable by far to the conditions of French or German peasants. The English labourer (though it must be admitted that commentators usually meant the London labourer) seemed well paid, well fed and extraordinarily independent and articulate. Most important of all perhaps was the emphasis laid by foreigners on the flexible definition of the English gentleman. Anyone, it appeared, who chose to dress like a gentleman was treated like one. Middle-class, even lower-class Londoners aped the fashions, manners, and opinions of polite society. This, it seems clear, was the authentic mark of a society in which all social values, distinctions, and customs gave way before the sovereign power of cash. England was the outstanding example in eighteenth-century Europe of a plutocratic society.

The nature of this plutocracy provides a crucial clue to the social stability of the period. On the face of it there was little evidence that the basic structure of property-ownership was changing dramatically. There was no striking surge of bourgeois

capital into land, no great expropriation of the landed aristocracy or gentry. The steady assimilation of small professional
and business families altered the precise make-up of the landed
class without significantly affecting its overall character.
Higher up the scale, the eighteenth century witnessed some
strengthening and consolidation of the great landowners. But
land was only one form of property and not necessarily the
most important. Even at the beginning of the century the
primacy of land was diminishing. Estimates of national income
at the time of the Glorious Revolution suggest that agriculture
contributed nearly a half of the total. But the proportion was
changing; by 1780 it was probably down to a third. In fact, the
land itself was merely part of the general commercialization of
the English economy; in its exploitation and its improvement, it
was increasingly treated exactly like an investment in stock, in
trade, and in manufacturing. It was noticeable that, whereas
temporary agrarian depressions had little significance for trade,
the converse did not hold; commercial recessions had extremely
grave implications for land prices. In the American War, when
overseas trade suffered a disastrous slump, the effect was instantly seen on property values, with serious political consequences. If the landed classes had owned the greater part
of non-landed property, the situation would have been very
different. But they plainly did not, whatever their importance
in certain sectors such as mining rights and government stocks.
Movable goods in the form of industrial capital, personal
wealth, and trading balances were overwhelmingly owned by
the broad mass of the middle class. On them, primarily,
depended the viability and growth of the national economy;
and on them too depended the social flexibility and stability
which were so much admired by foreigners.

The middle class or 'middling sort' was not, of course, a
socially self-conscious or particularly coherent grouping. It
remained diverse in point of both wealth and activity. A considerable distance stretched between the city bosses with great
mercantile fortunes who ruled the capital, and the small trades-

men or craftsmen who represented the backbone of commercial England—the new 'nation of shopkeepers', a phrase often attributed to Napoleon at the end of the century but in fact used by Adam Smith considerably earlier. Nor was there necessarily much resemblance between the middling countryman, a substantial tenant farmer soon to be dignified perhaps by the title of gentleman farmer, and his urban counterparts, the business man, doctor, and lawyer, who throve on early industrial society. None the less, such men had much in common. Frequently self-made and always dependent on aggressive use of their talents, they were genuine 'capitalists' in terms of the investment of their labour and their profits in entrepreneurial activity, whether commercial or professional. Together they owned, controlled, or operated the most dynamic portions of the economy. Politically, their supremacy was rarely challenged in towns of any size, and even in many rural parishes they more nearly represented the ruling class than the lofty oligarchs and lordly magnates who seemed so important at Whitehall and Westminster.

Everywhere the dominant tone of this class, with its pragmatic attitudes and its frankly commercial logic, was discernible. Not least was its influence apparent in education, a matter in which the eighteenth century has acquired a wretched reputation. Inspection of the great institutions of the Tudor and Stuart academic world, the grammar schools and the universities, is not reassuring in this respect. Grammar schools which continued vigorously to fulfil their function of offering a scholarly education to relatively humble children were few indeed. Most endowments proved inadequate to sustain the expenses or escape the cupidity of those who controlled them. The clergy who taught in them frequently did their best but rarely surmounted the discouraging effects of low salaries and poor support. The universities in England gave an impression of complacency and sloth, particularly by comparison with their Scottish counterparts. North of the border, academic life was characterized by religious strife and even bigotry. But it also displayed signs of immense vigour on which the Scottish Enlightenment prospered. The Scottish contribution to the European achievement of the age in fields as diverse as moral philosophy, political economy, and medical science was substantial. The English universities fell far short by this yardstick. Their function was partly to train their clergy, partly to offer a broad education to the genteel and the wealthy. This they performed with more zest than they are generally allowed. The disciplined and innovative instruction offered at a new foundation like Hertford in Oxford, or the genuine progress of mathematical scholarship at Cambridge by no means confirm the impression given by Rowlandson prints or anti-clerical propaganda. Even so, they plainly did not meet the demands of the middle class.

But the fact was that they were not expected to. In default of the grammar schools and the universities, the characteristically middle-class devices of subscription and fees were bringing into existence a great mass of practical, progressive education designed to fit the sons of the middling sort to staff the professions and the world of business. These schools were often short-lived, and when they passed they left so little behind them that it was easy for censorious Victorians to assume that they had never existed. Even the greatest of the eighteenth-century schools, including dissenting academies like those at Northampton and Warrington, among the best of their kind, withered before very long. But in the mean time they offered exactly the basic, unpretentious education on which the business classes depended.

The result was emphatically a middle-class culture, with an unmistakably pragmatic tone. If there was an English Enlightenment it was perhaps in this sense, an enlightenment of the practical mind. The fascination of the mid-eighteenth century was neither with theological polemics nor with philosophical speculation, but rather with applied technology. The Society of Arts, founded in 1758, was an appropriate expression of this spirit. Perhaps its most controversial project during its early years was a scheme to bring fish from the coast to London by road, thereby breaking the monopoly of the Thames fish dealers, and dramatically lowering the price of a valuable and (it was stressed) a nutritious commodity. It was faintly bizarre, no doubt, but its object was pre-eminently practical. The Society of Arts was a great national concern, but it was only the most famous of many formal and informal, enduring and ephemeral, clubs and associations which fed on the interest in scientific or pseudo-scientific knowledge. Such interest was at least as enthusiastic in the provinces as in the metropolis. Again, the Lichfield circle associated with Erasmus Darwin and the Lunar Society were only the most celebrated of many amateur groups with very earnest attitudes. The stream of literature which they helped to generate also provides a rough index to the growth of popular interest in matters scientific. Even the monthly magazines, designed primarily with a view to entertainment, featured the myriad inventions and speculations of an age deeply committed to the exploration of the physical world.

Middle-class work and study required middle-class play and diversions. The eighteenth century will for ever be associated with the amusements of a fashionable oligarchical society, represented most notably in the prime of the first of the great spa towns. Yet Bath would have been a shadow of its Georgian self without its middle-class clientele. The enterprise of the Woods as developers and of 'Beau' Nash as the first master of ceremonies was dependent not merely on the names of the great but also on the money of the middling. For every nobleman reported as taking the waters or attending the Assembly, there had to be a host of those paying for a share in the genteel atmosphere which was created. In this respect, as in so many others, it was the constant fidelity of the middling sort to the fashions and habits of their social superiors which sustained the commercial viability of leisure and luxury while maintaining the impression of a dominant and patronizing aristocratic élite. Bath, in any case, was hardly unique. The spas were after all a regional as well as a national phenomenon, offering in the provinces a number of fair imitations of their more celebrated model. When Daniel Defoe toured England in the early 1720s he discovered many spa towns. Tunbridge, he noted with surprise, was a town in which 'company and diversion is the main business of the place'. But Tunbridge had several competitors around the capital: Epsom, Dulwich, and Sydenham Wells all provided attractive resorts for Londoners seeking country air and mineral salts. In the Peak District, already a favourite area for the ancestor of the modern tourist, he found the demands of visitors outstripping the available accommodation at Buxton and Matlock. Buxton, especially, was to grow rapidly in the mid-eighteenth century, though by the 1780s its own rivalry with Tunbridge for second place to Bath was under pressure from a newcomer, Cheltenham.

Spa water, of course, was in limited supply, but there was no shortage of another valuable commodity, sea water. In this as in the case of the spas, the appropriate combination of health and recreation was provided by the co-operation of the medical profession, which hastened to testify to the inestimable benefits of salt water and sea air. Brighton was not developed to any extent until the 1790s. But the development of seaside resorts had begun long before. Dr Russell's *A Dissertation on the Use of Sea Water in the Diseases of the Glands*, published in 1749, was an important influence in this process. Weymouth, which made much of the high proportion of minerals in the waters of the English Channel, was already a flourishing resort by 1780. Margate and Ramsgate with easy access from London had established themselves even earlier, and offered more sophisticated and varied arrangements. Scarborough on the Yorkshire coast was equally advanced. The medical element in these developments was certainly important. But it is difficult not to see the essential impetus as deriving from more mundane social needs. Between fashionable society with its ritual divisions of the years and its court-orientated timetables, and the despised fairs and holidays of the lower sort, there was a considerable gap, a gap which the new resorts filled with immense success and profit. They were essentially middle-class, urban living transported temporarily to new surroundings, the bourgeois equivalent of the aristocrat's retreat to country-house life. Their underlying basis was the generally felt need for distinctively middle-class recreations. The use of fees or subscriptions ensured respectable company and a decently moneyed atmosphere. Particularly for women, in some ways the most obvious beneficiaries of the new affluence, such a flexible, yet protected environment was crucial. Long before the emergence of the resorts, its character had been fully displayed in what Defoe called the 'new fashion'd way of conversing by assemblies'. Assemblies, providing dancing, cards, tea-drinking, and general social mixing, were commonplace by the middle of the century. Even in many market towns they provided an invaluable focus for activities as businesslike as the marriage market, and as casual as country gossip. In the largest cities, spectacular displays of civic pride could be involved; at Norwich the theatre and the assembly hall erected in the 1750s featured striking designs by the local architect, Thomas Ivory. They went up at much the same time as a magnificent new dissenting church, a not inappropriate demonstration of the social link between religion and recreation. Many of those who paid for their admission to the almost daily 'routs' in the Assembly also made their way on Sunday to the chapel.

To force all the cultural developments of a complex age into a single pattern might seem incautious. Yet there is little doubt that the dominating tone of the mid-Georgian arts closely corresponded to the needs of a large, wealthy, and pretentious middle class. There was no simple retreat from austere aristocratic classicism to bourgeois romanticism. Rather the classical tradition continued to be interpreted as it had been for generations since the Renaissance. But about the ubiquitous Adam fireplaces and Wedgwood pottery there was a distinctly new and even anti-aristocratic spirit. The triumphs of the Augustan arts had been the triumphs of an élite, intended primarily for the consumption of an élite. Order, structure, and form were the hallmarks of early eighteenth-century art and a sophisticated sense of their classical significance the key to interpreting them. The Horatian satires of a Pope, the Palladian designs of a Burlington, and the still essentially formal landscape gardening beloved of classicists such as William Kent, belonged to the same world. But twenty years later few pragmatic products of a middle-class education would have appreciated the linguistic nuances of a satire and fewer still would have understood or identified with the Venetian Renaissance. By contrast the cultural achievements of the mid-century required neither sophistication nor subtlety. The picturesque gardening publicized by William Shenstone, and still more the vogue for 'natural' landscaping exploited by 'Capability' Brown, represented a major break with the early eighteenth-century passion for classical imitation and allusion. This was also markedly true of the new literary developments. The specifically bourgeois nature of the novel, whether in its picaresque or puritanical form, needs little emphasis. Sometimes, as in Richardson's jaundiced portrayal of rakish aristocrats in *Pamela* and *Clarissa* it was almost painfully prominent. At other times, as in the adventure stories of Smollett and Fielding, it took the form of a moralistic interest in the social life of the lower and middling sort. In any event these trends came together and produced their most characteristic expression in the triumph of sentiment in the 1760s. Laurence Sterne's *Tristram Shandy*, for example, invaded the palace as well as the parlour, and appealed to the plutocrat as well as the tradesman. But the widespread enthusiasm for the sentimental movement should not be allowed to obscure its significance as a vehicle of middle-class values and attitudes. Sentiment consummated in fantasy what the wealth of commercial England was bringing nearer in reality, the acquisition of gentility by a consumer society. Sentiment made 'natural' taste, the taste of the virtuous man, regardless of upbringing or breeding, the true criterion of gentility; it also boosted the domestic morality of the middle class with its stress on family life and its devotion to Calvinistic conceptions of virtue, against heroic but hierarchical notions of personal honour. After George II's death in 1760, the new king and queen were to prove altogether appropriate emblems of such ideals, giving to court society an air which can seem almost Victorian. In this, they faithfully reflected the mores of many of their subjects. Earlier middle classes had merely aped their social betters. Now there was, in theory at least, no need for aping them. Manners in this Brave New World needed no acquiring and a Man of Feeling, like the hero of Mackenzie's influential work of that name, was effectively classless.

If a middle-class culture was sentimental it was also marked by a certain insularity, tempered only by the anxiety of artists themselves to demonstrate their openness to external influences. But activities of intellectual trend-setters in this respect could be somewhat misleading. Sir Joshua Reynolds, the recognized maestro of English art in the new reign, consciously appealed to Continental models, and saw himself transmitting to a vulgar but expectant public superior traditions of European art. Yet in a way he embodied many of the new trends at home. For Reynolds, like his colleagues Hayman and Gainsborough, depended as much on a newly moneyed public as on more aristocratic patrons. In a way too, his influence neatly reflected both the national vitality and organized professionalism characteristic of the period. The emergence of the Royal Academy in 1768 saw at one level a representative association comparable to the professional bodies which were beginning to appear on behalf of doctors and lawyers. At another level it brought to a peak a vigorous native art such as Hogarth had heralded but never seen. Not that foreign influences were unimportant in this or in other fields of cultural endeavour. Angelica Kauffmann was the most sought-after decorator of fashionable London, Johann Zoffany one of its most successful portraitists. But neither played the part that foreigners had earlier in the century. There was no Verrio dominating the art of grand decoration, no Handel towering over English musicians, no Rysbrack or Roubiliac leading the way in monumental sculpture. Instead, there were the Adams to embellish the Englishman's house, a Burney or Boyce to educate his ear, a Wilton to commemorate his passing.

The new cultural confidence was nowhere more marked than among the painters themselves. What had been most striking about Hogarth's self-conscious attempts to create a truly native tradition had been his isolation in this grand enterprise. What was striking about his successors of the English school was the ease with which they felt free to appropriate Continental techniques without a sense of inferiority or dependence. In this respect Joseph Wright of Derby, not the most praised but perhaps the most innovative of mid-century artists, was also thoroughly representative. Appropriately he was a friend of Erasmus Darwin, grandfather of Charles and himself a distinguished physician, scientist, and even poet. Wright was at his best with his semi-educational studies of scientific experiments and discoveries. But he was also the skilled manipulator of light in ways which would not have shamed Caravaggio. Like everyone, Wright went to Italy, but after his major masterpieces not before; when he returned he seemed to many to have lost rather than gained inspiration.

The Politics of Protest

The social changes which made their mark on mid-Georgian England were profound, extensive, and of the utmost consequence for the future. But their immediate impact on the political structure, at a time when the power of prescription and force of custom were overriding, is difficult to assess. Superficially there were few changes in the character of politics around the middle of the century. The administrations of North (1770–82) and the younger Pitt (1783–1801) were to provoke comparisons in point of both technique and policy with those of Walpole and Pelham. Of great constitutional changes there were few indeed; the torrent of agitation and reform which threatened the *ancien régime* in the nineteenth century seems in retrospect an uncon-

scionable time arriving. Yet appearances in this respect were
deeply deceptive. The language, the objectives, even the mechanics of politics were all influenced by awareness of a large
political nation which lay beyond the immediate world of
Whitehall and Westminster. If nothing else the extent and bitterness of the polemical warfare which occurred in newspapers,
prints, and pamphlets in the 1750s and 1760s would be adequate testimony to the vitality of public debate and the concern
of politicians to engage in it. In this debate, one of the latter
seemed to occupy a special place. The elder Pitt's reputation is
such that, even after two centuries, it is difficult to give him the
critical treatment which such an influential figure requires. Before 1754 Pitt's career had been far from an unqualified success.
The younger son in a spendthrift and eccentric family, Pitt had
joined and eventually married into one of the great Whig
houses, that of Temple of Stowe. As a young man he made his
political name as a patriot orator of fearsome rhetoric and
imprudent vehemence. His anti-Hanoverian outbursts during
the War of the Austrian Succession acquired widespread publicity and earned him useful popularity, but they rendered him
almost permanently *persona non grata* with the king. When, in
1746, the Pelhams were able to offer him office it was on terms
which provided profit without prospects. As Paymaster-
General, Pitt was excluded from the making of high policy and
effectively muzzled in parliamentary debate. It seemed yet
another example of a patriot's progress, sacrificing principle to
promotion. But Pitt's fortunes were dramatically changed by
the events of the mid-1750s. The sudden death of Henry Pelham
in 1754 seemed even at the time a watershed, indicated not least
by the king's own observation on its significance: 'Now I shall
have no more peace.' Pelham's successor was his brother, Newcastle, a shrewd, experienced minister, and by no means the
ridiculous mediocrity portrayed by Whig legend. But in the
Lords he found it difficult to exercise the controlling influence
either of his brother or of Walpole. Pitt's principal rival in the
Commons, Henry Fox, lacked the political courage or weight

to replace Pelham. The 'old corps' of Whigs, the dominant force in Parliament since the Hanoverian accession, was almost without leadership. Their Tory opponents, by now increasingly restive under continuing proscription and no longer disposed to think seriously of a king over the water, also sought inspiration. Could not Pitt provide what both needed?

That he was able to do so owed much to circumstance, and in particular to the international situation. The War of Austrian Succession had identified major areas of conflict for the future without beginning to settle them. The principal focus overseas was no longer the fate of the Spanish Empire, but the world-wide conflict threatening between Britain and France, in a mercantilist age the most successful mercantilist powers. In North America, the French sought to forge a chain from Quebec to Louisiana, cutting off the English colonies. In the West Indies there was constant bickering over disputed sugar islands, as there was in West Africa over the trade in slaves and gum. In India the factiousness and feebleness of native princes combined with the rapacity of the French and English East India Companies to create a highly volatile situation. Everything pointed to a desperate and conclusive war for empire. When it came it began disastrously both for England and for Pitt's political rivals. In 1755–6, failure to deal the French navy a decisive blow in the Atlantic, and the loss of Minorca in the Mediterranean, if anything heightened by the ruthlessness with which the hapless Admiral Byng was sacrificed, left the old Whig regime discredited if not devastated. This was the making of Pitt, and perhaps of the First British Empire.

The ensuing years have taken their place in history as a period of exceptional importance and exceptional achievement. The successes of the Seven Years War, which decisively defeated France in North America and India, and turned back the Bourbon threat elsewhere, represented a high point of imperial achievement and made Pitt the most gloriously successful war minister in British history. Moreover, his triumph in trouncing the 'old corps' politicians seemed to suggest a new kind of politician and a new kind of politics, neatly encapsulated in Dr Johnson's contrast between Walpole as a 'minister given by the king to the people', and Pitt as a 'minister given by the people to the king'. Yet Pitt made his way to power more by shrewd political judgement and sheer luck than by public acclaim. His supposedly popular support was engineered by his friends in the City of London and by his new-found Tory associates in the provinces. His first essay in power, the Pitt–Devonshire ministry of 1756–7, was weak and short-lived; his second, the coalition of 1757, was much more successful, thanks partly to a deal with Newcastle, partly to the support of the Prince of Wales, the future George III. This combination of the reversionary interest and the 'old corps' was as cynical an exercise in political manœuvre as anything conceived by Pitt's predecessors and opponents; it corresponded closely with what Walpole had done in 1720 when he and Prince George (the later George II) had bullied and wheedled their way back to court.

Nor did the war quite present the unblemished record which Pitt's admirers were to make of it. The fundamental strategy which Pitt pursued was completely at variance with the patriot programme which he had previously espoused. His commitment to an expensive alliance with Prussia and his generous deployment of British resources both in money and men to maintain an army in Germany followed naturally from the diplomatic strategy of Pelham and Newcastle. Pitt's own most characteristic contribution to the war, his use of combined operations against the coast of France, designed to divert French attention from the war in Germany, was a desperate attempt to prove his patriot credentials to his friends the Tories, already increasingly dismayed by his 'Hanoverian' policies. In military terms, they were wasteful and largely ineffective. When victory eventually came, it owed much to forces over which Pitt had little control. In general, the French paid heavily for their failure to build up resources for naval and colonial warfare. In India, the advantage enjoyed by the British East India Company was marginal but it was decisive, particularly when the talents of Clive were thrown into the balance. Pitt's description of Clive as a 'heaven-born' general was a rhetorical admission that he could not claim the credit for Clive's appointment himself. Even Wolfe, whose heroic assault on Quebec captured the national imagination, was only the last of a number of commanders whose activities in North America by no means achieved uniform success. But victory solves all problems in war, at least until a peace has to be negotiated. Before the *annus mirabilis* of 1759, when the tide turned both in the West Indies and in North America, Pitt's coalition with Newcastle was precariously balanced on the brink of disintegration. Pitt's Tory supporters constantly talked of deserting a minister whose policies filled them with alarm, while his ally Newcastle repeatedly threatened to ditch a colleague who spent money like water in pursuit of costly defeats. In 1759 these difficulties dissolved.

Pitt did not fully deserve the credit for the fortunes of the Seven Years War but there were two important respects in which his historical reputation seems justified. For if Pitt's popular credentials have been exaggerated, his role in changing the character of eighteenth-century politics was none the less an important one. In the mid-1750s the mould was plainly cracking. The proscription of Toryism, and the ability of the Whig families to keep the control of patronage within a narrow circle, had a very short future. Pitt offered at least the hope of a break with the old politics, especially in the metropolis where his connections went deep into a genuinely popular electorate. Similarly, as a war leader he did provide one crucial quality which no rival possessed at this time, without which the war could not have been continued, let alone brought to a triumphant conclusion. Political courage, and with it a confidence which was difficult to distinguish from unthinking arrogance, gave other more competent and cautious men the moral base on which to fight and win a brilliant war. Pitt's faith in his own leadership provided a key component in the direction of the war at the very moment when the leaders of the old Whig gang,

Newcastle and Fox, had manifestly lost their nerve. If political laurels go in the last analysis to those prepared to risk everything, then in this sense at least Pitt deserved them.

Whatever the nature of Pitt's achievement, his controversial activities in these years formed a fitting prologue to the drama which was shortly to follow. The transformed character of politics in the 1760s will be for ever associated with the new king George III and with one of his most turbulent subjects, John Wilkes. So far as the king was concerned these years were to prove traumatic in the extreme. Yet much of what George III did was the logical culmination of trends in his grandfather's reign. This was particularly true of his supposedly revolutionary determination to abolish the old party distinctions. The validity of such distinctions had already been diminished by the success of Frederick Prince of Wales and Pitt in enlisting the aid of the Tories. The difference in 1760 was one of tone rather than substance with reluctant and grudging toleration being replaced by unavowed pride in the accessibility of the new regime to the old Tories. At court, they were welcomed back with open arms and with a judicious distribution of offices, honours, and peerages. In the counties, they returned, where they had not returned during the preceding decade, to the commissions of the peace; in the midland shires the commissions once again resembled a roll call of the country gentry, many of them of old Tory and even old royalist stock. One redoubtable Tory was granted a special place in the sun. Dr Johnson, the literary giant of the age, basked in the political approval of the new regime, signalized with a pension from Lord Bute in 1762. His new acceptability was not without irony. In the 1730s Johnson had written a bitter patriot attack on the pro-Spanish policy of Walpole in relation to the Caribbean, and British claims there. Now, under the new king, he was to pen an equally powerful and more compelling piece in defence of George III's supposed appeasement of Spain over the British claim to the Falkland Islands, which he described as 'a bleak and gloomy solitude, an island thrown aside from human use, stormy in winter, and barren in summer'. This was not the end of the Falkland Islands as an issue in the history of British foreign policy. What Johnson's progress as an individual signified was still more strikingly endorsed institutionally in the history of Oxford University. For forty-six years the home and shrine of sentimental Jacobitism had suffered in the political wilderness, as successive generations of Whig churchmen monopolized the places of honour and profit. The ecclesiastical masters of early Hanoverian England had generally been trained either at Cambridge or at the tiny minority of Whig colleges at Oxford. In the new reign, there was no doubt which university made its emotional home-coming. Oddly enough, Oxford had contributed more than one Prime Minister even to early Hanoverian government. But Pelham had made little attempt to prevent his brother's direction of ecclesiastical patronage to Cambridge, and Pitt had at one time stooped to making capital of his own university's Jacobite associations. Under George III, Oxford was to have in Lord North a Prime Minister who was also its Chancellor, and one who fittingly represented the old Tory families of the cavalier counties.

If the return to court of the Tories was unsurprising, George III's other new measures seem hardly less so. The reign began in a haze of good intentions and lofty aspirations. Any notion that a new 'patriot king' might seek to strengthen the royal prerogative was quickly crushed. The Demise of the Crown Act, which stipulated that judges would not as in the past resign their offices at the death of the sovereign, removed any suspicion that kings might use their legal rights to sweep away the Whig judicial establishment. At the same time, the Civil List Act provided for a strictly controlled royal allowance of £800,000 per annum; this was the same as that granted to George II but there was the important additional provision that any surplus produced by the civil list duties was for the future directed to the Exchequer not to the Crown. With inflation, this stipulation was seriously to impede the Crown's capacity to cope with the rising tide of court expenses and ironically proved to be a most damaging concession by the king in the name of patriotic propriety. This was the true legacy of the Leicester House party under Frederick Prince of Wales—not a fanciful scheme for the creation of a new benevolent despotism, but further limitation of the Crown's prerogative.

These, however, were minor matters compared with the most important of the new regime's priorities—peace. The old ministers, Pitt and Newcastle, both resigned from office, the former in 1761 because George III and Bute declined to extend the war to Spain at his insistence, the latter specifically in protest against the peace terms the next year. But most of the arguments which they deployed carry little weight in retrospect. Peace could not be secured without restoring to the Bourbons a proportion of the gains made during the war. The return of the principal French West Indian Islands and the preservation of French fishing rights in Canadian waters were not excessive concessions, nor would Pitt and Newcastle, in the diplomatic circumstances of 1762, have been able to make less without continuing the war to the bitter end. Moreover the immense successes of recent years had been gained at a fearful financial cost, which by 1761 was provoking widespread alarm. The case against further prosecution of the war, put repeatedly in newspapers and pamphlets and led by Israel Mauduit's *Considerations on the German War*, was a strong one. War *à outrance* would end in bankruptcy; moreover its object—continued support of Frederick the Great and the acquisition of some additional colonial possessions—seemed of doubtful value. It is possible that George III and Bute, moved in part by the reflection that the war, for all its glory, was not their war, and influenced also by the need to make a quick peace, surrendered rather more than they needed to, particularly in the terms they made with Spain. But in essentials their peace was a prudent, defensible measure and was overwhelmingly approved by parliamentary and public opinion.

Why, in these circumstances, did the new reign prove so controversial? Mainly, perhaps, it was because the new men

brought to their otherwise innocuous activities a degree of
personal animosity towards the old regime which was bound to
cause difficulties. The chosen instrument of George III's reforms
was his former tutor, Lord Bute, a Scottish peer of intellectual
bent whose experience and skills were slight. Most of the
instruction with which he had prepared the young king for
his task was more naïve than knavish. There was no great
conspiracy against liberty and the constitution, nor any determination to introduce a new authoritarian system. But there
was undoubtedly on the part of the new king and his minister
a deep-seated resentment of the men who had monopolized
power under George II and a readiness if not a determination
to dispense with, even to humiliate them. For 'black-hearted'
Pitt, who was seen as betraying the prince's court in 1757, there
was outright hatred, and it is difficult to see how Pitt and Bute
could have co-operated in the new circumstances. But Pitt was
a megalomaniac with whom only a saint could have co-
operated for long. The great Whig families were another matter. Their rank, weight, and inherited importance would make
them dangerous enemies. No doubt they treated the new king
with a measure of condescension. Families such as the
Cavendishes were apt to regard themselves as kingmakers, for
whom the electors of Hanover were at most *primi inter pares*.
Newcastle, after a lifetime in office, might be forgiven for expecting to have his advice taken seriously by a donnish, ineffectual
Scottish peer who was chiefly known for the shapeliness of his
legs and his patronage of botanists. There were, in short, good
reasons for proceeding cautiously, and above all reasons for
ensuring as smooth a transition as possible between the new
and the old politics. This was by no means out of the question.
The 'old corps' Whigs knew well that the substance of Bute's
demands must be granted. Most of them, in the absence of a
charismatic leader of their own, were content to labour on
under changed management. A typical figure was Lord North,
himself a cousin of the duke of Newcastle, a future Prime
Minister and in the new reign a passive adherent of George III's
court. Even the senior men, who saw themselves as victims of

the new order, were reluctant to declare war on it. Hardwicke, the doyen of Whig lawyers and one of the pillars of the Pelhamite system, sought only dignified provision for his friends and a continuing supply of places at court for his family. Given this background, it was maladroit of Bute and George III to drive out Newcastle and his friends. When they did so, ostensibly over the peace terms in the spring of 1762, they created one of the most enduring enmities in modern British politics.

Perhaps the alienation of the old political establishment would have been a price worth paying if the new plans had worked out. But Bute himself, having beset his young charge with powerful enemies, chose to resign from office after only a year, with the lordly intention of directing affairs from the back-benches, or rather (as it was inevitably seen) from the backstairs. And so to the folly of antagonizing the old Whig families was added that of providing them with a legend of intrigue and influence with which to sustain and inspire their opposition. This opposition and the equivocal conduct of Bute set the pattern for twenty years or more of politics. In the short run, the 1760s featured a nightmarish cycle of ministerial instab-ility, as George III sought a minister who was both congenial in the closet and capable of presiding in Parliament. In the process, the Whigs themselves under Lord Rockingham, Pitt, and the duke of Grafton were tried and found wanting, until in 1770 Lord North emerged as a figure capable of wearing the mantle of Walpole and Pelham. Running through these years of tortuous, factious politics there was always the *damnosa hered-itas* of Bute's inconsequential yet damaging flirtation with power, the suspicion of the Whig families, and the myth of a continuing improper secret influence. When Edmund Burke produced his comprehensive and classic analysis of the politics of the period, *Thoughts on the Cause of the Present Discon-tents* (1770), it was this influence which gave him the basis for a systematic onslaught on the new court and its system. The *Thoughts* were to pass into history as the authorized version of the Whig party, and for many later generations the standard account of the misdeeds of George III.

There was other inflammable material at hand in the 1760s. The war was succeeded by a serious economic slump which clearly demonstrates the uneven distribution of economic rewards in the age of enterprise. The period was marked by a series of violent industrial disputes which created widespread unrest in urban centres such as Manchester and Newcastle, and threatened to spill over into political agitation. Even in the countryside these were years of bad harvests, rising prices, and serious dearth. In this atmosphere the activities of John Wilkes found ample support. Wilkes's historical reputation as an amiable rogue has, to some extent, obscured his political shrewdness and inventiveness. Circumstances and opportunism were the making of Wilkes. The grievances which he took up would have made little impact ten years earlier. The general warrants, which permitted arbitrary arrest for political offences, and which caused so much controversy when Wilkes's journalistic activities provoked George III's ministers to deploy them, had been a familiar feature of Hanoverian government. They were used, for example, by both Pitt and Newcastle in their time. But then they had been justified by reference to the Jacobite threat, and they had been used against proscribed Tories rather than vociferous Whigs. Similarly when, in 1768, Wilkes stood for the county of Middlesex and found himself barred from his seat in the Commons there were tolerable precedents and adequate legal arguments for his exclusion. But the Middlesex election involved a popular county intimately connected with the feverish politics of the capital; the Middlesex electors could not be treated as if they were a handful of voters in a rotten borough. Three years later, when Wilkes and his friends attacked the right of the House of Commons to prevent the public reporting of its debates, they were attacking an old and jealously guarded privilege of the legislature. But the defence of that privilege proved hopelessly impracticable in the new climate. The Wilkesite radicals were typically small businessmen, craftsmen, and artisans. They represented the 'middling and inferior sort' at its most concentrated, its most articulate, and its most volatile.

When they took their grievance to the country they found support not only among provincial gentlemen worried by the threat to electoral rights but also among their own counterparts in towns up and down the country. The middle class, the crucial element in their campaign, had no unified politics, and protest was not necessarily their preferred political role. But their part in the Wilkesite movement unmistakably signalized their novel importance in the politics of George III's reign. Yet this importance was only in part of their own making. The rules by which the political game had been played under the early Hanoverians no longer applied, whatever precedents they offered; for the men who had found them advantageous now found it convenient to abandon them. The old Whigs, by their readiness to use any weapon of revenge against George III, did much to legitimize the new spirit of popular opposition to the court. Without this collaboration from highly respectable elements in the ruling class, the popular convulsions associated with Wilkes would have been a matter of much less consequence.

Rebellion and Reform

The early years of the new reign have always attracted attention for their colourful politics. Yet in some ways the most striking changes of the period concerned Britain's role overseas, especially the new awareness of empire which inevitably succeeded the Seven Years War. The effective hegemony of North America was especially entrancing. Imperial civil servants and ministers enjoyed a brief period of uninhibited inventiveness in the early 1760s as they planned a new and rosy future for the transatlantic colonies. Quebec was to provide a veritable cornucopia of fish and fur. The American colonies, reinforced by settlement in Canada and the Floridas, would form a vast, loyal market for British manufactures, a continuing source of essential raw materials, and even (enticing prospect for a debt-ridden mother country) a new source of revenue for the Treasury. The

West Indies, firmly entrenched in a more effectively policed mercantilist system, would maximize the benefits of a flourishing slave trade, provide a steady flow of tropical products, and form a valuable base for commercial incursions into the Spanish Empire. In the East still more speculative and still more exciting prospects appeared. After Clive's victory at Plassey in 1757 Britain had emerged as the dominant European power on the subcontinent. There was, technically, no territorial presence in the East Indies, but in reality from this time the British East India Company was inextricably involved in effective colonization. In this respect 1765, when Clive formally accepted the *diwani* (land revenues) of Bengal on behalf of the company and thereby committed it to direct political control rather than mere commercial activity, was a landmark as important as Plassey itself, though it followed logically from it. These events transformed the British perception of India. The exotic character of the new possessions and the fact that they brought to light a previously unappreciated culture made the impact of the new empire particularly powerful. This impact was early expressed by Francis Hayman's massive portrayal of Clive receiving the submission of native princes, erected at that pantheon of genteel amusements, Ranelagh, in 1765. Imports of Asian curiosities soared and for the first time something like an informed and genuine interest in Indian society began to take shape. Other aspects of the new acquisitions in the East were less refined and less affecting. In the general election of 1768, a noticeable feature of press reporting was the appearance in a number of constituencies of men who had returned from service in the East India Company and were using their allegedly ill-gotten wealth to buy their way into Parliament. The 'nabobs' had arrived. Their influence was invariably exaggerated, as were their misdeeds and villainies. Moreover, in principle they were no different from the West India planters, the 'Turkey merchants', the 'monied men', and others whose unconventional profits had incurred the enmity of older less 'diversified' families. But their appearance was inevitably a matter of intense curiosity and eventually concern. Clive himself was the embodiment of the rapacious 'nabob'; the ruthlessness and unashamedness with which he had acquired personal riches while in the service of the company seemed all too representative of an entire class of men who saw empire as the means to a fast and even felonious fortune. Nor, it seemed, were temptations restricted to India. The furious speculation in East India stock which followed the grant of the *diwani*, the consequent recurrent crises in the Company's financial affairs, and not least the government's growing interest in its activities all brought the complex and frequently corrupt character of East India politics into an unwelcome and glaring light.

America had no nabobs, but the economic and political problems caused by the preservation and extension of the American empire were greater even than the results of Eastern expansion, and their ramifications still wider. British ministers saw all too clearly the potential value of their transatlantic subjects, but they did not appreciate the extent to which the thirteen colonies had developed a highly independent attitude when it came to intervention from London. Nor did they grasp the capacity of a distant, wealthy, and resourceful population of some two and a half millions to obstruct and resist imperial power. The result was a decade of cyclical crisis in Anglo-American relations, beginning with the Stamp Act, which raised the American cry of 'no taxation without representation' in 1765, and finally culminating in rebellion and war in 1775. It is not easy to identify what, in the last analysis, was at issue from the British standpoint, even at two centuries' distance. By 1775 most of the aims of the post-war ministers had been explicitly or tacitly abandoned. Not even the most optimistic can have thought by 1775 that America was going to prove what Lord Rockingham called a 'revenue mine'. Quelling the colonies by force was bound to be as expensive as its ultimate consequences were bound to be unpredictable. European enemies would plainly see the War of Independence as an opportunity to redress that balance which had tilted so much to their disadvantage in the Seven Years War. Moreover there were those who challenged the entire basis of the war as a logical conclusion from mercantilist principles. Adam Smith's *Wealth of Nations*, published in the same year as the Declaration of Independence (and incidentally at the same time as the first volume of Edward Gibbon's pessimistic survey of the Roman Empire) systematically demolished the economic case for empire. Yet with a few exceptions, notably the radical politicians of the metropolis and some of the religious dissenters, Englishmen strongly supported the war against America. Its central principle, the defence of unlimited parliamentary sovereignty, was naturally important in this, the great age of that principle. William Blackstone's celebrated *Commentaries on the Laws of England*, published in 1765, had announced with uncompromising clarity the unbounded legal authority of the Crown-in-Parliament; the conflict with America was its clearest possible expression. Moreover, the economic arguments which seem so attractive in retrospect made little impression when they were first put. For most Englishmen the only viable concept of empire was the old mercantilist one. Colonies which declined to accept the full extent of parliamentary supremacy were not merely worthless, they were positively dangerous. Against this belief that an empire out of control was worse than no empire at all, more imaginative minds made little progress. Here, if ever, there was a clash of chronology and culture. Americans at heart were defending the rights of seventeenth-century Englishmen. For them, resistance to the stamp tax was on a par with Hampden's struggle against ship money; a sovereignty which overrode provincial assemblies and local rights was unthinkable. Englishmen, on the other hand, were deploying an eighteenth-century weapon, parliamentary supremacy, in what was one of the eighteenth century's most cherished doctrines, the indivisible and unlimited authority of metropolitan power in a mercantilist system. Only force would decide the outcome.

In due course, the outcome was determined in favour of the new United States. In the interim the war proved a disaster for

Britain—worse by far than anything since the Second Dutch War of 1665–7. It grew from being a colonial insurgency to an all-out war against the Bourbon monarchies, and eventually involved hostilities with the Dutch and a state of 'armed neutrality' with other powers. At the peace negotiations of 1782–3 a certain amount was saved from the wreckage. Although the thirteen colonies were lost irretrievably, a brilliant naval victory at 'the Saints' by Admiral Rodney in 1782 preserved the British West Indies and above all saved George III the embarrassment of surrendering what Cromwell had gained over a century before, the much-prized jewel of Jamaica. In the Mediterranean, Spain's attempt at the reconquest of Gibraltar was foiled. In India, Warren Hastings's desperate defence of Clive's acquisitions staved off both French *revanche* and princely rebellion. Contemporaries found the independence of America a bitter pill to swallow, but most of the empire outside the thirteen colonies remained intact, and at least the utter humiliation feared in the darkest days of the war was averted.

Almost more important than the overseas consequences of the American War were the domestic implications. The economic problems caused to a nascent industrial society by a world war and the accompanying embargoes on trade were immense. In the ensuing recession both the stock market and land values plunged to alarmingly low levels, unseen in many years. Unprecedentedly high taxes and the rapid growth of the National Debt reinforced the financial crisis and created serious economic problems. Fundamental questions were raised about government, Parliament, and the political system generally. In the ensuing chaos, relatively conservative forces, not least the country gentry, were swept into what looked like an open attack on the constitution, with the Association movement of 1779–80. The Associations had widespread support in the counties, the capital, and provincial cities, and in their demands for reform went further than all but the wilder radicals of the Wilkesite movement. Christopher Wyvill, the Yorkshire cleric and country gentleman, who came close to exercising national leadership of the movement, was hardly himself such a radical. Yet his demands for the elimination of rotten boroughs, the extension of the franchise, and the introduction of the secret ballot, had a futuristic ring about them. Moreover, there was about the Associations a hint, or in the mouths of metropolitan agitators such as John Jebb and Major Cartwright, a definite suggestion, that Parliament, if it resisted reform, should be superseded by the delegates of the counties. Contemporary fears of this new phenomenon were unnecessarily colourful. Yet in retrospect it is difficult not to be struck by the vigour and extent of the Association movement. It arguably brought reform nearer than at any time in the ensuing fifty years, and at its height in 1780 it achieved an extraordinary degree of national consensus. At this point even the House of Commons, notwithstanding the weight of vested interests in and out of government, passed a resolution declaring that the 'influence of the crown has increased, is increasing and ought to be diminished'. This was the signal for almost five years of intense political controversy and sustained ideological conflict.

Why, then, did the Association movement fail to fulfil its promise? When Lord North gave way to a brief period of Whig rule in 1782 Burke and his colleagues pushed through Parliament a handful of reforms abolishing some of the more notorious sinecure places and providing for a more intensive scrutiny of Crown finances. But parliamentary reform proved elusive. Even when the younger Pitt was granted supreme power in 1784 and reform was actually proposed from the Treasury bench with the Prime Minister's authority, there was nothing like a parliamentary majority for it. In large measure this had to do with the circumstances in which the Association movement was born. Genuine enthusiasm for root and branch reform was limited, and generally confined to the articulate and the urban. It sometimes made a disproportionately loud noise but real support even among the urban bourgeoisie was restricted. Association sprang from a national crisis in which any systematic critique of the existing politics would prove attractive. The outcry of the reformers against the waste and ineffici-

ency of the court system seemed particularly appropriate. The
same phenomenon was to appear for the same reason thirty
years later when the immense expenditure of the Napoleonic
Wars and the economic crisis associated with it produced
similar protests. But these conditions were short-lived and most
of the interest in reform died with them. By the mid-1780s
there was a growing sense of commercial revival and financial
recovery, not least due to the impact of the younger Pitt's
policies. Prosperity removed the stimulus to reform more
effectively than any argument could.

An additional consideration was the wide and growing concern at the measures of the extremists. The lunatic fringe of the
reform movement seemed to be challenging not merely the
corrupt politics of the court, but the constitutional framework
which supported it, and even the propertied order itself. What
was to become the 'Rights of Man' school was already visible
in the writings of the early reform movement. Men such as
Richard Price and Joseph Priestley were, by the standards of a
later age, moderate enough. But they were challenging some of
the most entrenched attitudes and commonplace ideas of their
day and it needed very little to force apart their fragile alliance
with backwoods gentry and provincial business men. In this
context the Gordon Riots proved particularly damaging. There
was no direct connection between the reformers and the Gordon rioters, who held London at their mercy for nearly a week
and engaged in an orgy of murder and destruction in the spring
of 1780. Their cause was unashamed religious prejudice, their
aim to repeal the liberal measure of relief for Roman Catholics
which had been passed with the support of both government
and opposition in 1778. As with the Jew Bill in 1754, it was
clear that the legislature could easily get out of step with
popular feeling. The leader of the anti-papists, Lord George
Gordon, called his movement the Protestant Association, and it
was easy enough for frightened men of property to make a
connection between the rioters and the political activities of
more respectable Associators. The conservative reaction so

marked in England during the following years could be traced back in origin to this episode.

The early 1780s were not only turbulent in the extra-parliamentary sense; they also provided the same spectacle of political instability as the 1760s. This, too, was an element in the failure of reform. Before 1782 reformers in Parliament had congregated loosely around the two main Whig groups, Lord Rockingham's party and those who followed Lord Shelburne. The two wings of recognized Whiggism represented distinct traditions going back to Newcastle and the old Whig clans in the case of Rockingham, and to the elder Pitt in that of Shelburne. The most promising talent in each was also a familiar name. Charles James Fox, one of Rockingham's most radical supporters and also his most popular, was the son of that Henry Fox who had been a rival to the elder Pitt, and in the new reign briefly a tool of Lord Bute. Among Shelburne's associates was the younger Pitt—in Burke's phrase, not 'a chip off the old block' but 'the block itself'. Both were authentic reformers, both seemed to offer a fresh approach to a jaded, yet optimistic age, both held out the hope of leadership against the discredited politics of the men who had mismanaged the American War. Unfortunately, if perhaps inevitably, they turned out to be rivals rather than allies, and in the complex, bitter politics which followed Lord North's resignation in 1782, their enmity proved crucially important. The initiative was taken by Fox, who sought nothing less than total control of the Cabinet, a monopoly of power which the king detested in one whom he also found personally objectionable. Fox's weapon in the battle which followed the death of Rockingham, in the summer of 1782, was an unholy alliance with his old enemy, North. It was a deeply offensive and widely despised alliance, but the prize, control of the Commons and, therefore, as Fox saw it, of the government, seemed big enough to override demands for consistency. But there were flaws in Fox's logic. His ministry, the notorious Fox–North coalition, was short-lived. It was strongly opposed by the king himself, who systematically plotted its destruction, and also by Pitt, who wanted no dependence on

Fox and cordially detested North. When Fox obligingly provided an issue on which Pitt and the king might appeal to the country, in the shape of a radical restructuring of the East India Company, in effect he committed political suicide. George III instructed the House of Lords to defeat the East India Bill, Pitt was placed in power, and in the spring of 1784 a general election was called. There could be no quarrelling with the result. Fox was roundly defeated not only where the Treasury could exert its influence, but also in the larger, more open constituencies where public opinion mattered and where the popular revulsion against him was manifest. When the dust settled, Pitt was Prime Minister on an outstandingly secure tenure, and the Whigs were thoroughly 'dished'. Above all, reform, the hoped-for product of a hoped-for alliance between Fox and Pitt against the combined forces of George III and North, was dead—killed, it seemed, by the irresponsible antics of Fox, that 'darling of the people'.

Perhaps reform was dead anyway. Once he had nodded in the direction of his youthful principles by putting a motion for reform which he knew could not be successful without the backing of the Crown, Pitt as Prime Minister showed little taste for radical political activity. A reformer he proved, but not in matters affecting the constitution in Church and State. Many of the demands of the 'economical reformers' for a reduction in the corruption and waste of the court were to be carried out under Pitt. Moreover, the first, extremely hesitant steps towards free trade were taken under his guidance, notably in the commercial treaty with France in 1787. Difficult imperial questions were also treated with a mixture of caution and innovation. The Irish had already, in the crisis of the American War, demanded parliamentary independence of Westminster, and after obtaining it in 1782 achieved a measure of home rule. Pitt would have given Ireland commercial equality with the mother country had the manufacturers of the Midlands and Lancashire allowed him to do so. His failure in this respect left Anglo-Irish relations in an equivocal and uncertain state. India was put to rest at least as a major issue in British politics with an East

India Act which finally gave government the ultimate say in the Company's affairs, at least when they did not exclusively concern trade. In 1791 Canada, with its incursion of loyalist settlers after the American War and its intractable 'ethnic' problem in Quebec, was given a settlement which was to endure, albeit uneasily, until 1867.

In many ways, Pitt's supremacy had a very traditional appearance. He was essentially a beneficiary of the court and of the king's support. His triumph in 1784 could be made to seem as much a triumph for the Crown as anything done by a Danby or a Sunderland. The opposition to Pitt looked traditional too. Fox depended much on the heir to the throne, the future George IV, whose antics, political, financial, and sexual, were as much the despair of the king as those of any heir to the Crown before him. But in other respects Pitt and his activities reflected the transformations of recent years. His administrative and economic reforms take their place among a great host of changes in contemporary attitudes which can easily be lost behind the political conservatism of the age. That most flourishing product of the Enlightenment mind—Utility—was already in sight. Jeremy Bentham and the philosophical radicals were yet to achieve a significant breakthrough in practical politics, but the flavour which they imparted or perhaps adopted was everywhere, as was the religious influence of Evangelicalism. The reforms which really did make an impact in this period were precisely those moral, humanitarian, pragmatic 'improvements' which delighted the Evangelical mind. John Howard's famous campaign belonged to the 1770s and 1780s. His 'voyage of discovery' or 'Circumnavigation of Charity', in Burke's words, provided a powerful stimulus to the work of prison reform, freely supported by many local magistrates. The Sunday Schools sprang from the same era of earnest endeavour, as did the widespread drive to establish friendly societies supervised by the clergy. Traditional recreations of the lower classes came increasingly under the disapproving inspection of their social superiors, particularly when, like cock-fighting and bull-baiting, they involved cruelty to animals. There was also a distinct shift in attitudes towards imperial responsibility. Burke's campaign against Warren Hastings, the saviour of British India, proved intolerably protracted and eventually unsuccessful; the impeachment had little to commend it despite Hastings' apparent guilt on some of the charges. But Hastings was the victim of changing standards of public morality. What would have been tolerated in a Clive was tolerated no longer. The treatment of subject peoples was no longer a matter of indifference at home. The interest in 'uncivilized' peoples from the Red Indians to Captain Cook's South Sea islanders, like Burke's indignation on behalf of more sophisticated but equally subjugated Asians, revealed a new sensitivity, tinged with romanticism, to the plight of the victims of empire. The most notorious target of the new sensibility was, of course, the slave trade. The campaign, led by Granville Sharp in the formative years of the 1770s, and by William Wilberforce in the 1780s, was to wait many years before success. But there were victories along the way. In the case of Sommersett, 1772, a Negro slave brought by a West Indian planter to London was freed on the grounds that no law of England authorized 'so high an act of dominion as slavery'. The publicity value of this decision was out of all proportion to its legal significance, but the interest which it aroused caught the essence of the late eighteenth-century mind, with its emphasis on human equality, religious redemption, and political conservatism. For Wilberforce and his friends were staunch defenders of the establishment in Church and State, and utterly uninterested in radical politics. In this they expressed the serious-minded, Evangelical enthusiasm of the business classes of the new industrial England. For all the supposedly unrepresentative nature of the political system it was these classes which Wilberforce's friend Pitt best represented. It was also their instinct for obstinate defence of the interests of property, combined with thrusting commercial aggressiveness and unlimited moral earnestness, which was to carry the England of the younger Pitt into the era of the French Revolution.

8. Revolution and the Rule of Law
(1789–1851)

CHRISTOPHER HARVIE

Reflections on the Revolutions

In 1881 the young Oxford historian Arnold Toynbee delivered his *Lectures on the Industrial Revolution*, and in so doing made it as distinct a 'period' of British history as the Wars of the Roses. This makes it easy, but misleading, to conceive of an 'age of the dual revolution'—political in France and industrial in Britain. But while the storming of the Bastille was obvious *fact*, industrialization was gradual and relative in its impact. It showed up only in retrospect, and notions of 'revolution' made less sense to the British, who shuddered at the word, than to the Europeans, who knew revolution at close quarters. A Frenchman was in fact the first to use the metaphor—the economist Adolphe Blanqui in 1827—and Karl Marx gave the concept general European currency after 1848.

This makes the historian's task awkward, balancing what is significant now against what was significant then. The first directs us to industrial changes, new processes developing in obscure workshops; the second reminds us how slowly the power of the pre-industrial élites ebbed, how tenacious religion proved in the scientific age. Only around 1830 were people conscious of substantial and permanent industrial change; it took another twenty years to convince even the middle class that it had all been for the better.

Should there not be a simple factual record of developments?

In theory, yes. But the age of the 'supremacy of fact' was so ever-changing and obsessively individualistic that recording and assessing facts was another matter. There was no official population Census until 1801; before then there had been real controversy about whether the population of Britain was growing or shrinking. Although the Census subsequently developed into a sophisticated implement of social analysis, covering occupations and housing conditions, this was as gradual a process as the systematic mapping of the country, carried out by the Ordnance Survey in stages between 1791 and the 1860s. The ideology of *laissez-faire* and actual government retrenchment adversely affected statistical compilation, as fewer goods or businesses were regulated or taxed. (Continental autocracies were, by comparison, enthusiastic collectors of data about their little industrial enterprises.) So controversy still rages over some elementary questions—notably about whether industrialization did the mass of the people any good.

At this point, modern politics casts its shadow. Toynbee's contemporaries agreed with Karl Marx that capitalist industrialization had, by 1848, failed to improve the condition of the working class. After 1917 Soviet Russia seemed to demonstrate a viable alternative: 'planned industrialization'. But the costs of this, in human life and liberty, soon became apparent and, with the 'developing world' in mind, liberal economists restated the case for industrialization achieved through the operation of the free market. Even in the short term, they argued, and faced with the problem of providing resources for investment, British capitalism had increased both investment and living standards. The results of this vehement dispute have been inconclusive. They have also been restricted in their geographical context, considering that British economic development had direct, and far from fortunate, effects on Ireland, India, and the Southern States of the USA.

If there are problems with statistics and context, there is also the question of consciousness. Industrialization as a concept was only germinating in the 1820s. Whatever the governing élite thought about economic doctrines, as magistrates and landowners their watchword was stability, their values were still pre-industrial. But by 1829 the trend to industrialization became, quite suddenly, unmistakable. Only eleven years after the last of Jane Austen's novels a raucous new voice pictured the 'Signs of the Times' in the *Edinburgh Review*:

We remove mountains, and make seas our smooth highway; nothing can resist us. We war with rude nature; and by our resistless engines, come off always victorious, and loaded with spoils.

Thomas Carlyle summed up, vividly and emotionally, a plethora of contemporary impressions: the change from heroic to economic politics that Sir Walter Scott had described in the Waverley novels, the planned factory community of Robert Owen's New Lanark, the visionary politics of desperate hand-loom weavers, the alarm and astonishment shown by European visitors. Only a few months later, his word was made iron in George Stephenson's *Rocket*.

But can we gain from such images a consistent set of concepts which are relevant both to us and to the age itself? G. M. Young, its pioneer explorer, in *The Portrait of an Age* (1936), saw his actors 'controlled, and animated, by the imponderable pressure of the Evangelical discipline and the almost universal faith in progress'. But Young's history—'the conversation of the people who counted'—was pretty élitist history, which neglected the mass of the people—miners and factory hands, Irish cotters, and London street arabs—or identified them solely as 'problems'. The perception, at its most acute in Tolstoy's *War and Peace*, that great movements stem from millions of individual decisions reached by ordinary people, was lacking. Few of the British contemporaries of his French and Russian soldiers shared the views of 'the people who counted': as far as we know, only a minority of them saw the inside of a church, and from what they wrote and read they had little enough faith in progress. Yet, however constrained their freedom of action, the decisions of those subjected to the 'monstrous condescension of posterity' are crucial. We have to attend to them.

E. P. Thompson, who coined this phrase, has argued that a continuing frame of interpretation did exist: the law. No matter how partial its administration—and in the eighteenth century this was often brutally apparent—'the rule of law' was still regarded as a common possession. This claim remained valid after the industrial impact. In 1832, as a young MP, Thomas Babington Macaulay argued in favour of political reform to protect the rule of law from the exercise of arbitrary power: 'People crushed by law have no hopes but from power. If laws are their enemies, they will be enemies to laws ...' Let the law 'incorporate' new groups, and these would defer to the state system. This philosophy balanced the 'revolutionary' consequences of industrial changes, and the frequent attempts to create from these a new politics.

The evolution of law, moreover, provided a model for other social and political changes. 'The most beautiful and wonderful of the natural laws of God', in an Oxford inaugural lecture of 1859, turned out to be economics, but they might as well have been jurisprudence or geology. Personal morality, technical innovation, the very idea of Britain: the equation of law with progress bore all these together on its strong current.

Among all classes, the old morality—bribery and unbelief, drinking, wenching, and gambling—gradually became regarded as archaic if not antisocial. As well as 'vital religion', rationalist enlightenment, retailed from Scotland or France, and cheaper consumer goods indicated that life could be longer and more refined. Where Samuel Pepys had regarded his Admiralty subordinates' wives as legitimate fringe benefits, James Boswell, equally amorous, agonized about his wife and family, foreshadowing new moral imperatives—whether engendered by the evils of corruption or slavery, proletarian unrest, the French, or the wrath of the God so dramatically depicted by William Blake.

The onus of proof was on the status quo. Did it elevate? Did it improve? The English traveller, who in 1839 was appalled to find that the Hungarians had no sailing boats on their waterways when their Muslim neighbours had *dhows* on the

Danube, was typical in regarding this, whatever the reasons for it—the interests of oarsmen and horsemen, the free transport entitlement of Hungarian nobles, sheer loathing of everything Turkish—as a case of 'sinister interests' blocking reform and progress.

Neither 'progress' nor the rule of law were inevitable but had to be fought for, against internal and external enemies: 'old corruption' and new disaffection at home, powerful rivals abroad. Progress meant moral development, not economic or political manipulation—the values expressed, say, by the hero of Mrs Craik's *John Halifax, Gentleman* (1857):

Nothing that could be done did he lay aside until it was done; his business affairs were kept in perfect order, each day's work being completed with the day. And in the thousand-and-one little things that were constantly arising, from his position as magistrate and land-owner, and his general interest in the movements of the time, the same system was invariably pursued. In his relations with the world outside, as in his own little valley, he seemed determined to 'work while it was day.' If he could possibly avoid it, no application was ever unattended to; no duty left unfinished; no good unacknowledged; no evil unremedied, or at least unforgiven.

The rule of law was an English tradition, but its role as an ideology of 'efficient' government had in part been created on Britain's internal frontiers. Dragging their country out of its backwardness, the Scots had used their distinctive legal institutions as instruments for consolidating landed capital, for exploring and ordering 'civil society'. In Edinburgh, Adam Smith, William Robertson, Adam Ferguson, and David Hume wove economics, history, sociology, and philosophy together with jurisprudence to produce the complex achievement of the Scots Enlightenment. Figures such as Patrick Colquhoun, James Mill, and the 'Edinburgh Reviewers' transmitted its values south. Ireland's contribution was quite different. 'The law', Dean Swift had written, 'presumes no Catholic to breathe in Ireland.' Protestant law had, by definition, to be coercive. Not surprisingly, Ireland saw the creation of Britain's first state-organized police force, in 1814.

Although legal campaigns helped to end the serfdom of Scots colliers and salt-workers in 1799, and the British Empire's slave trade in 1807, Scots and English cottars benefited little from their role in the 'improvement' of their countryside. Law was more than ever the tool of property: a function which unified the local élites of a still-disparate society when assault from Europe threatened. The clan chiefs and lairds who had rallied to the French-backed Charles Edward in 1745 were now land-owners who had no common cause with revolutionaries. Jacobinism was as alien to them as Jacobitism. But the ensuing use of law to enforce national solidarity and safeguard economic changes was to face it with its most formidable test.

Industrial Development

A greybeard in 1815, who could remember the panic in London as the Jacobites marched through Manchester in 1745, would be struck by one important international change—the reversal in the positions of Britain and France. This was not simply the result of over twenty years of war culminating in victory at Waterloo, but of consistent industrial development and the take-over of important markets. British blockade destroyed the economy of the great French seaports: grass grew in the streets of Bordeaux, and meanwhile Britain annexed something like 20 per cent of world trade, and probably about half the trade in manufactured goods.

Industrial development did not follow a predetermined, pre-dictable route to success. The process was gradual and casual. Adam Smith regarded industry with suspicion; even in the 1820s, economists doubted whether technology could improve general living standards. Britain had certainly advanced in the century which followed Gregory King's estimate, in 1688, that mining, manufacturing, and building produced a fifth of the gross national income of England and Wales. (The *British* figure would be less, as it included backward Scotland and Ireland.) By 1800, estimates put the British 'manufacturing' figure at 25 per cent of national income and trade and transport at 23 per cent. This sort of growth, however, was not beyond French capabilities. What marked Britain off were qualitative changes, notably in patterns of marketing, technology, and government intervention—and, at 33 per cent of national product in 1800, her capitalist agriculture. While revolution retarded French farming by enhancing peasant rights, in Britain feudal title became effective ownership, the key to commercial exploitation.

In 1745 France's population, at 21 million, was double that of Britain. Her economy, thanks to royal patronage and state control, had not only a huge output but was technologically inventive and grew as rapidly as Britain's. But technology in Britain was developed by new requirements, while in France it was checked not only by government interference but by the bounty of traditional resources. France still produced ample wood for charcoal: British ironmasters had to turn to coal. France had a huge woollen industry integrated with peasant farming; in Britain, enclosure and growing agricultural efficiency set limits to such domestic industries, and encouraged the building of large industrial plants which needed water or steam power or systematized production. Above all, Britain had already won the trade war by the 1770s, pushing France out of the Spanish territories, out of India and Canada—with even the loss of her American colonies soon made good by the rise of the cotton trade.

In 1801, the first official Census found that England had 8.3 million people, Scotland 1.63 million, Wales 587,000, and Ireland 5.22 million. This settled the debate on population: it seemed to have risen by about 25 per cent since 1750, a rate of increase 50 per cent greater than the European norm. Debate still continues about why. The death-rate fell some time before 1750 (as a result of improved food supplies and better hygiene, and a diminution in the killing power of epidemics) and this was then reflected in a rising birth-rate as the greater number of surviving children entered breeding age.

In Britain, increased manufacturing activity, and the vanishing of the family farm, made children a valuable source of income. 'Away, my boys, get children,' advised the agricultural writer Arthur Young, 'they are worth more than they ever were'. In Ireland, population growth surfed along on a different wave: the desire of landlords for greater rents, and the cultivation of potatoes from the 1720s on. The latter increased the nutritive output of a patch of land by a factor of three; the former realized that a rising population on additional farms meant that each acre might yield three times its rent. The population consequently doubled in the fifty years between 1780 and 1831.

Population (*in millions*)

	1780(est.)	1801	1831	1851
England	7.1	8.30	13.1	16.92
Wales	0.43	0.59	0.91	1.06
Scotland	1.4	1.63	2.37	2.90
Ireland	4.05	5.22	7.77	6.51
Total UK	12.98	15.74	24.15	27.39
England (as %)	54.7%	52.7%	54.2%	61.8%

A recent calculation has suggested that in the early nineteenth century British agriculture was 2.5 times more productive than that of France, itself much more efficient than the rest of Europe. The result was that a population on the move from country to town, and at the same time increasing, could be fed. In 1801 about 30 per cent of the mainland British lived in towns, and 21 per cent in towns of over 10,000 population—a far higher percentage than in any north European country. Industrial towns, however, accounted for less than a quarter of this figure. Their inhabitants were outnumbered by the numbers living in seaports, dockyard towns, and regional centres. London, already a metropolis without parallel, had around 1.1 millions, over a third of the entire urban population.

Otherwise, population was still fairly evenly distributed. The counties were still increasing in absolute numbers. The 'Celtic fringe' still accounted for nearly half (45 per cent) of United Kingdom population: Dublin (165,000) and Edinburgh (83,000) still followed London in the great towns league; Cork and Limerick were larger than most manufacturing towns. The complex organization of such regional centres reflected the predominant roles of local gentry, clergy, farmers, and professional people, and the result of decades of increasing trade.

Trade more than industry still characterized the British economy. Continental towns were—or had only recently ceased to be—stringently controlled, their trade limited and taxed in complex and frustrating ways. The medieval gates of little German cities still swung shut at nightfall to keep 'foreigners' from their markets. But in Britain, by contrast, there were scarcely any impediments to internal commerce, while 'mercantilist' governments had positively encouraged the acquisition of 'treasure by foreign trade'. The eighteenth century had seen important changes. Seemingly perpetual war in the Channel and the attraction of large-scale smuggling, centred on the Isle of Man, had shifted commerce routes north. Liverpool rose on grain and slaves, then on cotton, Glasgow on tobacco and linen, then on cotton and engineering. Gradually, their entrepôt function was being changed by the opening up of efficient transport links to their hinterland, and its transformation by manufacturing industry.

Trade and distribution provided the central impulses for industrialization. No other European country had 30 per cent of its population in towns, to be fed, clothed, and warmed, or controlled such vast overseas markets. The institutions through which British merchants handled all this—which the law allowed, if not encouraged them to set up—provided a framework in which increases in productivity could be translated into profit, credit, and further investment. At home, an expanding 'respectable class' provided a market for clothes, cutlery, building materials, china; this 'domestic' demand grew by some 42 per cent between 1750 and 1800. But in the same period the increase in export industries was over 200 per cent, most of this coming in the years after 1780.

Besides agriculture, three sectors were dominant—coal, iron, and textiles. The first two provided much of the capital equipment, infrastructure, and options for future development; but textiles made up over 50 per cent of exports by value in 1750, and over 60 per cent by 1800. Cotton, insignificant in 1750, was dominant with 39 per cent in 1810. Coal output doubled between 1750 and 1800, as steam pumps enabled deeper and more productive seams to be mined, and horse-worked railways bore coal ever-greater distances to water transport. Iron production, boosted by war demand, by the use of coal instead of charcoal for smelting, and by the perfecting in the 1780s of 'puddling' and 'rolling' wrought iron, rose by 200 per cent between 1788 and 1806. But textiles were the power which towed the glider of industrialization into the air.

Wool had always been England's great speciality, though linen, dominant on the Continent, was expanding under government patronage in Ireland and Scotland. Cotton rose largely through its adaptability to machine production, and the rapid increase in the supply of raw material that slavery in the American south made possible. The new machinery was primitive. But rising demand meant that resistance to its introduction by the labour force was overcome. John Kay's fly-shuttle loom (which doubled a weaver's output), destroyed when he tried to introduce it in the 1730s, was taken up in the 1770s, along with James Hargreaves's hand-operated spinning jenny (a multiple-spindle wheel) and Richard Arkwright's water-powered spinning frame. The last, and the great factories it required, spread from the Derbyshire valleys to Lancashire and Scotland. Before competition brought prices down—by two-thirds between 1784 and 1832—huge fortunes could be made. Arkwright's shrewd exploitation of his patent rights brought him £200,000 and a baronetcy. Sir Robert Peel, calico printer and father of the future Tory premier, ended up by employing 15,000. Robert Owen reckoned that between 1799 and 1829 his New Lanark mills netted him and his partners £300,000 profit *after* paying a 5 per cent dividend. For some twenty years a modest prosperity extended, too, to the handloom weavers, before the introduction of power-looms and the flooding of the labour market with Irish immigrants and, after 1815, ex-servicemen. This turned the weavers' situation into one of the starkest tragedies of the age.

Cotton technology spread to other textiles—speedily to Yorkshire worsteds, slowly to linen and wool. But it also boosted engineering and metal construction. Powerful and reliable machinery had to be built to drive thousands of spindles; mills—tinderboxes otherwise—had to be fireproofed with metal columns and joists. In 1770, Arkwright used millwrights and clockmakers to install his mainly wooden machinery at Cromford. But mill-design and machine-building soon became a specialized job, with water-wheels of up to 150 horsepower, complex spinning mules (a powered hybrid of the jenny and the frame, spinning very fine 'counts') and the increased use of steam-power.

James Watt patented his separate-condenser steam engine in 1774, and its rotative version in 1781. By 1800, cotton mills were its chief users, as it supplied reliable and continuous power for mule spinning. In its turn, the increasingly sophisticated technology required by the steam engine enhanced both its further application—to locomotives in 1804, to shipping in 1812—and the development of the machine-tool industry, particularly associated with Henry Maudslay and his invention of the screw-cutting lathe. This (and its associated invention, the micrometer) made possible the absolutely accurate machining of parts. From now on, machines could reproduce themselves and be constructed in ever-greater complexity. The standards of the eighteenth-century clockmaker were no longer an expensive skill, but part of the conventional wisdom of mechanical engineering.

The creation of a transport infrastructure made for a golden age of civil engineering, too, as men such as Brindley, Smeaton, Telford, and Rennie strove to exploit water-carriage and horse-power as efficiently as possible. In a parallel exploitation of wind-power, sailing ships became so sophisticated that they remained competitive with steam until the 1880s. The country's awful roads were repaired and regulated, and in some cases built from scratch, by turnpike trusts, even by government. It took nearly a fortnight to travel from London to Edinburgh in 1745, two and a half days in 1796, and around 36 hours by coach or steamer in 1830. Building on the steady growth of river navigation in the seventeenth century, 'dead-water' canals using pound locks were being built in Ireland in the 1730s. But it was the duke of Bridgewater's schemes to link Manchester with a local coalfield and Liverpool, 1760–71, that showed the importance of water transport for industrial growth. Bridgewater's engineer, Brindley, devised 'narrow' canals to prevent water loss in the 'dry' Midlands, and during the peace of 1764–72, when money was cheap, companies of gentry, merchants, manufacturers, and bankers managed to link all the major navigable rivers. Such private enterprise could pay, in the case of the Oxford canal, up to 30 per cent in dividend, but the average was about 8 per cent. The next boom, in the 1780s, pushed the system beyond what was commercially feasible, but Britain now had a transport network without parallel in Europe, while the unity of 'improvers', agricultural and industrial, in this cause overcame many of the barriers to further co-operation.

Reform and Religion

The British government did not play, or wish to play, a positive role in industrialization; as the Corn Laws of 1815 were to show, neither did it abstain in the interests of *laissez-faire*. But increasingly it observed principles which were more or less systematic, and less unfavourable to industrial capitalists than they were to any other class—except, of course, landowners, who were frequently capitalists themselves in mining, transport, and property development. The axioms of Blackstone and Burke: of continuity, the division of powers, the interpenetration of government, economy, and society—and above all the notion of government as a self-regulating mechanism—complemented the mechanics of classical economics, the discoveries of science, and even the cultivated deism of the upper classes.

But the ideal required renovation. Corruption and inefficiency had taken their toll at the time of the American War, and although the spectacle of mob violence—particularly in the Gordon Riots of 1780—made respectable reformers more circumspect, reform was an admitted necessity. The messages of Adam Smith and John Wesley had, in their various ways, seen to that. The problem was, how could it be kept within constitutional bounds? Attempts such as the Association movement to make politics more principled and symmetrical simply exposed the ramifications of 'interest' and downright corruption. The 'vast rotten borough' of Scotland, where only 4,000-odd electors returned 45 placemen MPs (only one man in 114 had the vote, compared with one in seven in England), got its reward in the patronage distributed by its 'managers' the Dundas family, notably in the East India Company and the Admiralty. Ireland's 'free' Parliament, after 1782, was still an institution for which no Catholic could vote.

The opinion of the great manufacturing towns had to be articulated by pressure groups such as the General Chamber of Manufacturers, because of the gross maldistribution of political power. In 1801 the 700,000 people of Yorkshire had only two county and 26 borough MPs, while the 188,000 people of Cornwall had two county and 42 borough MPs. Dissenters and Catholics were allowed to vote after 1793 but could not sit in Parliament. On the other hand, so restricted was the impact of politics, and so expensive the business of getting on in it, that for some exclusion was a positive benefit. Although their overall numbers were in decline, the elaborate family relationships of the Quakers (who could not 'marry out' and remain in the sect) underpinned widely scattered enterprises ranging from iron and lead-smelting works to banks and railways. The liberal-minded Unitarians, who 'believed in one God at most',

River navigations
'Broad' canals (14' x 70')*
'Narrow' canals (7' x 70')
'Northern' canals (14' x 60')
Coalfields
*Maximum beam and
length of boats

0   50 miles
0   50   100 km

Paisley • Glasgow • Edinburgh

Carlisle

Newcastle upon Tyne

Kendal

Ripon

Preston   Leeds and Liverpool 1770–1816   Leeds • York

Liverpool   Mersey   Manchester   Humber • Hull

Bridgewater 1761

Chester   Sheffield   Lincoln

Cromford

Llangollen   Stoke   Derby • Nottingham

Grand Trunk 1777   Trent

Newtown   Ironbridge   Birmingham   Leicester   King's Lynn

Severn   Grand Junction   Nene   Norwich

Stourport   Oxford 1790

Worcester   Grand Junction 1793   Cambridge

Brecon   Bedford

Hay • Hereford

Merthyr   Gloucester   Oxford   London

Tydfil   Wye   Severn   Thames

Cardiff   Thames & Severn 1792

Bristol   Kennet and Avon 1810

Tiverton   Wey and Arun 1816

Southampton • Portsmouth

Exeter   1802

Plymouth

THE CANAL SYSTEM IN THE EARLY NINETEENTH CENTURY

were energetic leaders of provincial enlightenment in science and education.

Somewhat different was the Evangelical revival. Populist and traditional high church in origin, this drew inspiration from the religious heritage of the seventeenth century—exemplified by Bunyan, and broadcast by John Wesley—and from the devotional literature of such as William Law. In contrast to 'Old Dissent' and Calvinist 'election', it stressed that grace was available to those who directed their life by biblical precept. It was respectable without being exclusive, ecumenical and diffusely 'enthusiastic' (many who were to become its severest agnostic and high-church critics started as devout Evangelicals)—a faith of crisis, valid against atheistic revolution, unfeeling industrial relationships, and brutal personal behaviour. Pitt drank and Fox gambled, but both were susceptible to the sort of pressure which well-placed Evangelicals could exert.

The Evangelical revival was politically conservative, yet it soon flowed into peculiar channels. In 1795 the 'Society of Methodists' founded by Wesley left the Church of England because they could no longer accept conventional ordination. Tories they remained, but further Methodist groups such as the Primitives (who seceded in 1811) became more autonomous and more radical. Methodism was northern—'the real religion of Yorkshire'—elsewhere the Baptists and Congregationalists expanded in industrial towns whose élites were frequently Unitarian or Quaker. George Eliot described dissenting values in her 'political novel' about 1832, *Felix Holt* (1867):

Here was a population not convinced that Old England was as good as possible; here were multitudinous men and women aware that their religion was not exactly the religion of their rulers, who might therefore be better than they were, and who, if better, might alter many things which now made the world perhaps more painful than it need be, and certainly more sinful.

'Vital religion' accomplished a religious revolution in Wales. In 1800 over 80 per cent of the population still adhered to the established Church whose mid-eighteenth-century missionary efforts, the 'circulating schools', had increased literacy (in Welsh) and enthusiasm beyond the point where it could sustain it. Into the vacuum flowed Calvinistic Methodism and the other nonconformist bodies; by 1851, Wales was 80 per cent chapel-going. In Scotland, the established Presbyterian Church, which controlled education and poor relief, was practically a subordinate legislature. Controlled by the landowners and their worldly, liberal clergy, it was coming under increasing assault not only from independent Presbyterians, but from those, usually Evangelicals, who wished to transfer power to the congregations. In Ireland, the dissenting tradition was initially liberal, its leaders comparing their legal disadvantages with those of the Catholics. But the events of the 1790s, and the recrudescence of Evangelical fundamentalism was ultimately to intensify the divide between the Protestant north-east and the rest of the country.

The Wars Abroad

The French Revolution was greeted with general enthusiasm in Britain. At worst, it would weaken the old enemy; at best it would create another constitutional state. Charles James Fox, James Watt, Joseph Priestley, the young Wordsworth, and Coleridge all celebrated it; Robert Burns was inspired to write 'Scots wha' hae'—which had obvious contemporary implications. Even the government was slow to echo Edmund Burke's severe censure in his *Reflections on the Revolution in France*, published in November 1790, while it still seemed a modest constitutional movement. Although Burke expressed what the establishment felt, especially when Paris lurched leftwards in June 1791: remove customary deference and force would rule. Reform should be permitted only on terms which retained the basic political structure. Burke both attacked France and dramatized Blackstone's defence of the British political system. The establishment became really alarmed by the

486 Revolution and the Rule of Law

Anglo-American radical Tom Paine's reply, *The Rights of Man* (1791–2), with its bold proposals for individualist, democratic reform. Burke may himself have started what he tried to avoid. If the *Reflections* sold 19,000 copies in six months, *The Rights of Man* sold 200,000—an incredible total for a society still only semi-literate. Pamphleteering had not demonstrated this range and impact since the Civil War.

The government was alarmed by two things above all—the impact of French notions of 'self-determination' on Britain's Low Country client states, and the contagion of ideas. The European monarchies, with even greater grounds for concern, abandoned the gentlemanly rules of eighteenth-century war in summer 1792 and treated the French as rabid dogs to be shot. The French reciprocated with the notion of war as a popular crusade: 'a nation in arms'. In Britain, the diplomatic threat worked on the political threat: warnings to France increased the conviction of some optimistic revolutionaries in Paris that war would lead to a British revolution. On 1 February 1793 France declared war.

Britain was unprepared. The army had only 45,000 men; scarcely a tenth of the battle-fleet could put to sea. Moreover, the war was quite different from earlier Anglo-French conflicts. The new style of army, the intensity of the revolutionary attack, the competence of France's new commanders: together these put Britain's allies in trouble from the start. By 1797 Austria had been knocked out and Britain stood alone against Bonaparte's Armée d'Angleterre.

Three things preoccupied the government in those early war years: the threat of invasion, the cost of the war, and the problem of combating internal dissension. The French made three invasion attempts, once via Wales and twice via Ireland. A landing in Pembrokeshire in 1797 found no support, but in autumn 1798 a force commanded by General Humbert landed at Killala in Mayo and, with local allies, campaigned for two weeks until defeated. The government hoped to defend the mainland by fortifying the coast with Martello towers, embodying the Militia (the home defence force), and extending the Militia Acts to Scotland and Ireland. All this gave ceaseless headaches to the part-time local officials involved. As subsidies to allies were running into tens of millions by 1795, taxation had to be radically increased and included, after 1799, the innovation of an income tax levied at 2s. (10p) in the pound. Finally the government acted drastically against groups which sought peace or solidarity with the French. 'Pitt's reign of terror' in 1793–4, supplemented by the local activities of magistrates, industrialists, and patriotic societies, destroyed many of the radical societies. The repression was particularly fierce in Scotland, where Lord Braxfield's brutal Doric humour arbitrarily upheld 'the most perfect constitution ever created'.

Braxfield's sarcasms—on being told by one of his victims that Jesus was a reformer, his reply was 'Muckle he made o' that. He waur hangit tae!'—symbolized the end of the upper-class liberalism of the Scottish enlightenment. Thirty years of fairly constant repression followed, wielded by Pitt's Scottish lawyer allies, the Dundas family.

In Ireland, the reversal was even more drastic. War led Pitt to pressurize the Irish Parliament into granting Catholics voting rights in 1793, in an attempt to win them from enthusiasm for 'godless' France. But the non-sectarian radicalism of the United Irishmen rapidly grew. By 1798, it was countered in Ulster by the ultra-Protestant Orange Lodges and by the local violence of a Catholic peasantry bitterly resentful at Protestant privileges, and in part influenced by French-trained priests imbued with revolutionary ideals. Shortly before Humbert landed there was a vicious, though short-lived, outburst in Wicklow, enough to convince the Protestant ascendancy of its isolation. In 1800 Ireland followed the example of the Scots in 1707, and entered into political union with England.

Apart from the brief interlude of 1801–3, the 'wars abroad' lasted until 1815. By then, Britain had spent £1,500 million on war; yet the effects were ambiguous and curiously limited. The war was soon erased from popular memory. Britain was an armed camp for much of the time: there were constant drafts into the militia, and at any stage about a sixth of the adult male population may have been under arms. Compared with France, few of these actually served abroad, although many—around 210,000—died. What was in France a demographic set-back— her population increased by 32 per cent, 1800–50, compared with Britain's 50 per cent—had a different, smaller impact on Britain. Yet British naval supremacy was never challenged after 1805, and through blockade it destroyed much of French industry, whose most dynamic sectors were based on the trading ports.

Adam Smith had written that war would distort demand and create a 'seller's market' among certain types of labour. It proceeded to do so. The iron trade boomed not only in its traditional base of the West Midlands, but in central Scotland and also in South Wales, where Merthyr Tydfil expanded twenty-fold in population between 1790 and 1820—a raw, re-mote city (accessible, incredibly, by canal) in a country whose largest mid-eighteenth-century town, Carmarthen, had con-tained scarcely 4,000 people. As blockade throttled her rivals, Britain's ever more commanding lead in textiles reached the stage where her manufacturers were clothing French armies. The huge naval dockyards of Chatham, Portsmouth, and Dev-onport were further expanded and became pioneers of mass production. Their creations, the sailing warships, were dramat-ically improved; steam-power, when it took over in the 1850s, was almost a lesser revolution.

The navy, in fact, typified many of government's problems. The wretched condition of the sailors provoked mutinies at Spithead and the Nore in 1797. These had little political con-tent; the mutineers, however aggrieved, remained overwhelm-ingly patriotic. They were dealt with by a mixture of coercion and concession—as indeed were the well-organized dock-yard workers. Elsewhere, government reacted ambiguously to attempts to remedy working-class distress. The Combination Laws of 1799 treated trade unions like revolutionary societies and outlawed them; government also successfully opposed attempts to secure legal minimum wages and restore older industrial relationships, even when these were backed by manufacturers (on the whole smaller ones). Such measures, and the depressions which resulted from the diversion of investment into government funds and the trade war, ensured that average real wages stagnated between 1790 and 1814. Yet the relatively generous poor relief scales adopted by many rural parishes after the 1790s—the so-called Speenhamland system—continued a traditional entitlement to relief, and undoubtedly mitigated even sharper social conflicts.

For most of the war Britain avoided European involvement, and paid subsidies instead to the members of the various coalitions she assembled, first against revolutionary France, then against Napoleon. This was simply a refinement of the mercenary principles of eighteenth-century wars. Only between 1811 and 1814, when she sent her own troops to the Peninsula, did her army take on a European role. The gains in other areas, however, were immense; her hold over India was strengthened, and she achieved effective dominance, through Singapore, of the Dutch East Indies; she conquered Ceylon between 1795 and 1816, took over South Africa from the Dutch, and established a claim on Egypt. Informally, she secured a trading hegemony over the former Spanish colonies of Central and South America.

Although Britain was victorious, the war's imprint on Europe was predominantly French. Wherever Napoleon's armies went, they left (or their opponents copied) the laws, the measurements, the administration—and above all the nationalistic ethos—of the revolution. The map had been totally changed. Before 1789, Britain had been part of a continental community. David Hume and Adam Smith were as much at home in Paris as they were in Edinburgh, and rather more, perhaps, than they were in London. After 1815, Britain, despite the economic progress which attracted hundreds of foreign visitors, remained at a distance from European life.

At home, war and depression polarized political ideas into 'revolutionary' and 'loyalist'. 'Pitt's reign of terror', patriotic societies, and church-and-king mobs pushed democratic thinkers, earlier commonplace enough, either into obscurity or into alliance with genuinely oppressed groups like the Irish or the working class. The 'Jacobin tradition' became as sensitive to industrial and economic change as it had been to the 'evils' of established government. A diffuse, volatile blend of everything from anarchism to religious millenarianism, it continued to mark working-class movements up to and including Chartism.

Paradoxically, however, the relentlessly practical approach of the governing élite, and the role of repression in exalting state power over contractual ideas of politics, conjured up its own radical rival. Evangelicalism, in the hands of William Wilberforce and the Clapham Sect, aimed at converting the élite; but so too did the reiterated schemes of Jeremy Bentham, a wealthy lawyer who believed, more or less, that society could be governed through a set of self-evident principles analogous to those of economics. Of these, the most easily grasped was 'utilitarianism'—that social action should aim at producing 'the greatest good for the greatest number'. The sworn foe to all ideals of 'social contract', Bentham opposed the French Revolution, and tried to interest successive British governments in his schemes, particularly of law and prison reform. He was probably more successful than he thought, but frustrations drove him towards the democratic reformers and by 1815 he was supporting universal suffrage. The 'philosophic radicals', as Bentham's disciples were called, offered the combination of institutional reform with political continuity—and, after 1815, offered it to both sides, as they built up a following of moderate working-class leaders. From this stemmed both a centralized pattern of state action, and a theory of public intervention, which remained powerfully influential for the rest of the century.

Benthamite theory saw local authorities raising rates and taking executive action in appropriately-sized districts. They would be supervised by salaried inspectors reporting to a central board. 'Old corruption' and popular profligacy would thus be supposedly checked; local responsibility would be retained. But, in fact, the officials were dominant. Bentham and his acolytes, the Mills, father and son, and Edwin Chadwick, may have been converted to democracy, but they were reluctant to let the people's representatives do more than veto the officials' actions. Not surprisingly, their most spectacular successes were gained in British India.

Law had shifted into a class pattern. Working men, accustomed to fight disabilities in the courts, lost traditional rights and had their independent action constrained. The alarm of the propertied classes gave teeth to hitherto ineffective sanctions. The 'making of the English working class' was, at least in part, a reaction to a combination of war, industrialization, and repression: it meant a hostility to inequitable law. There was little respect for 'the Thing' (the undeclared confederacy of the rich to exhaust the poor) in William Cobbett; practical ignorance of it, in Robert Owen. Even the Benthamites thought the legal establishment a 'vast sinister interest'. Although ultimately only the Irish stood out against it, the triumph of the rule of law, like Waterloo, proved 'a damned close-run thing'. It was probably only possible because popular expectations of it endured long enough to be sustained by a new wave of constitutional agitation.

Roads to Freedom

> Men of England, wherefore plough
> For the Lords who lay ye low?
> Wherefore weave with toil and care
> The rich robes your tyrants wear?
>
> .   .   .   .
>
> Shrink to your cellars, holes and cells;
> In halls ye deck another dwells.
> Why shake the chains ye wrought? Ye see
> The steel ye tempered glance on ye.
>
> Shelley, *To the Men of England*

The post-war Tory government after 1815 encountered a new set of literary radicals. Coleridge and Wordsworth, gathered to the bosom of the forces of order, were succeeded by Byron and Shelley. Lord Liverpool's administration of 1812–27 was in fact a pretty bourgeois affair, made up of minor gentry, the sons of doctors and merchants, and even (in the case of George Canning) an actress. Although condemned as reactionary—which some of its members certainly were—it sat edgily on the right centre. It was liberal (by the standards of Restoration Europe) abroad, and conciliatory at home. But it inherited a fearsome post-war slump and racking industrial tensions, on top of a war debt to be paid for, and demobilized servicemen to be settled. It was scarcely aided by an able Whig opposition, which lacerated it through the medium of the new literary reviews, and a rich culture of popular protest, from the 'unstamped' newspapers of Henry Hetherington and Richard Carlile to the bucolic radicalism of William Cobbett and the visionary millenarianism of William Blake. The landed interest pressed for, and obtained, the maintenance of subsidy on grain through the Corn Law of 1815; this probably staved off, for over a decade, discontent among those of the working population who tilled the land. But it was all at a cost. Even more than in 1811–12, the threat to order came from the new industrial towns, where the end of the post-war boom caused widespread unemployment and a steep fall in wages. The consciousness of the workers, more of their *industrial* than of their class position, had steadily sharpened since 1800, and the local representatives of government, industrialists and Justices of the Peace, felt their isolation acutely.

Do the fears that these gentry frequently expressed—of Jacobin mobs baying at their gates—and the explicitly revolutionary ideas of some leaders of the working classes, add up to a real threat to overthrow the regime, which was only narrowly averted? They might have done, had action been co-ordinated, had a common economic cause existed to bind industrial workers to the parliamentary radicals and the skilled trades of the capital, and had the governing classes really lost their nerve.

But this would have been very difficult to achieve. London was not an 'absolute' capital like Paris; there were few vital levers of power to be grasped—had the London radicals mobilized *en masse*.

London did not move with the provinces. The parliamentary opposition disowned and deprecated violence, and the Home Office under its repressive head, Viscount Sidmouth, and his local agents cowed resistance—but at a price. The climax came in Manchester on 16 August 1819, when the local magistracy ordered the yeomanry to apprehend speakers at a huge but peaceful reform demonstration in St. Peter's Fields. The soldiers turned on the crowd and eleven were killed at 'Peterloo'. Both the desire of radicals for revenge and the penetration of the radical movement by government spies and *agents provocateurs* were responsible for further outbreaks in the following year—a weavers' rising in Scotland and the 'Cato Street conspiracy' to assassinate the Cabinet in London. Repression—the gallows and transportation—was sharp, savage, and effective, but in the long term it strengthened constitutional resistance and steadily discredited the government.

The government itself looked askance at unbound industrialization. Moving towards free trade, systematic administration, and a reformed penal code, it still depended on the agricultural interest, and feared further working-class violence. Sir Walter Scott, its supporter, regretted the shift of industry to the towns, since he believed that in country mills the manufacturer 'exercised a salutary influence over men depending on and intimately connected with him and his prospects'. He probably had Robert Owen and New Lanark in mind. Propagandizing for self-governing industrial communities, Owen wanted to put a brake on industry and, through spade-cultivation, make agriculture again a great employer. His 'new moral world' fitted into the atmosphere of social peril and Utopian salvation which had been pervasive since the end of the war.

> The Strongest Poison ever known
> Came from Caesar's Laurel Crown.

Nought can deform the Human Race
Like to the Armour's iron brace.
When Gold & Gems adorn the Plow
To peaceful Arts shall Envy bow.

Artisans did not need to understand the artisan genius William Blake's cosmology to appreciate the message. The future must have seemed to many as apocalyptic as the huge but enormously detailed and didactic paintings of John Martin, which had a great vogue as engravings in the mid-1820s.

The Whig contribution to the political battle was, however, effective enough. In 1820 George IV's attempt to divorce his consort led to the royal family's dirty linen being washed in the courts. Henry Brougham, a leading contributor to the *Edinburgh Review*, championed Queen Caroline (not the most promising of martyrs) against king and ministry, to the plaudits of the public. Then in August 1822 Castlereagh, who as Foreign Secretary had managed to extricate Britain from the conservative powers represented in Metternich's Congresses, killed himself. The way was open for the more liberal side of the Liverpool government to show itself.

Castlereagh's successor at the Foreign Office, George Canning, sided with the American president Monroe in 1823 in guaranteeing the new republics of South America—and incidentally confirmed Britain's privileged access to a vast new market. Two years later the ministry repealed the Six Acts and anti-trade union legislation, and in 1826 it ended the 'management' of Scotland by the Dundases. The duke of Wellington's administration passed Catholic Emancipation in 1829. It bowed to Daniel O'Connell's expert management of Irish public opinion, and to the threat of a national uprising when O'Connell was elected as MP for County Clare in 1828 but, as a Catholic, was debarred from taking his seat.

Only parliamentary reform remained to be implemented, but here a direct party issue was involved. Pressure groups— the trade unions, the Scots, the Irish—could be bought off with judicious concessions. Reform, however, would mean a triumph for the Whigs, with all that meant in terms of parliamentary command and patronage. In 1828 the duke had dug his heels in, under pressure from his 'Ultras', but in the following year they parted from him over Catholic Emancipation. Meanwhile in the country agitation grew, and the Whigs did not scruple to encourage their radical rivals. Pressure rose to a peak after the Whigs under Earl Grey and Lord John Russell won the election which the death of George IV occasioned in 1830. When their Reform Bill was rejected by the Lords, well-organized 'Political Unions' held monster rallies in the cities; rioters attacked Nottingham Castle and the bishop's palace in Bristol, both seats of anti-Reform peers; in Merthyr riots were followed by the execution of a workers' leader, Dic Penderyn. In April 1832 the Lords gave way—by nine votes—much to the relief of Grey's government, which had shown its otherwise conservative nature by the brutal suppression of farm labourers' discontent—the 'Captain Swing' riots—in southern England.

Coping with Reform

Despite the near-revolutionary nature of the reform agitation, the act of 1832 incorporated the most potentially troublesome sectors of industrial and commercial power, but did little more. Scotland's electorate shot up from 4,579 to 64,447 (a 1,407 per cent increase), but that of Ireland increased by only 21 per cent; 41 large English towns—including Manchester, Bradford, and Birmingham—got representation for the first time, but the average size of an English borough electorate—and these returned almost half (324) of the total of 658 MPs—remained under 900. The 349 electors of Buckingham still returned as many MPs as the 4,172 electors of Leeds. England, with 54 per cent of the population, continued to return 71 per cent of the Commons. Before 1832 it had returned 74 per cent. 'Virtual representation', of interests rather than people, remained a principle, and

Parliament continued to be dominated by the landed interest for almost a further half-century.

Some conservatives now feared a Benthamite assault on the aristocracy and the Church. But there were few doctrinaires in Parliament, and the reforming zeal of the Whigs rapidly waned. Humanitarians got their way in 1833 with the abolition of slavery in the British Empire and the regulation of children's work in textile factories by the Factory Inspectorate. The Poor Law Amendment Act of 1834, which its architect Edwin Chadwick saw as the basis of a systematic and economical reconstruction of English local government, remained, however, an isolated monument—as much hated by the people as were its symbols, the gaunt Union Workhouses or 'bastilles'.

The Times, too, was loud in abuse of the New Poor Law, feeling perhaps that philosophical radicalism had gone far enough. For 1834 was a traumatic year. Ireland was quiet for once, the Whigs edging towards an understanding with O'Connell, which lasted for the rest of the decade, but on the mainland the 'alternative society' of the still-inchoate working class reached its apogee. The growth of trade unions, led by men such as John Doherty; the arguments of the 'unstamped' press; the frustration of radicals with the Reform Act; the return to politics of Robert Owen—all combined to produce a project for a Grand National Consolidated Trades Union which would destroy the capitalist system through a 'grand national holiday' or general strike. After this, society would be re-organized on a co-operative basis, with money values calculated in terms of hours of labour performed. Government counter-attacked in March with the victimization of six Dorset labourers—the 'Tolpuddle Martyrs'; the GNCTU undertook too many protests and strikes, which its organizers could not co-ordinate. Owen pulled out in August and effectively brought the movement to an end. On 16 October Parliament accidentally burned down; six months earlier this might have appeared more than simply symbolic.

The Whig triumph really came with local government reform. Scottish burgh councils, hitherto self-elected, were put under a rate-payer franchise in 1833; reform of the English towns followed two years later. In the larger towns, Whigs and radicals came into the fruits of office, and by and large stayed there. But the government was now badly split. In November 1834 the Tories, now under Peel and more or less pledged to work within the framework of reform, took office. A false dawn, this: the Whigs were back in April 1835, but under the deeply conservative Melbourne. When they fell from power in 1841 Peel seemed more acutely to reflect the spirit of gradualist reform, an outlook shared with the young queen's serious-minded consort, Albert of Saxe-Coburg-Gotha.

Peel, however, was threatened from two sides. Manufacturers, concerned at falling profits, demanded lower wages, and believed that they could only get them if the price of bread was reduced (bread was the staple diet of the working class—they ate about five pounds of it per head per week). This could only be done by permitting the free import of grain, in other words by repealing the Corn Law of 1815. Radicals, frustrated by Whig backsliding, climbed on to the band-waggon and grabbed the reins. Richard Cobden, a none-too-successful cotton merchant with transatlantic interests, John Bright, a Quaker carpet manufacturer from Rochdale, and James Wilson, the Scottish journalist who founded the *Economist* in 1843, became leading figures in the Anti-Corn Law League, inaugurated at a meeting in Manchester in October 1838. The League both represented, and in part created, the commercial-minded individualistic middle class—what the Germans called (and still call) 'Manchestertum'. By petitions, demonstrations, the mobilization of nonconformity, the imaginative use of the new penny post (1841), it created a widespread animus against the territorial aristocracy, and against Peel himself.

Peel had, in fact, followed most of the precepts of political economy in his public finance: duties on imports were drastically reduced, the Bank of England reorganized, railway promotion allowed to have its free enterprise head (despite the predilection of William Gladstone, the President of the Board of Trade, for outright nationalization). But the Leaguers acted with the fury of the desperate. They realized that their prosperity was borne on the back of an increasingly mutinous labour force. An extremely unorthodox Manchester cotton-master, the young German Friedrich Engels, watched the successive waves of discontent breaking against the mill-walls, and prophesied:

The moment the workers resolve to be bought and sold no longer, when, in the determination of the value of labour, they take the part of men possessed of a will as well as of working power, at that moment the whole Political Economy of today is at an end.

Engels's chosen instruments were the ultimate in economic depressions, and the power of the organized working class expressed in Chartism.

'I cares nothing about politics neither; but I'm a chartist' a London scavenger told Henry Mayhew, the pioneer social investigator, in 1848. The People's Charter, with its celebrated six points—manhood suffrage, the ballot, equal electoral districts, abolition of property qualifications for MPs, payment for MPs, and annual Parliaments—achieved the same immediate impact as the French Revolution and Daniel O'Connell's campaigns in Ireland. But this only gave a superficial and episodic unity to an immensely complex, highly localized movement. Formally it was ultra-democratic (although only as far as men were concerned—a proposal for female suffrage was an early casualty). In its most dramatic nation-wide phase it was also short-lived, lasting from 1838 to 1842. But organization, and heterodoxy, bubbled away in the regions, influenced by the local economic predicaments, political traditions, and the character of the leaders. The division between 'physical-' and 'moral-force' leaders was complicated by attitudes to the established parties, to the drink question, Ireland, property, and education. In Scotland and the English Midlands, leadership came from small tradesmen with a sprinkling of business and professional men. In Yorkshire it was militant, following heavy unemployment and the impact of the New Poor Law, but participated with the Tories in their campaign for factory reform. The 'frontier towns' of industrial Wales had already seen plenty of 'collective bargaining by riot', so it was possibly not surprising that a huge protest demonstration at Newport, on 4 November 1839, ended as a bloody confrontation with the military. Fourteen were killed, but subsequent trials led to transportation to Tasmania, not the gallows.

Peel was more humane and tactful than Melbourne in 1831 or Liverpool in 1819, and his policy succeeded. The economic boom of 1843 and 1844 sapped Chartism; its last revival in 1848 reflected the agony of Ireland rather than the ambitions of the English artisans, or any desire to emulate events in Europe. Late Chartism was more experimental and variegated, as well as more Irish. Feargus O'Connor projected land settlement schemes, Owenite and socialist ideas came back, along with ideas culled from European revolutionaries, many of whom ended up as exiles in Britain. But however fascinating intellectually the friendship of Julian Harney and Ernest Jones with Marx and Engels, the mass movement was dead. Old Chartists remained active in single-issue movements such as temperance, co-operation (the Rochdale Pioneer store of 1844 had Chartist origins), or trade unionism. Others emigrated. Many former Chartists ended up quite respectably integrated into mid-Victorian local government and the new provincial press.

'Unless the Lord build the City . . .'

In 1832 an appalling cholera epidemic, sweeping through Europe from the Middle East, probably killed 31,000 in Britain; in 1833 Parliament voted a £30,000 grant to elementary education, and John Keble preached at Oxford on 'national apostasy'. These events merely coincided with political reform—Parliament spent more time and money on the stables of Windsor Castle than on the education grant—but were important determinants of the direction that subsequent state action took, and the way in which the early Victorians rationalized their social position.

Cholera dramatized the problem of rapid urban growth, though its impact could be as deadly in the countryside. The new industrial towns were small in area, and densely packed, as walking to work was universal. Urban land usage accorded with economic power: the numerically tiny property-owning class, possibly less than 5 per cent of the population in a cotton town, often occupied 50 per cent of the land area. Working people lived where factories, roads, canals, and, later, railways allowed them to. The results were squalid—nineteenth-century towns smoked and stank—and, for the workers, expensive both in terms of rent and of human life. A tolerable house might take a quarter of a skilled man's weekly income, and few families were ever in a position to afford this. As a result, not only did slums multiply in the old inner-city area—the rooker-ies of London, the cellar-dwellings of Liverpool and Man-chester, the 'lands' of the Scottish burghs, 'China' in Merthyr Tydfil—but new regionally-specific types of slum were created by landlords and speculative builders—the 'back-to-backs' of Yorkshire and the tiny 'room and kitchen' or 'single-end' flats in which 70 per cent of Glasgow families lived by 1870.

If housing was bad, sanitation was worse. Better-off citizens could combine to create commissions to provide water and sewerage, light the streets, and provide some sort of policing, but if anything, this worsened the plight of their poorer neigh-bours. A middle-class area's new water-closets all too often drained into the working class's water supply.

Epidemics were the working class's revenge. Surrounded by masses of the very poor in the shape of servants and trades-people (whom they usually ignored) the wealthy suddenly became intensely vulnerable. A. C. Tait, a future Archbishop of Canter-bury, for example, lost five of his seven children to scarlet fever in Carlisle in 1856. In 1831 the government forced local not-ables to serve on temporary boards of health, in order to combat cholera. In 1840 Edwin Chadwick, concerned at the numbers driven into pauperism by the death of the bread-winner and ill-health, conducted on behalf of the Poor Law Commissioners an *Inquiry into the Sanatory Condition of the*

Labouring Population, published in 1842. As a result of this, and subsequent agitation, not to speak of the threat of another cholera outbreak, an act of 1848 gave municipalities powers to set up local boards of health, subject to three Public Health Commissioners, among them Chadwick himself. Besides the Benthamites, other forces had been mobilized—some Chartists and radicals, but probably more Tories, professional men, and philanthropists. Exemplifying the movement as a whole was Lord Ashley. The future earl of Shaftesbury could be a prejudiced low-church Tory—Macaulay referred to his style as 'the bray of Exeter Hall'—but he inherited Wilberforce's skills at manipulating public, and élite, opinion to secure effective government intervention. In the 1840s and 1850s these skills were used to help miners, factory hands, poor emigrants, and slum-dwellers. Some have argued that administrative reform took on a dynamic of its own, independent both of parliamentary action and ideology. 'The Tory interpretation of history' (as this view has somewhat unfairly been called) contrasted the power of officials—'the men on the spot'—and enthusiasts like Ashley virtually to create their own laws, with Parliament's indifference to social conditions. But this is only a partial explanation of the reform process. Standards of conduct among officials varied from department to department, and between individuals. Some were dedicated to the point of self-sacrifice, others reflected the easy-going ethos of a civil service still recruited by patronage. Anthony Trollope, as a senior official of the Post Office, still found time to hunt twice a week, and turn out a steady 1.7 novels per annum—one of which, *The Three Clerks* (1857), gives an engaging picture of a backwater of the unreformed civil service, and Trollope's own sour observations on its reformers.

As this was the golden age both of 'local self-government' and of professional evolution, the strongest initiatives came from the great cities, and from a new generation of largely Scottish-trained doctors, who were making the transition from lowly surgeon-apothecaries into a self-governing profession. Liverpool appointed the first Medical Officer of Health in 1847;

the City of London, a 'square mile' rich in every variety of
social peril, appointed the dynamic Dr John Simon a year later.
By 1854 the appointment of Medical Officers of Health was
compulsory, and proved critical not only in getting the cities to
undertake major water, drainage, and slum clearance schemes,
but to ensure that regulations on building and overcrowding
were enforced.

The new industrial society brought into question the organization of education. Opinions on this differed: the Evangelical Hannah More believed that to inculcate religion but preserve
order, children should learn to read but not write. Adam Smith,
fearing the intellectually stultifying impact of the division of
labour on the working class, sought to mitigate it by state
education. Although this existed in Scotland, as a result of the
Calvinist reformation of the Kirk, there was no English equivalent. Before the 1800s, there were grammar schools, frequently
of pre-reformation origin, independent or 'adventure' schools,
and charity schools. These varied enormously in quality, and
could never accommodate an expanding and youthful population, let alone service the new urban areas and improve standards. Around 1800, however, opinion—including even that of
George III—swung towards education as a prophylactic against
revolution—partly through the appearance of new, cheap, and
thus seductive forms of teaching. The 'monitorial' systems of
Lancaster and Bell, whereby senior pupils learned lessons by
rote and then instructed their juniors, led directly to the foundation of the British and Foreign Schools Society in 1808, and
the National Society in 1811. These two attempts at national
coverage, however, coincided with the exacerbation of hostilities between their respective sponsors, the nonconformists and
the established Church; religious animus continued to take
precedence over educational criteria for nearly a century.

Religious antagonisms in the reform of the endowed, or
'public', schools were internal to Anglicanism, and less fierce.
The schools' condition, peculiarly wretched in the last years of
the eighteenth century, had improved even before the radical

Broad-Churchman Thomas Arnold began his career at Rugby in 1829. His reforms, in fact, paralleled the essentially conservative political settlement of 1832, but lasted far longer. A 'liberal education' (Latin and Greek) remained dominant among those destined for the universities, but it was elevated from a totally meaningless ritual for young aristocrats into the subject-matter of competitive advancement, through scholarships and, at Oxford and Cambridge, college fellowships, for middle-class boys. Their goals were the prizes of subsidized entry into the professions, but their function was more profound: to act as bellwethers guiding other boys from the commercial middle class into a sanitized version of the values of the territorial aristocracy. By the time he died in 1842, Arnold was being imitated at the other older public schools, and the movement proceeded, aided by the expansion of the railway system and, in 1857, by Thomas Hughes's remarkably successful *Tom Brown's Schooldays*.

The remodelling of the public schools provided a paradigm for a new generation of reformers, many of whom had been educated there. Unlike the Benthamites, they developed no highly-integrated programme, but rather sought to convert institutions accessible only to the aristocracy and the Anglican clergy to serve the whole of society. This ideal of 'nationalization' with its corollary, the 'incorporation' of the working class into 'political society', was expressed in 1848 by the Christian Socialist followers of F. D. Maurice—including Tom Hughes—in their attempt to make the Church of England an arbiter between capital and labour. They were not alone. In Bradford William Edward Forster, a young radical woollen manufacturer, formerly a Quaker, wrote:

Unless some concessions be made to these masses, and unless all classes strive earnestly to keep them better fed, first or last there will be a convulsion; but I believe the best political method of preventing it is by the middle class sympathising with the operatives, and giving themselves power to oppose their unjust claims by helping them in those which are reasonable.

Forster's wife was the daughter of Arnold of Rugby, the sister of Matthew Arnold, inspector of schools and poet. The 'intellectual aristocracy' of high thinking and moderate reform was already shifting from evangelical religion to political intervention.

Arnold, the public schools, and most of the politicians belonged to the Broad Church or liberal Anglican tradition, whose principles envisaged the Church as partner of the State, a relationship to which theological doctrine was strictly subordinate. The Evangelicals exalted religious sanctions, but their simple theology was being corroded by liberal assaults, which seemed to reach a climax with the Reform Act of 1832. Clergymen feared that a tide of Benthamite, and hence atheistic, reform would be unleashed; John Keble in an Oxford sermon declared a clerical resistance which would be founded on the apostolic traditions of the Church of England. 'Tractarianism', or the Oxford Movement, did not oppose liberalism through social reform or through 'high-church' ceremonial. It was a conservative, intellectual appeal to Anglican tradition. After twelve years it split, in 1845, when some of its leaders, including John Henry Newman (partly in reaction to low-church persecution, partly out of sheer intellectual conviction) decided that nothing separated them from Rome, and 'went over'. Although its enemies forecast otherwise, the Oxford Movement served to strengthen the spirit of Anglicanism both through devout laymen such as W. E. Gladstone and through its influence on religious education and architecture. The Broad Church, being posited on a more sociological appreciation of religion, was in difficulties when it appeared that less than a fifth of the English attended their parish church. The unique religious Census of 1851 showed that only about 35 per cent of the English population went to Sunday service, and—although there were intense regional variations here—half of these 'sat under' dissenting ministers. In 1848 and after the Broad Church Christian Socialists tried energetically to reach out to working men, but for every working man convinced by the theology of the group's leader, F. D. Maurice, ten were impressed by the novels of his colleague Charles Kingsley, and many more helped practically by the work of J. M. Ludlow for the trade unions and E. V. Neale for the infant co-operative movement.

Anglicans at least possessed a tradition, wealth, and breadth of manœuvre denied to the nonconformists. Sectionally divided and always treated with suspicion by the ruling classes, several of their leaders—notably Jabez Bunting of the Methodist Conference—tried to integrate themselves through their conservatism. Political radicalism tended to be the hallmark of rural or mining area Dissenters—the change in South Wales was particularly drastic—or of urban élites such as the Unitarians or the Quakers. Only in the 1850s, after the success of the Corn Law campaign, did dissent begin to flex its muscles, align itself with the Liberal Party, and demand either improvements in its own civic status or—in the programme of the 'Liberation Society' (founded in 1844)—the dismantling of the established Church. Organized dissent came to play a major—and troublesome—institutional role within Liberalism, but it was a wasting asset, as the steady trickle of wealthy nonconformists over to the Church of England showed.

In Scotland the controversy over patronage came to a head in the 'ten years' conflict' of 1833–43, which ended with the 'Disruption' of the established Kirk and the creation of a new independent 'Free Church'. The secular role of the Kirk rapidly crumbled—a statutory poor law was enacted in 1845—but religious politics continued to obsess the Scots middle class for the rest of the century.

'The ringing grooves of change'

The 1840s remained, however, a decade of crisis, even in terms of classical economics. British industry was still dominated by textiles, and the market for them was both finite and subject to increasing competition from America and Europe. The industry was overcapitalized, and the adoption of each new invention meant that the return on capital decreased; each commercial depression was steeper and longer lasting than the last. Real wages increased only slowly, probably not sufficiently to counter the precipitate decline of the handwork trades and the high marginal costs of urban life. To Karl Marx, surveying Britain through the descriptions of his mill-owning friend Friedrich Engels, this was all part of one pattern. Capitalism was doomed to choke on its own surplus accumulations of capital; its increasingly underpaid labourers would, in the next economic depression, rise decisively against it. He would have echoed Shelley's challenge:

> Rise like Lions after slumber
> In unvanquishable number—
> Shake your chains to earth like dew
> Which in sleep had fallen on you—
> Ye are many—they are few.

In the 1840s events in Ireland seemed to bring the revolution perceptibly nearer. The potato blight of 1845, 1846, and 1848 destroyed the basis of the country's population growth; between 1845 and 1850 up to a million died of the consequences of malnutrition, two million emigrated between 1845 and 1855. The poor Irish immigrant, prepared to work for wages far below the English norm, had already been seen as an explosive force; Carlyle had written in *Chartism* (1839):

Every man who will take the statistic spectacles off his nose, and look, may discern in town or country . . . [that] the condition of the lower multitude of English labourers approximates more and more to the Irish competing with them in all markets. . . .

That this did not happen was substantially due to a dramatic industrial development which simultaneously soaked up surplus supplies of labour and capital and transformed them into a new and more varied economy. Its principal—and psychologically most spectacular—instrument was the railway.

Railways of various primitive types had since the early seventeenth century carried coal from mine to port or river; by 1800 there were perhaps two hundred miles of horse-worked track scattered throughout the country, built to various gauges and patterns, with wooden and later with iron rails. Cast iron was used from the 1770s, wrought iron 'edge-rail'—much more reliable—from the 1790s. Steam traction then appeared in two forms: stationary low-pressure engines dragged wagons up inclines, and light high-pressure 'locomotive' engines moved themselves on the rails. In 1804, Richard Trevithick demonstrated the locomotive in Wales, and it was soon adopted in the northern coalfield, where 'viewers' like George Stephenson were building large-capacity edge-railways whose demands stretched the capabilities of horse traction, as coal production doubled between 1800 and 1825. Throughout Britain by 1830, 375 miles of line, authorized by Parliament, had been built.

The commercial boom of the mid-1820s gave the next boost, with the promotion of the Liverpool and Manchester Railway. Cotton production had almost doubled between 1820 and 1830, and Manchester's population had risen by 47 per cent. Transport of the necessities for both was checked by the monopolistic Bridgewater Canal; a large-scale competitor was necessary. Its demands almost exceeded the technology available: only on the eve of its completion, and under pressure of an open competition, was an efficient enough locomotive produced by the Stephensons. The difference between the award-winning *Rocket* (1830) and the production-line *Patentee* (1834), however, was almost as great as that between the *Rocket* and its clumsy if reliable precursor, the *Locomotion*. Locomotive design did not subsequently change for half a century.

In the 1830s, railway development was buoyed up by another speculative boom. By 1840 nearly 2,400 miles of track connected London with Birmingham, Manchester, and Brighton. Some of the new lines were prosperous; others, overcapitalized and faced with penal land and legal charges, ran into trouble. There were few enough rules in the early days of joint-stock companies, and the reputation soared of those who succeeded in turning 'scrip into gold', such as George Hudson, 'the Railway King' who controlled a third of the system by 1845.

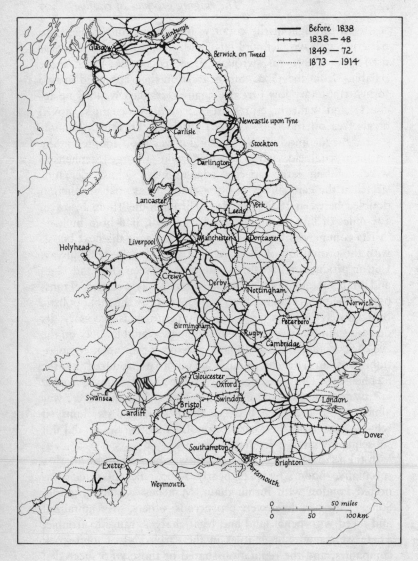

———	Before 1838
+++++	1838 — 48
———	1849 — 72
········	1873 — 1914

Edinburgh

Glasgow

Berwick on Tweed

Newcastle upon Tyne

Carlisle

Stockton

Darlington

Lancaster

Leeds York

Holyhead

Liverpool

Manchester Doncaster

Crewe

Derby

Nottingham

Norwich

Birmingham

Peterboro

Rugby

Cambridge

Swansea

Gloucester Oxford

Cardiff

Bristol Swindon

London

Dover

Southampton

Exeter

Brighton

Portsmouth

Weymouth

0   50 miles

0   50   100 km

RAILWAYS IN THE NINETEENTH CENTURY 1825–1914

Hudson made his attractive profits by paying the dividends of existing lines with capital raised for new branches; when the great mania of the 1840s, which he helped promote, faltered in 1848, he was exposed and fled the country—but not before mileage had risen to over 8,000, and the network had been extended from Aberdeen to Plymouth.

But the railway age produced its heroes as well: the self-taught Stephenson and his brilliant son Robert, Joseph Locke, Daniel Gooch, and the polymath Isambard Kingdom Brunel, whose vast projects—the seven-foot-gauge Great Western Railway, the pioneer iron-and-screw steamer *Great Britain*, and the 18,000 ton sea-leviathan *Great Eastern*—fascinated the public as much as they terrified his unfortunate financial backers. 'What poet-race', G. K. Chesterton would later ask, 'shot such cyclopean arches at the stars?' Such men—Carlyle called them 'captains of industry'—were more attractive entrepreneurs than the cotton-masters, and Samuel Smiles was subsequently to make them paragons of 'self-help'.

This new transport system had been created in less than a score of years, and without any modern construction techniques. The 'navvies'—of whom 250,000 were said to be at work in 1848, powered by beer and beef—created the huge earthworks which characterized early British railways. The image of the British working man in the 1830s had been of the pathetic factory slave or starving cotton-weaver. In the 1850s it was provided by the brawny labourers who ran up the Crystal Palace in six months, and who were shipped to the Crimea to make good—with railways and camps—the incompetence of the military. The railways had cost an unprecedented amount of money, however: by 1849 no less than £224.6 million had been invested. In 1849 total receipts remained low at only £11.4 million; although they rose by 1859 to £24.4 million, railways were never more than a modest and reliable investment, and in the case of some companies they were far from that. Until 1852, they made more money from passengers than freight and the subsequent expansion of goods traffic was obtained to a great

extent by a systematic process of buying over their chief competitors, the canals, whose owners, having hitherto enjoyed
inflated profits, were little inclined to see themselves beggared
by competition. By the mid-1850s, strategic sections of the
canal network were in railway ownership, and traffics were
ruthlessly transferred to rail. Already, in the most dynamic area
of industrial growth, the conspiracy of capitalists denounced by
Adam Smith had become a fact.

Politics and Diplomacy: Palmerston's Years

The railway boom coincided with a dramatic shift in politics.
The harvests of 1842, 1843, and 1844 had been good; grain was
plentiful and costs low. Then in 1845 the harvest was wrecked
by bad weather, and the first blights hit the Irish potato crop.
The arguments of the Anti-Corn Law League seemed confirmed. Peel attempted to carry free trade in Cabinet, failed,
and resigned, only to come back when the Whigs could not
form a ministry. In February 1846, he moved a package of
measures abolishing duties on imported corn over three years.
He thus bought—or hoped to buy—the support of the gentry
through grants towards the poor law and local police forces.
But his party was deeply split and only a minority supported
him when he was censured on Irish coercion in May. In the
ensuing election Russell came back with a Whig ministry, and
Whigs and later Liberals dominated politics thereafter. Badly
weakened by the shift of the Peelite élite, which included Gladstone, Aberdeen, and Sir James Graham, into the ambit of the
Whigs, the Tory gentry now found themselves led by the ex-
Whigs Lord Derby and Lord George Bentinck, and the exotic
ex-radical Benjamin Disraeli. The Tories stood firm as a party,
but held power for only five of the next thirty years.

There was a greater degree of party management, centred on
the new clubs of St. James's, the Reform and the (Tory) Carl-
ton, both founded in 1832, but to conceive of politics shading
from left to right means imposing the criteria of a later age.
National party organizations were as unknown as party pro-

grammes. Public speeches were rare. Leaders—still predominantly Whig magnates—would drop a few hints to their closest
colleagues, often their relatives, about policy just before elections (which took place every seven years). Prospective candidates travelled to likely seats, issued addresses, and canvassed
for the support of local notables, only 'going to the poll' if
promised respectable support.

Huge expenses made contested elections the exception rather
than the rule. The territorial nobility were impregnable in
their many surviving 'pocket boroughs'. A vote—delivered in
public—against, say, Blenheim Palace at Woodstock, was still
an almost suicidal move for a local farmer or tradesman. Counties, likewise, were dominated by the great families. The
medium-sized boroughs were more open but expensive; their
electors sometimes reached the levels of corruption depicted
at Eatanswill in Dickens's *Pickwick Papers*. The newly-
enfranchised great towns could sometimes elect active if
impecunious men—Macaulay sat for Leeds—but more often
favoured affluent local businessmen, who usually bore most of
the cost of the contest. Some things, however, remain familiar
today: England was more conservative, the 'Celtic fringe' more
radical.

Although Wellington's brief caretaker ministry of 1834
proved the last occasion on which a duke became first minister,
power lay with the landed interest, in which the Whigs were
still as well represented as the Tories, although in many cases
the elevation to this status was recent, a tribute to the flexibility
of the élite. Peel and Gladstone—both Oxford double-firsts—
were only a generation removed from provincial industry and
commerce, and even more remarkable was the rise of Benjamin
Disraeli, adventurer and novelist, stemming from a religion
whose members were only to obtain full civil equality in 1860.

Ministries spent little time over domestic legislation, but
much more over foreign and service affairs—not surprisingly,
since the latter claimed more than a third of the estimates.
Neither navy nor army had changed much since 1815. The navy
bought its first steamer, a tug called the *Monkey*, in 1822. With

enormous reluctance, others were ordered in 1828, the Lords of the Admiralty feeling that 'the introduction of steam is calculated to strike a fatal blow at the supremacy of the Empire'. Paddles meant a loss of broadside guns, and sailing ships could keep station for years, so Devonport was still launching all-sail three-deckers in 1848, although the successful use of screw-propulsion on smaller ships was numbering the days of the sailing fleet. The old long-service army of about 130,000 men— 42 per cent Irish and 14 per cent Scots in 1830—poorly paid and wretchedly accommodated, kept the peace in Ireland and the colonies. In many small campaigns it advanced Britain's spheres of influence and trade in India, and in the 'Opium War' of 1839–42 in China, although now on behalf of free-trading merchants rather than the fading Chartered Companies.

Britain's withdrawal from European commitments was reflected, too, in her diplomacy. After the defeat of Napoleon, the Continental conservative leaders, above all Tsar Alexander I of Russia, tried to establish a system of co-operation in Europe through regular congresses of the great powers. But even in 1814 British diplomats preferred security to be achieved by the traditional means of the balance of power, even if this meant resurrecting France as a counterweight to Russia. For much of the time between then and 1848, a tacit Anglo-French *entente* subsisted, though it was disturbed in 1830 when Catholic Belgium detached itself from Holland, and looked as if it might fall into the French sphere of influence. The solution to this was found in Belgian neutrality, and a new royal family with close links with Britain—all guaranteed by the Treaty of London (1839), whose violation by Germany in August 1914 brought the long peace to an end.

Other problems between Britain and France were less easily settled, as they were linked with the steady decline of the Turkish Empire, which Britain wished to maintain as a buffer against Austria and Russia in the Balkans. For much of this period, the dominant figure was Palmerston, who, coming late into foreign affairs in 1830 at the age of forty-six, burrowed himself into the grubby premises of the Foreign Office in Whitehall (which at the zenith of its power had a staff of only forty-five) and stayed there as the dominant force for over thirty years—aggressively patriotic, but still, within limits, liberal. In 1847, however, the most celebrated British politician in Europe was not Palmerston but Cobden, the apostle of free trade. He was fêted in capital after capital, and his hosts were sure of one thing—the conservative monarchies were doomed, and the day of liberalism would shortly dawn.

Early in 1848, Marx and Engels drafted the *Communist Manifesto* in London, prophesying, on behalf of a small group of German socialists, a European revolution, to be led by the workers of those countries most advanced towards capitalism. Paris rose up against Louis Philippe on 24 February, then Berlin, Vienna, and the Italian states erupted. But Britain did not follow. There was a momentary panic when the Chartists brought their last great petition to London on 14 April; 10,000 special constables were sworn in; the telegraphs bought over for the week by the Home Office. The constables were potentially more worrying than the Chartists, as middle-class volunteer forces had spearheaded the Continental risings. But their loyalty was absolute; revolutions were something that happened elsewhere. The Chartists dispersed from Kennington Common; Parliament laughed the great petition out.

But there was no repetition of 1793 either. The republican government in Paris wanted to maintain co-operation with Britain, acted firmly against its own radicals, and did not try to export revolution. Palmerston wanted no change in the balance of power, but favoured constitutional regimes and an Austrian withdrawal from Italy. This moderation was scarcely successful, and Britain was unable to guarantee any of the gains that the liberals briefly made. A combination of peasant support bought by land reform and Russian aid, which crushed Hungary and gave Austria a free hand elsewhere, brought the *anciens régimes* back to power—but Austria was now prostrate and the Russians worryingly dominant in Eastern Europe.

Incorporation

Repeal of the Corn Law, the handling of the 1848 emergency, and the rapid expansion of the railways not only made the economic situation more hopeful but underpinned it with a new political consensus. The agricultural interest had been checked, but its farming efficiency enabled it to ride out foreign competition. At the same time the bourgeoisie realized that it had both to co-operate with the old élite in controlling the industrial workers, and to concede enough to the latter to stave off political explosions. In this context (particularly compared with textiles), railways, steamers, and telegraphs were all useful and glamorous, attractive advertisements for industrialization. Functionally, they brought together land, commerce, and industry. And they made lawyers in particular very rich.

By the 1850s the law 'incorporated' the working classes—or, at least, their leading members. The 'New Model' trade unions of skilled workers, such as the Engineers and the Carpenters, pressed not for drastic state intervention but for contractual equality. They acted not through public demonstrations but through diplomatic pressure on MPs of both parties. Their procedures and iconography rejected the oaths and mysticism of the old quasi-conspiratorial societies for an almost pedantic legalism, concerned with defending their respectability at the top of the working class.

Economic and social theory moved towards the idea of 'incorporation'. Classical economics had earlier been subversive and pessimistic: one strand of it, in the hands of Marx, remained so. But John Stuart Mill in his *Logic* of 1840 and his *Political Economy* of 1848 reconciled utilitarianism with gradual reform and sympathy for the aims of moderate working-class leaders. Mill found to his surprise that the *Logic*, with its substantial borrowings from the French sociological tradition of Saint-Simon and Auguste Comte, became the orthodoxy of the older universities, which were recuperating from the traumas of the Oxford Movement. But the 'Saint of Rationalism' himself had, in his enthusiasm for the English Romantic poets, gone far to make his blend of utilitarianism, ethical individualism, and reformist 'socialism' acceptable to reformers within the establishment, who broadcast it in the high-minded literary reviews which burgeoned around the mid-century.

In the eyes of the candidates for political incorporation, 'the rule of law' was far from absolute. A. V. Dicey, who applied the phrase to nineteenth-century government, was himself to write in the 1860s: 'John Smith *qua* John Smith cannot be suppressed, but John Smith *qua* artisan can.' But he expected that the extension of the franchise would end such inequities. As, by and large, it did.

Who then remained 'without the law'? The Irish had been wounded too deeply. 'Repeal of the Union' was O'Connell's bequest to a new generation of patriots. Although the Catholic middle class, like the Scots, proved anxious to find niches in the British establishment, Irish nationalists were made more aggressive by the famine, and could in the future count on the aid of their embittered emigrant brethren in America. Settlers in the colonies may have prided themselves on their transplanting of British institutions, but as the Colonial Office was aware, settler notions of law found no place for the rights of the natives. High and low churchmen complained when the courts upheld the vague and all-embracing formulas of the Broad Church establishment. They could not dislodge it but they could indelibly affect the skyline of Victorian cities and the practice of piety.

The intellectuals accepted the notion of political and social evolution—Tennyson's 'freedom slowly broadens down/from precedent to precedent'—long before Darwin's *Origin of Species* appeared in 1859. Although no friend to liberalism, Thomas Carlyle's commendations of self-reliance and the work ethic gave individualism an almost religious quality. John Stuart Mill became a pillar of the mid-Victorian Liberal Party, eccentric only in his desire to extend 'incorporation' to the half of the population whom politics ignored—women (whose slow progress to civic and legal equality started, however, to accelerate during the 1850s). Two more troubled intellects were difficult to pin down. John Ruskin, 'the graduate of Oxford' whose *Modern Painters* was the sensation of 1843, combined reverence for aristocracy with increasingly subversive views on the economy and the environment; though his directly political impact was to be minimal compared to that of Robert Owen. No one savaged the law's delays and inequities more energetically than Charles Dickens, yet no one worried more about the results of revolution and lawlessness. The Circumlocution Office, the Tite Barnacles, Jarndyce *versus* Jarndyce, were balanced by Slackbridge, Madame Defarge, and Bill Sikes, though Dicey got it just about right when, on balance, he put Dickens alongside Shaftesbury as a force pushing public opinion towards 'positive' reforming legislation.

Militant dissent and old radicalism had their own world-view, remote from that of the establishment, but its tentacles reached out towards them. The middle class read 'industrial novels,' such as Disraeli's *Sybil*, in the 1840s, anxious about and intrigued by conditions in the great towns, trying to personalize their problems and reconcile them with individualist morality. But Mrs Gaskell in *Mary Barton* and Charles Kingsley in *Alton Locke* could not provide any such assurance; the only effective solution for their most heroic characters was emigration. Dickens's savage Carlylean satire on Manchester, *Hard Times*, wavered and collapsed when it came to considering any better future for the inhabitants of Coketown.

But few of the Coketown people had time or money to read about what the literati thought of their plight, and little enough was known about what they read, although it was obviously affected by the co-option of the literary radicals by a middle-class public. Henry Mayhew, the pioneer social investigator of the *Morning Chronicle*, just about carried on the journalistic tradition of Cobbett and Hazlitt into the 1860s; Dickens, from the same Bohemian milieu, shifted away from it. We know that the 'labour aristocracy' in the trade unions read what their betters wanted them to read; that the religious kept their Bibles and their *Pilgrim's Progress*; but what of the 'roughs', and 'tavern society'? A folk tradition survived and developed in the fishing ports, among the weavers, and on the farms. Later in the nineteenth century, an American professor discovered two-thirds of the great traditional English ballads still being sung in the 'Farmtouns' of north-east Scotland, where the more plebeian 'bothy ballads' acted as a means of spreading information about farmers among the ploughmen and carters, and the 'Society of the Horseman's Word' conserved a primitive, but effective, trade unionism.

In his novel *Except the Lord* (1953) about the mid-Victorian youth of a radical politician, Joyce Cary takes his hero, Chester Nimmo, into a fairground tent. A troupe of actors are performing *Maria Marten, or the Murder in the Red Barn*, a staple of nineteenth-century melodrama, loosely based on an actual murder which occurred in 1830—the eve of 'Captain Swing'. This was Nimmo's reaction:

The drama that we saw, and that millions had seen, was a story of the cruellest hurt of many inflicted by the rich on the poor. Throughout the play everything possible was done to show the virtue, innocence and helplessness of the poor, and the abandoned cruelty, the heartless self-indulgence of the rich.

And this was one among hundreds of such plays. I have wondered often how such propaganda failed to bring to England also, as to France, Italy, Germany, almost every other nation, a bloody revolution, for its power was incredible. As I say, it was decisive in my own life . . .

Cary, a subtle and historically aware novelist, seems to have sensed here a resentment and grievance deep enough to be concealed by the respectability and self-help of formal working-class politics but for which political 'incorporation', the repetitive rows of sanitarily adequate workmen's dwellings, the increasingly opulent chapels, the still-locked Sunday parks, offered no consolation.

9. The Liberal Age
(1851–1914)

H. C. G. MATTHEW

Free Trade: an Industrial Economy Rampant

THE Great Exhibition of 1851 celebrated the ascendancy of
the United Kingdom in the market-place of the world, though
many of the Coninental exhibits, especially those from the
German states, gave British manufacturers pause when the high
quality of their technology was examined. The Exhibition,
sponsored by the court and organized by the aristocracy,
reflected Britain's commitment to economic progress and hence
to Liberalism. It touched an enthusiastic nerve in the popular
mind. For many ordinary people, it was the first occasion for
a visit to London, an exhausting but exhilarating long day-
trip on one of the special trains which brought visitors from
all over the country. The success of the Exhibition astonished
contemporaries. Figures for attendance were published daily in
the press; by the end, over six million tickets had been sold,
and on one day over 109,000 persons visited the 'blazing arch
of lucid glass', Joseph Paxton's Crystal Palace which housed the
Exhibition in Hyde Park. Its substantial profits were later used
to build the museums at South Kensington. The huge crowds
were well behaved and openly monarchic. Members of the
propertied classes congratulated themselves: the nervous, brittle
atmosphere of the 1840s was giving way to the calmer tone of
the 1850s, which by the 1860s had become positively self-
confident. A street ballad sold at the Exhibition emphasized the

curious blend of artisan self-reliance, free-trade internationalism, and monarchic chauvinism which was to define the language of much of British public life for the rest of the century:

> O, surely England's greatest wealth,
> Is an honest working man....
> It is a glorious sight to see
> So many thousands meet,
> Not heeding creed or country,
> Each other friendly greet.
> Like children of one mighty sire,
> May that sacred tie ne'er cease,
> May the blood stain'd sword of War give way
> To the Olive branch of Peace.
>
> But hark! the trumpets flourish,
> Victoria does approach,
> That she may long be spared to us
> Shall be our reigning toast.
> I trust each heart, it will respond,
> To what I now propose—
> Good will and plenty to her friends,
> And confusion to her foes.

The tone of ballads such as this explains the popularity of Henry Temple, Lord Palmerston. When Lord Aberdeen's coalition government of 1852 foundered into war against Russia in the Crimea (1854–6) and then disintegrated when the ineptitude of the war effort was revealed, Palmerston emerged from its ruins as Prime Minister. He held this post, leading the Liberal coalition, with one short interruption until his death in October 1865. Palmerston personified the bombastic self-confidence of Britain as the only world power, and succeeded in being simultaneously an aristocrat, a reformer, a free-trader, an internationalist, and a chauvinist.

The society which the Great Exhibition of 1851 revealed was given more statistical analysis in the Census of the same year. Two facts captured the public imagination. For the first time, more people in the mainland of the United Kingdom lived in towns—albeit often quite small ones—than in the countryside: a dramatic contrast with the past and with any other economy. The free-trade movement accompanied rather than anticipated the commitment of the British economy to manufacturing, transport, and service industries with an urban base. That dream of the Liberal Tories of the 1820s, that the economy could be somehow held in balance between agriculture and industry, was forgotten with the free trade dawn. Agriculture remained easily the largest single industry and indeed increased its competence and output markedly in the 1850s and 1860s. But the growth of population was in the towns, and labourers left the land for the cities. When agriculture faced its crisis in the 1870s with the opening of the North American prairies, there were relatively few left to defend it. The 'Revolt of the Field' in the 1870s was a motley affair as out-of-work labourers struggled to organize themselves as wages fell and magistrates and farmers brought in the troops to harvest the crops. By the 1850s, British—and especially northern and midland England, South Wales, and southern Scotland—was thus, through the working of Adam Smith's 'invisible hand' of world trade rather than by any conscious political decision, committed to a ride on the roller-coaster of international capitalism, a ride where the travellers could not see beyond the rise or dip ahead of them: no one had been there before. An urban nation had no precedent: perhaps that was why the British dwelt so tenaciously on rural images and traditions.

The other statistic of the 1851 Census that caught the attention of contemporaries was its revelations about religion. It was the only Census ever to attempt to assess English religious attendance, or the lack of it. There were difficulties about the statistics, but the main emphasis was indisputable and surprising: England and Wales were only partly church-going, and Anglicans were in only a bare majority of those who attended. Of a total population of 17,927,609, the church-goers were:

Church of England	5,292,551
Roman Catholics	383,630
Protestant Dissenters	4,536,265

Of potential church-goers, over five and a quarter million stayed at home. The Census was a triumph for non-Anglicans. Their claim to greater political representation and attention was now backed by that most potent of all mid-Victorian weapons, so approved of by Mr Gradgrind, Charles Dickens's Lancastrian manufacturer: 'a fact'.

England in the 1850s was thus increasingly urban, perhaps increasingly secular, certainly increasingly non-Anglican in tone. Mid-Victorian politics reflected these tendencies, all of which pointed towards Liberalism.

Between 1847 and 1868, the Tories (the rump of the party left as protectionists after the 1846 split) lost six general elections running (1847, 1852, 1857, 1859, 1865, 1868). It is clear that the Tories lost these elections; it is less easy to say who won them. Majority governments relied on support from four main groups: the Whigs, the radicals, the Liberals and the Peelites (the followers of Sir Robert Peel in 1846). This support was always liable to disintegration. The classic mid-Victorian political pattern was as follows: a coalition government was made up of all or most of the above groups, compromising and bargaining until they could agree no more and a point of breakdown was reached: the government would go out of office without dissolving Parliament; the Tories would then form a minority government, during which the non-Tory groups would resolve their differences, defeat the Tories, force a dissolution, win the general election, and resume power. This overall pattern explains the minority Tory (Derby/Disraeli) ministries of 1852, 1958–9, and 1866–8.

The political system between 1846 and 1868 thus excluded the Tories from power, while allowing them occasional periods of minority office. During the same period, the majority coalition first formed by Lord Aberdeen in 1852 gradually fused itself into 'the liberal party', though even when it became regularly referred to by that name in the 1860s it remained fissiparous and liable to disintegration. At the executive level, the Whigs, the Peelites, and Lord Palmerston predominated. To a considerable extent they ruled on sufferance. That great surge of middle-class political awareness exemplified in the Anti-Corn Law League in the 1840s had made it clear to politicians that the old political structure could be maintained only if it came to terms with middle-class expectations. The series of great budgets introduced by the Peelite Chancellor of the Exchequer, William Ewart Gladstone, in the years 1853–5 and 1859–65 went far towards meeting these expectations fiscally. The manufacturing classes wanted free trade: Gladstone saw that they got it.

'Free trade' of course meant much more than simply the abolition of protective tariffs. 'Free trade' or *laissez-faire* were shorthand terms exemplifying a whole philosophy of political, social, and economic organization. John Stuart Mill's *Principles of Political Economy*, first published in 1848, the handbook of mid-Victorian liberalism, put the point in a nutshell: '*Laisser-faire*, in short, should be the general practice: every departure from it, unless required by some great good, is a certain evil.' The presumption was that the State should stand aside. The division which Mill and others made between 'the State' on the one hand and society on the other was based on the assumption that the individual could and should stand alone. Individualism, self-respect, self-reliance, and the organization of voluntary and co-operative societies, these were the keynotes of mid-Victorian liberalism. Thus the economy should be self-regulating, and the individual whether consumer or producer, holding his copy of Samuel Smiles's *Self-Help* (1859), should be free to make what way he could in it.

This view of individualism gained from the widely popular writings of the social evolutionists. Charles Darwin's *On The Origin of Species* (1859) was not a bolt from the blue: it fitted naturally into, as well as transcending, a corpus of writing on evolution. The concept of evolution, and consequently of 'progress', whether on the individual, national, or global level, came to permeate every aspect of Victorian life and thought. Because evolution was determined by laws of science (a view usually described as 'positivism'), man's duty was to discover and obey such laws, not meddle with them. Hence most positivists (such as Walter Bagehot, editor of the influential weekly *Economist*, and Herbert Spencer, author of many works on sociology) were strong *laissez-faire* supporters.

If the individual was to make his way productively, he or she must be prepared and equipped with knowledge: the availability of knowledge and the freedom to comment on it was thus central to a liberal society. Moral choices must be informed choices: self-awareness and self-development in the context of human sympathy were the themes of the novels of George Eliot (Mary Ann Evans) and her own life was a testimony to the trials as well as the liberation of the free spirit in mid-Victorian society.

The abolition in 1855 and 1861 of the 'Taxes on Knowledge' (the stamp duties on newspapers, and the customs and excise duties on paper) epitomized the sort of liberal legislation which was particularly prized. The repeal of these taxes made possible the phenomenon which was both the epitome and the guarantor of liberal Britain—the liberal metropolitan and provincial press. The 1850s and 1860s saw a spectacular expansion of daily and Sunday newspapers, especially in the provinces, overwhelmingly liberal in politics and in general outlook. By 1863, there were over 1,000 newspapers in Britain, the vast majority of very recent foundation. For example, in Yorkshire in 1867, 66 of the 86 local newspapers had been founded since 1853. In London, the *Daily Telegraph*, re-founded in 1855 as a penny daily and as the flagship of the liberal press, had a circulation of almost 200,000 in 1871, far outstripping *The Times*. The new provincial press took its tone from the *Telegraph*, and that tone was unabashedly and enthusiastically progressive. A typical example is this leader commenting on Gladstone's tour of the Newcastle shipyards in 1862:

When we pull a political pansy for Lord Derby [the Tory leader], and tell him 'that's for remembrance', it is because the violent fallacies and frenzies of Protection are not to be forgotten simply because they are forgiven . . . With ten years' honour upon her green laurels, and the French treaty [of free trade signed in 1860] in her hand—the emblem of future conquests—we have enshrined Free Trade at last in a permanent seat.

By the 1860s, free trade—in its specific sense of an absence of protective tariffs—had become a central orthodoxy of British politics, almost as entrenched as the Protestant succession. The triumph of the classical political economists was complete, in the sense that the cardinal tenet of their faith was established as a political principle so widely accepted that only a deliberately perverse or self-confessedly unreconstructed politician would deny it. Front-bench Tory politicians quickly took the view that if their party was again to become a majority party, they must accept that protection was 'not only dead but damned', as Disraeli said. Tory budgets became as impeccably free-trading as Liberal ones.

Outside the area of fiscal policy, there was less agreement about how far 'free trade' should go. Pressure groups within the Liberal movement in the 1850s and 1860s promoted a large range of 'negative' free-trade measures: the abolition of established Churches, the abolition of compulsory church rates, the abolition of religious tests for entry into Oxford and Cambridge and public offices, the removal of restrictions upon the transfer or use of land, the end of a civil service based on patronage. In addition to these, there was in the 1860s a general movement in the constituencies for further parliamentary reform—a demand welcomed by many but not all of the Liberal MPs. The Liberal Party legislating on such matters was not really a 'party' in the modern sense of the word. It was rather a loose coalition of complex, interlocking allegiances, the most basic of which was its commitment to a free-trading economy. Within the coalition nestled many reforming interests, especially of a religious sort. A great religious revival in the 1860s added to the number of religious activists within the Liberal Party, and to the enthusiasm with which they both aired their opinions and worked for the party's success. Roman Catholics, nonconformists, and even secularists found voices within this broadly-based movement for progress—the voices were given a common accent by their hostility to Anglicanism and the established Church. Non-Anglicanism was, throughout the century, perhaps the most important social reason for voting Liberal. Paradoxically, however, the leadership of the coalition was uniformly Anglican, though of a moderate and reforming kind. There was, therefore, considerable dispute between the leadership of the coalition and its more militant supporters about the speed of reform. On the whole, the leadership—Palmerston, Lord John Russell, Gladstone—wanted moderate reform which would strengthen the Anglican Church overall, while the radical rank and file wanted step-by-step reform which would lead to the eventual disestablishment of the Anglican Church. Both groups could thus agree on limited measures such as the abolition of compulsory church rates while disagreeing on the ultimate ends of their policies. The crowning success of this sort of approach to politics was the disestablishment of the Anglican Church in Ireland in 1869.

The participation of the articulate members of the working classes within the Liberal Party, especially at the constituency level, was of great importance. In the 1830s and early 1840s, the six points of the Chartists had constituted a demand which, in terms of the politics of the day, could not be incorporated by the classes holding political power. By the late 1850s, radical movement for constitutional reform, often led by ex-Chartists, demanded only changes in the franchise, and of these enfranchisement of the male head of each household at most ('household suffrage'). It was not difficult for political leaders in both parties, but especially in the Liberal Party, to come to

terms with such requests. They also had their own reasons for
wanting to change the system. Some Tories wanted to change it
because their experience from 1847 onwards showed that they
could not win a general election within the existing system.
Some Liberals, including Gladstone and Lord John Russell,
wanted to make marginal extensions to the franchise so as to
include more liberal artisans, sturdy individualists who would
support the Liberal's programme of retrenchment and reform.
Some radicals, such as John Bright, wanted a 'household
suffrage' to give a more full-blooded basis to Liberalism,
though even they were quick to point out that they did not
want votes given to what was known as 'the residuum' (that is,
paupers, the unemployed, the 'thriftless', men with no property
at all). Some Liberals such as Robert Lowe, radical enough on
ordinary legislation, distrusted any change leading to 'democracy' as they believed the 'intelligent class' would be swamped
by it. Some Tories such as the future Lord Salisbury feared a
household suffrage would lead to an attack on property
through increased direct taxes such as the income tax. Some
Whigs saw no reason to change a system which always returned
non-Tory Parliaments.

Palmerston reflected the views of this last group, and won a
great election victory in 1865 without a pledge to franchise
reform. He died that autumn. Russell, his successor as Prime
Minister, brought in with Gladstone in 1866 a very moderate
reform bill dealing mainly with towns, on which their ministry
broke up, some of their party withdrawing support because the
bill did too much, others because it did too little. The third of
the Derby/Disraeli minority Tory administrations then brought
in its own bill for the towns, thus selling the pass of the
anti-reformers' position. Reform of some sort became certain:
the Liberals had begun their customary regrouping when Disraeli unexpectedly announced his acceptance of a household
suffrage amendment: the bill then passed, in a form a great deal
more dramatic and sweeping than the Russell–Gladstone bill of
the previous year. The franchise system of 1832 was ended: the

parameters of urban politics until 1918 were established (similar voting privileges were granted to men in the counties in 1884–5). In an extremely confused situation in 1868, the Liberals seemed to reconfirm their 1865 election position as the dominant party by winning the general election with the huge majority of 112. In fact, the 1867 Reform Act had changed the rules of the political game in such a way that a majority Tory government again became possible—but it was to be a Tory government under Disraeli in 1874 which made no serious attempt to reverse any of the main Liberal achievements of the previous thirty years, certainly not the centre-piece of free trade.

The early years of Gladstone's first government (1868–74) were the culmination of these reforming pressures: by 1874 many of the demands of mid-century Liberalism were fulfilled. In addition to disestablishing the Irish Church, the Liberals in the 1860s and early 1870s had abolished compulsory church rates, the 'taxes on knowledge', religious tests for Oxford and Cambridge, and the purchase of commissions in the army; they had legislated on Irish land, and on education for England and Scotland; they had opened the civil service to entrance by competition and they had made capitalism relatively safe for the investor by introducing limited liability—all this in addition to their preoccupation with free trade finance, proper government accounting, minimum budgets, and retrenchment.

Though there was the usual tug and tussle of political bargaining, this great reforming surge had not been seriously opposed. Even the establishment of the Anglican Church—whose defence *in toto* had been a central rallying point of Toryism in the first half of the century—had been ended in part clearly and efficiently: what had in the 1830s been merely a radical dream had by the 1870s become reality, and almost without apparent struggle. The Tories' ultimate card, the unelected House of Lords, had been played in only a limited way—to delay repeal of the paper duties, to delay church rate repeal, the ballot, and the abolition of religious tests at the universities. The propertied and labouring classes had collaborated in a great clearing of the decks of the Liberal ship of state.

The advent of 'free trade' as the prevailing ethos coincided with an economic boom, lasting from the early 1850s to the early 1870s. Contemporaries saw the first as causing the second; economic historians have been more sceptical. The removal of tariff barriers probably had only a marginal impact on the British economy, but the ascendancy of 'free trade', in its larger sense of a national commitment to economic progress, was closely related to an entrepreneurial enthusiasm which all classes seem to have shared. The mid-century boom was not, in percentage terms, very spectacular, and it was linked to a mild inflation. But it was none the less extremely important, for it seemed to show that the 'condition of England' question which had been so much a preoccupation of the 1820–50 period could be solved—was being solved—by market forces working within the existing social and political structure. Even the distress caused by the 'cotton famine' of the 1860s in Lancashire—when the cotton mills were cut off by the American Civil War from their traditional source of raw material, the plantations in the Southern States—produced little prolonged political reaction, and the propertied classes congratulated themselves that local initiative and voluntary subscriptions had seemed to be sufficient to allow the Westminster government to avoid accepting any direct responsibility for the sufferings of the Lancastrian work-force (though in fact a government loan scheme had also been important).

Compared with any other country, the British economy in the period 1850–70 was extraordinary in its complexity and in the range of its products and activities. It was strong in the basic raw materials of an early industrial economy—coal and iron—and it increased its world ascendancy in these two commodities as Continental countries imported British coal and iron to supply the basic materials for their own industrialization. An energetic manufacturing sector pressed forward with a huge range of items, from ships and steam engines through textiles to the enormous variety of small manufactured goods which adorned Victorian houses and, by their export in British ships, 'Victorianized' the whole trading world. This intense industrial activity rested on a sound currency and on a banking system which, though it had its failures, was comparatively stable and was, especially from the 1870s, gaining an increasingly important role in the economy.

A Shifting Population: Town and Country

This surge of economic progress produced a nation and an economy whose preoccupations were by 1870 largely industrial and urban. The growth of towns, which some had thought in 1851 could hardly be continued, intensified. By 1901, only one-fifth of the population of England and Wales lived in what may be called 'rural areas'; that is, 80 per cent of the population was urbanized, a far greater proportion than in any European country, and one which remained little changed until the 1970s. By 1901, there were seventy-four towns with over 50,000 inhabitants and London, 'the metropolis' as Victorians called it, grew from 2.3 million in 1851 to 4.5 million in 1911 (or 7.3 million if we include all its suburbs). The most rapid growth was not in the already established 'industrial revolution' cities, such as Liverpool and Manchester, but in the clusters of towns around the industrial heartland, towns such as Salford. These areas of urban sprawl went to make up what Patrick Geddes, the late-Victorian theorist of town planning, called 'conurbations', that is large areas of industrial and urban land in which several cities merge to form what is really a single non-rural unit. By 1911, Britain had seven such areas, at a time when no European country had more than two. These were: Greater London (7.3 million), south-east Lancashire (2.1 million), the West Midlands (1.6 million), West Yorkshire (1.5 million), Merseyside (1.2 million), Tyneside (0.8 million), and central Clydeside (about 1.5 million)—all this in a nation with a population of only 40 million on the mainland in 1911. Some towns, such as the iron and steel town of Middlesbrough, grew from virtually nothing to a population of 120,000 in half a century. Most of these conurbations contained a significant Irish community, and their politics consequently tended to be more 'orange and green' than elsewhere. At the end of the century London and Leeds also absorbed large Jewish communities, the victims of an Eastern European 'rural depopulation' as ferocious as the Irish famine.

Urban growth at this sort of pace was, of course, to be a common phenomenon in underdeveloped countries in the twentieth century, but in the nineteenth it had no precedent. It is not easy to generalize about these towns. Styles and standards of architecture varied enormously, from the indestructible stone tenements of Glasgow, through the 'back-to-back, two-up, two-down' little houses in the mining towns, often built of poor-quality brick, to the decorous suburbs of the lower and upper middle classes. A common feature of this housing was that it was almost all leased or rented—owner-occupiers were rare, though becoming more common by the end of the century. Some towns were well planned by civically-minded local councils, with parks, libraries, concert halls, and baths; others were left to the mercy of the speculative builder.

These growing towns were dominated by the railways, which created for the first time a nationally integrated economy. They transformed the centres of towns by the space which their stations and marshalling yards took up, they made it possible for better-off people to live away from the town centre by providing cheap transport from the suburbs, and they covered everything with soot. Filth and noise characterized Victorian cities—filth from the trains, the chimneys of factories and houses, and the horses, noise from the carts and carriages and horses on the cobblestones. When motor transport began to replace horses in the early twentieth century, everyone noticed how relatively quiet and clean town centres became. But noise, filth, and bad housing are relative to what people are accustomed to: it was only slowly that the demand for improvement in urban life became a powerful one. For many Victorians, production was its own justification, a view well expressed by Florence, Lady Bell, in her book *At The Works*, a classic study of a classic industrial town, Middlesbrough, a town given over to one pursuit and one only, the making of iron:

In default of a romantic past, of a stately tradition, the fact of this swift gigantic growth has given to Middlesbrough a romance and dignity of another kind, the dignity of power, of being able to stand erect by its sheer strength on no historical foundation, unsupported by the pedestals of Time . . . And although it may not have the charm and beauty of antiquity, no manufacturing town . . . can fail to have an interest and picturesqueness all its own . . . Tall chimneys, great uncouth shapes of kilns and furnaces that appear through the smoke of a winter afternoon like turrets and pinnacles . . . Twilight and night are the conditions under which to see an ironmaking town, the pillars of cloud by day, the pillars of fire by night.

The dynamism of the towns was, in the twenty years after the Great Exhibition, and partly inspired by the machinery exhibited at it, mirrored in the countryside. 'High farming'—capital spending on fertilizers, drainage, buildings, farm machinery such as reapers and threshers, roads linking with the new railways—apparently belied the argument that free trade spelt doom for the countryside, and led to considerable modernization, moral as well as physical, and even in the countryside there were fears for the continuance of traditional religion, as many turned to nonconformity and some to materialism.

An energetic and aggressive farming generation won the profits which maintained the sedate, leisured, county society depicted in Anthony Trollope's novels of Barsetshire. In 1868, 80 per cent of food consumed in the United Kingdom was still home-produced. But despite 'high farming', many areas, especially in Ireland and Scotland, remained woefully under-capitalized, the foot-plough and hand-winnowing still being common in the north and west Highlands in the early twentieth century.

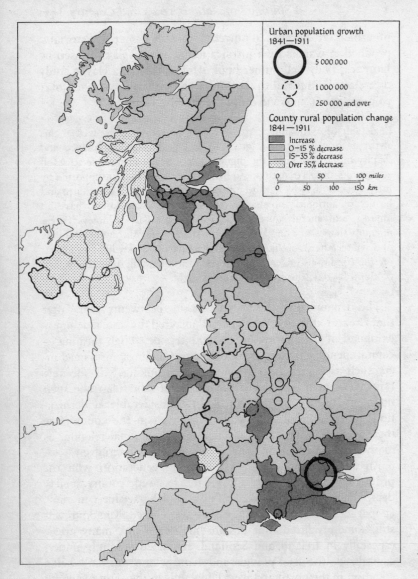

URBAN POPULATION GROWTH 1841–1911

In the 1870s, a series of bad harvests, the opening of the North American prairies, faster and cheaper shipping thence and from the overseas wool-growing areas, led to 'the great depression'. Only milk, hay, and straw production were not open to harsh foreign competition. In particular, the price of grain, the characteristic product of the eastern side of the country, fell dramatically, but farmers, especially the smaller ones, were slow to accept the permanence of this fall, or to adapt to the new demand for dairy products. The pastoral west was less severely affected. The significance of agriculture in the economy declined as towns grew, a decline made swifter by the depression: in 1851 agriculture accounted for 20.3 per cent of the national income, in 1901 only 6.4 per cent, and the majority of British food and agricultural raw materials such as wool were imported—a fact which was to be of considerable strategic importance. Cries for the protection of agriculture received little response, even within the Tory Party—certainly not to the point of an alteration to the fiscal system of free trade. Some Liberal land reformers—for whom protection was axiomatically ruled out—advocated smallholdings (the 'three acres and a cow' campaign of 1885) as a solution; the establishment of the Crofting Commission (1886) for the Scottish Highlands, empowered to establish crofting communities free from landlord interference, was the only substantial achievement on the mainland, though a notable one in its long-term results.

The attraction of higher wages for fewer hours in the towns, mechanization in the 1850s and 1860s, depression in the last quarter of the century, all led to extensive rural depopulation— a great exodus mostly to the Scottish and English towns, some to the coalfields (especially in Wales), some to the colonies, some to the army. Between 1861 and 1901 the decrease in the total of rural male labourers in England and Wales was just over 40 per cent; the total of women, less easily employable in the towns, decreased less dramatically, leaving a marked imbalance of the sexes in the countryside, though many unmarried women found their way into domestic service in the towns aided by such agencies as the Girls' Friendly Society.

All this left rural society demoralized and neglected, with the passivity characteristic of communities in decay. Thomas Hardy's novels, whose span of publication (1872–96) covered almost exactly the years of the agricultural depression, captured majestically the uncontrollable and distant forces which seemed to determine the fate of the country communities and their inhabitants. Hardy wrote of country habits and traditions which had passed away but, though historical in form, the novels had a contemporary overtone. *The Mayor of Caster-bridge* described the fate of Michael Henchard, a corn merchant whose failure to adapt to new methods of trading brought him to ruin. Hardy observed of him at the moment of his financial crash: 'The movements of his mind seemed to tend to the thought that some power was working against him.' The 'general drama of pain' which the Wessex novels depict was the disintegration of a civilization. Surveying his novels as a whole in 1895 Hardy observed: 'The change at the root of this has been the recent supplanting of the class of stationary cottagers, who carried on the local traditions and humours, by a population of more or less migratory labourers, which has led to a break of continuity in local history, more fatal than any other thing to the preservation of legend, folk-lore, close intersocial relations, and eccentric individualities. For these the indispensable conditions of existence are attachment to the soil of one particular spot by generation after generation.' Fortunately, Cecil Sharp, Marjorie Kennedy-Fraser, and other folklore and folk-song and dance historians recorded something of the quality of British rural life before it was wholly lost.

The breaking up of country customs was encouraged by Whitehall and Westminster. Educational measures—for example the 1872 Scottish Education Act—worked to Anglicize the Gaelic-speakers of Scotland and Ireland and the Welsh-speakers of Wales, and to equip the peasantry for urban life. Between 1850 and 1900 rural change and education policy dealt those languages a powerful and in Scotland almost a fatal blow. In Wales, however, local initative secured the teaching of Welsh in schools from 1889.

In some areas, there was a good deal of movement between town and country, as migrant workers left the towns for the harvest, and poaching by the inhabitants of small towns in the surrounding countryside was common. Some industrial workers, especially coal-miners, lived in villages with moors and fields at their doors and their sports such as whippet and pigeon racing had rural associations. Middle-class people took advantage of low land values to buy up a country place. For the financially sharp members of the propertied classes, the countryside became an expensive playground, a place for 'week-ending'; but for many urban-dwellers in the great cities it became a remote, even dangerous, place populated by a curious people with antique accents, clothes, and manners. Oscar Wilde's comedy, *The Importance of Being Earnest* (1895), caught the metropolitan tone:

LADY BRACKNELL....land has ceased to be either a profit or a pleasure. It gives one position, and prevents one from keeping it up. That's all that can be said about land.

JACK. I have a country house with some land, of course, attached to it, about fifteen hundred acres, I believe; but I don't depend on that for my real income. In fact, as far as I can make out, the poachers are the only people who make anything out of it.

LADY BRACKNELL. A country house!... You have a town house, I hope? A girl with a simple, unspoilt nature, like Gwendolen, could hardly be expected to reside in the country.

None the less, the image of a happy rural past lingered in the town-dweller's mind: regardless of class, whenever he (or she) could, he lived in a house with a garden, and perhaps rented an allotment: he recreated the country in the town while ignoring the reality of its sufferings. Architecture and town-planning increasingly reflected nostalgia for the village, culminating in the Bournville experiment of Cadbury's, the Quaker employers, and in the 'Garden City' movement at the end of the century.

The Masses and the Classes: the Urban Worker

The urbanization of the mass of the population and the decline of rural areas not surprisingly had profound social consequences for all classes of the population. The greatest fear of the propertied classes in the first half of the century had been of a revolutionary working class or classes: that no such class emerged is perhaps the most striking feature of the second half of the century. Most industrial labourers left no memorial save the products of their labours: the details of their lives, their aspirations, hopes, beliefs, likes, dislikes, habits, and enthusiasms are largely lost. In the empire, detailed reports on all such things were drawn up with all the efficiency of the trained civil servant fascinated by an alien race, but at home it was only at the end of the century that systematic observation of the living customs of the British urban poor began. Henry Mayhew's impressionistic *London Labour and the London Poor: a Cyclopaedia of the Condition and Earnings of those that will work, those that cannot work, and those that will not work* (1861–2) made a start, but an unsystematic one, and one which was not followed up. What we do know suggests highly complex and varied patterns of life, with regionalism and religion often playing an important part.

The standard of living of some members of the labouring population began to increase quite fast. Between 1860 and 1914 real wages doubled. The years of particularly rapid growth were the boom years of 1868–74, and the period 1880–96; during the latter period real wages went up by almost 45 per cent. By the 1880s, for the first time in the century, a significant number began to enjoy leisure time. Some money (though not much) was coming to be available for more than the essentials of food, housing, and clothing. Strikingly, this surplus coincided not with a rise but with a fall in the birth-rate, which affected the propertied classes from the 1870s, the working classes, mirroring their social superiors, a little later. The extra cash was thus not absorbed by extra children. This was a startling and unprecedented development which falsified the predictions of the classical political economists from Malthus to Marx, that the labouring classes were condemned to subsistence levels of living through the 'iron law of wages' because any surplus wealth would be absorbed by extra children. Control of family size opened the way to the relative prosperity of the British working class since the 1880s. How and why this happened is hardly known. Men and women married later; they may have made some use of the rather unreliable birth-control devices popularized from the 1870s; women may have used abortion as a regular means of birth-prevention.

The term 'working classes' (the Victorians almost always used the plural) of course covered a wide spectrum. Charles Booth's survey of *Life and Labour of the People in London*, begun in the late 1880s, found six main categories: 'highpaid labour'; 'regular standard earnings'; 'small regular earnings'; 'intermittent earnings'; 'casual earnings'; and what Booth called the 'lowest class'. 'Regular standard earners' made up the largest group—as much as the total of the other five categories put together—and it was this group of men and women which particularly reduced the size of their families, saw their real incomes rise, and began to be aware of their potential power within the economy.

The growing prosperity of the 'regular standard earners' led them to join trade unions as a means of safeguarding their gains and of negotiating for better wages and conditions of work. The unions of the mid-century were for the most part rather narrowly-based 'craft unions', made up of men who jealously guarded the privileged and hard-won ascendancy among their fellow employees given them by their qualifications through apprenticeship or their responsibility for skilled machine-working. The steady demand for skilled labour reinforced the influence and status of the craft unions, and some technical developments, for example in the building of iron ships, expanded rather than diminished their importance. In the 1870s and especially in the 1880s these began to be supplemented to include many more of the workmen in regular employment. Rising living standards made this possible, for trade union membership was quite expensive. The unions existed not only, or even chiefly, for purposes of wage negotiation, but also for a wide variety of 'self-help' benefits and the trade unions were closely linked to, and sometimes synonymous with, the Friendly Societies. The first of these benefits for any self-respecting workman was the burial benefit—the avoidance of a funeral paid for by the workhouse—but many unions also had sickness and unemployment benefits, for the State as yet offered no help for victims of temporary calamity, still less did it assist those more permanently disadvantaged, save for the ultimate safety net of the workhouse.

Trade union activity grew in a context which seems most curious to the post-1945 observer. The twenty years after 1874 were characterized by a sharp and substantial deflation—that is, prices (and, to a lesser extent, wages) fell. On the other hand, *real* wages, for those in regular exployment, rose. But this was hard for trade unionists to come to terms with: a man will hardly believe that an employer who reduces his wages may still be leaving him better off. The new trade unionism was thus concerned to defend working-class wages: it was a reaction, as much as a positive force. It had little ideology except for the concept of solidarity. Some socialists played a part in the most publicized strikes of the period—the strike at Bryant and May's match factory in 1888, and the London Dock Strike for the 'dockers' tanner' in 1889, both of which attracted much middle-class interest, probably because they both occurred in London under the noses of the radicals. But these were not typical strikes (indeed the London Dock Strike was not conducted by a union: the union was formed *after* the strike finished); nor should the role of the 'socialists' who led them, such as John Burns, be over-stressed. Even most of the trade union leadership was staunchly Gladstonian: Karl Marx and his works were virtually unknown, outside a small circle, in the country where he had spent almost all his working life; the writings of the socialist groups which sprang up in the 1880s reached only a tiny audience. Indeed, the resistance of the working classes to socialist ideas made them the despair of middle-class intellectuals.

If the trade union was the institutional expression of a growing working-class self-awareness, shared leisure activities, especially for the male wage-earner, further encouraged this sense of solidarity. Watching Association Football—a game founded by public schools and university amateur clubs, but essentially professional by the mid-1880s—became the regular relaxation of males (and almost without exception only males) in industrial towns from Portsmouth to Aberdeen. In the last quarter of the nineteenth century a football club was established in every self-respecting industrial town. Some of these teams reflected the religious schisms of the cities (Catholic Celtic and Protestant Rangers in Glasgow, Catholic Everton and Protestant Liverpool on Merseyside). All of them encouraged a local patriotism, enthusiasm, and self-identification on the part of the followers, which was the envy of many a political organizer. Football was the product of a highly-organized urban society: the regularity and complexity of the Cup (from 1871) and League (from 1888) competitions, the need for sustained as well as immediate interest, the budgeting for the weekly entrance fee and, perhaps, train fare for the away match, the large, self-regulating crowds, all reflected a disciplined and ordered workforce, content to pay for its leisure watching *others* play for a club organized usually by local businessmen. Sustaining attention over the whole of the football 'season' gave the working man something of the wider perspective of time familiar to his agricultural counterpart from the climatic seasons.

The growing popularity of the much lengthier, more idiosyncratic and socially integrative game of cricket, organized through the County Championship from 1873, defies any such simple explanation; it was, perhaps, a testimony to the survival of individuality despite industrialization and the division of labour. W. G. Grace, the Gloucestershire physician whose autocratic command of the pitches and players of the day allowed him to set many batting, bowling, and fielding records still hardly surpassed, became almost as much of a national hero as Fred Archer, the champion jockey in 1874–86. Grace's great and much-caricatured beard caused him to be confused in the popular mind with Lord Salisbury—a confusion probably of some advantage to the latter.

Travel for the working class had hitherto taken place in the context of a desperate search for new employment or accommodation. By the 1880s it was starting to be recreational: the trip to the seaside organized individually or by the firm on one of the new Bank Holidays became for many an annual excursion. Resorts—Blackpool, Morecambe, Scarborough, Southend, Eastbourne, Portobello—rose to meet the demand and to stimulate it further. For the holidays of the working classes were almost always spent in towns: 'the beach' meant the pier, sideshows, and bathing cabins, backed by hotels, boarding houses, and shops. Radicals and socialists in the 1890s attempted to broaden this tradition through rambling and cycling clubs which made trips into the countryside, but the appeal of these was more to the lower middle class than to the working class.

The development of a popular press and the rapid nationwide communication made possible by the electric telegraph encouraged the other great working-class recreation: betting, especially on horses, and, through the nascent pools industry, on football. Betting offered the pot of gold at the end of the rainbow: leisure could be fun, but it might also be profitable—though, of course, it rarely was.

The more prosperous sections of the working classes thus began to share a little the prosperity and expectations which the industrial revolution had brought the propertied classes half a century earlier. Diets improved a little, with meat, milk, and vegetables in addition to bread, potatoes, and beer. The quality of housing was a little better; houses and people were cleaner as soap became cheaper and generally available. Books, photographs, the odd item of decorative furniture, began to adorn the regularly employed workman's home. Respectability, in the sense of having the use of money to demonstrate some degree of control of living style, some sense of settled existence, some raising of the horizon beyond the weekly wage packet, became a goal, encouraged by the spread of hire-purchase companies, which managed much of the spending of the working classes' surplus.

The rise in the standard of living of the wage-earning population was important, but it must be kept in perspective. The second half of the nineteenth century was punctuated by short-term dislocations of the economy in each decade. Many contemporaries believed that the years from the mid-1870s to the mid-1890s constituted a 'great depression', when profits fell. As we have seen, this phrase is certainly true with respect to agriculture. With respect to industry as a whole, it was a period of readjustment rather than depression, but for the working person 'readjustment' usually meant misery. It was during the 1880s that the word 'unemployment' was given its modern meaning.

Religion, in the sense of church-going, played little direct part in the life of most working people in the towns. 'It is not that the Church of God has lost the great towns; it has never had them,' wrote A. F. Winnington-Ingram (an Anglican clergyman) in 1896. Protestant churches both Anglican and nonconformist were unsuccessful in persuading rural labourers to continue as church-goers as they entered the towns, and they failed to reach the majority of those born in towns, despite the indirect allurements of charitable hand-outs and the provision of education in Sunday Schools, and the direct approach of missions, revival crusades, and the Salvation and Church Armies. In London in 1902–3 only about 19 per cent of the population regularly went to church, and those that did came largely from the socially superior areas. The figures would probably be a little better in provincial cities and considerably better in small towns. Only the Roman Catholics attracted significant working-class attendance: their organization was geared to this, and they skilfully appealed through church social organizations and clubs to the Irishness as much as to the Catholicism of their congregations.

This is not to say that the working classes were wholly ignorant of religion. 'Rites of passage' (especially weddings and funerals) remained popular even when secular alternatives became available. Nor do non-church-goers appear to have been actively hostile to religion except when it took on a Romish or ritualistic form and became linked with the abrasive relations between Irish immigrants and the host community. Rather, especially in the case of Anglicanism, they resented a religion so obviously linked to the status and power of the propertied classes. Not going to church, in a society whose articulate members so strongly advocated the practice, was a protest as well as a sign of indifference.

Clerks and Commerce: the Lower Middle Class

For the middle classes, the decades after 1850 offered a golden age of expansion. In 1851 the middle class was a fairly small and reasonably easily identified group: the professions, business men, bankers, large shopkeepers, and the like. The gulf between this group and the working classes was deep. By the end of the century, a far more complex pattern had emerged. A large, intermediate group, which may be called the lower middle class, was called into being by economic change. The service sector of the economy had become much greater and more complex. As the British economy became gradually as much commercial as industrial, it created a vast army of white-collar workers to manage and serve in the retailing, banking, accounting, advertising, and trading sectors. The management of factories passed from a paternal family tradition to a new class of professional managers, and the bureaucracies of manufacturing industry grew swiftly. The civil service, both local and central, began to expand rapidly as government spent more on new responsibilities, especially on the education system created by the Act of 1870. Shops, offices, and telephone exchanges offered new opportunities for the employment of women. London was particularly affected by the changes which created a vast army of City workers, trained at the new polytechnics, commuting by train or by the new underground railways from the suburbs being built on what was then the edge of the city, or from towns such as Croydon which developed rapidly from the 1870s as dormitories for City clerks. Suburbanization was the characteristic innovation of city life in the second half of the century: rows of neat houses, terraced or semi-detached, with small gardens, often both at front and rear of the house, testified to the successful propertied aspirations of this new society.

These were families which had done well out of the Liberal age: Liberalism called for individual achievement, and this class had responded. It valued merit, competition, respectability, efficiency, and a sense of purpose. It respected achievement, money, and success. Uncertain of its own position in the social order, it responded to those confident of their own right to command: it respected hierarchy. In this, it differed considerably from the sturdy individualism of Liberals in the 1850s, sustained by the pre-industrial ethos of 'the good old cause' and the rallying cries of the seventeenth century; its search for a secure place in the social order made it the vehicle by which the Conservatives became a party with a stake in the cities. In some places, particularly in small towns with a nonconformist tradition such as the market towns of Wales and Scotland, it ran the town, and the self-confidence this gave it, together with its nonconformity, helped to keep it Liberal. In large towns, it tended to act as a collaborating class, offering the aristocracy and the upper middle class the means of power in exchange for recognition and status.

The *Daily Mail*, founded by the Harmsworth brothers in 1896, with its highly efficient national distribution, soon had the provincial press on the run, and was the archetypal reading matter for the lower middle class; initially liberal–imperialist in tone, it crossed over to the Unionists during the Boer War. 'By office boys for office boys', Lord Salisbury contemptuously remarked of it and its clientele.

The Propertied Classes

The upper middle classes divided into two. Those working in the professions—doctors, lawyers, the clergy of the established church, civil servants of the administrative grade—shared a common background of education at university and, increasingly, at one of the public schools. In many towns, they lived more exclusively than in the first half of the century, moving out of the town centre to imposing villas in the suburbs. The habit of sending children away to boarding school increased the national outlook of this class and weakened the roots of its individual members in the localities. The spirit of Thomas Arnold of Rugby, as interpreted and modified by his successors, pervaded the outlook of the professions. Educated through a syllabus dominated by Greek, Latin, and ancient history, moralized at by Broad-Church Anglicanism, 'fitted for life' by incessant games (rugby football in the winter, cricket and athletics in the summer) designed to occupy every idle moment, the ethos of the professional classes was worthy but sterile. Increasingly designed to provide men to run an empire, it neglected the needs of an industrial state.

The manufacturing middle class was to some extent affected by this. Instead of sending their children early into the family firm, manufacturers increasingly sent them into the educational process designed for the professional classes. Sons of the owners of cotton mills and shipyards learnt Greek and rugby football, and not, as their German counterparts were doing, science and accounting. Sons educated in this way often showed little interest in returning to manufacturing life, and the preservation of the entrepreneurial and manufacturing ethos which had been one of the chief motors of industrial progress in the first half of the century became increasingly difficult. Such men found commerce more congenial than industry, and went into the expanding banking sector where the sweat and gore of the factory floor and labour relations were sterilized into columns of figures.

The British economy came to rely more and more on the competence of such men. A huge balance of payments deficit on imports and exports of commodities began to open (£27 million in 1851, £134 million by 1911). This was turned into an overall surplus by 'invisible earnings'—the profits of banking, insurance, shipping, and the income from British capital invested abroad. Income from services (£24 million in 1851, £152 million in 1911) and from overseas dividends (£12 million in 1851, £188 million in 1911) seemed to become the vital elements in British prosperity, and with them came a middle class whose chief expertise was in handling money, not men or products.

This important development in British social and economic life was as unplanned as the earlier phase of manufacturing industrialization. It was the product of that industrialization in two ways. As the 'workshop of the world' sold its products abroad, it stimulated other economies which cried out for capital they could not themselves supply. Competition with such economies, and depression in some sectors of manufacturing in the 1880s, lowered the rate of profit on British manufacturing, and the 'invisible hand' thus pointed the way to the expansion of the service industries.

Again, this tendency must not be exaggerated, nor its novelty over-stressed. The easy fusion of land, industry, and commerce was a well-established English tradition. It had prevented the aristocracy becoming a caste in the Continental style, and it had offered the reward of status to the manufacturer. Some took this reward, others, especially nonconformists, did not seek it. Manufacturing and manufacturers remained a powerful force in England. But the primacy of manufacturers, 'the monarchy of the middle classes', so much expected and feared in the first half of the century, did not occur. In part this must be explained by the extent to which the aristocracy neutralized the political and social effects of 'trade' by absorbing it.

The middle classes were Protestant, and actively so. They were increasingly important within the hierarchy of the Anglican Church and the universities: the latter now catered largely for them as the passing of professional and civil-service examinations became required through the series of reforms consequent upon the Northcote–Trevelyan Report of 1854. Respectability, the need to maintain the house, and to pay the servants and school and university fees, encouraged restriction in the size of middle-class families from the 1870s, that is, rather earlier than the same phenomenon among the working classes.

Smaller families were also sought by middle-class women who were beginning to expect more from life than the privilege of breeding children and running the household. Women, thus partially liberated, played an important role in charities, churches, local politics, and the arts, especially music. With great difficulty, some forced themselves upon the universities (they were allowed to attend lectures and take examinations, but not degrees), and from the late 1870s women's colleges were founded at Oxford, Cambridge, and London. The professions remained barred to women, but a few succeeded in practising as doctors. The upper levels of nursing were, however, the nearest most women could get to a professional career.

Pomp and Circumstance

The aristocracy (and gentry) was only partly affected by these changes. Of the three great classes in British social life, it probably changed the least in Victoria's reign. The aristocracy was, as the socialist writer Beatrice Webb observed, 'a curiously tough substance'. It continued to wield considerable political power, supplying much of the membership of both political parties at Westminster, occupying almost all the upper posts in the empire, running local government in the counties, and officering the army—the navy was less socially exclusive. The aristocracy and gentry gained from prosperous farming in the 1850s–1870s, and lost by the agricultural depression; but it recovered some of its losses by skilful investment in urban land, and by the windfall of urban expansion, as what had been agricultural lands of declining value made their owners wealthy as suburbs were built upon them. The British aristocracy had always been involved in industrialization, especially in the development of mining, canals, and railways. It now shrewdly associated itself with the new wave of commercial expansion: most banks and insurance companies had a Lord to add tone to the managerial board. It also shored up its fortunes by astute marriages, notably with the new aristocracy of wealth in the United States: the best-known example was the marriage of the ninth duke of Marlborough to Consuelo Vanderbilt. By these means, many of the great aristocratic estates were preserved despite agricultural decline. But they were playthings as much as engines of wealth, and came to be treated as such. The aristocracy came to be known to the urban population chiefly through their representation in the popular press and magazines as men and women of leisure: racing, hunting, shooting and fishing in the country, gambling and attending the season in London. In a population for which leisure was becoming increasingly important, this did not make the aristocracy unpopular. The court led the way. The gravity which Albert applied to court life in the south was applied with equal pertinacity to the serious business of recreation in the north. Victoria and Albert's development of Balmoral on Deeside in the 1850s, their obvious and highly publicized enjoyment of peasant life and lore, their patronage of Sir Edwin Landseer, the hugely popular artist of rural slaughter, made Scotland respectable, and likewise similar moors and mountains in the north and west of England and in Wales. The court linked itself to the Romantic movement, now in its declining and consequently most popular phase, and by doing so re-established its popularity and represented the control of nature by an urban civilization. *The Monarch of the Glen*, Landseer's portrait of a stag, one of the most reproduced of all Victorian paintings, is not monarch of all he surveys, but a stag at bay, within the gun sights of the stalker: no glen was safe, nature was tamed.

Victoria and Albert's life at Balmoral was enjoyable but high-minded: duty to the peasantry was consistently emphasized. The Prince of Wales, Victoria's son Edward who succeeded her in 1901, was merely hedonistic. A series of scandals alarmed his mother but gratified the press by the copy they yielded. The Prince with his coterie of rich friends such as Sir Thomas Lipton, who made a fortune from the new retail trade in groceries, epitomized the 'plutocracy'. The evangelicalism and tractarianism which made such a mark on the aristocracy in post-Regency days and which made Palmerston's dandyism in the 1850s and 1860s seem conspicuously out of place, appeared to give way to ostentatious consumption and a general moral laxity. Some aristocrats, such as Lord Salisbury, the Tory Prime Minister, continued the old fashion of simple living despite magnificent surroundings, with a household noted for its religious tone. But Salisbury, the last Prime Minister to wear a beard, was becoming an anachronism by his last decade, the 1890s. Arthur Balfour, his nephew and successor as Prime Minister, was seen as a free-thinker. Balfour and Edward VII characterized the new fashion—the one apparently sceptical, the other openly sybaritic.

Despite the marked difference in style between Victoria and her son, the monarchy—the apex of the court and of polite society generally—flourished under both. Victoria in her long reign (1837–1901) jealously guarded its prerogatives which increasingly she saw as best safeguarded by a Conservative government. Her long disappearances from public life after Albert's death in 1861 were unpopular, and made possible quite a serious republican movement stimulated by the Paris Commune, which was headed off with some skill by the Liberal Party leadership in the early 1870s. It was the absence and idleness of the monarch that caused widespread adverse comment, not her presence. In a rapidly-changing society with important elements strongly receptive to the appeal of hierarchy, the monarchy, carefully presented by the growing mass-communications industry, seemed something of a fixed point, with its emphasis on family, continuity, and religion. Walter Bagehot in his classic study, *The English Constitution* (1867), pointed out that the English 'defer to what we may call the *theatrical show* of society ... the climax of the play is the Queen'. The monarchy helped to legitimize power: it is 'commonly hidden like a mystery, and sometimes paraded like a pageant', as it was with great success at the Jubilees in 1887 and 1897. The obvious ordinariness of Victoria herself, her well-publicized sufferings ('the widow of Windsor', bravely performing her duties), and the fact that she was a woman, old and often ill, pointed up the contrast between human frailty and the majesty of institutions, much increasing respect for the latter.

The monarchy represented the timeless quality of what was taken to be a pre-industrial order. In an increasingly urbanized society, it balanced the Industrial Revolution: the more urban Britain became, the more stylized, ritualized, and popular became its monarchy, for the values which it claimed to personify stood outside the competitive egalitarianism of capitalist society.

'A Great Change in Manners'

Britain (with the exception of Ireland) between the 1850s and the 1890s was a society of remarkable order and balance, given its extraordinary underlying tensions of industrial and social change. Though political rioting did not altogether disappear, it became infrequent enough to encourage widespread comment. Crime on the mainland, both in the form of theft and of acts of violence, declined absolutely as well as relatively—an extraordinary development in a rapidly-expanding population, firmly contradicting the adage that industrialization and urbanization necessarily lead to higher rates of criminality. The Criminal Registrar noted in 1901 that, since the 1840s, 'we have witnessed a great change in manners: the substitution of words without blows for blows with or without words; an approximation in the manners of different classes; a decline in the spirit of lawlessness.' This largely self-regulating society relied on voluntary organizations—the Churches, the Friendly Societies, a vast network of charitable organizations—to cater for spiritual and physical deprivation. In one important area—education—it was already admitted by the 1860s that voluntary effort by the Churches could not supply an elementary education system adequate to the needs of an industrial state, and in 1870 the Liberal government passed an Act to set up Education Boards with a duty to build board schools where there were no church schools (though children were not *required* to attend them until 1880, and had to pay to do so until 1891). Local initiative, especially in London and some of the northern manufacturing towns, grafted on to the elementary schools a quite effective and wide-ranging system of technical education for teenagers and even adults—but because it depended on the imagination of each school board, this system was patchy and in no way matched its German equivalent. Manufacturing towns, notably Manchester and Birmingham, set up civic universities much less orientated towards a classical education for those entering the traditional professions than Oxford and Cambridge. Government responsibility for education was seen by contemporaries as one of Mill's exceptions to the rule, not as the start of a wider acceptance of responsibility for social organization.

'Villa Tories': the Conservative Resurgence

By increasing the electorate from 20 per cent to 60 per cent of adult men in the towns, and to 70 per cent in the counties, the Reform Acts of 1867 and 1884 posed problems for politicians.

Household suffrage presented them with a much larger, though by no means universal, body of voters (far short of a universal suffrage, even for men) and elections were by secret ballot, whereas previously each individual's vote had been published.

For the Liberal coalition, accustomed never to losing general elections, the question was, could their amorphous system of informal alliances continue to be successful? It was a question posed the more starkly when Gladstone's first government disintegrated in the traditional Liberal style in 1873–4, and then, untraditionally, lost the election, thus yielding power to the Tories for the first time since 1846. The Liberals' response was twofold. In certain urban areas, and especially in Birmingham, where Joseph Chamberlain was the dominant political figure, a tight 'caucus' system of party organization was introduced. The 'caucus' was a group of self-appointed local notables, often nonconformist business men, and usually strongly critical of the Liberal Party leadership as being too cautious and too aristocratic. The National Liberal Federation, formed in 1877, attempted to give a degree of bureaucratic unity to the sundry local caucuses. On the other hand, the Liberal leadership, still predominantly aristocratic, reacted with alarm. Spanning the two groups was the commanding figure of W. E. Gladstone, son of a Liverpool (originally Scottish) corn merchant, but educated at Eton and Christ Church, Oxford; himself strongly Anglican but in the later phases of his career sympathetic to nonconformist aspirations, he was thus able to appeal to a wide spectrum of Victorian society. Gladstone had no 'caucus' to back him up: he aspired to a national rather than a local basis of power. He appealed over the heads of the local organizations to the body of Liberal opinion at large, and his means was the political speech and pamphlet. The new and vast network of national and provincial newspapers, linked by the telegraph, allowed for the first time an instant national debate: a politician's speech could be on the breakfast table of every middle-class household in the land the morning after it was given. Thus in the general election campaign of 1868, in his campaign against the Disraeli government's supine reaction to massacres of Christians by Turks in Bulgaria in 1876, and in his campaign against the moral and financial delinquency of the imperialistic exploits of the Conservatives in 1879–80 (the 'Midlothian Campaign'), Gladstone blazed a new trail in an attempt to create a great popular front of moral outrage. 'The Platform' became the characteristic form of late Victorian politics: Gladstone invented a new forum of political debate, and his contemporaries, both Liberal and Tory, were obliged to join in.

The 1867 Reform Act brought the Tories new opportunities. Accustomed, almost habituated to losing, they began to win. In 1867 the National Union of Conservative and Constitutional Associations was founded, and in 1870 a Central Office began to improve the co-ordination of electoral strategy. The target for the Tories was the boroughs: to obtain political power they had to enlarge their base from the counties to the expanding towns and suburbs. This they did with very considerable success in the 1870s and 1880s. Under the leadership of Disraeli they won the general election of 1874 convincingly; under the leadership of Salisbury after Disraeli's death in 1881 they became the predominant party. They achieved this by linking an essentially hierarchic, aristocratic, and Anglican party with the aspirations of the expanding middle and lower middle classes in the great cities: the Tories became the party of property and patriotism. Disraeli saw that political success was becoming as much a question of presentation as of policy. In famous speeches in Lancashire and at the Crystal Palace in 1872, he portrayed the Liberals as unpatriotic, a danger to property, a threat to the institutions of the nation, betrayers of Britain's world and imperial interests. In a more positive vein, he advocated a policy of social reform, supposedly of particular appeal to such members of the working classes as had recently become voters. The themes of these speeches—especially the patriotic ones—were quickly taken up by other Conservatives. They were the prototype for most Tory election addresses for the next century.

The early years of the Conservative government of 1874–80 were marked by a burst of social reforms mostly promoted by R. A. Cross, the Home Secretary: artisans' dwellings, public health, Friendly Societies, river pollution, the sale of food and drugs, merchant shipping, trade unions, factories, drink licensing, and education were all the subject of legislation. Many of these reforms were 'in the pipeline' and owed a strong debt to the Peelite–Liberal traditions which had also motivated the previous Gladstone government. They affected middle-class perhaps more than working-class interests and because the social measures were permissive rather than compulsory their effect was more limited than might have been expected (for example, by 1880, only ten of eighty-seven Welsh and English towns had decided to implement the Artisans' Dwellings Act). None the less, these reforms were important in Conservative mythology. They showed that the Tories could be a party which dealt effectively with urban questions, and they offered the basis for the claim that 'Tory democracy' was a reality. Contrasted with German conservative answers to the problems of urban life, they appeared integrative, conciliatory, and constructive.

But the real interest of Conservatism was the consolidation of an urban middle-class base: working-class support was a bonus. The bogy of Liberal lack of patriotism was only partially successful, for the Tories' claim to be the party of competent imperialism was severely dented by their mishandling of events in South Africa and Afghanistan in the late 1870s, and by the high costs of their military exploits. It was hard simultaneously to be imperialists and to appeal to the middle-class virtue of financial retrenchment: a self-contradiction which Gladstone's Midlothian speeches skilfully exposed.

The Tories lost the 1880 general election, borne down partly by Gladstone's oratory, partly by the trade recession of that year. The succeeding Gladstone government of 1880–5 was the nadir of Liberalism, the party restless, the Cabinet divided. In imperial affairs, Tory claims seemed borne out: hesitation and confusion led to a series of disasters, culminating in the death of Charles Gordon at Khartoum in 1885. Too habituated to the way the 'official mind' of the colonial office thought to decline to extend imperial responsibilities, the Liberals occupied territory while declaring their regrets: electorally, they lost both ways, alienating anti-imperialists by doing too much, and imperialists by seeming reluctant. In domestic affairs, Gladstone's determination to control and reduce expenditure made positive reform difficult. In marked contrast to 1868–74, the government was noted for only one great reform, the county franchise reform of 1884. The enfranchisement of agricultural labourers was expected to deliver the county seats into the Liberals' hands and Salisbury used the blocking power of the House of Lords to extract a great prize as a 'tit-for-tat': a redistribution bill allowed the boundaries of borough seats to be drawn much more favourably to the Tories. Thus the Tories were able to use a Liberal reform to create a political structure of single-member, middle-class urban and suburban constituencies on which the basis of their subsequent political success has since consistently rested.

The effect of this was to make the Liberals increasingly dependent on the 'Celtic fringe', the Irish, Scottish, and Welsh MPs. The concerns and priorities of these three countries thus moved on to the centre of the British imperial stage.

Ireland, Scotland, Wales: Home Rule Frustrated

That there was an 'Irish problem', nobody could deny: what it was, hardly anybody could agree. Disraeli caught the tone of metropolitan bewilderment:

I want to see a public man come forward and say what the Irish question is. One says it is a physical question; another, a spiritual. Now it is the absence of the aristocracy, then the absence of railroads. It is the Pope one day, potatoes the next.

Irish agriculture was overwhelmingly the country's largest industry and was overwhelmingly owned by Protestants, who mostly, contrary to popular myth, lived on or near their estates. It flourished in the boom of the 1850s and 1860s and achieved a modest degree of technical improvement, but it remained, compared with England, grossly under-capitalized. Ireland could not produce her own capital, and could not attract much from England. Her economy could not sustain her population: unknown numbers moved to the mainland, where no town of any size was without its Irish community; between 1841 and 1925 gross 'overseas' emigration included four and three-quarter million to the USA, 70,000 to Canada, and more than 370,000 to Australia.

The legacy of the 1798 rebellion, the failure of Daniel O'Connell's attempt in the 1830s and 1840s to repeal the 1800 Act of Union, and the catastrophe of the famine of 1845–6, produced the Fenian Irish independence movement of the 1860s which attempted risings in the USA and in Canada and in Ireland. In 1867 it astonished England by a series of bomb explosions, notably one at Clerkenwell Prison in London, in which over one hundred innocent persons were killed. The Fenian movement in no sense represented Irish opinion generally, but the danger that it might come to do so encouraged Liberal politicians, especially Gladstone, to concessionary action. Disestablishment of the Anglican Church in Ireland in 1869, the Land Act of 1870, and an abortive educational reform in 1873 (rejected by the Irish members themselves) were intended to show that Westminster could give the mass of the Irish what they wanted. But these reforms were not enough. Isaac Butt's Home Government Association flourished, and the Liberal Party, hitherto the dominant party in Irish politics, was on the run. The agricultural depression from the early 1870s to the mid 1890s greatly worsened the situation. Charles Stewart Parnell (like Butt, a Protestant) became leader of the Home Rule Party in 1877, a position he held until his ruin in a divorce scandal in 1890. Parnell was prepared to exploit every political situation without reluctance or embarrassment—but even this tougher line was to some extent outflanked by the Land League which sought personal ownership of the land for the peasantry. Parnell, somewhat ambivalently, became its president in 1879. The Land League—a potent blend of 'physical force' Fenians and 'moral force' Parnellites fused into a popular front of nationalistic Catholicism—fought a sustained campaign against evictions in the 'Land War' of 1879–82 at the height of the depression, meeting them with violence and their perpetrators with 'boycotting' (named after Captain Charles Boycott, whose nerve cracked when faced with social and economic ostracism). Violence in the Irish countryside, and the murder in 1882 of the Irish secretary, Lord Frederick Cavendish, Gladstone's nephew by marriage, astonished and appalled the propertied classes in England which, as we have seen, had become accustomed to a very low level of violent crime.

The Gladstone Government of 1880 met this crisis on the one hand with coercion and on the other with concession, in the form of the 1881 Land Act, which gave much to the peasants, but did not give them ownership. The Home Rule Party increased its hold on Ireland (helped by the county franchise reform of 1884) and at the election of December 1885 won 86 seats, thus holding the balance of power between the Liberals and Tories at Westminster.

Gladstone cut the Gordian knot by coming out for Home Rule; a private appeal to Salisbury to treat the question on a bipartisan basis was rejected. Gladstone's decision was quite consistent with the main thrust of Liberal thinking, but its timing recognized political necessity: only once subsequently, in 1906, were the Liberals to gain power without the need for the support of Home Rule MPs in the lobbies. Most Liberals championed devolution and the rights of nations 'struggling rightly to be free', as Gladstone put it; it was hard to deny in 1886 that Ireland had proved itself to be such a nation. The question was, was its nationality to be recognized or crushed? Moreover, the moderate Home Rule Bill produced by Gladstone in 1886 did not grant independence, though it was the argument of its opponents first, that despite Parnell's assurances it would in the long run lead to Irish independence, and, second, that it gave no safeguard against 'Rome Rule' to the Protestant population, mostly concentrated in Belfast, the industrial capital of the province of Ulster.

This complex series of events led to a major crisis in British politics. The Liberal Party, faced with Gladstone's Home Rule Bill in the summer of 1886, split: 93 MPs, most of them Whigs under Lord Hartington but with some radicals under Joseph Chamberlain, voted with the Tories against the bill, thus bringing down the Liberal government and introducing twenty years of Conservative (or Unionist, as the anti-Home Rule Coalition was called) hegemony. With the Liberal-Unionists (the defectors from Liberalism) went a significant proportion of the Liberal press and almost all those landed aristocrats who traditionally paid most of the party's electoral expenses. This loss of influence and money was probably of more importance to the Liberals than the actual numbers of defecting MPs, though in the Lords the Liberals were now a tiny minority.

The split of 1886 weakened the party, but left Gladstone in control of it and of the National Liberation Federation, a hold he consolidated at its Newcastle meeting in 1891 when he accepted its radical programme. Home Rule thus shackled Liberalism to Gladstone. Before 1886, Ireland blocked the way to the passage of second-rank measures, so Home Rule was necessary as well as right. But after 1886, Home Rule was impossible, given the existence of the House of Lords. Home Rule thus both stimulated Liberals to battle for the right, and condemned them to a generation of frustration.

Naturally enough, events in Ireland affected Scotland and Wales. In both, disestablishment of the Church also became a political issue, and both experienced land campaigns. These had little of the violence characteristic of parts of Ireland, though in the Isle of Skye troops were used in 1882 to suppress crofter demonstrations. Certain Liberals in both countries demanded 'Home Rule All Round' and this movement, buoyed up by the cultural renaissance that Wales and Scotland shared

with Ireland in the late nineteenth century, achieved consider-
able influence in the Liberal Party in the late 1880s and 1890s.
Unlike Ireland, however, the Liberal Party was able to contain
within itself the quasi-nationalistic movements in Scotland and
Wales, partly because the dominant industrial sector in Scot-
land and the growing predominance in Wales of the South
Wales coalfield bound those countries far more intimately than
Ireland to the imperial economy; in southern Scotland and
South Wales Liberal imperialism trumped nationalism.

With the Liberal Party split, and unable to reunite despite
various attempts in the late 1880s, the Tories consolidated their
hold. They were not active reactionaries. Salisbury made no
attempt to reverse the Liberal achievements of the 1850s–1870s
which at the time he had so bitterly opposed. Their position
and their alliance with the Liberal-Unionists depended on
preventing things being done, not on doing them. Thus though
some legislation was passed, particularly the establishment of
elected County Councils in 1888, a measure to improve
working-class housing in 1890, and, later, the Education Act of
1902, which went some way to establishing a system of secondary education, the Unionist hegemony of 1886–1905 was not a
period of legislative significance, nor was it intended to be.
The urban electorate which the Tories essentially relied upon
wanted the continuation of the Liberal state of the 1850s and
1860s, without the new accretions to Liberalism such as Home
Rule. It rejected Gladstonian Liberalism, not because it had
turned its back on the gains of the free-trade years in the
mid-century, but because the Gladstonian Liberals seemed to
have progressed too far beyond the objectives of that period.
The anti-Gladstonian coalition thus relied heavily on Home
Rule to keep the coalition together and to keep the Liberals
out. It ventured beyond its anti-Home Rule stance at its
electoral peril, as it was to find out in the early years of the
twentieth century. The continuing Liberal commitment to
Home Rule helped in this. The short Liberal minority
government of 1892–5 (Gladstone's last administration, with

Rosebery as its Prime Minister after his retirement in 1894) spent much effort upon the second Home Rule Bill, which it succeeded in passing through the Commons only to see it thrown out by the Lords. The Liberals could mount a disparate majority made up of the English counties, Scotland, Wales, and Ireland, but they could not sustain it or repeat it. The Unionists won convincingly in 1895 and confirmed their majority in 1900, taking advantage of temporary successes in the South African war to hold the 'Khaki election'.

Reluctant Imperialists?

The Unionist case against Home Rule had always had an imperial dimension: imperial power must not be devolved, the very circumstances of the passing of the Act of Union in 1800 showing the strategic importance of Ireland, which Home Rule would again put at risk. In the last third of the century, imperial issues became much more of a public preoccupation; we must now look at their effect on Britain's position in the world.

The British did not as a whole look for increased direct imperial authority, and pressure groups for its extension were of little popular or political significance. Indeed, in the old areas of white settlement, they successfully sought to devolve authority, passing the Dominion of Canada Act in 1867 and the Commonwealth of Australia Act in 1900. Yet the last forty years of the century saw the annexation of vast areas of land in Africa, the Far East, and the Pacific. In 1851 Britain was the world's trader, with an overwhelming dominance of world shipping, which continued even when Britain's dominance in manufactured goods was declining after 1870. British interests were thus to be found wherever there was trade, even though British imperial authority might not be *formally* present. *Informal* imperialism thus preceded formal annexation: nothing could be less true than the adage, 'trade follows the flag'. In almost every case, it was the opposite. As Joseph Conrad's

THE EXPANSION
OF THE
BRITISH EMPIRE
1815–1914

CANADA

NEWFOUNDLAND

~ Bermuda*

∴ Bahamas*

St Lucia*
Barbados*
Tobago*
Trinidad*

Jamaica

BR. HONDURAS
*Mosquito Coast
(British until 1850)

BRITISH
GUIANA

Bermuda*	Extent by 1815
Gilbert Is	Additions to 1914

Falkland Is

novels illustrate, there was no creek, however distant, without its British representative, organizing the shipping of paraffin oil and local goods.

In East and Central Africa, the first European presence was often religious, as evangelical medical missionaries such as David Livingstone preached the gospel, healed the sick, and exposed the inhumanity of the inland slave trade. H. M. Stanley's 'rescue' of Livingstone in 1871, skilfully self-publicized, became one of the great adventure stories of Victorian times, and greatly increased interest in 'the dark continent.'

In some areas, British attempts to trade were supported by arms—a notable example being the opium monopoly of the Indian government and the general free-trading access which was forced upon the Chinese government by the British in a series of 'opium wars' culminating in the treaty of Tien-tsin (1858), the most disreputable of all Britain's imperialistic exploits,

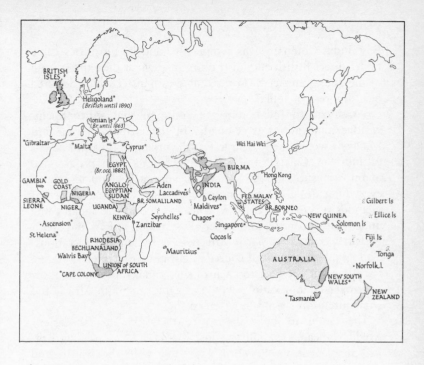

because it was a considered and consistent policy, not the accidental result of a local crisis. Governmental involvement of an oblique sort was sometimes used to develop small beginnings through the device of the Chartered Company—a trading company with governmentally guaranteed rights to trade and administer an area; Nigeria, East Africa, and Rhodesia all came under eventual British rule in this way, for when a Company went bankrupt (or effectively so—Cecil Rhodes's British South Africa Company never paid a dividend before 1920 and was taken over in 1923) the British government had little option but to assume its administrative responsibilities.

In addition to this huge and largely informal network of trade was the centre-piece of India, 'the chief jewel in the imperial crown', now no longer so profitable, but the assumed focal point of British thinking about security outside the European context. Following the Indian mutiny of 1857–8, the old

East India Company was wound up, and its territories came under direct British administration. In 1876, at the express wish of the queen, an Act was passed at Westminster which declared her 'Empress of India'.

To safeguard India, and the route to that subcontinent, various annexations were made. In the vicinity, Burma and Malaysia were annexed, largely at the urging of the government of India in Calcutta, which conducted its own programme of imperialism with the systematic approach characteristic of everything it did, and quite dissimilar to the haphazard methods of London. On the route, Egypt and the Sudan came under British control, and imperial expansion in East and South Africa was at least partly affected by Indian considerations. This simple statement of course disguises an extremely complex narrative with respect to each of these annexations. The most controversial annexations were in Egypt and South Africa, and some attention should be given to these.

The route to India had made security in the eastern Mediterranean, especially against Russia, a long-standing British preoccupation. Between 1854 and 1856 the British and French, with some assistance from Piedmont-Sardinia, had sent substantial fleets and armies to prop up Turkey. The Crimean War had a complex series of causes, but the root one was Russian aggrandizement against the sprawling and feeble Ottoman Empire. The performance of Britain and France, the two most 'advanced' European nations, against 'backward' Russia was disappointing and in certain respects inept, although the supply by sea of large armies at a considerable distance created new problems. The newspaper-reporting by telegraph of the hardships of the troops starkly illustrated the problems and the paradox of war-making by a liberal state, and Florence Nightingale made a name for herself as the 'lady with the lamp'. The immobility of the campaign, which consisted largely of a series of sieges, bloodily resolved in the Crimea and in the area of Kars in Asiatic Turkey, looked forward to the 1914–18 war. Turkey was successfully defended, and the British thus shored up the Ottoman Empire of which Egypt was a part.

The hope was that Turkey would reform and behave like a modern, liberal state. This hope was not fulfilled. By the 1870s, Turkey was again disintegrating, and under attack from Russia. The Disraeli government of 1874–80 continued the Crimean policy of defending Turkish integrity: the Liberal opposition under Gladstone argued that this was no longer feasible and supported the division of much of 'Turkey in Europe' into separate, Christian states. The 'Concert of Europe' present at the Congress of Berlin in 1878 reached agreement on this and Disraeli returned to London bringing 'peace with honour' and the imperial gain of the island of Cyprus, thought to be of strategic importance for the Eastern Mediterranean, but in fact useless as a naval base.

As Turkey disintegrated, so Egypt became increasingly self-reliant, organizing the building of the Suez Canal, opened in 1870, and of great importance to Britain's links with India. The inflow of capital to build the canal destabilized Egypt, which began to disintegrate socially and politically. In 1875 Disraeli bought the Khedive's large holding in the shares of the company which ran the canal. Thus when Egypt reached the point of bankruptcy, and a military coup was attempted, Britain had not only a general strategic interest in the situation but also a direct financial one. After attempts to find alternatives, Gladstone reluctantly invaded and occupied Egypt on behalf of the canal's creditors in 1882, and the British remained until 1954, though the country was never formally annexed and was thus similar in status to the theoretically independent princely states in India. Formal annexation of the rebellious Sudan naturally followed in a series of campaigns in the 1880s and 1890s, the Mahdi, the slayer of the maverick Gordon in 1885, being finally and ruthlessly crushed by Kitchener at the battle of Omdurman in 1898. Turkish decay thus drew Britain into becoming the major power in the Eastern Mediterranean and in North-eastern Africa.

Events in South Africa were not dissimilar, but were complicated by the presence of the Boers. The Cape was occupied in 1795 to safeguard the route to India. The security of the hinterland, whither the Boers had trekked in the 1830s, affected the Cape. Various plans for incorporating the Boers in a federation were suggested, and confederation was imposed upon the Boers by the Disraeli government in 1877 at a moment when the Boers were weakened by the Zulus. Incompetent generalship (a feature of British military operations in South Africa) led to the death of 800 British troops at Isandhlwana, one of the very few occasions in colonial wars in which spears triumphed over guns. This was, of course, only a temporary set-back, and the Zulus were liquidated at Ulundi (1879). The Boers then wished to regain their independence. After a short war when the defeat of a small group of British soldiers at Majuba Hill in 1881 gave a propaganda value to the Boers out of all proportion to its military significance, an ill-defined agreement was reached: the Transvaal and Orange Free State to have independence, but under British suzerainty. Increasing exploitation of diamonds and the discovery of gold in the Transvaal in 1886 transformed the situation. In financial terms, Southern Africa became literally Britain's chief imperial jewel. The influx of capital directed by men such as Cecil Rhodes destabilized the rural economy of the Boers, as it had that of Egypt. The Transvaal, like Egypt, went bankrupt, but the Boers, under Paul Kruger, retained strict political control. An attempt by Dr Jameson, a crony of Rhodes, to encourage a rising by the Uitlanders (the British in the Transvaal without political rights) failed in 1896. Alfred Milner, the new High Commissioner, asserted British rights over the Boer republics and determined to break Kruger by war. Milner goaded Kruger into attacking Cape Colony in 1899, and what was expected to be a short, limited war began. The Boers, however, were well stocked with German arms; the British, used to fighting colonial wars against undisciplined natives without guns, proceeded ineptly, and a series of disasters followed before weight of armaments captured the main Boer cities in 1900. The war seemed over, and Chamberlain, the Colonial Secretary, persuaded Salisbury to hold the 'Khaki election', easily won by the

Unionists. But the Boers refused to accept defeat, and harassed the British with guerrilla tactics. The British replied by burning Boer farms, clearing the veldt, and systematically herding Boer families into 'concentration camps'. High death-rates in the camps led to radical protests in Britain. 'When is a war not a war?' asked Sir Henry Campbell-Bannerman, Rosebery's successor as Liberal leader, answering himself: 'When it is carried on by methods of barbarism in South Africa'. In 1902, peace was negotiated: Milner had failed in his aim of smashing the social and political structure of Afrikanerdom.

The fin-de-siècle *Reaction: New Views of the State*

The Boer War was immensely expensive, costing far more than all Britain's other imperial exploits in the nineteenth century put together. It failed to smash the Boers, but it did smash the Gladstonian system of finance, raising government expenditure to a new plateau from which it never descended. The war also put into stark and dramatic popular form a number of concerns which were already preoccupying the intelligentsia. The war showed the strength and loyalty of the empire, for the white colonies sent troops to help, but it also showed its weaknesses. The empire seemed over-extended and under-coordinated. The British navy was no longer pre-eminent. The French navy was being joined as a threat by the Germans, the Italians, the Americans, and the Japanese. The policy of 'splendid isolation' began to look dangerous. Imperial rivalry had meant that in the 1870s–1890s France had usually seemed Britain's most likely enemy and Germany her most likely friend. Germany's navy plan of 1898, and her bid for 'a place in the sun' which coincided with her encouragement to Kruger during the Boer War, now made Germany seem a potent threat, the contemporary feeling about which is well captured in Erskine Childers's classic spy story *The Riddle of the Sands* (1903). Naval security in the Indian Ocean and the Pacific was gained by the Anglo-Japanese alliance of 1902. This attempt to limit imperial responsibility was followed up by agreements (*Ententes*) resolving imperial differences with France in 1904 over North Africa and with Russia in 1907 over Persia. The Boer War thus led to a 'new course' in British foreign policy. For while these *Ententes* were formally about extra-European areas, their real importance came to lie within Europe; although they were not alliances, they committed Britain, to some extent, to the side of the Franco-Russian alliance against Germany and Austria in the rising tension in Europe. What that extent was, was not yet clear.

Anxieties about world security raised by the Boer War also popularized discussion about Britain's relative economic position, for it was upon that that national strength ultimately rested. The overwhelming superiority of the British economy of the 1850s was much diminished. The USA, Germany, France, and Russia were now all substantial industrial powers, with the first two superior to the British in certain sectors of their economies. Britain was now one among several, no longer the unaccompanied trail-blazer. Yet for the most part British society and government behaved as if nothing had changed. The liberal state of the 1850s and 1860s, with its precepts of free trade, minimal government spending, an economy autonomous and self-regulating, lingered on, almost as carefully guarded under Conservative as under Liberal management. The *per capita* expenditure of central government in 1851 was £2.00; by 1891 it had only increased to £2.50 (by 1913 it was to be £4.00). In the 1880s and 1890s this situation came under increasing criticism, much of which the Boer War seemed to confirm and popularize.

Slow military progress in the Crimean War of the 1850s led to criticism of the competence of the ruling èlite; military ineffectiveness and the poor quality of recruits in the South African war led to a public cry among the propertied classes for a reappraisal of the economic, social, and even political arrangements of the nation as a whole.

Before considering the various schools of criticism of traditional Liberalism, a general influence should be noted, that of 'social Darwinism'. We saw earlier that positivists were strong supporters of *laissez-faire*. In the 1880s and 1890s the influence of social Darwinism began to take a different form. The struggle for 'the survival of the fittest' began to be seen less in terms of individuals in the market-place and more in terms of competition between nations. This dramatically reduced the number of units under discussion, and raised the question, prompted also by the imperialism which was related to this national competition, of whether individual 'races' were not better subjects for inquiry than a myriad of individuals, and whether 'advanced races' could control their destinies by governmental, social, or perhaps even genetic organization. This concept—a marrying of the British science of evolution and the German concept of the organic state—powerfully affected contemporary thought: the language of 'race' became the common coin of reformers right across the political spectrum, from Rudyard Kipling, ostensibly the poet of the right, through J. A. Hobson and L. T. Hobhouse, the philosophers of the new liberals, to G. B. Shaw, regarded as the playwright of the left. The popular form of social Darwinism readily became a facile assumption of racial superiority, linked to imperialism, as the popular press reported the successes of the many small-scale colonial military expeditions. Popular reporting of these emphasized the importance of individual daring, character, and initiative, 'deeds that won the Empire', rather than the enormous technical disparity between a disciplined European army armed with rifles and from the 1890s the occasional machine-gun, and local forces relying on massed use of spears or, at best, sporadic musket fire.

Criticism of the liberal state in its classic Victorian form came from three chief political directions: from discontented Conservatives and Unionists who believed their political leadership was excessively hidebound by the canons of Peel–Gladstone fiscal policy, from Liberals who believed Liberalism must move on to meet new challenges, and from socialists who, at least at first glance, challenged the whole order of the state. Elements from each of these came together to demand 'national efficiency', a slogan intended to suggest a willingness to use government power to organize and legislate for an 'Imperial race' fit to meet the challenges of the world.

The free-trade state had always had its critics. The most influential of these in the second half of the nineteenth century was John Ruskin, art critic and social commentator. Politically impossible to categorize, Ruskin's powerful prose in works such as *Unto this Last* (1862) attacked the aesthetics of industrial society, but he offered no very systematic critique. His aesthetic criticisms were taken up by the Pre-Raphaelite Brotherhood, a group of painters, writers, and craftsmen who emphasized, especially through the writings and designs of William Morris, the values of pre-industrial England, a mythical land of craftsmen, contented peasants, and romance. From such influences sprang wide-ranging changes in design and architecture, epitomized by the 'English style' of domestic architecture of Norman Shaw and, at the turn of the century, Lutyens, which characterized the best of the building of the new suburbs. From Morris also sprang a socialist rhetoric of enduring potency: the image of a rural, self-sufficient, egalitarian society of sturdy yeomen. Morris did not confront industrialization, he by-passed it.

The aestheticism of the Pre-Raphaelites, and their general critique of middle-class morality, was given fresh impetus by the aesthetes of the 1880s and 1890s, the most notable of whom was the wit and playwright Oscar Wilde, ruined, like his fellow Irishman Parnell, by the public exposure of his sexual habits. Wilde's remarkable essay, 'The Soul of Man under Socialism', exemplified the links between aestheticism and individualist rather than collectivist socialism.

From 1884 these leanings towards socialism were supplemented by the London-based Fabian Society whose members included Sidney and Beatrice Webb, George Bernard Shaw, H. G. Wells, and, later, the young Ramsay MacDonald, all strong social evolutionists. The Fabians' criticism of the Liberal economic order was not so much that it was unjust, but that it was inefficient and wasteful: a centrally-planned economy and labour market, administered by an élite of trained professionals, would eliminate inefficiency, the trade cycle, and its by-products such as unemployment and poverty. It would attain this end gradually through legislation and not by revolution (hence the name Fabian, after the Roman general whose tactics the society emulated). Perhaps the chief contribution of the Fabians was to assist in the development of a fresh concept of 'progress' on the British left which in the 1880s was becoming limited in its horizons by the persistent wrangles over Home Rule. For the Fabians addressed themselves to the existing intelligentsia: they were not a popular movement. But popular discontent with the limitations of Gladstonian Liberalism was also developing; Keir Hardie, a coal-miner from the Ayrshire coalfield, represented the view that the increasingly unionized working class must have its own representatives in the House of Commons (where MPs were still not paid). Hardie, elected for West Ham in 1892, helped form the Scottish Parliamentary Labour Party in 1888 and, in 1893, founded the Independent Labour Party in Bradford. The ILP saw itself as a socialist party, but it had difficulty in establishing a popularly-supported organization. It shared with the Liberals an anti-imperialist rhetoric, supported 'Home Rule All Round', but called also for nationalization. H. M. Hyndman's Social Democratic Federation was more vigorous in its quasi-Marxist ideology, but gained very little popular foothold.

Old Liberalism, New Liberalism, Labourism, and Tariff Reform

All these movements were limited in their impact; the Liberals remained overwhelmingly the dominant party of the 'left' (the use of the word became common in British political discussion for the first time in the 1880s). None the less, the ideas being put forward, and the threat of their organizational success, concentrated Liberal minds. Liberals made their own contribution to the intellectual debates of the last two decades of the century. Always the party of land reform, their enthusiasm for it was rekindled by works such as the American Henry George's *Progress and Poverty* (1880). Posing the question, 'what *does* produce poverty amid advancing wealth?', George's answer was, crudely stated, the rents of the landed proprietor and the exclusion of workmen from free access to land, both rural and urban. The solution was a thoroughgoing and efficient land tax, known as 'the single tax'. The land campaign was a major theme of radicalism until the First World War, and beyond.

'Why do we sit and quietly behold degradation worse than that from which we have rescued women and children in mines and factories?' asked Arnold Toynbee, the liberal Christian historian and radical and, with T. H. Green, a great radical influence in the Oxford of the 1870s and early 1880s. Toynbee's followers (such as Canon Barnett, founder of Toynbee Hall in East London in 1884) encouraged, first, personal (often religious) commitment on the part of the intelligentsia to on-the-spot observation of working-class problems, and, second and later, an acceptance that voluntary effort would not be sufficient by itself to solve those problems. 'Advanced radicals' came to anticipate much greater government involvement in the economy, and much more 'positive liberalism' to see that each individual had the means by which he or she could make the most of his or her individual abilities. This was bound to cost money, and Liberals believed this money should be raised by increasing direct taxation, in particular death duties and a graduated income tax, to achieve a measure of redistribution at the same time as raising revenue. An important step in this direction was taken by the 1892–5 minority Liberal government which paid for increased social reform and naval expenditure by imposing for the first time an effective death duty. 'New

Liberalism', as this movement came to be called, was an attempt to justify the free-market system by making it work 'fairly'; it attempted a rationalization of capitalism, not its replacement. The movement, whose most effective author was J. A. Hobson, also a strong critic of 'immoral' imperialism, hoped to convert the Liberal Party to 'New Liberalism' and thus to allow the continuation of the Liberals as a broadly-based party, capable of continuing to assimilate and integrate the urban working class. This would avoid the German situation, where the working class had formed its own class-based Marxist party which rejected the legitimacy of the German State. This view was reinforced by political expediency on the Liberals' part. Following a series of adverse legal decisions which questioned their legal right to picket and their freedom from damages culminating in the famous Taff Vale case (1900–1), some trade unions, now in the late 1890s growing fast, joined with the ILP to form the Labour Representation Committee in 1900. The Liberals, split three ways by the Boer War, were at their weakest, and seemed to be able to offer the trade unionists, hitherto Liberal, little chance of redress. The secretary of the LRC, Ramsay MacDonald, negotiated an electoral agreement with the Liberals in February 1903, by which Liberal and Labour constituency parties would not split the progressive vote to let in a Unionist, but would reach local agreements by which a number of Labour candidates would have a good chance of being elected.

This accommodation between the two parties of the left showed the considerable area of agreement that existed between them: the Labour Party (as the LRC became in 1906) was part of the 'party of progress', at least for the time being, sharing many of its reforming aspirations, and its commitment to free trade.

The Unionists (as the coalition of Tories and Liberal-Unionists should be called after 1895 when Joseph Chamberlain and Lord Hartington, the Liberal-Unionist leaders, entered Salisbury's Cabinet) wished to conserve the British constitution as it then stood. But most of them also conserved its fiscal arrangements and remained free traders. Lord Salisbury gave no effective support to protection despite his large majority in both Houses. The imperialist faction within his party, however, increasingly came to see some form of imperial protection as essential. Their reasons for this were threefold. First, they believed that the growing success of the American and German economies was due to the protection of young industries, and that in the new era of technically sophisticated industry—chemicals, electricals, automobiles—Britain would lose out unless there was protection, a degree of planning, and much more co-operation between industry and education, all things that only government could supervise. Second, they believed that an Imperial Customs Union (analogous to the German *Zollverein* of the early nineteenth century) could integrate the empire's economy, Britain producing manufactured goods, the colonies raw materials. Third, they saw tariffs, including duties on food, as the only alternative to direct taxation to pay for the social reforms necessary to make the imperial race fit for the increasingly harsh competition between nations which they believed the future would bring. This programme was embodied in the Tariff Reform campaign launched by Joseph Chamberlain in 1903 while still Colonial Secretary, much to the embarrassment of the Prime Minister, Arthur Balfour, who had succeeded his uncle, Lord Salisbury, the previous year. Well financed, sophisticatedly organized and presented, Tariff Reform divided the Unionist Party (though the young Winston Churchill was one of the few MPs who actually left it). It was renounced by the electorate in a series of by-elections and then in the general election of 1906, when the Liberals together with 29 Labour MPs returned with a huge overall majority. England had turned from Home Rule in the 1880s and 1890s, but not from free trade. The Peel–Gladstone tradition of open markets and cheap food still carried great weight: 'the big loaf and the little loaf' was the Liberals' effective catch-phrase.

But although the 1906 Liberal success was the result mainly of negative factors—hostility to Tariff Reform, the dislike of Balfour's 1902 Education Act by nonconformists (their ranks swollen by a great religious revival), general criticism of the Unionists' handling of imperial affairs—the atmosphere had changed. There was much 'old Liberalism' (and 'old Toryism') still around, but the critiques of the Victorian liberal state made from the left, the right, and by Liberals themselves, bit deep.

The opening years of the twentieth century (there was much debate as to whether it began on 1 January 1900 or 1901) brought the widespread use by the better-off of its characteristic appliances, available in the 1890s but slow to find markets because of technical inadequacies—electric light in the houses, telephones, typewriters, gramophones, automobiles —and, soon, wireless and aeroplanes. The first building in the world specially designed as a cinema was opened in Colne, Lancashire, in 1907. Quite suddenly, the Victorian years and their preoccupations began to seem worlds away. The deaths of the three most notable public figures of those years—Gladstone in 1898, Victoria herself in 1901, Salisbury in 1903—emphasized the change.

Edwardian Years: a Crisis of the State Contained

Reappraisals of the nineteenth-century state were reinforced by a series of social enquiries in the 1890s and early 1900s into the working of the labour market and into social conditions— investigations such as Charles Booth's *Life and Labour of the People in London* (which appeared in four series of thirty-three volumes in all, 1889–1903) and Seebohm Rowntree's *Poverty: a study of town life* (1901). Booth and Rowntree for the first time attempted to define 'poverty' as a social phenomenon (as opposed to the Poor Law's definition of pauperism which was a legal category). Rowntree found over 27 per cent of the population of York living in what he called 'primary or secondary poverty'. Standards of living might have risen for employed working people since the 1880s, but a significant proportion of the population was shown still to live in 'poverty' (a relative term) and on the brink of economic disaster. This contrasted markedly with the flamboyant 'plutocratic' living, noted earlier, of some members of the court and aristocracy.

Almost 30 per cent living in poverty was shocking, and it shocked contemporaries. But it also meant that 70 per cent were living in relative affluence, a proportion inconceivable in the days of the 'iron law of wages' of the mid-century. In the 1860s, Gladstone as Chancellor had admitted that the economy necessarily functioned with an 'enormous mass of paupers', and Victorians had been aware, in an ill-defined and helpless way, of the waste and suffering around them. Matthew Arnold's *Culture and Anarchy* (1869) described London's East End as containing 'those vast, miserable, unmanageable masses of sunken people'. Their reactions to it had been consequently local and personal, in the form of personal, charitable endeavour to alleviate the lot of those actually known to them or of particular categories of the so-called 'deserving poor', for example, distressed gentlefolk. Now, at the turn of the century, systematic investigation not only raised alarm that an 'imperial race' could be so impoverished, but, by providing figures, suggested manageability and means of redress: until the scale of the problem was known, it could not be tackled. 'While the problem of 1834 was the problem of pauperism, the problem of 1893 is the problem of poverty' remarked Alfred Marshall, the leading free-trade economist; he implied that the problem of poverty had become both definable and solvable.

The Liberal governments of 1905–14, especially after Asquith became Prime Minister in 1908 on Campbell-Bannerman's death, made a considerable attempt to begin to come to terms with these questions. Free school meals (1907), old age pensions (a scheme drawn up in 1908 by Asquith before becoming Prime Minister, though seen through the Commons by David Lloyd George, his successor as Chancellor of the Exchequer); the Development Act (1909) anticipating Keynesian deficit financing; Winston Churchill's labour exchanges (1909); and Lloyd George's National Insurance Bill (1911) giving compulsory insurance to certain workers for benefits in times of sickness and unemployment, paid for by the State, the employer, and the employee—these and a host of smaller measures constituted the first legislative milestones of the modern welfare state. They were based on the rejection of the Victorian principle that individual probity and diligence would ensure modest prosperity: the reforms accepted that capitalism was wasteful, inefficient, and punishing to individuals regardless of personal merit, and that 'voluntaryism' was not enough. But they were none the less the reforms of free-traders who believed that marginal adjustments to the system could phase out the injustices of capitalism and make it 'fair'.

These reforms were expensive but based on a wide measure of consensus; it was the raising of revenue to pay for them which caused particular controversy, a controversy compounded by the need to raise large sums to pay for a fleet of 'Dreadnought' ships to match German naval expansion. The Tariff Reformers advocated protective indirect taxes to raise such revenues: the Liberals legislated for expanded direct taxes. Lloyd George's budget of 1909 brought a long-festering issue to a head by introducing a 'super-tax' on the incomes of the very rich and an attempt at an effective tax on land. Balfour and the Unionists used the House of Lords to throw out the budget.

This was the culmination of increasing use of the Lords to frustrate Liberal legislation: the Home Rule Bill of 1893 and a series of measures in 1906–8 had been either mutilated or destroyed. The rejection of the budget, traditionally the prerogative of the Commons, struck at a central tenet of British representative government. The Unionists argued that the conventional exemption of financial legislation meant that Liberals were using it to 'tack' on what was really social legislation—but all taxation was, and always had been, ultimately social in its consequences. Two general elections in 1910 left the Liberals dependent on Labour and Irish support, but none the less with a clear majority against the Lords: the Unionist leadership—though not all its followers—eventually conceded the point and the Parliament Act of 1911 limited the Lords' veto to two years.

This great institutional battle had begun with a basic question about social organization: where would the extra tax burden fall—on the rich through the super-tax or on the poor through food taxes? Its progress raised another, about constitutional organization. For the Liberals, as required by their Irish supporters, now introduced the third Home Rule Bill which, together with disestablishment of the Anglican Church in Wales, became law under the provisions of the Parliament Act in 1914, though suspended in practice for the duration of the war.

The Unionists reluctantly swallowed the budget, but Home Rule they would not stomach. With implicit encouragement from their new leader, Andrew Bonar Law (who replaced Balfour in 1911), they took literally the slogan coined by Lord Randolph Churchill in 1886: 'Ulster will fight and Ulster will be right.' Guns, many of them German, were shipped to Northern Ireland. There was doubt about the loyalty of the army to the State. Three times denied possession of power by the electorate of the United Kingdom as a whole, the Unionists brought Ireland to the edge of civil war in 1914 despite substantial Liberal concessions on the Ulster question, which might have been introduced rather earlier. The outbreak of the First World War prevented posterity from knowing whether the Unionists would have gone over that edge.

Edwardian Britain was thus a turbulent time for politics and politicians. The resurgence of Liberalism and the Liberals' willingness to come to terms with many problems long delayed or frustrated was a painful business for the Unionists, who continue to regard themselves, in or out of power, as the natural rulers of the nation.

But if an old élite's decline caused the greatest trouble, new, rising forces were also very active. The movement for women's suffrage went back to J. S. Mill's attempt to amend the 1867

Reform Bill to give women the vote. Some progress was made, for some women gained the vote for local elections, and for the synod of the Church of England, and could stand as candidates for local councils, school boards, and the poor law board. But the marginal public role given to middle-class women in the 1870s and 1880s—helping the priest, the doctor, or the MP; being secretary to the charity whose chairman was almost always a man; taking university examinations but not degrees—was no longer enough. Exclusion from voting for elections of the imperial Parliament exemplified what had come to be seen as deprivation; the campaign for women's votes was a campaign for a new concept of citizenship. Mrs Fawcett's National Union of Women's Suffrage Societies, uniting in 1897 a number of well-established organizations, was a broadly-based movement of impeccably liberal credentials which made considerable headway. It was, however, outflanked and outshone by the Pankhursts' Women's Social and Political Union (1903). The WSPU increasingly advocated violence against both property and individual politicians, as well as inflicting through imprisonment and hunger strikes considerable hardship and even occasionally death upon its members. Whether the WSPU helped or hindered the cause is hard to say: on the one hand, it dramatized it, on the other, its support for violence alienated many potential supporters among MPs and in particular Asquith, the Prime Minister, and made its legislative success less likely. Despite committed support within the Liberal and Labour Parties, and from a few Unionists, no legislation had been passed by 1914.

The Edwardian years also saw a very considerable expansion of the trade union movement, from 2.0 million members in 1901 to 4.1 million in 1913. In the years after 1908, price inflation and stationary wages encouraged this burgeoning movement to exert its strength; and there was a series of major strikes in 1910–12, culminating in the first general railway strike in 1911, which Lloyd George, as Chancellor, defused—also something of a precedent. Since Labour Party membership could only be held through being a trade union member, and since most trade unions came to be affiliated to the Labour Party (the affiliation in 1909 of the coal-miners, the chief union still hitherto supporting the Liberals, was a particular triumph), the Labour Party grew considerably in strength. A wide network of constituency parties was established with a ferment of ideological discussion, much of it necessarily Utopian in character (much of it inspired by William Morris), for the means of implementation was as yet very limited. The party had a secure base in the Commons, but of a limited size, and considerably dependent on its pact with the Liberals which brought it some thirty seats at the 1906 election. Its limited success at elections was not surprising, given that in the sort of industrial seats in which it would expect to succeed, about 60 per cent of adult men were not enfranchised. As yet, the party in the Commons saw itself largely as a pressure group for trade union interests, successfully amending the original Liberal bill so as to prevent the legal incorporation of the unions through the 1906 Trade Disputes Act, the consequence of the Taff Vale case. The Labour Party also intervened on social questions and on foreign policy. This slow progress at Westminster led some trade unionists (notably some of the Welsh miners) to turn to syndicalism, that is, 'direct action' by trade unions to promote workers' control, circumventing MPs, Parliament, and the mechanisms of representative government.

The Labour Party's existence and success, closely linked to the expansion and difficulties of trade unionism, reflected a social, as much as an intellectual, difference from the Liberals. The solidarity of the Labour movement was based on cultural and social affinities, the shared experiences of working people in work and leisure, as much as any articulated perception of themselves as a separate class. Working people did not feel themselves to be alienated from the propertied classes, but they did feel themselves to be different. The Liberals reinforced this by their failure to adopt working men as candidates: however broad the agreement on policy matters, the middle-class members of the Liberal Associations—the people who called the tune in the constituencies—would not adopt as candidates men whom they would expect to enter their houses by the servants' door.

'Your English summer's done'

The refurbished Liberalism of the Edwardian years thus faced many difficulties. Legislatively, it met these dynamically and imaginatively with the first of the two great reforming governments of the century. It successfully contained and in large measure resolved the crisis over fiscal policy, welfare policy, socialism, and militarism which had brought many Continental nations to a political impasse by 1914 (though Ireland remained potentially an exception to this). It was not domestic divisions which were to bring Liberal governments in Britain to an end, but foreign affairs. We noted earlier the ambivalent consequences of the *Entente* policy pursued by Lord Lansdowne, Balfour's Foreign Secretary, and between 1905 and 1914 by Sir Edward Grey for the Liberals. Britain was committed implicitly and emotionally, but not in terms spelt out, to the French–Russian side of the European equation. Secret military conversations after 1905 between the British and the French increased this commitment. Although the greatest imperial power, Britain could bring little direct influence to bear on Continental affairs. R. B. Haldane's army reforms developed an Expeditionary Force intended for Europe, but, though efficient, it was tiny compared to the vast, conscript armies of the Continental powers. Indeed, the Germans simply discounted it, to their cost. As the concept of the 'Concert of Europe' gave way to overtly nationalistic self-assertion, the British contribution waned. Though personally strongly anti-German, Grey continued to avoid formal alliances, but by 1910 it was clear that Germany would be Britain's adversary, if she were to have one. In a series of incidents in North Africa, the Balkans, and Turkey, and in the continuing escalation of the navy building programme (despite British attempts, especially in 1911–12, to negotiate a limitation agreement) Anglo-German hostility became confirmed. It began to take on a cultural as well as a diplomatic and military aspect. The respect mixed with concern characteristic of British views of German achievements in the 1890s began to change to alarm and fear.

When events in the Balkans and Central Europe in June and July 1914 led rapidly to war, as Germany estimated that the moment for her bid for mastery had come, the British could bring little influence to bear. Britain had less to gain from war than any of the other major European powers except perhaps Russia. Whether the Liberal Cabinet would have entered the war at all had the Germans not invaded Belgium is open to doubt. But the Germans ignored both the traditional British concern for the strategic importance of the Low Countries, and the implications of guarantee of Belgian independence which they as well as the British had signed in 1870 to last during the Franco-Prussian War. The attack on Belgium decided the matter, and Asquith led his Cabinet into war with only two resignations—John Morley and John Burns. He did so with a heavy heart: the blithe spirit which infused the enthusiastic rush to the colours to join the war that was to be 'over by Christmas' was not shared by Britain's political leadership.

Britain was remarkably unprepared psychologically and, on the whole, physically for a Continental land war. War on land, even in the Crimea and South Africa, had been seen as a marginal matter, to be fought by professionals and a few volunteers. Military values were influential amongst the aristocracy and gentry and increasingly in the public schools, but elsewhere made little impact. Attempts by groups on the right to militarize society—from the Militia of the 1850s through the Riflemen and the Volunteers, to Lord Roberts's National Service League in the 1900s—had conspicuously failed. 'Trafalgar Day' was the annual martial celebration, reflecting the essentially naval and defensive cast of the public mind—the 'blue water' policy, as it was called. Except in certain rural areas, 'to go for a sodger', 'to take the King's shilling', had for ordinary people been an act of desperation in a time of unemployment or personal catastrophe. The British public liked bands and bright uniforms because they were entertainments, the exact opposite of harbingers of war. Pomp and domesticity was the British style. Government contracts for guns and ships were by the Edwardian years considerable in value and an important part of the economy of the northeast of England, but, in general, military matters seldom impinged on the thinking of government and society. Certainly, they had not penetrated the very fabric of the political, social, and economic order as they had in virtually every Continental state. The first industrial nation had offered the world a remarkable public experiment in liberal, capitalist democracy whose success was premised upon free trade and world peace. Tuesday, 4 August 1914 brought that experiment to an abrupt halt.

There's a whisper down the field where the year has shot her yield,
And the ricks stand grey to the sun,
Singing:—'Over then, come over, for the bee has quit the clover,
And your English summer's done.'

Rudyard Kipling, 'The Long Trail'

10. *The Twentieth Century*

(1914–1998)

KENNETH O. MORGAN

The First World War

AT the Lord Mayor of London's annual banquet at the Mansion House on 17 July 1914, the Chancellor of the Exchequer, David Lloyd George, issued stern warnings about the ominous condition of British society. At home, the 'triple alliance' of miners, railwaymen, and transport workers was threatening a mass united strike to back up the railwaymen's claim for union recognition and a 48-hour week. Alongside this prospect of nation-wide industrial paralysis, there was across the Irish Sea a state of near civil war in Ireland, with 200,000 or more men under arms in Protestant Ulster and the Catholic south, and the likelihood of the age-long saga of Irish nationalism being brought to a grim and bloody resolution. Abroad, there were nationalist troubles in India and in Egypt. Nearer home in south-east Europe, the ethnic nationalities of the Balkans were in renewed turmoil following the assassination of the Austrian Archduke, Franz Ferdinand, at Sarajevo in Bosnia on 28 June.

On the eve of world war, therefore, Britain seemed to present a classic picture of a civilized liberal democracy on the verge of dissolution, racked by tensions and strains with which its sanctions and institutions were unable to cope. And yet, as so often in the past, once the supreme crisis of war erupted, these elements of conflict subsided with remarkable speed. An underlying mood of united purpose gripped the nation. The first few weeks of hostilities, after Britain declared war on 4 August, were, inevitably, a time of some panic. Only dramatic measures by the Treasury and the Bank of England preserved the national currency and credit. Manufacturing and commerce tried desperately to adjust to the challenges of war against the background of an ethic that proclaimed that it was 'business as usual'. The early experiences of actual fighting were almost disastrous as the British Expeditionary Force, cobbled together in much haste and dispatched to Flanders and France, met with a severe reverse at Ypres, and had to retreat from Mons, in disarray and suffering heavy losses. Reduced to only three corps in strength, its fighting force was gravely diminished almost from the start. Only a stern resistance by the French forces on the river Marne prevented a rapid German advance on Paris and an early victory for Germany and its Austrian allies.

After the initial disasters, however, the nation and its leaders settled down for a long war. Vital domestic issues such as Irish home rule were suspended for the duration of hostilities. The political parties declared an indefinite truce. The industrial disturbances of the summer of 1914 petered out, with the TUC out-doing the employers in voicing the conventional patriotism of the time. A curious kind of calm descended, founded on a broad—though very far from universal—consensus about the justice of the war. The one element required to make it acceptable to a liberal society was some kind of broad, humane justification to explain what the war was really about. This was provided by Lloyd George, once a bitter opponent of the Boer War in South Africa in 1899, and for many years the most outspokenly left-wing member of the Asquith Liberal government. Lloyd George remained suspiciously silent during the early weeks. But in an eloquent address to a massed audience of his Welsh fellow-countrymen at the Queen's Hall, London, on 19 September 1914, he committed himself without reserve to a fight to the finish. He occupied, or claimed to occupy, the highest moral ground. It was, he declared, a war on behalf of liberal principles, a crusade on behalf of the 'little five-foot-five nations', like Belgium, flagrantly invaded by the Germans, or Serbia and Montenegro, now threatened by Austria-Hungary. It was not surprising that a claim that the war was a holy cause, backed up not only by the leaders of all the Christian churches but by all the Liberal pantheon of heroes from Fox to Gladstone, met with instant response, not least in the smaller nations of Scotland and Wales within Britain itself.

This broad consensus about the rightness of the war was not fundamentally eroded over the next four terrible years. Of course, it went through many changes, especially after the unpopular decision to impose conscription for the armed services was instituted in May 1916. Eventually, by 1917, sheer war-weariness was taking its toll, quite apart from other factors such as the growing militancy from organized labour and the Messianic appeal of the Bolshevik revolution in Russia. Of course, too, this consensus was sustained by subtle or crude manipulation of the news services, censorship of the press, government-sponsored legends of atrocities allegedly committed by 'the Huns'. There was much persecution of radical or anti-war critics. In spite of government pressures, bodies such as the Christian pacifist 'No-Conscription Fellowship' and the Union of Democratic Control (which sought a negotiated peace) were by 1917 making some impact on public opinion. Lord Lansdowne's appeal for peace (29 November 1917) caused a great stir. Nevertheless, the available evidence for the war years suggests that the broad mass of the population retained its faith that the war was just and necessary, and that it must be fought until the total surrender of the German enemy, whatever the cost. Recruitment to the armed services from volunteers was heavy and enthusiastic: indeed voluntary recruitment proved more successful in swelling the ranks of the army in France in 1914–16 than was the compulsory method of conscription thereafter. The long years of military and naval conflict that dragged on from the initial stalemate on the

The First World War 585

western front in the autumn of 1914, until the final Allied breakthrough in August–September 1918 were accepted with resignation and a kind of grim endurance.

The psychological and moral impact of those appalling years sank deep into the memory and the outlook of the British people. They profoundly coloured the literary sensibilities of a whole generation. They helped shape responses to the threat of foreign war for twenty years after the Great War came to an end. The war on the western front took the unfamiliar form of a prolonged slogging match between heavily-defended forces on either side, dug into slit trenches, and unable to exploit the new techniques of mobile striking power so dramatically tested in the Franco-Prussian war of 1870. For almost four years, the war in France showed little movement. There were occasional British attempts to seize the initiative. Always they ended in huge casualties on a scale scarcely comprehensible to a nation which lived on the luxurious memories of a century of almost unbroken peace. The British offensive at Loos was beaten back in September 1915. More damaging still, in June 1916 a new British advance on the Somme proved a calamitous failure with 60,000 men falling on the first day. British casualties here alone amounted to 420,000. The most terrible of these experiences came at Passchendaele in August–September 1917, when over 300,000 British troops were recorded as dead or wounded, many of them drowned in the mud of Flanders amidst torrential rain. Both the cavalry and mechanical inventions such as the 'tanks' made no impact in so immobile a campaign. The new fighter aircraft had little effect. As on other occasions, the class divide that cut off commanding officers from the rank-and-file infantrymen and hindered communication between them was fatal throughout. In effect, the British ceased to be a viable offensive force for the next few months. March and April 1918 saw the British army desperately striving to ward off a new German advance in the Amiens sector. Nor until the ultimate dramatic breakthrough by Haig that August did the war show signs of coming to a resolution. Meanwhile attempts, advocated by Lloyd George and Churchill amongst others, to circumvent the stalemate on the western front by a more peripheral 'eastern' strategy also led to successive débâcles. The Dardanelles expedition in the summer of 1915 was a colossal exercise in military mismanagement and led to further huge losses; so did the expedition to Salonika a year later. The Dardanelles in particular did immense harm to Churchill's reputation as a rational politician, from which he took years to recover. Even on the high seas, Britain's traditional area of supremacy, the one major battle, the encounter off Jutland in June 1916, was at best a draw between the British and German high fleets. The British Grand Fleet lost three battle cruisers, three other cruisers, and eight destroyers in an ill-conducted engagement.

Later anti-war propaganda depicted an angry populace displaying fierce hostility towards the military and naval commanders responsible for this terrible catalogue of disaster in almost every theatre. 'War poets' such as Wilfred Owen and Isaac Rosenberg (who fell in battle) and Siegfried Sassoon and Robert Graves (who survived), stirred particularly by the carnage of Passchendaele, all encouraged the view that a mass renunciation took place of the very idea of war itself, of the carnage that could result in half an entire generation of young men being wiped out. The bare statistics of the war— 750,000 killed, another 2,500,000 wounded, many permanently disabled—reinforced this belief in a mass rejection of militarism. That was not, however, how it appeared to most people at the time, even if it should have done so. While the British commander-in-chief on the western front, Sir John French, was indeed removed from command at the end of 1915, his successor, Sir Douglas Haig, a grim, taciturn Lowland Scot, steadily built up a massive public reputation for courage and integrity, a reputation matched by Sir Edwin Lutyens's towering war memorial to commemorate the British dead at Thiepval. Other naval and military leaders, such as Admiral Beatty and General Allenby (who conducted a brilliant campaign from Egypt, through Palestine into Syria in 1917–18, to eliminate the Turks as significant allies for the Germans) became almost popular heroes. The trenches became the symbol of stern, but inescapable, resolution. Bruce Bairnsfather's famous cartoon of 'Old Bill', urging his comrade that if he knew of 'a better 'ole' he should go to it, symbolized a popular mood of almost humorous tolerance of the terrors of trench warfare. When, after desperate military crises and with the immense military and financial aid of the United States, the British and French armies forced their way through the German lines to reach the borders of Germany itself by the time of the armistice on 11 November 1918, mass enthusiasm for the war appeared at its zenith. Britain seemed in danger of inventing a new military cult unknown in these islands since the days of Marlborough.

A major factor in the widespread popularity of the war—and also in its subsequent bitter unpopularity—was the involvement of the whole population and the entire social and economic fabric in total war. After a leisurely start, in 1915–16 the war brought about a massive industrial and social transformation; it erected a leviathan of state power and collectivist control without precedent. The forces of production and distribution in industry and agriculture were all harnessed to fuel the needs of a mighty war machine. The model was set by the new Ministry of Munitions of which Lloyd George assumed control in May 1915. Created to deal with bottle-necks in the supply of arms and ammunition, the Ministry became the engine of a massive central machine which invigorated the entire industrial structure through its 'men of push and go'. It achieved an immense impact as well on such different areas as social welfare, housing policy, and the status of women. The coal mines, the railways, merchant and other shipping were all taken under state control. The old pre-war shibboleths of *laissez-faire*, including the hallowed principle of free trade itself, were bypassed or ignored. Equally, the traditional system of industrial relations was wrenched into totally new patterns. The Treasury Agreement of March 1915, negotiated between the government and the trade unions (except for the miners), forbade strikes but also guaranteed collective bargaining and, indirectly, a new access to government for trade union leaders. The Treasury Agreement certainly did not achieve its aim of universal industrial peace during the war years. There were major disputes in the coal industry, notably a successful official strike by the South Wales Miners in July 1915. The work of the Ministry of Munitions in trying to 'dilute' the work-force by introducing unskilled workers (especially women) into engineering factories, and in trying to control the movements of labour in the armaments industry brought much trouble, notably on Clydeside. The unofficial activities of shop stewards in Scotland and also in Sheffield in 1916–17 remind us that the consensus of the war years was a shallow one and very far from unanimous. Nevertheless, the war did ensure a continuing corporate status for the unions—and also for employers, newly combined in the Federation of British Industry. A new organic, planned system of industrial relations appeared to be possible. It was significant that powerful businessmen such as Sir Eric Geddes and Sir Joseph Maclay, Lord Devonport and Lord Rhondda, appeared in key departments of central government. This symbolized the transformation in the relationship of industrial and political leadership that was taking place. Edward VII's Liberal England was being turned into a corporate state, almost what a later generation would term 'Great Britain Limited'.

Over a vast range of social and cultural activities, the collective impact of the Great War was profound indeed. Left-wing opponents of the war such as Ramsay MacDonald of the Labour Party noted ironically that the imperatives of war were achieving far more for social reform than had all the campaigns of the trade unions and of progressive humanitarians in half a century past. New vistas of governmental activity were being opened up. Fresh layers were being added to the techno-cratic, professional, and civil service élite that had governed Britain in the years of peace. The administrative and managerial class expanded massively. Social reformers such as William Beveridge or Seebohm Rowntree, even the socialist Beatrice Webb, became influential and even honoured figures in the recesses of central government, especially after Lloyd George succeeded Asquith as Prime Minister in December 1916. Wages went up; working conditions improved. The 1917 Corn Production Act revitalized British agriculture and gave a fresh lease of life to tenant farmers and their labourers. Attention was also paid to technical and other education, notably through H. A. L. Fisher's Act of 1918 which made free elementary education general and sought to create a ladder of opportunity from the elementary to the secondary and higher levels of education. Governmental inquiries, one of them headed by as conservative a figure as Lord Salisbury, opened up new vistas for state housing schemes, an area almost totally neglected by the New Liberalism before 1914. The principle was laid down for a system of subsidized local-authority houses, to provide the hundreds of thousands of working-class dwellings for rent that were required, and to remove the blight of slums in city centres and older industrial areas. Concern was voiced, too, for public health. The supreme irony was that a war which brought the loss of human life on such a colossal scale also saw the preservation of life at home through improved medical arrangements, better conditions for children and old people and nursing mothers, and such innovations as the Medical Research Council. By the end of 1918, the government was committed to the idea of a new Ministry of Health to co-ordinate the services for health and national insurance, and to take over the duties of the Local Government Board.

One important element of British society above all other gained from the wartime experience—indeed for them (a majority of the population, in fact) this was an era of emancipation. Women in Britain were supreme beneficiaries of the war years. Thousands of them served at the front, often in medical field hospitals. The spectacle of Nurse Edith Cavell martyred by the Germans for assisting in the escape of British and French prisoners of war in Belgium added powerfully to the public esteem of women in general. At home, suffragette leaders such as Mrs Pankhurst and her elder daughter Christabel (though not her socialist younger daughter, Sylvia) aided in recruiting campaigns for the government. More widely, women found vast new opportunities in clerical and administrative work, in munitions and other engineering factories, and in many other unfamiliar tasks previously reserved for men only. The very dissolution wrought by total war exerted powerful pressures in eroding the sex barriers which had restricted British women over the decades. It was hardly possible to argue now that women were incapable of exercising the rights of citizenship to the full; in the 1918 Representation of the People Act, therefore, women aged 30 and over were given the vote. It was almost anti-climactic. A long, bitter saga of persecution and prejudice ended with a whimper. Here as elsewhere, by emphasizing the positive, progressive consequences of the war, with the full panoply of 'reconstruction' (ill-defined) which was supposed to be launched when peace returned, the government contrived, perhaps unintentionally, to extend and fortify the consensus of the time.

For British politics, the Great War produced massive and tumultuous changes. At the outbreak of war, the House of Commons was still largely dominated by the Gilbertian rivalry of Liberals and Conservatives (or Unionists). However, for the Liberal Party the war brought disaster. Partly this was because of the serious inroads into individual and civil liberties that war entailed. Partly it was due to a deep-seated ambiguity about the very merits of the war that many Liberals harboured. The turning of Asquith's Liberal administration into a three-party coalition in May 1915 marked a new stage in the downfall of Liberalism. Thereafter, Asquith's own apparently lethargic and fumbling leadership was accompanied by severe internal party divisions over the fundamental issue of military conscription.

Lloyd George and Churchill both endorsed conscription as the symbol of whole-hearted commitment to 'a fight to the finish'. More traditional Liberals such as Simon and McKenna were hesitant. Asquith himself dithered unhappily. In the end, conscription came for all adult males aged between eighteen and forty-five, but criticism of Asquith and the Liberal ethic generally continued to mount.

In December 1916 the final crisis came. There had been complaints for months over government failures, not only in the field, but also over the inability to resolve the Irish question and to settle labour disputes at home. Between 1 and 9 December 1916 there followed political manœuvres of Byzantine complexity over which historians continue to dispute like so many medieval schoolmen. Lloyd George joined with two leading Unionists, Bonar Law and the Irishman, Sir Edward Carson, in proposing to Asquith a new supreme War Committee to run the war. After days of uncertainty, Asquith refused. Lloyd George then resigned and, in a crucial trial of strength between 4 and 9 December, emerged as Prime Minister of something like an all-party coalition. It included not only all the Unionists but also (by a very narrow majority on the National Executive) the Labour Party as well, in addition to roughly half the Liberals in the House of Commons. Henceforth, between December 1916 and November 1918, Lloyd George built himself up into a semi-presidential position of near-impregnability. He was the Prime Minister of a supreme War Cabinet, backed up by a new Cabinet office and a 'garden suburb' or kitchen cabinet of private secretaries. Beneath this apex extended a mighty machine of centralized power. Lloyd George's triumph helped to win the war—but for his own Liberal Party it meant a débâcle. The party remained split, weakened at the grass roots, ineffective and divided in Parliament, shorn of much of its morale and impetus in the press and in intellectual circles. The New Liberalism, which had animated so much social reform before 1914, just spluttered out. When the war ended in November 1918, the Liberals were a divided, much weakened rump, a supreme casualty of total war.

Their place was taken, quite unexpectedly, by the Labour Party. This party had also been much divided by the outbreak of war. In contrast to the patriotism of trade union leaders, Ramsay MacDonald and many on the socialist left had been opponents of entering the war. MacDonald had to resign his leadership of the parliamentary Labour Party in consequence. Issues during the war such as the impact of conscription (military and possible industrial), and the decision over whether or not to serve under Lloyd George also plagued the Labour Party. Nevertheless, the long-term consequences of the war for the party were wholly beneficial. The trade unions on which Labour depended were much strengthened by the war experience. Their membership roughly doubled to reach over eight million by the start of 1919. The party was also given new stimulus by the revolution in Russia, and by the wider anti-war radicalism in the last two years of the war. In effect, Labour was serving in government and acting as the formal opposition at one and the same time. It was ideally placed to exploit the internal difficulties of the Liberals. Finally, the 1918 franchise reforms extended the electorate from about 8 million to over 21 million. This meant a huge increase in the working-class vote and an encouragement of the tendency to polarize politics on grounds of class. The 1918 party constitution gave the party a new socialist commitment and, more important, a reorganized structure in the constituencies and in Head Office, dominated throughout by the trade unions. The advance of Labour was a powerful political consequence of the war, though quite unforeseen at the time.

The real beneficiaries were the Conservatives. The war encouraged a process by which they became the natural majority party. Apart from being united by the call by war, as the patriots they claimed to be, after being divided over tariffs and other questions before 1914, the Conservatives became increasingly dominated by business and manufacturing interests. They were now largely urban or suburban in their base, not a party of squires. At the end of the war, with new business-orientated figures such as Stanley Baldwin and Neville Chamberlain coming through, the Conservatives were poised, like the Labour Party, to destroy the Edwardian political system. When the war ended on 11 November 1918, Lloyd George assumed total command. His rump of Coalition Liberals were in electoral alliance with the Conservatives, in opposition to the 'pacifists' of the anti-government Liberals and the 'Bolsheviks' of the Labour Party. A new era of right-wing domination was in the making.

Externally, the war years encouraged further changes. It was, in all senses, a profoundly imperial war, fought for empire as well as for king and country. Much was owed to military and other assistance from Australia, New Zealand, Canada, South Africa, and India. Anzac Day (with memories of Suvla Bay, Gallipoli) became a tragic, symbolic event in the Australian calendar. In 1917 Lloyd George actually convened an Imperial War Cabinet of Prime Ministers to assist the Cabinet of the mother country. A powerful empire statesman like Smuts of South Africa was even called upon to participate in the deliberations of the British Cabinet. In commerce, imperial preference was becoming a reality. The imperial mystique was a powerful one at this time. The main architect of the day, Edwin Lutyens, had been in his younger days a disciple of the arts and crafts movement inspired by William Morris. Now he and Herbert Baker were turning their talents to pomp and circumstance by rebuilding the city of Delhi. It was to be dominated by a massive Viceroy's residence and Secretariat buildings as symbols of classical authority. During the war years, the imperial idea was taken further than ever before. Indeed, the secret treaties of the war years ensured that at the peace the mandate system or other stratagems would leave Britain with an imperial domain larger than ever, with vast new territories in the Middle East and up from the Persian Gulf. Buoyed up by the eccentric operations of individualists such as 'Lawrence of Arabia' and fired by the heady prospects of vast oil riches in Mesopotamia and elsewhere in the Middle East, the bounds of the British Empire extended ever wider.

Yet in reality it was all becoming increasingly impractical to maintain. Long before 1914, the financial and military constraints upon an effective imperial policy were becoming clear, especially in India with its growing Congress movement. There was something else now—new and increasingly effective nationalist uprisings against British rule. Unlike Wales, which was almost mindlessly patriotic with Lloyd George at the helm, Ireland offered a disturbing spectacle of colonial revolt. The Easter rising of April 1916, conducted by a few republicans and Sinn Fein partisans, seemed to be a fiasco. But, aided by the brutal reaction of Asquith's government, by mid-1918 Sinn Fein and its republican creed had won over almost all the twenty-six southern Irish counties. A veteran home ruler such as John Dillon was being swept aside by new nationalist radicals like Michael Collins and Eamon de Valera. By the end of the war, southern Ireland was virtually under martial law, resistant to conscription, in a state of near rebellion against the Crown and the Protestant ascendancy, or what was left of it. The long march of Irish nationalism, constitutional and largely peaceful in the decades from O'Connell to Parnell and Redmond, seemed on the verge of producing a new and violent explosion. One clear moral of the war years, therefore, was that the political and social consensus, fragile enough for Clydeside and the Welsh mining valleys, did not extend at all to southern Ireland. With the powerful thrust of Irish republicanism, a new kind of nationalist revolt against the constraints of imperial rule was well under way. Indians and Egyptians, among others, were likely to pay careful heed. The war left a legacy of a more integrated but also a more isolated Britain, whose grandiose imperial role was already being swamped by wider transformations in the post-war world.

The Twenties

When peace returned, it seemed that little had changed. The continuity between war and peace was confirmed by Lloyd George's overwhelming electoral triumph at the 'coupon election' of December 1918, a ratification of the patriotism and unity of the war years. The Prime Minister was acclaimed, almost universally, as 'the man who won the war', the most dominant political leader since Cromwell. The electoral verdict was indeed an overpowering one. The supporters of the coalition government numbered no less than 526 (of whom 136 were Liberals and almost all the rest Unionist), against a mere 57 Labour MPs and 26 Independent Liberals. The results were not so conclusive under closer examination. The Labour Party's tally of 57 MPs concealed the fact that the party had polled two and a half million votes, and was on the verge of a massive electoral breakthrough. In Ireland, Sinn Fein captured 73 seats out of 81 in the south; its representatives withdrew from Westminster and set up their own unofficial parliament or 'Dáil' in Dublin. Even so, the mandate on behalf of the Prime Minister and his wartime associates seemed quite irrefutable. The election seemed to confirm, too, that socio-economic normality in many respects was being rapidly restored. Many of the wartime controls and the apparatus of state collectivism disappeared as if they had never been. Major industries were returned to private hands—the railways, shipping, even the coal mines whose owners were perhaps the most hated group in the entire capitalist world. The government also began a consistent financial policy to ensure an eventual return to the gold standard; this would entail a deflationary approach, with a steady contraction of the note issue expanded so rapidly during the war. The City of London, the class system, private capitalism appeared destined to continue their unchallenged reign. To indicate that this was capitalism with a human face, the government also began with a flurry of reforming activity in

1919–20. Indeed, Lloyd George had campaigned far more vigorously at the election as a social reformer anxious to build a 'land fit for heroes', than as a chauvinist determined to hang the Kaiser or 'squeeze Germany till the pips squeaked'. So there followed a vigorous, if short-lived, programme to extend health and educational services, to raise pensions, and spread universal unemployment insurance. Most spectacular of all was the subsidized housing programme launched by the Liberal minister, Dr Christopher Addison, which, with reluctant treasury support, achieved a total of over 200,000 publicly-built houses in the 1919–22 period, a limited but valuable start in dealing with one of the major social scandals in the land.

But it soon became disturbingly clear that life was not normal and that the comforting framework of pre-1914 could not easily be restored. There were new and disruptive economic problems that resulted from the loss of foreign markets and the sale of overseas investments to pay for the war. The most ominous aspect of this, on which newspaper headlines focused attention, was the huge increase in the national debt. The unredeemed capital of the debt stood at £706 million in 1914. Six years later it had soared to £7,875 millions. This resulted in a passionate cry for 'economy', the ending of 'waste' in public expenditure, and a return to a balanced budget and a firm currency after the rapid inflation of 1918–19. Politically, too, things were very far from normal. Lloyd George's coalition had come to power in unhappy circumstances, with a background of conspiracy surrounding the calling of the 1918 'coupon' general election. Its moral title to power was in doubt. Furthermore, as a coalition it was prey to internal disputes, and constant tension between the Liberal Prime Minister and his Conservative colleagues over domestic, foreign, and imperial affairs. Lloyd George himself, a remote, Olympian figure, preoccupied with international peace conferences, aloof from the House of Commons, a Prime Minister without a party, an adventurer careless in his financial and sexual activities, was not one who inspired universal trust or affection. So the con-

sensus of the armistice period soon evaporated and new conflicts took its place.

A series of challenges was launched which gradually undermined the coalition's claim to govern. New patterns were being
formed which would shape the course of British history for the
next twenty years. On the left, Lloyd George was bitterly
attacked by many Liberals over his casualness towards old and
hallowed principles such as free trade. His policy in Ireland
appeared even more shocking since the British government pursued war against the IRA in 1919–21 with an unrestrained
policy of retaliation which led to bloody atrocities being committed by the auxiliary forces that were maintained by the
Crown to back up the army and the constabulary. In December
1921, Lloyd George, always by instinct a negotiator, eventually
made peace with the Sinn Fein leaders, Arthur Griffith and
Michael Collins. From January 1922, an Irish Free State, con-
sisting of the twenty-six Catholic counties of southern
Ireland, was created, with just the six Protestant counties of
Ulster in the north-east left within the United Kingdom. But
this volte-face was too late to repair Lloyd George's tarnished
image amongst liberal opinion. In the Labour Party and trade
union world, the Prime Minister totally lost the reputation he
had long enjoyed as a patron of labour. His government used
tough methods, including emergency powers and the use of
troops as strike-breakers, in dealing with national strikes by
miners, railwaymen, and many other workers (including even
the police) in 1919–21. Thereafter, the government failed to
prevent massive unemployment (soon rising to over a million
workers) from growing up and casting a blight over the older
industrial areas. Episodes like the apparent deceiving of the
coal-miners over the Sankey report and the proposed nationalization of the mines in 1919, and the further undermining of
the 'Triple Alliance' to frustrate the miners again on 'Black
Friday' (15 April 1921) sank deep into the consciousness of the
working class. A government elected to promote national solidarity and social unity had made the class divide wider than

ever before. If the coalition was attacked on the left, it was increasingly under fire on the right as well. Conservatives longed for the return of a healthy system of independent party politics, freed from the buccaneering methods of an autocratic Prime Minister and his retainers. Although the coalition hung on for almost four years, it was in dire straits and Lloyd George himself a Prime Minister at bay.

Above and beyond all this, there was a wider mood of disillusion with the peace treaties and the 'system of Versailles'. The peace settlement was increasingly unpopular. It was linked with covert secret treaties concluded during the war between Britain and its allies, and with unjust terms, for financial reparation and frontier arrangements, imposed on the defeated Germans. No book more effectively expressed this mood than did the economist J. M. Keynes's *Economic Consequences of the Peace* (1919). The work of a financial adviser to the Treasury who had resigned in protest during the Paris peace conference, it rapidly became a best seller on both sides of the Atlantic. It seemed to show conclusively that the reparations imposed on Germany would lead to its financial ruin and thereby to the permanent weakening of European economy. Keynes also evoked, in memorable and picturesque language, the frenzied, corrrupt atmosphere in which the various covert bargains were struck by the peacemakers in Versailles. Lloyd George was condemned as a man 'rooted in nothing'. The premier's efforts to act as the peacemaker of Europe in successive international conferences became unpopular. Britain refused any longer to act, in Bonar Law's striking phrase, as 'the policeman of the world'. The empire might be larger than ever, but it must be accompanied by a withdrawal from commitments in Europe. Otherwise another tragedy would afflict the land as it had done in August 1914. The final blow for Lloyd George's coalition came in October 1922 when it seemed that Britain was on the verge of war with Turkey over the defence of the Greek position in Asia Minor and protection of the Straits. Conservatives as well as the British left revolted against this rekindling of jingoism. The right-wing basis of the government collapsed. Lloyd George fell from power on 19 October 1922, a political pariah for the rest of his life.

Two kinds of reaction against Lloyd George's government followed. They were symbolized respectively by Ramsay MacDonald and Stanley Baldwin, both prominent in the movements that led to the downfall of the coalition in October 1922. MacDonald, with his heady Utopian internationalism and 'Brave New World' idealism, was the perfect voice for the growing Labour Party, whose tally of seats rose rapidly in the 1922 and 1923 general elections. He could straddle both the socialism of Clydeside and the social conventions of the London establishment. Alternatively, and more influential still, Stanley Baldwin led the Conservative forces of suburban middle-class respectability and of orthodox patriotism, all alarmed at Lloyd George's political experiments and the international adventurism of British foreign policy after the war. Baldwin, Prime Minister in 1923–4, 1924–9, and 1935–7, was an appropriate leader for a Britain desperate for a return to tranquillity and social peace.

There was constant flux and upheaval in other spheres of public life as well. Many of the settled patterns of pre-war now seemed under assault. In Wales and Scotland there were small movements of intellectuals, which suggested that the very unity of the kingdom could itself be threatened. Two small nationalist parties were formed on the Irish model, Plaid Cymru in Wales in 1925 and the National Party of Scotland in 1928. However, their significance was to lie in a distant future. In the arts, in literature, music, painting, and architecture, the surviving presence of pre-war giants such as Kipling and Hardy, Elgar and Lutyens masked the underlying challenge of avant-garde movements expressive of 'modernism' and revolt. Amongst the novelists, the main work of Joyce and of D. H. Lawrence had already been written; indeed after *Women in Love* appeared in 1920, with its echoes of the *malaise* of the war years, Lawrence's later work seemed relatively unimpressive.

More innovative were the writings of the coterie of intellectuals and artists linked with the 'Bloomsbury group'. In particular, the remarkable series of 'stream of consciousness' novels produced by Virginia Woolf, with their subtle delineation of human character and strangely fluid form, testified to the vitality of 'modernism' in the novel. More orthodox was E. M. Forster's *Passage to India* (1924), the work of a novelist indirectly associated with Bloomsbury, which, in its treatment of the interaction of Western and Eastern cultures, portrays the declining self-confidence of Western liberal humanism. The most notable pioneering development in poetry was T. S. Eliot's 'The Waste Land' (1922) with its disturbing rhythms and imagery; its pervading tone of Christian resignation and private melancholy captures one powerful aspect of the culture of the twenties. It was not a creative time for the theatre other than Shaw's *St. Joan*, his most powerful philosophic affirmation. Nor was it an age of great imagination in art, design, and architecture either; painters like Ben Nicholson were still seeking a new style, while others such as Paul Nash were apparently marking time. In the world of art, the Bloomsbury group again provided a few notable rebels, Roger Fry, the art critic and patron, painters such as Duncan Grant and Vanessa Bell, trying to break out of the mould of realism in pictorial representation. Bloomsbury, indeed, with its writers and artists, and associated figures like the economist J. M. Keynes, the essayist Lytton Strachey, and its philosopher-mentor G. E. Moore, embodied many of the strengths and limitations of the British cultural scene in the twenties. It genuinely attempted to infuse British art with the inspiration of the modernist poets and surrealist artists of continental Europe. It combined the cult of the new with an effective iconoclasm, most popularly conveyed in Lytton Strachey's satirical studies of the feet of clay of leading Victorian personalities, from the queen downwards. More negatively, Bloomsbury encouraged an inbred, almost tribal, view of artistic communication; it became in time a sheltered enclave with dynastic overtones. Writers in the thirties were to criticize the Bloomsbury group as a new cultural establishment. They attacked them for laying insufficient emphasis on moral (rather than purely aesthetic) sensibility and for their supposed lack of political or public concern. Probably the Bloomsbury ethos encouraged a tendency for the art of the classes and masses to grow further and further apart.

Developments in the arts, however, with their expressions of revolt and emancipation, chimed in with wider social movements of the time. The women who gained the vote, partially in 1918 and then (conclusively) in 1928, were able to enjoy other freedoms as well, the right to smoke, to enjoy new leisure interests such as the films, to pursue a more open and less constrained 'sex life', and to wear clothes that were spectacularly far less drab or puritanical. The 'bright young things' extolled in memoirs of the twenties, for whom the satires and plays of Noël Coward appeared to have been specifically written, were limited enough in their outlook. They were usually of middle- to upper-class background. They, or their friends, were strongly associated with the public schools, with Oxford and Cambridge. Oxford, in particular, became linked with a kind of free cultural self-expression, tending to decadence, nihilism, or both, just as it was to be identified (equally wrongly) in the thirties with anti-war protest. The older universities were probably far less influential in society at large than later myth-mongers alleged, but they merged into the experimental climate of a more formless, rootless world.

Certainly, the older arbiters of moral standards seemed to be suffering a crisis of authority after the war. Nowhere was this more apparent than amongst the churches, manifestly among the casualties of total war, with the possible exception of the Roman Catholics with their strongly Irish membership. The nonconformist chapels, moral beacons to many in the Victorian heyday, were now suffering from falling membership, declining funds, diminished authority. Even in their strongholds in Wales and the North, the chapels were in steady retreat. Not least, the challenges to Puritanism and Sabbatarianism that the war had produced severely undermined what sanctions the chapels could muster. The Church of England, too, maintained its established, national role with much difficulty after the war. Archbishops such as Randall Davidson and Cosmo Lang spoke in terms of the old cohesion and disciplines, but their message appeared increasingly ineffective. In a formal sense, Britain was still a recognizably Christian country. Its Church leaders were still honoured and respected, indissolubly bound to Crown and landed aristocracy. Sunday was still a day of tranquillity and gloom when the trains did not run, and shops and theatres were closed, as also were public houses in Wales and Scotland. The revision of the Anglican Prayer Book in 1927–8 produced furious public debate; the old battles between Anglo-Catholic and evangelical wings of the established Church were vigorously resumed. The identification of religion with middle-class values, with the family, the community, and a safe form of patriotism was still maintained. So, too, was the link of religion with the empire, notably through youth movements such as the Boy Scouts and the Church Brigade. The war itself encouraged a kind of secular religiosity, symbolized in the Cenotaph erected by Lutyens in Whitehall as a memorial to the war dead. And yet, for all the formal trappings to remind the people of their religious inheritance through the centuries, the impact and mystique of Christianity was clearly on the wane, especially among the post-war generation and ex-servicemen.

The inability of the churches significantly to influence the course of events was dramatically shown during the 1926 general strike. In that year, the terrible cycle of industrial decline, unemployment, and social bitterness led to the worst explosion of class conflict that Britain had yet known. The great strikes of 1919–21 had now passed away. The Prime Minister, Baldwin, called for 'Peace in our Time, O Lord'. But in the greatest industry in the land, coal-mining, tension remained high, with a background of wage cuts, dismissals, and falling living standards for mining families. In April 1926 the government refused to renew a subsidy to the mining industry. On 2 May Baldwin broke off negotiations with the TUC delegation. Almost by accident, the unions lurched into a general strike. For nine days (3–12 May) Britain was at a virtual standstill. Never before had the potential economic strength of the unions in challenging the government and the constitutional order been shown with more powerful effect. The Church leaders, with their call for conciliation, were impotent in the wings.

In practice, the general strike was peaceful enough. There was no violence directed against the many blacklegs (including many Oxford and Cambridge students who forsook their studies for the purpose) who drove buses and engaged in other strike-breaking activities. There was no violence either from, or directed against, the police or the armed forces. In the end the TUC suddenly called the strike off on 12 May, with industrial areas in Yorkshire, Cumbria, Tyneside, South Wales, and Scotland as solid as ever, and with several groups of key workers (such as power engineers) never called out at all. It was a complete defeat for the unions, and especially for the miners, who remained out on stike for several more bitter months. Britain's class war had been a brief, bloodless skirmish. For middle-class bystanders it had even been painless, and almost great fun.

Still, it is obvious that the divisiveness revealed and reinforced by the general strike was one powerful factor that survived to plague the unity of the nation over the next twenty years or more. In Britain's coalfields, memories of 1926, its triumphs and betrayals, were still a living reality as late as the national miners' strike of 1984–5. The general strike may have been shown to be ineffective in the circumstances of 1926, with the unions half-hearted and the government well prepared and (in the case of such ministers as Winston Churchill, the Chancellor) even belligerent. Nevertheless, 1926—'Year One' in the later recollection of one Welsh miner—did demonstrate the extraordinary loyalty and class solidarity within the working-class communities of Britain, not only in older mining, steel, and shipbuilding areas but also among the newer service workers of a 'semi-skilled' category in road or rail transport and distribution. The class divisions of the country were starkly revealed, even if they did not spill over into physical violence. A deep suspicion also was displayed about the alleged neutrality of the police or the civil service, even perhaps of the newly-formed BBC, which had in fact fought hard to preserve its independence in the face of governmental pressure. In mining districts, the general strike brought a legacy of victimization by mine-owners, swingeing wage cuts, and attempts to undermine the basic role of the Miners Federation as voices of the workers. If demagogic miners' leaders such as Arthur Cook moved on to the sidelines, their successors in the unions and the Labour Party were no more accommodating towards a social system so manifestly distorted in its rewards and opportunities, and which made such a mockery of the supposed social unity of the war years. As Britain continued to limp through the depression years, memories of the general strike endured, and a heritage of class protest along with it.

In the later twenties, the land settled down into a pattern that endured until the 1940s. The population continued to grow, if more slowly; it rose from 40,831,000 in 1911 to 42,769,000 in 1921, and to 44,795,000 by the 1931 Census. But within it there were deep and growing contrasts, as younger writers such as George Orwell were later to emphasize. For much of southern England and the Midlands, the twenties were a time of growing contentment and prosperity. There were many housing developments in the form of suburban middle-class estates, stemming from the abortive Addison housing programme of 1919–21 and later schemes by Neville Chamberlain which gave a direct subsidy to private house-builders. A larger proportion of the population emerged from the war with middle-class aspirations—home ownership; a quiet family environment; more leisure pursuits (there were, for instance, over a million cars in private hands by 1930 of which the most celebrated was the 'Baby' Austin); domestic comforts and mechanical aids such as Hoovers. The power of broadcasting through the BBC brought entertainment and instruction into the privacy of the home. For the junior managers, civil servants, schoolteachers, skilled workers, and others, members of the white-collar administrative and professional groups that had expanded so dramatically between 1880 and 1918, the twenties were not such a bad time, with prices starting to fall, houses more freely available on easy terms, and more leisure interests to pursue. Newer technologically-advanced industries were mushrooming, notably the modern car plants of Herbert Austin at Longbridge and William Morris at Cowley, both in the Midlands. New patterns of suburban residential life flourished around them. For such people, the humdrum, reassuring values symbolized by the nature-loving Prime Minister, Stanley Baldwin, embodying in his own person the message of 'safety first', seemed attractive after all the unwanted excitements of the war and the general strike.

Yet for many other areas, it was a time of growing despair and disillusion. The countryside, for instance, was sunk in depression in the twenties after the brief, heady revival of the war years. The rural population steadily declined, especially in the more mechanized agricultural sector of the wheat-growing areas of southern England. Prices of farm products fell; the level of rural incomes declined; the vitality of small country towns, from the Highlands to Cornwall, became impoverished. British country life preserved its traditional unchanging appearance on the surface; the 'green revolution' vastly enlarged the number of small landowners in the 1918–26 period, the greatest transformation in landholding since the Norman Conquest. But beneath the surface was a pattern of indebtedness, burdens of mortgages and bank loans, and visible decay which saw the gap in the quality of life between town and country growing wider. Since much of British literature took the countryside as its basic point of reference, this could have serious cultural, as well as social, implications.

In the older industrial communities, especially in the north and north-east of England, industrial South Wales, and the

Clydeside belt of mid-Scotland, and in the slums of Belfast across the Irish Sea, it was a time of mounting despair. The inadequacy and squalor of working-class housing and living conditions became increasingly well documented in the twenties, as did the environmental decay that cast a pall over older areas such as Jarrow or Wigan or Merthyr Tydfil. Along with damp, insanitary housing and poor schools and public services went appalling figures of child illness and mortality, tuberculosis for the middle-aged, lung disease for miners, physical deformity for the old. There was a markedly lower life expectancy in the older industrial regions of the north, Wales, and Scotland, contrasted with the county towns and spas of the English south-east and the West Midlands. The social gulf grew ever wider in the twenties, made more severe still by the endless unemployment which afflicted older industries such as steel-making, shipbuilding, and coal-mining, all of them starved of capital investment. The decision to return to the gold standard at the pre-war parity in 1925 was one taken by Churchill as Chancellor, in the face of biting criticism (after the event) from Keynes but with the broad endorsement of most orthodox economists and business men. It meant a serious overvaluing of British coal and steel exports, and a still higher rate of unemployment for the working men producing them. In terms of the quality of educational and medical facilities, of amenities such as libraries, swimming baths, or public parks, the social divisions were ever more apparent in the land over which Baldwin serenely presided. The era of 'safety first', with all its secularization, meant (according to some famous lectures by the socialist economic historian R. H. Tawney, published in 1929) the establishment of a new 'religion of inequality'. Among its features, two-thirds of the aggregate national wealth was owned by 400,000 people (less than one per cent of the population), along with immense disparities in the quality of life throughout British society.

Yet this growing social division occasioned surprisingly little revolt or protest at the time. In part, this was because of the warm solidarity of the working-class world which generated its own values, culture, and entertainment, even during the depression years. The relics of that period—the working-men's clubs and libraries; the vibrant world of the miners' lodge, the choir and brass band; the credit base provided by the 'co-op' in working-class communities—seem remote from the Britain of the 1980s. But they do testify to the strength and optimism of working-class life even in these gloomy years. The anodyne of mass entertainment was also encouraged by the rulers of the people to help promote patriotic loyalty. This 'bread and circuses' tradition dated from the Victorian music-hall. Many of its heroes such as George Robey (who had refused a knighthood) still flourished. But it was an art-form rapidly being outstripped by the new silent and talking pictures: Charlie Chaplin was now the darling of the halls. Beyond the innate resilience and dignity of working-class Britain, there were still qualities that kept the land relatively peaceful and integrated. These may have owed something to the much-maligned governments of the time. Neville Chamberlain's active and creative period as Minister of Health, 1924–9, which effectively saw the end of the old Poor Law, was one notable milestone in this process. The football crowds of the cloth-capped workers and the aspiring life-styles of the new middle class in the suburban housing developments were bound together by some semblance of common values. Familiar symbols could unite them all— perhaps the ever-popular figure of George V, perhaps the passive reassurance offered by Baldwin. The sporting hero of the decade was Jack Hobbs, opening batsman for Surrey and England, who in 1925 overtook the record number of centuries (125) scored by the legendary W. G. Grace. Modest, unprotesting, a devoted church-goer and teetotaller, a model family man, Jack Hobbs was the prototype of the loyal artisan dedicated to Crown and country. He was a professional 'player' content to be led by amateur public-school 'gentlemen' (who entered the Lord's playing arena by a different gate). He always played a straight bat and always accepted the umpire's verdict, however

disappointing or unfair, without complaint. Jack Hobbs's placid, kindly personality provided an acceptable touchstone for a
society struggling to preserve a traditional order in the swirling
tides of the post-war transformation.

The Thirties

The twenties ended in a confused haze of nostalgia and
innovation. The pomp and affluence of 'high society' and court
life were as resplendent as ever. Cigarette cards and magazines
acclaimed the personal appeal of social celebrities such as the
aged tea magnate 'Tommy' Lipton or hostesses such as Lady
Londonderry. Familiar giants still bestrode the land elsewhere.
Elgar survived as Master of the King's Musick until 1934;
Kipling remained actively writing until 1936; Thomas Hardy
died, full of years and honour, in 1928. The mood of 'safety
first' permitted only the most guarded forms of innovation. Its
political figurehead in the later twenties was the Labour leader,
Ramsay MacDonald, called upon to form a second Labour
government in 1929. MacDonald had a background of anti-
war protest in 1914–18, but as a reassuring figure in the general
strike, the hammer of socialist extremists, and intimate of
salons in high society, he seemed to be comfortingly locked
within the aristocratic embrace. A licensed rebel, he was a safe
enough symbol for a society committed to modest, but controlled, change. With Lloyd George now an isolated veteran
and Churchill actively excluding himself from the Tory
mainstream because of his 'die-hard' views on Indian self-
government, MacDonald appeared to be a reliable guide in
taking a few measured steps towards the apocalypse.

In fact, the second Labour government proved to be a disaster. In large part, this was because of forces far removed from
political control. The crash in the American stock exchange in
October 1929, followed by a downward spiral of trade and
employment, was beyond the reach of any government to

correct. For all that, it was all too apparent that the British Labour government had little to offer as a socialist or any other kind of palliative to unemployment that rose with alarming rapidity to reach nearly three million of the insured population at its peak in late 1932. Although unemployment gradually declined later in the thirties, in fact industrial stagnation and social decay continued. Beyond the world-wide forces of over-production and a slump in demand, there were factors peculiar to Britain alone. There was here an industrial structure unduly geared to a declining range of traditional industries, coal, steel, textiles, shipbuilding. There was a history of low investment, overmanning, and inefficient work practices, intensified by a culture that for decades had elevated humane disciplines and gentlemanly virtues in place of business education or entrepreneurial skills. The entire industrial and manufacturing base contracted with extreme violence. There was no sign of recovery visible until 1935. Long before then, the spectacle of hopelessness and despair in mining and other areas, of hunger marches and demonstrations by the unemployed, of the rigours of 'life on the dole' with all the helplessness and hopelessness that were implied had become one to which the great British public had become resigned or immune.

There were those who argued that a new kind of political initiative was required to regenerate and revitalize the nation and its economy, and to propel them in new directions. In the left centre, Lloyd George remained throughout the thirties an ageing, largely disregarded prophet, urging the need for a New Deal on the American model. On the far left, there were a variety of nostrums proposed, from the collectivism of the Socialist League, and later the Left Book Club, to the pure sectarianism of the tiny Communist Party. Sidney and Beatrice Webb claimed to see the future working in Soviet Russia. On the radical right, Sir Oswald Mosley left first the Conservative then the Labour Parties, and tried to create a British variant of Fascism with an admixture of corporate planning and anti-Semitism. Meanwhile the veteran socialist writers, Bernard

Shaw and H. G. Wells, in their different ways promoted the cause of a planned, antiseptic, scientific Utopia. But the most popular solutions were sought within the traditional mix of British politics. By August 1931 it was obvious that Mac-Donald's Labour government was in desperate straits. The climacteric arrived with a massive run on the pound accompanied by the publication of the May report which alleged that high government spending and an unbalanced budget were the root causes of industrial collapse. The government was urged to cut social spending, including the social benefit which was all that the unemployed had in order to subsist at all. The Cabinet was hopelessly divided, buffeted between the bankers and the TUC. On 23 August MacDonald resigned.

The next morning, however, instead of a Conservative–Liberal administration taking his place, it emerged that Mac-Donald was to stay on as Prime Minister of a new 'National' government from which almost all his own Labour Party colleagues would be excluded. At a subsequent general election in October, this government (which had latterly taken Britain off the gold standard and devalued the pound) was returned with a huge majority, with 556 supporters, and the Labour Party reduced to a mere 51, with almost all its leading former ministers defeated at the polls. This 'National Government' was to set the tone for Britain in the thirties. MacDonald, its figurehead, gradually faded from the scene, an increasingly pathetic personality. Baldwin lingered on until 1937. He was still able to summon up immense reserves of political and tactical skill, as when he pushed through a bill to grant more self-government to India in 1935, or in his total outmanœuvring of Edward VIII in 1936 when that uncrowned monarch flouted popular convention by seeking in vain to retain his crown and also to marry a divorced American woman, Mrs Simpson. But the main energy within the government came from a new technocratic style of Conservative, freed from the rural stereotypes of Victorian days. Dominant among them was Neville Chamberlain, heir to a famous Birmingham dynasty,

the outstanding figure in political life in the thirties, at home
and (later) abroad. Chamberlain it was who led a half-recovery
of the economy in the earlier part of the decade, with much
investment in housing and in consumer durables, and new
affluence for advanced industrial zones of the East Midlands
and southern England. Emigration from older regions such as
South Wales, Durham, Cumberland, and Scotland was
balanced by new growth in the suburbs and the centres of light
industry. There was a distinctive managerial regulatory style in
government, Britain's 'middle way' in economic policy. There
were benefits for farmers in the form of milk and other
marketing schemes and production quotas, and advantages for
urban and suburban residents such as improved transportation
(the London 'tube' being a notable example), extended gas and
electricity services, and cheap housing. A century of free trade
was buried at the Ottawa conference in 1932 when a new
commercial system of tariffs and imperial preference, due to
last until the 1970s, was inaugurated. The effect of tariffs upon
the British economy was deeply controversial, but the cartelized
steel industry was one industrial giant that appeared to show
some benefit. The voters were duly grateful. They returned the
National Government—now almost wholly Conservative—with
a comfortable majority in the 1935 general election, and gave
Chamberlainite managerial Conservatism a broad support until
new divisions emerged over foreign policy at the end of the
decade.

The politics of the National Government were based,
unequivocally and unapologetically, on class and regional
division. The older industrial areas were placed under the aegis
of the 'special areas' schemes. In popular parlance, industrial
Scotland, the north-east, Cumbria, much of Yorkshire and
Lancashire, and South Wales were the 'depressed areas', self-
contained societies only visible to the outside world when their
refugees appeared in London and Birmingham to take part in
hunger marches or to beg for coppers from theatre queues.
There was an ironic, self-sustaining pattern about life in

these so-called 'depressed' communities. There, industry was contracting, which meant that their rateable income fell further; this meant that amenities decayed still more, industrial decline was accelerated, and the entire, repetitive cycle became ever more severe. Some of the most powerful literature of the time— George Orwell's somewhat ambiguous saga of *The Road to Wigan Pier*, Walter Greenwood's pathetic account of *Love on the Dole*, Lewis Jones's moving treatment of life in Welsh mining villages in *Cwmardy* and *We Live*—evokes poignantly the consequences of this structural poverty upon the social and cultural sensibilities of the time. But little was done to remedy the causes. There were local philanthropic gestures by the Quakers and other idealists. There was some assistance from the government through the special areas commissions, although virtually nothing was done to diversify or overhaul the industrial base of these areas by a new regional policy. Thomas Jones ironically proposed that they might be turned into open-air archaeological museums, while trains carried off their inhabitants to the delights of employment at Dagenham or Hounslow. There were also novelties such as trading estates which offered inducements to industrialists to group together and move into older industrial areas by offering cheap rates or investment grants. The town of Slough in Buckinghamshire, for instance, became a focus for much industrial activity in the thirties—while its architectural horrors became the target for the unwontedly bitter satire of John Betjeman. But, in general, a combination of the constraints imposed by the Treasury and the Bank of England, and of a lack of urgency by government kept the areas of staple industry effectively without support. Not until the impact of rearmament in the period that followed the 1935 Defence White Paper, with its emphasis on engineering and aircraft production, was there a significant rise in employment.

But the main reason why so little stimulus was provided for the industrial regions crucified by depression was that they were self-contained and limited in extent. The majority of the population in other parts of Britain found that life after the holocaust was acceptable and in many ways agreeable. The thirties were a time of very low inflation, cheap private housing, and of a growing choice for consumers. An average of 345,000 houses was built annually between 1933 and 1937. The motor car industries, electrical, chemical, and textile concerns continued to thrive. In the Midlands, towns like Leicester and Coventry experienced unprecedented growth and affluence. The rewards of life were ever more apparent. Professional footballers for Herbert Chapman's Arsenal, though poorly paid, enjoyed a diet which included steak and champagne. In outer London, the spread of the 'tube', north towards Cockfosters on the edge of Hertfordshire, or west towards Uxbridge on the borders of Buckinghamshire, illustrated the expansion of the service and professional sectors of the white-collar population. In growing suburban communities such as Hendon, Harrow, or Kingsbury, there were smart shopping precincts, many new cinemas and football grounds. The untidy ribbon of semi-detached middle-class housing stretched far along arterial roads and bit deep into the surrounding countryside, relatively unhampered by environmental controls designed to preserve the 'green belts' around cities. The Western Avenue out of London became a byword for uncontrolled industrial and residential development, with a miscellany of factories in debased historicist styles (which a later generation, incongruously enough, often regarded as monuments of modern art). If one explanation for the lack of social change in Britain amidst the unemployment and depression of the thirties lies in the lack of political and economic power vested in the older industrial areas, another lies in the growing commitment to a pleasing and acceptable form of suburban life by larger and larger sections of the population left relatively unscathed by the bleak years.

Britain in the thirties, then, displayed a surprising degree of stability in a European continent which saw totalitarianism engulf Germany, Italy, and Austria, and the French and Spanish republics cast into disarray. The social and cultural hierarchy changed very little. The prestige of Parliament, of the law courts, of a highly stratified educational system headed by Oxford and Cambridge that remained almost totally a public-school preserve, all remained as high as ever. The monarchy retained its esteem by responding subtly to marginal changes in the outlook of the mass democracy: George V's attendance at the annual working-class festival of the Wembley Cup Final was one instance. The king's silver jubilee in 1935 provoked widespread national rejoicing. Even the brief crisis associated with the abdication of Edward VIII left the monarchy as an institution essentially unimpaired. The nation remained comfortably isolated from a strife-torn Continent, inhabited by far-away peoples of whom the British knew little.

In the arts, the thirties were in many ways a remarkably flourishing and creative period. In poetry, the most important figure remained T. S. Eliot, a conservative Anglo-Catholic of American birth, whose 'Four Quartets' appeared from 1930 onwards. Eliot, in fact, increasingly found the drama a more congenial art form, starting with *Murder in the Cathedral* (1935), a powerful commentary on the martyrdom of Thomas Becket. The most influential writers of the period, however, reacted strongly against what appeared to them to be the withdrawal and detachment of the Bloomsbury ethos in the twenties. In the maelstrom of the time, younger poets such as W. H. Auden, Stephen Spender, Cecil Day Lewis, and Louis MacNeice reflected the political excitements of the time. Auden's celebrated poem 'Spain' (1937), inspired by his brief period of service in the Civil War, epitomized the current literary mood. It is significant that all these young poets flirted with a kind of neo-Marxism, if they did not actually become Communists. Conversely, two of the abler young novelists of the time, Evelyn Waugh and Graham Greene, were converts to Roman Catholicism, albeit with very different political and other outlooks. British music was less volatile, though the romantic strains of Holst and Delius had to contend with the experimental endeavours, atonal, even unstructural, of the followers of Stravinsky and Schoenberg. Vaughan Williams, a contemporary enough figure in his diatonic compositional techniques, yet deeply English in his reliance on traditional airs and themes, demonstrated how modernity could be safely reconciled with the native musical tradition. In the visual arts, the thirties was a period of great excitement and innovation, both in sculpture and in painting. A new vitality for British sculpture was heralded by the work of Henry Moore, son of a Yorkshire miner, and the disciple of Epstein; another pioneer was Barbara Hepworth, the wife of the painter Ben Nicholson. British painting was also unusually vigorous at this period, ranging from the rustic Christian symbolism of Stanley Spencer to Paul Nash's successful engagements with French surrealism. Britain was generally a better country to look at in the thirties, with a much-needed innovation in architecture and design, without precedent since the heyday of Norman Shaw, Voysey, and Mackintosh before 1914. From dramatic set-piece public buildings which manifested the influence of Gropius and the German Bauhaus, through industrial factories and cinemas with *art nouveau* or art deco overtones, down to mundane but important landmarks such as Pick and Holden's attractive new underground railway stations for London Transport, British architecture offered many departures and a real sense of liberation. At a more accessible level, the new life shown by the Royal Academy and by such accepted popular arts festivals as Sir Henry Wood's London 'proms' suggested some qualified cultural advance, if hardly a cultural revolution.

In a variety of ways, then, Britain in the thirties showed distinct signs, outside the older industrial areas, of being a land at peace with itself, and enlivened by some cultural imagination. But the mood began to change abruptly in 1937, not through any immediate domestic disunity or reappraisal, but through the external impact of foreign affairs. Much of Britain's internal harmony in the twenties and thirties had been founded on a quiescent foreign policy. The mood dictated by

Keynes in 1919, the mood that had dislodged Lloyd George in 1922, had permeated the whole society. Right-wing reluctance to engage in overseas military adventures was countered by a profound belief on the left that the 1919 peace settlement was in any case vindictive and morally indefensible, the product of national and imperial rivalries rather than of a yearning for a more harmonious world. In the twenties, Britain's defences were gradually run down, with little public protest, based on the 'ten year' premiss that no major war would be fought within the next decade. The battle fleet was especially cut back in this period, most enthusiastically by Churchill himself while at the Treasury. The giant new naval base at Singapore, recently completed, already seemed an anachronism. The main military commitment was to the Raj in India, but a gradual, partial accommodation with Gandhi and the Congress movement enabled the British garrison in the subcontinent to be reduced slowly from 57,000 in 1925 to 51,000 in 1938. Equally, the increasingly harmonious relations with the Irish Free State, culminating in the 'agreements' of 1936 and the virtual wiping out of all debts owed to Britain by Ireland minimized another potential source of military or naval difficulty. The public mood in the early thirties remained a passive one, even after the advent of Hitler in Germany in January 1933. The British labour movement was pacifist-inclined, with a few exceptions such as Ernest Bevin of the Transport Workers. It opposed voting arms estimates on behalf of a right-wing National government. On the socialist left, there were advocates of a Popular Front such as Sir Stafford Cripps who urged the need for an alliance with the Soviet Union and argued that socialism alone was the true remedy for international discord. Conversely, most Conservatives had no wish for an adventurous foreign policy, especially since Baldwin had assured the people that there was no real defence possible in a future war which would be determined largely by air power. The bomber would always get through. There was scant Conservative enthusiasm for upholding the authority of the League of Nations in crises in Manchuria in 1931 or Abyssinia in 1935. There were those on the right, notably some press lords, who declared that there was common ground between Great Britain and Hitler's Germany, bound together by Teutonic racial origins and anti-Communism. A miscellaneous group of politicians and journalists found a haven in Lord and Lady Astor's mansion at Cliveden, by the Thames, near Marlow. It was widely believed to be turning the mind of the Foreign Office in these fellow-travelling directions.

When the opportunity for action came, public opinion was resistant. Hitler marched into the Rhineland in early 1936, in direct contravention of the Versailles settlement. But only a few voices, like the isolated and unpopular Winston Churchill, called for a military response from Great Britain. Earlier, the British public had generally endorsed, though with much embarrassment, the appeasement policy of the Foreign Office following the Italian invasion of Abyssinia. In effect, the Italians were allowed to occupy this ancient empire in the Horn of Africa with the minimum of British involvement, economic or military. Formal commitments were made to the League and to the spirit of collective security, but they added up to little enough. Sir Samuel Hoare, the Foreign Secretary, was offered up as a public sacrifice during the Abyssinian crisis, but it was clear that the appeasement of Mussolini's Italy was a collective government decision. Cabinet records now available confirm the point. In any event, Hoare re-entered the government a few months later with little controversy. Again, in Spain where a left-wing, democratically-elected Republican government was subjected to invasion by a right-wing Nationalist force led by General Franco, with later armed assistance from Italy and Germany, the British government adhered rigidly to 'non-intervention', even if this meant the eventual downfall of democracy in Spain. The advent of the powerful figure of Neville Chamberlain in October 1937, a confident man committed to an active, positive pursuit of a working accommodation with the Fascist dictators, as opposed to Baldwin's passive style of appeasement, confirmed a growing mood of non-involvement in Europe. Key figures in the civil service such as Sir Horace Wilson and Sir Nevile Henderson (ambassador to Berlin) pushed this policy forward.

At various levels, however, the public mood suddenly began to change. Even the government began to turn its mind to the need to overhaul the national defences, especially in the air. From 1935 onwards, a new fighter-based air force was in the making, backed up by the latest technology invested in 'radar' and other anti-aircraft and defence systems. Through men like Tizard and his rival Lindemann, the voice of scientific innovation was again sporadically heard in the corridors of power. By 1937 the rearmament programme was visibly under way, despite pressure from the Treasury which voiced concern at the effect on the balance of payments. Privately, it is now known that a wider range of financial relationships was entered into with the United States which alone could underwrite the arms programme capable of being launched by a Britain still in economic difficulties. More widely, the public psychology was deeply stirred by events in the Spanish Civil War. Not only poets such as Auden or prose writers like George Orwell, but many scores of British working-class volunteers who fought with the International Brigade were being propelled towards a new commitment to internationalism. Jewish refugees from Germany brought the reality of Hitler's regime and of anti-Semitism home to British opinion. Even on the Labour left, trade union leaders such as Bevin and Citrine turned vigorously against neo-pacifist Labour politicians who denied armed assistance to trade union and labour groups crushed in Fascist Germany and Austria. Chamberlain's equilibrism was harder to sustain, especially for a Prime Minister so lacking in the skills of flexibility.

The German advance in 1938, the seizure of Austria and the subsequent threat to Czechoslovakia, ostensibly on behalf of the Sudeten Germans in the western fringe of Bohemia, produced a national crisis of conscience. Chamberlain responded

with managerial decisiveness. At Berchtesgaden, Bad Godes-
berg, and finally at Munich in September 1938, he came to
terms with Hitler. In effect, he allowed the Germans to annex
Sudetenland on the basis of any timetable they chose, without
British or French armed retaliation. For a brief moment, it
seemed that this policy of surrender had mirrored the public's
response. Chamberlain returned in triumph, announcing, in
an ominous phrase, that it was to be peace in our time.
But this abdication of responsibility could no longer
adequately be justified. Those who have claimed that Chamberlain was seeking a breathing-space, in order for Britain to
challenge Germany more effectively in military terms later on,
do not find support from the records of Cabinet deliberations.
The criticisms of Churchill and his associates, and even of
Anthony Eden who had recently resigned from the Foreign
Office in protest at Chamberlain's conduct of foreign affairs,
now accorded far more precisely with popular sentiment. By
the end of 1938, as it became clear that Munich had really
meant the sacrifice of Czechoslovak democracy to armed
aggression, nation-wide anger was overwhelming. Chamberlain, so impregnable a figure a few months earlier, the most
powerful Prime Minister since Lloyd George in 1916, suddenly
looked like a man on the run. Rearmament was stepped up and
new negotiations begun with the engineering trade unions to
try to build up munitions and aircraft production. When Hitler
finally invaded Prague in March 1939, public anger exploded.
Chamberlain was forced by outside pressure to enter into a
military commitment to defend Poland, a land in Eastern
Europe far away from British shores, with no guarantee that
the Soviet Union would assist in protection of Poland's eastern
frontiers. A century of almost unbroken British non-
involvement in continental Europe, dating from the winding up
of the Peninsular War in 1812, was abruptly reversed. The
government was stampeded by a horrified public opinion.
There was even a formal attempt to conclude an alliance with
the Soviet Union, although things went so slowly that in the

end Russia formed a pact with Germany instead in August. During the summer, there was evident a new mood of determination to resist German aggression with the full combined resources of the nation and the empire. On 1 September 1939 Hitler took the fateful step of invading Poland. After a few desperate attempts to patch up a last-minute compromise, Chamberlain announced in a broadcast on 3 September that Britain had declared war on Germany. There was scarcely any dissent, even from the tiny Communist Party, many of whose leading figures opposed the official Moscow line and took up the anti-Fascist cause. In the House of Commons, it was a Labour member, Arthur Greenwood, who 'spoke for England', and, as events showed, for virtually all of Wales, Scotland, Northern Ireland, and the dominions as well.

In the later stages of the appeasement controversy, the climate of public debate became unprecedentedly bitter. The complacency of the early thirties was set aside. There was the continuing hostility between the National government and the Labour Party over the unending tragedy of unemployment, and the scandals of the 'dole' and the operation of the 'means test'. Added to this was a powerful rift on the right between the 'men of Munich', Chamberlain, Simon, Hoare, and their followers, and the nationalist critics headed by Churchill who denounced the policy of craven appeasement as dishonourable. Episodes such as the distant impact of events in Czechoslovakia brought left- and right-wing protest together, as Spain or Abyssinia could never have done. Domestic and international conflicts merged into one passionate, turbulent whole. Chamberlain, the architect of much of the prosperity of the thirties, the titan of the suburban middle class, the dominant leader of the decade, suddenly became the hated symbol of a fraudulent, decadent political order. He became foremost among the 'guilty men' so brilliantly denounced by two young radical journalists, Michael Foot and Frank Owen, in a fierce polemic in 1940, perhaps the greatest feat of political pamphleteering since the days of Wilkes.

Any society ruled by Neville Chamberlain at such a time

should have found it hard to unite behind a common cause. Yet, as in August 1914, Britain did so. Indeed, when war broke out in 1939 there was a unanimity that pervaded all regions and classes. As in 1914, the war was represented publicly as a crusade on behalf of oppressed nationalities and persecuted races—which, indeed, it largely was, and far more plausibly so than in 1914. Middle and working class, capitalist and worker, socialist and conservative entered the war for different motives, or perhaps for different priorities along the political spectrum. But broad imperatives survived to create a new consensus. As twenty years earlier, Britain regained its sense of unity and national purpose amidst the challenge and turmoil of total war.

The Second World War

The public mood after the outbreak of the Second World War was notably less passionate or strident than after August 1914. Neither the militarism nor the pacifism of that earlier conflict was echoed now. In large measure, this was because of the curious features of the early months of the war. During the so-called 'phoney war' period down to April 1940, the fighting seemed remote, almost academic. It is a curious, twilight phase well portrayed in Evelyn Waugh's novel, *Put Out More Flags*. There were massive air-raid precautions, trenches in public parks, barrage balloons aloft, anti-aircraft weaponry deployed on public buildings. Thirty-eight million gas masks were distributed to men, women, and children; hundreds of thousands of schoolchildren were evacuated from major cities to distant, and presumably safer, rural areas (though many later drifted back home). Rationing of food, clothing, petrol, and other commodities suddenly became commonplace. The war itself was uneventful, with traditional pleasures such as the long-range enjoyment of a British naval victory, when the German battleship *Graf Spee* was fatally cornered by three smaller British vessels in the estuary of the River Plate off Montevideo harbour in late 1939. The uncertainty of the public

mood was mirrored by the ambiguous nature of the government. Although the Cabinet had been reconstructed, to include
Churchill himself, back at the Admiralty as in 1914, it was still
the regime of the old gang, the National government of 1931
writ large. The trade unions in particular looked with deep
suspicion at an administration still headed by their old
adversary and class enemy, Chamberlain. Then in April 1940
the cold war hotted up. The Germans invaded Norway,
scattering before them the British naval and military forces at
Narvik. Soon afterwards, the Netherlands and Belgium were
overrun, and the French army broke up in disorderly retreat.
The security of the British Isles themselves was now under clear
and pressing threat.

The old regime of the thirties could survive no longer. In
a fateful division in the Commons on 7–8 May 1940, eighty
Conservatives rebelled against the leadership of Chamberlain.
Two days later he resigned, and Winston Churchill now emerged as wartime Prime Minister, with Labour and Liberals both
joining the government. The change of premier was generally
free of the apparent conspiratorial intrigue of December 1916.
Indeed, Churchill had a vastly broader base of support in press
and Parliament, and distinctly more loyalty from the military,
naval, and air high command than Lloyd George had ever
experienced. Churchill embodied a traditional sense of patriotic
unity as no one else amongst his contemporaries could ever do.
War gave his career a new impetus and relevance. His inspiring
oratory over the radio and in the Commons conjured up new
reserves of national will-power in this 'finest hour' for his
country. He was able to exploit a humiliating military disaster
in the retreat from Dunkirk as a kind of triumph for British
ingenuity and determination. With France surrendering to the
German forces by mid-June, British territorial security was
threatened as never before since the days of Napoleon I in 1804.

The extent to which Britain was prepared to defend itself in
military and naval terms is debatable. On the home front, apart
from mobilized reserves, the 'home guard' of civilians was later

to be effectively parodied as a 'dad's army' of amateurs muddling through with good humour. Its military effectiveness was, perhaps fortunately, never put to the test. But the real battle lay in the air, where the reserves of Spitfire and Hurricane fighter aircraft were rapidly built up by the press lord, Beaverbrook, now the Minister of Aircraft Production. From mid-August onwards, the German *Luftwaffe* launched wave after wave of blitz attacks, first on British airfields and aircraft factories, later on London, Coventry, Plymouth, Liverpool, Hull, Swansea, and other ports and major cities. Almost miraculously, civilian morale and national defences stood firm against this terrifying bombardment. In the air, the 'few', the legendary pilots of the Spitfires and Hurricanes, took heavy toll of the *Luftwaffe* in August–October. By Christmas, the threat of imminent invasion had effectively passed, though the 'blitz' on London and elsewhere continued. Churchill's personal reputation soared; the united spirit of his people grew with it. Dunkirk and the Battle of Britain in the air launched a thousand myths. They helped to encourage a latent isolationism and an unjustified feeling of national self-sufficiency, which led to a coolness towards Western European unity after the war. The British were aware that they alone of the belligerent Western democracies had escaped enemy occupation, as they had done consistently since 1066. For all that, the rhetoric of the 'finest hour' of 1940 captured the pride and the passion of what was felt to be a supreme moment of historic achievement.

The later course of the war on land, and more especially on sea and in the air, had a major long-term effect on the international and imperial status of Great Britain. It had begun by being a traditional European conflict to preserve national security and the balance of power in the West, to keep control of the Channel by extensive deployment of the British navy in the North Sea and in the northern Atlantic, along the western approaches. In effect, this aspect of the war reached a successful outcome by the summer of 1941, with the frustration of German threats to invade Britain (about which Hitler was always in any case hesitant) and the beating off of the *Luftwaffe* attacks. With the operations of the British merchant navy and (from early 1941) American lease-lend ensuring tolerable supplies of food and raw materials for the rest of the war, there was no imminent danger to the British Isles themselves, even though sinkings by German U-boats continued apace. Churchill kept a close eye on the ports of neutralist Eire and its anti-British premier, de Valera. The further hazards of guided missile attack by V1 and V2 machines, launched from bases in Holland in the summer and autumn of 1944, while deeply alarming and the source of much damage to life and property in south-east England, did not seriously imperil the security of nation either.

However, from late 1940, the war soon demonstrated wider, imperial themes. From being initially a conflict to preserve Western and Central Europe from the aggressive menace of German Fascism, the war rapidly turned into a broader effort to sustain the Commonwealth and empire as they had endured over the decades. The white dominions—Australia, New Zealand, Canada, and, far more hesitantly, South Africa—lent immediate support in terms of raw materials and armed naval and other assistance. In addition, the credits run up with India and Egypt in particular, the so-called 'sterling balances' which gave much trouble after the war, were vital in assisting with British payments for supplies, and in partially redressing the loss of overseas assets and the fall in 'invisible' income. The entry of the Soviet Union into the war in June 1941, and even more that of the United States in December 1941, following the Japanese assault on the US fleet at Pearl Harbor, ensured that the war would remain a worldwide one, fought in every continent and every ocean, and that the cosmic structure of the British Empire would come under acute threat.

Much British military, naval, and air-force effort was put into preserving the traditional lines of communication in the Middle East, centred on the Suez Canal, and the bases of the Persian Gulf and its hinterland, with their huge oil reserves.

British forces fought with much success to put pressure on the Italians in Abyssinia and Somaliland, after Italy entered the war in August 1940. Even more endeavour went into preserving Egypt and the north African littoral. In 1941 the British forces under Wavell captured the whole of Cyrenaica and advanced towards Tripoli, but were later forced to retreat back towards Egypt. The fall of Tobruk in early 1942 led to a major political crisis at home, in which Churchill's own position appeared under threat. The most important military engagement of later 1942 concerned the struggles of the British Eighth Army, under first Auchinleck then Montgomery, to resist a German advance towards Cairo and Suez. However, the final breakthrough by Montgomery at El Alamein in November 1942 resulted in a successful and sustained British drive across modern Libya, through Tripoli, and into Tunisia. Here, Montgomery linked up with the American armies under Bradley which had moved eastwards from the initial landing near Algiers. Subsequent allied campaigns, including the capture of Sicily and a prolonged drive through Italy, from the Anzio beach-head to the Alps, again had a strong concern with the imperial lines of strategic communication, and with control of the eastern Mediterranean. Those who argued that a second front should be launched in France in 1943, to relieve pressure on the Red Army in Russia, viewed this concentration in the Mediterranean with much frustration and anger. However, Churchill's Mediterranean commitment prevailed. In 1944, British forces again landed in Greece both to drive out the Germans and to beat down a native left-wing movement, ELAS.

In the Far East also, the war involved desperate efforts to shore up the empire at its base. The invasion of the Japanese through China into Indo-China and the Dutch East Indies, including the capture of all the American bases in the Philippines, led Churchill to place the Far East, with the approaches to the Indian subcontinent, even higher than the Middle East in the military priorities. There were dreadful losses. The most fateful of all involved the sinking of the battleships *Prince of Wales* and *Repulse* by Japanese bombs and torpedoes on 10 December 1941. There followed a rapid Japanese advance through Malaya and on 15 February 1942 the surrender of over 80,000 British and empire troops in Singapore. This disaster, the result of grave miscalculations by the commanding officer, General Percival, and by Churchill himself (who under-estimated Japanese fighting power), was described by the Prime Minister in the House as 'the worst capitulation in British history'. It was a landmark in the fall of empire. Henceforth, for instance, Australia and New Zealand were to look to the USA for protection in the Pacific rather than to the imperial mother country. However, the disasters went no further. Japanese advances into Burma were held off, with such forces as Orde Wingate's 'Chindits' gaining immense acclaim. British rule in India, threatened by disaffection by the Congress movement within the subcontinent as well as by Japanese assault from Burma, was sustained. By late 1944, the British position in eastern Asia and the Pacific, even with the loss of Malaya, Singapore, and Hong Kong, was still a powerful one, even if dependent on American land and naval assistance.

At last in June 1944, with the final invasion of France from the Normandy beach-heads by Allied forces under the com-mand of Eisenhower and Montgomery, the war again assumed a European aspect. British military tactics in this last phase have led to some controversy amongst military historians, especially the delays in pushing through northern France and the Low Countries. The airborne landing at Arnhem was a débâcle. Even so, in the end it was a rapid and triumphant campaign. It was General Montgomery who formally received the unconditional surrender of the German forces at Lüneburg Heath on 9 May 1945. Hitler himself had committed suicide a few days earlier. Japan also surrendered on 15 August after two atomic bombs had wrought huge devastation at Hiroshima and Nagasaki, killing over 110,000 people.

Throughout, the war etched deep into the national psy-chology, without raising either the doubts or the euphoric jingoism of the Great War of 1914–18. The most satisfying fact of all was that casualties were so much lighter in the six years of the Second World War than in the four years of slogging trench warfare in 1914–18. This time a total of 270,000 servicemen were lost in six years, as well as over 60,000 civilians killed on the home front in German air raids. The campaigns had been more peripheral, more episodic, and in the end far more effectively conducted on a technical basis. Even veterans of the peace movement such as the philosopher Bertrand Russell felt that here was almost a good war. At the same time, all the vital questions surrounding Britain's external role remained unanswered. In the Middle and Far East, supreme strains had been put on the imperial system, even if Britain assumed control again of territories such as Hong Kong, Sarawak, Malaya, and Singapore in Asia, and British Somaliland in Africa. The Americans were concerned, at war-time conferences and at the Potsdam peace conference of July–August 1945, to speed up the process of decolonization. Churchill was led to observe anxiously that he had not become the king's minister, or fought a bloody war for six years, in order to achieve the dissolution of the British Empire. But already his outlook was being overtaken by events.

On the home front, the impact of total war was scarcely less momentous. As in the earlier war, there was a vast upheaval in the pattern and structure of the population, and a new juggernaut of centralization and state control to regulate social and economic life. Unlike 1914–18, however, the apparatus this time seemed to operate with far more justice—and more likelihood of the momentum being continued into the post-war world. The war clearly expressed a profound spirit of egalitarianism, of a type previously unknown in British history at any period. George Orwell felt that a social revolution was taking place. The ration books, gas masks, identity cards, and other wartime controls afflicted the people equally and implied a mood of 'fair shares'. So did the communal sufferings during the blitz. A notable impact was achieved by the 'evacuees', the

school-children removed from London, Birmingham, Liverpool, and other cities to take refuge in rural communities in
England and Wales. For the first time, large sections of the
nation got to know each other. The medical and food provision
for the evacuated children of the urban slums meant a great
improvement in their physical and mental well-being. For their
parents, war miraculously meant that full employment was
restored, after the terrible decay of the thirties. Egalitarianism
also encouraged a new faith in social planning, even if the links
between shop floor and pit-head and the drawing-board
deliberations of London-based bureaucrats were not necessarily
obvious or automatic. The result, however, was that, in the
wartime mood of unity and equality of sacrifice, novel
questions began to be asked about public policy. A profound
conviction arose, equally amongst the armed forces, that this
time the 'land fit for heroes' would not be so wantonly set aside
as it was widely felt to have been in the years after 1918. This
mood was captured with much precision by the wartime
illustrated magazine, *Picture Post*, edited by Tom Hopkinson,
by the newspaper the *Daily Mirror*, and by the popular radio
talks of the Yorkshire author J. B. Priestley, whose Cobbett-like
style of native radicalism achieved widespread appeal.

The most celebrated document of this mood was the
Beveridge report of November 1942. The work of an austere
academic economist, it outlined an exciting scheme of comprehensive social security, financed from central taxation,
including maternity benefits and child allowances, universal
health and unemployment insurance, old age pension and death
benefits. It was, in the phrase of the time, provision 'from the
cradle to the grave'. An ecstatic public response gave the
uncharismatic Beveridge a new celebrity as another 'People's
William'; it ensured that social policy would remain high on
the public agenda after the war, along with other priorities such
as a free national health service. The Barlow report (actually
issued in 1940) visualized a complete overhaul of the stagnant
'depressed areas'. Subsequently the 1945 Distribution of

Industry Act began a long-overdue process of reversing the economic decline of areas such as north-east England and South Wales by diversifying and modernizing their economic infrastructure. The Uthwatt report of 1942 outlined a new dynamic approach to town planning with 'green belt' provision around major conurbations, new controls over land use, and 'new towns' to cater for the overspill of older cities. Underlying all these wartime blueprints was a commitment to full employment, spelt out in the 1943 budget and a government White Paper of 1944. The tragedy of stagnation and economic and human waste that had crucified many communities in the thirties would not be repeated. Spokesmen for the unemployed marchers then, people like 'Red Ellen' Wilkinson, MP for Jarrow and leader of the 1936 Hunger March, were now active in government. Underpinning this vogue for social innovation was the transformation of fiscal policy, with a commitment to counter-cyclical policies, a manpower budget, and the management of demand. These were taken up even by such traditionalist wartime Chancellors as Kingsley Wood and Sir John Anderson. Keynes himself served at the Treasury and greatly influenced the powerful Economic Section of the Cabinet. The leading critic of the post-war settlement of 1919, he was now a key figure, not only in domestic budgetary policies, but also in external financial arrangements including the attempt to rationalize international trade and currency through the Bretton Woods agreement. The most radical nostrums were now proposed in the most staid of circles: nationalization of major industries and the Bank of England; a levy on inherited capital; a salaried state-directed medical profession. They all provoked growing arguments between Conservative and Labour Cabinet ministers, with angry sniping from the back-benches by freebooters such as Emanuel Shinwell, a forthright Glasgow Jew, and Aneurin Bevan, a brilliant Welsh ex-miner. But such a flowering of social and intellectual debate, far more precisely conceived and of far wider appeal than the 'reconstruction' discussions of 1917–18, under the aegis of such a traditional wartime leader as Churchill, was indeed a sign of a new climate.

In culture and the arts, the war gave some new life to old values. Literature, significantly enough, was not stimulated to anything like the same degree as in 1914–18; there was nothing remotely resembling the generation of 'war poets' of that earlier period. Some encouragement was given to war artists, officially sponsored to depict experiences in the blitz and elsewhere: Henry Moore, John Piper, and Graham Sutherland are three notable examples. Interestingly, music was one art form given a powerful stimulus, especially through the patronage of the wartime creation of CEMA (Council for the Encouragement of Music and the Arts). Lunchtime piano concerts in London during the blitz by Dame Myra Hess suggested a new popular enthusiasm for music. The composers' response came in powerful creations by Michael Tippett (a pacifist who produced a moving and humane work, *A Child of Our Time*) and the work of Benjamin Britten. The latter's *Peter Grimes*, first performed in June 1945, gave a remarkable new vitality to English opera, still largely derived from the light concoctions of Gilbert and Sullivan fifty years earlier. During the war also, the cinema became more recognizable as an innovative art form. Films such as *In Which we Serve* and *Brief Encounter* drew effectively upon wartime themes—separation, loss, sacrifice—to imbue a commercially-inclined industry with some creative realism. Of all the media for cultural communication, however, it was BBC radio which loomed largest in the public mind. Comedians like Tommy Handley, popular singers like Vera Lynn, war reporters like Richard Dimbleby and Wynford Vaughan Thomas, became the great mass entertainers and communicators of their time. In a world convulsed by unfamiliar social and intellectual ideas, the BBC remained a basically conservative, reassuring institution, committed to God, the king, and the family, to the continuities of life and the permanence of the national heritage. In the holocaust of six years of war, that appeared to be what the mass populace required and demanded.

It was, in any case, an increasingly aware and educated populace. British education had not undergone any major overhaul since 1918; its expansion had been cruelly cut back by the Geddes economies of 1922. Large sections of the working-class community had virtually no secondary schooling at all, while the proportion attending university or other higher education down to 1939 was extraordinarily small by international standards, and almost entirely of wealthy or middle-class background, save only in Wales. Hence the Butler Education Act of 1944, another social landmark of the war years, laid the framework of a new comprehensive secondary system for all, divided like Gaul into three parts, secondary modern, grammar, and technical. At the same time by giving new life to the grammar schools, and outlining a vast future investment in school building and equipment, it helped ensure a far greater degree of literacy and of social and occupational mobility. In the post-war world, the age of the grammar-bred boy and girl would surely dawn, whatever doubts surrounded the standards of the 'modern' schools which the unsuccessful majority would attend.

The First World War had produced an official commitment to the restitution of traditional values and ideas, whatever the mass popular enthusiasm for social change, or even revolution, both in working-class circles and intellectual coteries. The Second World War saw far less division between aspiration and reality. Indeed, the congruence between a public commitment to change and a private administrative recognition that pre-war society was dangerously unjust and divisive was the most important legacy of the Second World War for the British people. One major aspect of this was that the trade unions were now very far from being the outsiders that they had been after 1918. The most powerful union leader of the day, Ernest Bevin of the Transport and General Workers, was the dominant government minister on the home front, after Churchill appointed him Minister of Labour in May 1940. Under his aegis, the unions worked with government in regulating working practices, in improving industrial conditions, and in the strategy of economic planning with an intimacy never before achieved. Walter Citrine, secretary of the TUC, became virtually an ancillary member of the government. There were indeed strikes during the war, notably among miners in Kent in 1942 and among boy apprentices on the Clyde in 1941 and in South Wales in 1942–3. But they were relatively minor events contrasted with the wider consensus that was emerging. By the end of the war in 1945, the TUC had drafted a revised list of public priorities, including the nationalization of major industries and public services, the maintenance of full employment, a welfare state on the lines of the Beveridge report, and a more egalitarian financial policy based on the wartime ethos of 'fair shares'.

At all levels this feeling chimed in with a noticeable mood of political radicalism. Indeed, in the years 1940–5, Britain may be said to have moved more rapidly to the left than at any other period of its history. In government, Labour ministers of the Churchill administration loomed large on the home front. Ernest Bevin; Clement Attlee, the deputy Prime Minister; Herbert Morrison, the Home Secretary; Greenwood, Dalton, and others became familiar and trusted figures. They were talismans of the faith that post-war reconstruction would indeed be carried into effect. So, too, were reformist Conservative ministers such as R. A. Butler, author of the Education Act. Their outlook harmonized with the new orthodoxies of the planners, many of them Liberal theoreticians such as Keynes or Beveridge, or simply apolitical technocrats. Beyond the confines of Westminster and Whitehall, it was clear that the public was becoming more radical—at least, it should have been clear, since this was documented in Gallup polls in the newspapers, though little attention was paid by contemporaries to these unfamiliar forms of sociological evidence, of transatlantic origin. In by-elections, there were several successes for the vaguely Christian socialist Common Wealth Party. There was the widespread public enthusiasm for the Red Army, newly popular after Stalingrad and the advance towards Berlin. Even in the armed forces, so it was murmured, left-wing or novel ideas were being bandied about in current affairs groups and discussion circles. Letters home from servicemen in the western desert or the Far East voiced the angry determination for a better deal in the post-war world.

Reconstruction, then, was a far more coherent and deep-rooted concept as the war came to its close. In 1918, many of the blueprints had been poorly-conceived and destined for rapid oblivion at the hands of the Treasury. This time it had been more plausibly a people's war. The ideas were more precise and had both more democratic impetus and more intellectual ballast behind them. The outcome was revealed with dramatic effect as soon as the war ended. The Churchill coalition broke up with unexpected suddenness in May 1945, a few days after the German surrender and with hostilities still continuing in the Far East against the Japanese. To Churchill's dismay, the Labour Party's national executive, voicing the wishes of the rank and file, insisted that Labour's ministers leave the government. A general election was called for July. The 'coupon election' of 1918 had been an unreal exercise throughout. Even if not polluted by the hysterical 'hang-the-Kaiser' jingoism to the extent that Keynes had suggested, that element was undoubtedly present. A general patriotic exaltation made the campaign of November–December 1918 a poor guide to the public mood. In June–July 1945, however, the spirit was more sober and focused more precisely on housing and health, full employment, and industrial regeneration, on post-war social imperatives rather than on external or imperial themes. In this sense, the power and prestige of Winston Churchill, the revered war leader, were an irrelevance, even an embarrassment to the Conservative Party. The result, to the general astonishment, was a political landslide without precedent since 1906. Labour made 203 gains and won, in all, 394 seats to the Conservatives' 210. Clement Attlee, the prosaic, reticent leader of the Labour Party, found himself propelled into 10 Downing Street, at the head of a government elected with a massive majority. Alongside were such experienced figures as Ernest Bevin as Foreign Secretary, Herbert Morrison as deputy Prime Minister, Hugh Dalton at the Treasury, and Sir Stafford Cripps at the Board of Trade. It was a striking comment on the changed atmosphere of the war years, and no doubt a delayed verdict on the bitterness of the thirties, with its memories of Munich and Spain, Jarrow and the hunger marches. For a rare moment in its history, Britain appeared to present a spectacle of discontinuity and disjunction. It left ministers and the mass electorate at the same time exhilarated and bewildered. As James Griffiths, one new Labour minister, exclaimed in genuine bewilderment at the deluge, 'After this—what?'

The Post-War World

In fact, one phase of continuity was to be followed by another. The Labour government of 1945–51, while productive of much domestic partisanship and occasional bitterness during its six years of office, launched a new kind of consensus, a social democracy based on a mixed economy and a welfare state which took Britain well enough through the difficult post-war transformations and endured in its essence for another generation or more. Not until the very different political and economic climate of the later 1970s did the Attlee-based consensus which emerged from the post-war period come to be challenged. Until then, the balance between innovation and stability that the post-1945 regime introduced seemed to conform to the general will.

At one level, the Attlee government certainly brought about a remarkable programme of sustained reformist activity. Major industries and institutions were brought into public ownership—coal, railways, road transport, civil aviation, gas, electricity, cable and wireless, even the Bank of England. In all, 20 per cent of the nation's industry was taken into the 'public sector'. Remote groups of corporate private capitalists were replaced by remote boards of corporate public bureaucrats. Not until the nationalization of iron and steel in 1948–9 brought differences within the government to the surface did the main premisses of public ownership, as spelt out in the 1945 Labour manifesto, come to be challenged. There was also the great extension of publicly-financed social welfare, popularly dubbed 'the welfare state'. The most spectacular and controversial feature of this was the National Health Service introduced by Aneurin Bevan in 1946, and coming into effect in July 1948. The Health Service generated much debate at the time, and much resistance by the doctors who viewed with alarm attempts to implement a salaried system to make them state employees, and to abolish the sale of private practices. However, the public consensus after the war was sufficiently powerful to force the bill through, and to enable free medical attention for all citizens to come into effect. Other notable measures included the national insurance system introduced in 1946, very much on the lines of Beveridge's wartime proposals; a new drive for state-subsidized 'council' houses which yielded well over a million new and temporary dwellings up to 1952; increased old age pensions; a raising of the school-leaving age; and child allowances. These measures were by no means greeted with such unanimous acclaim at the time as is sometimes alleged. The government made many concessions to its critics. Bevan himself had to allow the retention of private practice by the medical profession, and 'pay beds' within the nationalized hospitals, a typically British compromise. In secondary education, the public schools flourished side by side with the state grammar schools. Indeed, the years of socialist rule after 1945 saw Eton and other privately-endowed educational institutions never more thriving, with their charitable status protected by the Inland Revenue. Public housing schemes were whittled down by pressures to encourage homes for sale and the principle of a 'property-owning democracy'. With all its limitations, however, the welfare state gained a broad measure of support, and was accepted as a vital attribute of the balanced, compassionate society over the next twenty years. Despite a ministerial fracas in April 1951, which led to the resignation of Aneurin Bevan and two other ministers over charges on dentures and spectacles, the underlying principles of a publicly-supported, comprehensive welfare state survived largely unscathed. So, too, did the commitment to full employment and new regional policies that gave renewed life to once derelict areas such as the Welsh valleys, Durham, Cumberland, and the central industrial belt of Scotland. In the light of these benefits, trade unionists were prepared to accept wage freezes, devaluation, and disagreeable hardships. Their loyalty to their own government survived all rebuffs.

Later legend made this era one of austerity and general gloom. So in some ways it was. From the outset, Britain faced a huge post-war debt. There were continuous shortages of raw materials and of basic food supplies, made worse by the lack of dollars which led to a severe imbalance of trade with North America. There were moments of near-panic like the run on sterling, following convertibility of the exchanges, in July 1947; the decision to impose devaluation of the pound against the dollar in September 1949; the balance of payments difficulties during the Korean War in July–August 1951. Rationing for food, clothing, petrol, and many domestic commodities survived until 1954. Planning and controls, administered by faceless bureaucrats in Whitehall (and circumvented by 'spivs' and the 'black market'), became part of the conventional stereotypes of the time. For all that, most working-class people, the vast majority of the population, viewed the years since 1945 as much the best that had been generally known since the late-Victorian heyday. Wages rose to 30 per cent above their 1938 level. There were higher living standards, guaranteed employment, more satisfying environmental and educational facilities. In a world, too, where popular sport such as football and cricket, and also the cinema and the dance-hall, were readily accessible, the leisure aspects of the good life were catered for as well. Football stadiums such as Highbury, Villa Park, or Old

Trafford attracted each week over 60,000 enthusiastic (and entirely peaceable) spectators. In 1951, in its last few months in office, the Labour government launched a Festival of Britain, to commemorate the centenary of the Great Exhibition of 1851. At a time of economic shortages and much gloom in overseas affairs, it seemed to some jaundiced critics hardly the right time for a festival of national rejoicing. But the Festival proved a triumphant occasion. It led, amongst other benefits, to a dramatic cleaning-up of the derelict south bank of the Thames, focusing on a superb new Festival Hall for music and other arts. It released new powers of creativity for architects, sculptors, and designers. At the same time, it suggested also some of the technological and manufacturing skills latent in the British people. Along the Thames at Battersea, the fun fair was a riot of gaiety and invention. The Festival was testimony to a people still vital and vigorous in its culture, still at peace with itself and secure in its heritage.

In fact, the buoyancy implied by the Festival of Britain was more than sustained by the Conservatives after 1951. Churchill, Eden, Macmillan, and Douglas-Home, the Prime Ministers during the period of unbroken Tory rule from 1951 to 1964, pursued a policy of social peace. The trade unions were generally permitted to develop their freedoms and collective bargaining powers that they had strengthened during the war. There were few major strikes, and no domestic violence, even in Northern Ireland. The welfare state was reinforced, with relatively few incursions into its provisions. Full employment remained a broad priority; indeed, it was thought to be ensured in perpetuity by the Keynesian methods of demand management symbolized in the financial creed of 'Mr Butskell' (a hybrid of the Tory Butler and the Labour leader, Gaitskell, which suggested the centrist policies of the time). When unemployment again reared its head in 1959–60, the Conservatives were as vigorous in promoting interventionist regional policies as their Labour predecessors had been. The Prime Minister of this period, Harold Macmillan, was dubbed

'Supermac' by the (half-admiring) left-wing newspaper cartoon-ist, 'Vicky'. There was, therefore, no major departure from Attlee-style consensus between 1951 and 1964. The return of another Labour government under Harold Wilson by a narrow majority in 1964—confirmed by a much larger majority in 1966—suggested no great deviation from the broadly-accepted political and social framework of the past twenty years.

Political harmony at home gave scope to experiment and innovation in the arts. After a barren decade in the 1940s, the fifties saw major works from many novelists of distinction, several of whom had begun writing before the war: Joyce Cary, Lawrence Durrell, Angus Wilson, and Iris Murdoch were among the most significant. British drama also experienced a renaissance at this period, from the avant-garde work of the Irishman Samuel Beckett, and of Harold Pinter, to the social realism of committed figures such as John Osborne. The latter's *Look Back in Anger* (1956), performed at the radical strong-hold of the Royal Court theatre in Sloane Square, created a stir with its contemptuous rejection of social change in Britain since 1945. The ambiguous, romantic phenomenon of the 'angry young man' was born. In *The Outsider*, Colin Wilson captured the dilemma of the alienated intellectual. Poetry also showed much vitality, notably through the Welsh poet Dylan Thomas, until he drank himself to death in New York in 1953 while on a trip to the United States. There was also the 'Ulster Renais-sance' in Northern Ireland. Beyond the shores of Britain, British visitors to the United States noted the near-monopoly of British dramatists and actors on Broadway. The illusion was nourished that Britain, for all its acknowledged economic weakness and technical backwardness, could still, through its cultural attain-ments, play Greece to America's Rome.

British music was also unusually lively, with Britten in par-ticular active both in composition and in opera, and older figures like Walton also vigorous. What was perhaps more encouraging was that music-making showed clear signs of being a less esoteric or middle-class activity. School orchestras and amateur music groups flourished. Local festivals were springing up apace, with the one launched at Edinburgh in 1947 the most distinguished. A major factor in all this was state patronage through the Arts Council, however much controversy its presence and influence aroused. One area where there was less evidence of advance, unfortunately, was architecture and town planning. The 'new towns' were mostly bywords for grim, Stalinist uniformity, while opportunities to rebuild older cities ravaged in the blitz were too often cast aside, notably in Manchester and the City of London around St. Paul's. Ugly, high-rise flats pierced the skyline. New civic buildings and universities were often severe and unattractive. 'Plate glass' was not a concept that commanded enthusiasm, and the design of major urban centres and older cathedral cities suffered accordingly.

Elsewhere in the arts world, the BBC, in both radio and, to a much lesser degree, television, showed signs of being cultural pioneers. The Third Programme became from 1946 a powerful stimulus to music and drama. Television became a nation-wide phenomenon after 1950, and, with all its admitted limitations, served a useful social role in introducing the nation to itself. The BBC was also valuable in catering for the interests of minorities, including intellectuals, speakers of Welsh, and Asian and other coloured immigrants. The cinema also gradually became a medium for renewed artistic experimentation. It was fortified by the mass audiences that its low prices and informal atmosphere were able to attract, and its immediate freedom from the rival challenge of television. The most notable film events of the late 1940s were the Ealing Studios' comedies, distinctive for their reinterpretation of traditional British themes with restrained humour and gentle tolerance. *Passport to Pimlico*, *Kind Hearts and Coronets* and others of this genre were testimony to the continuities and coherence of British society. Far less interesting were endless films produced in the shadow of the British class system, which depicted the working class in the affectionate, patronizing, uncomprehending terms familiar to West-End theatre-goers over the generations.

Foreigners were usually suspect or simply comic (as they were in the children's books of Enid Blyton which poured forth at this time). Enduring symbols such as the friendly village 'bobby' were given sentimental currency in the film *The Blue Lamp* or in television serials. More positively, in the later fifties, some of the new tides sweeping through the French, Italian, and (to some degree) the American cinema had some real impact on Britain also. A wave of socially realistic films, often with sharp social comment to offer, suggested a shift in cultural attitudes. The popularity of *A Taste of Honey* or *Saturday Night and Sunday Morning*, with their searching penetration of working-class values and the human relationships moulded by them, implied a new depth and sensitivity in the British cinema industry. At a wider level, it suggested the security and stability of Britain at this transitional period in its history.

The stability of the domestic scene was much assisted by the general quietude of external policy. Britain in 1945 was still a great power, one of the 'Big Three' at the international peace conferences. It demonstrated the fact by manufacturing its own atomic and hydrogen bombs. Until the cumulative effect of economic decline took its inevitable toll, this façade was preserved up to the Moscow Test-Ban Treaty of 1963. Britain had its own powerful defence systems, its own supposedly independent nuclear weaponry, its own sterling area, its private strategic, trading, and financial ties with a mighty, if dissolving, empire. In medical, physical, and chemical science, Britain was still pre-eminent, as the international acclaim for such Nobel prize-winning pioneers as Fleming and Florey, Crick and Watson suggested.

However, Britain's international position was qualified by the gradual, but necessary, retreat from empire that the post-war period witnessed. It was a relentless process, even during the regime of such a veteran imperialist as Sir Winston Churchill. The granting of self-government to India, Pakistan, Burma, and Ceylon (Sri Lanka) by the Attlee government in 1947–9 was the key moment in the transfer of power. It was an unambiguous statement of Britain's military and financial inability and above all lack of will, to retain possession of distant lands by force. The process of decolonization gained in momentum in the fifties, with territories in West and East Africa and elsewhere receiving their independence, even Kenya and Cyprus, where there were bloody engagements against native nationalist forces. In southern Africa, the eventual break-up of the Central African Federation in 1963 meant independence for Northern Rhodesia (Zambia) and Nyasaland (Malawi) also. By the early 1960s, only a scattered handful of miscellaneous territories—British Honduras, the barren wastes of the Falkland Islands, Gibraltar, Hong Kong, Aden, Fiji, and a few other outposts—were still under direct British rule. There was little enough nostalgic hankering for the mystique of empire now. Empire Day disappeared from the calendar of state schools; Indian civil servants anonymously returned home; the king ceased to be Emperor of India. Then in October 1956, the Prime Minister of the time, Anthony Eden, astonishingly engaged in covert moves with the French and the Israelis to invade the Suez Canal Zone, after the Egyptians had declared that that crucial waterway was henceforth to be nationalized. World opinion turned against Britain, even in the United States. Sterling was threatened; oil supplies dried up; the British troops withdrew ignominiously, censured by the United Nations. There were few signs of prolonged public anger; the voices of the older imperialism were relatively muted. In the 1959 general election, the Conservatives fought, and comfortably won, on the basis of domestic prosperity—'You've never had it so good', in the argot of Macmillan. On the other hand, the American politician, Daniel Moynihan, could write of the new prestige of Britain in the Afro-Asian Third World for having liberated so large a proportion of the world's population without the bitterness of the French in Algeria, the Dutch in Indonesia, or the Belgians in the Congo. A world that had once listened to the liberal nostrums of Bentham and Ricardo, Mill and Gladstone, now hearkened to the social democratic creed

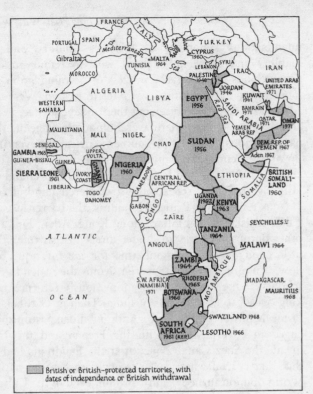

British or British-protected territories, with
dates of independence or British withdrawal

proclaimed by Laski and Tawney of the London School of
Economics, the *New Statesman*, and (even in opposition) the
Labour Party.

In its post-imperial phase, Britain became a more intro-
spective power, one whose role in world affairs was uncertain.
As the Commonwealth connection became more ceremonial
—though with important practical aspects like the imperial
preferences for Commonwealth products such as butter and
meat—the relationship with America, bitter-sweet in many
ways, loomed ever larger. From 1949 the United States and
Britain were bound together, strategically and geo-politically, in
NATO. Another organization SEATO, for South-East Asia,

followed on shortly. Thereafter, British and American policies
marched closely together, whether a Conservative or a Labour
government was in power. The British prided themselves that
this meant an equal 'special relationship' between the English-
speaking peoples. It is clear, however, that in practice this
relationship involved Britain striving desperately to maintain an
illusory posture of independence. In the Korean War, in dealings with Communist China (other than its formal recognition),
in the Middle East, above all in Europe in the face of Russian
threats, British and American policies were similar, if not ident-
ical. A rare attempt at rebellion such as the British involvement
in the Suez operation in 1956 was quickly snuffed out. The

Nassau agreements led to defence and economic dependence on the United States being more pronounced than ever.

Nearer home, there were attempts from 1947 onwards to form a political and economic union of Western Europe. From the dawn of this idea just after the war, British governments were suspicious, if not openly hostile. They cited the Commonwealth connection, the special relationship with the United States, the distinctiveness of the British constitutional and legal system, the autonomy of British socialist planning. More powerfully, most British people regarded other Western Europeans as incomprehensible aliens, with few natural ties linking them across the English Channel. The first British attempt to join the European Common Market was rebuffed by President de Gaulle of France in 1963; years passed before another effort was made. It cannot be said that the British showed any overwhelming sense of grief at this failure to be admitted to an alien institution which would mean dearer food and a threat to national sovereignty. The Euro-enthusiasts were swimming against the clear tide of public opinion.

In this self-contained, somewhat insular, society, the general pattern was set by consumer-led affluence. Beneath the surface, economists, the new soothsayers of the age, detected slow rates of growth and falling productivity. Sociologists unearthed deep inequalities and class divisions which prevented the modernizing of a 'stagnant society'. Attitudes to British institutions and conventions were maked by an overpowering complacency. For the British, life seemed now distinctly better. A falling birth-rate meant smaller and more affluent households. Homes were better furnished. Families increasingly had cars; they could buy their homes on cheap mortgages; they managed each summer a decent holiday abroad in Spain, France, or Italy. Nor were these growing delights confined to the semi-detached middle class in the suburbs. Working-class people also enjoyed air-lifted package holidays to the sunny Mediterranean coast, and revelled, in pubs, clubs, and elsewhere, in the freedom of choice afforded by higher wages and shorter working hours. The working-class young became a favourite target for sociological analysis and conventional head-shaking, with their more eccentric life-styles and a more expansive pop culture. A sporting hero such as the long-haired Northern Ireland and Manchester United footballer, George Best, suggested very different values from those of Jack Hobbs in the twenties. The musical breakthrough effected in the early 1960s by the Beatles, a group of Liverpudlian youths, made Britain the harbinger of the supposedly 'permissive' society, in which drink and drugs were freely available, skirts spectacularly shorter, sexual restraint much less in evidence. England's football World Cup victory in 1966 added an aura of patriotism to the new aggressiveness of the young.

In addition, middle-class reformers pioneered other social changes, assisted by the hedonistic outlook of a Prime Minister such as Harold Macmillan, and the civilized tolerance of a Labour Home Secretary, Roy Jenkins. Sexual offences, homosexual and otherwise, were less liable to the rigours of the law. Abortion, along with the pill and other easily obtainable contraceptives, offered scope for endless sexual indulgence; there were far more divorces, and one-parent families. The youth cult seemed for a time to be sweeping the land, allegedly fostered by President Kennedy's 'New Frontier' in America. In particular, a variety of cultures mingled in British universities. Here a growing number of uprooted working-class students merged with more aggressive middle-class contemporaries to fortify the appeal to youth with the protection of mere numbers. Many new universities sprang up in the ten years after 1963, while older universities were much expanded. 'More meant worse' complained some critics. Others countered that British potential was scarcely being exploited when only 5 per cent of the relevant age-group went on to higher education of any kind. Since the basic problems of subsistence were apparently being resolved by the economics of abundance, the articulate university young could turn their energies to new crusades.

The Campaign for Nuclear Disarmament in the later fifties owed much to the idealism of the middle-class young. For a time, it threatened to undermine the Labour Party as a potential party of government. Later in the sixties, the same kind of passion flowed into protest against the American war in Vietnam. Student rebellion, familiar abroad in Berkeley or the Sorbonne, briefly flared up in British campuses, and then equally mysteriously, petered out.

These movements had wider implications. Beneath the veneer of public contentment, there were in reality a variety of divisive forces that were deeply entrenched. A wide range of different groups were, in the period of Harold Wilson's first premiership (1964–70), exploding into revolt. The young, as has been seen, were finding the values of consumerism and conformism unappealing in a world whose ecology was being disturbed and whose very existence was threatened by weapons of unimaginable horror. Elsewhere, young people in Wales and Scotland generated a tide of nationalist protest, more familiar in the Basque regions of Spain or in French Quebec. Wales and Scotland had not fully enjoyed the economic growth of the 1950s. Their national aspirations were hardly fulfilled by such formal institutions as the Secretaries of State created for Scotland and much later (in 1964) for Wales. Scottish nationalists complained, with justice, that the very title of Elizabeth II was a misnomer in their country. In Wales, there was the added theme of an ancient language and culture threatened with extinction in the unequal battle against anglicized 'admass' culture. Victory for a Welsh Nationalist at Carmarthen in a by-election in 1966 was followed by renewed civil disobedience (and a few bombing attempts) on behalf of the Welsh language. In Scotland, the Nationalists captured the Hamilton seat, and several local authorities; a new anti-English mood seemed to be sweeping Highlands and Lowlands alike. Less constitutional or placid were the demands of the black or brown minorities, over a million of whom had migrated to Britain from India, Pakistan, West Africa, and the West Indies since

1950. In addition to dilapidated housing and racial discrimination in employment and (sometimes) at the hands of the police, there was the added hazard of racial bigotry in older urban areas. This was fanned by the inflammatory rhetoric of a maverick right-wing Cassandra, Enoch Powell. 'Rivers of blood' were forecast in British cities on the lines of the race riots of the United States.

More disturbing still, in Northern Ireland, an artificial state kept in being by the control of the Protestant majority from 1920 onwards was in disarray. A powerful civil rights movement arose on behalf of the Roman Catholic (and usually nationalist) minority. But, in practice, attempts to maintain religious and racial harmony clearly broke down. Troops were moved into Belfast and Londonderry to preserve order. An alarming wave of bombing attacks in English cities signified that the IRA and Sinn Fein were taking the age-old struggle of Irish nationalism into a new and sinister phase. In the later sixties, with minorities on the march from Brixton to Belfast, liberal consensual Britain seemed to be breaking down, as it had almost done in 1910–14.

Hitherto the social fabric had been kept intact, at least in part, because of high and advancing living standards for the population as a whole. But clear evidence mounted up in the 1960s that increasing economic pressures were adding to the new social tensions. Britain lurched in that miserable decade from one financial expedient to another, with frequent balance of payments crises and many runs on sterling. Devaluation of the pound in 1967 did not produce any lasting remedy. Inflation began to rise significantly, especially in the early 1970s when a Conservative government under Edward Heath recklessly expanded the money supply, a misguided version of Keynesianism. All the predictions of Keynesian economists were now overturned as rising inflation was accompanied by a growing toll of unemployment as well. At first this was confined to the older industrial regions of the north-east, Scotland, and South Wales. The rise of nationalism in the last two was much associated with the closure of collieries and factories and the laying off of labour. But by 1973 it was clear that the economic problems of Britain were having far more general consequences. The nation's capacity to generate wealth, along with its share of world trade and production, were in serious, perhaps terminal, decline. Britain seemed to have replaced Turkey as the legendary 'sick man of Europe'. In retaliation for declining living standards, the unions replied with collective industrial power. Strikes mounted up, most acutely in the case of the coal mines. A national miners' strike was called in February 1972 and was wholly successful. The Heath government experienced the full extent of the miners' ability to disrupt national production and energy supplies, despite all the contraction of the coal industry since the 1950s. Another miners' strike in February 1974 saw the government call an election on the theme of: 'Who governs Britain?' The answer was a small swing to Labour and the government duly fell. The miners again won all their demands and their former place high in the wages table. This background of a widening mood of protest, a reluctance to accept traditional sanctions and disciplines, institutional power from the unions thrust against a declining productive base— these formed the ominous backcloth as Britain emerged from its brief, heady acquaintance with 'affluence' to confront the unfamiliar challenges of a new international order.

From the Seventies to the Nineties

In the nineteen-seventies, Britain offered a permanent, painful case for macro-economic and sociological treatment. Its economic decline continued, comparatively in relation to almost all other developed nations, and even in absolute terms compared with earlier production levels. It was much aggravated by the dramatic change in the energy situation in 1973-4 as a result of which Britain and other Western nations suffered a fourfold increase in the price of Middle East oil. This gave new impetus to Britain's own major development in this decade, the exploitation of the oil reserves in the North Sea, and of North Sea natural gas also. With nuclear power stations and hydro-electric schemes, as well as abundant supplies of coal, Britain was in many ways far better prepared to confront these new difficulties than many of its competitors. But the huge rise in the price of oil inevitably fuelled inflation on a scale unknown since 1919. It was reinforced by trade union pressure for enormous wage increases of anything up to 30 per cent until late 1975. British inflation continued to run at a historically high level, reaching over 20 per cent for a time in 1980, before it sank in 1982–3 to a more manageable figure of less than half that amount. Thereafter, curbs on the money supply, aided by a slow-down in wage increases and a relative fall in the real price of many commodities, saw the inflation rate subside to around 4 per cent by the autumn of 1987. With surging price rises and pressure from wage and other unit costs, unemployment re-emerged as the major domestic scourge. By 1980 it was over two million, a total unknown since the thirties. With government investment and the money supply curtailed, un-employment had advanced to well over three million by the spring of 1983. It remained at that alarming total for the next three years, even creeping up somewhat, until some renewed economic growth saw a slight fall to below three million in 1987. There seemed to be a deep rot at the heart of the economy, with hundreds of thousands, many of them teenagers or other young people, doomed to perhaps years on national assistance, while public welfare services were steadily curtailed. There was evidence of decline elsewhere as well. Although the population continued to increase, from over 50 million in 1951 to over 56 million in 1981, it was noted that there was actually a fall in the period 1975–8. The birth-rate fell sharply during the recession, while a larger proportion of the population were elderly, placing strains on the social services and necessarily reliant on the wealth created by the able-bodied still in employment.

The outcome was most disruptive for the social fabric. An

initial period of runaway inflation in 1974–5 was stemmed by a period of an uneasy so-called 'social contract' with the unions, negotiated by the Labour governments of Wilson and then Callaghan in 1975–8. Unions agreed to moderate their wage demands in return for specified government policies geared to their needs, and especially to job protection. There were no serious strikes thereafter, until the so-called 'winter of discontent' in 1978–9, when a rash of strikes by public service workers, including even council grave-diggers, helped to ensure a Conservative election victory. Thereafter, the unions continued to be assertive in 'right-to-work' demonstrations in protest at cuts in public spending and the high rate of unemployment. Not only traditionally vulnerable areas such as Scotland, Merseyside, and the north-east but even once thriving regions such as the West Midlands showed rates of joblessness amounting to over 20 per cent. In the steel industry, mighty plants like Consett, Shotton, and Corby were closed down for ever. More indirectly, the quality of life was impoverished by declining investment in health and educational services (including the universities) and by reduced expenditure on art and the environment. Britain now provided a classic example of the post-Keynesian phenomenon of 'stagflation', with industrial recession and high inflation at one and the same time.

These economic pressures led to severe strains being placed on the stability of society in the seventies. They fuelled other social, communal, or ethnic tensions already much in evidence. The most disturbing case was still Northern Ireland where deep-seated racial and religious animosities between Protestants and Roman Catholics were aggravated by the most acute rate of unemployment in the United Kingdom. Throughout the seventies, the state of Northern Ireland became more and more alarming. The success of the civil rights movement dislodged the old Unionist ascendancy; the Stormont assembly was wound up in 1972 in favour of direct rule by Westminster. But renewed violence by the IRA was paralleled by the aggressive anti-Papist demagogy of the Reverend Ian Paisley. The end of

Stormont certainly brought communal peace no nearer. Troops continued to patrol the Bogside and the Falls Road. There were tense border incidents between Ulster and the Irish Republic to the south, from where the IRA derived funds and weapons. On occasion, the endemic violence of Northern Ireland stretched across the sea in the form of terrifying bomb attacks on English cities, and even assassinations of politicians. The Queen's relative, the distinguished admiral and statesman, Lord Mountbatten, was murdered, blown up on his yacht by an IRA bomb. A new effort to involve the Dublin government in the affairs of Northern Ireland directly, the first since 1922, came with the Anglo-Irish Hillsborough Agreement, concluded between the British Prime Minister, Mrs Thatcher, and the Irish Fine Gael Premier, Dr Garret FitzGerald, in November 1985. But this led to bitter protests from Unionists in Ulster who then boycotted Westminster. A genuine all-Ireland spirit of unity in that unhappy island remained far off. The age-old racial feuds of Ireland were not yet pacified. Repeated acts of violence, including an abortive mortar attack by the IRA on 10 Downing Street in February 1991, drove the point home for the general public.

Other tensions of the period were less violent but equally disturbing. Scottish and Welsh nationalists continued to express themselves though usually in constitutional form. After the failure of 'devolution' measures in 1979, Celtic nationalism seemed to be in retreat, but in Wales especially there continued to be much political and cultural conflict. The defence of the Welsh language still attracted much passionate loyalty, and even threats of fasts unto death by angry patriots. Englishmen who owned a 'second home' in the Welsh countryside sometimes found it burned down by local incendiarists. Pressure for governmental devolution remained powerful in Scotland, fuelled by the relative decline of its economic base in the 1980s. Wales and Scotland, however, remained, on balance, peaceful societies, less torn apart by nationalist anguish than their Celtic neighbour across the sea. More alarming were the troubles afflicting the large black community, much of it resident in

poor, dilapidated ghetto areas in large cities. There were sporadic troubles in the Notting Hill area of London and the St.
Paul's district of Bristol. In the summer of 1981 it seemed for a
time that Britain was experiencing the full horrors of race riots
on the American pattern, as black youths in the Toxteth area of
Liverpool and the Brixton district of south London engaged in
prolonged rioting, all faithfully recorded (and perhaps whipped
up) by television reporting. Another violent flare-up saw disturbances on the Broadwater Farm housing estate in Tot-
tenham, north London, and the murder of a policeman there by
black youths. A lack of trust between the immigrant community
and the police force was one notable aspect of these events.
But, with unemployment especially serious for young blacks
and a pervasive background of discrimination in jobs, housing,
and social opportunity, the relations between the races was a
mounting cause for concern and alarm.

Other troubles piled up. Some examples of trade union protest, for instance the demonstrations against the Grunwick
works in north London, seemed to go far beyond the usual
limits of industrial protest in the intimidation that characterized
them. Football matches and other sporting occasions were scar-
red by mindless violence by teenage spectators. Britain's traditional stability appeared, therefore, increasingly under fire from
many sources. An American congressman gloomily observed
that Britain was becoming as 'ungovernable as Chile', an
alarming parallel for Americans. This proved to be an absurd
exaggeration. Few societies would have survived high unemployment, rising inflation, and public retrenchment with as
much equanimity as did the British. Despite evidence of hallowed institutions being treated with less than their historic
respect—Oxford University being subjected to 'sit-ins'; police,
judges, Church leaders (and football referees) failing to sustain
their former authority; even members of the royal family being
subjected to public criticism or harassment—the broad fabric of
institutional and civic life held firm. But, without doubt, the
points of friction and potential dissolution were so numerous

that age-old sanctions and restraints would have to be re-examined and re-defined for British civilization to survive at all.

During this period of some turmoil, Britain's view of the outside world underwent a phase of introspection. In practice, a deep psychology of insularity dictated popular attitudes, as it had frequently done since 1918. The formal alliance with the Americans in NATO continued, but attracted little passionate commitment. Indeed, the revival in the late 1970s of the Campaign for Nuclear Disarmament, a singularly peaceful form of protest, suggested that the dependence of this alliance on a mounting arsenal of nuclear weapons of a quite horrific kind aroused much public disquiet. The proposed Cruise missiles aroused still more. After much diplomatic infighting, Britain entered the European Common Market in 1973. A unique referendum in 1975 saw a large majority, almost two-thirds in all, recording its support for British membership. But 'Europe' attracted affection largely in non-political contexts. Continental package holidays, the popularity of Continental cars and food products, European football matches did not make the British love their neighbours across the Channel any more fervently. British attitudes towards the Common Market continued after 1975 to be governed by sullen hostility; opinion polls recorded consistent opposition to membership of the EEC. In any case, an organization which consisted largely of a massive, anonymous, bureaucratic juggernaut, with scant democratic constraint, located far away in Brussels and Strasbourg could hardly win public love in as independent a nation as Britain. The linking of the Common Market with higher food prices, butter mountains, wine lakes and the like, was widely condemned, inevitably so by a people which had known a policy of cheap food since the repeal of the Corn Laws in 1846. The British were reluctant Europeans as they were reluctant Atlanticists.

On the other hand, there were signs by the later eighties that the British were becoming more reconciled to the fact that membership of the European community and that anti-Europeanism was diminishing. By the June 1987 general election, the Labour Party no longer proposed to negotiate British withdrawal from the EEC, especially since the latter now included socialist governments in France, Spain and Greece. The agreement concluded in 1986 between Mrs Thatcher and President Mitterrand of France to complete a high-speed rail tunnel under the English Channel to link Britain and France, a tunnel due to be operating in 1993, was a dramatic indication of at least a partial retreat from British isolationism. Britain agreed to enter the European Single Market in 1992, a momentous change. Finally, after much internal argument in her Cabinet, Mrs Thatcher was forced to enter the European Exchange Rate Mechanism in October 1990. Nevertheless the economic and political relationship with Europe remained a deeply divisive issue at several levels of the Conservative party and government. It played a major part in Mrs Thatcher being forced to step down as Prime Minister in November 1990, after over eleven years in power.

Commonwealth sentiment still retained some force with the Queen as its figurehead. Yet the Commonwealth ties were becoming more and more intangible, too. Whether in the forms of coloured immigrants into British cities or arguments over how to respond to *apartheid* in South Africa, they could produce friction rather than goodwill. Meanwhile the agreement with China in 1989 to withdraw the British presence in Hong Kong eight years later confirmed the irreversible retreat from a world role.

The withdrawal from empire continued apace with little public resentment. Economic and military weakness dictated a policy of controlled retreat. The most difficult surviving problem was that of Southern Rhodesia, where a racial holocaust was threatened in a land adjacent to South Africa with its apartheid system. In a dramatic reversal, Mrs Thatcher's Conservative government granted total self-government to Rhodesia (renamed Zimbabwe) in December 1979; the protests of white settlers were ignored. Parliament and public greeted this imperial retreat with a fanfare of acclamation. The spirit of Kipling and Rhodes had finally been exorcized. It seemed unlikely that empire would disturb the British psyche any further.

Then, quite unexpectedly, the distant barren outpost of the Falkland Islands was invaded by the Argentines in late March 1982. The British government responded vigorously in the face of a huge public outcry. The two remaining aircraft-carriers and dozens of other war vessels, many fighter planes, and 10,000 troops were assembled in a task force and dispatched 8,000 miles away to the stormy seas of the South Atlantic. In a swift and successful campaign, the islands were soon recaptured; the Union Jack again flew in Port Stanley on 14 June. The Falklands War was immensely popular; dissidents, CND or otherwise, were unable to gain a fair hearing. At the same time, it seemed most improbable that a war to retain these distant and almost valueless outposts, scarcely known to British people before the fighting began other than from postage stamps, would encourage a revived mystique of imperial grandeur. There was no more popular anxiety to commit naval strength or financial resources to the South Atlantic after the war than there had been before. What the Falklands episode possibly did was to confirm a rising tide of impatient insularity amongst the British people. In the face of international scepticism, Britain could still display great-power status, and demonstrate its military, naval, and technological superiority over a Fascist dictatorship such as the Argentine republic. National pride was refurbished.

But the jingoism of the Falklands petered out almost as soon as it began. Britain returned to the familiar domestic scene of strikes, economic decline, and social discontent, exemplified by a bitter miners' strike from March 1984 which lasted a whole year. There were violent clashes between the police and miners' pickets. However, the National Union of Mineworkers was itself divided, with important Midlands' coalfields continuing to work, and the result was a profound defeat for the NUM and the closure of many more pits. The power of the miners to coerce a British government into submission, a major feature of history and folklore since the First World War, was no longer apparent when coal was less essential to Britain's energy supplies, and with oil, gas, electricity, and nuclear power readily available. The miners' strike, however, was followed by a series of strikes by white-collar and public service workers, notably a lengthy dispute by Britain's schoolteachers which led to much disruption in schools in England and Wales in 1985–7.

The problems of the early eighties were intensified by a Conservative government under Mrs Thatcher which seemed to be the most right-wing that Britain had known in the twentieth century. At the same time, the Labour Party, with Tony Benn spearheading a grass-roots movement towards fundamentalist socialism, appeared to be moving equally far to the left. Consensus seemed to have disappeared. Pedants quoted W. B. Yeats to the effect that 'the best lacked all conviction and the worst were full of passionate intensity'. Some found solace in a new political party formed by dissident right-wing members of the Labour Party; this was the 'Social Democratic Party', committed to Keynes-style economic centrism, to an incomes policy, Europeanism, and the nuclear deterrent. Remarkably, despite much fatalism about the economy, the June 1983 general election provided an immense triumph for Mrs Thatcher and the Conservatives. They captured 397 seats, as against 209 for a visibly declining Labour Party, 17 for the Liberals, and only 6 for the SDP. But renewed fears for moderate middle-ground opinion being swept away in the maelstrom were somewhat assuaged by other, more hopeful developments. The economic changes in the country were not without compensation. In part, they were the result of a beneficial change in the national economy, with Britain becoming self-sufficient in North Sea oil, and thus in a unique position of strength in its energy base. The balance of payments suddenly moved (until 1986) into a large and continuing surplus. This also meant that the dominance of manufacturing industry in the British economy would be far less paramount henceforth. Certainly the technological wonders of oil, electronics, and aerospace, of Concorde, the Humber Bridge, the High-Speed Train, the Channel Tunnel, and the

computerized microchip age suggested that the native reserves
of innovation and scientific ingenuity had not run dry.

In the mid-eighties, there were some signs, too, that these
developments were helping to generate a renewal of affluence, at
least for southern England, parts of the Midlands, and East
Anglia, the last an area of particular growth. The British economy
began to advance rapidly and reached a rate of 4 per cent growth
in early 1987, assisted by the fall in the value of the pound and of
some imported commodities. It was noticeable that this advance
rested less on Britain's traditional strength in manufacturing,
which continued to lag far below pre-1970 levels of production,
than on credit, investment, and a consumer boom. A notable
event here was the so-called 'Big Bang' in the City of London
27 October 1986, which replaced the age-old spectacle of jobbers
milling on the Stock Exchange floor with an almost invisible,
highly sophisticated computer-based network for dealers. This
reflected the new internationalism of the capital market. It also
contributed, incidentally, to repairing decades of neglect and
dereliction in adjacent areas of London's East End. The social
phenomenon of the 'yuppy' (young upwardly-mobile professional), a money-making youth engaged in stock-broking, investment or merchant banking, was widely discussed. For many
British citizens, life suddenly appeared easier after the crises of the
seventies and early eighties. Home ownership continued to spread
until by the end of 1987, two-thirds of the population owned their
own home. Share-owning also became more widespread. The
government's policy of 'privatizing' state-owned enterprises such
as the telecommunications system, British Gas, Britoil and the
airports (with water and electricity to follow at the end of the
decade) helped towards this last end. Conversely, the trade unions
appeared to be declining in public esteem and even more in
membership which slumped from around 13 million in 1980 to
9 million in 1987 and to below 7 million by 1999.

The land was not proving to be culturally barren or intellectually unadventurous at this time. British novelists and dramatists remained remarkably creative. Several leading British

architects achieved international renown. The British musical scene was never more flourishing than in the 1980s with London plausibly claimed to be the musical capital of the world, and important new orchestral and operatic developments in Leeds, Cardiff, and elsewhere. British weekly literary periodicals remained of high quality. The BBC remained a major communications agency, though much distracted by disputes with the Thatcher government, and weakened by falling morale and revenue. Universities still maintained a flow of creative achievement in the arts and pure and applied science, including medicine, despite a policy of severe government cuts imposed from 1981 onwards. One American commentator, Bernard Nossiter, had even claimed in the late seventies, that the apparent economic rundown and unemployment in Britain masked something more positive—a deliberately creative use of leisure in which the British middle and skilled working class rebelled against the norms of ever-increasing mass production, and opted for greater freedom from the drudgery of automated labour. This view was probably too optimistic and ignored long-held traditions in antique working practices and managerial inertia which held the economy, and to some extent society, in thrall. In addition, the material base on which British culture rested was threatened by a renewed failure in technological innovation and enterprise. The problems of British universities and research institutes aroused great concern in the mid-eighties, with the 'brain drain' of gifted young scientists across the Atlantic. Two hundred years after the dawn of the Industrial Revolution, the British were still strangely reluctant to modernize and promote their scientific genius. Yet, despite this glaring weakness, British talents were not necessarily unequipped to cope with the new stresses of sociological upheaval and relative industrial weakness any more than with the burdens of commercial leadership and international power in past centuries.

These and other developments helped give a new lease of life to the Conservative government of Mrs Margaret Thatcher. In the

June 1987 general election, despite a vigorous Labour campaign under a new leader, Neil Kinnock, the Conservatives again won an easy victory with 375 seats as against 229 for Labour and only 22 for a flagging and disintegrating Liberal/Social Democrat Alliance. Mrs Thatcher thus became the first Prime Minister since Lord Liverpool in 1812–27 to win three successive general elections, an extraordinary achievement. The Conservatives made much in the campaign for their claims to have restored national prosperity, and also to be reliable protectors of national security. Labour's policy of unilateral nuclear disarmament did not command wide support. On the other hand, the regional gulf in Britain revealed by the election returns was very plain. The sweeping Conservative gains came in the South and the Midlands. They lost ground in the industrial cities of the North; there was a 5 per cent swing to Labour in Wales; and a 7.5 per cent swing in Scotland. There was much talk of a basic social divide in the land, between an increasingly prosperous and complacent South, and a decaying, declining North, with endemic unemployment, urban dereliction, and collapsing public services. The 'two nations', described in Disraeli's novels in the 1840s, were still much in evidence well over a century later.

Britain in the 1980s manifested a remarkable skein of elements of dissolution and stability, in fragile coexistence. The forces of disruption were evident enough. There were physical reminders in the troubles in Northern Ireland, in the industrial world, and in the black ghettos in the cities. There was the new challenge to the political consensus posed in their various guises by the neo-Marxist Labour left headed by Benn, by the racialist perversities of the quasi-Fascist National Front, perhaps by the patrician élitism displayed at times by some Social Democrats. Traditional relationships—the young towards their parents, 'feminist' wives towards their husbands, workers towards their employers and union leaders, students towards their teachers, citizens towards the custodians of law and order—seemed to be in flux. *Is Britain Dying?* was one evocative book title in 1979. British stability was too often expressed, by contrast, in an almost religious reverence for ancient forms and ancestor worship, as in the veneration of the royal family, or the ambiguous notion of 'heritage', which often entailed a distinctly selective and sentimental reading of British history.

Public instability was markedly reinforced by the disarray into which Mrs Thatcher's government lurched after the 1987 general election. For most of the decade, with its creed of monetarism, privatization, and the primacy of market forces; with its challenge to institutions such as the Church, the universities, and local government; with the almost invincible personal ascendancy of the Prime Minister herself, 'Thatcherism' seemed triumphant. But over the next three years it ran into severe difficulties. At home, some of its more radical proposals met with major opposition. Attempts to introduce market forces into education and even more into the National Health Service aroused great public anger. A proposal to abolish the system of household rates with a community charge (or 'poll tax') led to an upsurge of revolt across the nation. After all, freeborn Englishmen, headed by Wat Tyler, had rebelled against a poll tax back in 1381 (pp. 206–7) and the memory of it remained in popular legend. Most serious of all, the apparent revival in the economy began to lose credibility. The tax-cutting policy of the Chancellor, Nigel Lawson, was now seen to have led to a huge balance of payments deficit, at £20 billion the worst figure on record. Unemployment rose sharply and the pound came under pressure. Worse still, the conquest of inflation, the government's main boast, was now threatened by a consumer-credit and spending boom. Bank rate soared to 15 per cent, and the impact was felt by every mortgaged home-owner in the land. To make matters worse, the Chancellor, Nigel Lawson, locked in bitter argument with the Prime Minister over European policy, resigned. Mrs Thatcher herself now became increasingly unpopular. Her intensely personal, imperious style of leadership now seemed more of a liability. Her reputation for 'strength' in foreign affairs, dating from the Falklands War, also seemed less credible, especially with repeated rows over monetary union with our European partners. At the same time, the Labour Party, responding to Neil Kinnock's 'new realism' became increasingly moderate and therefore more electable. It dropped its commitment to mass nationalization and unilateral nuclear disarmament, and its hostility towards Europe, and turned on the hard-left Bennite remnants in the process. In the summer of 1990 it seemed that a sea change in British politics might be at hand.

In the autumn, the transformation duly occurred. Faced with Cabinet resignations, by-election losses, and difficulties over Europe and the economy, Mrs Thatcher seemed beleaguered as never before. She was then challenged for the party leadership (in effect, for the premiership) in November by Michael Heseltine, one of the many former Cabinet colleagues who had resigned from her government. Although Mrs Thatcher won the first ballot (204 votes to Heseltine's 152), the opposition to her within her party was sufficient to force her to resign. Like Lloyd George in 1922 and Neville Chamberlain in 1940, it was the Tory backbenchers, not the voters, who brought her down. In the second ballot, the victor was John Major, the little-known Chancellor of the Exchequer, and a man of apparently moderate views. He thus became Prime Minister, to guide the nation through the transition from the storms of 'Thatcherism' to a more consensual social and political order.

Towards the Millennium

The fall of Mrs Thatcher in 1990 like that of Lloyd George in 1922 was a traumatic event. As with the departure of that earlier leader, it seemed to usher in a period of greater tranquillity. John Major spoke of 'a nation at ease with itself'. As a unifying move, he brought Mrs Thatcher's main adversary, Michael Heseltine, into his Cabinet. For a while, there was a quieter phase. The unpopular poll tax was scrapped. British involvement in the Gulf War in February 1991, when its armoured troops and jet fighters were prominent in helping the Americans and other 'coalition' forces to drive Saddam Hussein's Iraqi armies out of Kuwait, shored up the government's popularity for a time, even if there was no 'Falklands factor' now to boost the Tory cause. Above all, John Major appeared to make progress in reconciling the divisions in his party over Europe. In the negotiations over the Maastricht treaty in December 1991, which spurred on European integration including a common currency due to start in 1999, the British government appeared to achieve a diplomatic success. It won from its European partners an 'opt-out' both from future monetary union and also the 'social chapter' of workers' rights and a minimum wage. A façade of Conservative unity was successfully maintained. On the other hand, the basic difficulties of Mrs Thatcher's later period still remained in full. In particular, the economy remained in recession. This time it was the middle classes of middle England who were conspicuously suffering, from job insecurity, dear mortgages, and falling house prices.

With all these problems confronting their natural supporters and their endless difficulties over Europe, it was generally expected that the Conservatives would finally lose to Labour in the general election of April 1992. Certainly that is what the opinion polls said. But they were simply wrong. John Major projected himself effectively as a plain, honest citizen without artifice. He won an unexpected victory, with the Conservatives winning 336 seats to Labour's 271 and the Liberal Democrats' 20. The government gained the support of 'Essex man', the patriotic, *Sun*-reading, skilled or semi-skilled worker in new towns such as Basildon. In fact, with 41.85 per cent of the votes to Labour's 34.16 per cent, the Conservatives had done better than their tally of seats suggested. Their total of 14,200,000 votes was their highest ever. It seemed that the electors did not really trust either Labour or its leader, Neil Kinnock, for economic competence. Labour to most electors still seemed the class-conscious party of a dying past, not a prosperous future. The Conservatives, having won four general elections running, the best performance since the Whig-Liberals after the repeal of the Corn Laws (p. 521), seemed destined for a further period of comfortable ascendancy.

Yet, in fact, the election was to bring a prolonged phase of division and torment that tore the Conservatives asunder. The collapse began on 'Black Wednesday', 16 September 1992, a traumatic day from which neither party nor premier was to recover. After intense pressure on sterling, Britain was forced to leave the European Exchange Rate Mechanism and to devalue the pound against all major currencies. It was a shattering blow for Major and his Chancellor, Norman Lamont, which destroyed at a stroke the Conservatives' reputation for competent economic management. They slumped massively in the opinion polls; Labour's lead, which rose at times even to a record margin of over 30 per cent, remained immense for the next four and a half years. There seemed little that the government could do to recover. Economic revival brought the voters cut-backs and higher taxes. Kenneth Clarke succeeded Lamont as Chancellor in 1993 and things slowly improved. There were other unpopular policies. The privatization of industries and utilities, the flagship of Thatcherite policies, lost its sheen. The public saw privatized trains which did not run on time, and privatized water services which led to shortages during dry summer months and huge salary increases for the company executives. There was, indeed, some progress in Northern Ireland for a time. John Major succeeded in negotiating a Downing Street agreement with the Irish prime minister in late 1993; the following year Sinn Fein declared a cease-fire which lasted for almost two years. Peace returned to the troubled streets of Belfast and the British army scaled down its presence. But a massive bomb blast in Canary Wharf in east London in February 1996 meant that the fragile peace was over. The political gulf between Protestant Loyalists and Catholic Nationalists remained as wide as it had been ever since the partition of Ireland back in 1922. John Major, like all his predecessors since Gladstone, had failed to overcome the ancestral sectarian divisions and bitterness of Northern Ireland.

Above all, the Conservative Party was plagued by relations with Europe. The Maastricht treaty proved to be not a platform for harmony but a ticking time-bomb that led inexorably to electoral disaster. Under leaders like Macmillan and Heath, the Conservatives had always been the more pro-European party since the 1950s, while Labour had been far more hostile. Now the positions were totally reversed. Labour felt wholly committed to a British role at the centre of Europe, including the social chapter which the unions warmly endorsed, while the Conservatives were ripped apart as the Euro-scepticism or Europhobia of Mrs Thatcher's later period built up into a kind of frenzy. It was no longer the siren call of empire that promoted anti-European sentiment, but threats to British national independence. Maastricht, with its perceived challenge to the sovereignty of the Crown in parliament, with its pressure towards a European superstate and a 'Euro' currency which would wipe out the historic primacy of the pound sterling, became the source of massive contention. The Conservative Cabinet was as divided over Europe as a previous Cabinet in 1903–5 had been over tariff reform and empire (pp. 572–3). John Major seemed as helpless and indecisive now as Arthur Balfour then—and in 1906 the outcome had been a massive electoral defeat.

Battle raged year after year in the Commons between different Conservative factions over Maastricht and Europe generally. Party divisions led to huge losses in by-elections and local government elections until the party at the grass roots seemed close to extinction. In the European elections of June 1994, Labour won 64 seats to the Conservatives' 18 and the Liberal Democrats' 2; after that, things got worse still. A variety of disputes about food added to the turmoil. Veal, lamb, the right to fish in British territorial waters all were said to be threatened by Brussels. Worst of all, the advent of BSE, a new disease among cattle which led to a few people dying and posed a major threat to public health, led to the European Union, headed by Germany, banning British beef exports to the Continent. It was the result of Thatcherite policies of deregulating animal feed, but it led to a massive outcry amongst British beef farmers, Tory backbenchers, and Europhobes in general. In the summer of 1996 there was a revival of anti-German prejudice of a kind unknown since the 1950s. The tabloid press, especially the Murdoch-owned *Sun*, fanned populist xenophobia. But the beef ban went on. John Major, goaded almost beyond reason by his Europhobe critics, actually resigned the party leadership in May 1995 and defeated a right-wing challenger, John Redwood, with some ease. But the episode only served to emphasize his long-term political weakness.

The tone and style of public life, perhaps more than the substance of policy, added to a mood of disillusion and cynicism in the mid-1990s. The government plunged into an extraordinary morass of sexual or financial scandals reminiscent of the early 1960s, an earlier period of lengthy one-party rule. An obscure word, 'sleaze', dominated public perceptions of political life, fanned remorselessly by a tabloid press that turned against John Major and his government. A series of minor government ministers were involved in a variety of sexual peccadilloes and had to resign. Even in an age of moral permissiveness, such behaviour was held to be politically unacceptable. It was especially so for a party which had unwisely proclaimed its attachment to 'family values' and its urge moralistically to 'go back to basics', a phrase in whose very ambiguity perils lurked. Worse still, a growing range of covert links between business and finance and Tory politicians appeared to suggest a deep rot of corruption in Westminster. Ministers or backbenchers were shown to have received undeclared payments from private firms or intermediary lobbyists. A number of ministerial resignations followed. There were also serious moral problems with aspects of policy. Cabinet ministers were publicly censured in the Scott inquiry for misleading or deceiving parliament in the sale of arms to Iraq down to 1991 (arms used against British troops in the Gulf War), while the Nolan Committee censured the standards of public life and called for far greater transparency. By the standards of American or perhaps Italian politics, the transgressions seemed relatively small-scale. In British terms, where the rooting out of corrupt practices had begun in the late eighteenth century, they seemed shocking. The government appeared casual, if not corrupt, and John Major a leader who either did not know or did not care about what was happening.

The atmosphere of Conservative decline and widespread 'sleaze' made the mid-nineties apparently a time of much public disillusion. Works of criticism like Will Hutton's *The State we're in* (1995) condemned the social inequality, centralization and declining community sense in post-Thatcher Britain; Hutton called for a revived citizenship and republican solidarity. Many institutions were now under fire. Even the monarchy found itself facing a wave of popular criticism unknown since Regency times. It was fuelled by private family troubles such as the separation and later divorce of Prince Charles and Princess Diana, and by criticism over the monarch's wealth, lifestyle, and inability to adapt to modern times. In 1992 the Queen spoke of the year as having been 'an *annus horribilis*'. Republicanism showed signs of making headway, just as it was doing in Australia. Elsewhere faith in the City of London was undermined by the Robert Maxwell pensions scandal and troubles in Lloyd's insurance. The criminal justice system showed up police abuses in cases such as the Birmingham Six where evidence had been tampered with. The Home Office was criticized for attacks on civil liberties and political interference with the law. There was also much public disgust with the state of British society. In east London, elegant postmodernist tower blocks, an ecological park, and a marina built by the Docklands Corporation around Canary Wharf contrasted starkly with young homeless people sleeping rough in the Strand or Lincoln's Inn Fields. Disparities in wealth, income, health, and lifestyle had grown ever-wider. Long departed diseases like tuberculosis returned to haunt the poor, quite apart from newer scourges like Aids. There were other sources of instability, too. Family breakdown went on apace: one marriage in three broke down and Britain had the highest divorce rate in the EU, higher even than the Scandinavian countries. There was long-term youth unemployment in areas like Merseyside, many troubled housing estates, and an endemic drug culture in urban areas, portrayed in the film *Train-spotting*, based on a disturbing novel by the Edinburgh writer, Irvine Welsh. British society, never more affluent, seemed spiritually impoverished and socially divided.

Yet in many ways, this feeling was unbalanced and the despair exaggerated. In spite of all its problems, John Major's Britain was increasingly prosperous and most of its citizens content with their lot. Ethnic minorities had made progress after the racial disturbances of the Thatcher years. Family incomes rose as a majority of women, married as well as single, now found employment; domestic servants such as nannies or child-minders rose in number for the first time since the Edwardian era. Amongst the young, entry into university rose sharply to include a third of the age group, while part-time or 'continuous' education became widespread. At the other end of the age scale, the expectation of life rose steadily (to 77 for women), while early retirement on personal pensions often meant a more comfortable old age. Foreign holidays were commonplace, helped by the Channel Tunnel being opened for road and rail in 1994. The vast majority of households had comforts such as central heating, microwaves, videos, or personal computers. Information technology, including the Internet, meant that more and more people were able to work from their own homes. There were 8 million mobile phones. City life showed a recovery, with towns such as Glasgow, Cardiff, Newcastle, or Leeds booming, with more cheerful pubs and more cosmopolitan restaurants and cafés. The excitement of gambling on the National Lottery (which generated much money for charitable causes) was very popular. Leisure activities reflected a wider affluence. Football in particular became hugely successful, with immense funding from satellite television and star foreign players imported from the Continent or South America. Among other things, the success of black footballers, athletes, or cricketers materially helped in race relations. Much of British culture remained vigorously alive. London was still a great literary centre; architects like Norman Foster and Richard Rogers were internationally celebrated.

The cinema became especially thriving and creative, with multi-screen theatres attracting many more filmgoers. Successful films ranged from a historical classic like *The Madness of King George* (made by Channel Four television) to *The Full Monty* (1997), a bracing account of six unemployed Sheffield steelworkers who turned their talents to striptease. The press was full of the vitality of British art and design; pop icons like the Spice Girls testified both to 'girl power' and a new ersatz patriotism. There was talk of 'Cool Britannia' and the country being a market leader in popular fashion as it had been in the heyday of the Beatles and the 'swinging sixties'. As the economy began to recover with an export-led growth in 1995–7, commentators puzzled over the apparent absence of a 'feel-good factor'. The public mood appeared downbeat.

Politics were the source of much of this disillusion. It also seemed to be politics that brought a hope of revival. The Labour Party, apparently doomed to permanent opposition as the symbol of the old socialism and union troubles of the past, unexpectedly became the hope of a better world. The recovery had begun under Neil Kinnock when left-wing policies were abandoned. His successor, John Smith, continued a process of modernization by cutting down of the power of the unions and the introduction of 'one man, one vote' into party conference. But the real change came after Smith died in 1994. His successor, Tony Blair, a 42-year-old public school and Oxford-educated barrister who travelled light ideologically, led a dramatic revival. Giving an impression of youthful freshness and a sense of the new, he became the most successful party leader in modern British history. He spoke not of 'Labour' but of 'New Labour'. He appealed less to the older working classes of Labour's heartland than to the mortgaged home-owning middle classes of middle England. He spoke the language of British patriotism and brandished the Union flag. Britain, he declared, was essentially a young country. He projected himself with a remarkably sophisticated apparatus of modern communications technology to keep the party 'on message' and magnify the role of the leader. John Major was taunted by Blair in the Commons: 'you follow your party, I lead mine.'

New Labour was much more inclusive. Tony Blair appealed openly to business leaders in the CBI; he courted the Murdoch press which had traduced his party in the past; he even spoke well of Mrs Thatcher's achievements in privatizing nationalized industries, spreading home ownership, and ending the stranglehold of the unions. His model appeared to be not the old Labour Party which had spanned the century from Keir Hardie to James Callaghan, but the 'market socialism' of Australian Labour or perhaps the American Democratic Party under President Bill Clinton. The effect was a remarkably undoctrinaire Labour Party which rejected the state planning, the nationalization, the universalized welfare benefits, the income redistribution, or the links with the unions which had characterized Attlee's party in 1945. Blair announced himself with a successful campaign for Labour to throw out Clause Four, the commitment to nationalization, in early 1995. Buoyed up by Tory failures and an immense lead in the polls, he dominated British politics.

The effect was seen in the 1997 general election. The opinion polls this time were amply confirmed. The Conservatives suffered an electoral débâcle worse even than 1945 or 1906, indeed their worst since the Duke of Wellington had resisted the great Reform Act in 1832. There was a 10.9 per cent swing to Labour, which won 419 seats against the Conservatives' 165, with the Liberals capturing 46, their best score since the 1920s. Five Cabinet ministers lost their seats; suburban seats in England swung massively to Labour including Mrs Thatcher's seat in Finchley. The major cities all went Labour, while Scotland and Wales returned not one Conservative between them. Another remarkable feature of the election was the election of no fewer than 120 women MPs; over 100 of them were Labour, all middle-class, while the trade union element in the party largely disappeared. It was one of the most remarkable electoral upheavals in British history, a delayed reaction against Conservative rule which had been welling up since the poll tax revolt against Mrs Thatcher ten years earlier. Tony Blair thus became at 44 the youngest premier since Victorian times.

Labour's transition to high office was remarkably smooth. The economy had been improving rapidly of late; here was the first Labour government in history to come to power without being met by a financial crisis. The new Chancellor followed a prudent financial policy, carrying out a pre-election pledge to maintain Conservative taxing and spending limits. The stock exchange boomed to new levels in early 1998. There was a mood of caution, even conservatism in domestic policies, especially in whittling down the welfare system so as to reduce dependency on the state, but protests from the left were brushed aside. There was a deliberate policy of friendship towards business, a tough stance on law and order, and the first charges for university tuition, all of these remarkable for a government supposedly of the left. On Europe, the government seemed much more positive than its predecessor. But Tony Blair was no more inclined to join a single European currency in the first wave than John Major had been. His instincts seemed transatlantic rather than European. In Northern Ireland, however, the government did appear to achieve a rare political breakthrough after decades of violence. Sinn Fein and Unionist politicians were brought together around the same table, and on Good Friday, April 1998, they came together to reach an agreement. It would involve setting up a 108-member elected assembly on the lines of that proposed for Scotland; a cross-border Ministerial Council for ministers fom Dublin and Belfast to handle security and other matters; and a British–Irish Council of the Isles. It appeared to be much the closest that Ulster's politicians had come to a meeting of minds since the partition of Ireland in 1922, and represented among other things a remarkable diplomatic achievement for Tony Blair. The agreement was endorsed by a majority of over 71 per cent (including a majority of Protestants) in the referendum held in Northern Ireland a month later.

The potential federalism inherent in the Northern Irish agreement chimed in with one domestic area where the Labour government did prove remarkably radical. In a tranche of proposed constitutional reforms, it introduced referendums for Scottish and Welsh devolution in September 1997. Scotland voted overwhelmingly for a Scottish parliament with taxing powers; Wales by contrast endorsed an elected assembly by the narrowest of margins. The outcome, perhaps, would be a dramatic change in the centralized governance of the United Kingdom as it had existed since the Act of Union in 1707. It might even, some speculated, remain united no longer. The advent of a Scottish parliament in 1999, possibly with an SNP majority, along with British involvement in a much more integrated European Union, seemed likely to generate major changes. Pluralism at home and integration in Europe could lead to a much looser structure in which the roles of the law, parliament, and Cabinet were transformed, to produce a very different view of the British identity. A few responded to this with a fierce kind of English nationalism. But most people, recognizing a post-imperial world, the information revolution, and a global economy, appeared to accept the prospect of major changes ahead with traditional equanimity.

As the Blair government settled in, British people contemplated the advent of a new millennium. They appeared to do so in a mood of distinctly greater tranquillity, even self-confidence than had seemed likely after Mrs Thatcher's fall from power. The economy had shown recovery; society (even perhaps in Northern Ireland) was more tranquil; ethnic minorities were more widely integrated; the Scots and the Welsh busied themselves constructively in preparations for devolution. Britain seemed to have found a style and a leadership with which, for the moment, it felt comfortable. Certainly there were ample signs of massive upheavals in recent decades. The interaction of classes, genders, and generations, social keystones like marriage, family, and parenthood experienced massive strains and became less structured. Historic institutions could find it hard to cope. The Church of England had much difficulty in adapting itself to a secular age; issues like the ordination of women priests added to its anxieties. Religious observance was confined to a small minority. The Nonconformist conscience was a relic of Victorian times, while the Catholic church was under fire for its views on issues such as abortion. Except in the furthest Calvinist recesses of the Scottish western isles, Sunday was a relaxed day for shopping, motoring, and mass sport.

The monarchy had been an even greater victim of recent turmoil. Many speculated that Prince Charles might not even inherit the throne when Queen Elizabeth II eventually died. But an extraordinary popular catharsis occurred on 31 August 1997 with the death in a car crash in Paris of Princess Diana, the divorced wife of Prince Charles. At her funeral, there was an outpouring of grief by a people for whom she had been both a glamorous show-business icon who dominated the tabloid press, and also a kind of establishment outsider who showed empathy with social victims such as Aids sufferers, the homeless, single mothers, and Asian minorities. Her funeral encouraged a renewed attachment to the monarchy, even if expressed in a more casual, less deferential manner. In a way, Tony Blair took her place, a beacon of authority rather than a candle in the wind. The opinion polls recorded, in the face of much processed gloom in the media, a popular commitment to being British and an enthusiasm for country rare in the Western world. No one much wanted to emigrate. As the millennium approached, a large, mysterious plastic dome arose at Greenwich. It was heir to the Crystal Palace of 1851 and the Festival Hall of 1951. It generated debate as they had once done, but without bitterness. Like the monarchy, the millennium could be used to reinforce a basic commitment to a civic culture to which newer immigrant citizens could also respond.

Britain in the years from 1914 to 1998 had gone through seismic transformations. Yet it was recognizably the same society. Despite two world wars, the mass unemployment of the thirties, and the social turmoil of the seventies and eighties, the face of Great Britain, like Snowdonia or Thomas Hardy's Egdon Heath, might show surface changes of light or pattern; but the underlying geology remained the same. In 1998 as in 1914 there remained a profound, non-exclusive sense of place. A loyalty to London (due to have its own elected mayor), to 'the North' or Tyneside or East Anglia or Cornwall, to the separate nationalities of Scotland or Wales was still a reality. Indeed, with Scottish and Welsh devolution perhaps to be followed by extended regional government in England, a sense of definable local community might even become stronger. The population remained intensely various, distinct, individual. In a largely ur-banized society, the countryside retained a fierce (perhaps exag-gerated) sense of its own needs and identity. Much of Britain in the late nineties was still the same relatively neighbourly society where people cherished their gardens and entertained in their own homes. Most powerfully of all, the British retained a pride in their collective past—even if 'British history' might have to be redefined in a pluralist, polycultural sense to take account variously of Celtic devolution, Commonwealth immigration, and membership of Europe. Debates over the significance of Diana's death or the meaning of the millennium offered insights into this abiding folk memory. An awareness of the past shone through in innumerable local festivals, in the civility of old cathedral cities and spa towns, in the Welsh national *eisteddfod*, the Highland games, even in the multi-ethnic Notting Hill carnival now 30 years old. Public institutions like parliament embodied this sense of history. So, too, more painfully, did the sense of resolve generated by the crisis of war or external threat. In the mass media, historical or other productions on television or film revived the mystique of ancient identity. In spite of decades of almost unbearable upheaval, Britain remained an organic, comparatively peaceful, close-knit society, capable of self-renewal. Its very forms of native protest often testified to an innate tolerance, a respect for individuality and eccentricity including in difficult areas such as sexual preference, a rejection of coercion and uniformity. The 'Liberty tree' was still being nurtured by environmental pressure groups in 1998. 'Swampy' was the natural dissenting heir of the Levellers or Tom Paine. At the dawn of the new millennium, as in times of greater pomp and power in the past, the values of being British could still be affirmed and sustained. So might they be again, in centuries yet to unfold.

FURTHER READING

1. ROMAN BRITAIN

BEFORE THE ROMAN CONQUEST

Richard Bradley, *The Prehistoric Settlement of Britain* (London, 1978), particularly readable.

Barry Cunliffe, *Iron Age Communities in Britain* (2nd edn. London, 1978), general account of the centuries immediately before the Roman Conquest.

John Brailsford, *Early Celtic Masterpieces from Britain in the British Museum* (London, 1975).

GENERAL SURVEYS

Sheppard Frere, *Britannia: a History of Roman Britain* (3rd edn. London, 1987), a standard work.

Peter Salway, *Roman Britain* (*Oxford History of England*, vol. 1a) (Oxford, 1981), large-scale general history, with essays on major themes.

Malcolm Todd, *Roman Britain 55 BC–AD 400: the Province beyond Ocean* (*Fontana History of England*) (London, 1981), perceptive and up-to-date narrative.

John Wacher, *Roman Britain* (London, 1978).

Peter A. Clayton (ed.), *A Companion to Roman Britain* (Oxford, 1980), exceptionally well-illustrated essays.

Roger J. A. Wilson, *A Guide to the Roman Remains in Britain* (3rd edn. London, 1988), recommended to those wishing to visit the accessible material remains of the period.

Ordnance Survey, *Map of Roman Britain* (4th edn. Southampton, 1978), 2 sheets, scale 1 : 625,000, and gazetteer.

Philip Dixon, *Barbarian Europe* (*The Making of the Past*) (Oxford, 1976), excellent, well-illustrated background reading, helping to place the end of Roman Britain in its European context.

SPECIAL ASPECTS

Anthony Birley, *The People of Roman Britain* (London, 1979), illuminating study based on the people known by name in Roman Britain.

A. L. F. Rivet and Colin Smith, *The Place-Names of Roman Britain*
(London, 1979), major work of reference: gazetteer, accompanied by
linguistic and geographical analysis.

P. A. Holder, *The Roman Army in Britain* (London, 1982), welcome
first modern account.

David J. Breeze, *The Northern Frontiers of Roman Britain* (London,
1982), current thought, well-presented.

Ralph Merrifield, *London: City of the Romans* (London, 1983).

J. M. C. Toynbee, *Art in Britain under the Romans* (Oxford, 1964),
enormously learned, wide-ranging, and clear.

Charles Thomas, *Christianity in Britain to AD 500* (London, 1981),
thought-provoking re-examination.

Ralph Merrifield, *The Archaeology of Ritual and Magic* (London,
1987), includes much illuminating reinterpretation of Romano-
British material.

2.   THE ANGLO-SAXON PERIOD

GENERAL HISTORY

F. M. Stenton, *Anglo-Saxon England* (3rd edn. Oxford, 1971), the
standard history.

J. Campbell (ed.), *The Anglo-Saxons* (Oxford, 1982), an outstandingly
good recent book, with many new ideas and splendid illustrations.

P. Hunter Blair, *An introduction to Anglo-Saxon England* (Cambridge,
1956), summarizes the main events and themes.

ORIGINAL SOURCES

The Anglo-Saxon Chronicle, trans. G. N. Garmonsway (London,
1953); the late Anglo-Saxon vernacular chronicle, providing contemporary comment from Alfred's reign onwards.

Bede, *Ecclesiastical History of the English People*, trans. L. Sherley-
Price (rev. edn. Harmondsworth, 1968), a brilliant and vivid narrative account written in the early eighth century, the most important
single source for earlier Anglo-Saxon history.

ARCHAEOLOGY, ART, AND LITERATURE

R. L. Bruce-Mitford, *The Sutton Hoo Ship Burial: a Handbook* (3rd
edn. London, 1979), a well-illustrated account of the most important
archaeological discovery from the Anglo-Saxon period.

The Earliest English Poems, trans. M. Alexander (2nd edn. Harmondsworth, 1977), translations of the more important Anglo-Saxon
poems, including *The Battle of Maldon* and selections from
Beowulf.

H. M. and Joan Taylor, *Anglo-Saxon Architecture*, i–iii (Cambridge,
1965–78), a comprehensive account of the surviving Anglo-Saxon
churches.

D. Talbot Rice, *English Art 871–1100* (Oxford, 1952), a well-
illustrated general account.

D. M. Wilson (ed.), *The archaeology of Anglo-Saxon England* (Cambridge, 1976), chapters by several authors on the various kinds of
physical evidence for the period.

THE MERCIAN SUPREMACY

A. Dornier (ed.), *Mercian Studies* (Leicester, 1977), a collection of
essays relating to the Mercian region, especially during the eighth
century.

LATE ANGLO-SAXON KINGSHIP AND GOVERNMENT

F. Barlow, *Edward the Confessor* (London, 1970), the standard biography.

D. Hill (ed.), *Ethelred the Unready: papers from the Millenary Conference* (Oxford, 1978), a recent collection of important and original
studies on the late tenth and early eleventh centuries.

THE CHURCH

H. Mayr-Harting, *The coming of Christianity to Anglo-Saxon England*
(London, 1972), the best general account of the conversions.

P. Hunter Blair, *The world of Bede* (London, 1970), religion and
learning in eighth-century Northumbria.

M. Deanesly, *The pre-Conquest church in England* (London, 1961), a
general survey of ecclesiastical institutions.

SCOTLAND AND WALES: GENERAL HISTORY

A. A. M. Duncan, *Scotland: the making of the kingdom* (Edinburgh,
1975).

W. Davies, *Wales in the early Middle Ages* (Leicester, 1982).

3.   THE EARLY MIDDLE AGES

GENERAL

M. T. Clanchy, *England and its Rulers 1066–1272* (Glasgow, 1983), a thought-provoking combination of political and cultural history.

G. W. S. Barrow, *Feudal Britain 1066–1314* (London, 1956), especially good on Scotland and Wales.

F. Barlow, *The Feudal Kingdom of England 1042–1216* (4th edn. London, 1988), an excellent outline.

D. M. Stenton, *English Society in the Early Middle Ages 1066–1307* (2nd edn. Harmondsworth, 1952), a brief social survey.

M. Chibnall, *Anglo-Norman England 1066–1166* (Oxford, 1986), judicious.

STUDIES OF SOME MAJOR POLITICAL THEMES

H. R. Loyn, *The Norman Conquest* (3rd edn. London, 1982), a brief and balanced survey of a standard problem.

J. Le Patourel, *The Norman Empire* (Oxford, 1976), magisterial. The starting-point for all future studies of this subject.

J. C. Holt, *Magna Carta* (Cambridge, 1965), indispensable for the political and social context of the charter.

G. O. Sayles, *The King's Parliament of England* (London, 1975), a distillation of 40 years of research and argument by Richardson and Sayles.

ROYAL BIOGRAPHIES

D. C. Douglas, *William the Conqueror* (London, 1964), a splendidly traditional biography.

F. Barlow, *William Rufus* (London, 1983), not just a life, also a fine study of the times.

R. H. C. Davis, *King Stephen* (London 1967), lively and stimulating. What could be better?

W. L. Warren, *Henry II* (London, 1973), somehow contrives to be both massive and readable.

J. Gillingham, *Richard the Lionheart* (2nd edn. London, 1989), emphasizes the importance of the Angevin dominions in France.

W. L. Warren, *King John* (Harmondsworth, 1961), seeks to rescue John from the damning verdict of thirteenth-century chroniclers.

OTHER BIOGRAPHIES

F. Barlow, *Thomas Becket* (London, 1986), a detached and detailed narrative.

C. R. Cheney, *Hubert Walter* (London, 1967), a lucid account of the career of the most powerful churchman of the age.

S. Painter, *William Marshal* (Baltimore, 1933), the story of a tournament knight who becomes regent of England.

CHURCH

F. Barlow, *The English Church 1066–1154* (London, 1979), a lively analysis of a radical and tumultuous age.

D. Knowles, *The Monastic Order in England 940–1216* (2nd edn. Cambridge, 1963), a scholarly history of monasticism by a scholar monk.

—— *The Religious Orders in England*, vol. 1 (Cambridge, 1962), important for the coming of the friars.

SCOTLAND

G. W. S. Barrow, *Kingship and Unity. Scotland 1000–1316* (London, 1981), an invaluable brief survey.

WALES

R. R. Davies, *Conquest, Coexistence and Change: Wales 1063–1415* (Oxford, 1987), economy, society, and politics: a major study.

IRELAND

R. Frame, *Colonial Ireland 1169–1369* (Dublin, 1981), an admirable sketch.

ECONOMY

J. L. Bolton, *The Medieval English Economy 1150–1500* (London, 1980), the most helpful general introduction.

E. Miller and J. Hatcher, *Medieval England: Rural Society and Economic Change 1086–1348* (London, 1978), a judicious survey of the rural economy.

S. Reynolds, *An Introduction to the History of English Medieval Towns* (2nd edn. Oxford, 1982), the thinking man's introduction to English urban history.

G. A. Williams, *Medieval London: from Commune to Capital*

(London, 1963), a vivid and detailed account of thirteenth and early fourteenth-century London.

LANGUAGE AND LITERACY

M. T. Clanchy, *From Memory to Written Record: England 1066–1307* (London, 1979), a fascinating analysis of the development of literacy and the literate mentality.

ART

T. S. R. Boase, *English Art 1100–1216* (Oxford, 1953).
P. Brieger, *English Art 1216–1307* (Oxford, 1957): two classic surveys of art and architecture.

4. THE LATER MIDDLE AGES

GENERAL SURVEYS

F. R. H. DuBoulay, *An Age of Ambition* (London, 1970), a stimulating look at themes (e.g. class, marriage, sex) often neglected.
S. B. Chrimes, C. D. Ross, and R. A. Griffiths (eds.), *Fifteenth-century England, 1399–1509: Studies in Politics and Society* (Manchester, 1972), up-to-date essays on central topics.
J. R. Lander, *Conflict and Stability in Fifteenth-century England* (3rd edn. London, 1977), an overall (if gloomy) view of the century.
M. Prestwich, *The Three Edwards* (London, 1980), clear and succinct.
Anthony Tuck, *Crown and Nobility, 1272–1461* (London, 1985), a clear and sound narrative.

PARTICULAR THEMES

A. R. Bridbury, *Economic Growth: England in the Later Middle Ages* (London, 1962).
K. B. McFarlane, *The Nobility of Later Medieval England* (Oxford, 1973), essays by a master-historian.
R. H. Hilton, *The English Peasantry in the Later Middle Ages* (Oxford, 1975).
C. Platt, *The English Medieval Town* (London, 1976), a pleasant, illustrated book.
J. Bellamy, *Crime and Public Order in England in the Later Middle Ages* (London, 1973).

R. G. Davies and J. H. Denton (eds.), *The English Parliament in the Middle Ages* (Manchester, 1981), nicely integrated essays.

J. C. Dickinson, *An Ecclesiastical History of England: the Later Middle Ages* (London, 1979).

K. B. McFarlane, *John Wycliffe and the Beginnings of English Nonconformity* (London, 1952).

J. Evans, *English Art, 1307–1461* (Oxford, 1949).

V. J. Scattergood and J. W. Sherborne (eds.), *English Court Culture in the Later Middle Ages* (London, 1983), expert essays on a variety of themes.

S. Medcalf (ed.), *The Context of English Literature: The Later Middle Ages* (London, 1981), a rare attempt to integrate cultural and social history.

J. Brown (ed.), *Scottish Society in the Fifteenth Century* (London, 1977), essays on central topics.

Alexander Grant, *Independence and Nationhood: Scotland, 1306–1469* (London, 1984), a comprehensive and often original survey.

G. Williams, *Recovery, Orientation, and Reformation: Wales c.1415–1642* (*History of Wales*, vol. 3) (Oxford, 1987).

J. F. Lydon, *Ireland in the Later Middle Ages* (Dublin, 1973).

C. D. Ross, *The Wars of the Roses* (London, 1976), wise and well illustrated.

A. E. Goodman, *The Wars of the Roses* (London, 1981), good on military matters.

RECENT ROYAL AND POLITICAL STUDIES

E. L. G. Stones, *Edward I* (Oxford, 1978).

R. Barber, *Edward, Prince of Wales and Aquitaine* (London, 1978).

J. A. Tuck, *Richard II and the English Nobility* (London, 1973).

J. L. Kirby, *Henry IV of England* (London, 1970).

K. B. McFarlane, *Lancastrian Kings and Lollard Knights* (Oxford, 1972), two major themes explored with insight.

G. L. Harriss (ed.), *Henry V: The Practice of Kingship* (Oxford, 1985), essays which amount to a new study of the king and his reign.

R. A. Griffiths, *The Reign of King Henry VI* (London, 1981), more than a biography of the king.

C. D. Ross, *Edward IV* (London, 1974).

—— *Richard III* (London, 1981).

5.   THE TUDOR AGE

GENERAL WORKS

John Guy, *Tudor England* (Oxford, 1988), the most up-to-date and comprehensive account of the period.

P. Williams, *The Tudor Regime* (Oxford, 1979), the most enlightened general survey of Tudor government.

C. S. L. Davies, *Peace, Print and Protestantism, 1450–1558* (London, 1976), a lucid introduction especially useful on social and economic history.

G. R. Elton, *Reform and Reformation: England 1509–1558* (London, 1977), the best-informed account of the early Tudors.

G. Donaldson, *All the Queen's Men: Power and Politics in Mary Stewart's Scotland* (London, 1983), an encyclopaedic who's who.

J. Wormald, *Court, Kirk and Community, 1470–1625* (London, 1981), the best survey of early modern Scotland.

D. M. Palliser, *The Age of Elizabeth: England under the Later Tudors, 1547–1603* (London, 1983), the best synthesis of social and economic conditions.

D. M. Loades, *The Tudor Court* (London, 1986), a solid anatomy of the political and cultural focus of the State.

BIOGRAPHIES

S. B. Chrimes, *Henry VII* (London, 1972), a sound synthesis of recent research.

J. J. Scarisbrick, *Henry VIII* (London, 1968), an enthralling and original biography accepted as standard.

E. W. Ives, *Anne Boleyn* (Oxford, 1986), a lively introduction to the factional politics of Henry VIII's reign.

A. F. Pollard, *Wolsey* (London, 1929), a dated but indispensable work.

R. Marius, *Thomas More* (London, 1985), the best biography.

D. M. Loades, *The Reign of Mary Tudor* (London, 1979), a solid but essential conspectus.

C. Read, *Mr. Secretary Cecil and Queen Elizabeth, Lord Burghley and Queen Elizabeth* (London, 1955, 1960), a two-volume study valuable on diplomacy, but which pays insufficient attention to domestic patronage and faction.

P. Johnson, *Elizabeth I: a Study in Power and Intellect* (London, 1974), a fair-minded assessment by a professional biographer, but Elizabeth's influence is overrated.

STUDIES OF SPECIAL TOPICS

G. R. Elton, *Reform and Renewal: Thomas Cromwell and the Common Weal* (Cambridge, 1973), the most convincing portrait of Thomas Cromwell by the leading authority.

A. G. Dickens, *The English Reformation* (London, 1964), a dispassionate and comprehensive account.

J. Loach and R. Tittler (eds.), *The Mid-Tudor Polity* (London, 1980), a provocative collection of essays by revisionist historians.

P. Collinson, *The Elizabethan Puritan Movement* (London, 1967), an authoritative study by the acknowledged expert.

C. Haigh (ed.), *The Reign of Elizabeth I* (London, 1984), revisionist essays on the reign.

G. Mattingley, *The Defeat of the Spanish Armada* (London, 1959), an absorbing book by a writer who knew Spanish as well as English sources.

L. Stone, *The Crisis of the Aristocracy* (Oxford, 1965), an important if controversial study of Tudor high society.

K. Thomas, *Religion and the Decline of Magic* (London, 1971), a sparkling and original study of the mentality of Tudor Englishmen.

R. Strong, *The Cult of Elizabeth: Elizabethan Portraiture and Pageantry* (London, 1977), a cultural backcloth by the leading expert.

M. James, *Society, Politics and Culture* (Cambridge, 1986), related case-studies tracing the social, political, and cultural roots of conformity and obedience in the State.

C. Haigh (ed.), *The English Reformation Revised* (Cambridge, 1987), incorporates the recent historiography on the Reformation.

6. THE STUARTS

POLITICAL AND CONSTITUTIONAL HISTORY

B. Coward, *The Stuart Age* (London, 1980), the best introductory survey.

A. B. Worden (ed.), *Stuart England* (London, 1986).

C. Russell, *The Crisis of Parliaments 1509–1660* (Oxford, 1971).

D. Hirst, *Authority and Conflict 1603–1658* (London, 1985).

J. R. Jones, *Country and Court 1658–1714* (London, 1979).

F. M. G. Higham, *Catholic and Reformed: A Study of the Church of England 1559–1662* (London, 1962), excellent study of religious thought.

J. P. Kenyon, *The Stuarts* (London, 1958).

S. J. Houston, *James I* (London, 1973).

R. Ollard, *The Image of the King: Charles I and Charles II* (London, 1979).

J. Miller, *James II: A Study in Kingship* (London, 1978).

J. S. Morrill, *The Revolt of the Provinces* (London, 1976).

A. Woolrych, *Battles of the English Civil War* (London, 1961).

G. E. Aylmer, *The Levellers in the English Revolution* (London, 1975), a brief essay and key texts.

C. Hill, *The World Turned Upside Down* (Harmondsworth, 1973), re-creates the world of the religious radicals of the 1650s.

C. H. Firth, *Oliver Cromwell and the Rule of the Puritans* (Oxford, 1900).

J. P. Kenyon, *The Popish Plot* (London, 1972).

J. R. Jones, *The Revolution of 1688 in England* (London, 1972).

G. Donaldson, *Scotland: James V to James VII* (Edinburgh, 1965).

T. W. Moody, F. X. Martin, F. J. Byrne (eds.), *A New History of Ireland*, vol. iii 1534–1691 (Oxford, 1976), a long narrative.

M. MacCurtain, *Tudor and Stuart Ireland* (Dublin, 1972) a short analysis.

SOCIAL, ECONOMIC, CULTURAL

D. C. Coleman, *The Economy of England 1450–1750* (Oxford, 1977), a brilliantly crisp synthesis.

K. Wrightson, *English Society 1580–1680* (London, 1982), re-creates the mental world of the seventeenth-century villager.

C. Clay, *Economic Expansion and Social Change: England 1500–1700* (Cambridge, 1984).

P. Laslett, *The World We Have Lost* (London, 1971).

L. Stone, *The Crisis of the Aristocracy* (abridged version, Oxford, 1967).

J. Hook, *The Baroque Age* (London, 1976).

R. Strong, *Van Dyck: Charles I on Horseback (London, 1972).

C. Webster, *The Great Instauration* (London, 1970).

K. V. Thomas, *Religion and the Decline of Magic* (London, 1971).

M. Spufford, *Small Books and Pleasant Histories: Popular Fiction and its Readers in 17th Century England* (London, 1981).

C. Hill, *Society and Puritanism in Pre-Revolutionary England* (London, 1964).

J. Bossy, *The English Catholic Community 1570–1850* (London, 1975).
T. C. Smout, *A History of the Scottish People 1560–1830* (London, 1969).

DOCUMENTS AND CONTEMPORARY TEXTS

Samuel Pepys, *Diary*, various editions, but all previous ones superseded by that of R. C. Latham and W. Matthews, 11 vols. (London, 1970–83).
The Illustrated Pepys, ed. R. C. Latham (London, 1978), a marvellous sampler.
John Evelyn, *Diary*, various editions and extracts, principally the edition by E. S. de Beer, 6 vols. (Oxford, 1955).
J. Aubrey, *Brief Lives* (again many editions but e.g. Harmondsworth, 1962).
R. Gough, *The History of Myddle* (Harmondsworth, 1981), a splendid evocation of life in a seventeenth-century parish, written by a local farmer.
J. P. Kenyon, *The Stuart Constitution* (Cambridge, 1962), for texts and stimulating commentary.
J. Thirsk and J. P. Cooper, *Seventeenth-century Economic Documents* (Oxford, 1972).

BIBLIOGRAPHY

M. F. Keeler, *Bibliography of British History: Stuart Period, 1603–1714* (Oxford, 1970), a comprehensive guide to publications up to 1960.
J. S. Morrill, *Critical Bibliographies in Modern History: Seventeenth Century Britain* (Folkestone, 1980), complements Keeler and offers comments on the works discussed.

7. THE EIGHTEENTH CENTURY

GENERAL WORKS

J. R. Jones, *Country and Court: England, 1658–1714* (London, 1978);
W. A. Speck, *Stability and Strife: England, 1714–1760* (London, 1977);
I. R. Christie, *Wars and Revolutions: Britain 1760–1815* (London, 1982): three books in Arnold's *New History of England* which together provide a general survey of the period.
J. B. Owen, *The Eighteenth Century, 1714–1815* (London, 1974), one

of the more recent and most useful of the many outline histories of
the eighteenth century.

POLITICS

J. H. Plumb, *The Growth of Political Stability in England 1675–1725*
(London, 1967), one of the most influential studies.

J. Cannon (ed.), *The Whig Ascendancy: Colloquies on Hanoverian
England* (London, 1981), discusses the recent literature on stability
and on many other themes.

H. T. Dickinson, *Politics and Literature in the Eighteenth Century*
(London, 1974), includes representative selections from contemporary works.

—— *Liberty and Property: Political Ideology in Eighteenth-Century
Britain* (London, 1977), a useful account for those interested in the
history of ideas.

J. Cannon, *Parliamentary Reform 1640–1832* (Cambridge, 1973, rev.
edn. 1982), deals with a particularly important theme.

J. R. Jones, *Britain and the World 1649–1815* (London, 1980), describes international relations in a British context.

I. R. Christie and B. W. Labaree, *Empire or Independence 1760–1776*
(London, 1976);

P. J. Marshall, *Problems of Empire: Britain and India 1757–1813*
(London, 1968); discussions of two particularly important imperial
problems, America and India, respectively.

L. Namier, *The Structure of Politics at the Accession of George III*
(London, 1967).

P. G. M. Dickson, *The Financial Revolution in England* (London,
1967).

ECONOMIC AND SOCIAL

E. Pawson, *The Early Industrial Revolution: Britain in the Eighteenth
Century* (London, 1979), a useful addition to the many economic
history textbooks on the eighteenth century.

R. Porter, *English Society in the Eighteenth Century* (London, 1982),
presents a colourful picture of social conditions, opportunities, and
developments.

G. E. Mingay, *English Landed Society in the Eighteenth Century*
(London, 1963), deals with the gentry.

R. W. Malcolmson, *Life and Labour in England 1700–1780* (London, 1981), deals with the lower orders.

J. Stevenson, *Popular Disturbances in England 1700–1870* (London, 1979), also useful on popular politics.

P. Corfield, *The Impact of English Towns 1700–1800* (Oxford, 1982), a survey of eighteenth-century urban growth.

D. Hay, P. Linebaugh, E. P. Thompson, *Albion's Fatal Tree: Crime and Society in Eighteenth Century England* (London, 1975), a pioneering study in the now flourishing history of crime.

J. Cannon, *Aristocratic Century: The Peerage of Eighteenth-Century England* (Cambridge, 1984), argues for aristocratic dominance of the period.

N. McKendrick, J. Brewer, and J. H. Plumb, *The Birth of a Consumer Society: The Commercialisation of Eighteenth-Century England* (London, 1982).

M. D. George, *London Life in the Eighteenth Century* (London, 1925), a classic of social and urban history.

P. Deane, *The First Industrial Revolution* (Cambridge, 1965), remains the best analytical introduction to its subject.

J. D. Chambers and G. E. Mingay, *The Agricultural Revolution 1750–1880* (London, 1966).

J. M. Beattie, *Crime and the Courts in England, 1660–1800* (Oxford, 1986), provides a definitive study of the operations of the criminal law.

RELIGIOUS AND CULTURAL

M. R. Watts, *The Dissenters: From the Reformation to the French Revolution* (Oxford, 1978).

N. Sykes, *Church and State in England in the Eighteenth Century* (London, 1932).

J. Redwood, *Reason, Ridicule and Religion: The Age of Enlightenment in England, 1660–1750* (London, 1976).

A. Armstrong, *The Church of England, the Methodists and Society 1700–1850* (London, 1973), a brief summary of the religious history of the period.

R. Paulson, *Emblem and Expression: Meaning in English Art of the Eighteenth Century* (London, 1975), transmits something of the flavour as well as some of the most important aspects of cultural controversy.

The English Satirical Print 1600–1823 in seven volumes (Cambridge,

1986), reproduces a wealth of contemporary cartoons and illustrations on diverse aspects of the age.

8.   REVOLUTION AND THE RULE OF LAW

GENERAL

Elie Halévy, *England in 1815* (Paris, 1913, London, 1924), an early but still authoritative account.

G. M. Young, *Victorian England: the Portrait of an Age* (Oxford, 1936), a key reappraisal, rescuing the nineteenth century from the likes of Lytton Strachey.

J. Steven Watson, *The Reign of George III, 1760–1815* (Oxford, 1960).

E. L. Woodward, *The Age of Reform, 1815–70* (Oxford, 1960).

G. S. Kitson Clark, *The Making of Victorian England* (London, 1962), like G. M. Young a high Tory, but unusually sensitive to the nature of middle-class reforming movements.

J. F. C. Harrison, *Early Victorian England, 1835–1850* (London, 1973), particularly strong on protest and radical movements.

C. Cook and Brian Keith, *British Historical Facts, 1830–1900* (London, 1975), includes economic as well as election and ministerial data.

ECONOMIC

Paul Mantoux, *The Industrial Revolution of the Eighteenth Century* (1911, London, 1961), pioneer and still perceptive study by a French historian.

J. H. Clapham, *An Economic History of Modern Britain* (Cambridge, 1933), some of Clapham's conclusions—notably over the standard of living—must be revised, but still conveys a wealth of detailed information. Best used as a supplement to Peter Mathias.

Peter Mathias, *The First Industrial Nation* (2nd rev. edn. London, 1983), reasonably up-to-date synthesis.

François Crouzet, *The Victorian Economy* (London, 1982), a synthesis of recent research by the leading French authority on the British economy.

Michael Robbins, *The Railway Age* (London, 1962), thematic study of railways and society.

Charles Hadfield, *British Canals* (London, 1950), an introduction to his great series of regional histories.

L. T. C. Rolt, *Victorian Engineering* (Harmondsworth, 1970), stress on mechanical engineering.

R. J. Morris and John Langton (eds.), *Atlas of Industrializing Britain* (London, 1986).

POLITICS AND GOVERNMENT

Oliver MacDonagh, *A Pattern of Government Growth* (London, 1961), a study of passenger ship regulation as an example of administrative development.

Michael Brock, *The Great Reform Bill* (London, 1973), the 1832 Reform Act.

E. J. Hobsbawm and George Rudé, *Captain Swing* (London, 1968), the labourers' revolts of 1831.

S. E. Finer, *Edwin Chadwick* (London, 1952), study of the great Benthamite reformer.

Norman McCord, *The Anti-Corn-Law League* (London, 1975).

Asa Briggs (ed.), *Chartist Studies* (London, 1974), emphasizes geographical diversity of movement.

Beatrice and Sidney Webb, *The History of Local English Government* (London, 1908–29).

Jasper Ridley, *Palmerston* (London, 1970).

A. V. Dicey, *The Relation between Law and Public Opinion in England in the Nineteenth Century* (London, 1906), lucid, influential but simplistic approach.

Dorothy Thompson, *The Chartists* (Aldershot, 1986).

SOCIETY

J. F. C. Harrison, *Robert Owen and the Owenites* (London, 1969).

Clive Emsley, *British Society and the French Wars, 1793–1815* (London, 1979), draws on much untapped archive material.

E. P. Thompson, *The Making of the English Working Class* (London, 1963), a controversial masterpiece.

—— *Whigs and Hunters* (London, 1975), law and society in the eighteenth century.

Harold Perkin, *The Origins of Modern English Society, 1780–1880* (London, 1969).

Roy Porter, *English Society in the 18th Century* (Harmondsworth, 1982).

W. R. Ward, *Religious Society in England, 1790–1950* (London, 1972), changes in family organization, mores, and emotions.

Lawrence Stone, *The Family, Sex and Marriage, 1500–1800* (London, 1977), changes in family organization, mores, and emotions.

Brian Simon, *Studies in the History of Education, 1780–1870* (London, 1960), strong on nonconformity and educational innovation.

Owen Chadwick, *The Victorian Church* (3rd edn. London, 1971), definitive; despite title, deals with all the churches.

Donald Read, *The English Provinces* (London, 1964), social background to industrial revolution and Anti-Corn Law League.

John Foster, *The Class Struggle in the Industrial Revolution* (London, 1974), well-researched Marxist interpretation of industry and politics in South Shields, Northampton, and Oldham.

Lawrence and Jeanne C. Fawtier Stone, *An Open Elite? England 1540–1880* (Oxford, 1984).

SCOTLAND, IRELAND, WALES

T. C. Smout, *A History of the Scottish People* (London, 1969).

—— *A Century of the Scottish People, 1830–1950* (London, 1986).

E. D. Evans, *A History of Wales, 1600–1815* (Cardiff, 1976).

Gearóid O'Tuathaigh, *Ireland before the Famine, 1798–1848* (Dublin, 1972).

CULTURE

Francis D. Klingender, *Art and the Industrial Revolution* (London, 1972), Marxist interpretation of art and industry, from optimism to doubt, *c.*1750–1850.

Raymond Williams, *Culture and Society, 1780–1950* (London, 1958), study of the social critical condition: Burke, Cobbett, Carlyle, Ruskin.

9. THE LIBERAL AGE

GENERAL SURVEYS

Asa Briggs, *The Age of Improvement* (London, 1959), a good political and social survey of the period up to 1867.

D. Read, *England 1868–1914* (London, 1979), a competent, detailed survey.

Geoffrey Best, *Mid-Victorian Britain 1851–1870* (London, 1971), a predominantly social account.

R. C. K. Ensor, *England, 1870–1914* (Oxford, 1936, often reprinted), still has material and analysis of value.

E. Halévy, *History of the English People in the Nineteenth Century*, vols. 5 (*Imperialism and the Rise of Labour, 1895–1905*) and 6 (*The Rule of Democracy, 1905–1914*) (rev. edn. London, 1951–2), a classic account, based on contemporary published material, which still holds its own.

ECONOMIC HISTORY

P. Mathias, *The First Industrial Nation* (2nd rev. edn. London, 1983), a clear and concise account.

E. Hobsbawm, *Industry and Empire* (London, 1968), an incisive argument, stressing the socio-economic shift from industry to commerce.

D. Landes, *The Unbound Prometheus. Technological Change, 1750 to the Present* (Cambridge, 1969), the relationship of technology to industry.

SOCIAL LIFE

H. J. Dyos and M. Wolff (eds.), *The Victorian City*, 2 vols. (London, 1973), splendidly comprehensive illustrations.

G. Mingay (ed.), *The Victorian Countryside*, 2 vols. (London, 1981), the complementary work.

Robert Roberts, *The Classic Slum* (London, 1971), childhood in Salford.

Florence, Lady Bell, *At the Works* (London, 1911 edn.), vivid and acute analysis of social life in Middlesbrough.

Flora Thompson, *Lark Rise to Candleford* (Oxford, 1945, often reprinted), the Oxfordshire countryside in decline.

Owen Chadwick, *The Victorian Church*, 2 vols. (3rd edn. London, 1971), a powerful survey, rather favourable to Anglicanism.

Asa Briggs, *Victorian Cities* (London, 1963), and *Victorian People* (2nd edn. London, 1965), stimulating essays.

The Batsford series, *Victorian and Edwardian Life* in photographs (many vols. by city and county) is excellent; an important source.

V. A. C. Gatrell, B. Lenman, and G. Parker, *Crime and the Law: the Social History of Crime in Western Europe since 1500* (London, 1980).

POLITICAL LIFE

John Vincent, *The Formation of the Liberal Party, 1857–1868* (London, 1966), a brilliant if sometimes excessively paradoxical analysis.

Martin Pugh, *The Making of Modern British Politics 1867–1939*
(London, 1982), an intelligent synthesis of recent research.
Robert Blake, *Disraeli* (London, 1966), the standard life.
H. C. G. Matthew, *Gladstone, 1809–1874* (Oxford, 1986).
Robert Blake, *The Conservative Party from Peel to Thatcher* (new edn.
London, 1982), the party's fall and rise.
Paul Smith, *Disraelian Conservatism and Social Reform* (London,
1967), sets Conservative social policy in context.
Kenneth O. Morgan, *The Age of Lloyd George* (3rd edn. London,
1978), the best introduction to Liberalism after Gladstone.
José Harris, *Unemployment and Politics. A Study in English Social
Policy 1886–1914* (Oxford, 1972; paperback 1984), a powerful cri-
tique of the early years of the welfare state.
Ross McKibbin, *The Evolution of the Labour Party, 1910–1924*
(Oxford, 1974, paperback 1983), the standard work on the party's
early years.
H. A. Clegg, A. Fox , and A. F. Thompson, *A History of British Trade
Unions since 1889*, vol. i. *1889–1910* (Oxford, 1964), indispensable
account of the complexities of politics and industrial relations.
Henry Pelling, *Popular Politics and Society in Late Victorian Britain*
(London, 1968), a volume of challenging reinterpretations.
A. Rosen, *Rise Up Women!* (London, 1974), places the suffragette
movement in a searching light, with unflattering consequences.
Asa Briggs (ed.), *William Morris. Selected Writings and Designs*
(London, 1962), gives a useful introduction to the art and craft
movement.

SCOTLAND, IRELAND, WALES

F. S. L. Lyons, *Ireland since the Famine* (London, 1971), authoritative,
from an Anglo-Irish viewpoint.
Kenneth O. Morgan, *Rebirth of a Nation: Wales 1880–1980* (Oxford
and Cardiff, 1981), a sympathetic account from a moderately
nationalist perspective.
Christopher Harvie, *Scotland and Nationalism* (London, 1977), lively
and original.

IMPERIALISM

D. K. Fieldhouse, *The Colonial Empires* (London, 1966), an excellent
survey.

R. Robinson and J. Gallagher, *Africa and the Victorians* (London, 1961), a bold thesis, arguing the superiority of strategic over economic motivation.

A. P. Thornton, *The Imperial Idea and its Enemies* (London, 1959), gives an elegant and witty account of the imperial debate.

A. J. P. Taylor, *The Troublemakers* (London, 1956, reprinted 1969), a heartfelt account of a tradition which failed.

Paul Kennedy, *The Realities behind Diplomacy* (London, 1981), offers a useful survey of the relationship of diplomacy to power.

A. J. P. Taylor, *The Struggle for Mastery in Europe, 1848–1918* (Oxford, 1954, often reprinted), a powerful analysis of the consequences of Germany's bid for power.

10. THE TWENTIETH CENTURY

GENERAL

Peter Clarke, *Hope and Glory: Britain 1900–1990* (London, 1996).

T. O. Lloyd, *Empire to Welfare State. English History, 1906–1992* (4th edn. Oxford, 1993), a good general survey.

C. L. Mowat, *Britain between the Wars* (London, 1955), excellent on social and economic themes.

Kenneth O. Morgan, *The People's Peace: British History since 1945* (Oxford, 1999).

SOCIAL AND ECONOMIC

A. H. Halsey (ed.), *Trends in British Society since 1900* (London, 1972), comprehensive and factual.

Arthur Marwick, *The Deluge* (London, 1965), covers the effects of the First World War.

William Ashworth, *An Economic History of Britain, 1870–1939* (London, 1960).

Sidney Pollard, *The Development of the British Economy, 1914–1980* (3rd edn. London, 1983).

R. Floud and D. McCloskey (eds.), *The Economic History of Britain since 1700*, vol. iii (Cambridge, 1994).

Alec Cairncross, *Years of Recovery: British Economic Policy, 1945–51* (London, 1985), a fine study of the Attlee years.

J. R. C. Dow, *The Management of the British Economy, 1945–60* (Cambridge, 1964).

E. H. Phelps Brown, *The Growth of British Industrial Relations, 1906–14* (London, 1963).

Henry Pelling, *A History of British Trade Unionism* (2nd edn. London, 1971).

Harold Perkin, *The Rise of Professional Society: England since 1880* (London, 1989).

John Stevenson, *British Society, 1914–1945* (London, 1984).

Ross McKibbin, *Culture and Classes: England 1918–1951* (Oxford, 1998).

G. C. Peden, *British Economic and Social Policy: Lloyd George to Margaret Thatcher* (Deddington, Oxon., 1985).

Rodney Lowe, *The Welfare State since 1945* (London, 1993).

Jane Lewis, *Women in Britain since 1945* (London, 1992).

POLITICAL

Martin Pugh, *The Making of Modern British Politics, 1867–1939* (London, 1982), a helpful survey for the student.

Samuel Beer, *Modern British Politics* (new edn. London, 1982), a stimulating thematic approach.

Robert Blake, *The Conservative Party from Peel to Major* (new edn. London, 1997).

John Ramsden, *An Appetite for Power* (London, 1998). The modern history of the Conservatives.

Trevor Wilson, *The Downfall of the Liberal Party, 1914–1935* (London, 1966).

Ross McKibbin, *The Evolution of the Labour Party, 1910–1924* (Oxford paperback, 1983).

Cameron Hazlehurst, *Politicians at War, July 1914 to May 1915* (London, 1971).

Robert Skidelsky, *Politicians and the Slump* (London, 1968), the second Labour government.

David Reynolds, *Britannia Overruled: British Policy and World Power in the Twentieth Century* (London, 1991), a fine overview.

R. A. C. Parker, *Chamberlain and Appeasement* (London, 1993), a powerful reassessment.

Paul Addison, *The Road to 1945* (London, 1975), a stimulating account of consensus and conflict in wartime politics.

Kenneth O. Morgan, *Labour in Power, 1945–1951* (Oxford, 1984).

—— *Labour People: Leaders and Lieutenants, Hardie to Kinnock* (new edn. Oxford, 1992).

Dennis Kavanagh, *Thatcherism and British Politics* (Oxford, 1984).

David Marquand, *The Unprincipled Society* (London, 1988), a perceptive critique of the British political economy.

BIOGRAPHIES

Robert Blake and Roger Louis (eds.), *Churchill* (Oxford, 1993), authoritative essays.

José Harris, *William Beveridge* (Oxford, 1977).

Roy Foster, *W. B. Yeats: A Life*, vol. i (Oxford, 1997).

Christopher Hussey, *The Life of Sir Edwin Lutyens* (London, 1950).

Hermione Lee, *Virginia Woolf* (London, 1996).

Alan Bullock, *The Life and Times of Ernest Bevin*, 3 vols. (London, 1960, 1967, 1983).

David Marquand, *Ramsay MacDonald* (London, 1977).

David Dilks, *Neville Chamberlain*, vol. i (Cambridge, 1984).

Kenneth Harris, *Attlee* (London, 1982).

Ben Pimlott, *Hugh Dalton* (London, 1985).

Robert Skidelsky, *John Maynard Keynes*, vols. i and ii (London, 1983, 1992).

Bernard Crick, *George Orwell: A Life* (London, 1980).

Brian Brivati, *Hugh Gaitskell* (London, 1996).

John Campbell, *Edward Heath* (London, 1993).

Kenneth O. Morgan, *Callaghan: A Life* (Oxford, 1997).

Hugo Young, *One of Us* (London, 1989), on Mrs Thatcher.

SCOTLAND, IRELAND, WALES

Kenneth O. Morgan, *Rebirth of a Nation: Wales 1880–1980* (Oxford and Cardiff, 1981).

Christopher Harvie, *Scotland and Nationalism* (new edn. London, 1994).

—— *No Gods and Precious Few Heroes: Scotland 1914–1980* (new edn. London, 1998).

F. S. L. Lyons, *Ireland since the Famine* (rev. edn. London, 1973), a definitive survey from the 1840s to the 1970s.

Joseph Lee, *Ireland, 1922–1985: Politics and Society* (Cambridge, 1989).

CULTURE AND THE ARTS

W. W. Robson, *Modern English Literature* (Oxford, 1970), the best brief account.

B. Ford (ed.), *The Pelican Guide to English Literature*, vol. vii. *From James to Eliot* (rev. edn. London, 1983).

—— *The Pelican Guide to English Literature*, vol. viii. *The Present* (London, 1983).

B. Bergonzi (ed.), *The Twentieth Century: Sphere History of Literature in the English Language*, vol. vii (London, 1970).

John Gross, *The Rise and Fall of the English Man of Letters* (London, 1969), a brilliant study.

Percy Young, *A History of British Music* (London, 1967).

P. Kidson, P. Murray, and P. Thompson (eds.), *A History of English Architecture* (London, 1979).

Dennis Farr, *English Art, 1870–1940* (Oxford, 1978), including architecture.

Boris Ford (ed.), *The Cambridge Guide to the Arts in Britain*, vol. viii (Cambridge, 1989), comprehensive.

Arthur Marwick, *Culture in Britain since 1945* (London, 1991).

—— *The Sixties* (Oxford, 1998).

Robert Hewison, *In Anger: Culture and the Cold War* (London, 1981).

—— *Too Much: Art and Society in the Sixties, 1960–1975* (London, 1988).

Raphael Samuel, *Theatres of Memory* (London, 1994).

CHRONOLOGY

* Entries in *italics* denote events belonging to the history of the Roman Empire.

	Marcus Aurelius (161–80); major wars on the Danube
? c.163	Hadrian's Wall restored
193	Clodius Albinus proclaimed in Britain
	Severan Emperors (193–235)
196–213	Britain becomes two provinces
208–11	Campaigns of Septimius Severus and Caracalla in Scotland
235–70	*Imperial crisis: civil wars and invasions in East and West*
260–73	'Gallic Empire'
270s	Renewed growth in Britain
	Diocletian (284–305)
	'The Tetarchy'
287–96	Carausius and Allectus
296	Britain recovered by Constantius
after 296	Britain becomes a civil diocese of four provinces
	House of Constantius (305–63)
306	Campaign of Constantius I in Scotland; Constantine the Great proclaimed at York
324	*Constantine sole emperor; foundation of Constantinople*
340–69	Period of severe stress: internal troubles, harassment by barbarians
350	*Magnentius proclaimed in Gaul*
353	*Constantius II sole emperor*
353	Purge by Paul the Chain
	House of Valentinian (364–92)
367–9	'Barbarian Conspiracy', recovery and restoration of Britain by the elder Theodosius
	House of Theodosius (379–455)
	Theodosius the Great (379–95)
383	Magnus Maximus proclaimed in Britain; victory over Picts
	Honorius (395–423)
398–400	Victories over Picts, Scots, Saxons
400–2	Possible troop withdrawals by Stilicho
402/3	*Western imperial court withdrawn from Milan to Ravenna*
406	Britain revolts from Honorius: two emperors proclaimed

407	Constantine III proclaimed in Britain
	Constantine III rules from Arles (407–11)
409	Britain revolts from Constantine III: end of Roman rule in Britain
410	'Rescript of Honorius': letter to Britons (?), significance disputed
429	St. Germanus visits Britain
c.450	The *adventus Saxonum*: Hengest and Horsa settle in Kent (traditional date)
455	Hengest rebels against Vortigern (traditional date)
477	Saxon settlement of Sussex (traditional date)
495	Saxon settlement of Wessex (traditional date)
c.500	Battle of *Mons Badonicus*
560	Æthelberht, later over-king, becomes king in Kent
577	The West Saxons capture Gloucester, Cirencester and Bath
597	St. Augustine's mission arrives in Kent
616	Raedwald of East Anglia, as over-king, makes Edwin king of Northumbria
c.624	Death of Raedwald, and his probable burial in the Sutton Hoo barrow
627	Conversion of Edwin and the Northumbrian court
633	Battle of Heavenfield; Oswald of Northumbria becomes over-king
635	Conversion of King Cynegils of Wessex
642	Oswald is killed at Oswestry by King Penda of Mercia
655	Penda is defeated and killed at the *Winwaed* by Oswy of Northumbria, who becomes over-king
664	Synod of Whitby
669	Arrival of Archbishop Theodore
672	Synod of Hertford; battle of the Trent, marking the beginnings of the rise of Mercia
685–8	Expansion of Wessex under Caedwalla to include Kent, Surrey and Sussex
716	Æthelbald become king of Mercia
731	Bede completes his *Ecclesiastical History*
746–7	First Council of Clofesho
757	Death of Æthelbald; Offa becomes king of Mercia
786	Legatine Council held under Offa

793–5	Danish raids on Lindisfarne, Jarrow, and Iona
796	Death of Offa
825	Egbert of Wessex defeats Mercia and annexes Kent, Essex, Surrey, and Sussex
835	Big Danish raid on Kent
865	The Danish 'Great Army' lands
867	Northumbria falls to the Danes
870	East Anglia falls to the Danes; murder of St. Edmund
871	The Danes attack Wessex; Alfred becomes king
874	Mercia falls to the Danes
878	(March) The Danes drive Alfred into the Somerset marshes
	(May) Alfred defeats the Danes at Edington; Guthrum is baptized
899	Death of Alfred; Edward 'the Elder' becomes king of Wessex
910–20	Edward and Æthelflaed reconquer most of the Danelaw
919	Norse kingdom of York is founded by Raegnald
924	Death of Edward; Athelstan becomes king
937	Athelstan defeats the Norse, Scots and Strathclyde Welsh at Brunanburh
939	Death of Athelstan; Edmund become king
940	Dunstan begin to refound Glastonbury as a regular monastic house
946	Death of Edmund
954	The last king of York is deposed
959	Edgar becomes king
960	Dunstan becomes Archbishop of Canterbury
c.970	*Regularis Concordia* is compiled
973	Edgar is crowned and consecrated, and receives the submission of British princes
975	Death of Edgar; Edward 'the Martyr' becomes king
979	Murder of Edward; Æthelred 'the Unready' becomes king
991	The Danes defeat Alderman Byrhtnoth and the Essex levies at Maldon; treaty between England and Normandy
1002	Æthelred orders the massacre of all Danes in England

1003	Danish invasion led by King Swein
1013	Swein returns with a new army; the Danelaw accepts him as king
1014	Swein dies; the Danish army in England elect Cnut as their king
1016	(April) Æthelred dies; Edmund 'Ironside' becomes king
	(autumn) Cnut defeats Edmund at Ashingdon; Edmund dies and Cnut becomes King of all England
1017	Cnut divides England into four earldoms
1035	Death of Cnut
1037	Harold becomes king
1040	Death of Harold; Harthacnut becomes king
1042	Death of Harthacnut; Edward 'the Confessor' becomes king
1051-2	Conflict between King Edward and Godwin earl of Wessex
1053	Death of Godwin; his son Harold becomes earl of Wessex
1064-5	Earl Harold visits Duke William in Normandy
1066	(January) Death of King Edward; Earl Harold becomes king
	(September) King Harold of England defeats and kills King Harold of Norway at Stamford Bridge
1066	(October) Duke William of Normandy defeats and kills King Harold of England at Hastings
	(December) William is consecrated king
1067-70	English rebellions
1069-70	The harrying of the north
1086	Domesday Survey carried out
1087	Death of William I; accession of William II Rufus
1088	Rebellion in support of Robert Curthose
1093	Anselm appointed Archbishop of Canterbury
1096	Robert pawns Normandy ot Rufus
1100	Death of William Rufus; accession of Henry I
1101	Invasion of Robert Curthose
1106	Battle of Tinchebray; Curthose imprisoned; Henry I takes Normandy
1107	Settlement of Investiture Dispute in England
1120	Wreck of the White Ship

1128	Marriage of Empress Matilda to Geoffrey of Anjou
1135	Death of Henry I; accession of Stephen
1139–53	Civil war in England
1141	Battle of Lincoln; Stephen captured; later exchanged for Robert of Gloucester
1141–5	Geoffrey of Anjou conquers Normandy
1149	Cession of Northumbria to David of Scotland
1152	Henry of Anjou (later Henry II) marries Eleanor of Aquitaine
1153	Henry invades England; he and Stephen come to terms
1154	Death of Stephen; accession of Henry II
1157	Henry regains Northumbria
1162	Becket appointed Archbishop of Canterbury
1164	Council and Constitutions of Clarendon; Becket goes into exile
1166	Assize of Clarendon
1169–72	English conquest of Ireland begins
1170	Coronation of the young king; murder of Becket
1173–4	Rebellion against Henry II; William 'the Lion' (king of Scotland) invades the north
1183	Death of the young king
1189	Death of Henry II; accession of Richard I
1190–92	Richard I on crusade
1193–4	Richard in prison in Germany
1193–1205	Hubert Walter, Archbishop of Canterbury (justiciar 1194–8; chancellor 1199–1205)
1197	Death of Rhys of Deheubarth
1199	Death of Richard I; accession of John; establishment of Chancery Rolls
1203–4	Philip Augustus conquers Anjou and Normandy
1208–14	Interdict in England
1214	Battle of Bouvines: French victory
1215	Magna Carta; civil war in England
1216	Louis (later Louis VIII) invades; death of John; accession of Henry III
1217	Battles of Lincoln and Dover; Louis withdraws
1221–4	Arrival of Dominican and Franciscan Friars in England
1224	Louis VIII completes conquest of Poitou
1232	Dismissal of Hubert de Burgh

1240	Death of Llywelyn the Great
1254	Henry III accepts papal offer of throne of Sicily
1258	Barons take over royal government; provisions of Oxford
1259	Treaty of Paris between England and France
1264	Battle of Lewes; Henry III captured; government of Simon de Montfort
1265	Battle of Evesham; killing of Simon de Montfort
1267	Henry recognizes Llywelyn ap Gruffydd as Prince of Wales
1272	Death of Henry III; accession of Edward I
1276–7	First Welsh War
1282–3	Edward's conquest of Wales
1286–9	Edward I in Gascony
1291	Edward I asserts his overlordship over Scotland
1294	War with France begins
1295	Franco-Scottish alliance
1296	Edward I invades Scotland; his conflict with the Church
1297	Edward I's conflict with his magnates; his expedition to Flanders
1306	Rebellion of Robert Bruce
1307	Death of Edward I; accession of Edward II
1314	Scottish victory at Bannockburn
1315–16	Great famine
1321–2	Civil war in England
1327	Deposition and death of Edward II; accession of Edward III
1330	Edward III takes the reins of government
1337	The Hundred Years War begins
1339–41	Political crisis in England
1346	English victories at Crécy and Neville's Cross
1347	English capture Calais
1348	First occurrence of plague in England
1356	English victory at Poitiers
1361	Second major occurrence of plague
1376	'Good Parliament' meets; death of Edward, the Black Prince
1377	Death of Edward III; accession of Richard II

1381	The Peasants' Revolt
1382	Condemnation of John Wycliffe's works
1388	'Merciless Parliament' meets; battle of Otterburn against the Scots
1389	Richard II declares himself of age
1394–5	Richard II's expedition to Ireland
1396	Anglo-French treaty
1397–9	Richard II's 'tyranny'
1399	Deposition of Richard II; accession of Henry IV
1400	Rebellion of Owain Glyndŵr begins (to 1410)
1403	Henry Hotspur defeated at Shrewsbury
1405	Execution of Archbishop Scrope of York
1408	Defeat of the earl of Northumberland at Bramham Moor
1413	Death of Henry IV; accession of Henry V
1415	English victory at Agincourt
1419–20	English conquest of Normandy
1420	Anglo-French treaty of Troyes
1422	Death of Henry V; accession of Henry VI
1435	Death of John, duke of Bedford; Franco-Burgundian treaty of Arras
1436–7	Henry VI comes of age
1445	Henry VI marries Margaret of Anjou
1449–50	French overrun Normandy
1450	Murder of the duke of Suffolk; John Cade's rebellion
1453	French overrun Gascony; Henry VI becomes ill
1455	Battle of St. Albans between Richard, duke of York and the royalist forces
1459	Defeat of the duke of York at Blore Heath and Ludford Bridge
1461	Deposition of Henry VI; accession of Edward IV
1465	Capture of Henry VI
1469	Rebellion of Richard, earl of Warwick and George, duke of Clarence
1470	Deposition of Edward IV; return of Henry VI
1471	Return of Edward IV; death of the earl of Warwick at Barnet; death of Henry VI
1475	Edward IV's expedition to France; Anglo-French treaty of Picquigny

1477	William Caxton's first printed book in England
1483	Death of Edward IV; accession, deposition, and death of Edward V; accession of Richard III; rebellion of Henry, duke of Buckingham
1485	Death of Richard III at Bosworth; accession of Henry VII
1487	Rebellion of Lambert Simnel
1491	Birth of Prince Henry
1509	Accession of Henry VIII
1510	Execution of Empson and Dudley
1512	War with France and Scotland
1513	Battle of Flodden: English victory over Scotland
1515	Wolsey appointed Lord Chancellor
1522	War with France
1525	Peace with France
1527	Divorce crisis begins
1528	War with Spain
1529	Peace of Cambrai; fall of Wolsey: Sir Thomas More succeeds as Lord Chancellor
1532	More resigns
1533	Henry VIII marries Anne Boleyn; Act of Appeals; birth of Princess Elizabeth
1534	Act of Supremacy
1535	Execution of More and Fisher
1536	Dissolution of the Monasteries; Pilgrimage of Grace; union of England and Wales
1542	Battle of Solway Moss; English victory over invading Scottish army
1543	War with France
1547	Succession of Edward VI; ascendancy of Protector Somerset; battle of Pinkie: English victory over Scotland
1549	First Book of Common Prayer; Northumberland's coup
1553	Accession of Mary
1554	Pole returns; reunion with Rome; Wyatt's rebellion
1555	Persecution of Protestants begins
1557	War with France
1558	New Book of Rates; accession of Elizabeth I

1559	Peace of Cateau-Cambrésis; religious Settlement in England
1566	Archbishop Parker's *Advertisements* demand religious conformity
1568	Mary Stuart flees to England
1569	Northern Rebellion
1570	Papal bull declares Elizabeth excommunicated and deposed
1580	Jesuit missionaries arrive in England
1585	War with Spain
1587	Execution of Mary Stuart
1588	Defeat of the Spanish Armada
1594	Bad harvests begin
1601	Essex's rebellion
1603	Death of Elizabeth; accession of James VI of Scotland as James I; peace in Ireland; Millenary Petition of the Puritans
1604	Peace with Spain (treaty of London); Hampton Court Conference (king, bishops, Puritans)
1605	Gunpowder Plot, the last major Catholic conspiracy
1606–7	Failure of James's plans for union of kingdoms
1607	Settlement of Virginia
1609	Rebellion of the Northern Earls in Ireland; beginnings of the Planting of Ulster by Scots and English Protestants
1610	Failure of Great Contract (reform of royal finance)
1611	Publication of Authorized Version of the Bible (Anglican–Puritan co-operation)
1612	Death of Prince Henry, James's promising elder son
1613	Marriage of Princess Elizabeth to Elector Palatine, Protestant zealot, enmeshed Britain in continental politics
1617–29	Ascendancy of George Villiers, duke of Buckingham
1919–22	Inigo Jones designs the Banqueting House, the first major royal public building since the reign of Henry VIII
1620	Pilgrim Fathers inaugurate religious migration to New England
1622–3	Prince Charles and Buckingham go to Spain to woo the king's daughter and are rebuffed

1624–30	War with Spain
1625	Death of James I; accession of Charles I and marriage to Henrietta Maria, sister of Louis XIII of France
1626–9	War with France
1628	Petition of Right; publication of Harvey's work on the circulation of the blood; assassination of Buckingham
1629	Charles I dissolves Parliament, determines to govern without one
1630	Large-scale emigration to Massachusetts begins
1633	William Laud translated to be Archbishop of Canterbury
1634–40	Ship Money case
1637	Hampden's case supports Charles I's claim to collect Ship Money
1637–40	Breakdown of Charles's government of Scotland and two attempts to impose his will by force
1640	Long Parliament summoned
1641	Remodelling of government in England and Scotland; abolition of conciliar courts, abolition of prerogative taxation, triennial bill, Grand Remonstrance; rebellion of Ulster Catholics
1642	King's attempt on the Five Members; his withdrawal from London; the 19 Propositions; the resort of arms: Civil War
1643	King's armies prosper; Scots invade on side of Parliament
1644	Parliamentary armies prosper, especially in the decisive battle of the war, Marston Moor (June)
1645	'Clubmen' risings of armed neutrals threaten both sides; Royalist armies disintegrate, but parliamentary forces reorganized (New Model Army)
1646	King surrenders to the Scots; bishops and Book of Common Prayer abolished, Presbyterian Church established
1647	Army revolt; radical movements criticize parliamentary tyranny; king prevaricates
1648	Second Civil War: Scots now side with the king and are defeated; provincial risings (Kent, Colchester, South Wales, Yorks., etc.) crushed

1649	Trial and execution of Charles I: England a Republic
1649–53	Government by sovereign single-chamber assembly, the 'Rump' Parliament thoroughly purged of royalists and moderates
1649–50	Oliver Cromwell conquers Ireland (Drogheda massacre)
1650–2	Oliver Cromwell conquers Scotland (battles of Dunbar and Worcester)
1651	Thomas Hobbes's *Leviathan* published
1652–4	First Dutch War
1653	Cromwell dissolves Rump, creates the Nominated or Barebones Assembly; it surrenders power back to him, and he becomes Lord Protector under a paper constitution (*The Instrument of Government*)
1655–60	War with Spain
1655	Royalist insurrection (Penruddock's rising) is a complete failure
1657	*Instrument of Government* replaced by a parliamentary paper constitution, the *Humble Petition and Advice*; Cromwell rejects title of King and remains Lord Protector, but nominates his own House of Lords
1658	Cromwell dies and is succeeded by his son Richard
1659	Richard overthrown by the army; Rump restored but displeases many in the army
1660	Charles II restored
1662	Church of England restored; Royal Society receives its Charter
1663	Failure of first royal attempt to grant religious toleration
1665–7	Second Dutch War
1665	Great Plague (final major outbreak)
1666	Great Fire of London
1667	Milton's *Paradise Lost* published
1672–3	Failure of second royal attempt to grant religious toleration
1672–4	Third Dutch War
1674	Grain bounties introduced (England self-sufficient in food)
1678	Titus Oates and the Popish Plot; Bunyan's *Pilgrim's Progress*, part I, published

1679–81	The Exclusion Crisis; emergence of Whig and Tory parties
1683	The Rye House Plot; Whigs proscribed
1685	Charles II dies; accession of James II; rebellion by Charles II's protestant bastard, the duke of Monmouth, fails
1687	James II's Declaration of Indulgence; Tories proscribed; Newton's *Principia Mathematica* published
1688	James II's son born
1688	William of Orange invades: James II takes flight, accession of William III (of Orange) and Mary
1689	Bill of Rights settles succession to the throne and declares illegal various grievances; Toleration Act grants rights to Trinitarian Protestant dissenters
1690	Battle of the Boyne: William III defeats Irish and French army
1694	Bank of England founded; death of Queen Mary; Triennial Act sets the maximum duration of a parliament at three years
1695	Lapse of Licensing Act
1697	Peace treaty of Ryswick between allied powers of the League of Augsburg and France; Civil List Act votes funds for the maintenance of the royal household
1701	War of Spanish Succession begins; Act of Settlement settles the royal succession on the descendants of Sophia of Hanover
1702	Death of William III; accession of Anne
1704	Battle of Blenheim: British, Dutch, German and Austrian troops defeat French and Bavarian forces; British capture of Gibraltar from Spain
1707	Union of England and Scotland
1710	Impeachment of Dr Sacheverell; Harley ministry
1713	Peace treaty of Utrecht concludes the War of Spanish Succession
1714	Death of Anne; accession of George I
1715	Jacobite rebellion aimed at overthrowing the Hanoverian succession fails
1716	Septennial Act sets the maximum duration of a parliament at seven years

1717	Whig split; suspension of convocation
1720	South Sea Bubble: many investors ruined after speculation in the stock of the South Sea Company
1721	Walpole ministry
1722	Atterbury Plot, the most notable Jacobite plot
1726	Jonathan Swift's *Gulliver's Travels* published
1727	Death of George I; accession of George II
1729	Alexander Pope's *Dunciad* published
1730	Walpole/Townshend split
1733	Excise crisis: Walpole has to abandon his plans to reorganize the customs and excise
1737	Death of Queen Caroline
1738	Wesley's 'conversion': the start of Methodism
1739	War of Jenkins' Ear: Anglo-Spanish naval war
1740	War of the Austrian Succession
1741	Samuel Richardson's *Pamela* published
1742	Fall of Walpole
1744	Ministry of Pelham
1745	Jacobite Rebellion led by 'Bonnie Prince Charlie'
1746	Battle of Culloden: the duke of Cumberland routs the Jacobite army
1748	Peace of Aix-la-Chapelle concludes War of the Austrian Succession
1752	Adoption of Gregorian Calendar
1753	Jewish Naturalization Bill
1754	Newcastle ministry
1756	Seven Years War: Britain allied with Frederick the Great of Prussian against France, Austria, and Russia
1757	Pitt–Newcastle ministry; battle of Plassey: British victory over Bengal
1759	Capture of Quebec: British victory over the French
1760	Death of George II; accession of George III
1761	Laurence Sterne's *Tristram Shandy* published
1762	Bute's ministry
1763	Peace of Paris concludes Seven Years War; Grenville ministry; Wilkes and General Warrants
1765	Rockingham ministry; American Stamp Act attempts to make the defence of the American colonies self-financing: repealed 1766

1766	Chatham ministry
1768	Grafton ministry; Middlesex election crisis
1769	James Watt's steam engine patented
1770	Lord North's ministry; Edmund Burke's *Thoughts on the Present Discontents* published; Falkland Islands crisis
1773	Boston Tea Party: American colonists protest against the East India Company's monopoly of tea exports to America
1774	Coercive Acts passed in retaliation for Boston Tea Party
1776	Declaration of American Independence; Edward Gibbon's *Decline and Fall* and Adam Smith's *Wealth of Nations* published
1779	Wyvill's Association movement
1780	Gordon Riots develop from a procession to petition parliament against the Catholic Relief Act
1781	Surrender at Yorktown: American victory over British troops
1782	Second Rockingham ministry
1783	Shelburne ministry; Peace of Versailles recognizes independence of American colonies; Fox–North coalition; Younger Pitt's ministry
1784	East India Act
1785	Pitt's motion for parliamentary reform defeated
1786	Eden commercial treaty with France
1789	French Revolution
1790	Edmund Burke's *Reflections on the Revolution in France* published
1791	Thomas Paine's *The Rights of Man* published
1792	Coal gas used for lighting; Mary Wollstonecraft's *Vindication of the Rights of Women* published
1793	Outbreak of war with France; voluntary Board of Agriculture set up; commercial depression
1795	'Speenhamland' system of outdoor relief adopted, making up wages to equal cost of subsistence
1796	Vaccination against smallpox introduced
1798	T. R. Malthus's *Essay on Population* published; tax of ten per cent on incomes over £200 introduced

1799	Trade Unions suppressed; Napoleon appointed First Consul in France
1799–1801	Commercial boom
1801	Union with Ireland; first British Census
1802	Peace with France; Peel introduces first factory legislation
1803	War with France; General Enclosure Act simplifies process of enclosure of common land
1805	Battle of Trafalgar: Nelson defeats the French and Spanish fleets
1809–10	Commercial boom
1811	Depression because of Orders in Council; 'Luddite' disturbances in Nottinghamshire and Yorkshire; George, Prince of Wales, made Prince Regent
1813	East India Company's monopoly abolished
1815	Battle of Waterloo: defeat of Napoleon; peace in Europe: Congress of Vienna; Corn Law passed setting price of corn at 80s. per quarter
1815–17	Commercial boom
1817	Slump; the Blanketeers' march and other disturbances
1819	Peterloo massacre: troops intervene at mass reform meeting, killing 11 and wounding 400
1820	Death of George III; accession of George IV
1821–3	Famine in Ireland
1824	Commercial boom
1825	Trade Unions legalized; Stockton and Darlington railway opens; commercial depression
1829	Catholic Emancipation, ending most denials or restrictions of Catholic civil rights, ownership of property, and holding of public office
1830	Death of George IV; accession of William IV; Liverpool and Manchester railway opens
1830–2	First major cholera epidemic; Whigs in power under Grey
1831	'Swing' riots in rural areas against the mechanization of agriculture
1832	Great Reform Bill brings climax to period of political reform, enlarging the franchise and restructuring representation in Parliament

1833	Factory Act limits child labour; beginning of Oxford Movement in Anglican Church
1834	Slavery abolished in the British Empire; parish workhouses instituted; Robert Owen founds the Grand National Consolidated Trade Union: action by government against 'illegal oaths' in unionism results in failure of GNCTU and transportation of six 'Tolpuddle Martyrs'
1835	Municipal Reform Act extends local government franchise to all ratepayers
1835–6	Commercial boom: 'little' railway mania
1837	Death of William IV; accession of Queen Victoria
1838	Anti-Corn Law League established; People's Charter drafted
1839	Chartist riots
1840	Penny post instituted
1841	Tories in power: Peel ministry
1844	Bank Charter Act; Rochdale Co-operative Society founded; Royal Commission on Health of Towns
1844–5	Railway mania: massive speculation and investment leads to building of 5,000 miles of track; potato famine begins in Ireland
1846	Corn Law abolished; Whigs in power
1848	Revolutions in Europe; Public Health Act
1851	Great Exhibition
1852	Derby's first minority Conservative government
1852–5	Aberdeen's coalition government
1853	Gladstone's first budget
1854	Northcote–Trevelyan civil service report
1854–6	Crimean War, defending European interests in the Middle East against Russia
1855	Palmerston's first government
1857–8	Second Opium War opens China to European trade
1858–9	Derby's second minority Conservative government
1858	Indian Mutiny and India Act
1859	Publication of Darwin's *Origin of Species*
1859–65	Palmerston's second Liberal government
1860	Anglo-French 'Cobden' treaty and Gladstone's budget codify and extend principles of free trade

1861	Death of Albert, Prince Consort
1862	Limited Liability Act provides vital stimulus to accumulation of capital in shares
1865	Death of Palmerston (October)
1865–6	Russell's second Liberal government
1866	Russell–Gladstone moderate Reform Bill fails
1866–8	Derby's third minority Conservative government
1867	Derby–Disraeli Reform Act; Dominion of Canada Act
1868	Disraeli succeeds Derby as Prime Minister (February)
1868–74	Gladstone's first Liberal government
1869	Suez Canal opened; Irish Church disestablished
1870	Irish Land Act; Forster–Ripon English Elementary Education Act; Married Women's Property Act extends the rights of women in marriage
1872	Scottish Education Act
1873	Gladstone government resigns after defeat on Irish Universities Bill; Disraeli declines to take office
1874–80	Disraeli's second Conservative government
1875	Disraeli buys Suez Canal shares, gaining a controlling interest for Britain
1875	Agricultural depression deepens
1875–6	R. A. Cross's Conservative social reforms passed
1876	Victoria proclaimed Empress of India; massacres of Christians in Turkish Bulgaria provoke anti-Turkish campaign in Britain, led by Gladstone
1877	Confederation of British and Boer states in South Africa
1878	Congress of Berlin; Disraeli announces 'peace with honour'
1879	Trade depression; Zulu War: British defeated at Isandhlwana, win at Ulundi
1879–80	Gladstone's Midlothian campaign denounces imperialism in Afghanistan and South Africa
1880–5	Gladstone's second Liberal government
1880–1	First Anglo-Boer War
1881	Irish Land and Coercion Acts
1882	Britain occupies Egypt; Triple Alliance between Germany, Austria, and Italy
1884–5	Reform and Redistribution Acts

1885   Death of Gordon at Khartoum; Burma annexed;
            Salisbury's first (minority) Conservative government
1886   Royal Niger Company chartered; gold found in
            Transvaal; Gladstone's third Liberal government
            introduces first Home Rule Bill for Ireland: Liberal
            Party splits
1886–92   Salisbury's second (Conservative–Liberal-Unionist)
            government
1887   British East Africa Company chartered
1888   County Councils Act establishes representative county
            authorities
1889   London dock strike; British South Africa Company
            chartered
1892–4   Gladstone's fourth (minority) Liberal government
1893   Second Home Rule Bill rejected by the Lords;
            Independent Labour Party founded
1894–5   Rosebery's minority Liberal government
1895–1902   Salisbury's third Unionist ministry
1896–8   Sudan conquered
1898   German naval expansion begins
1899–1902   Second Anglo-Boer War
1899   (autumn)British disasters in South Africa
1900   Khaki election won by Salisbury; formation of Labour
            Representation Committee; Commonwealth of
            Australia Act
1901   Death of Victoria; accession of Edward VII
1902   Balfour's Education Act; Anglo-Japanese alliance
1902–5   Balfour's Unionist government
1903   Chamberlain's Tariff Reform campaign starts
1904   Anglo-French *Entente*
1905–8   Campbell-Bannerman's Liberal government
1906   Liberals win general election (January); Labour Party
            formed
1907   Anglo-Russian *Entente*
1908–15   Asquith's Liberal government
1908   Asquith's Old Age Pensions plan introduced
1909   Churchill's Employment Exchanges introduced; Lloyd
            George's budget rejected by Lords; Union of South
            Africa Act

1910	(January) General election: Liberal government retains office
	(May) Death of Edward VII; accession of George V
	(December) General election: Liberal government again retains office
1911	Parliament Act curtails power of the House of Lords, establishes five-yearly elections; Lloyd George's National Insurance Act; Moroccan crisis
1911–12	Railway, mining, and coal strikes
1912	Anglo-German navy talks fail
1912–14	Third Home Rule Act (for Ireland) and Welsh Church Disestablishment Act passed, but suspended
1914	(28 June) Assassination of Archduke Ferdinand at Sarajevo
	(4 August) British Empire enters the First World War
1915–16	Dardanelles expedition, ending in British withdrawal from Gallipoli
1916	Battle of the Somme; battle of Jutland; Lloyd George succeeds Asquith as Prime Minister
1917	Battle of Passchendaele
1918	End of First World War (11 November); Lloyd George coalition government returned in 'coupon election' (December)
1919	Treaty of Versailles establishes peace in Europe
1921	Miners seek support of dockers' and railwaymen's unions (the 'Triple Alliance') in major strike: on 'Black Friday' the dockers and railwaymen back down, and the alliance is broken; Lloyd George concludes treaty with Sinn Fein
1922	Fall of Lloyd George; Bonar Law heads Conservative government
1923	Baldwin becomes Conservative Prime Minister; general election
1924	(January) MacDonald leads first Labour government
	(November) Conservatives return to office under Baldwin
1925	Britain goes back on the gold standard
1926	General Strike (3–12 May)

1929   General election; MacDonald leads second Labour
        government
1931   Financial crisis and run on the pound; Britain
        abandons the gold standard; MacDonald resigns and
        is returned in the election to head National
        government
1932   Ottawa Conference on imperial trade institutes
        protective tarriffs
1935   Conservatives win general election: Baldwin succeeds
        MacDonald as Prime Minister; Hoare–Laval pact
        on Abyssinia; Government of India Act
1936   Death of King George V; abdication of Edward VIII:
        George VI becomes king
1937   Neville Chamberlain succeeds Baldwin as Conservative
        Prime Minister
1938   Chamberlain meets Hitler at Berchtesgaden,
        Godesberg, and Munich
1939   British guarantee to Poland; British Empire declares
        war on Germany (3 September)
1940   Churchill succeeds Chamberlain as Prime Minister;
        withdrawal from Dunkirk; Battle of Britain
1941   *Luftwaffe* 'blitz' on many British cities; Soviet Union
        and United States enter the war
1942   Loss of Singapore; Montgomery's victory at El
        Alamein; battle of Stalingrad; Beveridge Report on
        social security
1943   Successful campaign in North Africa; Anglo-American
        armies invade Italy
1944   D-day invasion of France; Butler's Education Act
1945   End of war in Europe (8 May) and in far East (15
        August); general election: massive Labour victory
        and Attlee becomes Prime Minister
1947   Coal and other industries nationalized; convertibility
        crisis; transfer of power to independent India,
        Pakistan, and Burma
1949   NATO founded; devaluation of the pound by Cripps
1950   General election: Labour retains power by narrow
        majority; outbreak of war in Korea
1951   Festival of Britain; general election: Conservatives

	defeat Labour, and Churchill again becomes Prime Minister
1952	Death of King George VI; Queen Elizabeth II proclaimed
1954	British troops withdraw from Egypt
1955	Eden becomes Prime Minister; general election won by Conservatives
1956	Anglo-French invasion of Suez, followed by withdrawal
1957	Eden resigns; Macmillan becomes Prime Minister
1959	General election: Conservatives win with larger majority
1963	French veto Britain's application to join the European Common Market; test-ban treaty in Moscow limits nuclear testing; Douglas-Home succeeds Macmillan as Prime Minister
1964	General election: Labour under Harold Wilson win narrow majority
1966	General election: Labour win with much larger majority
1967	Devaluation of the pound
1970	General election: Conservatives under Edward Heath returned to office
1972	National miners' strike; Stormont government abolished in Northern Ireland
1973	Britain enters European Common Market
1974	National miners' strike; two general elections: Labour under Harold Wilson win both with narrow majorities
1975	Popular referendum confirms British membership of the Common Market
1976	Economic crisis: Britain obtains help from International Monetary Fund
1979	Devolution referendums in Wales and Scotland; general election: Conservatives under Mrs Thatcher returned to office; independence granted to Zimbabwe (Rhodesia)
1980	Britain becomes self-sufficient in North Sea oil
1981	Social Democratic Party founded
1982	Britain defeats Argentina in war over the Falkland Islands

1983	General election: Mrs Thatcher's Conservative government returned with massive majority; Cruise missiles installed
1984	Miners' strike
1985	Miners' strike ends after a year; Anglo-Irish Hillsborough Agreement signed
1986	Channel Tunnel treaty signed; 'Big Bang' in Stock Exchange
1987	General election: Mrs Thatcher's Conservative government again returned with a majority of over 100; Stock Exchange collapse in the autumn
1989	Poll tax introduced first in Scotland
1990	Resignation of Mrs Thatcher; John Major becomes Prime Minister
1991	Gulf War against Iraq
1992	Conservatives unexpectedly retain power at general election
	'Black Wednesday': Britain leaves the ERM
1994	IRA declares cease-fire in Northern Ireland
1996	Prince Charles and Diana divorce
1997	Labour wins general election with majority of 179: Tony Blair becomes Prime Minister
	Death of Princess Diana in car crash in Paris
	Scotland and Wales vote for devolution in referendums
	Britain leaves Hong Kong
1998	British presidency of EU
	Good Friday agreement in Northern Ireland
1999	EMU begins (1 January), without Britain
	First elections for Scottish parliament and Welsh assembly

THE HOUSE OF WESSEX
802–1066

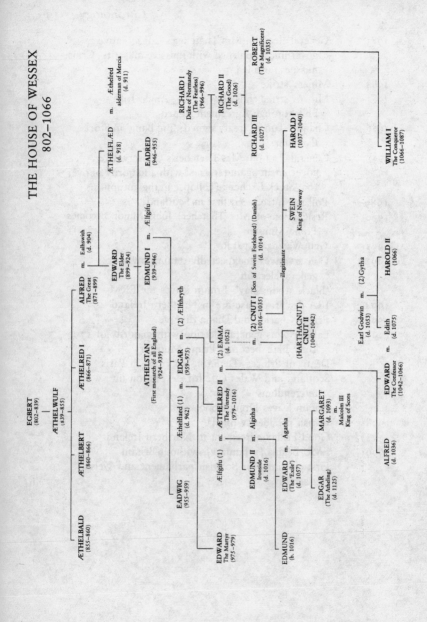

NORMAN AND PLANTAGENET
1066–1327

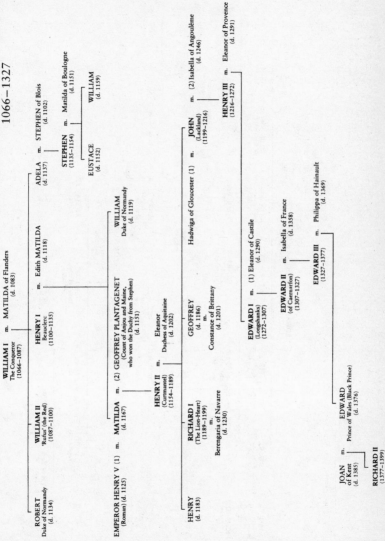

LANCASTER AND YORK
1327–1485

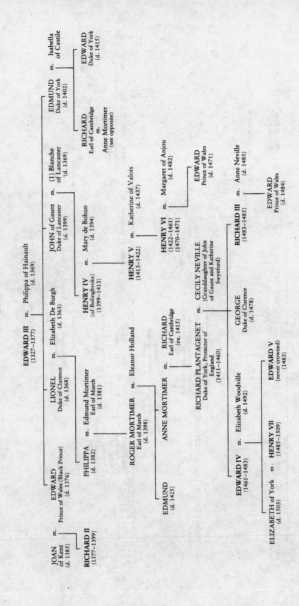

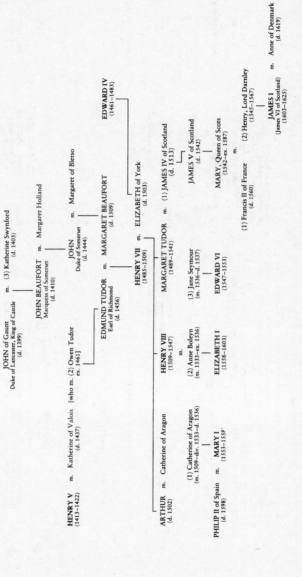

STUARTS AND HANOVERIANS
1603–1837

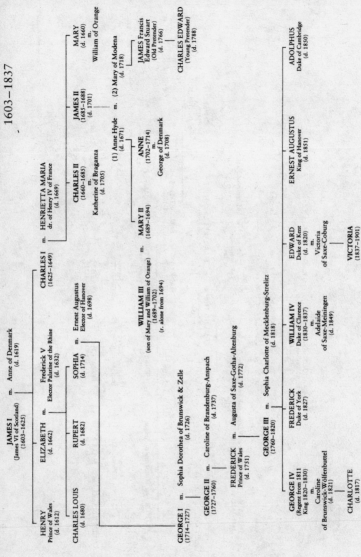

DESCENDANTS OF QUEEN VICTORIA

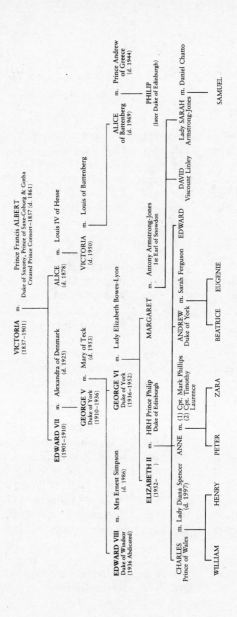

VICTORIA (1837–1901) m. Prince Francis ALBERT
Duke of Saxony, Prince of Saxe-Coburg & Gotha
Created Prince Consort–1857 (d. 1861)

EDWARD VII (1901–1910) m. Alexandra of Denmark (d. 1925)

ALICE (d. 1878) m. Louis IV of Hesse

GEORGE V Duke of York (1910–1936) m. Mary of Teck (d. 1953)

VICTORIA (d. 1950) m. Louis of Battenberg

EDWARD VIII Duke of Windsor (1936 Abdicated) m. Mrs Ernest Simpson (d. 1986)

GEORGE VI Duke of York (1936–1952) m. Lady Elizabeth Bowes-Lyon

ALICE of Battenberg (d. 1969) m. Prince Andrew of Greece (d. 1944)

ELIZABETH II (1952–) m. HRH Prince Philip Duke of Edinburgh

MARGARET m. Antony Armstrong-Jones 1st Earl of Snowdon

PHILIP (later Duke of Edinburgh)

CHARLES Prince of Wales m. Lady Diana Spencer (d. 1997)

ANNE m. (1) Cpt. Mark Phillips (2) Cpt. Timothy Laurence

ANDREW Duke of York m. Sarah Ferguson

EDWARD

DAVID Viscount Linley

Lady SARAH m. Daniel Chatto Armstrong-Jones

WILLIAM

HENRY

PETER

ZARA

BEATRICE

EUGENIE

SAMUEL

PRIME MINISTERS 1721–1998

Sir Robert Walpole	Apr. 1721	Viscount Melbourne	Apr. 1835
Earl of Wilmington	Feb. 1741	Sir Robert Peel	Aug. 1841
Henry Pelham	Aug. 1743	Lord John Russell	June 1846
Duke of Newcastle	Mar. 1754	Earl of Derby	Feb. 1852
Duke of Devonshire	Nov. 1756	Earl of Aberdeen	Dec. 1852
Duke of Newcastle	July 1757	Viscount Palmerston	Feb. 1855
Earl of Bute	May 1762	Earl of Derby	Feb. 1858
George Grenville	Apr. 1763	Viscount Palmerston	June 1859
Marquess of		Earl Russell	Oct. 1865
Rockingham	July 1765	Earl of Derby	June 1866
Earl of Chatham	July 1766	Benjamin Disraeli	Feb. 1868
Duke of Grafton	Oct. 1768	William Ewart	
Lord North	Jan. 1770	Gladstone	Dec. 1868
Marquess of		Benjamin Disraeli	Feb. 1874
Rockingham	Mar. 1782	William Ewart	
Earl of Shelburne	July 1782	Gladstone	Apr. 1880
Duke of Portland	Apr. 1783	Marquess of Salisbury	June 1885
William Pitt	Dec. 1783	William Ewart	
Henry Addington	Mar. 1801	Gladstone	Feb. 1886
William Pitt	May 1804	Marquess of Salisbury	July 1886
William Wyndham		William Ewart	
Grenville	Feb. 1806	Gladstone	Aug. 1892
Duke of Portland	Mar. 1807	Earl of Rosebery	Mar. 1894
Spencer Perceval	Oct. 1809	Marquess of Salisbury	June 1895
Earl of Liverpool	June 1812	Arthur James Balfour	July 1902
George Canning	Apr. 1827	Sir Henry Campbell-	
Viscount Goderich	Aug. 1827	Bannerman	Dec. 1905
Duke of Wellington	Jan. 1828	Herbert Henry	
Earl Grey	Nov. 1830	Asquith	Apr. 1908
Viscount Melbourne	July 1834	David Lloyd George	Dec. 1916
Duke of Wellington	Nov. 1834	Andrew Bonar Law	Oct. 1922
Sir Robert Peel	Dec. 1834	Stanley Baldwin	May 1923

James Ramsay		Harold Macmillan	Jan. 1957
MacDonald	Jan. 1924	Sir Alec Douglas-	
Stanley Baldwin	Nov. 1924	Home	Oct. 1963
James Ramsay		Harold Wilson	Oct. 1964
MacDonald	June 1929	Edward Heath	June 1970
Stanley Baldwin	June 1935	Harold Wilson	Mar. 1974
Neville Chamberlain	May 1937	James Callaghan	Apr. 1976
Winston Churchill	May 1940	Margaret Thatcher	May 1979
Clement Attlee	July 1945	John Major	Nov. 1990
Winston Churchill	Oct. 1951	Tony Blair	May 1997
Sir Anthony Eden	Apr. 1955		

INDEX

PERSONS are indexed under the name or title used in the text, with cross-references where necessary to alternative names. In longer entries, secondary references are grouped together after the word '*also*'. Page numbers in *italics* refer to maps.

OXFORD

MORE OXFORD PAPERBACKS

This book is just one of nearly 1000 Oxford Paper-
backs currently in print. If you would like details of
other Oxford Paperbacks, including titles in the
World's Classics, Oxford Reference, Oxford
Books, OPUS, Past Masters, Oxford Authors, and
Oxford Shakespeare series, please write to:

UK and Europe: Oxford Paperbacks Publicity Man-
ager, Arts and Reference Publicity Department,
Oxford University Press, Walton Street, Oxford
OX2 6DP.

Customers in UK and Europe will find Oxford
Paperbacks available in all good bookshops. But in
case of difficulty please send orders to the Cash-
with-Order Department, Oxford University Press
Distribution Services, Saxon Way West, Corby,
Northants NN18 9ES. Tel: 01536 741519; Fax:
01536 746337. Please send a cheque for the total cost
of the books, plus £1.75 postage and packing for
orders under £20; £2.75 for orders over £20. Customers outside the UK should add 10% of the cost
of the books for postage and packing.

USA: Oxford Paperbacks Marketing Manager,
Oxford University Press, Inc., 200 Madison Avenue, New York, N.Y. 10016.

Canada: Trade Department, Oxford University
Press, 70 Wynford Drive, Don Mills, Ontario M3C
1J9.

Australia: Trade Marketing Manager, Oxford University Press, G.P.O. Box 2784Y, Melbourne 3001,
Victoria.

South Africa: Oxford University Press, P.O. Box
1141, Cape Town 8000.

HISTORY IN OXFORD PAPERBACKS
TUDOR ENGLAND
John Guy

Tudor England is a compelling account of political and religious developments from the advent of the Tudors in the 1460s to the death of Elizabeth I in 1603.

Following Henry VII's capture of the Crown at Bosworth in 1485, Tudor England witnessed far-reaching changes in government and the Reformation of the Church under Henry VIII, Edward VI, Mary, and Elizabeth; that story is enriched here with character studies of the monarchs and politicians that bring to life their personalities as well as their policies.

Authoritative, clearly argued, and crisply written, this comprehensive book will be indispensable to anyone interested in the Tudor Age.

'lucid, scholarly, remarkably accomplished . . . an excellent overview' *Sunday Times*

'the first comprehensive history of Tudor England for more than thirty years' Patrick Collinson, *Observer*

ILLUSTRATED HISTORIES IN
OXFORD PAPERBACKS

THE OXFORD ILLUSTRATED HISTORY
OF ENGLISH LITERATURE

Edited by Pat Rogers

Britain possesses a literary heritage which is almost unrivalled in the Western world. In this volume, the richness, diversity, and continuity of that tradition are explored by a group of Britain's foremost literary scholars.

Chapter by chapter the authors trace the history of English literature, from its first stirrings in Anglo-Saxon poetry to the present day. At its heart towers the figure of Shakespeare, who is accorded a special chapter to himself. Other major figures such as Chaucer, Milton, Donne, Wordsworth, Dickens, Eliot, and Auden are treated in depth, and the story is brought up to date with discussion of living authors such as Seamus Heaney and Edward Bond.

'[a] lovely volume . . . put in your thumb and pull out plums' Michael Foot

'scholarly and enthusiastic people have written inspiring essays that induce an eagerness in their readers to return to the writers they admire' *Economist*

HISTORY IN OXFORD PAPERBACKS

THE STRUGGLE FOR THE MASTERY OF EUROPE 1848–1918

A. J. P. Taylor

The fall of Metternich in the revolutions of 1848 heralded an era of unprecedented nationalism in Europe, culminating in the collapse of the Hapsburg, Romanov, and Hohenzollern dynasties at the end of the First World War. In the intervening seventy years the boundaries of Europe changed dramatically from those established at Vienna in 1815. Cavour championed the cause of *Risorgimento* in Italy; Bismarck's three wars brought about the unification of Germany; Serbia and Bulgaria gained their independence courtesy of the decline of Turkey—'the sick man of Europe'; while the great powers scrambled for places in the sun in Africa. However, with America's entry into the war and President Wilson's adherence to idealistic internationalist principles, Europe ceased to be the centre of the world, although its problems, still primarily revolving around nationalist aspirations, were to smash the Treaty of Versailles and plunge the world into war once more.

A. J. P. Taylor has drawn the material for his account of this turbulent period from the many volumes of diplomatic documents which have been published in the five major European languages. By using vivid language and forceful characterization, he has produced a book that is as much a work of literature as a contribution to scientific history.

'One of the glories of twentieth-century writing.'
Observer

THE OXFORD AUTHORS

General Editor: Frank Kermode

THE OXFORD AUTHORS is a series of authoritative editions of major English writers. Aimed at both students and general readers, each volume contains a generous selection of the best writings—poetry, prose, and letters—to give the essence of a writer's work and thinking. All the texts are complemented by essential notes, an introduction, chronology, and suggestions for further reading.

Matthew Arnold
William Blake
Lord Byron
John Clare
Samuel Taylor Coleridge
John Donne
John Dryden
Ralph Waldo Emerson
Thomas Hardy
George Herbert and Henry Vaughan
Gerard Manley Hopkins
Samuel Johnson
Ben Jonson
John Keats
Andrew Marvell
John Milton
Alexander Pope
Sir Philip Sidney
Oscar Wilde
William Wordsworth

Oxford
Paperback
Reference

OXFORD PAPERBACK REFERENCE

From *Art and Artists* to *Zoology*, the Oxford Paperback Reference series offers the very best subject reference books at the most affordable prices.

Authoritative, accessible, and up to date, the series features dictionaries in key student areas, as well as a range of fascinating books for a general readership. Included are such well-established titles as Fowler's *Modern English Usage*, Margaret Drabble's *Concise Companion to English Literature*, and the bestselling science and medical dictionaries.

The series has now been relaunched in handsome new covers. Highlights include new editions of some of the most popular titles, as well as brand new paperback reference books on *Politics*, *Philosophy*, and *Twentieth-Century Poetry*.

With new titles being constantly added, and existing titles regularly updated, Oxford Paperback Reference is unrivalled in its breadth of coverage and expansive publishing programme. New dictionaries of *Film*, *Economics*, *Linguistics*, *Architecture*, *Archaeology*, *Astronomy*, and *The Bible* are just a few of those coming in the future.

Oxford
Paperback
Reference

THE CONCISE OXFORD COMPANION TO ENGLISH LITERATURE

Edited by Margaret Drabble and Jenny Stringer

Derived from the acclaimed *Oxford Companion to English Literature*, the concise maintains the wide coverage of its parent volume. It is an indispensable, compact guide to all aspects of English literature. For this revised edition, existing entries have been fully updated and revised with 60 new entries added on contemporary writers.

* **Over 5,000 entries on the lives and works of authors, poets and playwrights**

* **The most comprehensive and authoritative paperback guide to English literature**

* **New entries include Peter Ackroyd, Martin Amis, Toni Morrison, and Jeanette Winterson**

* **New appendices list major literary prize-winners**

From the reviews of its parent volume:

'It earns its place at the head of the best sellers: every home should have one'
Sunday Times